Student Quick Tips

Use this Student Quick Tips guide for a quick and easy start with McGraw-Hill Connect. You'll get valuable tips on registering, doing assignments, and accessing resources, as well as information about the support center hours.

Getting Started

TIP: To get started in Connect, you will need the following:

- Your instructor's Connect Web Address

  Sample of Connect Web Address:

  http://www.mcgrawhillconnect.com/class/instructorname_section_name

- Connect Access Code

TIP: If you do not have an access code or have not yet secured your tuition funds, you can click "Free Trial" during registration. This trial will provide temporary Connect access (typically three weeks) and will remind you to purchase online access before the end of your trial.

Registration and Sign In

1. Go to the Connect Web Address provided by your instructor
2. Click on **Register Now**
3. Enter your email address

TIP: If you already have a McGraw-Hill account, you will be asked for your password and will not be required to create a new account.

4. Enter a registration code or choose **Buy Online** to purchase access online

5. Follow the on-screen directions

TIP: Please choose your Security Question and Answer carefully. We will ask you for this information if you forget your password.

6. When registration is complete, click on **Go to Connect Now**

7. You are now ready to use **Connect**

Trouble Logging In?

- Ensure you are using the same email address you used during registration

- If you have forgotten your password, click on the "Forgot Password?" link at your Instructor's Connect Course Web Address

- When logged into Connect, you can update your account information (e.g. email address, password, and security question/answer) by clicking on the *"My Account"* link located at the top-right corner

Home (Assignments)

TIP: If you are unable to begin an assignment, verify the following:

- The assignment is available (start and due dates)

- That you have not exceeded the maximum number of attempts

- That you have not achieved a score of 100%

- If your assignment contains questions that require manual grading, you will not be able to begin your next attempt until your instructor has graded those questions

TIP: Based on the assignment policy settings established by your Instructor, you may encounter the following limitations when working on your assignment(s):

* Ability to Print Assignment

* Timed assignments – once you begin a "*timed assignment*," the timer will not stop by design

TIP: "*Save & Exit*" vs. "*Submit*" button

* If you are unable to complete your assignment in one sitting, utilize the "*Save & Exit*" button to save your work and complete it at a later time

* Once you have completed your assignment, utilize the "*Submit*" button in order for your assignment to be graded

Library

TIP: The *Library* section of your Connect account provides shortcuts to various resources.

* If you purchased ConnectPlus, you will see an *eBook* link, which can also be accessed from the section information widget of the *Home* tab

* *Recorded Lectures* can be accessed if your instructor is using *Tegrity Campus* to capture lectures. You may also access recorded lectures when taking an assignment by clicking on the projector icon in the navigation bar

* Many McGraw-Hill textbooks offer additional resources such as narrated slides and additional problems, which are accessible through the *Student Resources* link

Reports

TIP: Once you submit your assignment, you can view your available results in the *Reports* tab.

- If you see a dash (-) as your score, your instructor has either delayed or restricted your ability to see the assignment feedback

- Your instructor has the ability to limit the amount of information (e.g. questions, answers, scores) you can view for each submitted assignment

Need More Help?

CONTACT US ONLINE

Visit us at:

www.mcgrawhillconnect.com/support

Browse our support materials including tutorial videos and our searchable Connect knowledge base. If you cannot find an answer to your question, click on "Contact Us" button to send us an email.

GIVE US A CALL

Call us at:

1-800-331-5094

Our live support is available:

Mon-Thurs: 8 am – 11 pm CT
Friday: 8 am – 6 pm CT
Sunday: 6 pm – 11 pm CT

Financial
Accounting
Information for Decisions

6TH EDITION

John J. Wild
University of Wisconsin at Madison

Portland Community College

McGraw Hill Education

8 9 10 11 12 13 DIG/DIG 15 14 13

ISBN-13: 978-0-07-776836-2
ISBN-10: 0-07-776836-1
Part of
ISBN-13: 978-0-07-776837-9
ISBN-10: 0-07-776837-X

Learning Solutions Consultant: Michelle Payne
Production Editor: Larry Jackson
Cover Images © 2012 JupiterImages Corporation

Dear Colleagues/Friends,

As we roll out the new edition of *Financial Accounting*, I wish to thank each of you who provided suggestions to improve our textbook. As teachers, we know how important it is to select the right book for our course. This new edition reflects the advice and wisdom of many dedicated reviewers, students, instructors, and symposium and workshop participants. Together, we have created the most readable, concise, current, accurate, and innovative accounting book available today.

Throughout the writing process, I steered this book in the manner you directed. Reviewers, instructors, and students say this book's enhanced presentation, graphics, and technology cater to different learning styles and help students better understand accounting. McGraw-Hill *Connect Accounting*® offers new features to improve student learning and to assist instructor teaching and grading. LearnSmart, Self-Quiz and Study, Guided Examples, and Interactive Presentations provide additional tools and resources needed to achieve success through faster learning, more efficient studying, and higher retention of knowledge. You and your students will find all these tools easy to apply.

I owe the success of this book to you and our colleagues who graciously took time to help us focus on the changing needs of today's instructors and students. I feel fortunate to have witnessed our profession's extraordinary devotion to teaching. Your feedback and suggestions are reflected in everything I write. Please accept my heartfelt thanks for your dedication in helping today's students learn, understand, and appreciate accounting.

With kindest regards,

John J. Wild

About the Author

JOHN J. WILD is a distinguished professor of accounting at the University of Wisconsin at Madison. He previously held appointments at Michigan State University and the University of Manchester in England. He received his BBA, MS, and PhD from the University of Wisconsin.

Professor Wild teaches accounting courses at both the undergraduate and graduate levels. He has received numerous teaching honors, including the Mabel W. Chipman Excellence-in-Teaching Award, the departmental Excellence-in-Teaching Award, and the Teaching Excellence Award from the 2003 and 2005 business graduates at the University of Wisconsin. He also received the Beta Alpha Psi and Roland F. Salmonson Excellence-in-Teaching Award from Michigan State University. Professor Wild has received several research honors and is a past KPMG Peat Marwick National Fellow and is a recipient of fellowships from the American Accounting Association and the Ernst and Young Foundation.

Professor Wild is an active member of the American Accounting Association and its sections. He has served on several committees of these organizations, including the Outstanding Accounting Educator Award, Wildman Award, National Program Advisory, Publications, and Research Committees. Professor Wild is author of *Fundamental Accounting Principles, Financial Accounting Fundamentals, Managerial Accounting,* and *College Accounting,* each published by McGraw-Hill/Irwin. His research articles on accounting and analysis appear in *The Accounting Review; Journal of Accounting Research; Journal of Accounting and Economics; Contemporary Accounting Research; Journal of Accounting, Auditing and Finance; Journal of Accounting and Public Policy;* and other journals. He is past associate editor of *Contemporary Accounting Research* and has served on several editorial boards including *The Accounting Review.*

In his leisure time, Professor Wild enjoys hiking, sports, travel, people, and spending time with family and friends.

Helping Students Achieve New Heights

Financial Accounting, 6e

Assist your students in achieving new heights by giving them what they need to succeed in today's financial accounting course.

Whether the goal is to become an accountant or a businessperson, or simply to be an informed consumer of accounting information, *Financial Accounting (FA)* has helped thousands of students succeed by giving them support in the form of leading-edge accounting content that engages students, paired with state-of-the-art technology that elevates their understanding of key accounting principles.

With *FA* on your side, you'll be provided with **engaging content** in a **motivating style** to help students see the relevance of accounting. Students are motivated when reading materials that are clear and pertinent. *FA* excels at engaging students. Its chapter-opening vignettes showcase dynamic, successful entrepreneurial individuals and companies guaranteed to **interest and excite students**. This edition's featured companies—**Research In Motion** (maker of BlackBerry), **Apple**, **Nokia**, and **Palm**—captivate students with their products and annual reports, which are a pathway for learning financial statements. Further, this book's coverage of the accounting cycle fundamentals is widely praised for its clarity and effectiveness.

FA also delivers innovative technology to help student performance. **Connect Accounting**® provides students with instant grading and feedback for assignments that are completed online. **Connect Accounting Plus**® integrates an online version of the textbook with *Connect Accounting*. Our algorithmic test bank offers infinite variations of numerical test bank questions. The Self-Quiz and Study, Guided Examples, Interactive Presentations, and LearnSmart all provide additional support to help reinforce concepts and keep students motivated.

We're confident you'll agree that *FA* **will help your students achieve new heights**.

Students' Connection to

McGraw-Hill *Connect Accounting®* is an online assignment and assessment solution that connects your students with the tools and resources needed to achieve success through faster learning, more efficient studying, and higher retention of knowledge.

Online Assignments: *Connect Accounting* helps students learn more efficiently by providing feedback and practice material when they need it, where they need it. *Connect* grades homework automatically and gives immediate feedback on any questions students may have missed.

Interactive Presentations: The interactive presentations provide engaging narratives of all chapter learning objectives in an interactive online format. The presentations are tied specifically to *Financial Accounting*, 6e. They follow the structure of the text and are organized to match the learning objectives within each chapter. While the interactive presentations are not meant to replace the textbook in this course, they provide additional explanation and enhancement of material from the text chapter, allowing students to learn, study, and practice with instant feedback at their own pace.

Student Resource Library: The *Connect Accounting* Student Study Center gives access to additional resources such as recorded lectures, online practice materials, an eBook, and more.

Achieve New Heights!

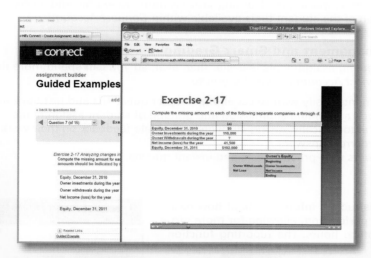

Guided Examples: The Guided Examples in *Connect Accounting* provide a narrated, animated, step-by-step walk-through of select exercise similar to those assigned. These short presentations provide reinforcement when students need it most.

LearnSmart: LearnSmart adaptive self-study technology within *Connect Accounting* helps students make the best use of their study time. LearnSmart provides a seamless combination of practice, assessment, and remediation for every concept in the textbook. LearnSmart's intelligent software adapts to students by supplying questions on a new concept when they are ready to learn it. With LearnSmart, students will spend less time on topics they understand and practice more on those they have yet to master.

Self-Quiz and Study: The Self-Quiz and Study (SQS) connects students to the learning resources students need to succeed in the course. For each chapter, students can take a practice quiz and immediately see how well they performed. A study plan then recommends specific readings from the text, supplemental study material, and practice exercises that will improve students' understanding and mastery of each learning objective.

For Better Learning

Chapter 6

New Belgium Brewing Company NEW opener with new entrepreneurial assignment

Revised SOX discussion of controls, including the role of COSO

Streamlined learning objectives

New material on drivers of human fraud

New graphic introducing a bank reconciliation with links to bank and book balances

Revised graphic on frequent cyber frauds

New graphic on drivers of financial misconduct

Chapter 7

Johnny Cupcakes NEW opener with new entrepreneurial assignment

Streamlined learning objectives

Reorganized recording of credit sales

Further clarification of interest formula

New boxes covering fraud risks with accounts receivable and some potential controls

Chapter 8

Games2U NEW opener with new entrepreneurial assignment

Reorganized learning objectives

Added entry to record impairment

Enhanced discussion of asset sales

Updated all real world examples and graphics

New box highlighting fraud risks with long-term assets

Chapter 9

SnorgTees NEW opener with new entrepreneurial assignment

New box highlighting fraud risks with payables

Updated tax illustrations and assignments using most recent government rates

New data on frauds involving employee payroll

New entry to reclassify long- to short-term debt

Updated all real world examples and graphics

Chapter 10

CakeLove NEW opener with new entrepreneurial assignment

Enhanced graphics for bonds and notes

Revised discussion of debt-to-equity

Enhanced explanation of how U.S. GAAP and IFRS determine fair value

New fraud discussion on hidden liabilities

Chapter 11

Clean Air Lawn Care NEW opener with new entrepreneurial assignment

Streamlined learning objectives

Inserted numerous key margin computations for entries involving equity

New box highlighting fraud risks with stock valuation

Updated all real world examples and graphics

Chapter 12

Animoto NEW opener with new entrepreneurial assignment

Streamlined learning objectives

New box highlighting fraud risks and cash controls

Updated discussion of different classifications for certain cash flows under IFRS

Increased number and range of assignments

Chapter 13

Motley Fool REVISED opener with new entrepreneurial assignment

Streamlined learning objectives

New discussion on analysis tools to help identify fraud

New companies—Research In Motion, Apple, Palm and Nokia—and new data throughout the chapter, exhibits, and illustrations

Enhanced horizontal and vertical analysis using new company and industry data

Enhanced discussion of common-size graphics

Revised ratio analysis using new company and industry data

Supplements

Instructor's Resource CD-ROM

ISBN13: 9780077429959
ISBN10: 0077429958

This is your all-in-one resource. It allows you to create custom presentations from your own materials or from the following text-specific materials provided in the CD's asset library:

- **Instructor's Resource Manual**

  Written by April Mohr, Jefferson Community and Technical College SW.

  This manual contains (for each chapter) a Lecture Outline, a chart linking all assignment materials to Learning Objectives, a list of relevant active learning activities, and additional visuals with transparency masters.

- **Solutions Manual**

  Prepared by John J. Wild.

  Includes detailed solutions and explanations for all assignments.

- **Test Bank, Computerized Test Bank**

  Prepared by Stacie Mayes, Rose State College, and Margaret Tanner, University of Arkansas-Fort Smith.

- **PowerPoint® Presentations**

  Prepared by Debra Schmidt, Cerritos College.

  Presentations allow for revision of lecture slides, and includes a viewer, allowing screens to be shown with or without the software.

- **Link to PageOut**

Working Papers

ISBN13: 9780077429980
ISBN10: 0077429982

Written by John J. Wild.

Blank solution and financial statement templates for students to complete that are specifically customized to each assignment throughout the book.

Assurance of Learning Ready

Many educational institutions today are focused on the notion of assurance of learning, an important element of some accreditation standards. *Financial Accounting* is designed specifically to support your assurance of learning initiatives with a simple, yet powerful solution. Each test bank question for *Financial Accounting* maps to a specific chapter learning objective listed in the text. You can use our test bank software, EZ Test and EZ Test Online, or *Connect Accounting* to easily query for learning objectives that directly relate to the learning objectives for your course. You can then use the reporting features of EZ Test to aggregate student results in similar fashion, making the collection and presentation of assurance of learning data simple and easy.

AACSB Statement

The McGraw-Hill Companies is a proud corporate member of AACSB International. Understanding the importance and value of AACSB accreditation, *Financial Accounting* recognizes the curricula guidelines detailed in the AACSB standards for business accreditation by connecting selected questions in the test bank to the six general knowledge and skill guidelines in the AACSB standards. The statements contained in *Financial Accounting* are provided only as a guide for the users of this textbook. The AACSB leaves content coverage and assessment within the purview of individual schools, the mission of the school, and the faculty. While *Financial Accounting* and the teaching package make no claim of any specific AACSB qualification or evaluation, we have within *Financial Accounting* labeled select questions according to the six general knowledge and skills areas.

The authors extend a special thanks to our contributing and technology supplement authors:

Contributing Author: Anita Kroll, University of Wisconsin–Madison

LearnSmart Authors: April Mohr, Jefferson Community and Technical College, SW; Anna Boulware, St. Charles Community College; Brenda Mattison, Tri County Technical College; and Dominique Svarc, William Rainey Harper College

Online Quizzes: Constance Hylton, George Mason University

Connect Self-Quiz and Study: Jeannine Metzler, Northampton Community College

Interactive Presentations: Jeannie Folk, College of DuPage

Guided Examples: Kathleen O'Donnell, Onondaga Community College

Acknowledgments

John J. Wild and McGraw-Hill/Irwin would like to recognize the following instructors for their valuable feedback and involvement in the development of *Financial Accounting,* 6e. We are thankful for their suggestions, counsel, and encouragement.

Dawn P. Addington, Central New Mexico Community College

Dave Alldredge, Salt Lake Community College

Sylvia Allen, Los Angeles Valley College

Sheryl Alley, Ball State University

Sheila Ammons, Austin Community College

Jack Aschkenazi, American Intercontinental University

Progyan Basu, University of Maryland

Joe Beams, University of New Orleans

Gerard L. Berardino, Community College of Allegheny County-Boyce Campus

Swati Bhandarkar, University of Georgia

Jaswinder Bhangal, Chabot College

David Borjarsky, California State University-Long Beach

Anna Marie Boulware, St. Charles Community College

Charles Boxell, Owens Community College

Mia Breen, DeAnza College

Philip Brown, Harding University

Eric Carstensen, MiraCosta College

Donna Chadwick, Sinclair Community College

Barbara Chaney, University of Montana

Betty Chavis, California State University Fullerton

Robert Churchman, Harding University

Marilyn Ciolino, Delgado Community College

Norman H. Colter, University of New Mexico

Laurie Dahlin, Worcester State College

Rosemond Desir, Colorado State University

Jap Efendi, University of Texas-Arlington

Terry Elliott, Morehead State University-Ashland

Stephanie Farewell, University of Arkansas-Little Rock

Carol Flowers, Orange Coast College

Mike Foland, Southwestern Illinois College

Jeannie Folk, College of DuPage

Amy Ford, Western Illinois University

Mitch Franklin, Syracuse University

Virginia Fullwood, Texas A&M University

Hubert Gill, University of North Florida

Saturnino Gonzalez Jr., El Paso Community College

Sherry L. Gordon, Palomar College

Marina Grau, Houston Community College

Jeannie Harrington, Middle Tennessee State University

Tracey Hawkins, University of Cincinnati, Clermont College

Roger G. Hehman, Raymond Walters College

Cecil Hill, Jackson State University

Tom Hrubec, Franklin University

Constance Hylton, George Mason University

Catherine Jeppson, California State University-Northridge

Christie W. Johnson, Montana State University

Vern Jorgensen, Southwestern Community College

Irene Kim, George Mason University

Phillip Korb, University of Baltimore

Anita Kroll, University of Wisconsin-Madison

David Krug, Johnson County Community College

Don Lucy, Indian River State College

Stacie Mayes, Rose State College

Allison McLeod, University of North Texas

Kathleen Michele, Sun Prairie College

Jeanne Miller, Cypress College

Tim Mills, Eastern Illinois University

Susan Minke, Indiana University/Purdue University at Ft. Wayne

April Mohr, Jefferson Community and Technical College, SW

Audrey S. Morrison, Pensacola Junior College

Matt Muller, Adirondack Community College

Kathleen Munter, Pima Community College

Karen Nunez, Elon University

Ash Patel, Normandale Community College

Reed Peoples, Austin Community College

Karin Petruska, Youngstown State University

Yvonne Phang, Borough of Manhattan Community College

Eric Primuth, Cuyahoga Community College Western-Parma

Allan M. Rabinowitz, Pace University

Ruthie Reynolds, Howard University

Lawrence A. Roman, Cuyahoga Community College

Lou Rosamilia, Hudson Valley Community College

Pamela Rouse, Butler University

Helen Roybark, Radford University

Joan Ryan, Clackamas Community College

Judith Sage, Texas A&M International University

Marilyn Sagrillo, University of Wisconsin-Green Bay

Christine Schalow, University of Wisconsin-Stevens Point

Albert Schepanski, University of Iowa

Debra Schmidt, Cerritos College

Randall Serrett, University of Houston-Downtown

Vicki Shipley, Ball State University

Gerald Smith, University of Northern Iowa

Nancy Snow, University of Toledo

Dale Spencer, New Mexico State University

Gloria Stuart, Georgia Southern University

Gracelyn V. Stuart-Tuggle, Palm Beach Community College-South

Diane Sturek, Indiana University-Indianapolis

Dominique Svarc, William Rainey Harper College

Diane Tanner, University of North Florida

Margaret Tanner, University of Arkansas-Fort Smith

Janet Tarase, Lorain County Community College

Karen Varnell, Tarleton State University

Donna J. Viens, Johnson & Wales University

Stephen J. Walsh, Clark College

Terri Walsh, Seminole State College of Florida

William J. Walsh, Syracuse University

James Weglin, North Seattle Community College

Dave Welch, Franklin University

Jean Wells, Howard Univeristy

Jane Wiese, Valencia Community College

Kenneth L. Wild, University of London

Gayle Williams, Sacramento City College

Scott Williams, County College of Morris

Karen Wisniewski, County College of Morris

Darryl Woolley, University of Idaho

Judith Zander, Grossmont College

In addition to the helpful and generous colleagues listed above, I thank the entire McGraw-Hill/Irwin *Financial Accounting,* 6e, team, including Tim Vertovec, Dana Woo, Christina Sanders, Aaron Downey of Matrix Productions, Lori Koetters, Matthew Baldwin, Carol Bielski, Patricia Plumb, Ron Nelms, and Brian Nacik. I also thank the great marketing and sales support staff, including Kathleen Klehr and Brad Parkins. Many talented educators and professionals worked hard to create the supplements for this book, and for their efforts we're grateful. Finally, many more people I either did not meet or whose efforts we did not personally witness nevertheless helped to make this book everything that it is, and we thank them all.

John J. Wild

Decision Insight

A **Decision Feature** launches each chapter showing the relevance of accounting for a real entrepreneur. An **Entrepreneurial Decision** problem at the end of the assignments returns to this feature with a mini-case.

Accounting for Twitter

"There is so much going on here . . ."
—**BIZ STONE** (RIGHT)

SAN FRANCISCO—"We came across the word 'twitter,' and it was just perfect," recalls Jack Dorsey (center of photo). "The definition was 'a short burst of inconsequential information,' and 'chirps from birds,' and that's exactly what the product was." Today, Twitter boasts over 200 million users. Founded by Jack, along with Biz Stone (right) and Evan Williams (left), **Twitter** (**Twitter.com**) is "facilitating connections between businesses and individuals in meaningful and relevant ways," says Jack. Along the way, the young entrepreneurs had to learn accounting and the details of preparing and interpreting financial statements.

"There is so much going on here," explains Biz when describing Twitter's business model. However, admits Evan, "We did a poor job of communicating." Important questions involving business formation, transaction analysis, and financial reporting arose. The entrepreneurs eventually met those challenges and, in the process, set Twitter apart. "If you stand pat," says Evan, "you risk being stagnant."

Information is the focus within Twitter's accounting records and systems. Jack recalls that when they launched Twitter, there were all these reasons why they would not succeed. He applied their similar "can-do" approach to accounting information. "My whole philosophy is making tech [and accounting] more accessible and human," says Jack. This includes using accounting information to make key business decisions.

Twitter is the language of micro-blogging, and accounting is the language of business. "Twitter is so many things: a messaging service, a customer-service tool, a real-time search," explains Biz, and the accounting system had to capture those things. Biz adds that Twitter is exploring additional "interesting ways to generate revenue." That revenue-stream is reflected in its financial statements, which are based on transaction analysis and accounting concepts.

Twitter's revenues exhibit growth and reflect what experts call the *monetizing* of its business. A recent study by the marketing firm SocialTwist found that the click-through rate was 19 for Twitter, which is the number of clicks on an embedded link. This compares with 3 clicks for Facebook links. Twitter's revenues in the recent year were estimated at $45 million, which are projected to exceed $100 million next year. Twitter also tracks its expenses and asset purchases. Twitter owners have an estimated valuation of between $5 and $10 billion!

The three entrepreneurs emphasize that accounting records must be in order for Twitter to realize its full potential. Many experts predict a public offering of its stock within the next two years, which could generate untold wealth. Still, Evan recognizes that "so many people here [at Twitter] contribute to that success." He also emphasizes that learning is a key to their business success. "I realized," insists Evan, "I could buy books and learn something that people spent years learning."

[Sources: Twitter Website, January 2012; *Entrepreneur,* December 2010; *USA Today,* May 2009; Smedio.com, June 2011; *San Francisco Chronicle,* March 2011; SocialTwist.com, October 2010; *The Wall Street Journal,* February 2011]

*A **Preview** opens each chapter with a summary of topics covered.*

Today's world is one of information—its preparation, communication, analysis, and use. Accounting is at the core of this information age. Knowledge of accounting gives us career opportunities and the insight to take advantage of them. This book introduces concepts, procedures, and analyses that help us make better decisions, including career choices. In this chapter we describe accounting, the users and uses of accounting information, the forms and activities of organizations, and several accounting principles. We also introduce transaction analysis and financial statements.

Introducing Accounting in Business

Importance of Accounting	Fundamentals of Accounting	Transaction Analysis	Financial Statements
• Accounting information users • Opportunities in accounting	• Ethics—key concept • Generally accepted accounting principles • International standards	• Accounting equation • Transaction analysis—illustrated	• Income statement • Statement of retained earnings • Balance sheet • Statement of cash flows

IMPORTANCE OF ACCOUNTING

C1 Explain the purpose and importance of accounting.

Why is accounting so popular on campuses? Why are there so many accounting jobs for graduates? Why is accounting so important to companies? Why do politicians and business leaders focus on accounting regulations? The answer is that we live in an information age, where that information, and its reliability, impacts the financial well-being of us all.

Accounting is an information and measurement system that identifies, records, and communicates relevant, reliable, and comparable information about an organization's business activities. *Identifying* business activities requires selecting transactions and events relevant to an organization. Examples are the sale of iPhones by **Apple** and the receipt of ticket money by **TicketMaster**. *Recording* business activities requires keeping a chronological log of transactions and events measured in dollars and classified and summarized in a useful format. *Communicating* business activities requires preparing accounting reports such as financial statements. It also requires analyzing and interpreting such reports. (The financial statements and notes of **Research In Motion**, the maker of BlackBerry, are shown in Appendix A near the end of this book. This appendix also shows the financial statements of **Apple**, **Palm**, and **Nokia**.) Exhibit 1.1 summarizes accounting activities.

Real company names are printed in bold magenta.

We must guard against a narrow view of accounting. Our most common contact with accounting is through credit approvals, checking accounts, tax forms, and payroll. These experiences are limited and tend to focus on the recordkeeping parts of accounting. **Recordkeeping,** or **bookkeeping,** is the recording of transactions and events, either manually or electronically. This is just one part of accounting. Accounting also identifies and communicates information on transactions and events, and it includes the crucial processes of analysis and interpretation.

EXHIBIT 1.1

Accounting Activities

Identifying — Select transactions and events · Recording — Input, measure, and classify · Communicating — Prepare, analyze, and interpret

Technology is a key part of modern business and plays a major role in accounting. Technology reduces the time, effort, and cost of recordkeeping while improving clerical accuracy. Some small organizations continue to perform various accounting tasks manually, but even they are impacted by technology. As technology has changed the way we store, process, and summarize masses of data, accounting has been freed to expand. Consulting, planning, and other financial services are now closely linked to accounting. These services require sorting through data, interpreting their meaning, identifying key factors, and analyzing their implications.

Point: Technology is only as useful as the accounting data available, and users' decisions are only as good as their understanding of accounting. The best software and recordkeeping cannot make up for lack of accounting knowledge.

Margin notes further enhance the textual material.

Users of Accounting Information

Accounting is often called the *language of business* because all organizations set up an accounting information system to communicate data to help people make better decisions. Exhibit 1.2 shows that the accounting information system serves many kinds of users (this is a partial listing) who can be divided into two groups: external users and internal users.

External users

Internal users

EXHIBIT 1.2

Users of Accounting Information

- Lenders   • Consumer groups
- Shareholders   • External auditors
- Governments   • Customers

- Officers   • Sales staff
- Managers   • Budget officers
- Internal auditors • Controllers

Infographics reinforce key concepts through visual learning.

External Information Users   **External users** of accounting information are *not* directly involved in running the organization. They include shareholders (investors), lenders, directors, customers, suppliers, regulators, lawyers, brokers, and the press. External users have limited access to an organization's information. Yet their business decisions depend on information that is reliable, relevant, and comparable.

C2   Identify users and uses of, and opportunities in, accounting.

Financial accounting is the area of accounting aimed at serving external users by providing them with *general-purpose financial statements*. The term *general-purpose* refers to the broad range of purposes for which external users rely on these statements.

Each external user has special information needs depending on the types of decisions to be made. *Lenders* (creditors) loan money or other resources to an organization. Banks, savings and loans, co-ops, and mortgage and finance companies are lenders. Lenders look for information to help them assess whether an organization is likely to repay its loans with interest. *Shareholders* (investors) are the owners of a corporation. They use accounting reports in deciding whether to buy, hold, or sell stock. Shareholders typically elect a *board of directors* to oversee their interests in an organization. Since directors are responsible to shareholders, their information needs are similar. *External* (independent) *auditors* examine financial statements to verify that they are prepared according to generally accepted accounting principles. *Nonexecutive employees* and *labor unions* use financial statements to judge the fairness of wages, assess job prospects, and bargain for better wages. *Regulators* often have legal authority over certain activities of organizations. For example, the Internal Revenue Service (IRS) and other tax authorities require organizations to file accounting reports in computing taxes. Other regulators include utility boards that use accounting information to set utility rates and securities regulators that require reports for companies that sell their stock to the public.

Accounting serves the needs of many other external users. *Voters, legislators,* and *government officials* use accounting information to monitor and evaluate government receipts and expenses. *Contributors* to nonprofit organizations use accounting information to evaluate the use and impact of their donations. *Suppliers* use accounting information to judge the soundness of a customer before making sales on credit, and *customers* use financial reports to assess the staying power of potential suppliers.

Internal Information Users   **Internal users** of accounting information are those directly involved in managing and operating an organization. They use the information to help improve the efficiency and effectiveness of an organization. **Managerial accounting** is the area of accounting that serves the decision-making needs of internal users. Internal reports are not subject to the same rules as external reports and instead are designed with the special needs of internal users in mind.

There are several types of internal users, and many are managers of key operating activities. *Research and development managers* need information about projected costs and revenues of any proposed changes in products and services. *Purchasing managers* need to know what, when, and how much to purchase. *Human resource managers* need information about employees' payroll, benefits, performance, and compensation. *Production managers* depend on information to monitor costs and ensure quality. *Distribution managers* need reports for timely, accurate, and efficient delivery of products and services. *Marketing managers* use reports about sales and costs to target consumers, set prices, and monitor consumer needs, tastes, and price concerns. *Service managers* require information on the costs and benefits of looking after products and services. Decisions of these and other internal users depend on accounting reports.

Both internal and external users rely on internal controls to monitor and control company activities. *Internal controls* are procedures set up to protect company property and equipment, ensure reliable accounting reports, promote efficiency, and encourage adherence to company policies. Examples are good records, physical controls (locks, passwords, guards), and independent reviews.

Decision Insight boxes highlight relevant items from practice.

Decision Insight

Virtuous Returns   Virtue is not always its own reward. Compare the S&P 500 with the Domini Social Index (DSI), which covers 400 companies that have especially good records of social responsibility. We see that returns for companies with socially responsible behavior are at least as high as those of the S&P 500. ■

Copyright © 2010 by KLD Research & Analytics, Inc. The "FTSE KLD 400 Social Index" is a service mark of KLD Research & Analytics.

Graphical displays are often used to illustrate key points.

Opportunities in Accounting

Accounting information affects many aspects of our lives. When we earn money, pay taxes, invest savings, budget earnings, and plan for the future, we are influenced by accounting. Accounting has four broad areas of opportunities: financial, managerial, taxation, and accounting-related. Exhibit 1.3 lists selected opportunities in each area.

EXHIBIT 1.3

Accounting Opportunities

Opportunities in Accounting

Financial	Managerial	Taxation	Accounting-related	
• Preparation	• General accounting	• Preparation	• Lenders	• FBI investigators
• Analysis	• Cost accounting	• Planning	• Consultants	• Market researchers
• Auditing	• Budgeting	• Regulatory	• Analysts	• Systems designers
• Regulatory	• Internal auditing	• Investigations	• Traders	• Merger services
• Consulting	• Consulting	• Consulting	• Directors	• Business valuation
• Planning	• Controller	• Enforcement	• Underwriters	• Forensic accounting
• Criminal investigation	• Treasurer	• Legal services	• Planners	• Litigation support
	• Strategy	• Estate plans	• Appraisers	• Entrepreneurs

Transaction 3: Purchase Equipment for Cash

FastForward spends $26,000 to acquire equipment for testing footwear. Like transaction 2, transaction 3 is an exchange of one asset, cash, for another asset, equipment. The equipment is an asset because of its expected future benefits from testing footwear. This purchase changes the makeup of assets but does not change the asset total. The accounting equation remains in balance.

	Cash	+	Supplies	+	Equipment	=	Liabilities	+	Equity
									Common Stock
Old Bal.	$27,500	+	$2,500			=			$30,000
(3)	−26,000			+	$26,000				
New Bal.	$ 1,500	+	$2,500	+	$ 26,000	=			$30,000
			$30,000						$30,000

Transaction 4: Purchase Supplies on Credit

Taylor decides more supplies of footwear and accessories are needed. These additional supplies total $7,100, but as we see from the accounting equation in transaction 3, FastForward has only $1,500 in cash. Taylor arranges to purchase them on credit from CalTech Supply Company. Thus, FastForward acquires supplies in exchange for a promise to pay for them later. This purchase increases assets by $7,100 in supplies, and liabilities (called *accounts payable* to CalTech Supply) increase by the same amount. The effects of this purchase follow:

Example: If FastForward pays $500 cash in transaction 4, how does this partial payment affect the liability to CalTech? What would be FastForward's cash balance? *Answers:* The liability to CalTech would be reduced to $6,600 and the cash balance would be reduced to $1,000.

	Cash	+	Supplies	+	Equipment	=	Accounts Payable	+	Common Stock
Old Bal.	$1,500	+	$2,500	+	$26,000	=			$30,000
(4)		+	7,100				+$7,100		
New Bal.	$1,500	+	$9,600	+	$26,000	=	$ 7,100	+	$30,000
			$37,100					$37,100	

Transaction 5: Provide Services for Cash

FastForward earns revenues by selling online ad space to manufacturers and by consulting with clients about test results on footwear and accessories. It earns net income only if its revenues are greater than its expenses incurred in earning them. In one of its first jobs, FastForward provides consulting services to a power-walking club and immediately collects $4,200 cash. The accounting equation reflects this increase in cash of $4,200 and in equity of $4,200. This increase in equity is identified in the far right column under Revenues because the cash received is earned by providing consulting services.

	Cash	+	Supplies	+	Equipment	=	Accounts Payable	+	Common Stock	+	Revenues
Old Bal.	$1,500	+	$9,600	+	$26,000	=	$7,100	+	$30,000		
(5)	+4,200									+	$4,200
New Bal.	$5,700	+	$9,600	+	$26,000	=	$7,100	+	$30,000	+	$ 4,200
			$41,300						$41,300		

Transactions 6 and 7: Payment of Expenses in Cash

FastForward pays $1,000 rent to the landlord of the building where its facilities are located. Paying this amount allows FastForward to occupy the space for the month of December. The rental payment is reflected in the following accounting equation as transaction 6. FastForward also pays the biweekly $700 salary of the company's only employee. This is reflected in the accounting equation as transaction 7. Both transactions 6 and 7 are December expenses for FastForward. The costs of both rent and salary are expenses, as opposed to assets, because their benefits are used in December (they

By definition, increases in expenses yield decreases in equity.

have no future benefits after December). These transactions also use up an asset (cash) in carrying out FastForward's operations. The accounting equation shows that both transactions reduce cash and equity. The far right column identifies these decreases as Expenses.

	Assets					=	Liabilities	+			Equity		
	Cash	+	Supplies	+	Equipment	=	Accounts Payable	+	Common Stock	+	Revenues	−	Expenses
Old Bal.	$5,700	+	$9,600	+	$26,000	=	$7,100	+	$30,000	+	$4,200		
(6)	−1,000											−	$1,000
Bal.	4,700	+	9,600	+	26,000	=	7,100	+	30,000	+	4,200	−	1,000
(7)	− 700											−	700
New Bal.	$4,000	+	$9,600	+	$26,000	=	$7,100	+	$30,000	+	$4,200	−	$ 1,700
			$39,600								$39,600		

Transaction 8: Provide Services and Facilities for Credit   FastForward provides consulting services of $1,600 and rents its test facilities for $300 to a podiatric services center. The rental involves allowing members to try recommended footwear and accessories at FastForward's testing area. The center is billed for the $1,900 total. This transaction results in a new asset, called *accounts receivable,* from this client. It also yields an increase in equity from the two revenue components reflected in the Revenues column of the accounting equation:

	Assets								=	Liabilities	+			Equity		
	Cash	+	Accounts Receivable	+	Supplies	+	Equipment	=	Accounts Payable	+	Common Stock	+	Revenues	−	Expenses
Old Bal.	$4,000	+		+	$9,600	+	$26,000	=	$7,100	+	$30,000	+	$4,200	−	$1,700
(8)		+	$1,900									+	1,600		
												+	300		
New Bal.	$4,000	+	$ 1,900	+	$9,600	+	$26,000	=	$7,100	+	$30,000	+	$6,100	−	$1,700
			$41,500										$41,500		

Transaction 9: Receipt of Cash from Accounts Receivable   The client in transaction 8 (the podiatric center) pays $1,900 to FastForward 10 days after it is billed for consulting services. This transaction 9 does not change the total amount of assets and does not affect liabilities or equity. It converts the receivable (an asset) to cash (another asset). It does not create new revenue. Revenue was recognized when FastForward rendered the services in transaction 8, not when the cash is now collected. This emphasis on the earnings process instead of cash flows is a goal of the revenue recognition principle and yields useful information to users. The new balances follow:

Point: Receipt of cash is not always a revenue.

	Assets								=	Liabilities	+			Equity		
	Cash	+	Accounts Receivable	+	Supplies	+	Equipment	=	Accounts Payable	+	Common Stock	+	Revenues	−	Expenses
Old Bal.	$4,000	+	$1,900	+	$9,600	+	$26,000	=	$7,100	+	$30,000	+	$6,100	−	$1,700
(9)	+1,900	−	1,900												
New Bal.	$5,900	+	$ 0	+	$9,600	+	$26,000	=	$7,100	+	$30,000	+	$6,100	−	$1,700
			$41,500										$41,500		

Transaction 10: Payment of Accounts Payable   FastForward pays CalTech Supply $900 cash as partial payment for its earlier $7,100 purchase of supplies (transaction 4), leaving $6,200 unpaid. The accounting equation shows that this transaction decreases FastForward's cash by $900 and decreases its liability to CalTech Supply by $900. Equity does not change. This event does not create an expense even though cash flows out of FastForward (instead the expense is recorded when FastForward derives the benefits from these supplies).

Assets						=	Liabilities	+		Equity			
	Cash	+	Accounts Receivable	+	Supplies	+	Equipment	=	Accounts Payable	+	Common Stock	+	Revenues	–	Expenses
---	---	---	---	---	---	---	---	---	---	---	---	---	---	---	---	---
Old Bal.	$5,900	+	$ 0	+	$9,600	+	$26,000	=	$7,100	+	$30,000	+	$6,100	–	$1,700
(10)	– 900								– 900						
New Bal.	$5,000	+	$ 0	+	$9,600	+	$26,000	=	$6,200	+	$30,000	+	$6,100	–	$1,700

$40,600 = $40,600

Transaction 11: Payment of Cash Dividend FastForward declares and pays a $200 cash dividend to its owner. Dividends (decreases in equity) are not reported as expenses because they are not part of the company's earnings process. Since dividends are not company expenses, they are not used in computing net income.

By definition, increases in dividends yield decreases in equity.

	Cash	+	Accounts Receivable	+	Supplies	+	Equipment	=	Accounts Payable	+	Common Stock	–	Dividends	+	Revenues	–	Expenses
Old Bal.	$5,000	+	$ 0	+	$9,600	+	$26,000	=	$6,200	+	$30,000			+	$6,100	–	$1,700
(11)	– 200												– $200				
New Bal.	$4,800	+	$ 0	+	$9,600	+	$26,000	=	$6,200	+	$30,000	–	$200	+	$6,100	–	$1,700

$40,400 = $40,400

Summary of Transactions

We summarize in Exhibit 1.9 the effects of these 11 transactions of FastForward using the accounting equation. First, we see that the accounting equation remains in balance after each transaction. Second, transactions can be analyzed by their effects on components of the

EXHIBIT 1.9

Summary of Transactions Using the Accounting Equation

	Cash	+	Accounts Receivable	+	Supplies	+	Equipment	=	Accounts Payable	+	Common Stock	–	Dividends	+	Revenues	–	Expenses
(1)	$30,000							=			$30,000						
(2)	– 2,500				+	$2,500											
Bal.	27,500			+	2,500			=			30,000						
(3)	–26,000						+	$26,000									
Bal.	1,500			+	2,500	+	26,000	=			30,000						
(4)					+	7,100				+$7,100							
Bal.	1,500			+	9,600	+	26,000	=	7,100	+	30,000						
(5)	+ 4,200													+	$4,200		
Bal.	5,700			+	9,600	+	26,000	=	7,100	+	30,000			+	4,200		
(6)	– 1,000															–	$1,000
Bal.	4,700			+	9,600	+	26,000	=	7,100	+	30,000			+	4,200	–	1,000
(7)	– 700															–	700
Bal.	4,000			+	9,600	+	26,000	=	7,100	+	30,000			+	4,200	–	1,700
(8)		+	$1,900											+	1,600		
														+	300		
Bal.	4,000	+	1,900	+	9,600	+	26,000	=	7,100	+	30,000			+	6,100	–	1,700
(9)	+ 1,900	–	1,900														
Bal.	5,900	+	0	+	9,600	+	26,000	=	7,100	+	30,000			+	6,100	–	1,700
(10)	– 900								– 900								
Bal.	5,000	+	0	+	9,600	+	26,000	=	6,200	+	30,000			+	6,100	–	1,700
(11)	– 200											–	$200				
Bal.	$ 4,800	+	$ 0	+	$ 9,600	+	$ 26,000	=	$ 6,200	+	$ 30,000	–	$200	+	$6,100	–	$ 1,700

Point: Knowing how financial statements are prepared improves our analysis of them. We develop the skills for analysis of financial statements throughout the book. Chapter 13 focuses on financial statement analysis.

accounting equation. For example, in transactions 2, 3, and 9, one asset increased while another asset decreased by equal amounts.

Quick Check   Answers — p. 30

17. When is the accounting equation in balance, and what does that mean?
18. How can a transaction not affect any liability and equity accounts?
19. Describe a transaction increasing equity and one decreasing it.
20. Identify a transaction that decreases both assets and liabilities.

FINANCIAL STATEMENTS

P2 Identify and prepare basic financial statements and explain how they interrelate.

This section introduces us to how financial statements are prepared from the analysis of business transactions. The four financial statements and their purposes are:

1. **Income statement**—describes a company's revenues and expenses along with the resulting net income or loss over a period of time due to earnings activities.
2. **Statement of retained earnings**—explains changes in retained earnings from net income (or loss) and from any dividends over a period of time.
3. **Balance sheet**—describes a company's financial position (types and amounts of assets, liabilities, and equity) at a point in time.
4. **Statement of cash flows**—identifies cash inflows (receipts) and cash outflows (payments) over a period of time.

We prepare these financial statements, in this order, using the 11 selected transactions of FastForward. (These statements are technically called *unadjusted*—we explain this in Chapters 2 and 3.)

Income Statement

FastForward's income statement for December is shown at the top of Exhibit 1.10. Information about revenues and expenses is conveniently taken from the Equity columns of Exhibit 1.9. Revenues are reported first on the income statement. They include consulting revenues of $5,800 from transactions 5 and 8 and rental revenue of $300 from transaction 8. Expenses are reported after revenues. (For convenience in this chapter, we list larger amounts first, but we can sort expenses in different ways.) Rent and salary expenses are from transactions 6 and 7. Expenses reflect the costs to generate the revenues reported. Net income (or loss) is reported at the bottom of the statement and is the amount earned in December. Stockholders' investments and dividends are *not* part of income.

Point: Net income is sometimes called *earnings* or *profit*.

Statement of Retained Earnings

The statement of retained earnings reports information about how retained earnings changes over the reporting period. This statement shows beginning retained earnings, events that increase it (net income), and events that decrease it (dividends and net loss). Ending retained earnings is computed in this statement and is carried over and reported on the balance sheet. FastForward's statement of retained earnings is the second report in Exhibit 1.10. The beginning balance is measured as of the start of business on December 1. It is zero because FastForward did not exist before then. An existing business reports the beginning balance equal to that as of the end of the prior reporting period (such as from November 30). Fast-Forward's statement shows the $4,400 of net income earned during the period. This links the income statement to the statement of retained earnings (see line ①). The statement also reports the $200 cash dividend and FastForward's end-of-period retained earnings balance.

Point: The statement of retained earnings is also called the *statement of changes in retained earnings.* Note: Beg. Retained Earnings + Net Income − Dividends = End. Retained Earnings

FASTFORWARD
Income Statement
For Month Ended December 31, 2011

Revenues		
Consulting revenue ($4,200 + $1,600)...............	$ 5,800	
Rental revenue..	300	
Total revenues		$ 6,100
Expenses		
Rent expense	1,000	
Salaries expense	700	
Total expenses		1,700
Net income		$ 4,400 ←

FASTFORWARD
Statement of Retained Earnings
For Month Ended December 31, 2011

Retained earnings, December 1, 2011..............................	$ 0	
Plus: Net income..	4,400 ←
	4,400	
Less: Dividends	200	
Retained earnings, December 31, 2011...........................	$ 4,200 ←	

FASTFORWARD
Balance Sheet
December 31, 2011

Assets		Liabilities	
Cash............	$ 4,800	Accounts payable.............	$ 6,200
Supplies	9,600	Total liabilities	6,200
Equipment........	26,000	**Equity**	
		Common stock	30,000
		Retained earnings	4,200 ←
		Total equity	34,200
Total assets	$ 40,400	Total liabilities and equity	$ 40,400

FASTFORWARD
Statement of Cash Flows
For Month Ended December 31, 2011

Cash flows from operating activities		
Cash received from clients ($4,200 + $1,900)..........	$ 6,100	
Cash paid for supplies ($2,500 + $900)...............	(3,400)	
Cash paid for rent	(1,000)	
Cash paid to employee	(700)	
Net cash provided by operating activities		$ 1,000
Cash flows from investing activities		
Purchase of equipment	(26,000)	
Net cash used by investing activities		(26,000)
Cash flows from financing activities		
Investments by stockholder	30,000	
Dividends to stockholder	(200)	
Net cash provided by financing activities		29,800
Net increase in cash		$ 4,800
Cash balance, December 1, 2011		0
Cash balance, December 31, 2011		$ 4,800

EXHIBIT 1.10

Financial Statements and
Their Links

Point: A statement's heading identifies the company, the statement title, and the date or time period.

Point: Arrow lines show how the statements are linked. ① Net income is used to compute equity. ② Retained earnings is used to prepare the balance sheet. ③ Cash from the balance sheet is used to reconcile the statement of cash flows.

Point: The income statement, the statement of retained earnings, and the statement of cash flows are prepared for a *period* of time. The balance sheet is prepared as of a *point* in time.

Point: A single ruled line denotes an addition or subtraction. Final totals are double underlined. Negative amounts are often in parentheses.

A list of key terms with page references concludes each chapter (a complete glossary is at the end of the book).

Key Terms

Accounting (p. 4)
Accounting equation (p. 15)
Assets (p. 15)
Audit (p. 13)
Auditors (p. 13)
Balance sheet (p. 20)
Bookkeeping (p. 4)
Business entity assumption (p. 11)
Common stock (p. 12)
Conceptual framework (p. 10)
Contributed capital (p. 15)
Corporation (p. 12)
Cost-benefit constraint (p. 13)
Cost principle (p. 11)
Dividends (p. 15)
Equity (p. 15)
Ethics (p. 8)
Events (p. 16)
Expanded accounting equation (p. 15)
Expense recognition principle (p. 11)
Expenses (p. 15)
External transactions (p. 16)

External users (p. 5)
Financial accounting (p. 5)
Financial Accounting Standards Board (FASB) (p. 9)
Full disclosure principle (p. 11)
Generally accepted accounting principles (GAAP) (p. 9)
Going-concern assumption (p. 11)
Income (p. 15)
Income statement (p. 20)
Internal transactions (p. 16)
Internal users (p. 6)
International Accounting Standards Board (IASB) (p. 9)
International Financial Reporting Standards (IFRS) (p. 9)
Liabilities (p. 15)
Managerial accounting (p. 6)
Matching principle (p. 11)
Materiality constraint (p. 13)
Measurement principle (p. 11)
Monetary unit assumption (p. 11)
Net income (p. 15)

Net loss (p. 15)
Partnership (p. 12)
Proprietorship (p. 11)
Recordkeeping (p. 4)
Retained earnings (p. 15)
Return (p. 28)
Return on assets (p. 24)
Revenue recognition principle (p. 11)
Revenues (p. 15)
Risk (p. 28)
Sarbanes–Oxley Act (p. 13)
Securities and Exchange Commission (SEC) (p. 9)
Shareholders (p. 12)
Shares (p. 12)
Sole proprietorship (p. 11)
Statement of cash flows (p. 20)
Statement of retained earnings (p. 20)
Stock (p. 12)
Stockholders (p. 12)
Time period assumption (p. 11)

Multiple Choice Quiz   Answers on p. 49   mhhe.com/wildFA6e

Additional quiz questions are available at the book's Website.

1. A building is offered for sale at $500,000 but is currently assessed at $400,000. The purchaser of the building believes the building is worth $475,000, but ultimately purchases the building for $450,000. The purchaser records the building at:
  a. $50,000
  b. $400,000
  c. $450,000
  d. $475,000
  e. $500,000

2. On December 30, 2010, KPMG signs a $150,000 contract to provide accounting services to one of its clients in 2011. KPMG has a December 31 year-end. Which accounting principle or assumption requires KPMG to record the accounting services revenue from this client in 2011 and not 2010?
  a. Business entity assumption
  b. Revenue recognition principle
  c. Monetary unit assumption
  d. Cost principle
  e. Going-concern assumption

3. If the assets of a company increase by $100,000 during the year and its liabilities increase by $35,000 during the same

year, then the change in equity of the company during the year must have been:
  a. An increase of $135,000.
  b. A decrease of $135,000.
  c. A decrease of $65,000.
  d. An increase of $65,000.
  e. An increase of $100,000.

4. Brunswick borrows $50,000 cash from Third National Bank. How does this transaction affect the accounting equation for Brunswick?
  a. Assets increase by $50,000; liabilities increase by $50,000; no effect on equity.
  b. Assets increase by $50,000; no effect on liabilities; equity increases by $50,000.
  c. Assets increase by $50,000; liabilities decrease by $50,000; no effect on equity.
  d. No effect on assets; liabilities increase by $50,000; equity increases by $50,000.
  e. No effect on assets; liabilities increase by $50,000; equity decreases by $50,000.

5. **Geek Squad** performs services for a customer and bills the customer for $500. How would Geek Squad record this transaction?

    a. Accounts receivable increase by $500; revenues increase by $500.

    b. Cash increases by $500; revenues increase by $500.

    c. Accounts receivable increase by $500; revenues decrease by $500.

    d. Accounts receivable increase by $500; accounts payable increase by $500.

    e. Accounts payable increase by $500; revenues increase by $500.

A(B) *Superscript letter A (B) denotes assignments based on Appendix 1A (1B).*

🔲 Icon denotes assignments that involve decision making.

Discussion Questions

1. What is the purpose of accounting in society?

2. Technology is increasingly used to process accounting data. Why then must we study and understand accounting?

3. 🔲 Identify four kinds of external users and describe how they use accounting information.

4. 🔲 What are at least three questions business owners and managers might be able to answer by looking at accounting information?

5. Identify three actual businesses that offer services and three actual businesses that offer products.

6. 🔲 Describe the internal role of accounting for organizations.

7. Identify three types of services typically offered by accounting professionals.

8. 🔲 What type of accounting information might be useful to the marketing managers of a business?

9. Why is accounting described as a service activity?

10. What are some accounting-related professions?

11. How do ethics rules affect auditors' choice of clients?

12. What work do tax accounting professionals perform in addition to preparing tax returns?

13. What does the concept of *objectivity* imply for information reported in financial statements? Why?

14. A business reports its own office stationery on the balance sheet at its $400 cost, although it cannot be sold for more than $10 as scrap paper. Which accounting principle and/or assumption justifies this treatment?

15. Why is the revenue recognition principle needed? What does it demand?

16. Describe the three basic forms of business organization and their key attributes.

17. Define (*a*) *assets*, (*b*) *liabilities*, (*c*) *equity*, and (*d*) *net assets*.

18. What events or transactions change equity?

19. Identify the two main categories of accounting principles.

20. What do accountants mean by the term *revenue?*

21. Define *net income* and explain its computation.

22. Identify the four basic financial statements of a business.

23. 🔲 What information is reported in an income statement?

24. Give two examples of expenses a business might incur.

25. What is the purpose of the statement of retained earnings?

26. 🔲 What information is reported in a balance sheet?

27. The statement of cash flows reports on what major activities?

28. 🔲 Define and explain return on assets.

29.ᴬ🔲 Define return and risk. Discuss the trade-off between them.

30.ᴮ Describe the three major business activities in organizations.

31.ᴮ Explain why investing (assets) and financing (liabilities and equity) totals are always equal.

32. Refer to the financial statements of **Research In Motion** in Appendix A near the end of the book. To *RIM* what level of significance are dollar amounts rounded? What time period does its income statement cover?

33. Identify the dollar amounts of **Apple**'s 2009 assets, liabilities, and equity as reported in its statements in *Apple* Appendix A near the end of the book.

34. Refer to **Nokia**'s balance sheet in Appendix A *NOKIA* near the end of the book. Confirm that its total assets equal its total liabilities plus total equity.

35. 🔲 Access the SEC EDGAR database (WWW.SEC. *Palm* gov) and retrieve **Palm**'s 2009 10-K (filed July 24, 2009; ticker PALM). Identify its auditor. What responsibility does its independent auditor claim regarding Palm's financial statements?

Connect reproduces assignments online, in static or algorithmic mode, which allows instructors to monitor, promote, and assess student learning. It can be used for practice, homework, or exams.

Quick Study exercises give readers a brief test of key elements.

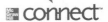

QUICK STUDY

QS 1-1

Identifying accounting terms **C1**

Reading and interpreting accounting reports requires some knowledge of accounting terminology. (*a*) Identify the meaning of these accounting-related acronyms: GAAP, SEC, FASB, IASB and IFRS. (*b*) Briefly explain the importance of the knowledge base or organization that is referred to for each of the accounting-related acronyms.

An important responsibility of many accounting professionals is to design and implement internal control procedures for organizations. Explain the purpose of internal control procedures. Provide two examples of internal controls applied by companies.

QS 1-2
Explaining internal control
C1

Identify the following users as either external users (E) or internal users (I).

a. Lenders　　　　**d.** Sales staff　　　　**g.** Brokers　　　　**j.** Managers

b. Controllers　　　**e.** FBI and IRS　　　**h.** Suppliers　　　**k.** Business press

c. Shareholders　　**f.** Consumer group　**i.** Customers　　　**l.** District attorney

QS 1-3
Identifying accounting users
C2

There are many job opportunities for those with accounting knowledge. Identify at least three main areas of opportunities for accounting professionals. For each area, identify at least three job possibilities linked to accounting.

QS 1-4
Accounting opportunities　C2

Accounting professionals must sometimes choose between two or more acceptable methods of accounting for business transactions and events. Explain why these situations can involve difficult matters of ethical concern.

QS 1-5
Identifying ethical concerns　C3
This icon highlights assignments that enhance decision-making skills.

Identify which accounting principle or assumption best describes each of the following practices:

a. If $51,000 cash is paid to buy land, the land is reported on the buyer's balance sheet at $51,000.

b. Alissa Kees owns both Sailing Passions and Dockside Supplies. In preparing financial statements for Dockside Supplies, Kees makes sure that the expense transactions of Sailing Passions are kept separate from Dockside's transactions and financial statements.

c. In December 2010, Ace Landscaping received a customer's order and cash prepayment to install sod at a new house that would not be ready for installation until March 2011. Ace should record the revenue from the customer order in March 2011, not in December 2010.

QS 1-6
Identifying accounting principles
C4

---

a. Total assets of Caldwell Company equal $40,000 and its equity is $10,000. What is the amount of its liabilities?

b. Total assets of Waterworld equal $55,000 and its liabilities and equity amounts are equal to each other. What is the amount of its liabilities? What is the amount of its equity?

QS 1-7
Applying the accounting equation
A1

Use the accounting equation to compute the missing financial statement amounts (*a*), (*b*), and (*c*).

QS 1-8
Applying the accounting equation
A1

Company	Assets	=	Liabilities	+	Equity
1	$ 30,000		$ (a)		$ 20,000
2	(b)		50,000		30,000
3	90,000		10,000		(c)

Accounting provides information about an organization's business transactions and events that both affect the accounting equation and can be reliably measured. Identify at least two examples of both (*a*) business transactions and (*b*) business events that meet these requirements.

QS 1-9
Identifying transactions and events　P1

Use **Apple**'s September 26, 2009, financial statements, in Appendix A near the end of the book, to answer the following:

a. Identify the dollar amounts of Apple's 2009 (1) assets, (2) liabilities, and (3) equity.

b. Using Apple's amounts from part *a*, verify that Assets = Liabilities + Equity.

QS 1-10
Identifying and computing assets, liabilities, and equity
P1

QS 1-11
Computing and interpreting return on assets

A2

In a recent year's financial statements, **Home Depot** reported the following results. Compute and interpret Home Depot's return on assets (assume competitors average a 5% return on assets).

Sales	$71,288 million
Net income	2,260 million
Average total assets	42,744 million

QS 1-12
Identifying items with financial statements

P2

Indicate in which financial statement each item would most likely appear: income statement (I), balance sheet (B), statement of retained earnings (RE), or statement of cash flows (CF).

a. Assets
b. Revenues
c. Liabilities
d. Equipment
e. Dividends
f. Expenses
g. Total liabilities and equity
h. Cash from operating activities
i. Net decrease (or increase) in cash

QS 1-13
International accounting standards C4

This icon highlights assignments that focus on IFRS-related content.

Answer each of the following questions related to international accounting standards.

a. The International Accounting Standards Board (IASB) issues preferred accounting practices that are referred to as what?
b. The FASB and IASB are working on a convergence process for what purpose?
c. The SEC has proposed a roadmap for use of IFRS by U.S. companies. What is the proposed adoption date for large U.S. companies to adopt IFRS?

■ connect

EXERCISES

Exercise 1-1
Classifying activities reflected in the accounting system

C1

Accounting is an information and measurement system that identifies, records, and communicates relevant, reliable, and comparable information about an organization's business activities. Classify the following activities as part of the identifying (I), recording (R), or communicating (C) aspects of accounting.

_____ **1.** Determining employee tasks behind a service.
_____ **2.** Establishing revenues generated from a product.
_____ **3.** Maintaining a log of service costs.
_____ **4.** Measuring the costs of a product.
_____ **5.** Preparing financial statements.
_____ **6.** Analyzing and interpreting reports.
_____ **7.** Presenting financial information.

Exercise 1-2
Identifying accounting users and uses

C2

Part A. Identify the following users of accounting information as either an internal (I) or an external (E) user.

_____ **1.** Shareholders
_____ **2.** Creditors
_____ **3.** Nonexecutive employee
_____ **4.** Research and development director
_____ **5.** Purchasing manager
_____ **6.** Human resources director
_____ **7.** Production supervisors
_____ **8.** Distribution managers

Part B. Identify the following questions as most likely to be asked by an internal (I) or an external (E) user of accounting information.

_____ **1.** What are the costs of our service to customers?
_____ **2.** Should we make a five-year loan to that business?
_____ **3.** Should we spend further research on our product?
_____ **4.** Do income levels justify the current stock price?
_____ **5.** What are reasonable payroll benefits and wages?
_____ **6.** Which firm reports the highest sales and income?
_____ **7.** What are the costs of our product's ingredients?

Exercise 1-3
Describing accounting responsibilities

C2

Many accounting professionals work in one of the following three areas:

A. Managerial accounting   **B.** Financial accounting   **C.** Tax accounting

Identify the area of accounting that is most involved in each of the following responsibilities:

_____ **1.** Reviewing reports for SEC compliance.
_____ **2.** Planning transactions to minimize taxes.
_____ **3.** Investigating violations of tax laws.
_____ **4.** Preparing external financial statements.
_____ **5.** Budgeting.
_____ **6.** Cost accounting.
_____ **7.** External auditing.
_____ **8.** Internal auditing.

Assume the following role and describe a situation in which ethical considerations play an important part in guiding your decisions and actions:

a. You are a student in an introductory accounting course.

b. You are an accounting professional with audit clients that are competitors in business.

c. You are an accounting professional preparing tax returns for clients.

d. You are a manager with responsibility for several employees.

Exercise 1-4
Identifying ethical concerns
C3

Match each of the numbered descriptions with the term or phrase it best reflects. Indicate your answer by writing the letter for the term or phrase in the blank provided.

A. Audit   **C.** Ethics   **E.** SEC   **G.** Net income

B. GAAP   **D.** Tax accounting   **F.** Public accountants   **H.** IASB

_____ **1.** Amount a business earns after paying all expenses and costs associated with its sales and revenues.

_____ **2.** An examination of an organization's accounting system and records that adds credibility to financial statements.

_____ **3.** Principles that determine whether an action is right or wrong.

_____ **4.** Accounting professionals who provide services to many clients.

_____ **5.** An accounting area that includes planning future transactions to minimize taxes paid.

Exercise 1-5
Learning the language
of business
C1–C3

Match each of the numbered descriptions with the principle or assumption it best reflects. Enter the letter for the appropriate principle or assumption in the blank space next to each description.

A. Cost principle   **E.** General accounting principle

B. Matching principle   **F.** Business entity assumption

C. Specific accounting principle   **G.** Revenue recognition principle

D. Full disclosure principle   **H.** Going-concern assumption

_____ **1.** Revenue is recorded only when the earnings process is complete.

_____ **2.** Information is based on actual costs incurred in transactions.

_____ **3.** Usually created by a pronouncement from an authoritative body.

_____ **4.** Financial statements reflect the assumption that the business continues operating.

_____ **5.** A company reports details behind financial statements that would impact users' decisions.

_____ **6.** A company records the expenses incurred to generate the revenues reported.

_____ **7.** Derived from long-used and generally accepted accounting practices.

_____ **8.** Every business is accounted for separately from its owner or owners.

Exercise 1-6
Identifying accounting principles
and assumptions
C4

The following describe several different business organizations. Determine whether the description refers to a sole proprietorship, partnership, or corporation.

a. A-1 pays its own income taxes and has two owners.

b. Ownership of Zeller Company is divided into 1,000 shares of stock.

c. Waldron is owned by Mary Malone, who is personally liable for the company's debts.

d. Micah Douglas and Nathan Logan own Financial Services, a financial services provider. Neither Douglas nor Logan has personal responsibility for the debts of Financial Services.

e. Bailey and Kay own Squeaky Clean, a cleaning service. Both are personally liable for the debts of the business.

f. Plasto Products does not pay income taxes and has one owner.

g. Ian LLC does not have separate legal existence apart from the one person who owns it.

Exercise 1-7
Distinguishing business
organizations
C4

Answer the following questions. (*Hint:* Use the accounting equation.)

a. Office Mart has assets equal to $123,000 and liabilities equal to $53,000 at year-end. What is the total equity for Office Mart at year-end?

b. At the beginning of the year, Logan Company's assets are $200,000 and its equity is $150,000. During the year, assets increase $70,000 and liabilities increase $30,000. What is the equity at the end of the year?

c. At the beginning of the year, Keller Company's liabilities equal $60,000. During the year, assets increase by $80,000, and at year-end assets equal $180,000. Liabilities decrease $10,000 during the year. What are the beginning and ending amounts of equity?

Exercise 1-8
Using the accounting
equation
A1 P1

Check (c) Beg. equity, $40,000

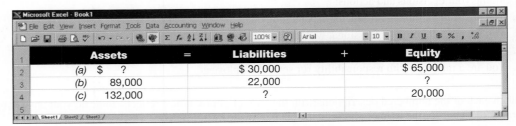
Exercise 1-9

Using the accounting equation

A1

Determine the missing amount from each of the separate situations a, b, and c below.

	Assets	=	Liabilities	+	Equity
(a)	$?		$ 30,000		$ 65,000
(b)	89,000		22,000		?
(c)	132,000		?		20,000

Exercise 1-10

Identifying effects of transactions on the accounting equation

P1

Provide an example of a transaction that creates the described effects for the separate cases a through g.

a. Increases an asset and decreases an asset.
b. Decreases an asset and decreases a liability.
c. Decreases a liability and increases a liability.
d. Increases an asset and increases a liability.

e. Decreases an asset and decreases equity.
f. Increases a liability and decreases equity.
g. Increases an asset and increases equity.

Exercise 1-11

Identifying effects of transactions using the accounting equation

P1

Lena Gold began a professional practice on June 1 and plans to prepare financial statements at the end of each month. During June, Gold (the owner) completed these transactions:

a. Owner invested $50,000 cash in the company along with equipment that had a $10,000 market value in exchange for common stock.
b. The company paid $1,600 cash for rent of office space for the month.
c. The company purchased $12,000 of additional equipment on credit (payment due within 30 days).
d. The company completed work for a client and immediately collected the $2,000 cash earned.
e. The company completed work for a client and sent a bill for $7,000 to be received within 30 days.
f. The company purchased additional equipment for $8,000 cash.
g. The company paid an assistant $2,400 cash as wages for the month.
h. The company collected $5,000 cash as a partial payment for the amount owed by the client in transaction e.
i. The company paid $12,000 cash to settle the liability created in transaction c.
j. The company paid $500 cash for dividends.

Required

Check   Net income, $5,000

Create a table like the one in Exhibit 1.9, using the following headings for columns: Cash; Accounts Receivable; Equipment; Accounts Payable; Common Stock; Dividends; Revenues; and Expenses. Then use additions and subtractions to show the effects of the transactions on individual items of the accounting equation. Show new balances after each transaction.

Exercise 1-12

Analysis using the accounting equation

P1

Zelda began a new consulting firm on January 5. The accounting equation showed the following balances after each of the company's first five transactions. Analyze the accounting equation for each transaction and describe each of the five transactions with their amounts.

	Assets						=	Liabilities	+	Equity		
Trans-action	Cash	+	Accounts Receiv-able	+	Office Sup-plies	+	Office Furni-ture	=	Accounts Payable	+	Common Stock	+	Revenues
a.	$20,000	+	$ 0	+	$ 0	+	$ 0	=	$ 0	+	$20,000	+	$ 0
b.	19,000	+	0	+	1,500	+	0	=	500	+	20,000	+	0
c.	11,000	+	0	+	1,500	+	8,000	=	500	+	20,000	+	0
d.	11,000	+	3,000	+	1,500	+	8,000	=	500	+	20,000	+	3,000
e.	11,500	+	3,000	+	1,500	+	8,000	=	500	+	20,000	+	3,500

The following table shows the effects of five transactions (*a* through *e*) on the assets, liabilities, and equity of Vera's Boutique. Write short descriptions of the probable nature of each transaction.

Exercise 1-13
Identifying effects of
transactions on accounting
equation
P1

	Assets								=	Liabilities	+		Equity			
	Cash	+	Accounts Receivable	+	Office Supplies	+	Land		=	Accounts Payable	+	Common Stock	+	Revenues	
	$ 10,500	+	$ 0	+	$1,500	+	$ 9,500		=	$ 0	+	$21,500	+	$ 0	
a.	− 2,000					+	2,000								
b.				+	500					+500					
c.		+	950										+	950	
d.	− 500									−500					
e.	+ 950	−	950												
	$ 8,950	+	$ 0	+	$2,000	+	$11,500		=	$ 0	+	$21,500	+	$950	

On October 1, Natalie King organized Real Solutions, a new consulting firm. On October 31, the company's records show the following items and amounts. Use this information to prepare an October income statement for the business.

Cash	$ 2,000	Cash dividends	$ 3,360
Accounts receivable	13,000	Consulting fees earned	15,000
Office supplies	4,250	Rent expense	2,550
Land	36,000	Salaries expense	6,000
Office equipment	28,000	Telephone expense	660
Accounts payable	7,500	Miscellaneous expenses	680
Common stock	74,000		

Check Net income, $5,110

Use the information in Exercise 1-14 to prepare an October statement of retained earnings for Real Solutions.

Exercise 1-15
Preparing a statement of
retained earnings P2

Use the information in Exercise 1-14 (if completed, you can also use your solution to Exercise 1-15) to prepare an October 31 balance sheet for Real Solutions.

Use the information in Exercise 1-14 to prepare an October 31 statement of cash flows for Real Solutions. Also assume the following:

a. The owner's initial investment consists of $38,000 cash and $36,000 in land in exchange for common stock.

b. The company's $28,000 equipment purchase is paid in cash.

c. The accounts payable balance of $7,500 consists of the $4,250 office supplies purchase and $3,250 in employee salaries yet to be paid.

d. The company's rent, telephone, and miscellaneous expenses are paid in cash.

e. $2,000 has been collected on the $15,000 consulting fees earned.

Check Net increase in cash, $2,000

Geneva Group reports net income of $20,000 for 2011. At the beginning of 2011, Geneva Group had $100,000 in assets. By the end of 2011, assets had grown to $150,000. What is Geneva Group's 2011 return on assets? How would you assess its performance if competitors average a 10% return on assets?

Indicate the section where each of the following would appear on the statement of cash flows.

A. Cash flows from operating activity

B. Cash flows from investing activity

C. Cash flows from financing activity

_____ **1.** Cash paid for wages

_____ **2.** Cash paid for dividends

_____ **3.** Cash purchase of equipment

_____ **4.** Cash paid for advertising

_____ **5.** Cash paid on an account payable

_____ **6.** Cash received from stock issued

_____ **7.** Cash received from clients

_____ **8.** Cash paid for rent

Exercise 1-19
Identifying sections of the
statement of cash flows
P2

Exercise 1-20^B

Identifying business activities

C5

Match each transaction or event to one of the following activities of an organization: financing activities (F), investing activities (I), or operating activities (O).

1. _____ An owner contributes resources to the business in exchange for stock.
2. _____ An organization purchases equipment.
3. _____ An organization advertises a new product.
4. _____ The organization borrows money from a bank.
5. _____ An organization sells some of its land.

Exercise 1-21

Preparing an income statement for a global company

P2

Nintendo Company reports the following income statement accounts for the year ended March 31, 2009. (Japanese yen in millions.)

Net sales	¥1,838,622
Cost of sales	1,044,981
Selling, general and administrative expenses	238,378
Other expenses	276,174

Use this information to prepare Nintendo's income statement for the year ended March 31, 2009.

Problem Set B located at the end of Problem Set A is provided for <u>each</u> problem to reinforce the learning process.

PROBLEM SET A

Problem 1-1A

Identifying effects of transactions on financial statements

A1 P1

Identify how each of the following separate transactions affects financial statements. For the balance sheet, identify how each transaction affects total assets, total liabilities, and total equity. For the income statement, identify how each transaction affects net income. For the statement of cash flows, identify how each transaction affects cash flows from operating activities, cash flows from financing activities, and cash flows from investing activities. For increases, place a "+" in the column or columns. For decreases, place a "−" in the column or columns. If both an increase and a decrease occur, place a "+/−" in the column or columns. The first transaction is completed as an example.

		Balance Sheet			Income Statement	Statement of Cash Flows		
	Transaction	Total Assets	Total Liab.	Total Equity	Net Income	Operating Activities	Financing Activities	Investing Activities
1	Owner invests cash for stock	+		+			+	
2	Incurs legal costs on credit							
3	Pays cash for employee wages							
4	Borrows cash by signing long-term note payable							
5	Receives cash for services provided							
6	Buys land by signing note payable							
7	Buys office equipment for cash							
8	Provides services on credit							
9	Collects cash on receivable from (8)							
10	Pays cash dividend							

The following financial statement information is from five separate companies:

	Company A	Company B	Company C	Company D	Company E
December 31, 2010					
Assets........................	$45,000	$35,000	$29,000	$80,000	$123,000
Liabilities	23,500	22,500	14,000	38,000	?
December 31, 2011					
Assets........................	48,000	41,000	?	125,000	112,500
Liabilities	?	27,500	19,000	64,000	75,000
During year 2011					
Stock issuances	5,000	1,500	7,750	?	4,500
Net income (loss)	7,500	?	9,000	12,000	18,000
Cash dividends	2,500	3,000	3,875	0	9,000

Problem 1-2A
Computing missing information using accounting knowledge
A1 P1

Required

1. Answer the following questions about Company A:
   a. What is the amount of equity on December 31, 2010?
   b. What is the amount of equity on December 31, 2011?
   c. What is the amount of liabilities on December 31, 2011?
2. Answer the following questions about Company B:
   a. What is the amount of equity on December 31, 2010?
   b. What is the amount of equity on December 31, 2011?
   c. What is net income for year 2011?
3. Calculate the amount of assets for Company C on December 31, 2011.
4. Calculate the amount of stock issuances for Company D during year 2011.
5. Calculate the amount of liabilities for Company E on December 31, 2010.

Check   (1*b*) $31,500

(2*c*) $2,500
(3) $46,875

The following is selected financial information for Affiliated Company as of December 31, 2011: liabilities, $34,000; equity, $56,000; assets, $90,000.

Required

Prepare the balance sheet for Affiliated Company as of December 31, 2011.

Problem 1-3A
Preparing a balance sheet
P2

The following is selected financial information for Sun Energy Company for the year ended December 31, 2011: revenues, $65,000; expenses, $50,000; net income, $15,000.

Required

Prepare the 2011 calendar-year income statement for Sun Energy Company.

Problem 1-4A
Preparing an income statement
P2

Following is selected financial information for Boardwalk for the year ended December 31, 2011.

Retained earnings, Dec. 31, 2011........	$15,000	Cash dividends	$2,000
Net income	9,000	Retained earnings, Dec. 31, 2010	8,000

Problem 1-5A
Preparing a statement of retained earnings
P2

Required

Prepare the 2011 statement of retained earnings for Boardwalk.

Problem 1-6A

Preparing a statement of cash flows

P2

Following is selected financial information of Trimark for the year ended December 31, 2011.

Cash used by investing activities	$(3,000)
Net increase in cash	200
Cash used by financing activities	(3,800)
Cash from operating activities	7,000
Cash, December 31, 2010	3,300

Check Cash balance, Dec. 31, 2011, $3,500

Required

Prepare the 2011 statement of cash flows for Trimark Company.

Problem 1-7A

Analyzing effects of transactions

C4 P1 P2 A1

Miranda Right started Right Consulting, a new business, and completed the following transactions during its first year of operations.

a. M. Right invests $60,000 cash and office equipment valued at $30,000 in the company in exchange for common stock.

b. The company purchased a $300,000 building to use as an office. Right paid $50,000 in cash and signed a note payable promising to pay the $250,000 balance over the next 10 years.

c. The company purchased office equipment for $6,000 cash.

d. The company purchased $4,000 of office supplies and $1,000 of office equipment on credit.

e. The company paid a local newspaper $1,000 cash for printing an announcement of the office's opening.

f. The company completed a financial plan for a client and billed that client $4,000 for the service.

g. The company designed a financial plan for another client and immediately collected an $8,000 cash fee.

h. The company paid $1,800 cash for dividends.

i. The company received $3,000 cash as partial payment from the client described in transaction *f*.

j. The company made a partial payment of $500 cash on the equipment purchased in transaction *d*.

k. The company paid $2,500 cash for the office secretary's wages for this period.

Required

1. Create a table like the one in Exhibit 1.9, using the following headings for the columns: Cash; Accounts Receivable; Office Supplies; Office Equipment; Building; Accounts Payable; Notes Payable; Common Stock; Dividends; Revenues; and Expenses.

Check (2) Ending balances: Cash, $9,200; Expenses, $3,500; Notes Payable, $250,000

(3) Net income, $8,500

2. Use additions and subtractions within the table created in part 1 to show the dollar effects of each transaction on individual items of the accounting equation. Show new balances after each transaction.

3. Once you have completed the table, determine the company's net income.

Problem 1-8A

Analyzing transactions and preparing financial statements

C4 P1 P2

mhhe.com/wildFA6e

J. D. Simpson started The Simpson Co., a new business that began operations on May 1. The Simpson Co. completed the following transactions during its first month of operations.

May	1	J. D. Simpson invested $60,000 cash in the company in exchange for common stock.
	1	The company rented a furnished office and paid $3,200 cash for May's rent.
	3	The company purchased $1,680 of office equipment on credit.
	5	The company paid $800 cash for this month's cleaning services.
	8	The company provided consulting services for a client and immediately collected $4,600 cash.
	12	The company provided $3,000 of consulting services for a client on credit.
	15	The company paid $850 cash for an assistant's salary for the first half of this month.
	20	The company received $3,000 cash payment for the services provided on May 12.
	22	The company provided $2,800 of consulting services on credit.
	25	The company received $2,800 cash payment for the services provided on May 22.
	26	The company paid $1,680 cash for the office equipment purchased on May 3.
	27	The company purchased $60 of advertising in this month's (May) local paper on credit; cash payment is due June 1.
	28	The company paid $850 cash for an assistant's salary for the second half of this month.
	30	The company paid $200 cash for this month's telephone bill.
	30	The company paid $480 cash for this month's utilities.
	31	The company paid $1,200 cash for dividends.

Required

1. Arrange the following asset, liability, and equity titles in a table like Exhibit 1.9: Cash; Accounts Receivable; Office Equipment; Accounts Payable; Common Stock; Dividends; Revenues; and Expenses.

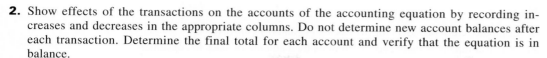

2. Show effects of the transactions on the accounts of the accounting equation by recording increases and decreases in the appropriate columns. Do not determine new account balances after each transaction. Determine the final total for each account and verify that the equation is in balance.

3. Prepare an income statement for May, a statement of retained earnings for May, a May 31 balance sheet, and a statement of cash flows for May.

Check   (2) Ending balances: Cash, $61,140; Expenses, $6,440

(3) Net income, $3,960; Total assets, $62,820

Curtis Hamilton started a new business and completed these transactions during December.

Dec. 1   Curtis Hamilton transferred $56,000 cash from a personal savings account to a checking account in the name of Hamilton Electric in exchange for common stock.
2   The company rented office space and paid $800 cash for the December rent.
3   The company purchased $14,000 of electrical equipment by paying $3,200 cash and agreeing to pay the $10,800 balance in 30 days.
5   The company purchased office supplies by paying $900 cash.
6   The company completed electrical work and immediately collected $1,000 cash for these services.
8   The company purchased $3,800 of office equipment on credit.
15   The company completed electrical work on credit in the amount of $4,000.
18   The company purchased $500 of office supplies on credit.
20   The company paid $3,800 cash for the office equipment purchased on December 8.
24   The company billed a client $600 for electrical work completed; the balance is due in 30 days.
28   The company received $4,000 cash for the work completed on December 15.
29   The company paid the assistant's salary of $1,200 cash for this month.
30   The company paid $440 cash for this month's utility bill.
31   The company paid $700 cash for dividends.

Problem 1-9A

Analyzing transactions and preparing financial statements

C4 P1 P2

mhhe.com/wildFA6e

Required

1. Arrange the following asset, liability, and equity titles in a table like Exhibit 1.9: Cash; Accounts Receivable; Office Supplies; Office Equipment; Electrical Equipment; Accounts Payable; Common Stock; Dividends; Revenues; and Expenses.

2. Use additions and subtractions to show the effects of each transaction on the accounts in the accounting equation. Show new balances after each transaction.

3. Use the increases and decreases in the columns of the table from part 2 to prepare an income statement, a statement of retained earnings, and a statement of cash flows—each of these for the current month. Also prepare a balance sheet as of the end of the month.

Check   (2) Ending balances: Cash, $49,960, Accounts Payable, $11,300

(3) Net income, $3,160; Total assets, $69,760

Analysis Component

4. Assume that the owner investment transaction on December 1 was $40,000 cash instead of $56,000 and that Hamilton Electric obtained another $16,000 in cash by borrowing it from a bank. Explain the effect of this change on total assets, total liabilities, and total equity.

Nolan manufactures, markets, and sells cellular telephones. The average total assets for Nolan is $250,000. In its most recent year, Nolan reported net income of $55,000 on revenues of $455,000.

Required

1. What is Nolan's return on assets?

2. Does return on assets seem satisfactory for Nolan given that its competitors average a 12% return on assets?

3. What are total expenses for Nolan in its most recent year?

4. What is the average total amount of liabilities plus equity for Nolan?

Problem 1-10A

Determining expenses, liabilities, equity, and return on assets

A1 A2

Check   (3) $400,000

(4) $250,000

Coca-Cola and PepsiCo both produce and market beverages that are direct competitors. Key financial figures (in $ millions) for these businesses over the past year follow.

Key Figures ($ millions)	Coca-Cola	PepsiCo
Sales	$30,990	$43,232
Net income	6,906	5,979
Average assets	44,595	37,921

Problem 1-11A

Computing and interpreting return on assets

A2

Check (1*a*) 15.5%; (1*b*) 15.8%

Required

1. Compute return on assets for (*a*) Coca-Cola and (*b*) PepsiCo.
2. Which company is more successful in its total amount of sales to consumers?
3. Which company is more successful in returning net income from its assets invested?

Analysis Component

4. Write a one-paragraph memorandum explaining which company you would invest your money in and why. (Limit your explanation to the information provided.)

Problem 1-12A^A

Identifying risk and return

A3 ♟

All business decisions involve aspects of risk and return.

Required

Identify both the risk and the return in each of the following activities:

1. Investing $1,000 in a 4% savings account.
2. Placing a $1,000 bet on your favorite sports team.
3. Investing $10,000 in Yahoo! stock.
4. Taking out a $10,000 college loan to earn an accounting degree.

Problem 1-13A^B

Describing organizational activities   C5

An organization undertakes various activities in pursuit of business success. Identify an organization's three major business activities, and describe each activity.

Problem 1-14A^B

Describing organizational activities

C5

A start-up company often engages in the following transactions in its first year of operations. Classify those transactions in one of the three major categories of an organization's business activities.

F. Financing   **I.** Investing   **O.** Operating

_____ **1.** Owner investing land in business.   _____ **5.** Purchasing equipment.
_____ **2.** Purchasing a building.   _____ **6.** Selling and distributing products.
_____ **3.** Purchasing land.   _____ **7.** Paying for advertising.
_____ **4.** Borrowing cash from a bank.   _____ **8.** Paying employee wages.

PROBLEM SET B

Problem 1-1B

Identifying effects of transactions on financial statements   A1 P1 ♟

Identify how each of the following separate transactions affects financial statements. For the balance sheet, identify how each transaction affects total assets, total liabilities, and total equity. For the income statement, identify how each transaction affects net income. For the statement of cash flows, identify how each transaction affects cash flows from operating activities, cash flows from financing activities, and cash flows from investing activities. For increases, place a "+" in the column or columns. For decreases, place a "−" in the column or columns. If both an increase and a decrease occur, place "+/−" in the column or columns. The first transaction is completed as an example.

	Transaction	Balance Sheet Total Assets	Balance Sheet Total Liab.	Balance Sheet Total Equity	Income Statement Net Income	Statement of Cash Flows Operating Activities	Statement of Cash Flows Financing Activities	Statement of Cash Flows Investing Activities
I	Owner invests cash for stock	+		+			+	
2	Buys building by signing note payable							
3	Pays cash for salaries incurred							
4	Provides services for cash							
5	Pays cash for rent incurred							
6	Incurs utilities costs on credit							
7	Buys store equipment for cash							
8	Pays cash dividend							
9	Provides services on credit							
10	Collects cash on receivable from (9)							

The following financial statement information is from five separate companies.

	Company V	Company W	Company X	Company Y	Company Z
December 31, 2010					
Assets........................	$45,000	$70,000	$121,500	$82,500	$124,000
Liabilities	30,000	50,000	58,500	61,500	?
December 31, 2011					
Assets........................	49,000	90,000	136,500	?	160,000
Liabilities	26,000	?	55,500	72,000	52,000
During year 2011					
Stock issuances	6,000	10,000	?	38,100	40,000
Net income or (loss)............	?	30,000	16,500	24,000	32,000
Cash dividends	4,500	2,000	0	18,000	6,000

Required

1. Answer the following questions about Company V:
   a. What is the amount of equity on December 31, 2010?
   b. What is the amount of equity on December 31, 2011?
   c. What is the net income or loss for the year 2011?
2. Answer the following questions about Company W:
   a. What is the amount of equity on December 31, 2010?
   b. What is the amount of equity on December 31, 2011?
   c. What is the amount of liabilities on December 31, 2011?
3. Calculate the amount of stock issuances for Company X during 2011.
4. Calculate the amount of assets for Company Y on December 31, 2011.
5. Calculate the amount of liabilities for Company Z on December 31, 2010.

Check   (1*b*) $23,000

(2*c*) $32,000

(4) $137,100

The following is selected financial information for RWB Company as of December 31, 2011.

Liabilities	$74,000	Equity	$40,000	Assets	$114,000

Required

Prepare the balance sheet for RWB Company as of December 31, 2011.

Selected financial information for Online Company for the year ended December 31, 2011, follows.

Revenues	$58,000	Expenses	$30,000	Net income	$28,000

Required

Prepare the 2011 income statement for Online Company.

Following is selected financial information of ComEx for the year ended December 31, 2011.

Retained earnings, Dec. 31, 2011	$47,000	Cash dividends	$ 8,000
Net income	6,000	Retained earnings, Dec. 31, 2010	49,000

Required

Prepare the 2011 statement of retained earnings for ComEx.

Problem 1-6B
Preparing a statement of cash flows
P2

Selected financial information of BuyRight Company for the year ended December 31, 2011, follows.

Cash from investing activities	$2,600
Net increase in cash	1,400
Cash from financing activities	2,800
Cash used by operating activities	(4,000)
Cash, December 31, 2010	1,300

Required

Prepare the 2011 statement of cash flows for BuyRight Company.

Problem 1-7B
Analyzing effects of transactions
C4 P1 P2 A1

Tiana Moore started a new business, Tiana's Solutions, and completed the following transactions during its first year of operations.

a. T. Moore invests $95,000 cash and office equipment valued at $20,000 in the company in exchange for common stock.

b. The company purchased a $120,000 building to use as an office. It paid $20,000 in cash and signed a note payable promising to pay the $100,000 balance over the next 10 years.

c. The company purchased office equipment for $20,000 cash.

d. The company purchased $1,400 of office supplies and $3,000 of office equipment on credit.

e. The company paid a local newspaper $400 cash for printing an announcement of the office's opening.

f. The company completed a financial plan for a client and billed that client $1,800 for the service.

g. The company designed a financial plan for another client and immediately collected a $2,000 cash fee.

h. The company paid $5,000 cash for dividends.

i. The company received $1,800 cash from the client described in transaction f.

j. The company made a payment of $2,000 cash on the equipment purchased in transaction d.

k. The company paid $2,000 cash for the office secretary's wages.

Required

1. Create a table like the one in Exhibit 1.9, using the following headings for the columns: Cash; Accounts Receivable; Office Supplies; Office Equipment; Building; Accounts Payable; Notes Payable; Common Stock; Dividends; Revenues; and Expenses.

Check (2) Ending balances: Cash, $49,400; Expenses, $2,400; Notes Payable, $100,000

(3) Net income, $1,400

2. Use additions and subtractions within the table created in part 1 to show the dollar effects of each transaction on individual items of the accounting equation. Show new balances after each transaction.

3. Once you have completed the table, determine the company's net income.

Problem 1-8B
Analyzing transactions and preparing financial statements
C4 P1 P2

Ken Stone launched a new business, Ken's Maintenance Co., that began operations on June 1. The following transactions were completed by the company during that first month.

June	1	K. Stone invested $120,000 cash in the company in exchange for common stock.
	2	The company rented a furnished office and paid $4,500 cash for June's rent.
	4	The company purchased $2,400 of equipment on credit.
	6	The company paid $1,125 cash for this month's advertising of the opening of the business.
	8	The company completed maintenance services for a customer and immediately collected $750 cash.
	14	The company completed $6,300 of maintenance services for City Center on credit.
	16	The company paid $900 cash for an assistant's salary for the first half of the month.
	20	The company received $6,300 cash payment for services completed for City Center on June 14.
	21	The company completed $3,500 of maintenance services for Skyway Co. on credit.
	24	The company completed $825 of maintenance services for Comfort Motel on credit.
	25	The company received $3,500 cash payment from Skyway Co. for the work completed on June 21.
	26	The company made payment of $2,400 cash for equipment purchased on June 4.
	28	The company paid $900 cash for an assistant's salary for the second half of this month.
	29	The company paid $2,000 cash for dividends.
	30	The company paid $120 cash for this month's telephone bill.
	30	The company paid $525 cash for this month's utilities.

Required

1. Arrange the following asset, liability, and equity titles in a table like Exhibit 1.9: Cash; Accounts Receivable; Equipment; Accounts Payable; Common Stock; Dividends; Revenues; and Expenses.

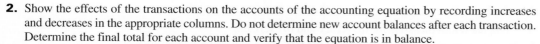

2. Show the effects of the transactions on the accounts of the accounting equation by recording increases and decreases in the appropriate columns. Do not determine new account balances after each transaction. Determine the final total for each account and verify that the equation is in balance.

3. Prepare a June income statement, a June statement of retained earnings, a June 30 balance sheet, and a June statement of cash flows.

Check   (2) Ending balances: Cash, $118,080; Expenses, $8,070

(3) Net income, $3,305; Total assets, $121,305

Swender Excavating Co., owned by Patrick Swender, began operations in July and completed these transactions during that first month of operations.

Problem 1-9B

Analyzing transactions and preparing financial statements

C4 P1 P2

July 1   P. Swender invested $60,000 cash in the company in exchange for common stock.
2   The company rented office space and paid $500 cash for the July rent.
3   The company purchased excavating equipment for $4,000 by paying $800 cash and agreeing to pay the $3,200 balance in 30 days.
6   The company purchased office supplies for $500 cash.
8   The company completed work for a customer and immediately collected $2,200 cash for the work.
10   The company purchased $3,800 of office equipment on credit.
15   The company completed work for a customer on credit in the amount of $2,400.
17   The company purchased $1,920 of office supplies on credit.
23   The company paid $3,800 cash for the office equipment purchased on July 10.
25   The company billed a customer $5,000 for work completed; the balance is due in 30 days.
28   The company received $2,400 cash for the work completed on July 15.
30   The company paid an assistant's salary of $1,260 cash for this month.
31   The company paid $260 cash for this month's utility bill.
31   The company paid $1,200 cash for dividends.

Required

1. Arrange the following asset, liability, and equity titles in a table like Exhibit 1.9: Cash; Accounts Receivable; Office Supplies; Office Equipment; Excavating Equipment; Accounts Payable; Common Stock; Dividends; Revenues; and Expenses.

2. Use additions and subtractions to show the effects of each transaction on the accounts in the accounting equation. Show new balances after each transaction.

Check   (2) Ending balances: Cash, $56,280; Accounts Payable, $5,120

(3) Net income, $7,580; Total assets, $71,500

3. Use the increases and decreases in the columns of the table from part 2 to prepare an income statement, a statement of retained earnings, and a statement of cash flows—each of these for the current month. Also prepare a balance sheet as of the end of the month.

Analysis Component

4. Assume that the $4,000 purchase of excavating equipment on July 3 was financed from an owner investment of another $4,000 cash in the business in exchange for more common stock (instead of the purchase conditions described in the transaction). Explain the effect of this change on total assets, total liabilities, and total equity.

Aspen Company manufactures, markets, and sells ATV and snowmobile equipment and accessories. The average total assets for Aspen is $2,000,000. In its most recent year, Aspen reported net income of $100,000 on revenues of $1,200,000.

Problem 1-10B

Determining expenses, liabilities, equity, and return on assets

A1 A2

Required

1. What is Aspen Company's return on assets?

2. Does return on assets seem satisfactory for Aspen given that its competitors average a 9.5% return on assets?

3. What are the total expenses for Aspen Company in its most recent year?

4. What is the average total amount of liabilities plus equity for Aspen Company?

Check   (3) $1,100,000

(4) $2,000,000

AT&T and Verizon produce and market telecommunications products and are competitors. Key financial figures (in $ millions) for these businesses over the past year follow.

Problem 1-11B

Computing and interpreting return on assets

A2

Key Figures ($ millions)	AT&T	Verizon
Sales	$123,018	$107,808
Net income	12,535	10,358
Average assets	266,999	214,937

Check (1*a*) 4.7%; (1*b*) 4.8%

Required

1. Compute return on assets for (*a*) AT&T and (*b*) Verizon.
2. Which company is more successful in the total amount of sales to consumers?
3. Which company is more successful in returning net income from its assets invested?

Analysis Component

4. Write a one-paragraph memorandum explaining which company you would invest your money in and why. (Limit your explanation to the information provided.)

Problem 1-12B^A
Identifying risk and return

A3

All business decisions involve aspects of risk and return.

Required

Identify both the risk and the return in each of the following activities:

1. Stashing $1,000 cash under your mattress.
2. Placing a $500 bet on a horse running in the Kentucky Derby.
3. Investing $10,000 in Nike stock.
4. Investing $10,000 in U.S. Savings Bonds.

Problem 1-13B^B
Describing organizational activities C5

Identify in outline format the three major business activities of an organization. For each of these activities, identify at least two specific transactions or events normally undertaken by the business's owners or its managers.

Problem 1-14B^B
Describing organizational activities

C5

A start-up company often engages in the following activities during its first year of operations. Classify each of the following activities into one of the three major activities of an organization.

A. Financing   **B.** Investing   **C.** Operating

_____ **1.** Providing client services.   _____ **5.** Supervising workers.
_____ **2.** Obtaining a bank loan.   _____ **6.** Owner investing money in business.
_____ **3.** Purchasing machinery.   _____ **7.** Renting office space.
_____ **4.** Research for its products.   _____ **8.** Paying utilities expenses.

This serial problem starts in this chapter and continues throughout most chapters of the book. It is most readily solved if you use the Working Papers that accompany this book (but working papers are not required).

SERIAL PROBLEM
Business Solutions

C4 P1

SP 1 On October 1, 2011, Santana Rey launched a computer services company, **Business Solutions,** that is organized as a corporation and provides consulting services, computer system installations, and custom program development. Rey adopts the calendar year for reporting purposes and expects to prepare the company's first set of financial statements on December 31, 2011.

Required

Create a table like the one in Exhibit 1.9 using the following headings for columns: Cash; Accounts Receivable; Computer Supplies; Computer System; Office Equipment; Accounts Payable; Common Stock; Dividends; Revenues; and Expenses. Then use additions and subtractions within the table created to show the dollar effects for each of the following October transactions for Business Solutions on the individual items of the accounting equation. Show new balances after each transaction.

Oct. 1 S. Rey invested $45,000 cash, a $20,000 computer system, and $8,000 of office equipment in the company in exchange for common stock.
    3 The company purchased $1,420 of computer supplies on credit from Harris Office Products.
    6 The company billed Easy Leasing $4,800 for services performed in installing a new Web server.
    8 The company paid $1,420 cash for the computer supplies purchased from Harris Office Products on October 3.
   10 The company hired Lyn Addie as a part-time assistant for $125 per day, as needed.
   12 The company billed Easy Leasing another $1,400 for services performed.
   15 The company received $4,800 cash from Easy Leasing as partial payment toward its account.
   17 The company paid $805 cash to repair computer equipment damaged when moving it.
   20 The company paid $1,728 cash for advertisements published in the local newspaper.
   22 The company received $1,400 cash from Easy Leasing toward its account.
   28 The company billed IFM Company $5,208 for services performed.
   31 The company paid $875 cash for Lyn Addie's wages for seven days of work this month.
   31 The company paid $3,600 cash for dividends.

Check Ending balances: Cash, $42,772; Revenues, $11,408; Expenses, $3,408

Beyond the Numbers (BTN) is a special problem section aimed to refine communication, conceptual, analysis, and research skills. It includes many activities helpful in developing an active learning environment.

Beyond the Numbers

BTN 1-1   Key financial figures for **Research In Motion**'s fiscal year ended February 27, 2010, follow.

Key Figure	In Millions
Liabilities + Equity.........	$10,204
Net income	2,457
Revenues	14,953

REPORTING IN ACTION

A1 A2 A3

RIM

Required

1. What is the total amount of assets invested in Research In Motion?
2. What is Research In Motion's return on assets? Its assets at February 28, 2009, equal $8,101 (in millions).
3. How much are total expenses for Research In Motion for the year ended February 27, 2010?
4. Does Research In Motion's return on assets seem satisfactory if competitors average an 18% return?

Check   (2) 26.8%

Fast Forward

5. Access Research In Motion's financial statements (Form 10-K) for fiscal years ending after February 27, 2010, from its Website (**RIM.com**) or from the SEC Website (**www.sec.gov**) and compute its return on assets for those fiscal years. Compare the February 27, 2010, fiscal year-end return on assets to any subsequent years' returns you are able to compute, and interpret the results.

BTN 1-2   Key comparative figures ($ millions) for both **Research In Motion** and **Apple** follow.

Key Figure	Research In Motion	Apple
Liabilities + Equity.........	$10,204	$47,501
Net income	2,457	8,235
Revenues and sales	14,953	42,905

COMPARATIVE ANALYSIS

A1 A2 A3

RIM

Apple

Required

1. What is the total amount of assets invested in (*a*) Research In Motion and (*b*) Apple?
2. What is the return on assets for (*a*) Research In Motion and (*b*) Apple? Research In Motion's beginning-year assets equal $8,101 (in millions) and Apple's beginning-year assets equal $36,171 (in millions).
3. How much are expenses for (*a*) Research In Motion and (*b*) Apple?
4. Is return on assets satisfactory for (*a*) Research In Motion and (*b*) Apple? (Assume competitors average an 18% return.)
5. What can you conclude about Research In Motion and Apple from these computations?

Check   (2b) 19.7%

BTN 1-3   Madison Thorne works in a public accounting firm and hopes to eventually be a partner. The management of Allnet Company invites Thorne to prepare a bid to audit Allnet's financial statements. In discussing the audit fee, Allnet's management suggests a fee range in which the amount depends on the reported profit of Allnet. The higher its profit, the higher will be the audit fee paid to Thorne's firm.

ETHICS CHALLENGE

C3 C4

Required

1. Identify the parties potentially affected by this audit and the fee plan proposed.
2. What are the ethical factors in this situation? Explain.
3. Would you recommend that Thorne accept this audit fee arrangement? Why or why not?
4. Describe some ethical considerations guiding your recommendation.

COMMUNICATING IN PRACTICE

A1 C2

BTN 1-4   Refer to this chapter's opening feature about Twitter. Assume that the owners desire to expand their online services to meet people's demands regarding online services. They eventually decide to meet with their banker to discuss a loan to allow Twitter to expand.

Required

1. Prepare a half-page report outlining the information you would request from the owners if you were the loan officer.
2. Indicate whether the information you request and your loan decision are affected by the form of business organization for Twitter.

TAKING IT TO THE NET

A2

BTN 1-5   Visit the EDGAR database at (www.sec.gov). Access the Form 10-K report of Rocky Mountain Chocolate Factory (ticker RMCF) filed on May 26, 2009, covering its 2009 fiscal year.

Required

1. Item 6 of the 10-K report provides comparative financial highlights of RMCF for the years 2005–2009. How would you describe the revenue trend for RMCF over this five-year period?
2. Has RMCF been profitable (see net income) over this five-year period? Support your answer.

TEAMWORK IN ACTION

C1

BTN 1-6   Teamwork is important in today's business world. Successful teams schedule convenient meetings, maintain regular communications, and cooperate with and support their members. This assignment aims to establish support/learning teams, initiate discussions, and set meeting times.

Required

1. Form teams and open a team discussion to determine a regular time and place for your team to meet between each scheduled class meeting. Notify your instructor via a memorandum or e-mail message as to when and where your team will hold regularly scheduled meetings.
2. Develop a list of telephone numbers and/or e-mail addresses of your teammates.

ENTREPRENEURIAL DECISION

A1 P1

BTN 1-7   Refer to this chapter's opening feature about Twitter. Assume that the owners decide to open a new Website devoted to micro-blogging for accountants and those studying accounting. This new company will be called AccounTwit.

Required

1. AccounTwit obtains a $500,000 loan and the three owners contribute $250,000 in total from their own savings in exchange for common stock in the new company.
   a. What is the new company's total amount of liabilities plus equity?
   b. What is the new company's total amount of assets?
2. If the new company earns $80,000 in net income in the first year of operation, compute its return on assets (assume average assets equal $750,000). Assess its performance if competitors average a 10% return.

Check   (2) 10.7%

HITTING THE ROAD

C2

BTN 1-8   You are to interview a local business owner. (This can be a friend or relative.) Opening lines of communication with members of the business community can provide personal benefits of business networking. If you do not know the owner, you should call ahead to introduce yourself and explain your position as a student and your assignment requirements. You should request a 30-minute appointment for a face-to-face or phone interview to discuss the form of organization and operations of the business. Be prepared to make a good impression.

Required

1. Identify and describe the main operating activities and the form of organization for this business.
2. Determine and explain why the owner(s) chose this particular form of organization.
3. Identify any special advantages and/or disadvantages the owner(s) experiences in operating with this form of business organization.

BTN 1-9 Nokia (www.Nokia.com) is a leading manufacturer of mobile devices and services, and it competes to some extent with both **Research In Motion** and **Apple**. Key financial figures for Nokia follow.

Key Figure*	Euro (EUR) in Millions
Average assets.................	37,660
Net income...................	260
Revenue	40,984
Return on assets..............	0.7%

* Figures prepared in accordance with International Financial Reporting Standards.

GLOBAL DECISION

A1 A2 A3

NOKIA

RIM

Apple

Required

1. Identify any concerns you have in comparing Nokia's income and revenue figures to those of Research In Motion and Apple (in BTN 1-2) for purposes of making business decisions.

2. Identify any concerns you have in comparing Nokia's return on assets ratio to those of Research In Motion and Apple (computed for BTN 1-2) for purposes of making business decisions.

ANSWERS TO MULTIPLE CHOICE QUIZ

1. c; $450,000 is the actual cost incurred.

2. b; revenue is recorded when earned.

3. d;

Assets	=	Liabilities	+	Equity
+$100,000	=	+35,000	+	?

Change in equity = $100,000 − $35,000 = $65,000

4. a

5. a

A Look Back

Chapter 1 defined accounting and introduced financial statements. We described forms of organizations and identified users and uses of accounting. We defined the accounting equation and applied it to transaction analysis.

A Look at This Chapter

This chapter focuses on the accounting process. We describe transactions and source documents, and we explain the analysis and recording of transactions. The accounting equation, T-account, general ledger, trial balance, and debits and credits are key tools in the accounting process.

A Look Ahead

Chapter 3 extends our focus on processing information. We explain the importance of adjusting accounts and the procedures in preparing financial statements.

2

Analyzing and Recording Transactions

Learning Objectives

CAP

CONCEPTUAL

C1 Explain the steps in processing transactions and the role of source documents. (p. 52)

C2 Describe an account and its use in recording transactions. (p. 53)

C3 Describe a ledger and a chart of accounts. (p. 56)

C4 Define *debits* and *credits* and explain double-entry accounting. (p. 57)

ANALYTICAL

A1 Analyze the impact of transactions on accounts and financial statements. (p. 61)

A2 Compute the debt ratio and describe its use in analyzing financial condition. (p. 72)

LP2

PROCEDURAL

P1 Record transactions in a journal and post entries to a ledger. (p. 58)

P2 Prepare and explain the use of a trial balance. (p. 67)

P3 Prepare financial statements from business transactions. (p. 68)

8. Provide Consulting and Rental Services on Credit

1 IDENTIFY FastForward provides consulting services of $1,600 and rents its test facilities for $300. The customer is billed $1,900 for these services.

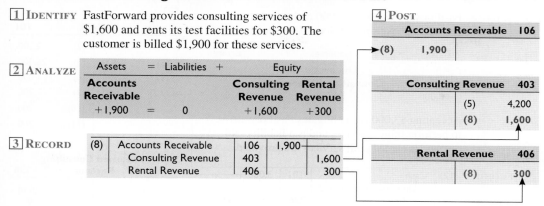

Point: Transaction 8 is a **compound journal entry,** which affects three or more accounts.

9. Receipt of Cash on Account

1 IDENTIFY FastForward receives $1,900 cash from the client billed in transaction 8.

Point: The *revenue recognition principle* requires revenue to be recognized when earned, which is when the company provides products and services to a customer. This is not necessarily the same time that the customer pays. A customer can pay before or after products or services are provided.

10. Partial Payment of Accounts Payable

1 IDENTIFY FastForward pays CalTech Supply $900 cash toward the payable of transaction 4.

11. Payment of Cash Dividend

1 IDENTIFY FastForward pays $200 cash for dividends

12. Receipt of Cash for Future Services

1 IDENTIFY   FastForward receives $3,000 cash in advance of providing consulting services to a customer.

2 ANALYZE

Assets	=	Liabilities	+	Equity
Cash		**Unearned Consulting Revenue**		
+3,000	=	+3,000	+	0

Accepting $3,000 cash obligates FastForward to perform future services and is a liability. No revenue is earned until services are provided.

3 RECORD

(12)	Cash	101	3,000	
	Unearned Consulting Revenue	236		3,000

4 POST

Cash		101	
(1)	30,000	(2)	2,500
(5)	4,200	(3)	26,000
(9)	1,900	(6)	1,000
(12)	3,000	(7)	700
		(10)	900
		(11)	200

Unearned Consulting Revenue			236
		(12)	3,000

Point: Luca Pacioli, a 15th-century monk, is considered a pioneer in accounting and the first to devise double-entry accounting.

13. Pay Cash for Future Insurance Coverage

1 IDENTIFY   FastForward pays $2,400 cash (insurance premium) for a 24-month insurance policy. Coverage begins on December 1.

2 ANALYZE

Assets		=	Liabilities	+	Equity
Cash	**Prepaid Insurance**				
−2,400	+2,400	=	0	+	0

Changes the composition of assets from cash to prepaid insurance. Expense is incurred as insurance coverage expires.

3 RECORD

(13)	Prepaid Insurance	128	2,400	
	Cash	101		2,400

4 POST

Prepaid Insurance		128	
(13)	2,400		

Cash		101	
(1)	30,000	(2)	2,500
(5)	4,200	(3)	26,000
(9)	1,900	(6)	1,000
(12)	3,000	(7)	700
		(10)	900
		(11)	200
		(13)	2,400

14. Purchase Supplies for Cash

1 IDENTIFY   FastForward pays $120 cash for supplies.

2 ANALYZE

Assets		=	Liabilities	+	Equity
Cash	**Supplies**				
−120	+120	=	0	+	0

3 RECORD

(14)	Supplies	126	120	
	Cash	101		120

4 POST

Supplies		126	
(2)	2,500		
(4)	7,100		
(14)	120		

Cash		101	
(1)	30,000	(2)	2,500
(5)	4,200	(3)	26,000
(9)	1,900	(6)	1,000
(12)	3,000	(7)	700
		(10)	900
		(11)	200
		(13)	2,400
		(14)	120

15. Payment of Expense in Cash

1 IDENTIFY — FastForward pays $230 cash for December utilities expense.

2 ANALYZE

Assets	=	Liabilities	+	Equity
Cash				**Utilities Expense**
−230	=	0		−230

3 RECORD

(15)	Utilities Expense	690	230	
	Cash	101		230

4 POST

Utilities Expense 690

(15)	230	

Cash			101
(1)	30,000	(2)	2,500
(5)	4,200	(3)	26,000
(9)	1,900	(6)	1,000
(12)	3,000	(7)	700
		(10)	900
		(11)	200
		(13)	2,400
		(14)	120
		(15)	230

16. Payment of Expense in Cash

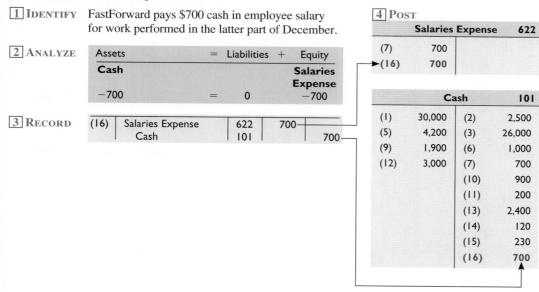

1 IDENTIFY — FastForward pays $700 cash in employee salary for work performed in the latter part of December.

2 ANALYZE

Assets	=	Liabilities	+	Equity
Cash				**Salaries Expense**
−700	=	0		−700

3 RECORD

(16)	Salaries Expense	622	700	
	Cash	101		700

4 POST

Salaries Expense 622

(7)	700	
(16)	700	

Cash			101
(1)	30,000	(2)	2,500
(5)	4,200	(3)	26,000
(9)	1,900	(6)	1,000
(12)	3,000	(7)	700
		(10)	900
		(11)	200
		(13)	2,400
		(14)	120
		(15)	230
		(16)	700

Point: We could merge transactions 15 and 16 into one *compound entry.*

Accounting Equation Analysis

Exhibit 2.13 shows the ledger accounts (in T-account form) of FastForward after all 16 transactions are recorded and posted and the balances computed. The accounts are grouped into three major columns corresponding to the accounting equation: assets, liabilities, and equity. Note several important points. First, as with each transaction, the totals for the three columns must obey the accounting equation. Specifically, assets equal $42,470 ($4,350 + $0 + $9,720 + $2,400 + $26,000); liabilities equal $9,200 ($6,200 + $3,000); and equity equals $33,270 ($30,000 − $200 + $5,800 + $300 − $1,400 − $1,000 − $230). These numbers prove the accounting equation: Assets of $42,470 = Liabilities of $9,200 + Equity of $33,270. Second, the common stock, dividends, revenue, and expense accounts reflect the transactions that change equity. The latter three account categories underlie the statement of retained earnings. Third, the revenue and expense account balances will be summarized and reported in the income statement. Fourth, increases and decreases in the cash account make up the elements reported in the statement of cash flows.

Debit and Credit Rules

Accounts	Increase (normal bal.)	Decrease
Asset	Debit	Credit
Liability	Credit	Debit
Common stock	Credit	Debit
Dividends	Debit	Credit
Revenue	Credit	Debit
Expense	Debit	Credit

Point: Technology does not provide the judgment required to analyze most business transactions. Analysis requires the expertise of skilled and ethical professionals.

EXHIBIT 2.13

Ledger for FastForward (in T-Account Form)

Assets				=	Liabilities				+	Equity		

Assets = **Liabilities** + **Equity**

Cash			101
(1)	30,000	(2)	2,500
(5)	4,200	(3)	26,000
(9)	1,900	(6)	1,000
(12)	3,000	(7)	700
		(10)	900
		(11)	200
		(13)	2,400
		(14)	120
		(15)	230
		(16)	700
Balance	4,350		

Accounts Receivable			106
(8)	1,900	(9)	1,900
Balance	0		

Supplies			126
(2)	2,500		
(4)	7,100		
(14)	120		
Balance	9,720		

Prepaid Insurance			128
(13)	2,400		

Equipment			167
(3)	26,000		

$42,470

Accounts Payable			201
(10)	900	(4)	7,100
		Balance	6,200

Unearned Consulting Revenue			236
		(12)	3,000

$9,200

Common Stock			307
		(1)	30,000

Dividends			319
(11)	200		

Consulting Revenue			403
		(5)	4,200
		(8)	1,600
		Balance	5,800

Rental Revenue			406
		(8)	300

Salaries Expense			622
(7)	700		
(16)	700		
Balance	1,400		

Rent Expense			640
(6)	1,000		

Utilities Expense			690
(15)	230		

Accounts in this white area reflect those reported on the income statement.

$33,270

Quick Check

Answers — p. 77

8. What types of transactions increase equity? What types decrease equity?

9. Why are accounting systems called *double-entry?*

10. For each transaction, double-entry accounting requires which of the following? (*a*) Debits to asset accounts must create credits to liability or equity accounts, (*b*) a debit to a liability account must create a credit to an asset account, or (*c*) total debits must equal total credits.

11. An owner invests $15,000 cash along with equipment having a market value of $23,000 in a company in exchange for common stock. Prepare the necessary journal entry.

12. Explain what a compound journal entry is.

13. Why are posting reference numbers entered in the journal when entries are posted to ledger accounts?

TRIAL BALANCE

Double-entry accounting requires the sum of debit account balances to equal the sum of credit account balances. A trial balance is used to confirm this. A **trial balance** is a list of accounts and their balances at a point in time. Account balances are reported in their appropriate debit or credit columns of a trial balance. A trial balance can be used to confirm this and to follow up on any abnormal or unusual balances. Exhibit 2.14 shows the trial balance for FastForward after its 16 entries have been posted to the ledger. (This is an *unadjusted* trial balance—Chapter 3 explains the necessary adjustments.)

EXHIBIT 2.14

Trial Balance (Unadjusted)

Peachtree Accounting: FastForward
File Edit Lists Maintain Tasks Analysis Options Reports & Forms Services Window Help

Company
  Business Status
  Customers & Sales
  Vendors & Purchases
  Inventory & Services
  Employees & Payroll
  Banking
  Company

Shortcuts   Customize
Sales Invoice
Receive Money from Customer
Bills - Pay Bill
Customer List
Vendor List
Find Transactions
General Journal Entry

FASTFORWARD
Trial Balance
December 31, 2011

	Debit	Credit
Cash	$ 4,350	
Accounts receivable	0	
Supplies	9,720	
Prepaid insurance	2,400	
Equipment	26,000	
Accounts payable		$ 6,200
Unearned consulting revenue		3,000
Common stock		30,000
Dividends	200	
Consulting revenue		5,800
Rental revenue		300
Salaries expense	1,400	
Rent expense	1,000	
Utilities expense	230	
Totals	$ 45,300	$ 45,300

Point: The ordering of accounts in a trial balance typically follows their identification number from the chart of accounts.

Preparing a Trial Balance

Preparing a trial balance involves three steps:

P2 Prepare and explain the use of a trial balance.

1. List each account title and its amount (from ledger) in the trial balance. If an account has a zero balance, list it with a zero in its normal balance column (or omit it entirely).
2. Compute the total of debit balances and the total of credit balances.
3. Verify (*prove*) total debit balances equal total credit balances.

▲ **Fraud** ▬▬▬▬▬▬▬▬▬

Heavenly accounting. Religious organizations are especially vulnerable to fraud. Due to "trust" among religious cohorts, the opportunity factor in the fraud triangle looms large for such entities. In many cases, the recording of transactions has few or no controls. For example, in 2011, a mother and son team from Morristown, Tennessee, pleaded guilty to defrauding a local church. They had recorded nearly 2,000 checks to "cash," amounting to more than $1.5 million, which they cashed and pocketed. An independent review of transactions or a requirement for documentation would have reduced the opportunity factor.

The total of debit balances equals the total of credit balances for the trial balance in Exhibit 2.14. Equality of these two totals does not guarantee that no errors were made. For example, the column totals still will be equal when a debit or credit of a correct amount is made to a wrong account. Another error that does not cause unequal column totals occurs when equal debits and credits of an incorrect amount are entered.

Point: A trial balance is *not* a financial statement but a mechanism for checking equality of debits and credits in the ledger. Financial statements do not have debit and credit columns.

Example: If a credit to Unearned Revenue was incorrectly posted from the journal as a credit to the Revenue ledger account, would the ledger still balance? Would the financial statements be correct? *Answers:* The ledger would balance, but liabilities would be understated, equity would be overstated, and income would be overstated (all because of overstated revenues).

Point: The IRS requires companies to keep records that can be audited.

Searching for and Correcting Errors If the trial balance does not balance (when its columns are not equal), the error (or errors) must be found and corrected. An efficient way to search for an error is to check the journalizing, posting, and trial balance preparation in *reverse order.* Step 1 is to verify that the trial balance columns are correctly added. If step 1 fails to find the error, step 2 is to verify that account balances are accurately entered from the ledger. Step 3 is to see whether a debit (or credit) balance is mistakenly listed in the trial balance as a credit (or debit). A clue to this error is when the difference between total debits and total credits equals twice the amount of the incorrect account balance. If the error is still undiscovered, Step 4 is to recompute each account balance in the ledger. Step 5 is to verify that each journal entry is properly posted. Step 6 is to verify that the original journal entry has equal debits and credits. At this point, the errors should be uncovered.[3]

If an error in a journal entry is discovered before the error is posted, it can be corrected in a manual system by drawing a line through the incorrect information. The correct information is written above it to create a record of change for the auditor. Many computerized systems allow the operator to replace the incorrect information directly.

If an error in a journal entry is not discovered until after it is posted, we do not strike through both erroneous entries in the journal and ledger. Instead, we correct this error by creating a *correcting entry* that removes the amount from the wrong account and records it to the correct account. As an example, suppose a $100 purchase of supplies is journalized with an incorrect debit to Equipment, and then this incorrect entry is posted to the ledger. The Supplies ledger account balance is understated by $100, and the Equipment ledger account balance is overstated by $100. The correcting entry is: debit Supplies and credit Equipment (both for $100).

Using a Trial Balance to Prepare Financial Statements

P3 Prepare financial statements from business transactions.

This section shows how to prepare *financial statements* from the trial balance in Exhibit 2.14 and from information on the December transactions of FastForward. These statements differ from those in Chapter 1 because of several additional transactions. These statements are also more precisely called *unadjusted statements* because we need to make some further accounting adjustments (described in Chapter 3).

EXHIBIT 2.15

Links between Financial Statements across Time

How financial statements are linked in time is illustrated in Exhibit 2.15. A balance sheet reports on an organization's financial position at a *point in time.* The income statement, statement of retained earnings, and statement of cash flows report on financial performance over a *period of time.* The three statements in the middle column of Exhibit 2.15 link balance sheets from the

---

[3] *Transposition* occurs when two digits are switched, or transposed, within a number. If transposition is the only error, it yields a difference between the two trial balance totals that is evenly divisible by 9. For example, assume that a $691 debit in an entry is incorrectly posted to the ledger as $619. Total credits in the trial balance are then larger than total debits by $72 ($691 − $619). The $72 error is *evenly* divisible by 9 (72/9 = 8). The first digit of the quotient (in our example it is 8) equals the difference between the digits of the two transposed numbers (the 9 and the 1). The number of digits in the quotient also tells the location of the transposition, starting from the right. The quotient in our example had only one digit (8), so it tells us the transposition is in the first digit. Consider another example where a transposition error involves posting $961 instead of the correct $691. The difference in these numbers is $270, and its quotient is 30 (270/9). The quotient has two digits, so it tells us to check the second digit from the right for a transposition of two numbers that have a difference of 3.

beginning to the end of a reporting period. They explain how financial position changes from one point to another.

Preparers and users (including regulatory agencies) determine the length of the reporting period. A one-year, or annual, reporting period is common, as are semiannual, quarterly, and monthly periods. The one-year reporting period is known as the *accounting,* or *fiscal, year.* Businesses whose accounting year begins on January 1 and ends on December 31 are known as *calendar-year* companies. Many companies choose a fiscal year ending on a date other than December 31. **Research In Motion** is a *noncalendar-year* company as reflected in the headings of its February 27 year-end financial statements in Appendix A near the end of the book.

Point: A statement's heading lists the 3 W's: **W**ho—name of organization, **W**hat—name of statement, **W**hen—statement's point in time or period of time.

Income Statement   An income statement reports the revenues earned less the expenses incurred by a business over a period of time. FastForward's income statement for December is shown at the top of Exhibit 2.16. Information about revenues and expenses is conveniently taken from the trial balance in Exhibit 2.14. Net income of $3,470 is reported at the bottom of the statement. Owner investments and dividends are *not* part of income.

EXHIBIT 2.16

Financial Statements and Their Links

FASTFORWARD		
Income Statement		
For Month Ended December 31, 2011		
Revenues		
Consulting revenue ($4,200 + $1,600)	$ 5,800	
Rental revenue	300	
Total revenues		$ 6,100
Expenses		
Rent expense	1,000	
Salaries expense	1,400	
Utilities expense	230	
Total expenses		2,630
Net income		$ 3,470

FASTFORWARD	
Statement of Retained Earnings	
For Month Ended December 31, 2011	
Retained earnings, December 1, 2011	$ 0
Plus: Net income	3,470
	3,470
Less: Cash dividends......................	200
Retained earnings, December 31, 2011	$ 3,270

Point: Arrow lines show how the statements are linked.

FASTFORWARD			
Balance Sheet			
December 31, 2011			
Assets		**Liabilities**	
Cash	$ 4,350	Accounts payable	$ 6,200
Supplies	9,720	Unearned revenue	3,000
Prepaid insurance ..	2,400	Total liabilities	9,200
Equipment	26,000	**Equity**	
		Common stock	30,000
		Retained earnings	3,270
		Total equity	33,270
Total assets	$42,470	Total liabilities and equity ..	$42,470

Point: To *foot* a column of numbers is to add them.

Use the information in each of the following separate cases to calculate the unknown amount.

a. During October, Shandra Company had $97,500 of cash receipts and $101,250 of cash disbursements. The October 31 Cash balance was $16,800. Determine how much cash the company had at the close of business on September 30.

b. On September 30, Mordish Co. had a $97,500 balance in Accounts Receivable. During October, the company collected $88,950 from its credit customers. The October 31 balance in Accounts Receivable was $100,500. Determine the amount of sales on account that occurred in October.

c. Nasser Co. had $147,000 of accounts payable on September 30 and $136,500 on October 31. Total purchases on account during October were $270,000. Determine how much cash was paid on accounts payable during October.

Exercise 2-6
Analyzing account entries and balances
A1

Prepare general journal entries for the following transactions of a new company called Pose for Pics.

Aug. 1 Kasey Madison, the owner, invested $7,500 cash and $32,500 of photography equipment in the company in exchange for common stock.
      2 The company paid $3,000 cash for an insurance policy covering the next 24 months.
      5 The company purchased office supplies for $1,400 cash.
     20 The company received $2,650 cash in photography fees earned.
     31 The company paid $875 cash for August utilities.

Exercise 2-7
Preparing general journal entries
P1

Use the information in Exercise 2-7 to prepare an August 31 trial balance for Pose for Pics. Begin by opening these T-accounts: Cash; Office Supplies; Prepaid Insurance; Photography Equipment; Common Stock; Photography Fees Earned; and Utilities Expense. Then, post the general journal entries to these T-accounts (which will serve as the ledger), and prepare the trial balance.

Exercise 2-8
Preparing T-accounts (ledger) and a trial balance   P2

Prepare general journal entries to record the transactions below for Dexter Company by using the following accounts: Cash; Accounts Receivable; Office Supplies; Office Equipment; Accounts Payable; Common Stock; Dividends; Fees Earned; and Rent Expense. Use the letters beside each transaction to identify entries. After recording the transactions, post them to T-accounts, which serves as the general ledger for this assignment. Determine the ending balance of each T-account.

a. Macy Dexter, owner, invested $12,750 cash in the company in exchange for common stock.
b. The company purchased office supplies for $375 cash.
c. The company purchased $7,050 of office equipment on credit.
d. The company received $1,500 cash as fees for services provided to a customer.
e. The company paid $7,050 cash to settle the payable for the office equipment purchased in transaction c.
f. The company billed a customer $2,700 as fees for services provided.
g. The company paid $525 cash for the monthly rent.
h. The company collected $1,125 cash as partial payment for the account receivable created in transaction f.
i. The company paid $1,000 cash for dividends.

Exercise 2-9
Recording effects of transactions in T-accounts
A1

Check   Cash ending balance, $6,425

After recording the transactions of Exercise 2-9 in T-accounts and calculating the balance of each account, prepare a trial balance. Use May 31, 2011, as its report date.

Exercise 2-10
Preparing a trial balance   P2

Examine the following transactions and identify those that create revenues for Jade Services, a company owned by Mia Jade. Prepare general journal entries to record those revenue transactions and explain why the other transactions did not create revenues.

a. Mia Jade invests $38,250 cash in the company in exchange for common stock.
b. The company provided $1,350 of services on credit.
c. The company provided services to a client and immediately received $1,575 cash.
d. The company received $9,150 cash from a client in payment for services to be provided next year.
e. The company received $4,500 cash from a client in partial payment of an account receivable.
f. The company borrowed $150,000 cash from the bank by signing a promissory note.

Exercise 2-11
Analyzing and journalizing revenue transactions
A1   P1

Exercise 2-12

Analyzing and journalizing expense transactions

A1 P1

Examine the following transactions and identify those that create expenses for Jade Services. Prepare general journal entries to record those expense transactions and explain why the other transactions did not create expenses.

a. The company paid $14,100 cash for payment on a 14-month old liability for office supplies.

b. The company paid $1,125 cash for the just completed two-week salary of the receptionist.

c. The company paid $45,000 cash for equipment purchased.

d. The company paid $930 cash for this month's utilities.

e. The company paid $5,000 cash for dividends.

Exercise 2-13

Preparing an income statement

C3 P3

Dominick Lopez operates a consulting firm called Tech Today, which began operations on August 1. On August 31, the company's records show the following accounts and amounts for the month of August. Use this information to prepare an August income statement for the business.

Cash	$ 8,360	Dividends	$ 3,000
Accounts receivable	17,000	Consulting fees earned	17,000
Office supplies	3,250	Rent expense	4,550
Land	46,000	Salaries expense	8,000
Office equipment	18,000	Telephone expense	560
Accounts payable	8,000	Miscellaneous expenses	280
Common Stock	84,000		

Check Net income, $3,610

Exercise 2-14

Preparing a statement of retained earnings P3

Check End. Ret. Earn., $610

Use the information in Exercise 2-13 to prepare an August statement of retained earnings for Tech Today. (The owner invested $84,000 cash in the company in exchange for common stock on August 1.)

Exercise 2-15

Preparing a balance sheet P3

Use the information in Exercise 2-13 (if completed, you can also use your solution to Exercise 2-14) to prepare an August 31 balance sheet for Tech Today.

Exercise 2-16

Computing net income

A1

A corporation had the following assets and liabilities at the beginning and end of this year.

	Assets	Liabilities
Beginning of the year	$ 70,000	$30,000
End of the year	115,000	46,000

Determine the net income earned or net loss incurred by the business during the year for each of the following *separate* cases:

a. Owner made no investments in the business and no dividends were paid during the year.

b. Owner made no investments in the business, but dividends were $1,250 cash per month.

c. No dividends were paid during the year, but the owner did invest an additional $45,000 cash in exchange for common stock.

d. Dividends were $1,250 cash per month and the owner invested an additional $25,000 cash in exchange for common stock.

Exercise 2-17

Analyzing changes in a company's equity

P3

Compute the missing amount for each of the following separate companies *a* through *d*.

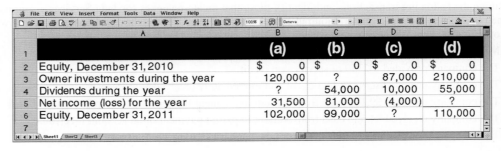

	A	(a)	(b)	(c)	(d)
1					
2	Equity, December 31, 2010	$ 0	$ 0	$ 0	$ 0
3	Owner investments during the year	120,000	?	87,000	210,000
4	Dividends during the year	?	54,000	10,000	55,000
5	Net income (loss) for the year	31,500	81,000	(4,000)	?
6	Equity, December 31, 2011	102,000	99,000	?	110,000
7					

Assume the following T-accounts reflect Joy Co.'s general ledger and that seven transactions *a* through *g* are posted to them. Provide a short description of each transaction. Include the amounts in your descriptions.

Exercise 2-18
Interpreting and describing transactions from T-accounts

A1

Cash			
(a)	7,000	(b)	3,600
(e)	2,500	(c)	600
		(f)	2,400
		(g)	700

Office Supplies		
(c)	600	
(d)	200	

Prepaid Insurance		
(b)	3,600	

Equipment		
(a)	5,600	
(d)	9,400	

Automobiles		
(a)	11,000	

Accounts Payable			
(f)	2,400	(d)	9,600

Common Stock		
	(a)	23,600

Delivery Services Revenue		
	(e)	2,500

Gas and Oil Expense		
(g)	700	

Use information from the T-accounts in Exercise 2-18 to prepare general journal entries for each of the seven transactions *a* through *g*.

Exercise 2-19
Preparing general journal entries

P1

Posting errors are identified in the following table. In column (1), enter the amount of the difference between the two trial balance columns (debit and credit) due to the error. In column (2), identify the trial balance column (debit or credit) with the larger amount if they are not equal. In column (3), identify the account(s) affected by the error. In column (4), indicate the amount by which the account(s) in column (3) is under- or overstated. Item (a) is completed as an example.

Exercise 2-20
Identifying effects of posting errors on the trial balance

A1 P2

	Description of Posting Error	(1) Difference between Debit and Credit Columns	(2) Column with the Larger Total	(3) Identify Account(s) Incorrectly Stated	(4) Amount that Account(s) Is Over- or Understated
a.	$2,400 debit to Rent Expense is posted as a $1,590 debit.	$810	Credit	Rent Expense	Rent Expense understated $810
b.	$4,050 credit to Cash is posted twice as two credits to Cash.				
c.	$9,900 debit to the Dividends account is debited to Common Stock.				
d.	$2,250 debit to Prepaid Insurance is posted as a debit to Insurance Expense.				
e.	$42,000 debit to Machinery is posted as a debit to Accounts Payable.				
f.	$4,950 credit to Services Revenue is posted as a $495 credit.				
g.	$1,440 debit to Store Supplies is not posted.				

You are told the column totals in a trial balance are not equal. After careful analysis, you discover only one error. Specifically, a correctly journalized credit purchase of a computer for $16,950 is posted from the journal to the ledger with a $16,950 debit to Office Equipment and another $16,950 debit to Accounts Payable. The Office Equipment account has a debit balance of $40,100 on the trial balance. Answer each of the following questions and compute the dollar amount of any misstatement.

Exercise 2-21
Analyzing a trial balance error

A1 P2

a. Is the debit column total of the trial balance overstated, understated, or correctly stated?

b. Is the credit column total of the trial balance overstated, understated, or correctly stated?

c. Is the Office Equipment account balance overstated, understated, or correctly stated in the trial balance?

d. Is the Accounts Payable account balance overstated, understated, or correctly stated in the trial balance?

e. If the debit column total of the trial balance is $360,000 before correcting the error, what is the total of the credit column before correction?

Exercise 2-22
Interpreting the debt ratio
and return on assets

A2

a. Calculate the debt ratio and the return on assets using the year-end information for each of the following six separate companies ($ thousands).

Case	Assets	Liabilities	Average Assets	Net Income
Company 1	$147,000	$56,000	$200,000	$21,000
Company 2	104,500	51,500	70,000	12,000
Company 3	90,500	12,000	100,000	20,000
Company 4	92,000	31,000	40,000	7,500
Company 5	64,000	47,000	40,000	3,800
Company 6	32,500	26,500	50,000	660

b. Of the six companies, which business relies most heavily on creditor financing?

c. Of the six companies, which business relies most heavily on equity financing?

d. Which two companies indicate the greatest risk?

e. Which two companies earn the highest return on assets?

f. Which one company would investors likely prefer based on the risk–return relation?

Exercise 2-23
Preparing a balance sheet
following IFRS

P3

BMW reports the following balance sheet accounts for the year ended December 31, 2009 (euro in millions). Prepare the balance sheet for this company as of December 31, 2009, following the usual IFRS formats.

Current liabilities	€ 8,350	Noncurrent liabilities	€10,943
Current assets	17,663	Noncurrent assets	6,984
Total equity	5,354		

connect

PROBLEM SET A

Problem 2-1A
Preparing and posting journal
entries; preparing a trial balance

C3 C4 A1 P1 P2

mhhe.com/wildFA6e

Gary Bauer opens a computer consulting business called Technology Consultants and completes the following transactions in April.

April 1 Bauer invested $100,000 cash along with $24,000 in office equipment in the company in exchange for common stock.

2 The company prepaid $7,200 cash for twelve months' rent for an office. (*Hint:* Debit Prepaid Rent for $7,200.)

3 The company made credit purchases of office equipment for $12,000 and office supplies for $2,400. Payment is due within 10 days.

6 The company completed services for a client and immediately received $2,000 cash.

9 The company completed an $8,000 project for a client, who must pay within 30 days.

13 The company paid $14,400 cash to settle the account payable created on April 3.

19 The company paid $6,000 cash for the premium on a 12-month insurance policy. (*Hint:* Debit Prepaid Insurance for $6,000.)

22 The company received $6,400 cash as partial payment for the work completed on April 9.

25 The company completed work for another client for $2,640 on credit.

28 The company paid $6,200 cash for dividends.

29 The company purchased $800 of additional office supplies on credit.

30 The company paid $700 cash for this month's utility bill.

Required

1. Prepare general journal entries to record these transactions (use the account titles listed in part 2).

2. Open the following ledger accounts—their account numbers are in parentheses (use the balance column format): Cash (101); Accounts Receivable (106); Office Supplies (124); Prepaid Insurance (128);

Prepaid Rent (131); Office Equipment (163); Accounts Payable (201); Common Stock (307); Dividends (319); Services Revenue (403); and Utilities Expense (690). Post the journal entries from part 1 to the ledger accounts and enter the balance after each posting.

3. Prepare a trial balance as of the end of April.

Shelton Engineering completed the following transactions in the month of June.

a. Shana Shelton, the owner, invested $105,000 cash, office equipment with a value of $6,000, and $45,000 of drafting equipment to launch the company in exchange for common stock.

b. The company purchased land worth $54,000 for an office by paying $5,400 cash and signing a long-term note payable for $48,600.

c. The company purchased a portable building with $75,000 cash and moved it onto the land acquired in *b*.

d. The company paid $6,000 cash for the premium on an 18-month insurance policy.

e. The company completed and delivered a set of plans for a client and collected $5,700 cash.

f. The company purchased $22,500 of additional drafting equipment by paying $10,500 cash and signing a long-term note payable for $12,000.

g. The company completed $12,000 of engineering services for a client. This amount is to be received in 30 days.

h. The company purchased $2,250 of additional office equipment on credit.

i. The company completed engineering services for $18,000 on credit.

j. The company received a bill for rent of equipment that was used on a recently completed job. The $1,200 rent cost must be paid within 30 days.

k. The company collected $7,200 cash in partial payment from the client described in transaction *g*.

l. The company paid $1,500 cash for wages to a drafting assistant.

m. The company paid $2,250 cash to settle the account payable created in transaction *h*.

n. The company paid $675 cash for minor maintenance of its drafting equipment.

o. The company paid $9,360 cash for dividends.

p. The company paid $1,500 cash for wages to a drafting assistant.

q. The company paid $3,000 cash for advertisements in the local newspaper during June.

Problem 2-2A

Preparing and posting journal entries; preparing a trial balance

C3 C4 A1 P1 P2

Required

1. Prepare general journal entries to record these transactions (use the account titles listed in part 2).

2. Open the following ledger accounts—their account numbers are in parentheses (use the balance column format): Cash (101); Accounts Receivable (106); Prepaid Insurance (108); Office Equipment (163); Drafting Equipment (164); Building (170); Land (172); Accounts Payable (201); Notes Payable (250); Common Stock (307); Dividends (319); Engineering Fees Earned (402); Wages Expense (601); Equipment Rental Expense (602); Advertising Expense (603); and Repairs Expense (604). Post the journal entries from part 1 to the accounts and enter the balance after each posting.

3. Prepare a trial balance as of the end of June.

The accounting records of Fabiano Distribution show the following assets and liabilities as of December 31, 2010 and 2011.

December 31	2010	2011
Cash	$ 52,500	$ 18,750
Accounts receivable	28,500	22,350
Office supplies	4,500	3,300
Office equipment	138,000	147,000
Trucks	54,000	54,000
Building	0	180,000
Land	0	45,000
Accounts payable	7,500	37,500
Note payable	0	105,000

Problem 2-3A

Computing net income from equity analysis, preparing a balance sheet, and computing the debt ratio

C2 A1 A2 P3

mhhe.com/wildFA6e

Late in December 2011, the business purchased a small office building and land for $225,000. It paid $120,000 cash toward the purchase and a $105,000 note payable was signed for the balance. Mr. Fabiano had to invest $35,000 cash in the business (in exchange for stock) to enable it to pay the $120,000 cash. The business also pays $3,000 cash per month for dividends.

Required

1. Prepare balance sheets for the business as of December 31, 2010 and 2011. (*Hint:* Report only total equity on the balance sheet and remember that total equity equals the difference between assets and liabilities.)

2. By comparing equity amounts from the balance sheets and using the additional information presented in this problem, prepare a calculation to show how much net income was earned by the business during 2011.

3. Compute the 2011 year-end debt ratio for the business.

Problem 2-4A

Preparing and posting journal entries; preparing a trial balance

C3 C4 A1 P1 P2

Santo Birch opens a Web consulting business called Show-Me-the-Money and completes the following transactions in its first month of operations.

March	1	Birch invests $150,000 cash along with office equipment valued at $22,000 in the company in exchange for common stock.
	2	The company prepaid $6,000 cash for twelve months' rent for office space. (*Hint:* Debit Prepaid Rent for $6,000.)
	3	The company made credit purchases for $3,000 in office equipment and $1,200 in office supplies. Payment is due within 10 days.
	6	The company completed services for a client and immediately received $4,000 cash.
	9	The company completed a $7,500 project for a client, who must pay within 30 days.
	13	The company paid $4,200 cash to settle the account payable created on March 3.
	19	The company paid $5,000 cash for the premium on a 12-month insurance policy. (*Hint:* Debit Prepaid Insurance for $5,000.)
	22	The company received $3,500 cash as partial payment for the work completed on March 9.
	25	The company completed work for another client for $3,820 on credit.
	29	The company paid $5,100 cash for dividends.
	30	The company purchased $600 of additional office supplies on credit.
	31	The company paid $200 cash for this month's utility bill.

Required

1. Prepare general journal entries to record these transactions (use account titles listed in part 2).

2. Open the following ledger accounts—their account numbers are in parentheses (use the balance column format): Cash (101); Accounts Receivable (106); Office Supplies (124); Prepaid Insurance (128); Prepaid Rent (131); Office Equipment (163); Accounts Payable (201); Common Stock (307); Dividends (319); Services Revenue (403); and Utilities Expense (690). Post journal entries from part 1 to the ledger accounts and enter the balance after each posting.

3. Prepare a trial balance as of March 31.

Problem 2-5A

Recording transactions; posting to ledger; preparing a trial balance

C3 A1 P1 P2

Business transactions completed by Eric Pense during the month of September are as follows.

a. Pense invested $23,000 cash along with office equipment valued at $12,000 in exchange for common stock of a new company named EP Consulting.

b. The company purchased land valued at $8,000 and a building valued at $33,000. The purchase is paid with $15,000 cash and a long-term note payable for $26,000.

c. The company purchased $600 of office supplies on credit.

d. Pense invested his personal automobile in the company in exchange for more common stock. The automobile has a value of $7,000 and is to be used exclusively in the business.

e. The company purchased $1,100 of additional office equipment on credit.

f. The company paid $800 cash salary to an assistant.

g. The company provided services to a client and collected $2,700 cash.

h. The company paid $430 cash for this month's utilities.

i. The company paid $600 cash to settle the account payable created in transaction *c*.

j. The company purchased $4,000 of new office equipment by paying $4,000 cash.

k. The company completed $2,400 of services for a client, who must pay within 30 days.

l. The company paid $800 cash salary to an assistant.

m. The company received $1,000 cash in partial payment on the receivable created in transaction *k*.

n. The company paid $1,050 cash for dividends.

Required

1. Prepare general journal entries to record these transactions (use account titles listed in part 2).
2. Open the following ledger accounts—their account numbers are in parentheses (use the balance column format): Cash (101); Accounts Receivable (106); Office Supplies (108); Office Equipment (163); Automobiles (164); Building (170); Land (172); Accounts Payable (201); Notes Payable (250); Common Stock (307); Dividends (319); Fees Earned (402); Salaries Expense (601); and Utilities Expense (602). Post the journal entries from part 1 to the ledger accounts and enter the balance after each posting.
3. Prepare a trial balance as of the end of September.

Check   (2) Ending balances: Cash, $4,020; Office Equipment, $17,100

(3) Trial balance totals, $74,200

Carlos Beltran started an engineering firm called Beltran Engineering. He began operations and completed seven transactions in May, which included his initial investment of $17,000 cash. After those seven transactions, the ledger included the following accounts with normal balances.

Problem 2-6A
Analyzing account balances and reconstructing transactions
C1 C3 A1 P2

Cash	$26,660
Office supplies	660
Prepaid insurance	3,200
Office equipment	16,500
Accounts payable	16,500
Common Stock	17,000
Dividends	3,740
Engineering fees earned	24,000
Rent expense	6,740

Required

1. Prepare a trial balance for this business as of the end of May.

Check   (1) Trial balance totals, $57,500

Analysis Components

2. Analyze the accounts and their balances and prepare a list that describes each of the seven most likely transactions and their amounts.
3. Prepare a report of cash received and cash paid showing how the seven transactions in part 2 yield the $26,660 ending Cash balance.

(3) Cash paid, $14,340

Shaw Management Services opens for business and completes these transactions in November.

PROBLEM SET B

Nov. 1   Kita Shaw, the owner, invested $30,000 cash along with $15,000 of office equipment in the company in exchange for common stock.

Problem 2-1B
Preparing and posting journal entries; preparing a trial balance
C3 C4 A1 P1 P2

2   The company prepaid $4,500 cash for six months' rent for an office. (*Hint:* Debit Prepaid Rent for $4,500.)
4   The company made credit purchases of office equipment for $2,500 and of office supplies for $600. Payment is due within 10 days.
8   The company completed work for a client and immediately received $3,400 cash.
12   The company completed a $10,200 project for a client, who must pay within 30 days.
13   The company paid $3,100 cash to settle the payable created on November 4.
19   The company paid $1,800 cash for the premium on a 24-month insurance policy.
22   The company received $5,200 cash as partial payment for the work completed on November 12.
24   The company completed work for another client for $1,750 on credit.
28   The company paid $5,300 cash for dividends.
29   The company purchased $249 of additional office supplies on credit.
30   The company paid $531 cash for this month's utility bill.

Required

1. Prepare general journal entries to record these transactions (use account titles listed in part 2).
2. Open the following ledger accounts—their account numbers are in parentheses (use the balance column format): Cash (101); Accounts Receivable (106); Office Supplies (124); Prepaid Insurance (128); Prepaid Rent (131); Office Equipment (163); Accounts Payable (201); Common Stock (307); Dividends (319); Services Revenue (403); and Utilities Expense (690). Post the journal entries from part 1 to the ledger accounts and enter the balance after each posting.
3. Prepare a trial balance as of the end of November.

Check   (2) Ending balances: Cash, $23,369; Accounts Receivable, $6,750; Accounts Payable, $249

(3) Total debits, $60,599

Problem 2-2B

Preparing and posting journal entries; preparing a trial balance

C3 C4 A1 P1 P2

At the beginning of April, Brooke Gable launched a custom computer solutions company called Softways. The company had the following transactions during April.

a. Brooke Gable invested $45,000 cash, office equipment with a value of $4,500, and $28,000 of computer equipment in the company in exchange for common stock.

b. The company purchased land worth $24,000 for an office by paying $4,800 cash and signing a long-term note payable for $19,200.

c. The company purchased a portable building with $21,000 cash and moved it onto the land acquired in *b*.

d. The company paid $6,600 cash for the premium on a two-year insurance policy.

e. The company provided services to a client and immediately collected $3,200 cash.

f. The company purchased $3,500 of additional computer equipment by paying $700 cash and signing a long-term note payable for $2,800.

g. The company completed $3,750 of services for a client. This amount is to be received within 30 days.

h. The company purchased $750 of additional office equipment on credit.

i. The company completed client services for $9,200 on credit.

j. The company received a bill for rent of a computer testing device that was used on a recently completed job. The $320 rent cost must be paid within 30 days.

k. The company collected $4,600 cash in partial payment from the client described in transaction *i*.

l. The company paid $1,600 cash for wages to an assistant.

m. The company paid $750 cash to settle the payable created in transaction *h*.

n. The company paid $425 cash for minor maintenance of the company's computer equipment.

o. The company paid $3,875 cash for dividends.

p. The company paid $1,600 cash for wages to an assistant.

q. The company paid $800 cash for advertisements in the local newspaper during April.

Required

1. Prepare general journal entries to record these transactions (use account titles listed in part 2).

Check (2) Ending balances: Cash, $10,650; Accounts Receivable, $8,350; Accounts Payable, $320

2. Open the following ledger accounts—their account numbers are in parentheses (use the balance column format): Cash (101); Accounts Receivable (106); Prepaid Insurance (108); Office Equipment (163); Computer Equipment (164); Building (170); Land (172); Accounts Payable (201); Notes Payable (250); Common Stock (307); Dividends (319); Fees Earned (402); Wages Expense (601); Computer Rental Expense (602); Advertising Expense (603); and Repairs Expense (604). Post the journal entries from part 1 to the accounts and enter the balance after each posting.

(3) Trial balance totals, $115,970

3. Prepare a trial balance as of the end of April.

Problem 2-3B

Computing net income from equity analysis, preparing a balance sheet, and computing the debt ratio

C2 A1 A2 P3

The accounting records of Schmit Co. show the following assets and liabilities as of December 31, 2010 and 2011.

December 31	2010	2011
Cash	$14,000	$ 10,000
Accounts receivable	25,000	30,000
Office supplies	10,000	12,500
Office equipment	60,000	60,000
Machinery	30,500	30,500
Building	0	260,000
Land	0	65,000
Accounts payable	5,000	15,000
Note payable	0	260,000

Late in December 2011, the business purchased a small office building and land for $325,000. It paid $65,000 cash toward the purchase and a $260,000 note payable was signed for the balance. Janet Schmit, the owner, had to invest an additional $25,000 cash (in exchange for common stock) to enable it to pay the $65,000 cash toward the purchase. The company also pays $1,000 cash per month for dividends.

Required

1. Prepare balance sheets for the business as of December 31, 2010 and 2011. (*Hint:* Report only total equity on the balance sheet and remember that total equity equals the difference between assets and liabilities.)

2. By comparing equity amounts from the balance sheets and using the additional information presented in the problem, prepare a calculation to show how much net income was earned by the business during 2011.

Check (2) Net income, $45,500

3. Calculate the December 31, 2011, debt ratio for the business.

(3) Debt ratio, 58.76%

Lummus Management Services opens for business and completes these transactions in September.

Problem 2-4B
Preparing and posting journal entries; preparing a trial balance

C3 C4 A1 P1 P2

Sept. 1 Rhonda Lummus, the owner, invests $28,000 cash along with office equipment valued at $25,000 in the company in exchange for common stock.
2 The company prepaid $10,500 cash for 12 months' rent for office space. (*Hint:* Debit Prepaid Rent for $10,500.)
4 The company made credit purchases for $9,000 in office equipment and $1,200 in office supplies. Payment is due within 10 days.
8 The company completed work for a client and immediately received $2,600 cash.
12 The company completed a $13,400 project for a client, who must pay within 30 days.
13 The company paid $10,200 cash to settle the payable created on September 4.
19 The company paid $5,200 cash for the premium on an 18-month insurance policy. (*Hint:* Debit Prepaid Insurance for $5,200.)
22 The company received $7,800 cash as partial payment for the work completed on September 12.
24 The company completed work for another client for $1,900 on credit.
28 The company paid $5,300 cash for dividends.
29 The company purchased $1,700 of additional office supplies on credit.
30 The company paid $460 cash for this month's utility bill.

Required

1. Prepare general journal entries to record these transactions (use account titles listed in part 2).

2. Open the following ledger accounts—their account numbers are in parentheses (use the balance column format): Cash (101); Accounts Receivable (106); Office Supplies (124); Prepaid Insurance (128); Prepaid Rent (131); Office Equipment (163); Accounts Payable (201); Common Stock (307); Dividends (319); Service Fees Earned (401); and Utilities Expense (690). Post journal entries from part 1 to the ledger accounts and enter the balance after each posting.

Check (2) Ending balances: Cash, $6,740; Accounts Receivable, $7,500; Accounts Payable, $1,700

3. Prepare a trial balance as of the end of September.

(3) Total debits, $72,600

Cooke Consulting completed the following transactions during June.

Problem 2-5B
Recording transactions; posting to ledger; preparing a trial balance

C3 A1 P1 P2

a. Chris Cooke, the owner, invested $80,000 cash along with office equipment valued at $30,000 in the new company in exchange for common stock.
b. The company purchased land valued at $30,000 and a building valued at $170,000. The purchase is paid with $40,000 cash and a long-term note payable for $160,000.
c. The company purchased $2,400 of office supplies on credit.
d. C. Cooke invested his personal automobile in the company in exchange for more common stock. The automobile has a value of $18,000 and is to be used exclusively in the business.
e. The company purchased $6,000 of additional office equipment on credit.
f. The company paid $1,500 cash salary to an assistant.
g. The company provided services to a client and collected $6,000 cash.
h. The company paid $800 cash for this month's utilities.
i. The company paid $2,400 cash to settle the payable created in transaction *c*.
j. The company purchased $20,000 of new office equipment by paying $20,000 cash.
k. The company completed $5,200 of services for a client, who must pay within 30 days.
l. The company paid $1,500 cash salary to an assistant.
m. The company received $3,800 cash in partial payment on the receivable created in transaction *k*.
n. The company paid $6,400 cash for dividends.

Required

1. Prepare general journal entries to record these transactions (use account titles listed in part 2).

2. Open the following ledger accounts—their account numbers are in parentheses (use the balance column format): Cash (101); Accounts Receivable (106); Office Supplies (108); Office Equipment (163); Automobiles (164); Building (170); Land (172); Accounts Payable (201); Notes Payable (250); Common Stock (307); Dividends (319); Fees Earned (402); Salaries Expense (601); and Utilities Expense (602). Post the journal entries from part 1 to the ledger accounts and enter the balance after each posting.

Check (2) Ending balances: Cash, $17,200; Office Equipment, $56,000

3. Prepare a trial balance as of the end of June.

(3) Trial balance totals, $305,200

Problem 2-6B
Analyzing account balances
and reconstructing
transactions

C1 C3 A1 P2

Michael Gould started a Web consulting firm called Gould Solutions. He began operations and completed seven transactions in April that resulted in the following accounts, which all have normal balances.

Cash	$12,485
Office supplies	560
Prepaid rent	1,500
Office equipment	11,450
Accounts payable	11,450
Common Stock	10,000
Dividends	6,200
Consulting fees earned	16,400
Operating expenses	5,655

Required

Check   (1) Trial balance total, $37,850

1. Prepare a trial balance for this business as of the end of April.

Analysis Component

2. Analyze the accounts and their balances and prepare a list that describes each of the seven most likely transactions and their amounts.

(3) Cash paid, $13,915

3. Prepare a report of cash received and cash paid showing how the seven transactions in part 2 yield the $12,485 ending Cash balance.

SERIAL PROBLEM
Business Solutions

A1 P1 P2

(This serial problem started in Chapter 1 and continues through most of the chapters. If the Chapter 1 segment was not completed, the problem can begin at this point. It is helpful, but not necessary, to use the Working Papers that accompany this book.)

SP 2   On October 1, 2011, Santana Rey launched a computer services company called **Business Solutions,** which provides consulting services, computer system installations, and custom program development. Rey adopts the calendar year for reporting purposes and expects to prepare the company's first set of financial statements on December 31, 2011. The company's initial chart of accounts follows.

Account	No.	Account	No.
Cash	101	Common Stock....................	307
Accounts Receivable	106	Dividends	319
Computer Supplies	126	Computer Services Revenue	403
Prepaid Insurance	128	Wages Expense....................	623
Prepaid Rent	131	Advertising Expense	655
Office Equipment	163	Mileage Expense	676
Computer Equipment	167	Miscellaneous Expenses	677
Accounts Payable	201	Repairs Expense—Computer.........	684

Required

1. Prepare journal entries to record each of the following transactions for Business Solutions.

Oct.   1   S. Rey invested $45,000 cash, a $20,000 computer system, and $8,000 of office equipment in the company in exchange for its common stock.

     2   The company paid $3,300 cash for four months' rent. (*Hint:* Debit Prepaid Rent for $3,300.)

     3   The company purchased $1,420 of computer supplies on credit from Harris Office Products.

     5   The company paid $2,220 cash for one year's premium on a property and liability insurance policy. (*Hint:* Debit Prepaid Insurance for $2,220.)

     6   The company billed Easy Leasing $4,800 for services performed in installing a new Web server.

     8   The company paid $1,420 cash for the computer supplies purchased from Harris Office Products on October 3.

     10   The company hired Lyn Addie as a part-time assistant for $125 per day, as needed.

     12   The company billed Easy Leasing another $1,400 for services performed.

15	The company received $4,800 cash from Easy Leasing as partial payment on its account.
17	The company paid $805 cash to repair computer equipment that was damaged when moving it.
20	The company paid $1,728 cash for advertisements published in the local newspaper.
22	The company received $1,400 cash from Easy Leasing on its account.
28	The company billed IFM Company $5,208 for services performed.
31	The company paid $875 cash for Lyn Addie's wages for seven days' work.
31	The company paid $3,600 cash for dividends.

Nov. 1   The company reimbursed S. Rey in cash for business automobile mileage allowance (Rey logged 1,000 miles at $0.32 per mile).

2   The company received $4,633 cash from Liu Corporation for computer services performed.

5   The company purchased computer supplies for $1,125 cash from Harris Office Products.

8   The company billed Gomez Co. $5,668 for services performed.

13   The company received notification from Alex's Engineering Co. that Business Solutions' bid of $3,950 for an upcoming project is accepted.

18   The company received $2,208 cash from IFM Company as partial payment of the October 28 bill.

22   The company donated $250 cash to the United Way in the company's name.

24   The company completed work for Alex's Engineering Co. and sent it a bill for $3,950.

25   The company sent another bill to IFM Company for the past-due amount of $3,000.

28   The company reimbursed S. Rey in cash for business automobile mileage (1,200 miles at $0.32 per mile).

30   The company paid $1,750 cash for Lyn Addie's wages for 14 days' work.

30   The company paid $2,000 cash for dividends.

2. Open ledger accounts (in balance column format) and post the journal entries from part 1 to them.

3. Prepare a trial balance as of the end of November.

Check   (2) Cash, Nov. 30 bal., $38,264

(3) Trial bal. totals, $98,659

Beyond the Numbers

BTN 2-1   Refer to **Research In Motion**'s financial statements in Appendix A for the following questions.

Required

1. What amount of total liabilities does it report for each of the fiscal years ended February 28, 2009, and February 27, 2010?

2. What amount of total assets does it report for each of the fiscal years ended February 28, 2009, and February 27, 2010?

3. Compute its debt ratio for each of the fiscal years ended February 28, 2009, and February 27, 2010.

4. In which fiscal year did it employ more financial leverage (February 28, 2009, or February 27, 2010)? Explain.

Fast Forward

5. Access its financial statements (10-K report) for a fiscal year ending after February 27, 2010, from its Website (**RIM.com**) or the SEC's EDGAR database (**www.sec.gov**). Recompute its debt ratio for any subsequent year's data and compare it with the debt ratio for 2009 and 2010.

REPORTING IN ACTION

A1 A2

RIM

BTN 2-2   Key comparative figures for **Research In Motion** and **Apple** follow.

($ millions)	Research In Motion		Apple	
	Current Year	Prior Year	Current Year	Prior Year
Total liabilities	$ 2,602	$ 2,227	$15,861	$13,874
Total assets	10,204	8,101	47,501	36,171

COMPARATIVE ANALYSIS

A1 A2

RIM

Apple

1. What is the debt ratio for Research In Motion in the current year and for the prior year?

2. What is the debt ratio for Apple in the current year and for the prior year?

3. Which of the two companies has the higher degree of financial leverage? What does this imply?

ETHICS CHALLENGE

C1

BTN 2-3   Review the *Decision Ethics* case from the first part of this chapter involving the cashier. The guidance answer suggests that you should not comply with the assistant manager's request.

Required

Propose and evaluate two other courses of action you might consider, and explain why.

COMMUNICATING IN PRACTICE

C1 C2 A1 P3

BTN 2-4   Mora Stanley is an aspiring entrepreneur and your friend. She is having difficulty understanding the purposes of financial statements and how they fit together across time.

Required

Write a one-page memorandum to Stanley explaining the purposes of the four financial statements and how they are linked across time.

TAKING IT TO THE NET

A1

BTN 2-5   Access EDGAR online (www.sec.gov) and locate the 2009 year 10-K report of Amazon.com (ticker AMZN) filed on January 29, 2010. Review its financial statements reported for years ended 2009, 2008, and 2007 to answer the following questions.

Required

1. What are the amounts of its net income or net loss reported for each of these three years?
2. Do Amazon's operating activities provide cash or use cash for each of these three years?
3. If Amazon has a 2009 net income of more than $900 million and 2009 operating cash flows of more than $3,000 million, how is it possible that its cash balance at December 31, 2009, increases by less than $700 million relative to its balance at December 31, 2008?

TEAMWORK IN ACTION

C1 C2 C4 A1

BTN 2-6   The expanded accounting equation consists of assets, liabilities, common stock, dividends, revenues, and expenses. It can be used to reveal insights into changes in a company's financial position.

Required

1. Form *learning teams* of six (or more) members. Each team member must select one of the six components and each team must have at least one expert on each component: (*a*) assets, (*b*) liabilities, (*c*) common stock, (*d*) dividends, (*e*) revenues, and (*f*) expenses.
2. Form *expert teams* of individuals who selected the same component in part 1. Expert teams are to draft a report that each expert will present to his or her learning team addressing the following:
   a. Identify for its component the (i) increase and decrease side of the account and (ii) normal balance side of the account.
   b. Describe a transaction, with amounts, that increases its component.
   c. Using the transaction and amounts in (*b*), verify the equality of the accounting equation and then explain any effects on the income statement and statement of cash flows.
   d. Describe a transaction, with amounts, that decreases its component.
   e. Using the transaction and amounts in (*d*), verify the equality of the accounting equation and then explain any effects on the income statement and statement of cash flows.
3. Each expert should return to his/her learning team. In rotation, each member presents his/her expert team's report to the learning team. Team discussion is encouraged.

ENTREPRENEURIAL DECISION

A1 A2 P3

BTN 2-7   Assume Susie Levitt and Katie Shea of CitySlips plan on expanding their business to accommodate more product lines. They are considering financing their expansion in one of two ways: (1) contributing more of their own funds to the business or (2) borrowing the funds from a bank.

Required

Identify at least two issues that Susie and Katie should consider when trying to decide on the method for financing their expansion.

BTN 2-8 Lisa Langely is a young entrepreneur who operates Langely Music Services, offering singing lessons and instruction on musical instruments. Langely wishes to expand but needs a $15,000 loan. The bank requests Langely to prepare a balance sheet and key financial ratios. Langely has not kept formal records but is able to provide the following accounts and their amounts as of December 31, 2011.

ENTREPRENEURIAL DECISION

A1 A2 P3

Cash	$ 1,800	Accounts Receivable	$4,800	Prepaid Insurance	$ 750
Prepaid Rent	4,700	Store Supplies	3,300	Equipment	25,000
Accounts Payable	1,100	Unearned Lesson Fees . . .	7,800	Total Equity*	31,450
Annual net income . . .	20,000				

* The total equity amount reflects all owner investments, dividends, revenues, and expenses as of December 31, 2011.

Required

1. Prepare a balance sheet as of December 31, 2011, for Langely Music Services. (Report only the total equity amount on the balance sheet.)
2. Compute Langely's debt ratio and its return on assets (the latter ratio is defined in Chapter 1). Assume average assets equal its ending balance.
3. Do you believe the prospects of a $15,000 bank loan are good? Why or why not?

BTN 2-9 Obtain a recent copy of the most prominent newspaper distributed in your area. Research the classified section and prepare a report answering the following questions (attach relevant classified clippings to your report). Alternatively, you may want to search the Web for the required information. One suitable Website is **CareerOneStop** (**www.CareerOneStop.org**). For documentation, you should print copies of Websites accessed.

HITTING THE ROAD

C1

1. Identify the number of listings for accounting positions and the various accounting job titles.
2. Identify the number of listings for other job titles, with examples, that require or prefer accounting knowledge/experience but are not specifically accounting positions.
3. Specify the salary range for the accounting and accounting-related positions if provided.
4. Indicate the job that appeals to you, the reason for its appeal, and its requirements.

BTN 2-10 Nokia (**www.Nokia.com**) is a leading global manufacturer of mobile devices and services, and it competes to some extent with both **Research In Motion** and **Apple**. Key financial ratios for the current fiscal year follow.

GLOBAL DECISION

A2

NOKIA

RIM

Apple

Key Figure	Nokia	Research In Motion	Apple
Return on assets	0.7%	26.8%	19.7%
Debt ratio	58.7%	25.5%	33.4%

Required

1. Which company is most profitable according to its return on assets?
2. Which company is most risky according to the debt ratio?
3. Which company deserves increased investment based on a joint analysis of return on assets and the debt ratio? Explain.

ANSWERS TO MULTIPLE CHOICE QUIZ

1. b; debit Utility Expense for $700, and credit Cash for $700.
2. a; debit Cash for $2,500, and credit Unearned Lawn Service Fees for $2,500.
3. c; debit Cash for $250,000, debit Land for $500,000, and credit Common Stock for $750,000.
4. d
5. e; Debt ratio = $400,000/$1,000,000 = <u>40%</u>

Depreciation   A special category of prepaid expenses is **plant assets,** which refers to long-term tangible assets used to produce and sell products and services. Plant assets are expected to provide benefits for more than one period. Examples of plant assets are buildings, machines, vehicles, and fixtures. All plant assets, with a general exception for land, eventually wear out or decline in usefulness. The costs of these assets are deferred but are gradually reported as expenses in the income statement over the assets' useful lives (benefit periods). **Depreciation** is the process of allocating the costs of these assets over their expected useful lives. Depreciation expense is recorded with an adjusting entry similar to that for other prepaid expenses.

Point: Plant assets are also called *Plant & Equipment,* or *Property, Plant & Equipment.*

Point: Depreciation does not necessarily measure decline in market value.

Point: An asset's expected value at the end of its useful life is called *salvage value.*

Step 1: Recall that FastForward purchased equipment for $26,000 in early December to use in earning revenue. This equipment's cost must be depreciated.

Step 2: The equipment is expected to have a useful life (benefit period) of four years and to be worth about $8,000 at the end of four years. This means the *net* cost of this equipment over its useful life is $18,000 ($26,000 − $8,000). We can use any of several methods to allocate this $18,000 net cost to expense. FastForward uses a method called **straight-line depreciation,** which allocates equal amounts of the asset's net cost to depreciation during its useful life. Dividing the $18,000 net cost by the 48 months in the asset's useful life gives a monthly cost of $375 ($18,000/48).

Step 3: The adjusting entry to record monthly depreciation expense, along with T-account postings, follows:

Depreciation
Dec. 3   Purchase equipment and record asset

Dec. 31   Allocate asset cost and record depreciation

	Adjustment (c)		
Dec. 31	Depreciation Expense	375	
	Accumulated Depreciation—Equipment		375
	To record monthly equipment depreciation.		

Assets = Liabilities + Equity
−375   −375

Depreciation Expense—Equipment	612		Equipment	167		Accumulated Depreciation—Equipment	168
Dec. 31 375			Dec. 3 26,000				Dec. 31 375

Explanation   After posting the adjustment, the Equipment account ($26,000) less its Accumulated Depreciation ($375) account equals the $25,625 net cost (made up of $17,625 for the 47 remaining months in the benefit period plus the $8,000 value at the end of that time). The $375 balance in the Depreciation Expense account is reported in the December income statement. *Not* making the adjustment at December 31 would (1) understate expenses by $375 and overstate net income by $375 for the December income statement and (2) overstate both assets and equity (because of income) by $375 in the December 31 balance sheet. The following table highlights the adjustment for depreciation.

Before Adjustment	Adjustment	After Adjustment
Equipment, net = $26,000	Deduct $375 from Equipment, net Add $375 to Depreciation Expense	Equipment, net = $25,625
Reports $26,000 in equipment.	Record $375 in depreciation and $375 as accumulated depreciation, which is deducted from equipment.	Reports $25,625 in equipment, net of accumulated depreciation.

Accumulated depreciation is kept in a separate contra account. A **contra account** is an account linked with another account, where the contra account has a normal balance opposite of the account it is linked with. It is reported as a subtraction from that other account's balance. For instance, FastForward's contra account of Accumulated Depreciation—Equipment is subtracted from the Equipment account in the balance sheet (see Exhibit 3.7). This contra account allows balance sheet readers to know both the full costs of assets and the total depreciation.

The title of the contra account, *Accumulated Depreciation,* reveals that this account includes total depreciation expense for all prior periods for which the asset was used. To illustrate, the Equipment and the Accumulated Depreciation accounts appear as in Exhibit 3.6 on February 28, 2012, after three months of adjusting entries. The $1,125 balance in the accumulated depreciation account can be subtracted from its related $26,000 asset cost. The difference ($24,875) between these two balances is the cost of the asset that has not yet been depreciated. This difference is

Point: The cost principle requires an asset to be initially recorded at acquisition cost. Depreciation causes the asset's book value (cost less accumulated depreciation) to decline over time.

EXHIBIT 3.6

Accounts after Three Months of
Depreciation Adjustments

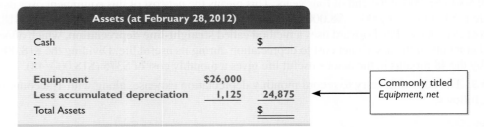

Equipment		167
Dec. 3	26,000	

Accumulated Depreciation—Equipment		168
	Dec. 31	375
	Jan. 31	375
	Feb. 28	375
	Balance	1,125

Point: The net cost of equipment is also called the *depreciable basis.*

called the **book value,** or the *net amount,* which equals the asset's costs less its accumulated depreciation.

These account balances are reported in the assets section of the February 28 balance sheet in Exhibit 3.7.

EXHIBIT 3.7

Equipment and Accumulated Depreciation on February 28 Balance Sheet

Assets (at February 28, 2012)		
Cash		$
⋮		
Equipment	$26,000	
Less accumulated depreciation	1,125	24,875
Total Assets		$

Commonly titled *Equipment, net*

Fraud

Where Are the Assets? The U.S. government seems to lose assets. The **Center for Disease Control and Prevention** (CDC) seems especially vulnerable. In a recent year, the CDC lost track of over $8 million in computer and video equipment. In another year it was unable to account for nearly $6 million in computers, microscopes, and vehicles. The president of *Citizens Against Government Waste* said "It's just a good thing they haven't lost any diseases!"

Unearned (Deferred) Revenues

The term **unearned revenues** refers to cash received in advance of providing products and services. Unearned revenues, also called *deferred revenues,* are liabilities. When cash is accepted, an obligation to provide products or services is accepted. As products or services are provided, the unearned revenues become *earned* revenues. Adjusting entries for unearned revenues involve increasing revenues and decreasing unearned revenues, as shown in Exhibit 3.8.

EXHIBIT 3.8

Adjusting for Unearned Revenues

	Decreased			Increased
	Liability			Revenue
Debit adjustment	Unadjusted balance			Credit adjustment

Dr. Liability..... #
Cr. Revenue... #

Point: To *defer* is to postpone. We postpone reporting amounts received as revenues until they are earned.

An example of unearned revenues is from **The New York Times Company,** which reports unexpired (unearned) subscriptions of $81 million: "Proceeds from ... subscriptions are deferred at the time of sale and are recognized in earnings on a pro rata basis over the terms of the subscriptions." Unearned revenues are nearly 10% of the current liabilities for the Times. Another example comes from the **Boston Celtics.** When the Celtics receive cash from advance ticket sales and broadcast fees, they record it in an unearned revenue account called *Deferred Game Revenues.* The Celtics recognize this unearned revenue with adjusting entries on a game-by-game basis. Since the NBA regular season begins in October and ends in April, revenue recognition is mainly limited to this period. For a recent season, the Celtics' quarterly revenues were $0 million for July–September; $34 million for October–December; $48 million for January–March; and $17 million for April–June.

Returning to FastForward, it also has unearned revenues. It agreed on December 26 to provide consulting services to a client for a fixed fee of $3,000 for 60 days.

Step 1: On December 26, the client paid the 60-day fee in advance, covering the period December 27 to February 24. The entry to record the cash received in advance is

Unearned Revenues

Dec. 26 Cash received in advance and record liability

Thanks for cash in advance. I'll work now through Feb. 24

Dec. 31 Provided services and record revenue

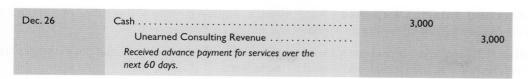

Dec. 26	Cash	3,000	
	Unearned Consulting Revenue		3,000
	Received advance payment for services over the next 60 days.		

Assets = Liabilities + Equity
+3,000   +3,000

This advance payment increases cash and creates an obligation to do consulting work over the next 60 days.

Step 2: As time passes, FastForward earns this payment through consulting. By December 31, it has provided five days' service and earned 5/60 of the $3,000 unearned revenue. This amounts to $250 ($3,000 × 5/60). The *revenue recognition principle* implies that $250 of unearned revenue must be reported as revenue on the December income statement.

Step 3: The adjusting entry to reduce the liability account and recognize earned revenue, along with T-account postings, follows:

Dec. 31	**Adjustment (d)**		
	Unearned Consulting Revenue	250	
	Consulting Revenue		250
	To record earned revenue that was received in advance ($3,000 × 5/60).		

Assets = Liabilities + Equity
−250   +250

Unearned Consulting Revenue			236
Dec. 31	250	Dec. 26	3,000
		Balance	2,750

Consulting Revenue			403
		Dec. 5	4,200
		12	1,600
		31	250
		Balance	6,050

Explanation   The adjusting entry transfers $250 from unearned revenue (a liability account) to a revenue account. *Not* making the adjustment (1) understates revenue and net income by $250 in the December income statement and (2) overstates unearned revenue and understates equity by $250 on the December 31 balance sheet. The following highlights the adjustment for unearned revenue.

Before Adjustment	Adjustment	After Adjustment
Unearned Consulting Revenue = $3,000	**Deduct $250 from Unearned Consulting Revenue** **Add $250 to Consulting Revenue**	**Unearned Consulting Revenue = $2,750**
Reports $3,000 in unearned revenue for consulting services promised for 60 days.	Record 5 days of earned consulting revenue, which is 5/60 of unearned amount.	Reports $2,750 in unearned revenue for consulting services owed over next 55 days.

Accounting for unearned revenues is crucial to many companies. For example, the **National Retail Federation** reports that gift card sales, which are unearned revenues for sellers, exceed $20 billion annually. Gift cards are now the top selling holiday gift.

Accrued Expenses

Accrued expenses refer to costs that are incurred in a period but are both unpaid and unrecorded. Accrued expenses must be reported on the income statement of the period when incurred. Adjusting entries for recording accrued expenses involve increasing expenses and increasing liabilities as shown in Exhibit 3.9. This adjustment recognizes expenses incurred in a period but not yet paid. Common examples of accrued expenses are salaries, interest, rent, and taxes. We use salaries and interest to show how to adjust accounts for accrued expenses.

Point: Accrued expenses are also called accrued liabilities.

EXHIBIT 3.9

Adjusting for Accrued Expenses

Accrued Salaries Expense FastForward's employee earns $70 per day, or $350 for a five-day workweek beginning on Monday and ending on Friday.

Step 1: Its employee is paid every two weeks on Friday. On December 12 and 26, the wages are paid, recorded in the journal, and posted to the ledger.

Step 2: The calendar in Exhibit 3.10 shows three working days after the December 26 payday (29, 30, and 31). This means the employee has earned three days' salary by the close of business

EXHIBIT 3.10

Salary Accrual and Paydays

Point: An employer records salaries expense and a vacation pay liability when employees earn vacation pay.

on Wednesday, December 31, yet this salary cost has not been paid or recorded. The financial statements would be incomplete if FastForward fails to report the added expense and liability to the employee for unpaid salary from December 29, 30, and 31.

Step 3: The adjusting entry to account for accrued salaries, along with T-account postings, follows:

Assets = Liabilities + Equity
        +210   −210

Explanation Salaries expense of $1,610 is reported on the December income statement and $210 of salaries payable (liability) is reported in the balance sheet. *Not* making the adjustment (1) understates salaries expense and overstates net income by $210 in the December income statement and (2) understates salaries payable (liabilities) and overstates equity by $210 on the December 31 balance sheet. The following highlights the adjustment for salaries incurred.

Before Adjustment	Adjustment	After Adjustment
Salaries Payable = $0	**Add $210 to Salaries Payable** **Add $210 to Salaries Expense**	**Salaries Payable = $210**
Reports $0 from employee salaries incurred but not yet paid in cash.	Record 3 days' salaries owed to employee, but not yet paid, at $70 per day.	Reports $210 salaries payable to employee but not yet paid.

Accrued Interest Expense Companies commonly have accrued interest expense on notes payable and other long-term liabilities at the end of a period. Interest expense is incurred with the passage of time. Unless interest is paid on the last day of an accounting period, we need to adjust for interest expense incurred but not yet paid. This means we must accrue interest cost from the most recent payment date up to the end of the period. The formula for computing accrued interest is:

Principal amount owed × Annual interest rate × Fraction of year since last payment date.

To illustrate, if a company has a $6,000 loan from a bank at 6% annual interest, then 30 days' accrued interest expense is $30—computed as $6,000 × 0.06 × 30/360. The adjusting entry would be to debit Interest Expense for $30 and credit Interest Payable for $30.

Point: Interest computations assume a 360-day year; known as the *bankers' rule.*

Future Payment of Accrued Expenses   Adjusting entries for accrued expenses foretell cash transactions in future periods. Specifically, accrued expenses at the end of one accounting period result in *cash payment* in a *future period*(s). To illustrate, recall that FastForward recorded accrued salaries of $210. On January 9, the first payday of the next period, the following entry settles the accrued liability (salaries payable) and records salaries expense for seven days of work in January:

Jan. 9	Salaries Payable (3 days at $70 per day)	210	
	Salaries Expense (7 days at $70 per day)	490	
	Cash		700
	Paid two weeks' salary including three days accrued in December.		

Assets = Liabilities + Equity
−700   −210   −490

The $210 debit reflects the payment of the liability for the three days' salary accrued on December 31. The $490 debit records the salary for January's first seven working days (including the New Year's Day holiday) as an expense of the new accounting period. The $700 credit records the total amount of cash paid to the employee.

Accrued Revenues

The term **accrued revenues** refers to revenues earned in a period that are both unrecorded and not yet received in cash (or other assets). An example is a technician who bills customers only when the job is done. If one-third of a job is complete by the end of a period, then the technician must record one-third of the expected billing as revenue in that period—even though there is no billing or collection. The adjusting entries for accrued revenues increase assets and increase revenues as shown in Exhibit 3.11. Accrued revenues commonly arise from services, products, interest, and rent. We use service fees and interest to show how to adjust for accrued revenues.

Point: Accrued revenues are also called *accrued assets.*

EXHIBIT 3.11

Adjusting for Accrued Revenues

Accrued Services Revenue   Accrued revenues are not recorded until adjusting entries are made at the end of the accounting period. These accrued revenues are earned but unrecorded because either the buyer has not yet paid for them or the seller has not yet billed the buyer. FastForward provides an example.

Step 1: In the second week of December, it agreed to provide 30 days of consulting services to a local fitness club for a fixed fee of $2,700. The terms of the initial agreement call for Fast-Forward to provide services from December 12, 2011, through January 10, 2012, or 30 days of service. The club agrees to pay FastForward $2,700 on January 10, 2012, when the service period is complete.

Step 2: At December 31, 2011, 20 days of services have already been provided. Since the contracted services have not yet been entirely provided, FastForward has neither billed the club nor recorded the services already provided. Still, FastForward has earned two-thirds of the 30-day fee, or $1,800 ($2,700 × 20/30). The *revenue recognition principle* implies that it must report the $1,800 on the December income statement. The balance sheet also must report that the club owes FastForward $1,800.

Accrued Revenues

Dec. 31   Record revenue and receivable for services provided but unbilled

Pay me next month

Jan. 10   Receive cash and reduce receivable

reversing entries. Steps 1 through 3 usually occur regularly as a company enters into transactions. Steps 4 through 9 are done at the end of a period. *Reversing entries* in step 10 are optional and are explained in Appendix 3C.

Quick Check
Answers — p. 130

14. What are the major steps in preparing closing entries?
15. Why are revenue and expense accounts called *temporary?* Identify and list the types of temporary accounts.
16. What accounts are listed on the post-closing trial balance?

CLASSIFIED BALANCE SHEET

Our discussion to this point has been limited to unclassified financial statements. This section describes a classified balance sheet. The next chapter describes a classified income statement. An **unclassified balance sheet** is one whose items are broadly grouped into assets, liabilities, and equity. One example is FastForward's balance sheet in Exhibit 3.14. A **classified balance sheet** organizes assets and liabilities into important subgroups that provide more information to decision makers.

C4 Explain and prepare a classified balance sheet.

Classification Structure

A classified balance sheet has no required layout, but it usually contains the categories in Exhibit 3.20. One of the more important classifications is the separation between current and noncurrent items for both assets and liabilities. Current items are those expected to come due (either collected or owed) within one year or the company's operating cycle, whichever is longer. The **operating cycle** is the time span from when *cash is used* to acquire goods and services until *cash is received* from the sale of goods and services. "Operating" refers to company operations and "cycle" refers to the circular flow of cash used for company inputs and then cash received from its outputs. The length of a company's operating cycle depends on its activities. For a service company, the operating cycle is the time span between (1) paying employees who perform the services and (2) receiving cash from customers. For a merchandiser selling products, the operating cycle is the time span between (1) paying suppliers for merchandise and (2) receiving cash from customers.

Point: Current and Noncurrent are also referred to as Short-Term and Long-Term, respectively.

Assets	Liabilities and Equity
Current assets	Current liabilities
Noncurrent assets	Noncurrent liabilities
Long-term investments	Equity
Plant assets	
Intangible assets	

EXHIBIT 3.20

Typical Categories in a Classified Balance Sheet

Most operating cycles are less than one year. This means most companies use a one-year period in deciding which assets and liabilities are current. A few companies have an operating cycle longer than one year. For instance, producers of certain beverages (wine) and products (ginseng) that require aging for several years have operating cycles longer than one year. A balance sheet lists current assets before noncurrent assets and current liabilities before noncurrent liabilities. This consistency in presentation allows users to quickly identify current assets that are most easily converted to cash and current liabilities that are shortly coming due. Items in current assets and current liabilities are listed in the order of how quickly they will be converted to, or paid in, cash.

EXHIBIT 3.21

Example of a Classified Balance Sheet

SNOWBOARDING COMPONENTS
Balance Sheet
January 31, 2011

Assets

Current assets

Cash	$ 6,500	
Short-term investments	2,100	
Accounts receivable, net	4,400	
Merchandise inventory	27,500	
Prepaid expenses	2,400	
Total current assets		$ 42,900

Long-term investments

Notes receivable	1,500	
Investments in stocks and bonds	18,000	
Land held for future expansion	48,000	
Total long-term investments		67,500

Plant assets

Equipment and buildings	203,200	
Less accumulated depreciation	53,000	
Equipment and buildings, net		150,200
Land		73,200
Total plant assets		223,400
Intangible assets		10,000
Total assets		$343,800

Liabilities

Current liabilities

Accounts payable	$ 15,300	
Wages payable	3,200	
Notes payable	3,000	
Current portion of long-term liabilities	7,500	
Total current liabilities		$ 29,000
Long-term liabilities (net of current portion)		150,000
Total liabilities		179,000

Equity

Common stock		50,000
Retained earnings		114,800
Total equity		164,800
Total liabilities and equity		$343,800

Classification Categories

This section describes the most common categories in a classified balance sheet. The balance sheet for Snowboarding Components in Exhibit 3.21 shows the typical categories. Its assets are classified as either current or noncurrent. Its noncurrent assets include three main categories: long-term investments, plant assets, and intangible assets. Its liabilities are classified as either current or long-term. Not all companies use the same categories of assets and liabilities for their balance sheets. **K2 Inc.**, a manufacturer of snowboards, reported a balance sheet with only three asset classes: current assets; property, plant and equipment; and other assets.

Current Assets **Current assets** are cash and other resources that are expected to be sold, collected, or used within one year or the company's operating cycle, whichever is longer. Examples are cash, short-term investments, accounts receivable, short-term notes receivable, goods for sale (called *merchandise* or *inventory*), and prepaid expenses. The individual prepaid expenses of a company are usually small in amount compared to many other assets and are often combined and shown as a single item. The prepaid expenses likely include items such as prepaid insurance, prepaid rent, office supplies, and store supplies. Prepaid expenses are usually listed last because they will not be converted to cash (instead, they are used).

Long-Term Investments A second major balance sheet classification is **long-term** (or *noncurrent*) **investments.** Notes receivable and investments in stocks and bonds are long-term assets when they are expected to be held for more than the longer of one year or the operating cycle. Land held for future expansion is a long-term investment because it is *not* used in operations.

Plant Assets Plant assets are tangible assets that are both *long-lived* and *used to produce* or *sell products and services.* Examples are equipment, machinery, buildings, and land that are used to produce or sell products and services. The order listing for plant assets is usually from most liquid to least liquid such as equipment and machinery to buildings and land.

Intangible Assets Intangible assets are long-term resources that benefit business operations, usually lack physical form, and have uncertain benefits. Examples are patents, trademarks, copyrights, franchises, and goodwill. Their value comes from the privileges or rights granted to or held by the owner. **K2, Inc.,** reported intangible assets of $228 million, which is nearly 20 percent of its total assets. Its intangibles included trademarks, patents, and licensing agreements.

Current Liabilities **Current liabilities** are obligations due to be paid or settled within one year or the operating cycle, whichever is longer. They are usually settled by paying out current assets such as cash. Current liabilities often include accounts payable, notes payable, wages payable, taxes payable, interest payable, and unearned revenues. Also, any portion of a long-term liability due to be paid within one year or the operating cycle, whichever is longer, is a current liability. Unearned revenues are current liabilities when they will be settled by delivering products or services within one year or the operating cycle, whichever is longer. Current liabilities are reported in the order of those to be settled first.

Long-Term Liabilities **Long-term liabilities** are obligations *not* due within one year or the operating cycle, whichever is longer. Notes payable, mortgages payable, bonds payable, and lease obligations are common long-term liabilities. If a company has both short- and long-term items in each of these categories, they are commonly separated into two accounts in the ledger.

Equity Equity is the owner's claim on assets. The equity section for a corporation is divided into two main subsections, common stock and retained earnings.

Point: Current is also called *short-term*, and noncurrent is also called *long-term*.

Point: Plant assets are also called *fixed assets; property, plant and equipment;* or *long-lived assets.*

Point: Many financial ratios are distorted if accounts are not classified correctly.

Point: Only assets and liabilities are classified as current or noncurrent.

Quick Check
Answers — p. 130

17. Classify the following assets as (1) current assets, (2) plant assets, or (3) intangible assets: (*a*) land used in operations, (*b*) office supplies, (*c*) receivables from customers due in 10 months, (*d*) insurance protection for the next 9 months, (*e*) trucks used to provide services to customers, (*f*) trademarks.
18. Cite at least two examples of assets classified as investments on the balance sheet.
19. Explain the operating cycle for a service company.

GLOBAL VIEW

We explained that accounting under U.S. GAAP is similar, but not identical, to that under IFRS. This section discusses differences in adjusting accounts, preparing financial statements, and reporting assets and liabilities on a balance sheet.

Adjusting Accounts   Both U.S. GAAP and IFRS include broad and similar guidance for adjusting accounts. Although some variations exist in revenue and expense recognition and other principles, all of the adjustments in this chapter are accounted for identically under the two systems. In later chapters we describe how certain assets and liabilities can result in different adjusted amounts using fair value measurements.

Preparing Financial Statements   Both U.S. GAAP and IFRS prepare the same four basic financial statements following the same process discussed in this chapter. Chapter 2 explained how both U.S. GAAP and IFRS require current items to be separated from noncurrent items on the balance sheet (yielding a classified balance sheet). U.S. GAAP balance sheets report current items first. Assets are listed from most liquid to least liquid, where liquid refers to the ease of converting an asset to cash. Liabilities are listed from nearest to maturity to furthest from maturity, maturity refers to the nearness of paying off the liability. IFRS balance sheets normally present noncurrent items first (and equity before liabilities), but this is not a requirement. Other differences with financial statements exist, which we identify in later chapters. Nokia provides the following example of IFRS reporting for its assets, liabilities, and equity within the balance sheet:

NOKIA

NOKIA				
Balance Sheet (in EUR millions)				
December 31, 2009				
Assets			**Equity and Liabilities**	
Noncurrent assets		Total equity		14,749
Goodwill and other intangibles	8,076	Noncurrent liabilities		
Property, plant and equipment	1,867	Long-term interest-bearing liabilities		4,432
Other noncurrent assets	2,182	Other long-term liabilities		1,369
Total noncurrent assets	12,125	Total noncurrent liabilities		5,801
Current assets		Current liabilities		
Inventories...........................	1,865	Current portion of long-term loans........		44
Accounts receivable, net	7,981	Short-term borrowings and other liabilities ...		972
Prepaid expenses and accrued income	4,551	Accounts payable		4,950
Other current assets	8,074	Accrued expenses		6,504
Cash	1,142	Provisions		2,718
Total current assets	23,613	Total current liabilities		15,188
Total assets	35,738	Total equity and liabilities		35,738

Closing Process   The closing process is identical under U.S. GAAP and IFRS. Although unique accounts can arise under either system, the closing process remains the same.

  IFRS _____

Revenue and expense recognition are key to recording accounting adjustments. IFRS tends to be more *principles-based* relative to U.S. GAAP, which is viewed as more *rules-based*. A principles-based system depends heavily on control procedures to reduce the potential for fraud or misconduct. Failure in judgment led to improper accounting adjustments at **Fannie Mae**, **Xerox**, **WorldCom**, and others. A KPMG 2009 survey of accounting and finance employees found that 13% of them had witnessed falsification or manipulation of accounting data within the past year. Internal controls and governance processes are directed at curtailing such behavior. ●

| Profit Margin and Current Ratio | | Decision Analysis |

A useful measure of a company's operating results is the ratio of its net income to net sales. This ratio is called **profit margin,** or *return on sales,* and is computed as in Exhibit 3.22.

A2 Compute profit margin and describe its use in analyzing company performance.

$$\text{Profit margin} = \frac{\text{Net income}}{\text{Net sales}}$$

EXHIBIT 3.22

Profit Margin

This ratio is interpreted as reflecting the percent of profit in each dollar of sales. To illustrate how we compute and use profit margin, let's look at the results of **Limited Brands, Inc.,** in Exhibit 3.23 for its fiscal years 2006 through 2010.

EXHIBIT 3.23

Limited Brands' Profit Margin

$ in millions	2010	2009	2008	2007	2006
Net income	$ 448	$ 220	$ 718	$ 676	$ 683
Net sales	$8,632	$9,043	$10,134	$10,671	$9,699
Profit margin	5.2%	2.4%	7.1%	6.3%	7.0%
Industry profit margin	0.9%	0.3%	1.1%	1.6%	1.5%

The Limited's average profit margin is 5.6% during this 5-year period. This favorably compares to the average industry profit margin of 1.1%. However, Limited's profit margin has declined in the most recent two years—from 7.1% in 2008 to 2.4% and 5.2% for the recent recessionary periods (see margin graph). Future success depends on Limited maintaining its market share and increasing its profit margin.

Current Ratio

An important use of financial statements is to help assess a company's ability to pay its debts in the near future. Such analysis affects decisions by suppliers when allowing a company to buy on credit. It also affects decisions by creditors when lending money to a company, including loan terms such as interest rate, due date, and collateral requirements. It can also affect a manager's decisions about using cash to pay debts when they come due. The **current ratio** is one measure of a company's ability to pay its short-term obligations. It is defined in Exhibit 3.24 as current assets divided by current liabilities.

A3 Compute the current ratio and describe what it reveals about a company's financial condition.

$$\text{Current ratio} = \frac{\text{Current assets}}{\text{Current liabilities}}$$

EXHIBIT 3.24

Current Ratio

Using financial information from **Limited Brands, Inc.,** we compute its current ratio for the recent four-year period. The results are in Exhibit 3.25.

EXHIBIT 3.25

Limited Brands' Current Ratio

$ in millions	2010	2009	2008	2007	2006
Current assets	$3,250	$2,867	$2,919	$2,771	$2,784
Current liabilities	$1,322	$1,255	$1,374	$1,709	$1,575
Current ratio	2.5	2.3	2.1	1.6	1.8
Industry current ratio	1.9	2.0	2.1	2.3	2.4

Limited Brands' current ratio averaged 2.1 for its fiscal years 2006 through 2010. The current ratio for each of these years suggests that the company's short-term obligations can be covered with its short-term assets. However, if its ratio would approach 1.0, Limited would expect to face challenges in covering liabilities. If the ratio were *less* than 1.0, current liabilities would exceed current assets, and the company's ability to pay short-term obligations could be in doubt.

Decision Maker Answer — p. 130

Analyst You are analyzing the financial condition of a company to assess its ability to meet upcoming loan payments. You compute its current ratio as 1.2. You also find that a major portion of accounts receivable is due from one client who has not made any payments in the past 12 months. Removing this receivable from current assets lowers the current ratio to 0.7. What do you conclude? ■

DEMONSTRATION PROBLEM 1

The following information relates to Fanning's Electronics on December 31, 2011. The company, which uses the calendar year as its annual reporting period, initially records prepaid and unearned items in balance sheet accounts (assets and liabilities, respectively).

a. The company's weekly payroll is $8,750, paid each Friday for a five-day workweek. Assume December 31, 2011, falls on a Monday, but the employees will not be paid their wages until Friday, January 4, 2012.

b. Eighteen months earlier, on July 1, 2010, the company purchased equipment that cost $20,000. Its useful life is predicted to be five years, at which time the equipment is expected to be worthless (zero salvage value).

c. On October 1, 2011, the company agreed to work on a new housing development. The company is paid $120,000 on October 1 in advance of future installation of similar alarm systems in 24 new homes. That amount was credited to the Unearned Services Revenue account. Between October 1 and December 31, work on 20 homes was completed.

d. On September 1, 2011, the company purchased a 12-month insurance policy for $1,800. The transaction was recorded with an $1,800 debit to Prepaid Insurance.

e. On December 29, 2011, the company completed a $7,000 service that has not been billed and not recorded as of December 31, 2011.

Required

1. Prepare any necessary adjusting entries on December 31, 2011, in relation to transactions and events *a* through *e*.

2. Prepare T-accounts for the accounts affected by adjusting entries, and post the adjusting entries. Determine the adjusted balances for the Unearned Revenue and the Prepaid Insurance accounts.

3. Complete the following table and determine the amounts and effects of your adjusting entries on the year 2011 income statement and the December 31, 2011, balance sheet. Use up (down) arrows to indicate an increase (decrease) in the Effect columns.

Entry	Amount in the Entry	Effect on Net Income	Effect on Total Assets	Effect on Total Liabilities	Effect on Total Equity

PLANNING THE SOLUTION

● Analyze each situation to determine which accounts need to be updated with an adjustment.

● Calculate the amount of each adjustment and prepare the necessary journal entries.

● Show the amount of each adjustment in the designated accounts, determine the adjusted balance, and identify the balance sheet classification of the account.

● Determine each entry's effect on net income for the year and on total assets, total liabilities, and total equity at the end of the year.

SOLUTION TO DEMONSTRATION PROBLEM 1

1. Adjusting journal entries.

(a) Dec. 31	Wages Expense	1,750	
	Wages Payable		1,750
	To accrue wages for the last day of the year ($8,750 × 1/5).		
(b) Dec. 31	Depreciation Expense—Equipment	4,000	
	Accumulated Depreciation—Equipment		4,000
	To record depreciation expense for the year ($20,000/5 years = $4,000 per year).		
(c) Dec. 31	Unearned Services Revenue	100,000	
	Services Revenue		100,000
	To recognize services revenue earned ($120,000 × 20/24).		
(d) Dec. 31	Insurance Expense	600	
	Prepaid Insurance		600
	To adjust for expired portion of insurance ($1,800 × 4/12).		
(e) Dec. 31	Accounts Receivable	7,000	
	Services Revenue		7,000
	To record services revenue earned.		

2. T-accounts for adjusting journal entries *a* through *e*.

Wages Expense	
(a) 1,750	

Wages Payable	
	(a) 1,750

Depreciation Expense—Equipment	
(b) 4,000	

Accumulated Depreciation—Equipment	
	(b) 4,000

Unearned Revenue	
	Unadj. Bal. 120,000
(c) 100,000	
	Adj. Bal. 20,000

Services Revenue	
	(c) 100,000
	(e) 7,000
	Adj. Bal. 107,000

Insurance Expense	
(d) 600	

Prepaid Insurance	
Unadj. Bal. 1,800	
	(d) 600
Adj. Bal. 1,200	

Accounts Receivable	
(e) 7,000	

3. Financial statement effects of adjusting journal entries.

Entry	Amount in the Entry	Effect on Net Income	Effect on Total Assets	Effect on Total Liabilities	Effect on Total Equity
a	$ 1,750	$ 1,750 ↓	No effect	$ 1,750 ↑	$ 1,750 ↓
b	4,000	4,000 ↓	$4,000 ↓	No effect	4,000 ↓
c	100,000	100,000 ↑	No effect	$100,000 ↓	100,000 ↑
d	600	600 ↓	$ 600 ↓	No effect	600 ↓
e	7,000	7,000 ↑	$7,000 ↑	No effect	7,000 ↑

DEMONSTRATION PROBLEM 2

Use the following adjusted trial balance to answer questions 1–3.

CHOI COMPANY Adjusted Trial Balance December 31		
	Debit	Credit
Cash	$ 3,050	
Accounts receivable	400	
Prepaid insurance	830	
Supplies	80	
Equipment	217,200	
Accumulated depreciation—Equipment		$ 29,100
Wages payable		880
Interest payable		3,600
Unearned rent		460
Long-term notes payable		150,000
Common stock.............................		10,000
Retained earnings		30,340
Dividends	21,000	
Rent earned		57,500
Wages expense	25,000	
Utilities expense	1,900	
Insurance expense	3,200	
Supplies expense	250	
Depreciation expense—Equipment	5,970	
Interest expense	3,000	
Totals	$281,880	$281,880

1. Prepare the annual income statement from the adjusted trial balance of Choi Company.

Answer:

CHOI COMPANY Income Statement For Year Ended December 31		
Revenues		
Rent earned		$57,500
Expenses		
Wages expense	$25,000	
Utilities expense	1,900	
Insurance expense	3,200	
Supplies expense	250	
Depreciation expense—Equipment	5,970	
Interest expense	3,000	
Total expenses		39,320
Net income		$18,180

2. Prepare a statement of retained earnings from the adjusted trial balance of Choi Company.

Answer:

CHOI COMPANY Statement of Retained Earnings For Year Ended December 31	
Retained earnings, December 31 prior year-end	$30,340
Plus: Net income	18,180
	48,520
Less: Dividends....................................	21,000
Retained earnings, December 31 current year-end	$27,520

3. Prepare a balance sheet from the adjusted trial balance of Choi Company.

Answer:

CHOI COMPANY
Balance Sheet
December 31

Assets

Cash		$ 3,050
Accounts receivable		400
Prepaid insurance		830
Supplies		80
Equipment	$217,200	
Less accumulated depreciation	29,100	188,100
Total assets		$192,460

Liabilities

Wages payable		$ 880
Interest payable		3,600
Unearned rent		460
Long-term notes payable		150,000
Total liabilities		154,940

Equity

Common stock		10,000
Retained earnings		27,520
Total equity		37,520
Total liabilities and equity		$192,460

Alternative Accounting for Prepayments

3A

This appendix explains an alternative in accounting for prepaid expenses and unearned revenues.

Recording Prepayment of Expenses <u>in Expense Accounts</u>   An alternative method is to record *all* prepaid expenses with debits to expense accounts. If any prepaids remain unused or unexpired at the end of an accounting period, then adjusting entries must transfer the cost of the unused portions from expense accounts to prepaid expense (asset) accounts. This alternative method is acceptable. The financial statements are identical under either method, but the adjusting entries are different. To illustrate the differences between these two methods, let's look at FastForward's cash payment of December 6 for 24 months of insurance coverage beginning on December 1. FastForward recorded that payment with a debit to an asset account, but it could have recorded a debit to an expense account. These alternatives are shown in Exhibit 3A.1.

> **P6** Explain the alternatives in accounting for prepaids.

		Payment Recorded as Asset	Payment Recorded as Expense
Dec. 6	Prepaid Insurance	2,400	
	Cash	2,400	
Dec. 6	Insurance Expense		2,400
	Cash		2,400

EXHIBIT 3A.1

Alternative Initial Entries for Prepaid Expenses

At the end of its accounting period on December 31, insurance protection for one month has expired. This means $100 ($2,400/24) of insurance coverage expired and is an expense for December. The adjusting entry depends on how the original payment was recorded. This is shown in Exhibit 3A.2.

EXHIBIT 3A.2

Adjusting Entry for Prepaid Expenses for the Two Alternatives

			Payment Recorded as Asset	Payment Recorded as Expense
Dec. 31	Insurance Expense		100	
	Prepaid Insurance		100	
Dec. 31	Prepaid Insurance			2,300
	Insurance Expense			2,300

When these entries are posted to the accounts in the ledger, we can see that these two methods give identical results. The December 31 adjusted account balances in Exhibit 3A.3 show Prepaid Insurance of $2,300 and Insurance Expense of $100 for both methods.

EXHIBIT 3A.3

Account Balances under Two Alternatives for Recording Prepaid Expenses

Payment Recorded as Asset					Payment Recorded as Expense			

Prepaid Insurance			128
Dec. 6	2,400	Dec. 31	100
Balance	2,300		

Prepaid Insurance		128
Dec. 31	2,300	

Insurance Expense			637
Dec. 31	100		

Insurance Expense			637
Dec. 6	2,400	Dec. 31	2,300
Balance	100		

Recording Prepayment of Revenues <u>in Revenue Accounts</u>   As with prepaid expenses, an alternative method is to record *all* unearned revenues with credits to revenue accounts. If any revenues are unearned at the end of an accounting period, then adjusting entries must transfer the unearned portions from revenue accounts to unearned revenue (liability) accounts. This alternative method is acceptable. The adjusting entries are different for these two alternatives, but the financial statements are identical. To illustrate the accounting differences between these two methods, let's look at FastForward's December 26 receipt of $3,000 for consulting services covering the period December 27 to February 24. FastForward recorded this transaction with a credit to a liability account. The alternative is to record it with a credit to a revenue account, as shown in Exhibit 3A.4.

EXHIBIT 3A.4

Alternative Initial Entries for Unearned Revenues

			Receipt Recorded as Liability	Receipt Recorded as Revenue
Dec. 26	Cash		3,000	
	Unearned Consulting Revenue		3,000	
Dec. 26	Cash			3,000
	Consulting Revenue			3,000

By the end of its accounting period on December 31, FastForward has earned $250 of this revenue. This means $250 of the liability has been satisfied. Depending on how the initial receipt is recorded, the adjusting entry is as shown in Exhibit 3A.5.

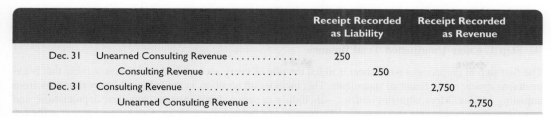

	Receipt Recorded as Liability	Receipt Recorded as Revenue
Dec. 31	Unearned Consulting Revenue	250	
	Consulting Revenue		250
Dec. 31	Consulting Revenue		2,750
	Unearned Consulting Revenue		2,750

EXHIBIT 3A.5

Adjusting Entry for Unearned Revenues for the Two Alternatives

After adjusting entries are posted, the two alternatives give identical results. The December 31 adjusted account balances in Exhibit 3A.6 show unearned consulting revenue of $2,750 and consulting revenue of $250 for both methods.

EXHIBIT 3A.6

Account Balances under Two Alternatives for Recording Unearned Revenues

Receipt Recorded as Liability

Unearned Consulting Revenue			236
Dec. 31	250	Dec. 26	3,000
		Balance	2,750

Consulting Revenue			403
		Dec. 31	250

Receipt Recorded as Revenue

Unearned Consulting Revenue			236
		Dec. 31	2,750

Consulting Revenue			403
Dec. 31	2,750	Dec. 26	3,000
		Balance	250

Work Sheet as a Tool

3B

Information preparers use various analyses and internal documents when organizing information for internal and external decision makers. Internal documents are often called **working papers.** One widely used working paper is the **work sheet,** which is a useful tool for preparers in working with accounting information. It is usually not available to external decision makers.

Benefits of a Work Sheet (Spreadsheet)   A work sheet is *not* a required report, yet using a manual or electronic work sheet has several potential benefits. Specifically, a work sheet:

P7 Prepare a work sheet and explain its usefulness.

- Aids the preparation of financial statements.
- Reduces the possibility of errors when working with many accounts and adjustments.
- Links accounts and adjustments to their impacts in financial statements.
- Assists in planning and organizing an audit of financial statements—as it can be used to reflect any adjustments necessary.
- Helps in preparing interim (monthly and quarterly) financial statements when the journalizing and posting of adjusting entries are postponed until the year-end.
- Shows the effects of proposed or "what if" transactions.

Use of a Work Sheet (Spreadsheet)   When a work sheet is used to prepare financial statements, it is constructed at the end of a period before the adjusting process. The complete work sheet includes a list of the accounts, their balances and adjustments, and their sorting into financial statement columns. It provides two columns each for the unadjusted trial balance, the adjustments, the adjusted trial balance, the income statement, and the balance sheet. To describe and interpret the work sheet, we

Point: Since a work sheet is *not* a required report or an accounting record, its format is flexible and can be modified by its user to fit his/her preferences.

use the information from FastForward. Preparing the work sheet has five important steps. Each step, 1 through 5, is color-coded and explained with reference to Exhibit 3B.1.

① Step 1. Enter Unadjusted Trial Balance

The first step in preparing a work sheet is to list the title of every account and its account number that is expected to appear on its financial statements. This includes all accounts in the ledger plus any new ones from adjusting entries. Most adjusting entries—including expenses from salaries, supplies, depreciation, and insurance—are predictable and recurring. The unadjusted balance for each account is then entered in the appropriate Debit or Credit column of the unadjusted trial balance columns. The totals of these two columns must be equal. Exhibit 3B.1 shows FastForward's work sheet after completing this first step. Sometimes blank lines are left on the work sheet based on past experience to indicate where lines will be needed for adjustments to certain accounts. Exhibit 3B.1 shows Consulting Revenue as one example. An alternative is to squeeze adjustments on one line or to combine the effects of two or more adjustments in one amount. In the unusual case when an account is not predicted, we can add a new line for such an account following the *Totals* line.

② Step 2. Enter Adjustments

The second step in preparing a work sheet is to enter adjustments in the Adjustments columns. The adjustments shown are the same ones shown in Exhibit 3.13. An identifying letter links the debit and credit of each adjusting entry. This is called *keying* the adjustments. After preparing a work sheet, adjusting entries must still be entered in the journal and posted to the ledger. The Adjustments columns provide the information for those entries.

③ Step 3. Prepare Adjusted Trial Balance

Point: To avoid omitting the transfer of an account balance, start with the first line (cash) and continue in account order.

The adjusted trial balance is prepared by combining the adjustments with the unadjusted balances for each account. As an example, the Prepaid Insurance account has a $2,400 debit balance in the Unadjusted Trial Balance columns. This $2,400 debit is combined with the $100 credit in the Adjustments columns to give Prepaid Insurance a $2,300 debit in the Adjusted Trial Balance columns. The totals of the Adjusted Trial Balance columns confirm the equality of debits and credits.

④ Step 4. Sort Adjusted Trial Balance Amounts to Financial Statements

This step involves sorting account balances from the adjusted trial balance to their proper financial statement columns. Expenses go to the Income Statement Debit column and revenues to the Income Statement Credit column. Assets and Dividends go to the Balance Sheet Debit column. Liabilities, Retained Earnings, and Common Stock go to the Balance Sheet Credit column.

⑤ Step 5. Total Statement Columns, Compute Income or Loss, and Balance Columns

Each financial statement column (from Step 4) is totaled. The difference between the totals of the Income Statement columns is net income or net loss. This occurs because revenues are entered in the Credit column and expenses in the Debit column. If the Credit total exceeds the Debit total, there is net income. If the Debit total exceeds the Credit total, there is a net loss. For FastForward, the Credit total exceeds the Debit total, giving a $3,785 net income.

The net income from the Income Statement columns is then entered in the Balance Sheet Credit column. Adding net income to the last Credit column implies that it is to be added to retained earnings. If a loss occurs, it is added to the Debit column. This implies that it is to be subtracted from retained earnings. The ending balance of retained earnings does not appear in the last two columns as a single amount, but it is computed in the statement of retained earnings using these account balances. When net income or net loss is added to the proper Balance Sheet column, the totals of the last two columns must balance. If they do not, one or more errors have been made. The error can either be mathematical or involve sorting one or more amounts to incorrect columns.

Work Sheet Applications and Analysis   A work sheet does not substitute for financial statements. It is a tool we can use at the end of an accounting period to help organize data and prepare financial statements. FastForward's financial statements are shown in Exhibit 3.14. Its income statement amounts are taken from the Income Statement columns of the work sheet. Similarly, amounts for its balance sheet and its statement of retained earnings are taken from the Balance Sheet columns of the work sheet.

Work sheets are also useful in analyzing the effects of proposed, or what-if, transactions. This is done by entering financial statement amounts in the Unadjusted (what-if) columns. Proposed transactions are then entered in the Adjustments columns. We then compute "adjusted" amounts from these proposed transactions. The extended amounts in the financial statement columns show the effects of these proposed transactions. These financial statement columns yield **pro forma financial statements** because they show the statements *as if* the proposed transactions occurred.

EXHIBIT 3B.1

Work Sheet

No.	Account	Unadjusted Trial Balance Dr.	Cr.	Adjustments Dr.	Cr.	Adjusted Trial Balance Dr.	Cr.	Income Statement Dr.	Cr.	Balance Sheet Dr.	Cr.
101	Cash	4,350				4,350				4,350	
106	Accounts receivable	0		(f)1,800		1,800				1,800	
126	Supplies	9,720			(b)1,050	8,670				8,670	
128	Prepaid insurance	2,400			(a) 100	2,300				2,300	
167	Equipment	26,000				26,000				26,000	
168	Accumulated depreciation—Equip.		0		(c) 375		375				375
201	Accounts payable		6,200				6,200				6,200
209	Salaries payable		0		(e) 210		210				210
236	Unearned consulting revenue		3,000	(d) 250			2,750				2,750
307	Common stock		30,000				30,000				30,000
318	Retained earnings		0				0				0
319	Dividends	200				200				200	
403	Consulting revenue		5,800		(d) 250		7,850		7,850		
					(f)1,800						
406	Rental revenue		300				300		300		
612	Depreciation expense—Equip.	0		(c) 375		375		375			
622	Salaries expense	1,400		(e) 210		1,610		1,610			
637	Insurance expense	0		(a) 100		100		100			
640	Rent expense	1,000				1,000		1,000			
652	Supplies expense	0		(b)1,050		1,050		1,050			
690	Utilities expense	230				230		230			
	Totals	45,300	45,300	3,785	3,785	47,685	47,685	4,365	8,150	43,320	39,535
	Net income							3,785			3,785
	Totals							8,150	8,150	43,320	43,320

List all accounts from the ledger and those expected to arise from adjusting entries.

Enter all amounts available from ledger accounts. Column totals must be equal.

A work sheet collects and summarizes information used to prepare adjusting entries, financial statements, and closing entries.

APPENDIX

Reversing Entries

3C

Reversing entries are optional. They are recorded in response to accrued assets and accrued liabilities that were created by adjusting entries at the end of a reporting period. The purpose of reversing entries is to simplify a company's recordkeeping. Exhibit 3C.1 shows an example of FastForward's reversing entries. The top of the exhibit shows the adjusting entry FastForward recorded on December 31 for its employee's earned but unpaid salary. The entry recorded three days' salary of $210, which increased December's total salary expense to $1,610. The entry also recognized a liability of $210. The expense is reported on December's income statement. The expense account is then closed. The ledger on January 1, 2012, shows a $210 liability and a zero balance in the Salaries Expense account. At this point, the choice is made between using or not using reversing entries.

Point: As a general rule, adjusting entries that create new asset or liability accounts are likely candidates for reversing.

EXHIBIT 3C.1

Reversing Entries for an
Accrued Expense

Accrue salaries expense on December 31, 2011

| Salaries Expense .... 210 | | | | |
| Salaries Payable .... 210 | | | | |

Salaries Expense

Date	Expl.	Debit	Credit	Balance
2011				
Dec. 12	(7)	700		700
26	(16)	700		1,400
31	(e)	210		1,610

Salaries Payable

Date	Expl.	Debit	Credit	Balance
2011				
Dec. 31	(e)		210	210

WITHOUT Reversing Entries	— OR —	**WITH Reversing Entries**
No reversing entry recorded on January 1, 2012		*Reversing entry recorded on January 1, 2012*

WITHOUT Reversing Entries

NO ENTRY

Salaries Expense

Date	Expl.	Debit	Credit	Balance
2012				

Salaries Payable

Date	Expl.	Debit	Credit	Balance
2011				
Dec. 31	(e)		210	210
2012				

WITH Reversing Entries

| Salaries Payable .... 210 | | | | |
| Salaries Expense .... 210 | | | | |

Salaries Expense*

Date	Expl.	Debit	Credit	Balance
2012				
Jan. 1			210	(210)

Salaries Payable

Date	Expl.	Debit	Credit	Balance
2011				
Dec. 31	(e)		210	210
2012				
Jan. 1		210		0

Pay the accrued and current salaries on January 9, the first payday in 2012

WITHOUT Reversing Entries

Salaries Expense 490				
Salaries Payable 210				
Cash 700				

Salaries Expense

Date	Expl.	Debit	Credit	Balance
2012				
Jan. 9		490		490

Salaries Payable

Date	Expl.	Debit	Credit	Balance
2011				
Dec. 31	(e)		210	210
2012				
Jan. 9		210		0

WITH Reversing Entries

| Salaries Expense .... 700 | | | | |
| Cash .... 700 | | | | |

Salaries Expense*

Date	Expl.	Debit	Credit	Balance
2012				
Jan. 1			210	(210)
Jan. 9		700		490

Salaries Payable

Date	Expl.	Debit	Credit	Balance
2011				
Dec. 31	(e)		210	210
2012				
Jan. 1		210		0

Under both approaches, the expense and liability accounts have
identical balances after the cash payment on January 9.

| Salaries Expense .... $490 | | | | |
| Salaries Payable .... $ 0 | | | | |

*Circled numbers in the *Balance* column indicate abnormal balances.

Accounting *without* Reversing Entries   The path down the left side of Exhibit 3C.1 is described in the chapter. To summarize here, when the next payday occurs on January 9, we record payment with a compound entry that debits both the expense and liability accounts and credits Cash. Posting that entry creates a $490 balance in the expense account and reduces the liability account balance to zero because the debt has been settled. The disadvantage of this approach is the slightly more complex entry required on January 9. Paying the accrued liability means that this entry differs from the routine entries made on all other paydays. To construct the proper entry on January 9, we must recall the effect of the December 31 adjusting entry. Reversing entries overcome this disadvantage.

P8 Prepare reversing entries
and explain their purpose.

Accounting *with* Reversing Entries   The right side of Exhibit 3C.1 shows how a reversing entry on January 1 overcomes the disadvantage of the January 9 entry when not using reversing entries.

A reversing entry is the exact opposite of an adjusting entry. For FastForward, the Salaries Payable liability account is debited for $210, meaning that this account now has a zero balance after the entry is posted. The Salaries Payable account temporarily understates the liability, but this is not a problem since financial statements are not prepared before the liability is settled on January 9. The credit to the Salaries Expense account is unusual because it gives the account an *abnormal credit balance.* We highlight an abnormal balance by circling it. Because of the reversing entry, the January 9 entry to record payment is straightforward. This entry debits the Salaries Expense account and credits Cash for the full $700 paid. It is the same as all other entries made to record 10 days' salary for the employee. Notice that after the payment entry is posted, the Salaries Expense account has a $490 balance that reflects seven days' salary of $70 per day (see the lower right side of Exhibit 3C.1). The zero balance in the Salaries Payable account is now correct. The lower section of Exhibit 3C.1 shows that the expense and liability accounts have exactly the same balances whether reversing entries are used or not. This means that both approaches yield identical results.

Summary

C1 **Explain the importance of periodic reporting and the time period assumption.** The value of information is often linked to its timeliness. To provide timely information, accounting systems prepare periodic reports at regular intervals. The time period assumption presumes that an organization's activities can be divided into specific time periods for periodic reporting.

C2 **Explain accrual accounting and how it improves financial statements.** Accrual accounting recognizes revenue when earned and expenses when incurred—not necessarily when cash inflows and outflows occur. This information is valuable in assessing a company's financial position and performance.

C3 **Identify steps in the accounting cycle.** The accounting cycle consists of 10 steps: (1) analyze transactions, (2) journalize, (3) post, (4) prepare an unadjusted trial balance, (5) adjust accounts, (6) prepare an adjusted trial balance, (7) prepare statements, (8) close, (9) prepare a post-closing trial balance, and (10) prepare (optional) reversing entries.

C4 **Explain and prepare a classified balance sheet.** Classified balance sheets report assets and liabilities in two categories: current and noncurrent. Noncurrent assets often include long-term investments, plant assets, and intangible assets. A corporation separates equity into common stock and retained earnings.

A1 **Explain how accounting adjustments link to financial statements.** Accounting adjustments bring an asset or liability account balance to its correct amount. They also update related expense or revenue accounts. Every adjusting entry affects one or more income statement accounts *and* one or more balance sheet accounts. An adjusting entry never affects cash.

A2 **Compute profit margin and describe its use in analyzing company performance.** *Profit margin* is defined as the reporting period's net income divided by its net sales. Profit margin reflects on a company's earnings activities by showing how much income is in each dollar of sales.

A3 **Compute the current ratio and describe what it reveals about a company's financial condition.** A company's current ratio is defined as current assets divided by current liabilities. We use it to evaluate a company's ability to pay its current liabilities out of current assets.

P1 **Prepare and explain adjusting entries.** *Prepaid expenses* refer to items paid for in advance of receiving their benefits. Prepaid expenses are assets. Adjusting entries for prepaids involve increasing (debiting) expenses and decreasing (crediting) assets. *Unearned (or prepaid) revenues* refer to cash received in advance of providing products and services. Unearned revenues are liabilities. Adjusting entries for unearned revenues involve increasing (crediting) revenues and decreasing (debiting) unearned revenues. *Accrued expenses* refer to costs incurred in a period that are both unpaid and unrecorded. Adjusting entries for recording accrued expenses involve increasing (debiting) expenses and increasing (crediting) liabilities. *Accrued revenues* refer to revenues earned in a period that are both unrecorded and not yet received in cash. Adjusting entries for recording accrued revenues involve increasing (debiting) assets and increasing (crediting) revenues.

P2 **Explain and prepare an adjusted trial balance.** An adjusted trial balance is a list of accounts and balances prepared after recording and posting adjusting entries. Financial statements are often prepared from the adjusted trial balance.

P3 **Prepare financial statements from an adjusted trial balance.** Revenue and expense balances are reported on the income statement. Asset, liability, and equity balances are reported on the balance sheet. We usually prepare statements in the following order: income statement, statement of retained earnings, balance sheet, and statement of cash flows.

P4 **Describe and prepare closing entries.** Closing entries involve four steps: (1) close credit balances in revenue (and gain) accounts to Income Summary, (2) close debit balances in expense (and loss) accounts to Income Summary, (3) close Income Summary to retained earnings, and (4) close dividends account to retained earnings.

P5 **Explain and prepare a post-closing trial balance.** A post-closing trial balance is a list of permanent accounts and their balances after all closing entries have been journalized and posted. Its purpose is to verify that (1) total debits equal total credits for permanent accounts and (2) all temporary accounts have zero balances.

P6ᴬ **Explain the alternatives in accounting for prepaids.** Charging all prepaid expenses to expense accounts when they are purchased is acceptable. When this is done, adjusting entries must transfer any unexpired amounts from expense accounts to asset accounts. Crediting all unearned revenues to revenue accounts when cash is received is also acceptable. In this case, the adjusting entries must transfer any unearned amounts from revenue accounts to unearned revenue accounts.

P7ᴮ Prepare a work sheet and explain its usefulness. A work sheet can be a useful tool in preparing and analyzing financial statements. It is helpful at the end of a period in preparing adjusting entries, an adjusted trial balance, and financial statements. A work sheet usually contains five pairs of columns: Unadjusted Trial Balance, Adjustments, Adjusted Trial Balance, Income Statement, and Balance Sheet & Statement of Equity.

P8ᶜ Prepare reversing entries and explain their purpose. Reversing entries are an optional step. They are applied to accrued expenses and revenues. The purpose of reversing entries is to simplify subsequent journal entries. Financial statements are unaffected by the choice to use or not use reversing entries.

Guidance Answers to Decision Maker and Decision Ethics

Investor Prepaid expenses are items paid for in advance of receiving their benefits. They are assets and are expensed as they are used up. The publishing company's treatment of the signing bonus is acceptable provided future book sales can at least match the $500,000 expense. As an investor, you are concerned about the risk of future book sales. The riskier the likelihood of future book sales is, the more likely your analysis is to treat the $500,000, or a portion of it, as an expense, not a prepaid expense (asset).

Loan Officer Your concern in lending to this store arises from analysis of current-year sales. While increased revenues and income are fine, your concern is with collectibility of these promotional sales. If the owner sold products to customers with poor records of paying bills, then collectibility of these sales is low. Your analysis must assess this possibility and recognize any expected losses.

Financial Officer Omitting accrued expenses and recognizing revenue early can mislead financial statement users. One action is to request a second meeting with the president so you can explain that accruing expenses when incurred and recognizing revenue when earned are required practices. If the president persists, you might discuss the situation with legal counsel and any auditors involved. Your ethical action might cost you this job, but the potential pitfalls for falsification of statements, reputation and personal integrity loss, and other costs are too great.

Analyst A current ratio of 1.2 suggests that current assets are sufficient to cover current liabilities, but it implies a minimal buffer in case of errors in measuring current assets or current liabilities. Removing the past due receivable reduces the current ratio to 0.7. Your assessment is that the company will have some difficulty meeting its loan payments.

Guidance Answers to Quick Checks

1. An annual reporting (or accounting) period covers one year and refers to the preparation of annual financial statements. The annual reporting period is not always a calendar year that ends on December 31. An organization can adopt a fiscal year consisting of any consecutive 12 months or 52 weeks.

2. Interim financial statements (covering less than one year) are prepared to provide timely information to decision makers.

3. The revenue recognition principle and the expense recognition (matching) principle lead most directly to the adjusting process.

4. No. Cash basis accounting is not consistent with the matching principle because it reports revenue when received, not necessarily when earned, and expenses when paid, not necessarily in the period when the expenses were incurred as a result of the revenues earned.

5. No expense is reported in 2012. Under cash basis accounting, the entire $4,800 is reported as an expense in April 2011 when the premium is paid.

6. If the accrued revenues adjustment of $200 is not made, then both revenues and net income are understated by $200 on the current year's income statement, and both assets and equity are understated by $200 on the balance sheet.

7. A contra account is an account that is subtracted from the balance of a related account. Use of a contra account provides more information than simply reporting a net amount.

8. An accrued expense is a cost incurred in a period that is both unpaid and unrecorded prior to adjusting entries. One example is salaries earned but not yet paid at period-end.

9. An unearned revenue arises when a firm receives cash (or other assets) from a customer before providing the services or products to the customer. A magazine subscription paid in advance is one example; season ticket sales is another.

10.

Salaries Payable	1,000	
Salaries Expense	6,000	
Cash		7,000

   Paid salary including accrual from December.

11. The probable adjusting entries of Jordan Air are:

Insurance Expense	300	
Prepaid Insurance		300

   To record insurance expired.

Salaries Expense	1,400	
Salaries Payable		1,400

   To record accrued salaries.

12. Revenue accounts and expense accounts.

13. Statement of retained earnings.

14. The major steps in preparing closing entries are to close (1) credit balances in revenue accounts to Income Summary, (2) debit balances in expense accounts to Income Summary,

(3) Income Summary to retained earnings, and (4) any dividends account to retained earnings.

15. Revenue (and gain) and expense (and loss) accounts are called *temporary* because they are opened and closed each period. The Income Summary and Dividends accounts are also temporary.

16. Permanent accounts make up the post-closing trial balance, which consist of asset, liability, and equity accounts.

17. Current assets: (*b*), (*c*), (*d*). Plant assets: (*a*), (*e*). Item (*f*) is an intangible asset.

18. Investment in common stock, investment in bonds, and land held for future expansion.

19. For a service company, the operating cycle is the usual time between (1) paying employees who do the services and (2) receiving cash from customers for services provided.

Key Terms

Accounting cycle (p. 114)
Accounting period (p. 96)
Accrual basis accounting (p. 97)
Accrued expenses (p. 103)
Accrued revenues (p. 105)
Adjusted trial balance (p. 108)
Adjusting entry (p. 98)
Annual financial statements (p. 96)
Book value (p. 102)
Cash basis accounting (p. 97)
Classified balance sheet (p. 115)
Closing entries (p. 110)
Closing process (p. 110)
Contra account (p. 101)
Current assets (p. 116)

Current liabilities (p. 117)
Current ratio (p. 119)
Depreciation (p. 101)
Expense recognition (or **matching**) principle (p. 98)
Fiscal year (p. 97)
Income summary (p. 111)
Intangible assets (p. 117)
Interim financial statements (p. 96)
Long-term investments (p. 117)
Long-term liabilities (p. 117)
Natural business year (p. 97)
Operating cycle (p. 115)
Permanent accounts (p. 110)
Plant assets (p. 101)

Post-closing trial balance (p. 112)
Prepaid expenses (p. 99)
Pro forma financial statements (p. 126)
Profit margin (p. 119)
Reversing entries (p. 127)
Straight-line depreciation method (p. 101)
Temporary accounts (p. 110)
Time period assumption (p. 96)
Unadjusted trial balance (p. 108)
Unclassified balance sheet (p. 115)
Unearned revenues (p. 102)
Working papers (p. 125)
Work sheet (p. 125)

Multiple Choice Quiz   Answers on p. 155   mhhe.com/wildFA6e

Additional quiz questions are available at the book's Website.

1. A company forgot to record accrued and unpaid employee wages of $350,000 at period-end. This oversight would
  a. Understate net income by $350,000.
  b. Overstate net income by $350,000.
  c. Have no effect on net income.
  d. Overstate assets by $350,000.
  e. Understate assets by $350,000.

2. Prior to recording adjusting entries, the Supplies account has a $450 debit balance. A physical count of supplies shows $125 of unused supplies still available. The required adjusting entry is:
  a. Debit Supplies $125; Credit Supplies Expense $125.
  b. Debit Supplies $325; Credit Supplies Expense $325.
  c. Debit Supplies Expense $325; Credit Supplies $325.
  d. Debit Supplies Expense $325; Credit Supplies $125.
  e. Debit Supplies Expense $125; Credit Supplies $125.

3. On May 1, 2011, a two-year insurance policy was purchased for $24,000 with coverage to begin immediately. What is the amount of insurance expense that appears on the company's income statement for the year ended December 31, 2011?
  a. $4,000
  b. $8,000

  c. $12,000
  d. $20,000
  e. $24,000

4. On November 1, 2011, Stockton Co. receives $3,600 cash from Hans Co. for consulting services to be provided evenly over the period November 1, 2011, to April 30, 2012—at which time Stockton credited $3,600 to Unearned Consulting Fees. The adjusting entry on December 31, 2011 (Stockton's year-end), would include a
  a. Debit to Unearned Consulting Fees for $1,200.
  b. Debit to Unearned Consulting Fees for $2,400.
  c. Credit to Consulting Fees Earned for $2,400.
  d. Debit to Consulting Fees Earned for $1,200.
  e. Credit to Cash for $3,600.

5. If a company had $15,000 in net income for the year, and its sales were $300,000 for the same year, what is its profit margin?
  a. 20%
  b. 2,000%
  c. $285,000
  d. $315,000
  e. 5%

6. Based on the following information from Repicor Company's balance sheet, what is Repicor Company's current ratio?

a. 2.10		**d.** 0.95	
b. 1.50		**e.** 0.67	
c. 1.00			

Current assets	$ 75,000	Current liabilities	$ 50,000
Investments	30,000	Long-term liabilities ...	60,000
Plant assets	300,000	Common stock	295,000

A(B,C) *Superscript letter A(B,C) denotes assignments based on Appendix 3A(3B,3C).*

  Icon denotes assignments that involve decision making.

Discussion Questions

1. What is the difference between the cash basis and the accrual basis of accounting?

2.   Why is the accrual basis of accounting generally preferred over the cash basis?

3. What type of business is most likely to select a fiscal year that corresponds to its natural business year instead of the calendar year?

4. What is a prepaid expense and where is it reported in the financial statements?

5.   What type of assets require adjusting entries to record depreciation?

6.   What contra account is used when recording and reporting the effects of depreciation? Why is it used?

7. Apple has unearned revenue. What is unearned revenue and where is it reported in financial statements? Apple

8. What is an accrued revenue? Give an example.

9.^AIf a company initially records prepaid expenses with debits to expense accounts, what type of account is debited in the adjusting entries for those prepaid expenses?

10.   Review the balance sheet of Research In Motion in Appendix A. Identify one asset account that requires adjustment before annual financial statements can be prepared. What would be the effect on the income statement if this asset account were not adjusted? *RIM*

11.   Review the balance sheet of Nokia in Appendix A. Identify the amount for property, plant, and equipment. What adjusting entry is necessary (no numbers required) for this account when preparing financial statements? NOKIA

12.   Refer to Palm's balance sheet in Appendix A. If it made an adjustment for unpaid wages at year-end, where would the accrued wages be reported on its balance sheet? Palm

13. What accounts are affected by closing entries? What accounts are not affected?

14.   What two purposes are accomplished by recording closing entries?

15. What are the steps in recording closing entries?

16. What is the purpose of the Income Summary account?

17.   Explain whether an error has occurred if a post-closing trial balance includes a Depreciation Expense account.

18.^B What tasks are aided by a work sheet?

19.^B Why are the debit and credit entries in the Adjustments columns of the work sheet identified with letters?

20. What is a company's operating cycle?

21. What classes of assets and liabilities are shown on a typical classified balance sheet?

22. How is unearned revenue classified on the balance sheet?

23. What are the characteristics of plant assets?

24.^C How do reversing entries simplify recordkeeping?

25.^C If a company recorded accrued salaries expense of $500 at the end of its fiscal year, what reversing entry could be made? When would it be made?

26.   Refer to the balance sheet for Research In Motion in Appendix A. What five main noncurrent asset categories are used on its classified balance sheet? *RIM*

27. Refer to Nokia's balance sheet in Appendix A. Identify and list its 9 current assets. NOKIA

28.   Refer to Apple's balance sheet in Appendix A. Identify the three accounts listed as current liabilities. Apple

29.   Refer to Palm's financial statements in Appendix A. What journal entry was likely recorded as of May 31, 2009, to close its Income Summary account? Palm

■ connect™

QUICK STUDY

QS 3-1

Identifying accounting adjustments

P1

Classify the following adjusting entries as involving prepaid expenses (PE), unearned revenues (UR), accrued expenses (AE), or accrued revenues (AR).

a. _____ To record revenue earned that was previously received as cash in advance.

b. _____ To record annual depreciation expense.

c. _____ To record wages expense incurred but not yet paid (nor recorded).

d. _____ To record revenue earned but not yet billed (nor recorded).

e. _____ To record expiration of prepaid insurance.

a. On July 1, 2011, Baxter Company paid $1,800 for six months of insurance coverage. No adjustments have been made to the Prepaid Insurance account, and it is now December 31, 2011. Prepare the journal entry to reflect expiration of the insurance as of December 31, 2011.

b. Tyrell Company has a Supplies account balance of $1,000 on January 1, 2011. During 2011, it purchased $3,000 of supplies. As of December 31, 2011, a supplies inventory shows $1,300 of supplies available. Prepare the adjusting journal entry to correctly report the balance of the Supplies account and the Supplies Expense account as of December 31, 2011.

QS 3-2
Adjusting prepaid expenses
P1

---

a. Carlos Company purchases $30,000 of equipment on January 1, 2011. The equipment is expected to last five years and be worth $5,000 at the end of that time. Prepare the entry to record one year's depreciation expense of $5,000 for the equipment as of December 31, 2011.

b. Chaves Company purchases $40,000 of land on January 1, 2011. The land is expected to last indefinitely. What depreciation adjustment, if any, should be made with respect to the Land account as of December 31, 2011?

QS 3-3
Adjusting for depreciation
P1

---

a. Eager Co. receives $20,000 cash in advance for 4 months of legal services on October 1, 2011, and records it by debiting Cash and crediting Unearned Revenue both for $20,000. It is now December 31, 2011, and Eager has provided legal services as planned. What adjusting entry should Eager make to account for the work performed from October 1 through December 31, 2011?

b. Rutherford Co. started a new publication called *Contest News*. Its subscribers pay $48 to receive 12 issues. With every new subscriber, Rutherford debits Cash and credits Unearned Subscription Revenue for the amounts received. The company has 100 new subscribers as of July 1, 2011. It sends *Contest News* to each of these subscribers every month from July through December. Assuming no changes in subscribers, prepare the journal entry that Rutherford must make as of December 31, 2011, to adjust the Subscription Revenue account and the Unearned Subscription Revenue account.

QS 3-4
Adjusting for unearned revenues
A1 P1

Marsha Moder employs one college student every summer in her coffee shop. The student works the five weekdays and is paid on the following Monday. (For example, a student who works Monday through Friday, June 1 through June 5, is paid for that work on Monday, June 8.) Moder adjusts her books monthly, if needed, to show salaries earned but unpaid at month-end. The student works the last week of July—Friday is August 1. If the student earns $100 per day, what adjusting entry must Moder make on July 31 to correctly record accrued salaries expense for July?

QS 3-5
Accruing salaries
A1 P1

Adjusting entries affect at least one balance sheet account and at least one income statement account. For the following entries, identify the account to be debited and the account to be credited. Indicate which of the accounts is the income statement account and which is the balance sheet account.

a. Entry to record revenue earned that was previously received as cash in advance.

b. Entry to record annual depreciation expense.

c. Entry to record wage expenses incurred but not yet paid (nor recorded).

d. Entry to record revenue earned but not yet billed (nor recorded).

e. Entry to record expiration of prepaid insurance.

QS 3-6
Recording and analyzing adjusting entries
A1

In its first year of operations, Harden Co. earned $39,000 in revenues and received $33,000 cash from these customers. The company incurred expenses of $22,500 but had not paid $2,250 of them at year-end. The company also prepaid $3,750 cash for expenses that would be incurred the next year. Calculate the first year's net income under both the cash basis and the accrual basis of accounting.

QS 3-7
Computing accrual and cash income
C2 A1

The following information is taken from Cruz Company's unadjusted and adjusted trial balances.

QS 3-8
Interpreting adjusting entries
C2 P2

	Unadjusted		Adjusted	
	Debit	Credit	Debit	Credit
Prepaid insurance.........	$4,100		$3,700	
Interest payable		$ 0		$800

Given this information, which of the following is likely included among its adjusting entries?

a. A $400 credit to Prepaid Insurance and an $800 debit to Interest Payable.

b. A $400 debit to Insurance Expense and an $800 debit to Interest Payable.

c. A $400 debit to Insurance Expense and an $800 debit to Interest Expense.

QS 3-9

Determining effects of adjusting entries

A1

In making adjusting entries at the end of its accounting period, Gomez Consulting failed to record $1,600 of insurance coverage that had expired. This $1,600 cost had been initially debited to the Prepaid Insurance account. The company also failed to record accrued salaries expense of $1,000. As a result of these two oversights, the financial statements for the reporting period will [choose one] (1) understate assets by $1,600; (2) understate expenses by $2,600; (3) understate net income by $1,000; or (4) overstate liabilities by $1,000.

QS 3-10

Preparing adjusting entries

P1

During the year, Lyle Co. recorded prepayments of expenses in asset accounts, and cash receipts of unearned revenues in liability accounts. At the end of its annual accounting period, the company must make three adjusting entries: (1) accrue salaries expense, (2) adjust the Unearned Services Revenue account to recognize earned revenue, and (3) record services revenue earned for which cash will be received the following period. For each of these adjusting entries (1), (2), and (3), indicate the account from *a* through *i* to be debited and the account to be credited.

a. Prepaid Salaries	**d.** Salaries Payable	**g.** Unearned Services Revenue
b. Salaries Expense	**e.** Equipment	**h.** Accounts Receivable
c. Services Revenue	**f.** Cash	**i.** Accounts Payable

QS 3-11

Analyzing profit margin   A2

Yang Company reported net income of $37,925 and net sales of $390,000 for the current year. Calculate the company's profit margin and interpret the result. Assume that its competitors earn an average profit margin of 15%.

QS 3-12^A

Preparing adjusting entries

P6

Diego Consulting initially records prepaid and unearned items in income statement accounts. Given this company's accounting practices, which of the following applies to the preparation of adjusting entries at the end of its first accounting period?

a. Earned but unbilled (and unrecorded) consulting fees are recorded with a debit to Unearned Consulting Fees and a credit to Consulting Fees Earned.

b. Unpaid salaries are recorded with a debit to Prepaid Salaries and a credit to Salaries Expense.

c. The cost of unused office supplies is recorded with a debit to Supplies Expense and a credit to Office Supplies.

d. Unearned fees (on which cash was received in advance earlier in the period) are recorded with a debit to Consulting Fees Earned and a credit to Unearned Consulting Fees.

QS 3-13

International accounting standards   P3

Answer each of the following questions related to international accounting standards.

a. Do financial statements prepared under IFRS normally present assets from least liquid to most liquid or vice-versa?

b. Do financial statements prepared under IFRS normally present liabilities from furthest from maturity to nearest to maturity or vice-versa?

QS 3-14

Identifying the accounting cycle

C3

List the following steps of the accounting cycle in their proper order.

a. Preparing the post-closing trial balance.
b. Posting the journal entries.
c. Journalizing and posting adjusting entries.
d. Preparing the adjusted trial balance.
e. Journalizing and posting closing entries.

f. Analyzing transactions and events.
g. Preparing the financial statements.
h. Preparing the unadjusted trial balance.
i. Journalizing transactions and events.

QS 3-15

Identifying current accounts and computing the current ratio

A3

Compute Jamar Company's current ratio using the following information.

Accounts receivable	$15,000	Long-term notes payable	$20,000
Accounts payable	10,000	Office supplies	1,800
Buildings	42,000	Prepaid insurance	2,500
Cash	6,000	Unearned services revenue	4,000

The following are common categories on a classified balance sheet.

A. Current assets   **D.** Intangible assets

B. Long-term investments   **E.** Current liabilities

C. Plant assets   **F.** Long-term liabilities

QS 3-16
Classifying balance sheet items
C4

For each of the following items, select the letter that identifies the balance sheet category where the item typically would appear.

_____ **1.** Trademarks   _____ **5.** Cash

_____ **2.** Accounts receivable   _____ **6.** Wages payable

_____ **3.** Land not currently used in operations   _____ **7.** Store equipment

_____ **4.** Notes payable (due in three years)   _____ **8.** Accounts payable

---

The ledger of Avril Company includes the following accounts with normal balances: Common Stock $6,000; Dividends $400; Services Revenue $10,000; Wages Expense $5,200; and Rent Expense $800. Prepare the necessary closing entries from the available information at December 31.

QS 3-17
Prepare closing entries from the ledger P4

Identify the accounts listed in QS 3-17 that would be included in a post-closing trial balance.

QS 3-18
Identify post-closing accounts P5

The ledger of Terrel Company includes the following unadjusted normal balances: Prepaid Rent $800, Services Revenue $11,600, and Wages Expense $5,000. Adjusting entries are required for **(a)** accrued rent expense $240; **(b)** accrued services revenue $180; and **(c)** accrued wages expense $160. Enter these unadjusted balances and the necessary adjustments on a work sheet and complete the work sheet for these accounts. *Note:* Also include the following accounts: Accounts Receivable, Wages Payable, and Rent Expense.

QS 3-19ᴮ
Preparing a partial work sheet
P7

On December 31, 2010, Lester Co. prepared an adjusting entry for $6,700 of earned but unrecorded management fees. On January 16, 2011, Lester received $15,500 cash in management fees, which included the accrued fees earned in 2010. Assuming the company uses reversing entries, prepare the January 1, 2011, reversing entry and the January 16, 2011, cash receipt entry.

QS 3-20ᶜ
Reversing entries
P8

---

connect

For each of the following separate cases, prepare adjusting entries required of financial statements for the year ended (date of) December 31, 2011. (Assume that prepaid expenses are initially recorded in asset accounts and that fees collected in advance of work are initially recorded as liabilities.)

a. One-third of the work related to $30,000 cash received in advance is performed this period.

b. Wages of $9,000 are earned by workers but not paid as of December 31, 2011.

c. Depreciation on the company's equipment for 2011 is $19,127.

d. The Office Supplies account had a $480 debit balance on December 31, 2010. During 2011, $5,349 of office supplies are purchased. A physical count of supplies at December 31, 2011, shows $587 of supplies available.

e. The Prepaid Insurance account had a $5,000 balance on December 31, 2010. An analysis of insurance policies shows that $2,200 of unexpired insurance benefits remain at December 31, 2011.

f. The company has earned (but not recorded) $750 of interest from investments in CDs for the year ended December 31, 2011. The interest revenue will be received on January 10, 2012.

g. The company has a bank loan and has incurred (but not recorded) interest expense of $3,500 for the year ended December 31, 2011. The company must pay the interest on January 2, 2012.

EXERCISES

Exercise 3-1
Preparing adjusting entries
P1

Check (e) Dr. Insurance Expense, $2,800; (f) Cr. Interest Revenue, $750

Prepare adjusting journal entries for the year ended (date of) December 31, 2011, for each of these separate situations. Assume that prepaid expenses are initially recorded in asset accounts. Also assume that fees collected in advance of work are initially recorded as liabilities.

a. Depreciation on the company's equipment for 2011 is computed to be $16,000.

b. The Prepaid Insurance account had a $7,000 debit balance at December 31, 2011, before adjusting for the costs of any expired coverage. An analysis of the company's insurance policies showed that $1,040 of unexpired insurance coverage remains.

c. The Office Supplies account had a $300 debit balance on December 31, 2010; and $2,680 of office supplies were purchased during the year. The December 31, 2011, physical count showed $354 of supplies available.

Exercise 3-2
Preparing adjusting entries
P1

Check (c) Dr. Office Supplies Expense, $2,626; (e) Dr. Insurance Expense, $4,600

d. One-half of the work related to $10,000 of cash received in advance was performed this period.

e. The Prepaid Insurance account had a $5,600 debit balance at December 31, 2011, before adjusting for the costs of any expired coverage. An analysis of insurance policies showed that $4,600 of coverage had expired.

f. Wage expenses of $4,000 have been incurred but are not paid as of December 31, 2011.

Exercise 3-3

Adjusting and paying accrued expenses

A1

Check (b) May 20 Dr. Interest Expense, $4,160

The following three separate situations require adjusting journal entries to prepare financial statements as of April 30. For each situation, present both the April 30 adjusting entry and the subsequent entry during May to record the payment of the accrued expenses.

a. On April 1, the company retained an attorney for a flat monthly fee of $2,500. This amount is paid to the attorney on the 12th day of the following month in which it was earned.

b. A $780,000 note payable requires 9.6% annual interest, or $6,240 to be paid at the 20th day of each month. The interest was last paid on April 20 and the next payment is due on May 20. As of April 30, $2,080 of interest expense has accrued.

c. Total weekly salaries expense for all employees is $9,000. This amount is paid at the end of the day on Friday of each five-day workweek. April 30 falls on Tuesday of this year, which means that the employees had worked two days since the last payday. The next payday is May 3.

Exercise 3-4

Determining cost flows through accounts

C1 A1

Determine the missing amounts in each of these four separate situations a through d.

	a	b	c	d
Supplies available—prior year-end	$ 300	$1,600	$1,360	?
Supplies purchased during the current year	2,100	5,400	?	$6,000
Supplies available—current year-end	750	?	1,840	800
Supplies expense for the current year	?	1,300	9,600	6,575

Exercise 3-5

Adjusting and paying accrued wages

C1 P1

Pablo Management has five part-time employees, each of whom earns $100 per day. They are normally paid on Fridays for work completed Monday through Friday of the same week. They were paid in full on Friday, December 28, 2011. The next week, the five employees worked only four days because New Year's Day was an unpaid holiday. Show (a) the adjusting entry that would be recorded on Monday, December 31, 2011, and (b) the journal entry that would be made to record payment of the employees' wages on Friday, January 4, 2012.

Exercise 3-6

Analyzing and preparing adjusting entries

A1 P3

Following are two income statements for Kendall Co. for the year ended December 31. The left column is prepared before any adjusting entries are recorded, and the right column includes the effects of adjusting entries. The company records cash receipts and payments related to unearned and prepaid items in balance sheet accounts. Analyze the statements and prepare the eight adjusting entries that likely were recorded. (*Note:* 30% of the $6,000 adjustment for Fees Earned has been earned but not billed, and the other 70% has been earned by performing services that were paid for in advance.)

KENDALL CO. Income Statements For Year Ended December 31	Unadjusted	Adjusted
Revenues		
Fees earned	$24,000	$30,000
Commissions earned	42,500	42,500
Total revenues	66,500	72,500
Expenses		
Depreciation expense—Computers	0	1,500
Depreciation expense—Office furniture	0	1,750
Salaries expense	12,500	14,950
Insurance expense	0	1,300
Rent expense	4,500	4,500
Office supplies expense	0	480
Advertising expense	3,000	3,000
Utilities expense	1,250	1,320
Total expenses	21,250	28,800
Net income	$45,250	$43,700

Use the following information to compute profit margin for each separate company *a* through *e*.

	Net Income	Net Sales		Net Income	Net Sales
a.	$ 5,390	$ 44,830	**d.**	$55,234	$1,458,999
b.	87,644	398,954	**e.**	70,158	435,925
c.	93,385	257,082			

Which of the five companies is the most profitable according to the profit margin ratio? Interpret that company's profit margin ratio.

Exercise 3-7
Computing and interpreting profit margin

A2

Corbel Company experienced the following events and transactions during July.

July 1 Received $2,000 cash in advance of performing work for Beth Oker.
     6 Received $8,400 cash in advance of performing work for Lisa Poe.
    12 Completed the job for Oker.
    18 Received $7,500 cash in advance of performing work for Henry Coe.
    27 Completed the job for Poe.
    31 None of the work for Coe has been performed.

a. Prepare journal entries (including any adjusting entries as of the end of the month) to record these events using the procedure of initially crediting the Unearned Fees account when payment is received from a customer in advance of performing services.

b. Prepare journal entries (including any adjusting entries as of the end of the month) to record these events using the procedure of initially crediting the Fees Earned account when payment is received from a customer in advance of performing services.

c. Under each method, determine the amount of earned fees reported on the income statement for July and the amount of unearned fees reported on the balance sheet as of July 31.

Exercise 3-8^A
Recording and reporting revenues received in advance
P6

Check (*c*) Fees Earned—using entries from part *b*, $10,400

On-The-Mark Construction began operations on December 1. In setting up its accounting procedures, the company decided to debit expense accounts when it prepays its expenses and to credit revenue accounts when customers pay for services in advance. Prepare journal entries for items *a* through *d* and the adjusting entries as of its December 31 period-end for items *e* through *g*.

a. Supplies are purchased on December 1 for $3,000 cash.

b. The company prepaid its insurance premiums for $1,440 cash on December 2.

c. On December 15, the company receives an advance payment of $12,000 cash from a customer for remodeling work.

d. On December 28, the company receives $3,600 cash from another customer for remodeling work to be performed in January.

e. A physical count on December 31 indicates that On-The-Mark has $1,920 of supplies available.

f. An analysis of the insurance policies in effect on December 31 shows that $240 of insurance coverage had expired.

g. As of December 31, only one remodeling project has been worked on and completed. The $6,300 fee for this project had been received in advance and recorded as unearned remodeling fees.

Exercise 3-9^A
Adjusting for prepaids recorded as expenses and unearned revenues recorded as revenues
P6

Check (*f*) Cr. Insurance Expense, $1,200; (*g*) Dr. Remodeling Fees Earned, $9,300

---

adidas AG reports the following balance sheet accounts for the year ended December 31, 2009 (euros in millions). Prepare the balance sheet for this company as of December 31, 2009, following usual IFRS practices.

Exercise 3-10
Preparing a balance sheet following IFRS

P3

Tangible and other assets	€1,410	Intangible assets	€2,980
Total equity	3,776	Total current liabilities	2,836
Receivables and financial assets	1,753	Inventories	1,471
Total noncurrent liabilities	2,263	Total liabilities	5,099
Cash and cash equivalents	775	Other current assets	486
Total current assets	4,485	Total noncurrent assets	4,390

Use the following adjusted trial balance of Webb Trucking Company to prepare the (1) income statement and (2) statement of retained earnings, for the year ended December 31, 2011. The retained earnings account balance is $151,000 at December 31, 2010.

Exercise 3-11
Preparing financial statements
C3   P3

Account Title	Debit	Credit
Cash	$ 7,000	
Accounts receivable	16,500	
Office supplies	2,000	
Trucks	170,000	
Accumulated depreciation—Trucks		$ 35,000
Land	75,000	
Accounts payable		11,000
Interest payable		3,000
Long-term notes payable		52,000
Common stock		10,000
Retained earnings		151,000
Dividends	19,000	
Trucking fees earned		128,000
Depreciation expense—Trucks	22,500	
Salaries expense	60,000	
Office supplies expense	7,000	
Repairs expense—Trucks	11,000	
Totals	$390,000	$390,000

Exercise 3-12
Preparing a classified balance sheet C4

Check Total assets, $235,500

Use the information in the adjusted trial balance reported in Exercise 3-11 to prepare Webb Trucking Company's classified balance sheet as of December 31, 2011.

Exercise 3-13
Computing the current ratio
A3

Use the information in the adjusted trial balance reported in Exercise 3-11 to compute the current ratio as of the balance sheet date (round the ratio to two decimals). Interpret the current ratio for the Webb Trucking Company. (Assume that the industry average for the current ratio is 1.5.)

Exercise 3-14
Computing and analyzing the current ratio
A3

Calculate the current ratio in each of the following separate cases (round the ratio to two decimals). Identify the company case with the strongest liquidity position. (These cases represent competing companies in the same industry.)

	Current Assets	Current Liabilities
Case 1	$ 78,000	$31,000
Case 2	104,000	75,000
Case 3	44,000	48,000
Case 4	84,500	80,600
Case 5	60,000	99,000

Exercise 3-15ᴬ
Preparing reversing entries
P8

The following two events occurred for Tanger Co. on October 31, 2011, the end of its fiscal year.

a. Tanger rents a building from its owner for $3,200 per month. By a prearrangement, the company delayed paying October's rent until November 5. On this date, the company paid the rent for both October and November.

b. Tanger rents space in a building it owns to a tenant for $750 per month. By prearrangement, the tenant delayed paying the October rent until November 8. On this date, the tenant paid the rent for both October and November.

Required

1. Prepare adjusting entries that the company must record for these events as of October 31.

2. Assuming Tanger does *not* use reversing entries, prepare journal entries to record Tanger's payment of rent on November 5 and the collection of rent on November 8 from Tanger's tenant.

3. Assuming that the company uses reversing entries, prepare reversing entries on November 1 and the journal entries to record Tanger's payment of rent on November 5 and the collection of rent on November 8 from Tanger's tenant.

Following are **Nintendo**'s revenue and expense accounts for a recent calendar year (yen in millions). Prepare the company's closing entries for its revenues and its expenses.

Sales	¥1,838,622
Cost of sales (expense)	1,044,981
Advertising expense	117,308
Other expense, net	397,244

Exercise 3-16
Preparing closing entries

P4

The following data are taken from the unadjusted trial balance of the Madison Company at December 31, 2011. Each account carries a normal balance and the accounts are shown here in alphabetical order.

Exercise 3-17
Completing a worksheet

P7

Accounts Payable.	$ 2	Prepaid Insurance . .	$ 6	Retained earnings	$11
Accounts Receivable	4	Revenue	25	Dividends	2
Accumulated Depreciation—Equip. . .	5	Salaries Expense	6	Unearned Revenue	4
Cash	7	Supplies	8	Utilities Expense	4
Equipment	13	Common stock.	3		

1. Use the data above to prepare a worksheet. Enter the accounts in proper order and enter their balances in the correct debit or credit column.

2. Use the following adjustment information to complete the worksheet.

  a. Depreciation on equipment, $1   **d.** Supplies available at December 31, 2011, $5

  b. Accrued salaries, $2   **e.** Expired insurance, $5

  c. The $4 of unearned revenue has been earned

▇ connect

Meyer Co. follows the practice of recording prepaid expenses and unearned revenues in balance sheet accounts. The company's annual accounting period ends on December 31, 2011. The following information concerns the adjusting entries to be recorded as of that date.

a. The Office Supplies account started the year with a $3,000 balance. During 2011, the company purchased supplies for $12,400, which was added to the Office Supplies account. The inventory of supplies available at December 31, 2011, totaled $2,640.

b. An analysis of the company's insurance policies provided the following facts.

PROBLEM SET A

Problem 3-1A
Preparing adjusting and subsequent journal entries

C1 A1 P1

Policy	Date of Purchase	Months of Coverage	Cost
A	April 1, 2010	24	$15,840
B	April 1, 2011	36	13,068
C	August 1, 2011	12	2,700

The total premium for each policy was paid in full (for all months) at the purchase date, and the Prepaid Insurance account was debited for the full cost. (Year-end adjusting entries for Prepaid Insurance were properly recorded in all prior years.)

c. The company has 15 employees, who earn a total of $2,100 in salaries each working day. They are paid each Monday for their work in the five-day workweek ending on the previous Friday. Assume that December 31, 2011, is a Tuesday, and all 15 employees worked the first two days of that week. Because New Year's Day is a paid holiday, they will be paid salaries for five full days on Monday, January 6, 2012.

d. The company purchased a building on January 1, 2011. It cost $855,000 and is expected to have a $45,000 salvage value at the end of its predicted 30-year life. Annual depreciation is $27,000.

e. Since the company is not large enough to occupy the entire building it owns, it rented space to a tenant at $2,400 per month, starting on November 1, 2011. The rent was paid on time on November 1, and the amount received was credited to the Rent Earned account. However, the tenant has not paid the December rent. The company has worked out an agreement with the tenant, who has promised to pay both December and January rent in full on January 15. The tenant has agreed not to fall behind again.

f. On November 1, the company rented space to another tenant for $2,175 per month. The tenant paid five months' rent in advance on that date. The payment was recorded with a credit to the Unearned Rent account.

The adjusted trial balance for Giovanni Co. as of December 31, 2011, follows.

Problem 3-8B
Preparing closing entries,
financial statements, and ratios
C4 A2 A3 P3 P4

GIOVANNI COMPANY
Adjusted Trial Balance
December 31, 2011

No.	Account Title	Debit	Credit
101	Cash	$ 6,400	
104	Short-term investments	10,200	
126	Supplies	3,600	
128	Prepaid insurance	800	
167	Equipment	18,000	
168	Accumulated depreciation—Equipment		$ 3,000
173	Building	90,000	
174	Accumulated depreciation—Building		9,000
183	Land	28,500	
201	Accounts payable		2,500
203	Interest payable		1,400
208	Rent payable		200
210	Wages payable		1,180
213	Property taxes payable		2,330
233	Unearned professional fees		650
251	Long-term notes payable		32,000
307	Common stock..............................		30,000
318	Retained earnings		61,800
319	Dividends	6,000	
401	Professional fees earned		47,000
406	Rent earned		3,600
407	Dividends earned		500
409	Interest earned		1,120
606	Depreciation expense—Building	2,000	
612	Depreciation expense—Equipment	1,000	
623	Wages expense	17,500	
633	Interest expense	1,200	
637	Insurance expense	1,425	
640	Rent expense	1,800	
652	Supplies expense	900	
682	Postage expense	310	
683	Property taxes expense	3,825	
684	Repairs expense	579	
688	Telephone expense	421	
690	Utilities expense............................	1,820	
	Totals	$196,280	$196,280

J. Giovanni invested $30,000 cash in the business in exchange for more common stock during year 2011 (the December 31, 2010, credit balance of retained earnings was $61,800). Giovanni Company is required to make a $6,400 payment on its long-term notes payable during 2012.

Required

1. Prepare the income statement and the statement of retained earnings for the calendar year 2011 and the classified balance sheet at December 31, 2011.

2. Prepare the necessary closing entries at December 31, 2011.

3. Use the information in the financial statements to calculate these ratios: (*a*) return on assets (total assets at December 31, 2010, were $150,000), (*b*) debt ratio, (*c*) profit margin ratio (use total revenues as the denominator), and (*d*) current ratio.

Check (1) Total assets (12/31/2011), $145,500; Net income, $19,440

SERIAL PROBLEM
Business Solutions
P1 P2 P3 P4 P5

(This serial problem began in Chapter 1 and continues through most of the book. If previous chapter segments were not completed, the serial problem can still begin at this point. It is helpful, but not necessary, to use the Working Papers that accompany the book.)

SP 3   After the success of the company's first two months, Santana Rey continues to operate Business Solutions. (Transactions for the first two months are described in the serial problem of Chapter 2.) The November 30, 2011, unadjusted trial balance of Business Solutions (reflecting its transactions for October and November of 2011) follows.

No.	Account Title	Debit	Credit
101	Cash	$38,264	
106	Accounts receivable	12,618	
126	Computer supplies	2,545	
128	Prepaid insurance	2,220	
131	Prepaid rent	3,300	
163	Office equipment	8,000	
164	Accumulated depreciation—Office equipment		$ 0
167	Computer equipment	20,000	
168	Accumulated depreciation—Computer equipment		0
201	Accounts payable		0
210	Wages payable		0
236	Unearned computer services revenue		0
307	Common stock		73,000
318	Retained earnings		0
319	Dividends	5,600	
403	Computer services revenue		25,659
612	Depreciation expense—Office equipment	0	
613	Depreciation expense—Computer equipment	0	
623	Wages expense	2,625	
637	Insurance expense	0	
640	Rent expense	0	
652	Computer supplies expense	0	
655	Advertising expense	1,728	
676	Mileage expense	704	
677	Miscellaneous expenses	250	
684	Repairs expense—Computer	805	
	Totals	$98,659	$98,659

Business Solutions had the following transactions and events in December 2011.

Dec.   2   Paid $1,025 cash to Hillside Mall for Business Solutions' share of mall advertising costs.
    3   Paid $500 cash for minor repairs to the company's computer.
    4   Received $3,950 cash from Alex's Engineering Co. for the receivable from November.
    10   Paid cash to Lyn Addie for six days of work at the rate of $125 per day.
    14   Notified by Alex's Engineering Co. that Business Solutions' bid of $7,000 on a proposed project has been accepted. Alex's paid a $1,500 cash advance to Business Solutions.
    15   Purchased $1,100 of computer supplies on credit from Harris Office Products.
    16   Sent a reminder to Gomez Co. to pay the fee for services recorded on November 8.
    20   Completed a project for Liu Corporation and received $5,625 cash.
22–26   Took the week off for the holidays.
    28   Received $3,000 cash from Gomez Co. on its receivable.
    29   Reimbursed S. Rey for business automobile mileage (600 miles at $0.32 per mile).
    31   The business paid $1,500 cash for dividends.

The following additional facts are collected for use in making adjusting entries prior to preparing financial statements for the company's first three months:

a. The December 31 inventory count of computer supplies shows $580 still available.

b. Three months have expired since the 12-month insurance premium was paid in advance.

c. As of December 31, Lyn Addie has not been paid for four days of work at $125 per day.

d. The computer system, acquired on October 1, is expected to have a four-year life with no salvage value.

e. The office equipment, acquired on October 1, is expected to have a five-year life with no salvage value.

f. Three of the four months' prepaid rent has expired.

Required

1. Prepare journal entries to record each of the December transactions and events for Business Solutions. Post those entries to the accounts in the ledger.

2. Prepare adjusting entries to reflect *a* through *f*. Post those entries to the accounts in the ledger.

3. Prepare an adjusted trial balance as of December 31, 2011.

4. Prepare an income statement for the three months ended December 31, 2011.

5. Prepare a statement of retained earnings for the three months ended December 31, 2011.

6. Prepare a balance sheet as of December 31, 2011.

7. Record and post the necessary closing entries for Business Solutions.

8. Prepare a post-closing trial balance as of December 31, 2011.

Check (3) Adjusted trial balance totals, $109,034

(6) Total assets, $83,460
Check Post-closing trial balance totals, $85,110

Beyond the Numbers

BTN 3-1 Refer to Research In Motion's financial statements in Appendix A to answer the following.

1. Identify and write down the revenue recognition principle as explained in the chapter.

2. Review Research In Motion's footnotes to discover how it applies the revenue recognition principle and when it recognizes revenue. Report what you discover.

3. What is Research In Motion's profit margin for fiscal years ended February 28, 2009, and February 27, 2010?

4. For the fiscal year ended February 27, 2010, what amount is credited to Income Summary to summarize its revenues earned?

5. For the fiscal year ended February 27, 2010, what amount is debited to Income Summary to summarize its expenses incurred?

6. For the fiscal year ended February 27, 2010, what is the balance of its Income Summary account before it is closed?

Fast Forward

7. Access RIM's annual report (10-K) for fiscal years ending after February 27, 2010, at its Website (RIM.com) or the SEC's EDGAR database (www.sec.gov). Assess and compare the February 27, 2010, fiscal year profit margin to any subsequent year's profit margin that you compute.

REPORTING IN ACTION
C1 C2 A1 A2 P4

RIM

BTN 3-2 Key figures for the recent two years of both Research In Motion and Apple follow.

($ millions)	Research In Motion		Apple	
	Current Year	Prior Year	Current Year	Prior Year
Net income	$ 2,457	$ 1,893	$ 8,235	$ 6,119
Net sales	14,953	11,065	42,905	37,491
Current assets	5,813	4,842	31,555	30,006
Current liabilities	2,432	2,115	11,506	11,361

COMPARATIVE ANALYSIS
A2 A3

RIM
Apple

Required

1. Compute profit margins for (*a*) Research In Motion and (*b*) Apple for the two years of data shown.
2. Which company is more successful on the basis of profit margin? Explain.
3. Compute the current ratio for both years for both companies.
4. Which company has the better ability to pay short-term obligations according to the current ratio?
5. Analyze and comment on each company's current ratios for the past two years.
6. How do RIM's and Apple's current ratios compare to their industry (assumed) average ratio of 2.4?

ETHICS CHALLENGE
C1 C2 A1

BTN 3-3   Jackie Bergez works for Sea Biscuit Co. She and Bob Welch, her manager, are preparing adjusting entries for annual financial statements. Bergez computes depreciation and records it as

Depreciation Expense—Equipment	123,000	
Accumulated Depreciation—Equipment		123,000

Welch agrees with her computation but says the credit entry should be directly to the Equipment account. Welch argues that while accumulated depreciation is technically correct, "it is less hassle not to use a contra account and just credit the Equipment account directly. And besides, the balance sheet shows the same amount for total assets under either method."

Required

1. How should depreciation be recorded? Do you support Bergez or Welch?
2. Evaluate the strengths and weaknesses of Welch's reasons for preferring his method.
3. Indicate whether the situation Bergez faces is an ethical problem. Explain.

COMMUNICATING IN PRACTICE
P4

BTN 3-4   Assume that one of your classmates states that a company's books should be ongoing and therefore not closed until that business is terminated. Write a half-page memo to this classmate explaining the concept of the closing process by drawing analogies between (1) a scoreboard for an athletic event and the revenue and expense accounts of a business or (2) a sports team's record book and retained earnings. (*Hint:* Think about what would happen if the scoreboard is not cleared before the start of a new game.)

TAKING IT TO THE NET
C1 A2

BTN 3-5   Access EDGAR online (www.sec.gov) and locate the 10-K report of The Gap, Inc., (ticker GPS) filed on March 26, 2010. Review its financial statements reported for the year ended January 30, 2010, to answer the following questions.

Required

1. What are Gap's main brands?
2. What is Gap's fiscal year-end?
3. What is Gap's net sales for the period ended January 30, 2010?
4. What is Gap's net income for the period ended January 30, 2010?
5. Compute Gap's profit margin for the year ended January 30, 2010.
6. Do you believe Gap's decision to use a year-end of late January or early February relates to its natural business year? Explain.

TEAMWORK IN ACTION
A1 P1

BTN 3-6   Four types of adjustments are described in the chapter: (1) prepaid expenses, (2) unearned revenues, (3) accrued expenses, and (4) accrued revenues.

Required

1. Form *learning teams* of four (or more) members. Each team member must select one of the four adjustments as an area of expertise (each team must have at least one expert in each area).

2. Form *expert teams* from the individuals who have selected the same area of expertise. Expert teams are to discuss and write a report that each expert will present to his or her learning team addressing the following:

   a. Description of the adjustment and why it's necessary.

   b. Example of a transaction or event, with dates and amounts, that requires adjustment.

   c. Adjusting entry(ies) for the example in requirement *b*.

   d. Status of the affected account(s) before and after the adjustment in requirement *c*.

   e. Effects on financial statements of not making the adjustment.

3. Each expert should return to his or her learning team. In rotation, each member should present his or her expert team's report to the learning team. Team discussion is encouraged.

BTN 3-7 Review the opening feature of this chapter dealing with Cheezburger Network.

ENTREPRENEURIAL DECISION

A2

Required

1. Assume that Cheezburger Network sells a $300 gift certificate to a customer, collecting the $300 cash in advance. Prepare the journal entry for the (*a*) collection of the cash for delivery of the gift certificate to the customer and (*b*) revenue from the subsequent delivery of merchandise when the gift certificate is used.

2. How can keeping less inventory help to improve Cheezburger Network's profit margin?

3. Ben Huh understands that many companies carry considerable inventory, and Ben is thinking of carrying additional inventory of merchandise for sale. Ben desires your advice on the pros and cons of carrying such inventory. Provide at least one reason for and one reason against carrying additional inventory.

BTN 3-8 Select a company that you can visit in person or interview on the telephone. Call ahead to the company to arrange a time when you can interview an employee (preferably an accountant) who helps prepare the annual financial statements. Inquire about the following aspects of its *accounting cycle:*

HITTING THE ROAD

C1

1. Does the company prepare interim financial statements? What time period(s) is used for interim statements?

2. Does the company use the cash or accrual basis of accounting?

3. Does the company use a work sheet in preparing financial statements? Why or why not?

4. Does the company use a spreadsheet program? If so, which software program is used?

5. How long does it take after the end of its reporting period to complete annual statements?

BTN 3-9 Nokia (www.Nokia.com) is a leading global manufacturer of mobile devices and services.

GLOBAL DECISION

A2 A3 C1 C2

NOKIA

Required

1. Locate the notes to its December 31, 2009, financial statements at the company's Website, and read note *1 Accounting Principles—Revenue Recognition,* first paragraph only. When is revenue recognized by Nokia?

2. Refer to Nokia's financials in Appendix A. What is Nokia's profit margin for the year ended December 31, 2009?

3. Compute Nokia's current ratio for both the current year and the prior year.

4. Comment on any change from the prior year to the current year for the current ratio.

ANSWERS TO MULTIPLE CHOICE QUIZ

1. b; the forgotten adjusting entry is: *dr.* Wages Expense, *cr.* Wages Payable.

2. c; Supplies used = $450 − $125 = $325

3. b; Insurance expense = $24,000 × (8/24) = $8,000; adjusting entry is: *dr.* Insurance Expense for $8,000, *cr.* Prepaid Insurance for $8,000.

4. a; Consulting fees earned = $3,600 × (2/6) = $1,200; adjusting entry is: *dr.* Unearned Consulting Fee for $1,200, *cr.* Consulting Fees Earned for $1,200.

5. e; Profit margin = $15,000/$300,000 = 5%

6. b

A Look Back

Chapter 3 focused on the final steps of the accounting process. We explained the importance of proper revenue and expense recognition and described the adjusting and closing processes. We also prepared financial statements.

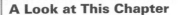

A Look at This Chapter

This chapter emphasizes merchandising activities. We explain how reporting merchandising activities differs from reporting service activities. We also analyze and record merchandise purchases and sales transactions, and explain the adjustments and closing process for merchandisers.

A Look Ahead

Chapter 5 extends our analysis of merchandising activities and focuses on the valuation of inventory. Topics include the items in inventory, costs assigned, costing methods used, and inventory estimation techniques.

4 Reporting and Analyzing Merchandising Operations

Learning Objectives

CAP

CONCEPTUAL

C1 Describe merchandising activities and identify income components for a merchandising company. (p. 158)

C2 Identify and explain the inventory asset and cost flows of a merchandising company. (p. 159)

ANALYTICAL

A1 Compute the acid-test ratio and explain its use to assess liquidity. (p. 174)

A2 Compute the gross margin ratio and explain its use to assess profitability. (p. 174)

LP4

PROCEDURAL

P1 Analyze and record transactions for merchandise purchases using a perpetual system. (p. 160)

P2 Analyze and record transactions for merchandise sales using a perpetual system. (p. 165)

P3 Prepare adjustments and close accounts for a merchandising company. (p. 168)

P4 Define and prepare multiple-step and single-step income statements. (p. 170)

P5 *Appendix 4A*—Record and compare merchandising transactions using both periodic and perpetual inventory systems. (p. 179)

Out of Africa

"We are changing history and . . . we are all going to make a whole lot of money."

—SELENA CUFFE

LOS ANGELES—Selena Cuffe was in Johannesburg as part of a student exchange program when she discovered wine at the Soweto Wine Festival. "They have wine here?" asked a puzzled Selena. That festival unleashed Selena's passion to pursue the merchandising of wine. But not just any wine—she would import and distribute wine produced by indigenous African vintners. She and her husband, Khary, launched **Heritage Link Brands (HeritageLinkBrands.com).** Our mission, says Selena, is "to showcase the very best wines from Africa and the African Diaspora."

But the start-up was a struggle. "Our business is a family business so whatever decisions we make have to be made with the best interest of my family and those we work with," explains Selena. She describes how the business required a merchandising accounting system to account for purchases and sales transactions and to effectively track the levels of the various wines. Inventory was especially important to account for and monitor. Khary explains, "It is very easy to underestimate expenses."

To succeed, Selena and Khary needed to make smart business decisions. They set up an accounting system to capture and communicate costs and sales information. Tracking merchandising activities was necessary to set prices and to manage discounts, allowances, and returns of both sales and purchases. A perpetual inventory system enabled them to stock the right kind and amount of merchandise and to avoid the costs of out-of-stock and excess inventory. Khary stressed that they monitored current assets and current liabilities (working capital). "Understand working capital," insists Khary. "If you don't understand working capital, stop right here and open an accounting book."

Mastering accounting for merchandising is a means to an end for Selena and Khary. "My training is really about how to run a successful business," says Selena. "How to get the most profit you can out of something." Still, Selena recognizes that her merchandising business is more than profits and losses. "What we're able to do and how we're able to make an impact with this business only matters in as much as the people here and on the continent are able to be successful and thrive."

[Sources: *Heritage Link Brands Website,* January 2012; *TIME,* September 2007; *Black Enterprise,* May 2009; *Inc,* March 2009; *SpreadLuv,* May 2011]

COMPLETING THE ACCOUNTING CYCLE

Exhibit 4.10 shows the flow of merchandising costs during a period and where these costs are reported at period-end. Specifically, beginning inventory plus the net cost of purchases is the merchandise available for sale. As inventory is sold, its cost is recorded in cost of goods sold on the income statement; what remains is ending inventory on the balance sheet. A period's ending inventory is the next period's beginning inventory.

EXHIBIT 4.10

Merchandising Cost Flow in the Accounting Cycle

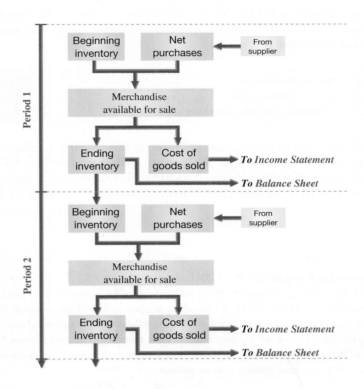

Adjusting Entries for Merchandisers

P3 Prepare adjustments and close accounts for a merchandising company.

Each of the steps in the accounting cycle described in the prior chapter for a service company applies to a merchandiser. This section and the next two further explain three steps of the accounting cycle for a merchandiser—adjustments, statement preparation, and closing.

Adjusting entries are generally the same for merchandising companies and service companies, including those for prepaid expenses (including depreciation), accrued expenses, unearned revenues, and accrued revenues. However, a merchandiser using a perpetual inventory system is usually required to make another adjustment to update the Merchandise Inventory account to reflect any loss of merchandise, including theft and deterioration. **Shrinkage** is the term used to refer to the loss of inventory and it is computed by comparing a physical count of inventory with recorded amounts. A physical count is usually performed at least once annually.

To illustrate, Z-Mart's Merchandise Inventory account at the end of year 2011 has a balance of $21,250, but a physical count reveals that only $21,000 of inventory exists. The adjusting entry to record this $250 shrinkage is

Point: About two-thirds of shoplifting losses are thefts by employees.

Assets = Liabilities + Equity
−250   −250

Dec. 31	Cost of Goods Sold	250	
	Merchandise Inventory		250
	To adjust for $250 shrinkage revealed by a		
	physical count of inventory.		

November 6, and the returned items sell for $800 and cost $600. The revenue part of this transaction must reflect the decrease in sales from the customer's return of merchandise as follows:

(f) Nov. 6	Sales Returns and Allowances	800	
	Accounts Receivable		800
	Customer returns merchandise of Nov. 3 sale.		

Assets = Liabilities + Equity
−800   −800

If the merchandise returned to Z-Mart is not defective and can be resold to another customer, Z-Mart returns these goods to its inventory. The entry to restore the cost of such goods to the Merchandise Inventory account is

Nov. 6	Merchandise Inventory	600	
	Cost of Goods Sold		600
	Returned goods added to inventory.		

Assets = Liabilities + Equity
+600   +600

This entry changes if the goods returned are defective. In this case the returned inventory is recorded at its estimated value, not its cost. To illustrate, if the goods (costing $600) returned to Z-Mart are defective and estimated to be worth $150, the following entry is made: Dr. Merchandise Inventory for $150, Dr. Loss from Defective Merchandise for $450, and Cr. Cost of Goods Sold for $600.

Fraud

Reversing Returns. On May 3, 2011, **Green Mountain Coffee Roasters** beat analysts' earnings estimates by $0.10 per share for the 13-week period ended March 26, 2011. The next day the stock price rose $11.91 per share to close at $75.98 per share, an 18.5% increase over the prior day's closing price. In the weeks that followed, some analysts raised questions about the quality of Green Mountain's earnings because of its accounting for sales returns. They allege that a large part of that earnings increase was due to an accounting adjustment that reversed much of a reserve that was set up for sales returns in prior periods.

Sales Allowances   To illustrate sales allowances, assume that $800 of the merchandise Z-Mart sold on November 3 is defective but the buyer decides to keep it because Z-Mart offers a $100 price reduction. Z-Mart records this allowance as follows:

Nov. 6	Sales Returns and Allowances	100	
	Accounts Receivable		100
	To record sales allowance on Nov. 3 sale.		

Assets = Liabilities + Equity
−100   −100

The seller usually prepares a credit memorandum to confirm a buyer's return or allowance. A seller's **credit memorandum** informs a buyer of the seller's credit to the buyer's Account Receivable (on the seller's books).

Point: The sender (maker) of a credit memorandum will *credit* the account of the receiver. The receiver of a credit memorandum will *debit* the sender's account.

Quick Check   Answers — p. 185

7. Why are sales discounts and sales returns and allowances recorded in contra revenue accounts instead of directly in the Sales account?

8. Under what conditions are two entries necessary to record a sales return?

9. When merchandise is sold on credit and the seller notifies the buyer of a price allowance, does the seller create and send a credit memorandum or a debit memorandum?

Preparing Financial Statements

The financial statements of a merchandiser, and their preparation, are similar to those for a service company described in Chapters 2 and 3. The income statement mainly differs by the inclusion of *cost of goods sold* and *gross profit*. Also, net sales is affected by discounts, returns, and allowances, and some additional expenses are possible such as delivery expense and loss from defective merchandise. The balance sheet mainly differs by the inclusion of *merchandise inventory* as part of current assets. The statement of retained earnings is unchanged. A work sheet can be used to help prepare these statements, and one is illustrated in Appendix 4B for Z-Mart.

Point: Staples's costs of shipping merchandise to its stores is included in its costs of inventories as required by the cost principle.

Closing Entries for Merchandisers

Closing entries are similar for service companies and merchandising companies using a perpetual system. The difference is that we must close some new temporary accounts that arise from merchandising activities. Z-Mart has several temporary accounts unique to merchandisers: Sales (of goods), Sales Discounts, Sales Returns and Allowances, and Cost of Goods Sold. Their existence in the ledger means that the first two closing entries for a merchandiser are slightly different from the ones described in the prior chapter for a service company. These differences are set in **red boldface** in the closing entries of Exhibit 4.11.

Point: The Inventory account is not affected by the closing process under a perpetual system.

EXHIBIT 4.11

Closing Entries for a Merchandiser

Step 1: Close Credit Balances in Temporary Accounts to Income Summary.

Dec. 31	Sales	321,000	
	Income Summary		321,000
	To close credit balances in temporary accounts.		

Step 2: Close Debit Balances in Temporary Accounts to Income Summary.

Dec. 31	Income Summary	308,100	
	Sales Discounts		4,300
	Sales Returns and Allowances		2,000
	Cost of Goods Sold		230,400
	Depreciation Expense		3,700
	Salaries Expense		43,800
	Insurance Expense		600
	Rent Expense		9,000
	Supplies Expense		3,000
	Advertising Expense		11,300
	To close debit balances in temporary accounts.		

Step 3: Close Income Summary to Retained Earnings.

The third closing entry is identical for a merchandising company and a service company. The $12,900 amount is net income reported on the income statement.

Dec. 31	Income Summary	12,900	
	Retained Earnings		12,900
	To close the Income Summary account.		

Step 4: Close Dividends Account to Retained Earnings.

The fourth closing entry is identical for a merchandising company and a service company. It closes the Dividends account and adjusts the Retained Earnings account to the amount shown on the balance sheet.

Dec. 31	Retained Earnings	4,000	
	Dividends		4,000
	To close the Dividends account.		

Summary of Merchandising Entries

Exhibit 4.12 summarizes the key adjusting and closing entries of a merchandiser (using a perpetual inventory system) that are different from those of a service company described in prior chapters (the Demonstration Problem 2 illustrates these merchandising entries).

EXHIBIT 4.12

Summary of Merchandising Entries

	Merchandising Transactions	Merchandising Entries	Dr.	Cr.
Purchases	Purchasing merchandise for resale.	Merchandise Inventory	#	
		Cash or Accounts Payable		#
	Paying freight costs on purchases; FOB shipping point.	Merchandise Inventory	#	
		Cash.........................		#
	Paying within discount period.	Accounts Payable	#	
		Merchandise Inventory		#
		Cash.........................		#
	Recording purchase returns or allowances.	Cash or Accounts Payable	#	
		Merchandise Inventory		#
Sales	Selling merchandise.	Cash or Accounts Receivable	#	
		Sales........................		#
		Cost of Goods Sold	#	
		Merchandise Inventory		#
	Receiving payment within discount period.	Cash.........................	#	
		Sales Discounts	#	
		Accounts Receivable		#
	Granting sales returns or allowances.	Sales Returns and Allowances	#	
		Cash or Accounts Receivable		#
		Merchandise Inventory	#	
		Cost of Goods Sold		#
	Paying freight costs on sales; FOB destination.	Delivery Expense	#	
		Cash		#

	Merchandising Events	Adjusting and Closing Entries		
Adjusting	Adjusting due to shrinkage (occurs when recorded amount larger than physical inventory).	Cost of Goods Sold	#	
		Merchandise Inventory		#
Closing	Closing temporary accounts with credit balances.	Sales..........................	#	
		Income Summary		#
	Closing temporary accounts with debit balances.	Income Summary	#	
		Sales Returns and Allowances		#
		Sales Discounts		#
		Cost of Goods Sold		#
		Delivery Expense		#
		"Other Expenses"		#

Quick Check

Answers — p. 185

10. When a merchandiser uses a perpetual inventory system, why is it sometimes necessary to adjust the Merchandise Inventory balance with an adjusting entry?

11. What temporary accounts do you expect to find in a merchandising business but not in a service business?

12. Describe the closing entries normally made by a merchandising company.

FINANCIAL STATEMENT FORMATS

P4 Define and prepare multiple-step and single-step income statements.

Generally accepted accounting principles do not require companies to use any one presentation format for financial statements so we see many different formats in practice. This section describes two common income statement formats: multiple-step and single-step. The classified balance sheet of a merchandiser is also explained.

Multiple-Step Income Statement

A **multiple-step income statement** format shows detailed computations of net sales and other costs and expenses, and reports subtotals for various classes of items. Exhibit 4.13 shows a multiple-step income statement for Z-Mart. The statement has three main parts: (1) *gross profit*, determined by net sales less cost of goods sold, (2) *income from operations*, determined by gross profit less operating expenses, and (3) *net income*, determined by income from operations adjusted for nonoperating items.

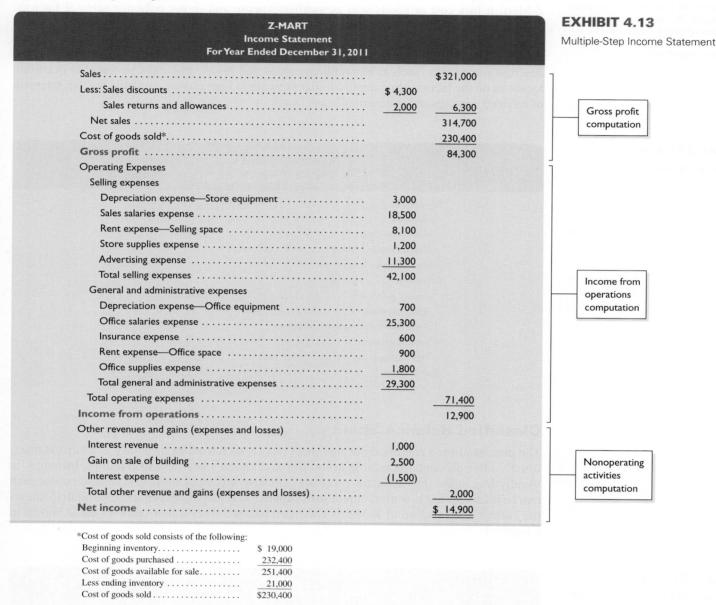

EXHIBIT 4.13

Multiple-Step Income Statement

*Cost of goods sold consists of the following:
Beginning inventory	$ 19,000
Cost of goods purchased	232,400
Cost of goods available for sale	251,400
Less ending inventory	21,000
Cost of goods sold	$230,400

Operating expenses are classified into two sections. **Selling expenses** include the expenses of promoting sales by displaying and advertising merchandise, making sales, and delivering goods to customers. **General and administrative expenses** support a company's overall operations and include expenses related to accounting, human resource management, and financial management. Expenses are allocated between sections when they contribute to more than one. Z-Mart allocates rent expense of $9,000 from its store building between two sections: $8,100 to selling expense and $900 to general and administrative expense.

Nonoperating activities consist of other expenses, revenues, losses, and gains that are unrelated to a company's operations. *Other revenues and gains* commonly include interest revenue,

Point: Z-Mart did not have any nonoperating activities; however, Exhibit 4.13 includes some for illustrative purposes.

[continued from previous page]

PERIODIC		
Closing Entries		
(1) Sales	321,000	
Merchandise Inventory	21,000	
Purchase Discounts	4,200	
Purchase Returns and Allowances	1,500	
Income Summary		347,700
(2) Income Summary	334,800	
Sales Discounts		4,300
Sales Returns and Allowances		2,000
Merchandise Inventory		19,000
Purchases		235,800
Transportation-In		2,300
Depreciation Expense		3,700
Salaries Expense		43,800
Insurance Expense		600
Rent Expense		9,000
Supplies Expense		3,000
Advertising Expense		11,300
(3) Income Summary	12,900	
Retained Earnings		12,900
(4) Retained Earnings	4,000	
Dividends		4,000

PERPETUAL		
Closing Entries		
(1) Sales	321,000	
Income Summary		321,000
(2) Income Summary	308,100	
Sales Discounts		4,300
Sales Returns and Allowances		2,000
Cost of Goods Sold		230,400
Depreciation Expense		3,700
Salaries Expense		43,800
Insurance Expense		600
Rent Expense		9,000
Supplies Expense		3,000
Advertising Expense		11,300
(3) Income Summary	12,900	
Retained Earnings		12,900
(4) Retained Earnings	4,000	
Dividends		4,000

shrinkage) in the first closing entry and removes the $19,000 beginning inventory balance from the account in the second closing entry.[2]

By updating Merchandise Inventory and closing Purchases, Purchase Discounts, Purchase Returns and Allowances, and Transportation-In, the periodic system transfers the cost of goods sold amount to Income Summary. Review the periodic side of Exhibit 4A.1 and notice that the **boldface** items affect Income Summary as follows.

Credit to Income Summary in the first closing entry includes amounts from:	
Merchandise inventory (ending)	$ 21,000
Purchase discounts	4,200
Purchase returns and allowances	1,500
Debit to Income Summary in the second closing entry includes amounts from:	
Merchandise inventory (beginning)	(19,000)
Purchases	(235,800)
Transportation-in	(2,300)
Net effect on Income Summary	$(230,400)

This $230,400 effect on Income Summary is the cost of goods sold amount. The periodic system transfers cost of goods sold to the Income Summary account but without using a Cost of Goods Sold account. Also, the periodic system does not separately measure shrinkage. Instead, it computes cost of goods available

---

[2] This approach is called the *closing entry method.* An alternative approach, referred to as the *adjusting entry method,* would not make any entries to Merchandise Inventory in the closing entries of Exhibit 4A.1, but instead would make two adjusting entries. Using Z-Mart data, the two adjusting entries would be: (1) Dr. Income Summary and Cr. Merchandise Inventory for $19,000 each, and (2) Dr. Merchandise Inventory and Cr. Income Summary for $21,000 each. The first entry removes the beginning balance of Merchandise Inventory, and the second entry records the actual ending balance.

for sale, subtracts the cost of ending inventory, and defines the difference as cost of goods sold, which includes shrinkage.

Preparing Financial Statements   The financial statements of a merchandiser using the periodic system are similar to those for a service company described in prior chapters. The income statement mainly differs by the inclusion of *cost of goods sold* and *gross profit*—of course, net sales is affected by discounts, returns, and allowances. The cost of goods sold section under the periodic system follows

Calculation of Cost of Goods Sold For Year Ended December 31, 2011	
Beginning inventory	$ 19,000
Cost of goods purchased	232,400
Cost of goods available for sale	251,400
Less ending inventory	21,000
Cost of goods sold	$230,400

The balance sheet mainly differs by the inclusion of *merchandise inventory* in current assets—see Exhibit 4.15. The statement of retained earnings is unchanged. A work sheet can be used to help prepare these statements. The only differences under the periodic system from the work sheet illustrated in Appendix 4B using the perpetual system are highlighted as follows in blue boldface font.

```
File  Edit  View  Insert  Format  Tools  Data  Accounting  Window  Help                                    _ |8| x|
```

	No.	Account	Unadjusted Trial Balance Dr.	Cr.	Adjustments Dr.	Cr.	Adjusted Trial Balance Dr.	Cr.	Income Statement Dr.	Cr.	Balance Sheet Dr.	Cr.
3	101	Cash	8,200				8,200				8,200	
4	106	Accounts receivable	11,200				11,200				11,200	
5	119	**Merchandise Inventory**	19,000				19,000		19,000	21,000	21,000	
6	126	Supplies	3,800			(b) 3,000	800				800	
7	128	Prepaid insurance	900			(a) 600	300				300	
8	167	Equipment	34,200				34,200				34,200	
9	168	Accumulated depr.—Equip.		3,700		(c) 3,700		7,400				7,400
10	201	Accounts payable		16,000				16,000				16,000
11	209	Salaries payable				(d) 800		800				800
12	307	Common stock		10,000				10,000				10,000
13	318	Retained earnings		32,600				32,600				32,600
14	319	Dividends	4,000				4,000				4,000	
15	413	Sales		321,000				321,000		321,000		
16a	414	Sales returns and allowances	2,000				2,000		2,000			
16b	415	Sales discounts	4,300				4,300		4,300			
16c	505	**Purchases**	235,800				235,800		235,800			
16d	506	**Purchases returns & allowance**		1,500				1,500		1,500		
17	507	**Purchases discounts**		4,200				4,200		4,200		
18	508	**Transportation-in**	2,300				2,300		2,300			
19	612	Depreciation expense—Equip.			(c) 3,700		3,700		3,700			
20	622	Salaries expense	43,000		(d) 800		43,800		43,800			
21	637	Insurance expense			(a) 600		600		600			
22	640	Rent expense	9,000				9,000		9,000			
23	652	Supplies expense			(b) 3,000		3,000		3,000			
24	655	Advertising expense	11,300				11,300		11,300			
25		Totals	389,000	389,000	8,100	8,100	393,500	393,500	334,800	347,700	79,700	66,800
26		Net income							12,900			12,900
27		Totals							347,700	347,700	79,700	79,700

```
Sheet1 / Sheet2 / Sheet3 /
```

Quick Check   Answers — p. 185

13. What account is used (for journalizing entries) in a perpetual inventory system but not in a periodic system?

14. Which of the following accounts are temporary accounts under a periodic system?
(*a*) Merchandise Inventory; (*b*) Purchases; (*c*) Transportation-In.

15. How is cost of goods sold computed under a periodic inventory system?

16. Do reported amounts of ending inventory and net income differ if the adjusting entry method of recording the change in inventory is used instead of the closing entry method?

APPENDIX

Work Sheet—Perpetual System

4B

Exhibit 4B.1 shows the work sheet for preparing financial statements of a merchandiser. It differs slightly from the work sheet layout in Chapter 3—the differences are in **red boldface**. Also, the adjustments in the work sheet reflect the following: (*a*) Expiration of $600 of prepaid insurance. (*b*) Use of $3,000 of supplies. (*c*) Depreciation of $3,700 for equipment. (*d*) Accrual of $800 of unpaid salaries. (*e*) Inventory shrinkage of $250. Once the adjusted amounts are extended into the financial statement columns, the information is used to develop financial statements.

EXHIBIT 4B.1

Work Sheet for Merchandiser (using a perpetual system)

No.	Account	Unadjusted Trial Balance Dr.	Cr.	Adjustments Dr.	Cr.	Adjusted Trial Balance Dr.	Cr.	Income Statement Dr.	Cr.	Balance Sheet Dr.	Cr.
101	Cash	8,200				8,200				8,200	
106	Accounts receivable	11,200				11,200				11,200	
119	Merchandise Inventory	21,250			(e) 250	21,000				21,000	
126	Supplies	3,800			(b) 3,000	800				800	
128	Prepaid insurance	900			(a) 600	300				300	
167	Equipment	34,200				34,200				34,200	
168	Accumulated depr.—Equip.		3,700		(c) 3,700		7,400				7,400
201	Accounts payable		16,000				16,000				16,000
209	Salaries payable				(d) 800		800				800
307	Common stock		10,000				10,000				10,000
318	Retained earnings		32,600				32,600				32,600
319	Dividends	4,000				4,000				4,000	
413	Sales		321,000				321,000		321,000		
414	Sales returns and allowances	2,000				2,000		2,000			
415	Sales discounts	4,300				4,300		4,300			
502	Cost of goods sold	230,150		(e) 250		230,400		230,400			
612	Depreciation expense—Equip.			(c) 3,700		3,700		3,700			
622	Salaries expense	43,000		(d) 800		43,800		43,800			
637	Insurance expense			(a) 600		600		600			
640	Rent expense	9,000				9,000		9,000			
652	Supplies expense			(b) 3,000		3,000		3,000			
655	Advertising expense	11,300				11,300		11,300			
	Totals	383,300	383,300	8,350	8,350	387,800	387,800	308,100	321,000	79,700	66,800
	Net income							12,900			12,900
	Totals							321,000	321,000	79,700	79,700

Summary

C1 **Describe merchandising activities and identify income components for a merchandising company.** Merchandisers buy products and resell them. Examples of merchandisers include Walmart, Home Depot, The Limited, and Barnes & Noble. A merchandiser's costs on the income statement include an amount for cost of goods sold. Gross profit, or gross margin, equals sales minus cost of goods sold.

C2 **Identify and explain the inventory asset and cost flows of a merchandising company.** The current asset section of a merchandising company's balance sheet includes *merchandise inventory,* which refers to the products a merchandiser sells and are available for sale at the balance sheet date. Cost of merchandise purchases flows into Merchandise Inventory and from there to Cost of Goods Sold on the income statement. Any remaining inventory is reported as a current asset on the balance sheet.

A1 **Compute the acid-test ratio and explain its use to assess liquidity.** The acid-test ratio is computed as quick assets (cash, short-term investments, and current receivables) divided by current liabilities. It indicates a company's ability to pay its current liabilities with its existing quick assets. An acid-test ratio equal to or greater than 1.0 is often adequate.

A2 **Compute the gross margin ratio and explain its use to assess profitability.** The gross margin ratio is computed as gross margin (net sales minus cost of goods sold) divided by net sales. It indicates a company's profitability before considering other expenses.

P1 **Analyze and record transactions for merchandise purchases using a perpetual system.** For a perpetual inventory system, purchases of inventory (net of trade discounts) are added to the Merchandise Inventory account. Purchase discounts and purchase returns and allowances are subtracted from Merchandise Inventory, and transportation-in costs are added to Merchandise Inventory.

P2 **Analyze and record transactions for merchandise sales using a perpetual system.** A merchandiser records sales at list price less any trade discounts. The cost of items sold is transferred from Merchandise Inventory to Cost of Goods Sold. Refunds or credits given to customers for unsatisfactory merchandise are recorded in Sales Returns and Allowances, a contra account to Sales. If merchandise is returned and restored to inventory, the cost of this merchandise is removed from Cost of Goods Sold and transferred back to Merchandise Inventory. When cash discounts from the sales price are offered and customers pay within the discount period, the seller records Sales Discounts, a contra account to Sales.

P3 **Prepare adjustments and close accounts for a merchandising company.** With a perpetual system, it is often necessary to make an adjustment for inventory shrinkage. This is computed by comparing a physical count of inventory with the Merchandise Inventory balance. Shrinkage is normally charged to Cost of Goods Sold. Temporary accounts closed to Income Summary for a merchandiser include Sales, Sales Discounts, Sales Returns and Allowances, and Cost of Goods Sold.

P4 **Define and prepare multiple-step and single-step income statements.** Multiple-step income statements include greater detail for sales and expenses than do single-step income statements. They also show details of net sales and report expenses in categories reflecting different activities.

P5ᴬ **Record and compare merchandising transactions using both periodic and perpetual inventory systems.** A perpetual inventory system continuously tracks the cost of goods available for sale and the cost of goods sold. A periodic system accumulates the cost of goods purchased during the period and does not compute the amount of inventory or the cost of goods sold until the end of a period. Transactions involving the sale and purchase of merchandise are recorded and analyzed under both the periodic and perpetual inventory systems. Adjusting and closing entries for both inventory systems are illustrated and explained.

Guidance Answers to Decision Maker and Decision Ethics

Entrepreneur For terms of 3/10, n/90, missing the 3% discount for an additional 80 days equals an implied annual interest rate of 13.69%, computed as (365 days ÷ 80 days) × 3%. Since you can borrow funds at 11% (assuming no other processing costs), it is better to borrow and pay within the discount period. You save 2.69% (13.69% − 11%) in interest costs by paying early.

Credit Manager Your decision is whether to comply with prior policy or to create a new policy and not abuse discounts offered by suppliers. Your first step should be to meet with your superior to find out if the late payment policy is the actual policy and, if so, its rationale. If it is the policy to pay late, you must apply your own sense of ethics. One point of view is that the late payment policy is unethical. A deliberate plan to make late payments means the company lies when it pretends to make payment within the discount period. Another view is that the late payment policy is acceptable. In some markets, attempts to take discounts through late payments are accepted as a continued phase of "price negotiation." Also, your company's suppliers can respond by billing your company for the discounts not accepted because of late payments. However, this is a dubious viewpoint, especially since the prior manager proposes that you dishonestly explain late payments as computer or mail problems and since some suppliers have complained.

Supplier A current ratio of 2.1 suggests sufficient current assets to cover current liabilities. An acid-test ratio of 0.5 suggests, however, that quick assets can cover only about one-half of current liabilities. This implies that the retailer depends on money from sales of inventory to pay current liabilities. If sales of inventory decline or profit margins decrease, the likelihood that this retailer will default on its payments increases. Your decision is probably not to extend credit. If you do extend credit, you are likely to closely monitor the retailer's financial condition. (It is better to hold unsold inventory than uncollectible receivables.)

Financial Officer   Your company's net profit margin is about equal to the industry average and suggests typical industry performance. However, gross margin reveals that your company is paying far more in cost of goods sold or receiving far less in sales price than competitors. Your attention must be directed to finding the problem with cost of goods sold, sales, or both. One positive note is that your company's expenses make up 19% of sales (36% − 17%). This favorably compares with competitors' expenses that make up 28% of sales (44% − 16%).

Guidance Answers to Quick Checks

1. Cost of goods sold is the cost of merchandise purchased from a supplier that is sold to customers during a specific period.
2. Gross profit (or gross margin) is the difference between net sales and cost of goods sold.
3. Widespread use of computing and related technology has dramatically increased the use of the perpetual inventory system.
4. Under credit terms of 2/10, n/60, the credit period is 60 days and the discount period is 10 days.
5. (b) trade discount.
6. *FOB* means "free on board." It is used in identifying the point when ownership transfers from seller to buyer. *FOB destination* means that the seller transfers ownership of goods to the buyer when they arrive at the buyer's place of business. It also means that the seller is responsible for paying shipping charges and bears the risk of damage or loss during shipment.
7. Recording sales discounts and sales returns and allowances separately from sales gives useful information to managers for internal monitoring and decision making.
8. When a customer returns merchandise *and* the seller restores the merchandise to inventory, two entries are necessary. One entry records the decrease in revenue and credits the customer's account. The second entry debits inventory and reduces cost of goods sold.
9. Credit memorandum—seller credits accounts receivable from buyer.
10. Merchandise Inventory may need adjusting to reflect shrinkage.
11. Sales (of goods), Sales Discounts, Sales Returns and Allowances, and Cost of Goods Sold (and maybe Delivery Expense).
12. Four closing entries: (1) close credit balances in temporary accounts to Income Summary, (2) close debit balances in temporary accounts to Income Summary, (3) close Income Summary to retained earnings, and (4) close dividends account to retained earnings.
13. Cost of Goods Sold.
14. (b) Purchases and (c) Transportation-In.
15. Under a periodic inventory system, the cost of goods sold is determined at the end of an accounting period by adding the net cost of goods purchased to the beginning inventory and subtracting the ending inventory.
16. Both methods report the same ending inventory and income.

Key Terms

Acid-test ratio (p. 174)
Cash discount (p. 161)
Cost of goods sold (p. 158)
Credit memorandum (p. 167)
Credit period (p. 161)
Credit terms (p. 161)
Debit memorandum (p. 162)
Discount period (p. 161)
EOM (p. 161)
FOB (p. 163)
General and administrative expenses (p. 171)

Gross margin (p. 159)
Gross margin ratio (p. 174)
Gross profit (p. 158)
Inventory (p. 159)
List price (p. 160)
Merchandise (p. 158)
Merchandise inventory (p. 159)
Merchandiser (p. 158)
Multiple-step income statement (p. 171)
Periodic inventory system (p. 160)
Perpetual inventory system (p. 160)

Purchase discount (p. 161)
Retailer (p. 158)
Sales discount (p. 161)
Selling expenses (p. 171)
Shrinkage (p. 168)
Single-step income statement (p. 172)
Supplementary records (p. 164)
Trade discount (p. 160)
Wholesaler (p. 158)

Multiple Choice Quiz   Answers on p. 203   mhhe.com/wildFA6e

Additional quiz questions are available at the book's Website.

1. A company has $550,000 in net sales and $193,000 in gross profit. This means its cost of goods sold equals
   a. $743,000
   b. $550,000
   c. $357,000
   d. $193,000
   e. $(193,000)

2. A company purchased $4,500 of merchandise on May 1 with terms of 2/10, n/30. On May 6, it returned $250 of that merchandise. On May 8, it paid the balance owed for merchandise, taking any discount it is entitled to. The cash paid on May 8 is
   a. $4,500
   b. $4,250
   c. $4,160
   d. $4,165
   e. $4,410

3. A company has cash sales of $75,000, credit sales of $320,000, sales returns and allowances of $13,700, and sales discounts of $6,000. Its net sales equal
   a. $395,000
   b. $375,300
   c. $300,300
   d. $339,700
   e. $414,700

4. A company's quick assets are $37,500, its current assets are $80,000, and its current liabilities are $50,000. Its acid-test ratio equals
   a. 1.600
   b. 0.750
   c. 0.625
   d. 1.333
   e. 0.469

5. A company's net sales are $675,000, its costs of goods sold are $459,000, and its net income is $74,250. Its gross margin ratio equals
   a. 32%
   b. 68%
   c. 47%
   d. 11%
   e. 34%

$^{A(B)}$ *Superscript letter A (B) denotes assignments based on Appendix 4A (4B).*

Icon denotes assignments that involve decision making.

Discussion Questions

1. In comparing the accounts of a merchandising company with those of a service company, what additional accounts would the merchandising company likely use, assuming it employs a perpetual inventory system?

2. What items appear in financial statements of merchandising companies but not in the statements of service companies?

3. Explain how a business can earn a positive gross profit on its sales and still have a net loss.

4. Why do companies offer a cash discount?

5. How does a company that uses a perpetual inventory system determine the amount of inventory shrinkage?

6. Distinguish between cash discounts and trade discounts. Is the amount of a trade discount on purchased merchandise recorded in the accounts?

7. What is the difference between a sales discount and a purchase discount?

8. Why would a company's manager be concerned about the quantity of its purchase returns if its suppliers allow unlimited returns?

9. Does the sender (maker) of a debit memorandum record a debit or a credit in the recipient's account? What entry (debit or credit) does the recipient record?

10. What is the difference between the single-step and multiple-step income statement formats?

11. Refer to the balance sheet and income statement for **Research In Motion** in Appendix A. What does the company title its inventory account? Does the company present a detailed calculation of its cost of sales? **RIM**

12. Refer to **Nokia**'s income statement in Appendix A. What title does it use for cost of goods sold? **NOKIA**

13. Refer to the income statement for **Apple** in Appendix A. What does Apple title its cost of goods sold account? **Apple**

14. Refer to the income statement of **Palm** in Appendix A. Does its income statement report a gross profit figure? If yes, what is the amount? **Palm**

15. Buyers negotiate purchase contracts with suppliers. What type of shipping terms should a buyer attempt to negotiate to minimize freight-in costs?

■ connect™

QUICK STUDY

QS 4-1

Applying merchandising terms

C1

Enter the letter for each term in the blank space beside the definition that it most closely matches.

A. Cash discount	**E.** FOB shipping point	**H.** Purchase discount
B. Credit period	**F.** Gross profit	**I.** Sales discount
C. Discount period	**G.** Merchandise inventory	**J.** Trade discount
D. FOB destination		

_____ 1. Ownership of goods is transferred when delivered to the buyer's place of business.

_____ 2. Time period in which a cash discount is available.

_____ 3. Difference between net sales and the cost of goods sold.

_____ 4. Reduction in a receivable or payable if it is paid within the discount period.

_____ 5. Purchaser's description of a cash discount received from a supplier of goods.

_____ 6. Ownership of goods is transferred when the seller delivers goods to the carrier.

_____ 7. Reduction below list or catalog price that is negotiated in setting the price of goods.

_____ 8. Seller's description of a cash discount granted to buyers in return for early payment.

_____ 9. Time period that can pass before a customer's payment is due.

_____ 10. Goods a company owns and expects to sell to its customers.

The cost of merchandise inventory includes which of the following:

a. Costs incurred to buy the goods.

b. Costs incurred to ship the goods to the store(s).

c. Costs incurred to make the goods ready for sale.

d. Both a and b.

e. a, b, and c.

QS 4-2
Identifying inventory costs
C2

Prepare journal entries to record each of the following purchases transactions of a merchandising company. Show supporting calculations and assume a perpetual inventory system.

Mar. 5   Purchased 500 units of product at a cost of $5 per unit. Terms of the sale are 2/10, n/60; the invoice is dated March 5.

Mar. 7   Returned 50 defective units from the March 5 purchase and received full credit.

Mar. 15   Paid the amount due from the March 5 purchase, less the return on March 7.

QS 4-3
Recording purchases—
perpetual system
P1

Prepare journal entries to record each of the following sales transactions of a merchandising company. Show supporting calculations and assume a perpetual inventory system.

Apr. 1   Sold merchandise for $2,000, granting the customer terms of 2/10, EOM; invoice dated April 1. The cost of the merchandise is $1,400.

Apr. 4   The customer in the April 1 sale returned merchandise and received credit for $500. The merchandise, which had cost $350, is returned to inventory.

Apr. 11   Received payment for the amount due from the April 1 sale less the return on April 4.

QS 4-4
Recording sales—
perpetual system
P2

Compute net sales, gross profit, and the gross margin ratio for each separate case _a_ through _d_. Interpret the gross margin ratio for case _a_.

QS 4-5
Computing and analyzing
gross margin

A2

	a	b	c	d
Sales	$130,000	$512,000	$35,700	$245,700
Sales discounts	4,200	16,500	400	3,500
Sales returns and allowances	17,000	5,000	5,000	700
Cost of goods sold	76,600	326,700	21,300	125,900

Nix'It Company's ledger on July 31, its fiscal year-end, includes the following selected accounts that have normal balances (Nix'It uses the perpetual inventory system).

QS 4-6
Accounting for shrinkage—
perpetual system
P3

Merchandise inventory	$ 34,800	Sales returns and allowances	$ 3,500
Retained earnings	115,300	Cost of goods sold	102,000
Dividends	7,000	Depreciation expense	7,300
Sales	157,200	Salaries expense	29,500
Sales discounts	1,700	Miscellaneous expenses	2,000

A physical count of its July 31 year-end inventory discloses that the cost of the merchandise inventory still available is $32,900. Prepare the entry to record any inventory shrinkage.

QS 4-7
Closing entries   **P3**

Refer to QS 4-6 and prepare journal entries to close the balances in temporary revenue and expense accounts. Remember to consider the entry for shrinkage that is made to solve QS 4-6.

QS 4-8
Computing and interpreting acid-test ratio

A1

Use the following information on current assets and current liabilities to compute and interpret the acid-test ratio. Explain what the acid-test ratio of a company measures.

Cash	$1,200	Prepaid expenses	$ 600
Accounts receivable	2,700	Accounts payable	4,750
Inventory	5,000	Other current liabilities	950

QS 4-9
Contrasting liquidity ratios   **A1**

Identify similarities and differences between the acid-test ratio and the current ratio. Compare and describe how the two ratios reflect a company's ability to meet its current obligations.

QS 4-10
Multiple-step income statement
P4

The multiple-step income statement normally includes which of the following:
a. Detailed computations of net sales.
b. Detailed computations of expenses, including subtotals for various expense categories.
c. Operating expenses are usually classified into (1) selling expenses and (2) general and administrative expenses.
d. Both a and c.
e. a, b, and c.

QS 4-11^A

QS 4-11ᴬ
Contrasting periodic and perpetual systems
P5

Identify whether each description best applies to a periodic or a perpetual inventory system.
a. Provides more timely information to managers.
b. Requires an adjusting entry to record inventory shrinkage.
c. Markedly increased in frequency and popularity in business within the past decade.
d. Records cost of goods sold each time a sales transaction occurs.
e. Updates the inventory account only at period-end.

QS 4-12ᴬ
Recording purchases—
periodic system   **P5**

Refer to QS 4-3 and prepare journal entries to record each of the merchandising transactions assuming that the periodic inventory system is used.

QS 4-13ᴬ
Recording purchases—
periodic system   **P5**

Refer to QS 4-4 and prepare journal entries to record each of the merchandising transactions assuming that the periodic inventory system is used.

QS 4-14
IFRS income statement presentation
P4

Income statement information for **adidas**, a German footwear, apparel, and accessories manufacturer, for the year ended December 31, 2009, follows. The company applies IFRS, as adopted by the European Union, and reports its results in millions of euros. Prepare its calendar year 2009 (1) multiple-step income statement and (2) single-step income statement.

Net income	€ 245
Financial income	19
Financial expenses	169
Operating profit	508
Cost of sales	5,669
Income taxes	113
Income before taxes	358
Gross profit	4,712
Royalty and commission income	86
Other operating income	100
Other operating expenses	4,390
Net sales	10,381

Answer each of the following questions related to international accounting standards.

a. Explain how the accounting for merchandise purchases and sales is different between accounting under IFRS versus U.S. GAAP.

b. Income statements prepared under IFRS usually report an item titled *finance costs*. What do finance costs refer to?

c. U.S. GAAP prohibits alternative measures of income reported on the income statement. Does IFRS permit such alternative measures on the income statement?

QS 4-15
International accounting standards

C1

connect

Prepare journal entries to record the following transactions for a retail store. Assume a perpetual inventory system.

Apr. 2   Purchased merchandise from Blue Company under the following terms: $3,600 price, invoice dated April 2, credit terms of 2/15, n/60, and FOB shipping point.
   3   Paid $200 for shipping charges on the April 2 purchase.
   4   Returned to Blue Company unacceptable merchandise that had an invoice price of $600.
   17   Sent a check to Blue Company for the April 2 purchase, net of the discount and the returned merchandise.
   18   Purchased merchandise from Fox Corp. under the following terms: $7,500 price, invoice dated April 18, credit terms of 2/10, n/30, and FOB destination.
   21   After negotiations, received from Fox a $2,100 allowance on the April 18 purchase.
   28   Sent check to Fox paying for the April 18 purchase, net of the discount and allowance.

EXERCISES

Exercise 4-1
Recording entries for merchandise purchases
P1

Check   April 28, Cr. Cash $5,292

Taos Company purchased merchandise for resale from Tuscon Company with an invoice price of $22,000 and credit terms of 3/10, n/60. The merchandise had cost Tuscon $15,000. Taos paid within the discount period. Assume that both buyer and seller use a perpetual inventory system.

1. Prepare entries that the buyer should record for (a) the purchase and (b) the cash payment.

2. Prepare entries that the seller should record for (a) the sale and (b) the cash collection.

3. Assume that the buyer borrowed enough cash to pay the balance on the last day of the discount period at an annual interest rate of 11% and paid it back on the last day of the credit period. Compute how much the buyer saved by following this strategy. (Assume a 365-day year and round dollar amounts to the nearest cent, including computation of interest per day.)

Exercise 4-2
Analyzing and recording merchandise transactions— both buyer and seller
P1 P2

Check   (3) $338.50 savings (rounded)

The operating cycle of a merchandiser with credit sales includes the following five activities. Starting with merchandise acquisition, identify the chronological order of these five activities.

a. _____ purchases of merchandise.

b. _____ credit sales to customers.

c. _____ inventory made available for sale.

d. _____ cash collections from customers.

e. _____ accounts receivable accounted for.

Exercise 4-3
Operating cycle for merchandiser
C2

Spare Parts was organized on May 1, 2011, and made its first purchase of merchandise on May 3. The purchase was for 1,000 units at a price of $10 per unit. On May 5, Spare Parts sold 600 of the units for $14 per unit to DeSoto Co. Terms of the sale were 2/10, n/60. Prepare entries for Spare Parts to record the May 5 sale and each of the following separate transactions *a* through *c* using a perpetual inventory system.

a. On May 7, DeSoto returns 200 units because they did not fit the customer's needs. Spare Parts restores the units to its inventory.

b. On May 8, DeSoto discovers that 50 units are damaged but are still of some use and, therefore, keeps the units. Spare Parts sends DeSoto a credit memorandum for $300 to compensate for the damage.

c. On May 15, DeSoto discovers that 72 units are the wrong color. DeSoto keeps 43 of these units because Spare Parts sends a $92 credit memorandum to compensate. DeSoto returns the remaining 29 units to Spare Parts. Spare Parts restores the 29 returned units to its inventory.

Exercise 4-4
Recording sales returns and allowances   P2

Check   (c) Dr. Merchandise Inventory $290

Refer to Exercise 4-4 and prepare the appropriate journal entries for DeSoto Co. to record the May 5 purchase and each of the three separate transactions *a* through *c*. DeSoto is a retailer that uses a perpetual inventory system and purchases these units for resale.

Exercise 4-5
Recording purchase returns and allowances   P1

Exercise 4-6

Analyzing and recording merchandise transactions—both buyer and seller

P1 P2

Check (1) May 20, Cr. Cash $27,936

On May 11, Smythe Co. accepts delivery of $30,000 of merchandise it purchases for resale from Hope Corporation. With the merchandise is an invoice dated May 11, with terms of 3/10, n/90, FOB shipping point. The goods cost Hope $20,000. When the goods are delivered, Smythe pays $335 to Express Shipping for delivery charges on the merchandise. On May 12, Smythe returns $1,200 of goods to Hope, who receives them one day later and restores them to inventory. The returned goods had cost Hope $800. On May 20, Smythe mails a check to Hope Corporation for the amount owed. Hope receives it the following day. (Both Smythe and Hope use a perpetual inventory system.)

1. Prepare journal entries that Smythe Co. records for these transactions.
2. Prepare journal entries that Hope Corporation records for these transactions.

Exercise 4-7

Sales returns and allowances

C1

Business decision makers desire information on sales returns and allowances. (1) Explain why a company's manager wants the accounting system to record customers' returns of unsatisfactory goods in the Sales Returns and Allowances account instead of the Sales account. (2) Explain whether this information would be useful for external decision makers.

Exercise 4-8

Recording effects of merchandising activities

P1 P2

The following supplementary records summarize Titus Company's merchandising activities for year 2011. Set up T-accounts for Merchandise Inventory and Cost of Goods Sold. Then record the summarized activities in those T-accounts and compute account balances.

Cost of merchandise sold to customers in sales transactions	$186,000
Merchandise inventory, December 31, 2010	27,000
Invoice cost of merchandise purchases	190,500
Shrinkage determined on December 31, 2011	700
Cost of transportation-in	1,900
Cost of merchandise returned by customers and restored to inventory	2,200
Purchase discounts received	1,600
Purchase returns and allowances	4,100

Check Year-End Merchandise Inventory Dec. 31, $29,200

Exercise 4-9

Computing revenues, expenses, and income

C1 C2

Using your accounting knowledge, fill in the blanks in the following separate income statements *a* through *e*. Identify any negative amount by putting it in parentheses.

	a	b	c	d	e
Sales	$60,000	$42,500	$36,000	$?	$23,600
Cost of goods sold					
Merchandise inventory (beginning)	6,000	17,050	7,500	7,000	2,560
Total cost of merchandise purchases	36,000	?	?	32,000	5,600
Merchandise inventory (ending)	?	(2,700)	(9,000)	(6,600)	?
Cost of goods sold	34,050	15,900	?	?	5,600
Gross profit	?	?	3,750	45,600	?
Expenses	9,000	10,650	12,150	2,600	6,000
Net income (loss)	$?	$15,950	$ (8,400)	$43,000	$?

Exercise 4-10

Preparing adjusting and closing entries for a merchandiser

P3

The following list includes selected permanent accounts and all of the temporary accounts from the December 31, 2011, unadjusted trial balance of Deacon Co., a business owned by Julie Deacon. Use these account balances along with the additional information to journalize (*a*) adjusting entries and (*b*) closing entries. Deacon Co. uses a perpetual inventory system.

	Debit	Credit
Merchandise inventory	$ 28,000	
Prepaid selling expenses	5,000	
Dividends	2,200	
Sales		$429,000
Sales returns and allowances	16,500	
Sales discounts	4,000	
Cost of goods sold	211,000	
Sales salaries expense	47,000	
Utilities expense	14,000	
Selling expenses	35,000	
Administrative expenses	95,000	

[continued on next page]

Additional Information

Accrued sales salaries amount to $1,600. Prepaid selling expenses of $2,000 have expired. A physical count of year-end merchandise inventory shows $27,450 of goods still available.

A retail company recently completed a physical count of ending merchandise inventory to use in preparing adjusting entries. In determining the cost of the counted inventory, company employees failed to consider that $2,000 of incoming goods had been shipped by a supplier on December 31 under an FOB shipping point agreement. These goods had been recorded in Merchandise Inventory as a purchase, but they were not included in the physical count because they were in transit. Explain how this overlooked fact affects the company's financial statements and the following ratios: return on assets, debt ratio, current ratio, and acid-test ratio.

Exercise 4-11
Interpreting a physical count error as inventory shrinkage

A1

Refer to the information in Exercise 4-11 and explain how the error in the physical count affects the company's gross margin ratio and its profit margin ratio.

Exercise 4-12
Physical count error and profits

A2

Compute the current ratio and acid-test ratio for each of the following separate cases. (Round ratios to two decimals.) Which company case is in the best position to meet short-term obligations? Explain.

Exercise 4-13
Computing and analyzing acid-test and current ratios

A1

	Case A	Case B	Case C
Cash......................	$ 800	$ 510	$3,200
Short-term investments	0	0	1,100
Current receivables............	0	790	800
Inventory	2,000	1,600	1,900
Prepaid expenses.............	1,200	600	300
Total current assets	$4,000	$3,500	$7,300
Current liabilities.............	$2,200	$1,100	$3,650

Journalize the following merchandising transactions for CSI Systems assuming it uses a perpetual inventory system.

1. On November 1, CSI Systems purchases merchandise for $1,400 on credit with terms of 2/5, n/30, FOB shipping point; invoice dated November 1.
2. On November 5, CSI Systems pays cash for the November 1 purchase.
3. On November 7, CSI Systems discovers and returns $100 of defective merchandise purchased on November 1 for a cash refund.
4. On November 10, CSI Systems pays $80 cash for transportation costs with the November 1 purchase.
5. On November 13, CSI Systems sells merchandise for $1,500 on credit. The cost of the merchandise is $750.
6. On November 16, the customer returns merchandise from the November 13 transaction. The returned items would sell for $200 and cost $100; the items were not damaged and were returned to inventory.

Exercise 4-14
Preparing journal entries—perpetual system

P1 P2

A company reports the following sales-related information: Sales (gross) of $100,000; Sales discounts of $2,000; Sales returns and allowances of $8,000; Sales salaries expense of $5,000. Prepare the net sales portion only of this company's multiple-step income statement.

Exercise 4-15
Multiple-step income statement

P4

Refer to Exercise 4-1 and prepare journal entries to record each of the merchandising transactions assuming that the periodic inventory system is used.

Exercise 4-16^A
Recording purchases—periodic system   P5

Refer to Exercise 4-2 and prepare journal entries to record each of the merchandising transactions assuming that the periodic inventory system is used by both the buyer and the seller. (Skip the part 3 requirement.)

Exercise 4-17^A
Recording purchases and sales—periodic system   P5

Exercise 4-18^A
Buyer and seller transactions—
periodic system   P5

Refer to Exercise 4-6 and prepare journal entries to record each of the merchandising transactions assuming that the periodic inventory system is used by both the buyer and the seller.

Exercise 4-19^A
Recording purchases—
periodic system   P5

Refer to Exercise 4-14 and prepare journal entries to record each of the merchandising transactions assuming that the periodic inventory system is used.

Exercise 4-20
Preparing an income statement
following IFRS

P4

L'Oréal reports the following income statement accounts for the year ended December 31, 2009 (euros in millions). Prepare the income statement for this company for the year ended December 31, 2009, following usual IFRS practices.

Net profit	€ 1,794.9	Income tax expense	€	676.1
Finance costs	76.0	Profit before tax expense		2,471.0
Net sales	17,472.6	Research and development expense		609.2
Gross profit	12,311.0	Selling, general and administrative expense		3,735.5
Other expense	30.6	Advertising and promotion expense		5,388.7
Cost of sales	5,161.6			

■ connect

PROBLEM SET A

Problem 4-1A
Preparing journal entries for
merchandising activities—
perpetual system

P1 P2

Check Aug. 9, Dr. Delivery
Expense, $120

Aug. 18, Cr. Cash $4,695

Aug. 29, Dr. Cash $2,970

Prepare journal entries to record the following merchandising transactions of Stone Company, which applies the perpetual inventory system. (*Hint:* It will help to identify each receivable and payable; for example, record the purchase on August 1 in Accounts Payable—Abilene.)

Aug. 1 Purchased merchandise from Abilene Company for $6,000 under credit terms of 1/10, n/30, FOB destination, invoice dated August 1.
      4 At Abilene's request, Stone paid $100 cash for freight charges on the August 1 purchase, reducing the amount owed to Abilene.
      5 Sold merchandise to Lux Corp. for $4,200 under credit terms of 2/10, n/60, FOB destination, invoice dated August 5. The merchandise had cost $3,000.
      8 Purchased merchandise from Welch Corporation for $5,300 under credit terms of 1/10, n/45, FOB shipping point, invoice dated August 8. The invoice showed that at Stone's request, Welch paid the $240 shipping charges and added that amount to the bill. (*Hint:* Discounts are not applied to freight and shipping charges.)
      9 Paid $120 cash for shipping charges related to the August 5 sale to Lux Corp.
     10 Lux returned merchandise from the August 5 sale that had cost Stone $500 and been sold for $700. The merchandise was restored to inventory.
     12 After negotiations with Welch Corporation concerning problems with the merchandise purchased on August 8, Stone received a credit memorandum from Welch granting a price reduction of $800.
     15 Received balance due from Lux Corp. for the August 5 sale less the return on August 10.
     18 Paid the amount due Welch Corporation for the August 8 purchase less the price reduction granted.
     19 Sold merchandise to Trax Co. for $3,600 under credit terms of 1/10, n/30, FOB shipping point, invoice dated August 19. The merchandise had cost $2,500.
     22 Trax requested a price reduction on the August 19 sale because the merchandise did not meet specifications. Stone sent Trax a $600 credit memorandum to resolve the issue.
     29 Received Trax's cash payment for the amount due from the August 19 sale.
     30 Paid Abilene Company the amount due from the August 1 purchase.

Problem 4-2A
Preparing journal entries for
merchandising activities—
perpetual system

P1 P2

Prepare journal entries to record the following merchandising transactions of Bask Company, which applies the perpetual inventory system. (*Hint:* It will help to identify each receivable and payable; for example, record the purchase on July 1 in Accounts Payable—Black.)

July 1 Purchased merchandise from Black Company for $6,000 under credit terms of 1/15, n/30, FOB shipping point, invoice dated July 1.
      2 Sold merchandise to Coke Co. for $800 under credit terms of 2/10, n/60, FOB shipping point, invoice dated July 2. The merchandise had cost $500.
      3 Paid $100 cash for freight charges on the purchase of July 1.

8   Sold merchandise that had cost $1,200 for $1,600 cash.

9   Purchased merchandise from Lane Co. for $2,300 under credit terms of 2/15, n/60, FOB destination, invoice dated July 9.

11   Received a $200 credit memorandum from Lane Co. for the return of part of the merchandise purchased on July 9.

12   Received the balance due from Coke Co. for the invoice dated July 2, net of the discount.

16   Paid the balance due to Black Company within the discount period.

19   Sold merchandise that cost $900 to AKP Co. for $1,250 under credit terms of 2/15, n/60, FOB shipping point, invoice dated July 19.

21   Issued a $150 credit memorandum to AKP Co. for an allowance on goods sold on July 19.

24   Paid Lane Co. the balance due after deducting the discount.

30   Received the balance due from AKP Co. for the invoice dated July 19, net of discount.

31   Sold merchandise that cost $3,200 to Coke Co. for $5,000 under credit terms of 2/10, n/60, FOB shipping point, invoice dated July 31.

Check   July 12, Dr. Cash $784
July 16, Cr. Cash $5,940

July 24, Cr. Cash $2,058
July 30, Dr. Cash $1,078

The following unadjusted trial balance is prepared at fiscal year-end for Rex Company.

Problem 4-3A
Preparing adjusting entries and income statements; and computing gross margin, acid-test, and current ratios

A1 A2 P3 P4

mhhe.com/wildFA6e

File Edit View Insert Format Tools Data Accounting Window Help

REX COMPANY
Unadjusted Trial Balance
January 31, 2011

		Debit	Credit
1			
2	Cash	$ 2,200	
3	Merchandise inventory	11,500	
4	Store supplies	4,800	
5	Prepaid insurance	2,300	
6	Store equipment	41,900	
7	Accumulated depreciation—Store equipment		$ 15,000
8	Accounts payable		9,000
9	Common stock		5,000
10	Retained earnings		27,000
11	Dividends	2,000	
12	Sales		104,000
13	Sales discounts	1,000	
14	Sales returns and allowances	2,000	
15	Cost of goods sold	37,400	
16	Depreciation expense—Store equipment	0	
17	Salaries expense	31,000	
18	Insurance expense	0	
19	Rent expense	14,000	
20	Store supplies expense	0	
21	Advertising expense	9,900	
22	Totals	$160,000	$160,000
23			

Sheet1 ⟨ Sheet2 ⟨ Sheet3 ⟩

Rent expense and salaries expense are equally divided between selling activities and the general and administrative activities. Rex Company uses a perpetual inventory system.

Required

1. Prepare adjusting journal entries to reflect each of the following:

   a. Store supplies still available at fiscal year-end amount to $1,650.

   b. Expired insurance, an administrative expense, for the fiscal year is $1,500.

   c. Depreciation expense on store equipment, a selling expense, is $1,400 for the fiscal year.

   d. To estimate shrinkage, a physical count of ending merchandise inventory is taken. It shows $11,100 of inventory is still available at fiscal year-end.

2. Prepare a multiple-step income statement for fiscal year 2011.

3. Prepare a single-step income statement for fiscal year 2011.

4. Compute the current ratio, acid-test ratio, and gross margin ratio as of January 31, 2011.

Problem 4-4A
Computing merchandising amounts and formatting income statements

C2 P4

BizKid Company's adjusted trial balance on August 31, 2011, its fiscal year-end, follows.

	Debit	Credit
Merchandise inventory	$ 31,000	
Other (noninventory) assets	120,400	
Total liabilities		$ 35,000
Common stock		10,000
Retained earnings.		91,650
Dividends	8,000	
Sales		212,000
Sales discounts	3,250	
Sales returns and allowances	14,000	
Cost of goods sold	82,600	
Sales salaries expense	29,000	
Rent expense—Selling space	10,000	
Store supplies expense	2,500	
Advertising expense	18,000	
Office salaries expense	26,500	
Rent expense—Office space	2,600	
Office supplies expense	800	
Totals	$348,650	$348,650

On August 31, 2010, merchandise inventory was $25,000. Supplementary records of merchandising activities for the year ended August 31, 2011, reveal the following itemized costs.

Invoice cost of merchandise purchases	$91,000
Purchase discounts received	1,900
Purchase returns and allowances	4,400
Costs of transportation-in	3,900

Required

1. Compute the company's net sales for the year.

2. Compute the company's total cost of merchandise purchased for the year.

3. Prepare a multiple-step income statement that includes separate categories for selling expenses and for general and administrative expenses.

4. Prepare a single-step income statement that includes these expense categories: cost of goods sold, selling expenses, and general and administrative expenses.

Problem 4-5A
Preparing closing entries and interpreting information about discounts and returns

C2 P3

Use the data for BizKid Company in Problem 4-4A to complete the following requirements.

Required

1. Prepare closing entries as of August 31, 2011 (the perpetual inventory system is used).

Analysis Component

2. The company makes all purchases on credit, and its suppliers uniformly offer a 3% sales discount. Does it appear that the company's cash management system is accomplishing the goal of taking all available discounts? Explain.

3. In prior years, the company experienced a 5% returns and allowance rate on its sales, which means approximately 5% of its gross sales were eventually returned outright or caused the company to grant allowances to customers. How do this year's results compare to prior years' results?

Refer to the data and information in Problem 4-3A.

Required

Prepare and complete the entire 10-column work sheet for Rex Company. Follow the structure of Exhibit 4B.1 in Appendix 4B.

Problem 4-6A[B]
Preparing a work sheet for a merchandiser
P3

Prepare journal entries to record the following merchandising transactions of Wave Company, which applies the perpetual inventory system. (*Hint:* It will help to identify each receivable and payable; for example, record the purchase on July 3 in Accounts Payable—CAP.)

July 3 Purchased merchandise from CAP Corp. for $15,000 under credit terms of 1/10, n/30, FOB destination, invoice dated July 3.

  4 At CAP's request, Wave paid $250 cash for freight charges on the July 3 purchase, reducing the amount owed to CAP.

  7 Sold merchandise to Morris Co. for $10,500 under credit terms of 2/10, n/60, FOB destination, invoice dated July 7. The merchandise had cost $7,500.

  10 Purchased merchandise from Murdock Corporation for $14,200 under credit terms of 1/10, n/45, FOB shipping point, invoice dated July 10. The invoice showed that at Wave's request, Murdock paid the $600 shipping charges and added that amount to the bill. (*Hint:* Discounts are not applied to freight and shipping charges.)

  11 Paid $300 cash for shipping charges related to the July 7 sale to Morris Co.

  12 Morris returned merchandise from the July 7 sale that had cost Wave $1,250 and been sold for $1,750. The merchandise was restored to inventory.

  14 After negotiations with Murdock Corporation concerning problems with the merchandise purchased on July 10, Wave received a credit memorandum from Murdock granting a price reduction of $2,000.

  17 Received balance due from Morris Co. for the July 7 sale less the return on July 12.

  20 Paid the amount due Murdock Corporation for the July 10 purchase less the price reduction granted.

  21 Sold merchandise to Ulsh for $9,000 under credit terms of 1/10, n/30, FOB shipping point, invoice dated July 21. The merchandise had cost $6,250.

  24 Ulsh requested a price reduction on the July 21 sale because the merchandise did not meet specifications. Wave sent Ulsh a credit memorandum for $1,500 to resolve the issue.

  30 Received Ulsh's cash payment for the amount due from the July 21 sale.

  31 Paid CAP Corp. the amount due from the July 3 purchase.

PROBLEM SET B

Problem 4-1B
Preparing journal entries for merchandising activities—perpetual system
P1 P2

Check July 17, Dr. Cash $8,575
July 20, Cr. Cash $12,678

July 30, Dr. Cash $7,425

Prepare journal entries to record the following merchandising transactions of Yang Company, which applies the perpetual inventory system. (*Hint:* It will help to identify each receivable and payable; for example, record the purchase on May 2 in Accounts Payable—Bots.)

May 2 Purchased merchandise from Bots Co. for $9,000 under credit terms of 1/15, n/30, FOB shipping point, invoice dated May 2.

  4 Sold merchandise to Chase Co. for $1,200 under credit terms of 2/10, n/60, FOB shipping point, invoice dated May 4. The merchandise had cost $750.

  5 Paid $150 cash for freight charges on the purchase of May 2.

  9 Sold merchandise that had cost $1,800 for $2,400 cash.

  10 Purchased merchandise from Snyder Co. for $3,450 under credit terms of 2/15, n/60, FOB destination, invoice dated May 10.

  12 Received a $300 credit memorandum from Snyder Co. for the return of part of the merchandise purchased on May 10.

  14 Received the balance due from Chase Co. for the invoice dated May 4, net of the discount.

  17 Paid the balance due to Bots Co. within the discount period.

  20 Sold merchandise that cost $1,450 to Tex Co. for $2,800 under credit terms of 2/15, n/60, FOB shipping point, invoice dated May 20.

  22 Issued a $400 credit memorandum to Tex Co. for an allowance on goods sold from May 20.

  25 Paid Snyder Co. the balance due after deducting the discount.

  30 Received the balance due from Tex Co. for the invoice dated May 20, net of discount and allowance.

  31 Sold merchandise that cost $4,800 to Chase Co. for $7,500 under credit terms of 2/10, n/60, FOB shipping point, invoice dated May 31.

Problem 4-2B
Preparing journal entries for merchandising activities—perpetual system
P1 P2

Check May 14, Dr. Cash $1,176
May 17, Cr. Cash $8,910

May 30, Dr. Cash $2,352

Decision Insight

A wireless portable device with a two-way radio allows clerks to quickly record inventory by scanning bar codes and to instantly send and receive inventory data. It gives managers access to up-to-date information on inventory and its location. ■

Determining Inventory Costs

Merchandise inventory includes costs of expenditures necessary, directly or indirectly, to bring an item to a salable condition and location. This means that the cost of an inventory item includes its invoice cost minus any discount, and plus any incidental costs necessary to put it in a place and condition for sale. Incidental costs can include import duties, freight, storage, insurance, and costs incurred in an aging process (for example, aging wine or cheese).

Accounting principles prescribe that incidental costs be added to inventory. Also, the *matching (expense recognition) principle* states that inventory costs should be recorded against revenue in the period when inventory is sold. However, some companies use the *materiality constraint (cost-to-benefit constraint)* to avoid assigning some incidental costs of acquiring merchandise to inventory. Instead, they expense them when incurred. These companies argue either that those incidental costs are immaterial or that the effort in assigning them outweighs the benefit.

C2 Identify the costs of merchandise inventory.

Internal Controls and Taking a Physical Count

The Inventory account under a perpetual system is updated for each purchase and sale, but events can cause the Inventory account balance to differ from the actual inventory available. Such events include theft, loss, damage, and errors. Thus, nearly all companies take a *physical count of inventory* at least once each year—informally called *taking an inventory*. This often occurs at the end of a fiscal year or when inventory amounts are low. This physical count is used to adjust the Inventory account balance to the actual inventory available.

Point: The Inventory account is a controlling account for the inventory subsidiary ledger. This *subsidiary ledger* contains a separate record (units and costs) for each separate product, and it can be in electronic or paper form. Subsidiary records assist managers in planning and monitoring inventory.

 Fraud

A company applies internal controls when taking a physical count of inventory that usually include the following:

- *Prenumbered inventory tickets* are prepared and distributed to the *counters*—each ticket must be accounted for.
- Counters of inventory are assigned and do not include those responsible for inventory.
- Counters confirm the validity of inventory, including its existence, amount, and quality.
- A second count is taken by a different counter.
- A manager confirms that all inventories are ticketed once, and only once.

Quick Check

Answers — p. 231

1. What accounting principle most guides the allocation of cost of goods available for sale between ending inventory and cost of goods sold?
2. If **Skechers** sells goods to **Target** with terms FOB shipping point, which company reports these goods in its inventory while they are in transit?
3. An art gallery purchases a painting for $11,400 on terms FOB shipping point. Additional costs in obtaining and offering the artwork for sale include $130 for transportation-in, $150 for import duties, $100 for insurance during shipment, $180 for advertising, $400 for framing, and $800 for office salaries. For computing inventory, what cost is assigned to the painting?

INVENTORY COSTING UNDER A PERPETUAL SYSTEM

Accounting for inventory affects both the balance sheet and the income statement. A major goal in accounting for inventory is to properly match costs with sales. We use the *matching principle* to decide how much of the cost of the goods available for sale is deducted from sales and how much is carried forward as inventory and matched against future sales.

Management decisions in accounting for inventory involve the following:

- Items included in inventory and their costs.
- Costing method (specific identification, FIFO, LIFO, or weighted average).
- Inventory system (perpetual or periodic).
- Use of market values or other estimates.

The first point was explained on the prior two pages. The second and third points will be addressed now. The fourth point is the focus at the end of this chapter. Decisions on these points affect the reported amounts for inventory, cost of goods sold, gross profit, income, current assets, and other accounts.

One of the most important issues in accounting for inventory is determining the per unit costs assigned to inventory items. When all units are purchased at the same unit cost, this process is simple. When identical items are purchased at different costs, however, a question arises as to which amounts to record in cost of goods sold and which amounts remain in inventory.

EXHIBIT 5.1

Frequency in Use of Inventory Methods

Other* 3%

FIFO 50%

Weighted Average 20%

LIFO 27%

*Includes specific identification.

Four methods are commonly used to assign costs to inventory and to cost of goods sold: (1) specific identification; (2) first-in, first-out; (3) last-in, first-out; and (4) weighted average. Exhibit 5.1 shows the frequency in the use of these methods.

Each method assumes a particular pattern for how costs flow through inventory. Each of these four methods is acceptable whether or not the actual physical flow of goods follows the cost flow assumption. Physical flow of goods depends on the type of product and the way it is stored. (Perishable goods such as fresh fruit demand that a business attempt to sell them in a first-in, first-out physical flow. Other products such as crude oil and minerals such as coal, gold, and decorative stone can be sold in a last-in, first-out physical flow.) **Physical flow and cost flow need not be the same.**

Inventory Cost Flow Assumptions

P1 Compute inventory in a perpetual system using the methods of specific identification, FIFO, LIFO, and weighted average.

This section introduces inventory cost flow assumptions. For this purpose, assume that three identical units are purchased separately at the following three dates and costs: May 1 at $45, May 3 at $65, and May 6 at $70. One unit is then sold on May 7 for $100. Exhibit 5.2 gives a visual layout of the flow of costs to either the gross profit section of the income statement or the inventory reported on the balance sheet for FIFO, LIFO, and weighted average.

(1) *FIFO assumes costs flow in the order incurred.* The unit purchased on May 1 for $45 is the earliest cost incurred—it is sent to cost of goods sold on the income statement first. The remaining two units ($65 and $70) are reported in inventory on the balance sheet.

(2) *LIFO assumes costs flow in the reverse order incurred.* The unit purchased on May 6 for $70 is the most recent cost incurred—it is sent to cost of goods sold on the income statement. The remaining two units ($45 and $65) are reported in inventory on the balance sheet.

(3) *Weighted average assumes costs flow at an average of the costs available.* The units available at the May 7 sale average $60 in cost, computed as ($45 + $65 + $70)/3. One unit's $60 average cost is sent to cost of goods sold on the income statement. The remaining two units' average costs are reported in inventory at $120 on the balance sheet.

Cost flow assumptions can markedly impact gross profit and inventory numbers. Exhibit 5.2 shows that gross profit as a percent of net sales ranges from 30% to 55% due to nothing else but the cost flow assumption.

Point: It is helpful to recall the cost flow of inventory from Exhibit 4.4.

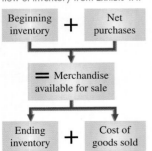

Beginning inventory + Net purchases

= Merchandise available for sale

Ending inventory + Cost of goods sold

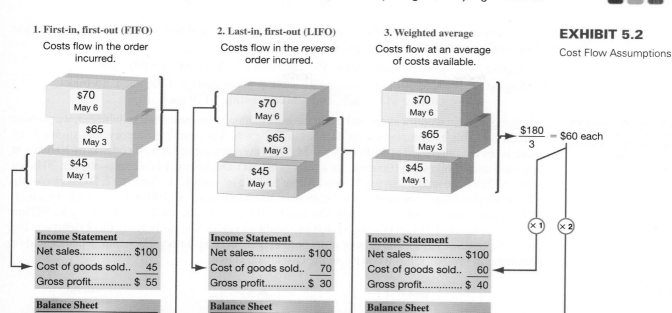

EXHIBIT 5.2

Cost Flow Assumptions

The following sections on inventory costing use the perpetual system. Appendix 5A uses the periodic system. An instructor can choose to cover either one or both systems. If the perpetual system is skipped, then read Appendix 5A and return to the section (six pages ahead) titled "Valuing Inventory at LCM and . . ."

Inventory Costing Illustration

This section provides a comprehensive illustration of inventory costing methods. We use information from Trekking, a sporting goods store. Among its many products, Trekking carries one type of mountain bike whose sales are directed at resorts that provide inexpensive mountain bikes for complimentary guest use. Its customers usually purchase in amounts of 10 or more bikes. We use Trekking's data from August. Its mountain bike (unit) inventory at the beginning of August and its purchases and sales during August are shown in Exhibit 5.3. It ends August with 12 bikes remaining in inventory.

Date	Activity	Units Acquired at Cost	Units Sold at Retail	Unit Inventory
Aug. 1	Beginning inventory	10 units @ $ 91 = $ 910		10 units
Aug. 3	Purchases	15 units @ $106 = $1,590		25 units
Aug. 14	Sales		20 units @ $130	5 units
Aug. 17	Purchases	20 units @ $115 = $2,300		25 units
Aug. 28	Purchases	10 units @ $119 = $1,190		35 units
Aug. 31	Sales		23 units @ $150	12 units
	Totals	**55 units** **$5,990**	**43 units**	

EXHIBIT 5.3

Purchases and Sales of Goods

Trekking uses the perpetual inventory system, which means that its merchandise inventory account is continually updated to reflect purchases and sales. **(Appendix 5A describes the assignment of costs to inventory using a periodic system.)** Regardless of what inventory method or system is used, cost of goods available for sale must be allocated between cost of goods sold and ending inventory.

Point: The perpetual inventory system is now the most dominant system for U.S. businesses.

Point: Cost of goods sold plus ending inventory equals cost of goods available for sale.

Specific Identification

When each item in inventory can be identified with a specific purchase and invoice, we can use **specific identification** (also called *specific invoice inventory pricing*) to assign costs. We also need sales records that identify exactly which items were sold and when. Trekking's internal documents reveal the following specific unit sales:

August 14   Sold 8 bikes costing $91 each and 12 bikes costing $106 each

August 31   Sold 2 bikes costing $91 each, 3 bikes costing $106 each, 15 bikes costing $115 each, and 3 bikes costing $119 each

Point: Three key variables determine the dollar value of ending inventory: (1) inventory quantity, (2) costs of inventory, and (3) cost flow assumption.

Applying specific identification, and using the information above and from Exhibit 5.3, we prepare Exhibit 5.4. This exhibit starts with 10 bikes at $91 each in beginning inventory. On August 3, 15 more bikes are purchased at $106 each for $1,590. Inventory available now consists of 10 bikes at $91 each and 15 bikes at $106 each, for a total of $2,500. On August 14 (see sales above), 20 bikes costing $2,000 are sold—leaving 5 bikes costing $500 in inventory. On August 17, 20 bikes costing $2,300 are purchased, and on August 28, another 10 bikes costing $1,190 are purchased, for a total of 35 bikes costing $3,990 in inventory. On August 31 (see sales above), 23 bikes costing $2,582 are sold, which leaves 12 bikes costing $1,408 in ending inventory. Carefully study this exhibit and the boxed explanations to see the flow of costs both in and out of inventory. Each unit, whether sold or remaining in inventory, has its own specific cost attached to it.

EXHIBIT 5.4

Specific Identification Computations

For the 20 units sold on Aug. 14, the company specifically identified that 8 of those had cost $91 and 12 had cost $106.

For the 23 units sold on Aug. 31, the company specifically identified each bike sold and its acquisition cost from prior purchases.

Date	Goods Purchased	Cost of Goods Sold		Inventory Balance	
		"goods in"	"goods out"	"what's left"	
Aug. 1	Beginning balance			10 @ $ 91	= $ 910
Aug. 3	15 @ $106 = $1,590			10 @ $ 91 15 @ $106 }	= $2,500
Aug. 14		8 @ $ 91 = $ 728 12 @ $106 = $1,272 }	= $2,000*	2 @ $ 91 3 @ $106 }	= $ 500
Aug. 17	20 @ $115 = $2,300			2 @ $ 91 3 @ $106 20 @ $115 }	= $2,800
Aug. 28	10 @ $119 = $1,190			2 @ $ 91 3 @ $106 20 @ $115 10 @ $119 }	= $3,990
Aug. 31		2 @ $ 91 = $ 182 3 @ $106 = $ 318 15 @ $115 = $1,725 3 @ $119 = $ 357 }	= $2,582* $4,582	5 @ $115 7 @ $119 }	= $1,408

* Identification of items sold (and their costs) is obtained from internal documents that track each unit from its purchase to its sale.

When using specific identification, Trekking's cost of goods sold reported on the income statement totals **$4,582**, the sum of $2,000 and $2,582 from the third column of Exhibit 5.4. Trekking's ending inventory reported on the balance sheet is **$1,408**, which is the final inventory balance from the fourth column of Exhibit 5.4.

Point: Specific identification is usually practical only for companies with expensive, custom-made inventory.

The purchases and sales entries for Exhibit 5.4 follow (the colored boldface numbers are those impacted by the cost flow assumption).

Purchases

Aug. 3	Merchandise Inventory	....	1,590	
	Accounts Payable	....		1,590
17	Merchandise Inventory	....	2,300	
	Accounts Payable	....		2,300
28	Merchandise Inventory	....	1,190	
	Accounts Payable	....		1,190

Sales

Aug. 14	Accounts Receivable	....	2,600	
	Sales	....		2,600
14	Cost of Goods Sold	....	2,000	
	Merchandise Inventory	....		2,000
31	Accounts Receivable	....	3,450	
	Sales	....		3,450
31	Cost of Goods Sold	....	2,582	
	Merchandise Inventory	....		2,582

First-In, First-Out

The **first-in, first-out (FIFO)** method of assigning costs to both inventory and cost of goods sold assumes that inventory items are sold in the order acquired. When sales occur, the costs of the earliest units acquired are charged to cost of goods sold. This leaves the costs from the most recent purchases in ending inventory. Use of FIFO for computing the cost of inventory and cost of goods sold is shown in Exhibit 5.5.

This exhibit starts with beginning inventory of 10 bikes at $91 each. On August 3, 15 more bikes costing $106 each are bought for $1,590. Inventory now consists of 10 bikes at $91 each and 15 bikes at $106 each, for a total of $2,500. On August 14, 20 bikes are sold—applying FIFO, the first 10 sold cost $91 each and the next 10 sold cost $106 each, for a total cost of $1,970. This leaves 5 bikes costing $106 each, or $530, in inventory. On August 17, 20 bikes costing $2,300 are purchased, and on August 28, another 10 bikes costing $1,190 are purchased, for a total of 35 bikes costing $4,020 in inventory. On August 31, 23 bikes are sold—applying FIFO, the first 5 bikes sold cost $530 and the next 18 sold cost $2,070, which leaves 12 bikes costing $1,420 in ending inventory.

Point: The "Goods Purchased" column is identical for all methods. Data are taken from Exhibit 5.3.

Date	Goods Purchased	Cost of Goods Sold	Inventory Balance
Aug. 1	Beginning balance		10 @ $91 = $910
Aug. 3	15 @ $106 = $1,590		10 @ $91 } 15 @ $106 } = $2,500
Aug. 14		10 @ $91 = $910 } 10 @ $106 = $1,060 } = $1,970	5 @ $106 = $530
Aug. 17	20 @ $115 = $2,300		5 @ $106 } 20 @ $115 } = $2,830
Aug. 28	10 @ $119 = $1,190		5 @ $106 } 20 @ $115 } 10 @ $119 } = $4,020
Aug. 31		5 @ $106 = $530 } 18 @ $115 = $2,070 } = $2,600 $4,570	2 @ $115 } 10 @ $119 } = $1,420

EXHIBIT 5.5

FIFO Computations—Perpetual System

For the 20 units sold on Aug. 14, the first 10 sold are assigned the earliest cost of $91 (from beg. bal.). The next 10 sold are assigned the next earliest cost of $106.

For the 23 units sold on Aug. 31, the first 5 sold are assigned the earliest available cost of $106 (from Aug. 3 purchase). The next 18 sold are assigned the next earliest cost of $115 (from Aug. 17 purchase).

Trekking's FIFO cost of goods sold reported on its income statement (reflecting the 43 units sold) is **$4,570** ($1,970 + $2,600), and its ending inventory reported on the balance sheet (reflecting the 12 units unsold) is **$1,420**.

The purchases and sales entries for Exhibit 5.5 follow (the colored boldface numbers are those affected by the cost flow assumption).

Point: Under FIFO, a unit sold is assigned the earliest (oldest) cost from inventory. This leaves the most recent costs in ending inventory.

	Purchases				Sales		
Aug. 3	Merchandise Inventory	1,590		Aug. 14	Accounts Receivable	2,600	
	Accounts Payable		1,590		Sales		2,600
17	Merchandise Inventory	2,300		14	Cost of Goods Sold	1,970	
	Accounts Payable		2,300		Merchandise Inventory		1,970
28	Merchandise Inventory	1,190		31	Accounts Receivable	3,450	
	Accounts Payable		1,190		Sales		3,450
				31	Cost of Goods Sold	2,600	
					Merchandise Inventory		2,600

Last-In, First-Out

The **last-in, first-out (LIFO)** method of assigning costs assumes that the most recent purchases are sold first. These more recent costs are charged to the goods sold, and the costs of the earliest purchases are assigned to inventory. As with other methods, LIFO is acceptable even when the physical flow of goods does not follow a last-in, first-out pattern. One appeal of LIFO is that by

2c. Weighted average perpetual method.

Date	Goods Purchased	Cost of Goods Sold	Inventory Balance
Jan. 1	Beginning balance		400 @ $14 = $ 5,600
Jan. 15		200 @ $14 = $2,800	200 @ $14 = $ 2,800
Mar. 10	200 @ $15 = $3,000		200 @ $14 } 200 @ $15 } = $ 5,800 (avg. cost is $14.5)
April 1		200 @ $14.5 = $2,900	200 @ $14.5 = $ 2,900
May 9	300 @ $16 = $4,800		200 @ $14.5 } 300 @ $16 } = $ 7,700 (avg. cost is $15.4)
Sept. 22	250 @ $20 = $5,000		200 @ $14.5 } 300 @ $16 } = $ 12,700 250 @ $20 } (avg. cost is $16.93)
Nov. 1		300 @ $16.93 = $5,079	450 @ $16.93 = $ 7,618.5
Nov. 28	100 @ $21 = $2,100		450 @ $16.93 } 100 @ $21 } = $9,718.5
Total cost of goods sold*		**$10,779**	

* The cost of goods sold ($10,779) plus ending inventory ($9,718.5) is $2.5 less than the cost of goods available for sale ($20,500) due to rounding.

2d. Specific identification method.

Date	Goods Purchased	Cost of Goods Sold	Inventory Balance
Jan. 1	Beginning balance		400 @ $14 = $ 5,600
Jan. 15		200 @ $14 = $2,800	200 @ $14 = $ 2,800
Mar. 10	200 @ $15 = $3,000		200 @ $14 } 200 @ $15 } = $ 5,800
April 1		200 @ $15 = $3,000	200 @ $14 = $ 2,800
May 9	300 @ $16 = $4,800		200 @ $14 } 300 @ $16 } = $ 7,600
Sept. 22	250 @ $20 = $5,000		200 @ $14 } 300 @ $16 } = $ 12,600 250 @ $20 }
Nov. 1		200 @ $14 = $2,800 100 @ $20 = $2,000	300 @ $16 } 150 @ $20 } = $ 7,800
Nov. 28	100 @ $21 = $2,100		300 @ $16 } 150 @ $20 } = $ 9,900 100 @ $21 }
Total cost of goods sold		**$10,600**	

3.

	FIFO	LIFO	Weighted Average	Specific Identification
Income Statement				
Sales*	$ 22,500	$22,500	$ 22,500	$22,500
Cost of goods sold	10,200	11,600	10,779	10,600
Gross profit	$ 12,300	$10,900	$ 11,721	$11,900
Balance Sheet				
Inventory	$10,300	$ 8,900	$9,718.5	$ 9,900

* Sales = (200 units × $30) + (200 units × $30) + (300 units × $35) = $22,500

4. Mistakenly using LIFO when FIFO should have been used overstates cost of goods sold in year 2011 by $1,400, which is the difference between the FIFO and LIFO amounts of ending inventory. It understates income in 2011 by $1,400. In year 2012, income is overstated by $1,400 because of the understatement in beginning inventory.

5. Analysis of the effects of alternative inventory methods.

	Cost of Goods Sold	Difference from FIFO Cost of Goods Sold	Effect on Net Income If Adopted Instead of FIFO
FIFO	$10,200	—	—
LIFO	11,600	+$1,400	$1,400 lower
Weighted average	10,779	+ 579	579 lower
Specific identification	10,600	+ 400	400 lower

APPENDIX

5A Inventory Costing under a Periodic System

> **P3** Compute inventory in a periodic system using the methods of specific identification, FIFO, LIFO, and weighted average.

The basic aim of the periodic system and the perpetual system is the same: to assign costs to inventory and cost of goods sold. The same four methods are used to assign costs under both systems: specific identification; first-in, first-out; last-in, first-out; and weighted average. We use information from Trekking to show how to assign costs using these four methods with a periodic system. Data for sales and purchases are in Exhibit 5A.1. Also, recall that we explained the accounting entries under a periodic system in Appendix 4A.

EXHIBIT 5A.1

Purchases and Sales of Goods

Date	Activity	Units Acquired at Cost	Units Sold at Retail	Unit Inventory
Aug. 1	Beginning inventory	10 units @ $ 91 = $ 910		10 units
Aug. 3	Purchases	15 units @ $106 = $ 1,590		25 units
Aug. 14	Sales		20 units @ $130	5 units
Aug. 17	Purchases	20 units @ $115 = $ 2,300		25 units
Aug. 28	Purchases.............	10 units @ $119 = $ 1,190		35 units
Aug. 31	Sales.................		23 units @ $150	12 units
	Totals	55 units $5,990	43 units	

Specific Identification　We use the above sales and purchases information and the specific identification method to assign costs to ending inventory and units sold. Trekking's internal data reveal the following specific unit sales:

August 14　Sold 8 bikes costing $91 each and 12 bikes costing $106 each

August 31　Sold 2 bikes costing $91 each, 3 bikes costing $106 each, 15 bikes costing $115 each, and 3 bikes costing $119 each

Applying specific identification and using the information above, we prepare Exhibit 5A.2. This exhibit starts with 10 bikes at $91 each in beginning inventory. On August 3, 15 more bikes are purchased at $106 each for $1,590. Inventory available now consists of 10 bikes at $91 each and 15 bikes at $106 each, for a total of $2,500. On August 14 (see specific sales data above), 20 bikes costing $2,000 are sold—leaving 5 bikes costing $500 in inventory. On August 17, 20 bikes costing $2,300 are purchased, and on August 28, another 10 bikes costing $1,190 are purchased, for a total of 35 bikes costing $3,990 in inventory. On August 31 (see specific sales above), 23 bikes costing $2,582 are sold, which leaves 12 bikes costing $1,408 in ending inventory. Carefully study Exhibit 5A.2 to see the flow of costs both in and out of inventory. Each unit, whether sold or remaining in inventory, has its own specific cost attached to it.

EXHIBIT 5A.2

Specific Identification Computations

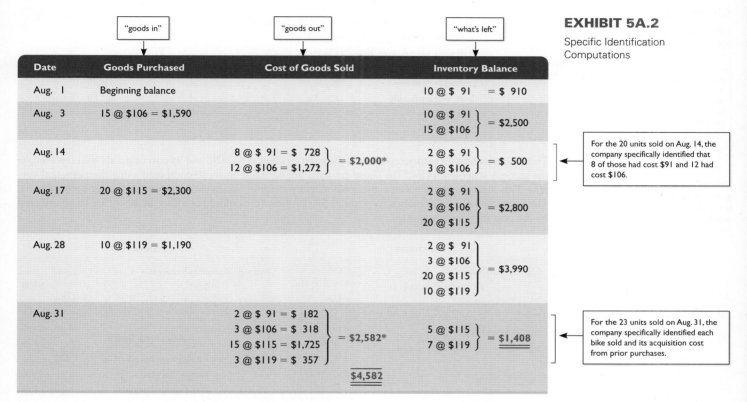

Date	Goods Purchased	Cost of Goods Sold	Inventory Balance
Aug. 1	Beginning balance		10 @ $ 91 = $ 910
Aug. 3	15 @ $106 = $1,590		10 @ $ 91 ⎱ = $2,500 15 @ $106 ⎰
Aug. 14		8 @ $ 91 = $ 728 ⎱ = $2,000* 12 @ $106 = $1,272 ⎰	2 @ $ 91 ⎱ = $ 500 3 @ $106 ⎰
Aug. 17	20 @ $115 = $2,300		2 @ $ 91 ⎱ 3 @ $106 ⎰ = $2,800 20 @ $115
Aug. 28	10 @ $119 = $1,190		2 @ $ 91 3 @ $106 20 @ $115 = $3,990 10 @ $119
Aug. 31		2 @ $ 91 = $ 182 3 @ $106 = $ 318 ⎱ = $2,582* 15 @ $115 = $1,725 3 @ $119 = $ 357 ⎰ $4,582	5 @ $115 ⎱ = $1,408 7 @ $119 ⎰

"goods in" → "goods out" → "what's left" →

For the 20 units sold on Aug. 14, the company specifically identified that 8 of those had cost $91 and 12 had cost $106.

For the 23 units sold on Aug. 31, the company specifically identified each bike sold and its acquisition cost from prior purchases.

* Identification of items sold (and their costs) is obtained from internal documents that track each unit from its purchase to its sale.

When using specific identification, Trekking's cost of goods sold reported on the income statement totals **$4,582**, the sum of $2,000 and $2,582 from the third column of Exhibit 5A.2. Trekking's ending inventory reported on the balance sheet is **$1,408**, which is the final inventory balance from the fourth column. The purchases and sales entries for Exhibit 5A.2 follow (the colored boldface numbers are those affected by the cost flow assumption).

Point: The assignment of costs to the goods sold and to inventory using specific identification is the same for both the perpetual and periodic systems.

	Purchases		
Aug. 3	Purchases	1,590	
	Accounts Payable		1,590
17	Purchases	2,300	
	Accounts Payable		2,300
28	Purchases	1,190	
	Accounts Payable		1,190

	Sales		
Aug. 14	Accounts Receivable	2,600	
	Sales.................		2,600
31	Accounts Receivable	3,450	
	Sales.................		3,450
	Adjusting Entry		
31	Merchandise Inventory	1,408	
	Income Summary.........		498
	Merchandise Inventory		910

First-In, First-Out The first-in, first-out (FIFO) method of assigning costs to inventory assumes that inventory items are sold in the order acquired. When sales occur, the costs of the earliest units acquired are charged to cost of goods sold. This leaves the costs from the most recent purchases in ending inventory. Use of FIFO for computing the cost of inventory and cost of goods sold is shown in Exhibit 5A.3.

This exhibit starts with computing $5,990 in total units available for sale—this is given to us at the start of this appendix. Applying FIFO, we know that the 12 units in ending inventory will be reported at the cost of the most recent 12 purchases. Reviewing purchases in reverse order, we assign costs to the 12 bikes in ending inventory as follows: $119 cost to 10 bikes and $115 cost to 2 bikes. This yields 12 bikes costing $1,420 in ending inventory. We then subtract this $1,420 in ending inventory from $5,990 in cost of goods available to get $4,570 in cost of goods sold.

EXHIBIT 5A.3

FIFO Computations—
Periodic System

Exhibit 5A.1 shows that the 12 units in ending inventory consist of 10 units from the latest purchase on Aug. 28 and 2 units from the next latest purchase on Aug. 17.

Total cost of 55 units available for sale (from Exhibit 5A.1)		$5,990
Less ending inventory priced using FIFO		
10 units from August 28 purchase at $119 each	$1,190	
2 units from August 17 purchase at $115 each	230	
Ending inventory		1,420
Cost of goods sold		$4,570

Point: The assignment of costs to the goods sold and to inventory using FIFO is the same for both the perpetual and periodic systems.

Trekking's ending inventory reported on the balance sheet is **$1,420**, and its cost of goods sold reported on the income statement is **$4,570**. These amounts are the same as those computed using the perpetual system. This always occurs because the most recent purchases are in ending inventory under both systems. The purchases and sales entries for Exhibit 5A.3 follow (the colored boldface numbers are those affected by the cost flow assumption).

Purchases				**Sales**		
Aug. 3	Purchases.....................	1,590		Aug. 14	Accounts Receivable	2,600
	Accounts Payable..........		1,590		Sales	2,600
17	Purchases.....................	2,300		31	Accounts Receivable	3,450
	Accounts Payable..........		2,300		Sales	3,450
28	Purchases.....................	1,190			**Adjusting Entry**	
	Accounts Payable..........		1,190			
				31	Merchandise Inventory	1,420
					Income Summary	510
					Merchandise Inventory	910

Last-In, First-Out   The last-in, first-out (LIFO) method of assigning costs assumes that the most recent purchases are sold first. These more recent costs are charged to the goods sold, and the costs of the earliest purchases are assigned to inventory. LIFO results in costs of the most recent purchases being assigned to cost of goods sold, which means that LIFO comes close to matching current costs of goods sold with revenues. Use of LIFO for computing cost of inventory and cost of goods sold is shown in Exhibit 5A.4.

This exhibit starts with computing $5,990 in total units available for sale—this is given to us at the start of this appendix. Applying LIFO, we know that the 12 units in ending inventory will be reported at the cost of the earliest 12 purchases. Reviewing the earliest purchases in order, we assign costs to the 12 bikes in ending inventory as follows: $91 cost to 10 bikes and $106 cost to 2 bikes. This yields 12 bikes costing $1,122 in ending inventory. We then subtract this $1,122 in ending inventory from $5,990 in cost of goods available to get $4,868 in cost of goods sold.

EXHIBIT 5A.4

LIFO Computations—
Periodic System

Exhibit 5A.1 shows that the 12 units in ending inventory consist of 10 units from the earliest purchase (beg. inv.) and 2 units from the next earliest purchase on Aug. 3.

Total cost of 55 units available for sale (from Exhibit 5A.1)		$5,990
Less ending inventory priced using LIFO		
10 units in beginning inventory at $91 each	$910	
2 units from August 3 purchase at $106 each.................	212	
Ending inventory		1,122
Cost of goods sold		$4,868

Ringo Company had $900,000 of sales in each of three consecutive years 2010–2012, and it purchased merchandise costing $500,000 in each of those years. It also maintained a $200,000 physical inventory from the beginning to the end of that three-year period. In accounting for inventory, it made an error at the end of year 2010 that caused its year-end 2010 inventory to appear on its statements as $180,000 rather than the correct $200,000.

1. Determine the correct amount of the company's gross profit in each of the years 2010–2012.
2. Prepare comparative income statements as in Exhibit 5.11 to show the effect of this error on the company's cost of goods sold and gross profit for each of the years 2010–2012.

Exercise 5-8
Analysis of inventory errors
A2 ♟

Check   2010 reported gross profit, $380,000

Chess Company uses LIFO for inventory costing and reports the following financial data. It also recomputed inventory and cost of goods sold using FIFO for comparison purposes.

	2011	2010
LIFO inventory	$150	$100
LIFO cost of goods sold	730	670
FIFO inventory	220	125
FIFO cost of goods sold	685	—
Current assets (using LIFO)	210	180
Current liabilities	190	170

1. Compute its current ratio, inventory turnover, and days' sales in inventory for 2011 using (a) LIFO numbers and (b) FIFO numbers. (Round answers to one decimal.)
2. Comment on and interpret the results of part 1.

Exercise 5-9
Comparing LIFO numbers to FIFO numbers; ratio analysis
A1 A3 ♟

Check   (1) FIFO: Current ratio, 1.5; Inventory turnover, 4.0 times

---

Use the following information for Ryder Co. to compute inventory turnover for 2011 and 2010, and its days' sales in inventory at December 31, 2011 and 2010. (Round answers to one decimal.) Comment on Ryder's efficiency in using its assets to increase sales from 2010 to 2011.

	2011	2010	2009
Cost of goods sold	$643,825	$426,650	$391,300
Ending inventory	96,400	86,750	91,500

Exercise 5-10
Inventory turnover and days' sales in inventory
A3 ♟

Refer to Exercise 5-3 and assume the periodic inventory system is used. Determine the costs assigned to ending inventory and to cost of goods sold using (a) specific identification, (b) weighted average, (c) FIFO, and (d) LIFO. (Round per unit costs to three decimals, but inventory balances to the dollar.)

Exercise 5-11[A]
Inventory costing—
periodic system P3

Refer to Exercise 5-5 and assume the periodic inventory system is used. Determine the costs assigned to ending inventory and to cost of goods sold using (a) FIFO and (b) LIFO. Then (c) compute the gross margin for each method.

Exercise 5-12[A]
Inventory costing—
periodic system P3

Lopez Co. reported the following current-year data for its only product. The company uses a periodic inventory system, and its ending inventory consists of 300 units—100 from each of the last three purchases. Determine the cost assigned to ending inventory and to cost of goods sold using (a) specific identification, (b) weighted average, (c) FIFO, and (d) LIFO. (Round per unit costs to three decimals, but inventory balances to the dollar.) Which method yields the highest net income?

Exercise 5-13[A]
Alternative cost flow
assumptions—periodic
P3

Jan.	1	Beginning inventory	200 units @ $2.00 = $	400
Mar.	7	Purchase	440 units @ $2.25 =	990
July	28	Purchase	1080 units @ $2.50 =	2,700
Oct.	3	Purchase	960 units @ $2.80 =	2,688
Dec.	19	Purchase	320 units @ $2.90 =	928
		Totals	3,000 units	$7,706

Check   Inventory; LIFO, $625;
FIFO, $870

Exercise 5-14ᴬ
Alternative cost flow
assumptions—periodic
P3

Candis Gifts reported the following current-year data for its only product. The company uses a periodic inventory system, and its ending inventory consists of 300 units—100 from each of the last three purchases. Determine the cost assigned to ending inventory and to cost of goods sold using (a) specific identification, (b) weighted average, (c) FIFO, and (d) LIFO. (Round per unit costs to three decimals, but inventory balances to the dollar.) Which method yields the lowest net income?

Jan. 1	Beginning inventory	280 units @ $3.00 = $	840
Mar. 7	Purchase	600 units @ $2.80 =	1,680
July 28	Purchase	800 units @ $2.50 =	2,000
Oct. 3	Purchase	1,100 units @ $2.30 =	2,530
Dec. 19	Purchase	250 units @ $2.00 =	500
	Totals	3,030 units	$7,550

Check Inventory: LIFO, $896;
FIFO, $615

Exercise 5-15ᴮ
Estimating ending inventory—
retail method
P4

In 2011, Wichita Company had net sales (at retail) of $130,000. The following additional information is available from its records at the end of 2011. Use the retail inventory method to estimate Wichita's 2011 ending inventory at cost.

	At Cost	At Retail
Beginning inventory	$ 31,900	$64,200
Cost of goods purchased	57,810	98,400

Check End. Inventory, $17,930

Exercise 5-16ᴮ
Estimating ending inventory—
gross profit method
P4

On March 1, KB Shop had $450,000 of inventory at cost. In the first quarter of the year, it purchased $1,590,000 of merchandise, returned $23,100, and paid freight charges of $37,600 on purchased merchandise, terms FOB shipping point. The company's gross profit averages 30%, and the store had $2,000,000 of net sales (at retail) in the first quarter of the year. Use the gross profit method to estimate its cost of inventory at the end of the first quarter.

Exercise 5-17
Accounting for inventory
following IFRS
P2

Samsung Electronics reports the following regarding its accounting for inventories.

> Inventories are stated at the lower of cost or net realizable value. Cost is determined using the average cost method, except for materials-in-transit which are stated at actual cost as determined using the specific identification method. Losses on valuation of inventories and losses on inventory obsolescence are recorded as part of cost of sales. As of December 31, 2008, losses on valuation of inventories amounted to ₩651,296 million (₩ is Korean won).

1. What cost flow assumption(s) does Samsung apply in assigning costs to its inventories?
2. What has Samsung recorded for 2008 as a write-down on valuation of its inventories?
3. If at year-end 2009 there was an increase in the value of its inventories such that there was a reversal of ₩900 million for the 2008 write-down, how would Samsung account for this under IFRS? Would Samsung's accounting be different for this reversal if it reported under U.S. GAAP? Explain.

■ connect

PROBLEM SET A

Problem 5-1A
Alternative cost
flows—perpetual
P1

Anthony Company uses a perpetual inventory system. It entered into the following purchases and sales transactions for March.

Date	Activities	Units Acquired at Cost	Units Sold at Retail
Mar. 1	Beginning inventory	50 units @ $50/unit	
Mar. 5	Purchase...................	200 units @ $55/unit	
Mar. 9	Sales		210 units @ $85/unit
Mar. 18	Purchase...................	60 units @ $60/unit	
Mar. 25	Purchase...................	100 units @ $62/unit	
Mar. 29	Sales		80 units @ $95/unit
	Totals	410 units	290 units

Required

1. Compute cost of goods available for sale and the number of units available for sale.
2. Compute the number of units in ending inventory.
3. Compute the cost assigned to ending inventory using (*a*) FIFO, (*b*) LIFO, (*c*) weighted average, and (*d*) specific identification. (Round per unit costs to three decimals, but inventory balances to the dollar.) For specific identification, the March 9 sale consisted of 40 units from beginning inventory and 170 units from the March 5 purchase; the March 29 sale consisted of 20 units from the March 18 purchase and 60 units from the March 25 purchase.
4. Compute gross profit earned by the company for each of the four costing methods in part 3.

Check (3) Ending Inventory: FIFO, $7,400; LIFO, $6,840, WA, $7,176

(4) LIFO gross profit, $8,990

Marlow Company uses a perpetual inventory system. It entered into the following calendar-year 2011 purchases and sales transactions.

Problem 5-2A
Alternative cost flows—perpetual

P1

Date	Activities	Units Acquired at Cost	Units Sold at Retail
Jan. 1	Beginning inventory	600 units @ $44/unit	
Feb. 10	Purchase...................	200 units @ $40/unit	
Mar. 13	Purchase...................	100 units @ $20/unit	
Mar. 15	Sales		400 units @ $75/unit
Aug. 21	Purchase...................	160 units @ $60/unit	
Sept. 5	Purchase...................	280 units @ $48/unit	
Sept. 10	Sales		200 units @ $75/unit
	Totals	1,340 units	600 units

Required

1. Compute cost of goods available for sale and the number of units available for sale.
2. Compute the number of units in ending inventory.
3. Compute the cost assigned to ending inventory using (*a*) FIFO, (*b*) LIFO, (*c*) specific identification—units sold consist of 500 units from beginning inventory and 100 units from the March 13 purchase, and (*d*) weighted average. (Round per unit costs to three decimals, but inventory balances to the dollar.)
4. Compute gross profit earned by the company for each of the four costing methods in part 3.

Check (3) Ending inventory: FIFO, $33,040; LIFO, $35,440; WA, $34,055;

(4) LIFO gross profit, $21,000

Analysis Component

5. If the company's manager earns a bonus based on a percent of gross profit, which method of inventory costing will the manager likely prefer?

A physical inventory of Helmke Company taken at December 31 reveals the following.

Problem 5-3A
Lower of cost or market

P2

		Per Unit	
Item	**Units**	**Cost**	**Market**
Audio equipment			
Receivers	335	$ 90	$ 98
CD players	250	111	100
MP3 players	316	86	95
Speakers	194	52	41
Video equipment			
Handheld LCDs	470	150	125
VCRs	281	93	84
Camcorders	202	310	322
Car audio equipment			
Satellite radios	175	70	84
CD/MP3 radios	160	97	105

Required

1. Calculate the lower of cost or market for the inventory applied separately to each item.
2. If the market amount is less than the recorded cost of the inventory, then record the LCM adjustment to the Merchandise Inventory account.

Check $263,024

Problem 5-4A

Analysis of inventory errors

A2

mhhe.com/wildFA6e

Doubletree Company's financial statements show the following. The company recently discovered that in making physical counts of inventory, it had made the following errors: Inventory on December 31, 2010, is understated by $50,000, and inventory on December 31, 2011, is overstated by $20,000.

For Year Ended December 31		2010	2011	2012
(a)	Cost of goods sold	$ 725,000	$ 955,000	$ 790,000
(b)	Net income....................	268,000	275,000	250,000
(c)	Total current assets	1,247,000	1,360,000	1,230,000
(d)	Total equity...................	1,387,000	1,580,000	1,245,000

Required

1. For each key financial statement figure—(a), (b), (c), and (d) above—prepare a table similar to the following to show the adjustments necessary to correct the reported amounts.

Figure: _____	2010	2011	2012
Reported amount			
Adjustments for: 12/31/2010 error			
12/31/2011 error			
Corrected amount			

Check (1) Corrected net income:
2010, $318,000; 2011, $205,000;
2012, $270,000

Analysis Component

2. What is the error in total net income for the combined three-year period resulting from the inventory errors? Explain.

3. Explain why the understatement of inventory by $50,000 at the end of 2010 results in an understatement of equity by the same amount in that year.

Problem 5-5A[A]

Alternative cost flows—periodic

P3

mhhe.com/wildFA6e

Viper Company began year 2011 with 20,000 units of product in its January 1 inventory costing $15 each. It made successive purchases of its product in year 2011 as follows. The company uses a periodic inventory system. On December 31, 2011, a physical count reveals that 35,000 units of its product remain in inventory.

Mar. 7	28,000 units @ $18 each
May 25	30,000 units @ $22 each
Aug. 1	20,000 units @ $24 each
Nov. 10	33,000 units @ $27 each

Required

1. Compute the number and total cost of the units available for sale in year 2011.

Check (2) Cost of goods sold:
FIFO, $1,896,000; LIFO, $2,265,000;
WA, $2,077,557

2. Compute the amounts assigned to the 2011 ending inventory and the cost of goods sold using (a) FIFO, (b) LIFO, and (c) weighted average. (Round per unit costs to three decimals, but inventory balances to the dollar.)

Problem 5-6A[A]

Income comparisons and cost flows—periodic

A1 P3

Botch Corp. sold 5,500 units of its product at $45 per unit in year 2011 and incurred operating expenses of $6 per unit in selling the units. It began the year with 600 units in inventory and made successive purchases of its product as follows.

Jan. 1	Beginning inventory	600 units @ $18 per unit
Feb. 20	Purchase	1,500 units @ $19 per unit
May 16	Purchase	700 units @ $20 per unit
Oct. 3	Purchase	400 units @ $21 per unit
Dec. 11	Purchase	3,300 units @ $22 per unit
	Total	6,500 units

Required

Check (1) Net income: FIFO,
$71,540; LIFO, $69,020; WA, $70,603

1. Prepare comparative income statements similar to Exhibit 5.8 for the three inventory costing methods of FIFO, LIFO, and weighted average. (Round per unit costs to three decimals, but inventory balances

SOX has markedly impacted companies, and the costs of its implementation are high. Importantly, **Section 404** of SOX requires that managers document and assess the effectiveness of all internal control processes that can impact financial reporting. The benefits include greater confidence in accounting systems and their related reports. However, the public continues to debate the costs versus the benefits of SOX as nearly all business activities of these companies are impacted by SOX. Section 404 of SOX requires that managers document and assess their internal controls *and* that auditors provide an opinion on managers' documentation and assessment. Costs of complying with Section 404 for companies is reported to average $4 million (source: Financial Executives Institute).

Principles of Internal Control

Internal control policies and procedures vary from company to company according to such factors as the nature of the business and its size. Certain fundamental internal control principles apply to all companies. The **principles of internal control** are to

1. Establish responsibilities.
2. Maintain adequate records.
3. Insure assets and bond key employees.
4. Separate recordkeeping from custody of assets.
5. Divide responsibility for related transactions.
6. Apply technological controls.
7. Perform regular and independent reviews.

This section explains these seven principles and describes how internal control procedures minimize the risk of fraud and theft. These procedures also increase the reliability and accuracy of accounting records. A framework for how these seven principles improve the quality of financial reporting is provided by the **Committee of Sponsoring Organizations (COSO)** (www.COSO.org). Specifically, these principles link to five aspects of internal control: control activities, control environment, risk assessment, monitoring, and communication.

Point: Sarbanes-Oxley Act (SOX) requires that each annual report contain an *internal control report,* which must: (1) state managers' responsibility for establishing and maintaining adequate internal controls for financial reporting; and (2) assess the effectiveness of those controls.

Establish Responsibilities   Proper internal control means that responsibility for a task is clearly established and assigned to one person. When a problem occurs in a company where responsibility is not identified, determining who is at fault is difficult. For instance, if two salesclerks share the same cash register and there is a cash shortage, neither clerk can be held accountable. To prevent this problem, one clerk might be given responsibility for handling all cash sales. Alternately, a company can use a register with separate cash drawers for each clerk. Most of us have waited at a retail counter during a shift change while employees swap cash drawers.

Point: Many companies have a mandatory vacation policy for employees who handle cash. When another employee must cover for the one on vacation, it is more difficult to hide cash frauds.

Maintain Adequate Records   Good recordkeeping is part of an internal control system. It helps protect assets and ensures that employees use prescribed procedures. Reliable records are also a source of information that managers use to monitor company activities. When detailed records of equipment are kept, for instance, items are unlikely to be lost or stolen without detection. Similarly, transactions are less likely to be entered in wrong accounts if a chart of accounts is set up and carefully used. Many preprinted forms and internal documents are also designed for use in a good internal control system. When sales slips are properly designed, for instance, sales personnel can record needed information efficiently with less chance of errors or delays to customers. When sales slips are prenumbered and controlled, each one issued is the responsibility of one salesperson, preventing the salesperson from pocketing cash by making a sale and destroying the sales slip. Computerized point-of-sale systems achieve the same control results.

Insure Assets and Bond Key Employees   Good internal control means that assets are adequately insured against casualty and that employees handling large amounts of cash and easily transferable assets are bonded. An employee is *bonded* when a company purchases an insurance policy, or a bond, against losses from theft by that employee. Bonding reduces the risk of loss. It also discourages theft because bonded employees know an independent bonding company will be involved when theft is uncovered and is unlikely to be sympathetic with an employee involved in theft.

Point: The Association of Certified Fraud Examiners (cfenet.com) estimates that employee fraud costs small companies more than $100,000 per incident.

Fraud

Tag Control. A novel technique exists for marking physical assets. It involves embedding a less than one-inch-square tag of fibers that creates a unique optical signature recordable by scanners. Manufacturers hope to embed tags in everything from compact discs and credit cards to designer clothes for purposes of internal control and efficiency.

Separate Recordkeeping from Custody of Assets   A person who controls or has access to an asset must not keep that asset's accounting records. This principle reduces the risk of theft or waste of an asset because the person with control over it knows that another person keeps its records. Also, a recordkeeper who does not have access to the asset has no reason to falsify records. This means that to steal an asset and hide the theft from the records, two or more people must *collude*—or agree in secret to commit the fraud.

Divide Responsibility for Related Transactions   Good internal control divides responsibility for a transaction or a series of related transactions between two or more individuals or departments. This is to ensure that the work of one individual acts as a check on the other. This principle, often called *separation of duties,* is not a call for duplication of work. Each employee or department should perform unduplicated effort. Examples of transactions with divided responsibility are placing purchase orders, receiving merchandise, and paying vendors. These tasks should not be given to one individual or department. Assigning responsibility for two or more of these tasks to one party increases mistakes and perhaps fraud. Having an independent person, for example, check incoming goods for quality and quantity encourages more care and attention to detail than having the person who placed the order do the checking. Added protection can result from identifying a third person to approve payment of the invoice. A company can even designate a fourth person with authority to write checks as another protective measure.

Apply Technological Controls   Cash registers, check protectors, time clocks, and personal identification scanners are examples of devices that can improve internal control. Technology often improves the effectiveness of controls. A cash register with a locked-in tape or electronic file makes a record of each cash sale. A check protector perforates the amount of a check into its face and makes it difficult to alter the amount. A time clock registers the exact time an employee both arrives at and departs from the job. Mechanical change and currency counters quickly and accurately count amounts, and personal scanners limit access to only authorized individuals. Each of these and other technological controls are an effective part of many internal control systems.

Point: There's a new security device—a person's ECG (electrocardiogram) reading—that is as unique as a fingerprint and a lot harder to lose or steal than a PIN. ECGs can be read through fingertip touches. An ECG also shows that a living person is actually there, whereas fingerprint and facial recognition software can be fooled.

Decision Insight

About Face   Face-recognition software snaps a digital picture of the face and converts key facial features—say, the distance between the eyes—into a series of numerical values. These can be stored on an ID or ATM card as a simple bar code to prohibit unauthorized access. ■

Perform Regular and Independent Reviews   Changes in personnel, stress of time pressures, and technological advances present opportunities for shortcuts and lapses. To counter these factors, regular reviews of internal control systems are needed to ensure that procedures are followed. These reviews are preferably done by internal auditors not directly involved in the activities. Their impartial perspective encourages an evaluation of the efficiency as well as the effectiveness of the internal control system. Many companies also pay for audits by independent, external auditors. These external auditors test the company's financial records to give an opinion as to whether its financial statements are presented fairly. Before external auditors decide on how much testing is needed, they evaluate the effectiveness of the internal control system. This evaluation is often helpful to a client.

☐ Decision Maker   Answer — p. 277

Entrepreneur   As owner of a start-up information services company, you hire a systems analyst. One of her first recommendations is to require all employees to take at least one week of vacation per year. Why would she recommend a "forced vacation" policy? ∎

Technology and Internal Control

The fundamental principles of internal control are relevant no matter what the technological state of the accounting system, from purely manual to fully automated systems. Technology impacts an internal control system in several important ways. Perhaps the most obvious is that technology allows us quicker access to databases and information. Used effectively, technology greatly improves managers' abilities to monitor and control business activities. This section describes some technological impacts we must be alert to.

Point: Information on Internet fraud can be found at these Websites: sec.gov/investor/pubs/cyberfraud.htm ftc.gov/bcp/consumer.shtm www.fraud.org

Reduced Processing Errors   Technologically advanced systems reduce the number of errors in processing information. Provided the software and data entry are correct, the risk of mechanical and mathematical errors is nearly eliminated. However, we must remember that erroneous software or data entry does exist. Also, less human involvement in data processing can cause data entry errors to go undiscovered. Moreover, errors in software can produce consistent but erroneous processing of transactions. Continually checking and monitoring all types of systems are important.

Point: Evidence of any internal control failure for a company reduces user confidence in its financial statements.

More Extensive Testing of Records   A company's review and audit of electronic records can include more extensive testing when information is easily and rapidly accessed. When accounting records are kept manually, auditors and others likely select only small samples of data to test. When data are accessible with computer technology, however, auditors can quickly analyze large samples or even the entire database.

Limited Evidence of Processing   Many data processing steps are increasingly done by computer. Accordingly, fewer hard-copy items of documentary evidence are available for review. Yet technologically advanced systems can provide new evidence. They can, for instance, record who made the entries, the date and time, the source of the entry, and so on. Technology can also be designed to require the use of passwords or other identification before access to the system is granted. This means that internal control depends more on the design and operation of the information system and less on the analysis of its resulting documents.

Point: We look to several sources when assessing a company's internal controls. Sources include the auditor's report, management report on controls (if available), management discussion and analysis, and financial press.

Crucial Separation of Duties   Technological advances in accounting information systems often yield some job eliminations or consolidations. While those who remain have the special skills necessary to operate advanced programs and equipment, a company with a reduced workforce risks losing its crucial separation of duties. The company must establish ways to control and monitor employees to minimize risk of error and fraud. For instance, the person who designs and programs the information system must not be the one who operates it. The company must also separate control over programs and files from the activities related to cash receipts and disbursements. For instance, a computer operator should not control check-writing activities. Achieving acceptable separation of duties can be especially difficult and costly in small companies with few employees.

Point: COSO organizes control components into five types:
• Control environment
• Control activities
• Risk assessment
• Monitoring
• Information and communication

Increased E-Commerce   Technology has encouraged the growth of e-commerce. Amazon and eBay are examples of companies that have successfully exploited e-commerce. Most companies have some e-commerce transactions. All such transactions involve at least three risks. (1) *Credit card number theft* is a risk of using, transmitting, and storing such data online. This increases the cost of e-commerce. (2) *Computer viruses* are malicious programs that attach themselves to innocent files for purposes of infecting and harming other files and programs. (3) *Impersonation* online can result in charges of sales to bogus accounts, purchases of inappropriate materials, and the unknowing giving up of confidential information to hackers. Companies use both firewalls and encryption to

"Worst case of identity theft I've ever seen!"
Copyright 2004 by Randy Glasbergen. www.glasbergen.com

combat some of these risks—firewalls are points of entry to a system that require passwords to continue, and encryption is a mathematical process to rearrange contents that cannot be read without the process code. Nearly 5% of Americans already report being victims of identity theft, and roughly 10 million say their privacy has been compromised.

Decision Insight

Cheery Fraud Victim Certified Fraud Examiners Website reports the following: Andrew Cameron stole Jacqueline Boanson's credit card. Cameron headed to the racetrack and promptly charged two bets for $150 on the credit card—winning $400. Unfortunately for Cameron the racetrack refused to pay him cash as its internal control policy is to credit winnings from bets made on a credit card to that same card. Cameron was later nabbed; and the racetrack let Ms. Boanson keep the winnings. ■

Limitations of Internal Control

All internal control policies and procedures have limitations that usually arise from either (1) the human element or (2) the cost–benefit principle.

Internal control policies and procedures are applied by people. This human element creates several potential limitations that we can categorize as either (1) human error or (2) human fraud. *Human error* can occur from negligence, fatigue, misjudgment, or confusion. *Human fraud* involves intent by people to defeat internal controls, such as *management override,* for personal gain. Fraud also includes collusion to thwart the separation of duties. The human element highlights the importance of establishing an *internal control environment* to convey management's commitment to internal control policies and procedures. Human fraud is driven by the *triple-threat* of fraud:

- **Opportunity**—refers to internal control deficiencies in the workplace.
- **Pressure**—refers to financial, family, society, and other stresses to succeed.
- **Rationalization**—refers to employees justifying fraudulent behavior.

The second major limitation on internal control is the *cost–benefit principle,* which dictates that the costs of internal controls must not exceed their benefits. Analysis of costs and benefits must consider all factors, including the impact on morale. Most companies, for instance, have a legal right to read employees' e-mails, yet companies seldom exercise that right unless they are confronted with evidence of potential harm to the company. The same holds for drug testing, phone tapping, and hidden cameras. The bottom line is that managers must establish internal control policies and procedures with a net benefit to the company.

Point: <u>Cybercrime.gov</u> pursues computer and intellectual property crimes, including that of e-commerce.

Address www.hacker'sguidetocyberspace.com **GO**

Hacker's Guide to Cyberspace

Pharming Viruses attached to e-mails and Websites load software onto your PC that monitors keystrokes; when you sign on to financial Websites, it steals your passwords.

Phishing Hackers send e-mails to you posing as banks; you are asked for information using fake Websites where they reel in your passwords and personal data.

WI-Phishing Cybercrooks set up wireless networks hoping you use them to connect to the Web; your passwords and data are stolen as you use their network.

Bot-Networking Hackers send remote-control programs to your PC that take control to send out spam and viruses; they even rent your bot to other cybercrooks.

Typo-Squatting Hackers set up Websites with addresses similar to legit outfits; when you make a typo and hit their sites, they infect your PC with viruses or take them over as bots.

Quick Check

Answers — p. 277

1. Principles of internal control suggest that (choose one): (*a*) Responsibility for a series of related transactions (such as placing orders, receiving and paying for merchandise) should be assigned to one employee; (*b*) Responsibility for individual tasks should be shared by more than one employee so that one serves as a check on the other; or (*c*) Employees who handle considerable cash and easily transferable assets should be bonded.

2. What are some impacts of computing technology on internal control?

CONTROL OF CASH

Cash is a necessary asset of every company. Most companies also own *cash equivalents* (defined below), which are assets similar to cash. Cash and cash equivalents are the most liquid of all assets and are easily hidden and moved. An effective system of internal controls protects these assets and it should meet three basic guidelines:

1. Handling cash is separate from recordkeeping of cash.
2. Cash receipts are promptly deposited in a bank.
3. Cash disbursements are made by check.

The first guideline applies separation of duties to minimize errors and fraud. When duties are separated, two or more people must collude to steal cash and conceal this action in the accounting records. The second guideline uses immediate (say, daily) deposits of all cash receipts to produce a timely independent record of the cash received. It also reduces the likelihood of cash theft (or loss) and the risk that an employee could personally use the money before depositing it. The third guideline uses payments by check to develop an independent bank record of cash disbursements. This guideline also reduces the risk of cash theft (or loss).

This section begins with definitions of cash and cash equivalents. Discussion then focuses on controls and accounting for both cash receipts and disbursements. The exact procedures used to achieve control over cash vary across companies. They depend on factors such as company size, number of employees, volume of cash transactions, and sources of cash.

Cash, Cash Equivalents, and Liquidity

Good accounting systems help in managing the amount of cash and controlling who has access to it. Cash is the usual means of payment when paying for assets, services, or liabilities. **Liquidity** refers to a company's ability to pay for its near-term obligations. Cash and similar assets are called **liquid assets** because they can be readily used to settle such obligations. A company needs liquid assets to effectively operate.

Cash includes currency and coins along with the amounts on deposit in bank accounts, checking accounts (called *demand deposits*), and many savings accounts (called *time deposits*). Cash also includes items that are acceptable for deposit in these accounts such as customer checks, cashier's checks, certified checks, and money orders. **Cash equivalents** are short-term, highly liquid investment assets meeting two criteria: (1) readily convertible to a known cash amount and (2) sufficiently close to their due date so that their market value is not sensitive to interest rate changes. Only investments purchased within three months of their due date usually satisfy these criteria. Examples of cash equivalents are short-term investments in assets such as U.S. Treasury bills and money market funds. To increase their return, many companies invest idle cash in cash equivalents. Most companies combine cash equivalents with cash as a single item on the balance sheet.

C2 Define cash and cash equivalents and explain how to report them.

Point: The most liquid assets are usually reported first on a balance sheet; the least liquid assets are reported last.

Point: Google reports cash and cash equivalents of $10,198 million in its balance sheet. This amount makes up nearly 25% of its total assets.

Cash Management

When companies fail, one of the most common causes is their inability to manage cash. Companies must plan both cash receipts and cash payments. The goals of cash management are twofold:

1. Plan cash receipts to meet cash payments when due.
2. Keep a minimum level of cash necessary to operate.

the account balance, the bank records it with a *credit* to that liability account. This means that debit memos from the bank produce *credits* on the depositor's books, and credit memos from the bank produce *debits* on the depositor's books.

Enclosed with a bank statement is a list of the depositor's canceled checks (or the actual canceled checks) along with any debit or credit memoranda affecting the account. Increasingly, banks are showing canceled checks electronically via online access to accounts. **Canceled checks** are checks the bank has paid and deducted from the customer's account during the period. Other deductions that can appear on a bank statement include (1) service charges and fees assessed by the bank, (2) checks deposited that are uncollectible, (3) corrections of previous errors, (4) withdrawals through automated teller machines (ATMs), and (5) periodic payments arranged in advance by a depositor. (Most company checking accounts do not allow ATM withdrawals because of the company's desire to make all disbursements by check.) Except for service charges, the bank notifies the depositor of each deduction with a debit memorandum when the bank reduces the balance. A copy of each debit memorandum is usually sent with the statement (again, this information is often available earlier via online access and notifications).

Transactions that increase the depositor's account include amounts the bank collects on behalf of the depositor and the corrections of previous errors. Credit memoranda notify the depositor of all increases when they are recorded. A copy of each credit memorandum is often sent with the bank statement. Banks that pay interest on checking accounts often compute the amount of interest earned on the average cash balance and credit it to the depositor's account each period. In Exhibit 6.6, the bank credits $8.42 of interest to the account.

Global: If cash is in more than one currency, a company usually translates these amounts into U.S. dollars using the exchange rate as of the balance sheet date. Also, a company must disclose any restrictions on cash accounts located outside the U.S.

Bank Reconciliation

When a company deposits all cash receipts and makes all cash payments (except petty cash) by check, it can use the bank statement for proving the accuracy of its cash records. This is done using a **bank reconciliation,** which is a report explaining any differences between the checking account balance according to the depositor's records and the balance reported on the bank statement. The figure below reflects this process, which we describe in the following sections.

P3 Prepare a bank reconciliation.

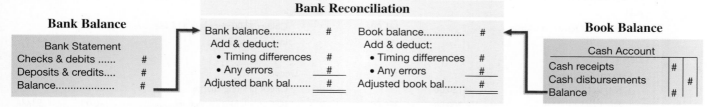

Purpose of Bank Reconciliation   The balance of a checking account reported on the bank statement rarely equals the balance in the depositor's accounting records. This is usually due to information that one party has that the other does not. We must therefore prove the accuracy of both the depositor's records and those of the bank. This means we must *reconcile* the two balances and explain or account for any differences in them. Among the factors causing the bank statement balance to differ from the depositor's book balance are these:

- **Outstanding checks. Outstanding checks** are checks written (or drawn) by the depositor, deducted on the depositor's records, and sent to the payees but not yet received by the bank for payment at the bank statement date.

- **Deposits in transit** (also called **outstanding deposits**). **Deposits in transit** are deposits made and recorded by the depositor but not yet recorded on the bank statement. For example, companies can make deposits (in the night depository) at the end of a business day after the bank is closed. If such a deposit occurred on a bank statement date, it would not appear on this period's statement. The bank would record such a deposit on the next business day, and it would appear on the next period's bank statement. Deposits mailed to the bank near the end of a period also can be in transit and unrecorded when the statement is prepared.

- **Deductions for uncollectible items and for services.** A company sometimes deposits another party's check that is uncollectible (usually meaning the balance in that party's account is not large enough to cover the check). This check is called a *non-sufficient funds (NSF)* check. The bank would have initially credited the depositor's account for the amount of the

Forms of Check Fraud (CkFraud.org)

- Forged signatures—legitimate blank checks with fake payer signature
- Forged endorsements—stolen check that is endorsed and cashed by someone other than the payee
- Counterfeit checks—fraudulent checks with fake payer signature
- Altered checks—legitimate check altered (such as changed payee or amount) to benefit perpetrator
- Check kiting—deposit check from one bank account (without sufficient funds) into a second bank account

check. When the bank learns the check is uncollectible, it debits (reduces) the depositor's account for the amount of that check. The bank may also charge the depositor a fee for processing an uncollectible check and notify the depositor of the deduction by sending a debit memorandum. The depositor should record each deduction when a debit memorandum is received, but an entry is sometimes not made until the bank reconciliation is prepared. Other possible bank charges to a depositor's account that are first reported on a bank statement include printing new checks and service fees.

- **Additions for collections and for interest.** Banks sometimes act as collection agents for their depositors by collecting notes and other items. Banks can also receive electronic funds transfers to the depositor's account. When a bank collects an item, it is added to the depositor's account, less any service fee. The bank also sends a credit memorandum to notify the depositor of the transaction. When the memorandum is received, the depositor should record it; yet it sometimes remains unrecorded until the bank reconciliation is prepared. The bank statement also includes a credit for any interest earned.

- **Errors.** Both banks and depositors can make errors. Bank errors might not be discovered until the depositor prepares the bank reconciliation. Also, depositor errors are sometimes discovered when the bank balance is reconciled. Error testing includes: (a) comparing deposits on the bank statement with deposits in the accounting records and (b) comparing canceled checks on the bank statement with checks recorded in the accounting records.

Point: Small businesses with few employees often allow recordkeepers to both write checks and keep the general ledger. If this is done, it is essential that the owner do the bank reconciliation.

Point: The person preparing the bank reconciliation should not be responsible for processing cash receipts, managing checks, or maintaining cash records.

Illustration of a Bank Reconciliation We follow nine steps in preparing the bank reconciliation. It is helpful to refer to the bank reconciliation in Exhibit 6.7 when studying steps ① through ⑨.

EXHIBIT 6.7

Bank Reconciliation

	VIDEOBUSTER Bank Reconciliation October 31, 2011						
①	Bank statement balance		$ 2,050.00	⑤	Book balance		$ 1,404.58
②	Add			⑥	Add		
	Deposit of Oct. 31 in transit		145.00		Collect $500 note less $15 fee	$485.00	
			2,195.00		Interest earned	8.42	493.42
							1,898.00
③	Deduct						
	Outstanding checks			⑦	Deduct		
	No. 124	$150.00			Check printing charge	23.00	
	No. 126	200.00	350.00		NSF check plus service fee	30.00	53.00
④	**Adjusted bank balance**		**$1,845.00**	⑧	**Adjusted book balance**		**$1,845.00**
			↑				↑
				⑨ Balances are equal (reconciled)			

1 Identify the bank statement balance of the cash account (*balance per bank*). VideoBuster's bank balance is $2,050.

2 Identify and list any unrecorded deposits and any bank errors understating the bank balance. Add them to the bank balance. VideoBuster's $145 deposit placed in the bank's night depository on October 31 is not recorded on its bank statement.

Point: Outstanding checks are identified by comparing canceled checks on the bank statement with checks recorded. This includes identifying any outstanding checks listed on the *previous* period's bank reconciliation that are not included in the canceled checks on this period's bank statement.

3 Identify and list any outstanding checks and any bank errors overstating the bank balance. Deduct them from the bank balance. VideoBuster's comparison of canceled checks with its books shows two checks outstanding: No. 124 for $150 and No. 126 for $200.

4 Compute the *adjusted bank balance,* also called the *corrected* or *reconciled balance.*

5 Identify the company's book balance of the cash account (*balance per book*). VideoBuster's book balance is $1,404.58.

6 Identify and list any unrecorded credit memoranda from the bank, any interest earned, and errors understating the book balance. Add them to the book balance. VideoBuster's bank statement includes a credit memorandum showing the bank collected a note receivable for the company on October 23. The note's proceeds of $500 (minus a $15 collection fee) are credited to the company's account. VideoBuster's bank statement also shows a credit of $8.42 for interest earned on the average cash balance. There was no prior notification of this item, and it is not yet recorded.

7 Identify and list any unrecorded debit memoranda from the bank, any service charges, and errors overstating the book balance. Deduct them from the book balance. Debits on Video-Buster's bank statement that are not yet recorded include (a) a $23 charge for check printing and (b) an NSF check for $20 plus a related $10 processing fee. (The NSF check is dated October 16 and was included in the book balance.)

8 Compute the *adjusted book balance*, also called *corrected* or *reconciled balance*.

9 Verify that the two adjusted balances from steps 4 and 8 are equal. If so, they are reconciled. If not, check for accuracy and missing data to achieve reconciliation.

> **Point:** Adjusting entries can be combined into one compound entry.

Adjusting Entries from a Bank Reconciliation   A bank reconciliation often identifies unrecorded items that need recording by the company. In VideoBuster's reconciliation, the adjusted balance of $1,845 is the correct balance as of October 31. But the company's accounting records show a $1,404.58 balance. We must prepare journal entries to adjust the book balance to the correct balance. It is important to remember that only the items reconciling the *book balance* require adjustment. A review of Exhibit 6.7 indicates that four entries are required for VideoBuster.

Collection of note.   The first entry is to record the proceeds of its note receivable collected by the bank less the expense of having the bank perform that service.

Oct. 31	Cash	485	
	Collection Expense	15	
	Notes Receivable		500
	To record the collection fee and proceeds		
	for a note collected by the bank.		

Assets = Liabilities + Equity
+485   −15
−500

Interest earned.   The second entry records interest credited to its account by the bank.

Oct. 31	Cash	8.42	
	Interest Revenue		8.42
	To record interest earned on the cash		
	balance in the checking account.		

Assets = Liabilities + Equity
+8.42   +8.42

Check printing.   The third entry records expenses for the check printing charge.

Oct. 31	Miscellaneous Expenses..........................	23	
	Cash		23
	Check printing charge.		

Assets = Liabilities + Equity
−23   −23

NSF check.   The fourth entry records the NSF check that is returned as uncollectible. The $20 check was originally received from T. Woods in payment of his account and then deposited. The bank charged $10 for handling the NSF check and deducted $30 total from VideoBuster's account. This means the entry must reverse the effects of the original entry made when the check was received and must record (add) the $10 bank fee.

> **Point:** The company will try to collect the entire NSF amount of $30 from customer.

Oct. 31	Accounts Receivable—T. Woods	30	
	Cash		30
	To charge Woods' account for $20 NSF check		
	and $10 bank fee.		

Assets = Liabilities + Equity
+30
−30

Point: The Demo Problem 1 shows an adjusting entry for an error correction.

Cash			
Unadj. bal.	1,404.58		
⑥	485.00	⑦	23.00
⑥	8.42	⑦	30.00
Adj. bal.	1,845.00		

After these four entries are recorded, the book balance of cash is adjusted to the correct amount of $1,845 (computed as $1,404.58 + $485 + $8.42 − $23 − $30). The Cash T-account to the side shows the same computation, where entries are keyed to the numerical codes in Exhibit 6.7.

Fraud

Fraud. A survey reports that 74% of employees had 'personally seen' or had 'firsthand knowledge of' fraud or misconduct in their company within the past year. These employees also identified factors that would drive employees and managers to engage in misconduct. They cited pressures to meet targets, lack of standards, and other root causes—see graphic (KPMG 2009).

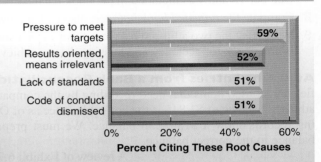

Quick Check
Answers — p. 277

11. What is a bank statement?

12. What is the meaning of the phrase *to reconcile a bank balance?*

13. Why do we reconcile the bank statement balance of cash and the depositor's book balance of cash?

14. List at least two items affecting the *bank balance* side of a bank reconciliation and indicate whether the items are added or subtracted.

15. List at least three items affecting the *book balance* side of a bank reconciliation and indicate whether the items are added or subtracted.

GLOBAL VIEW

This section discusses similarities and differences between U.S. GAAP and IFRS regarding internal controls and in the accounting and reporting of cash.

Internal Control Purposes, Principles, and Procedures   Both U.S. GAAP and IFRS aim for high-quality financial reporting. That aim translates into enhanced internal controls worldwide. Specifically, the purposes and principles of internal control systems are fundamentally the same across the globe. However, culture and other realities suggest different emphases on the mix of control procedures, and some sensitivity to different customs and environments when establishing that mix. Nevertheless, the discussion in this chapter applies internationally. Nokia provides the following description of its control activities.

NOKIA

Nokia has an internal audit function that acts as an independent appraisal function by examining and evaluating the adequacy and effectiveness of the company's system of internal control.

Control of Cash   Accounting definitions for cash are similar for U.S. GAAP and IFRS. The need for control of cash is universal and applies globally. This means that companies worldwide desire to apply cash management procedures as explained in this chapter and aim to control both cash receipts and disbursements. Accordingly, systems that employ tools such as cash monitoring mechanisms, verification of documents, and petty cash processes are applied worldwide. The basic techniques explained in this chapter are part of those control procedures.

Banking Activities as Controls   There is a global demand for banking services, bank statements, and bank reconciliations. To the extent feasible, companies utilize banking services as part of their effective control procedures. Further, bank statements are similarly used along with bank reconciliations to control and monitor cash.

 IFRS _____

Internal controls are crucial to companies that convert from U.S. GAAP to IFRS. Major risks include misstatement of financial information and fraud. Other risks are ineffective communication of the impact of this change for investors, creditors and others, and management's inability to certify the effectiveness of controls over financial reporting. ●

| Days' Sales Uncollected | **Decision Analysis** |

An important part of cash management is monitoring the receipt of cash from receivables. If customers and others who owe money to a company are delayed in payment, then that company can find it difficult to pay its obligations when they are due. A company's customers are crucial partners in its cash management. Many companies attract customers by selling to them on credit. This means that cash receipts from customers are delayed until accounts receivable are collected.

A1 Compute the days' sales uncollected ratio and use it to assess liquidity.

One measure of how quickly a company can convert its accounts receivable into cash is the **days' sales uncollected,** also called *days' sales in receivables*. This measure is computed by dividing the current balance of receivables by net credit sales over the year just completed and then multiplying by 365 (number of days in a year). Since net credit sales usually are not reported to external users, the net sales (or revenues) figure is commonly used in the computation as in Exhibit 6.8.

$$\text{Days' sales uncollected} = \frac{\text{Accounts receivable}}{\text{Net sales}} \times 365$$

EXHIBIT 6.8

Days' Sales Uncollected

We use days' sales uncollected to estimate how much time is likely to pass before the current amount of accounts receivable is received in cash. For evaluation purposes, we need to compare this estimate to that for other companies in the same industry. We also make comparisons between current and prior periods.

To illustrate, we select data from the annual reports of two toy manufacturers, Hasbro and Mattel. Their days' sales uncollected figures are shown in Exhibit 6.9.

EXHIBIT 6.9

Analysis Using Days' Sales Uncollected

Company	Figure ($ millions)	2009	2008	2007	2006	2005
Hasbro	Accounts receivable	$1,039	$612	$655	$556	$523
	Net sales	$4,068	$4,022	$3,838	$3,151	$3,088
	Days' sales uncollected	93 days	56 days	62 days	64 days	62 days
Mattel	Accounts receivable	$749	$874	$991	$944	$761
	Net sales	$5,431	$5,918	$5,970	$5,650	$5,179
	Days' sales uncollected	50 days	54 days	61 days	61 days	54 days

Days' sales uncollected for Hasbro in 2009 is computed as ($1,039/$4,068) × 365 days = 93 days. This means that it will take about 93 days to collect cash from ending accounts receivable. This number reflects one or more of the following factors: a company's ability to collect receivables, customer financial health, customer payment strategies, and discount terms. To further assess days' sales uncollected for Hasbro, we compare it to four prior years and to those of Mattel. We see that Hasbro's days' sales uncollected has worsened in 2009 as it takes much longer to collect its receivables relative to the prior four years. In comparison, Mattel fluctuated on days' sales uncollected for each of those years—from 54 days, to 61 days for two years, then back down to 54 days, and then down to the current 50 days. For all years, Mattel is superior to Hasbro on this measure of cash management. The less time that money is tied up in receivables often translates into increased profitability.

Days
Days' Sales Uncollected: ■ Mattel □ Hasbro

 Decision Maker   Answer – p. 277

Sales Representative   The sales staff is told to take action to help reduce days' sales uncollected for cash management purposes. What can you, a salesperson, do to reduce days' sales uncollected? ■

DEMONSTRATION PROBLEM 1

Prepare a bank reconciliation for Jamboree Enterprises for the month ended November 30, 2011. The following information is available to reconcile Jamboree Enterprises' book balance of cash with its bank statement balance as of November 30, 2011:

a. After all posting is complete on November 30, the company's book balance of Cash has a $16,380 debit balance, but its bank statement shows a $38,520 balance.

b. Checks No. 2024 for $4,810 and No. 2026 for $5,000 are outstanding.

c. In comparing the canceled checks on the bank statement with the entries in the accounting records, it is found that Check No. 2025 in payment of rent is correctly drawn for $1,000 but is erroneously entered in the accounting records as $880.

d. The November 30 deposit of $17,150 was placed in the night depository after banking hours on that date, and this amount does not appear on the bank statement.

e. In reviewing the bank statement, a check written by Jumbo Enterprises in the amount of $160 was erroneously drawn against Jamboree's account.

f. A credit memorandum enclosed with the bank statement indicates that the bank collected a $30,000 note and $900 of related interest on Jamboree's behalf. This transaction was not recorded by Jamboree prior to receiving the statement.

g. A debit memorandum for $1,100 lists a $1,100 NSF check received from a customer, Marilyn Welch. Jamboree had not recorded the return of this check before receiving the statement.

h. Bank service charges for November total $40. These charges were not recorded by Jamboree before receiving the statement.

PLANNING THE SOLUTION

● Set up a bank reconciliation with a bank side and a book side (as in Exhibit 6.7). Leave room to both add and deduct items. Each column will result in a reconciled, equal balance.

● Examine each item *a* through *h* to determine whether it affects the book or the bank balance and whether it should be added or deducted from the bank or book balance.

● After all items are analyzed, complete the reconciliation and arrive at a reconciled balance between the bank side and the book side.

● For each reconciling item on the book side, prepare an adjusting entry. Additions to the book side require an adjusting entry that debits Cash. Deductions on the book side require an adjusting entry that credits Cash.

SOLUTION TO DEMONSTRATION PROBLEM 1

JAMBOREE ENTERPRISES
Bank Reconciliation
November 30, 2011

Bank statement balance		$ 38,520	Book balance		$ 16,380
Add			Add		
Deposit of Nov. 30	$17,150		Collection of note	$30,000	
Bank error (Jumbo)	160	17,310	Interest earned	900	30,900
		55,830			47,280
Deduct			Deduct		
Outstanding checks			NSF check (M. Welch)	1,100	
No. 2024	4,810		Recording error (# 2025) ...	120	
No. 2026	5,000	9,810	Service charge	40	1,260
Adjusted bank balance ...		**$46,020**	**Adjusted book balance**		**$46,020**

Required Adjusting Entries for Jamboree

Nov. 30	Cash	30,900	
	Notes Receivable		30,000
	Interest Earned		900
	To record collection of note with interest.		
Nov. 30	Accounts Receivable—M. Welch	1,100	
	Cash		1,100
	To reinstate account due from an NSF check.		
Nov. 30	Rent Expense	120	
	Cash		120
	To correct recording error on check no. 2025.		
Nov. 30	Bank Service Charges	40	
	Cash		40
	To record bank service charges.		

Point: Error correction can alternatively involve (1) reversing the error entry, and (2) recording the correct entry.

DEMONSTRATION PROBLEM 2

Bacardi Company established a $150 petty cash fund with Dean Martin as the petty cashier. When the fund balance reached $19 cash, Martin prepared a petty cash payment report, which follows.

Petty Cash Payments Report				
Receipt No.	**Account Charged**		**Approved by**	**Received by**
12	Delivery Expense	$ 29	Martin	A. Smirnoff
13	Merchandise Inventory	18	Martin	J. Daniels
15	(Omitted)	32	Martin	C. Carlsberg
16	Miscellaneous Expense	41	(Omitted)	J. Walker
	Total	$120		

Required

1. Identify four internal control weaknesses from the payment report.
2. Prepare general journal entries to record:
   a. Establishment of the petty cash fund.
   b. Reimbursement of the fund. (Assume for this part only that petty cash receipt no. 15 was issued for miscellaneous expenses.)
3. What is the Petty Cash account balance immediately before reimbursement? Immediately after reimbursement?

SOLUTION TO DEMONSTRATION PROBLEM 2

1. Four internal control weaknesses are
   a. Petty cash ticket no. 14 is missing. Its omission raises questions about the petty cashier's management of the fund.
   b. The $19 cash balance means that $131 has been withdrawn ($150 − $19 = $131). However, the total amount of the petty cash receipts is only $120 ($29 + $18 + $32 + $41). The fund is $11 short of cash ($131 − $120 = $11). Was petty cash receipt no. 14 issued for $11? Management should investigate.
   c. The petty cashier (Martin) did not sign petty cash receipt no. 16. This omission could have been an oversight on his part or he might not have authorized the payment. Management should investigate.
   d. Petty cash receipt no. 15 does not indicate which account to charge. This omission could have been an oversight on the petty cashier's part. Management could check with C. Carlsberg and the petty cashier (Martin) about the transaction. Without further information, debit Miscellaneous Expense.

2. Petty cash general journal entries.

a. Entry to establish the petty cash fund.

Petty Cash	150	
Cash		150

b. Entry to reimburse the fund.

Delivery Expense	29	
Merchandise Inventory	18	
Miscellaneous Expense ($41 + $32)	73	
Cash Over and Short	11	
Cash		131

3. The Petty Cash account balance *always* equals its fund balance, in this case $150. This account balance does not change unless the fund is increased or decreased.

APPENDIX

6A

Documentation and Verification

This appendix describes the important business documents of a voucher system of control.

P4 Describe the use of documentation and verification to control cash disbursements.

Purchase Requisition Department managers are usually not allowed to place orders directly with suppliers for control purposes. Instead, a department manager must inform the purchasing department of its needs by preparing and signing a **purchase requisition,** which lists the merchandise needed and requests that it be purchased—see Exhibit 6A.1. Two copies of the purchase requisition are sent to the purchasing department, which then sends one copy to the accounting department. When the accounting department receives a purchase requisition, it creates and maintains a voucher for this transaction. The requesting department keeps the third copy.

EXHIBIT 6A.1

Purchase Requisition

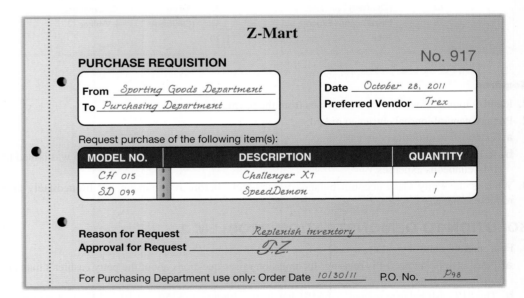

Point: A voucher system is designed to uniquely meet the needs of a specific business. Thus, we should read this appendix as one example of a common voucher system design, but *not* the only design.

Purchase Order A **purchase order** is a document the purchasing department uses to place an order with a **vendor** (seller or supplier). A purchase order authorizes a vendor to ship ordered merchandise at the stated price and terms—see Exhibit 6A.2. When the purchasing department receives a purchase requisition, it prepares at least five copies of a purchase order. The copies are distributed as follows: *copy 1* to the vendor as a purchase request and as authority to ship merchandise; *copy 2,* along with a copy of the purchase requisition, to the accounting department, where it is entered in the voucher and used in approving payment of the invoice; *copy 3* to the requesting department to inform its manager that action is being taken; *copy 4* to the receiving department without order quantity so it can compare with goods received and provide independent count of goods received; and *copy 5* retained on file by the purchasing department.

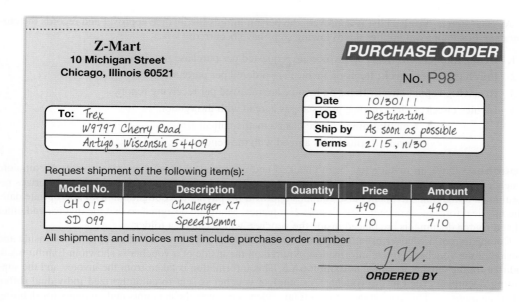

EXHIBIT 6A.2

Purchase Order

Invoice   An **invoice** is an itemized statement of goods prepared by the vendor listing the customer's name, items sold, sales prices, and terms of sale. An invoice is also a bill sent to the buyer from the supplier. From the vendor's point of view, it is a *sales invoice*. The buyer, or **vendee,** treats it as a *purchase invoice*. When receiving a purchase order, the vendor ships the ordered merchandise to the buyer and includes or mails a copy of the invoice covering the shipment to the buyer. The invoice is sent to the buyer's accounting department where it is placed in the voucher. (Refer back to Exhibit 4.5, which shows Z-Mart's purchase invoice.)

Receiving Report   Many companies maintain a separate department to receive all merchandise and purchased assets. When each shipment arrives, this receiving department counts the goods and checks them for damage and agreement with the purchase order. It then prepares four or more copies of a **receiving report,** which is used within the company to notify the appropriate persons that ordered goods have been received and to describe the quantities and condition of the goods. One copy is sent to accounting and placed in the voucher. Copies are also sent to the requesting department and the purchasing department to notify them that the goods have arrived. The receiving department retains a copy in its files.

Invoice Approval   When a receiving report arrives, the accounting department should have copies of the following documents in the voucher: purchase requisition, purchase order, and invoice. With the information in these documents, the accounting department can record the purchase and approve its payment. In approving an invoice for payment, it checks and compares information across all documents. To facilitate this checking and to ensure that no step is omitted, it often uses an **invoice approval,** also called *check authorization*—see Exhibit 6A.3. An invoice approval is a checklist of steps necessary for approving an invoice for recording and payment. It is a separate document either filed in the voucher or preprinted (or stamped) on the voucher.

INVOICE APPROVAL

DOCUMENT			BY	DATE
Purchase requisition		917	TZ	10/28/11
Purchase order		P98	JW	10/30/11
Receiving report		R85	SK	11/03/11
Invoice:		4657		11/12/11
Price			JK	11/12/11
Calculations			JK	11/12/11
Terms			JK	11/12/11
Approved for payment			BC	

EXHIBIT 6A.3

Invoice Approval

Point: Recording a purchase is initiated by an invoice approval, not an invoice. An invoice approval verifies that the amount is consistent with that requested, ordered, and received. This controls and verifies purchases and related liabilities.

As each step in the checklist is approved, the person initials the invoice approval and records the current date. Final approval implies the following steps have occurred:

1. **Requisition check:** Items on invoice are requested per purchase requisition.
2. **Purchase order check:** Items on invoice are ordered per purchase order.
3. **Receiving report check:** Items on invoice are received per receiving report.
4. **Invoice check: Price:** Invoice prices are as agreed with the vendor.
   Calculations: Invoice has no mathematical errors.
   Terms: Terms are as agreed with the vendor.

Voucher   Once an invoice has been checked and approved, the voucher is complete. A complete voucher is a record summarizing a transaction. Once the voucher certifies a transaction, it authorizes recording an obligation. A voucher also contains approval for paying the obligation on an appropriate date. The physical form of a voucher varies across companies. Many are designed so that the invoice and other related source documents are placed inside the voucher, which can be a folder.

Completion of a voucher usually requires a person to enter certain information on both the inside and outside of the voucher. Typical information required on the inside of a voucher is shown in Exhibit 6A.4, and that for the outside is shown in Exhibit 6A.5. This information is taken from the invoice and the supporting documents filed in the voucher. A complete voucher is sent to an authorized individual (often called an *auditor*). This person performs a final review, approves the accounts and amounts for debiting (called the *accounting distribution*), and authorizes recording of the voucher.

EXHIBIT 6A.4

Inside of a Voucher

After a voucher is approved and recorded (in a journal called a **voucher register**), it is filed by its due date. A check is then sent on the payment date from the cashier, the voucher is marked "paid," and the voucher is sent to the accounting department and recorded (in a journal called the **check register**). The person issuing checks relies on the approved voucher and its signed supporting documents as proof that an obligation has been incurred and must be paid. The purchase requisition and purchase order confirm the purchase was authorized. The receiving report shows that items have been received, and the invoice approval form verifies that the invoice has been checked for errors. There is little chance for error and even less chance for fraud without collusion unless all the documents and signatures are forged.

EXHIBIT 6A.5

Outside of a Voucher

Control of Purchase Discounts

6B

This appendix explains how a company can better control its cash *disbursements* to take advantage of favorable purchases discounts. Chapter 4 described the entries to record the receipt and payment of an invoice for a merchandise purchase with and without discount terms. Those entries were prepared under what is called the **gross method** of recording purchases, which initially records the invoice at its *gross* amount ignoring any cash discount.

The **net method** is another means of recording purchases, which initially records the invoice at its *net* amount of any cash discount. The net method gives management an advantage in controlling and monitoring cash payments involving purchase discounts.

To explain, when invoices are recorded at *gross* amounts, the amount of any discounts taken is deducted from the balance of the Merchandise Inventory account when cash payment is made. This means that the amount of any discounts lost is not reported in any account or on the income statement. Lost discounts recorded in this way are unlikely to come to the attention of management. When purchases are recorded at *net* amounts, a **Discounts Lost** expense account is recorded and brought to management's attention. Management can then seek to identify the reason for discounts lost such as oversight, carelessness, or unfavorable terms. (Chapter 4 explains how managers assess whether a discount is favorable or not.)

P5 Apply the net method to control purchase discounts.

Perpetual Inventory System To illustrate, assume that a company purchases merchandise on November 2 at a $1,200 invoice price with terms of 2/10, n/30. Its November 2 entries under the gross and net methods are

Gross Method—Perpetual		
Merchandise Inventory	1,200	
Accounts Payable		1,200

Net Method—Perpetual		
Merchandise Inventory	1,176	
Accounts Payable		1,176

If the invoice is paid on November 12 within the discount period, it records the following:

Gross Method—Perpetual		
Accounts Payable	1,200	
Merchandise Inventory		24
Cash		1,176

Net Method—Perpetual		
Accounts Payable	1,176	
Cash		1,176

If the invoice is *not* paid within the discount period, it records the following November 12 entry (which is the date corresponding to the end of the discount period):

Gross Method—Perpetual			**Net Method—Perpetual**		
No entry			Discounts Lost	24	
			Accounts Payable		24

Then, when the invoice is later paid on December 2, outside the discount period, it records the following:

Gross Method—Perpetual			**Net Method—Perpetual**		
Accounts Payable	1,200		Accounts Payable	1,200	
Cash		1,200	Cash		1,200

(The discount lost can be recorded when the cash payment is made with a single entry. However, in this case, when financial statements are prepared after a discount is lost and before the cash payment is made, an adjusting entry is required to recognize any unrecorded discount lost in the period when incurred.)

Periodic Inventory System   The preceding entries assume a perpetual inventory system. If a company is using a periodic system, its November 2 entries under the gross and net methods are

Gross Method—Periodic			**Net Method—Periodic**		
Purchases	1,200		Purchases	1,176	
Accounts Payable		1,200	Accounts Payable		1,176

If the invoice is paid on November 12 within the discount period, it records the following:

Gross Method—Periodic			**Net Method—Periodic**		
Accounts Payable	1,200		Accounts Payable	1,176	
Purchases Discounts		24	Cash		1,176
Cash		1,176			

If the invoice is *not* paid within the discount period, it records the following November 12 entry:

Gross Method—Periodic			**Net Method—Periodic**		
No entry			Discounts Lost	24	
			Accounts Payable		24

Then, when the invoice is later paid on December 2, outside the discount period, it records the following:

Gross Method—Periodic			**Net Method—Periodic**		
Accounts Payable	1,200		Accounts Payable	1,200	
Cash		1,200	Cash		1,200

Summary

C1 Define internal control and identify its purpose and principles. An internal control system consists of the policies and procedures managers use to protect assets, ensure reliable accounting, promote efficient operations, and urge adherence to company policies. It can prevent avoidable losses and help managers both plan operations and monitor company and human performance. Principles of good internal control include establishing responsibilities, maintaining adequate records, insuring assets and bonding employees, separating recordkeeping from custody of assets, dividing responsibilities for related transactions, applying technological controls, and performing regular independent reviews.

C2 Define cash and cash equivalents and explain how to report them. Cash includes currency, coins, and amounts on (or acceptable for) deposit in checking and savings accounts. Cash equivalents are short-term, highly liquid investment assets readily convertible to a known cash amount and sufficiently close to their maturity date so that market value is not sensitive to interest rate changes. Cash and cash equivalents are liquid assets because they are readily converted into other assets or can be used to pay for goods, services, or liabilities.

A1 **Compute the days' sales uncollected ratio and use it to assess liquidity.** Many companies attract customers by selling to them on credit. This means that cash receipts from customers are delayed until accounts receivable are collected. Users want to know how quickly a company can convert its accounts receivable into cash. The days' sales uncollected ratio, one measure reflecting company liquidity, is computed by dividing the ending balance of receivables by annual net sales, and then multiplying by 365.

P1 **Apply internal control to cash receipts and disbursements.** Internal control of cash receipts ensures that all cash received is properly recorded and deposited. Attention focuses on two important types of cash receipts: over-the-counter and by mail. Good internal control for over-the-counter cash receipts includes use of a cash register, customer review, use of receipts, a permanent transaction record, and separation of the custody of cash from its record-keeping. Good internal control for cash receipts by mail includes at least two people assigned to open mail and a listing of each sender's name, amount, and explanation. (Banks offer several services that promote the control and safeguarding of cash.)

P2 **Explain and record petty cash fund transactions.** Petty cash disbursements are payments of small amounts for items such as postage, courier fees, minor repairs, and supplies. A company usually sets up one or more petty cash funds. A petty cash fund cashier is responsible for safekeeping the cash, making payments from this fund, and keeping receipts and records. A Petty Cash account

is debited only when the fund is established or increased in amount. When the fund is replenished, petty cash disbursements are recorded with debits to expense (or asset) accounts and a credit to cash.

P3 **Prepare a bank reconciliation.** A bank reconciliation proves the accuracy of the depositor's and the bank's records. The bank statement balance is adjusted for items such as outstanding checks and unrecorded deposits made on or before the bank statement date but not reflected on the statement. The book balance is adjusted for items such as service charges, bank collections for the depositor, and interest earned on the account.

P4^A **Describe the use of documentation and verification to control cash disbursements.** A voucher system is a set of procedures and approvals designed to control cash disbursements and acceptance of obligations. The voucher system of control relies on several important documents, including the voucher and its supporting files. A key factor in this system is that only approved departments and individuals are authorized to incur certain obligations.

P5^B **Apply the net method to control purchase discounts.** The net method aids management in monitoring and controlling purchase discounts. When invoices are recorded at gross amounts, the amount of discounts taken is deducted from the balance of the Inventory account. This means that the amount of any discounts lost is not reported in any account and is unlikely to come to the attention of management. When purchases are recorded at net amounts, a Discounts Lost account is brought to management's attention as an operating expense. Management can then seek to identify the reason for discounts lost, such as oversight, carelessness, or unfavorable terms.

Guidance Answers to Decision Maker and Decision Ethics

Entrepreneur A forced vacation policy is part of a good system of internal controls. When employees are forced to take vacations, their ability to hide any fraudulent behavior decreases because others must perform the vacationers' duties. A replacement employee potentially can uncover fraudulent behavior or falsified records. A forced vacation policy is especially important for employees in sensitive positions of handling money or in control of easily transferable assets.

Sales Representative A salesperson can take several steps to reduce days' sales uncollected. These include (1) decreasing the ratio of sales on account to total sales by encouraging more cash sales, (2) identifying customers most delayed in their payments and encouraging earlier payments or cash sales, and (3) applying stricter credit policies to eliminate credit sales to customers that never pay.

Guidance Answers to Quick Checks

1. (c)
2. Technology reduces processing errors. It also allows more extensive testing of records, limits the amount of hard evidence, and highlights the importance of separation of duties.
3. A company holds liquid assets so that it can purchase other assets, buy services, and pay obligations.
4. It owns cash equivalents because they yield a return greater than what cash earns (and are readily exchanged for cash).
5. Examples of cash equivalents are 90-day (or less) U.S. Treasury bills, money market funds, and commercial paper (notes).
6. (a)
7. A voucher system is used when an owner/manager can no longer control purchasing procedures through personal supervision and direct participation.

8. If all cash payments are made by check, numerous checks for small amounts must be written. Since this practice is expensive and time-consuming, a petty cash fund is often established for making small (immaterial) cash payments.
9. If the petty cash fund is not reimbursed at the end of an accounting period, the transactions involving petty cash are not yet recorded and the petty cash asset is overstated.
10. First, petty cash transactions are recorded when the petty cash fund is reimbursed. Second, reimbursement provides cash to allow the fund to continue being used. Third, reimbursement identifies any cash shortage or overage in the fund.
11. A bank statement is a report prepared by the bank describing the activities in a depositor's account.

12. To reconcile a bank balance means to explain the difference between the cash balance in the depositor's accounting records and the cash balance on the bank statement.

13. The purpose of the bank reconciliation is to determine whether the bank or the depositor has made any errors and whether the bank has entered any transactions affecting the account that the depositor has not recorded.

14. Unrecorded deposits—added
Outstanding checks—subtracted

15. Interest earned—added   Debit memos—subtracted
Credit memos—added   NSF checks—subtracted
Bank service charges—subtracted

Key Terms

Bank reconciliation (p. 265)
Bank statement (p. 264)
Canceled checks (p. 265)
Cash (p. 255)
Cash equivalents (p. 255)
Cash Over and Short (p. 257)
Check (p. 262)
Check register (p. 274)
Committee of Sponsoring Organizations (COSO) (p. 251)
Days' sales uncollected (p. 269)
Deposit ticket (p. 262)

Deposits in transit (p. 265)
Discounts lost (p. 275)
Electronic funds transfer (EFT) (p. 263)
Gross method (p. 275)
Internal control system (p. 250)
Invoice (p. 273)
Invoice approval (p. 273)
Liquid assets (p. 255)
Liquidity (p. 255)
Net method (p. 275)
Outstanding checks (p. 265)
Petty cash (p. 260)

Principles of internal control (p. 251)
Purchase order (p. 272)
Purchase requisition (p. 272)
Receiving report (p. 273)
Sarbanes-Oxley Act (p. 250)
Section 404 (of SOX) (p. 251)
Signature card (p. 262)
Vendee (p. 273)
Vendor (p. 272)
Voucher (p. 259)
Voucher register (p. 274)
Voucher system (p. 258)

Multiple Choice Quiz   Answers on p. 291   mhhe.com/wildFA6e

Additional quiz questions are available at the book's Website.

1. A company needs to replenish its $500 petty cash fund. Its petty cash box has $75 cash and petty cash receipts of $420. The journal entry to replenish the fund includes
 a. A debit to Cash for $75.
 b. A credit to Cash for $75.
 c. A credit to Petty Cash for $420.
 d. A credit to Cash Over and Short for $5.
 e. A debit to Cash Over and Short for $5.

2. The following information is available for Hapley Company:
 • The November 30 bank statement shows a $1,895 balance.
 • The general ledger shows a $1,742 balance at November 30.
 • A $795 deposit placed in the bank's night depository on November 30 does not appear on the November 30 bank statement.
 • Outstanding checks amount to $638 at November 30.
 • A customer's $335 note was collected by the bank in November. A collection fee of $15 was deducted by the bank and the difference deposited in Hapley's account.
 • A bank service charge of $10 is deducted by the bank and appears on the November 30 bank statement.

 How will the customer's note appear on Hapley's November 30 bank reconciliation?
 a. $320 appears as an addition to the book balance of cash.
 b. $320 appears as a deduction from the book balance of cash.
 c. $320 appears as an addition to the bank balance of cash.
 d. $320 appears as a deduction from the bank balance of cash.
 e. $335 appears as an addition to the bank balance of cash.

3. Using the information from question 2, what is the reconciled balance on Hapley's November 30 bank reconciliation?
 a. $2,052
 b. $1,895
 c. $1,742
 d. $2,201
 e. $1,184

4. A company had net sales of $84,000 and accounts receivable of $6,720. Its days' sales uncollected is
 a. 3.2 days
 b. 18.4 days
 c. 230.0 days
 d. 29.2 days
 e. 12.5 days

5.^B A company records its purchases using the net method. On August 1, it purchases merchandise on account for $6,000 with terms of 2/10, n/30. The August 1 journal entry to record this transaction includes a
 a. Debit to Merchandise Inventory for $6,000.
 b. Debit to Merchandise Inventory for $5,880.
 c. Debit to Merchandise Inventory for $120.
 d. Debit to Accounts Payable for $5,880.
 e. Credit to Accounts Payable for $6,000.

A(B) *Superscript letter A(B) denotes assignments based on Appendix 6A (6B).*
🎲 Icon denotes assignments that involve decision making.

Discussion Questions

1. List the seven broad principles of internal control.

2. 🎲 Internal control procedures are important in every business, but at what stage in the development of a business do they become especially critical?

3. 🎲 Why should responsibility for related transactions be divided among different departments or individuals?

4. 🎲 Why should the person who keeps the records of an asset not be the person responsible for its custody?

5. 🎲 When a store purchases merchandise, why are individual departments not allowed to directly deal with suppliers?

6. What are the limitations of internal controls?

7. Which of the following assets is most liquid? Which is least liquid? Inventory, building, accounts receivable, or cash.

8. What is a petty cash receipt? Who should sign it?

9. Why should cash receipts be deposited on the day of receipt?

10. **Research In Motion**'s statement of cash flows in Appendix A describes changes in cash and cash **RIM** equivalents for the year ended February 27, 2010. What total amount is provided (used) by investing activities? What amount is provided (used) by financing activities?

11. Refer to **Apple**'s financial statements in Appendix A. Identify Apple's net income for the year ended December 31, 2009. Is its net income equal to the increase in cash and cash equivalents for the year? Explain the difference between net income and the increase in cash and cash equivalents. **Apple**

12. 🎲 Refer to **Nokia**'s balance sheet in Appendix A. How does its cash (titled "bank and cash") compare with its other current assets (both in amount and percent) as of December 31, 2009? Compare and assess its cash at December 31, 2009, with its cash at December 31, 2008. **NOKIA**

13. 🎲 **Palm**'s balance sheet in Appendix A reports that cash and equivalents decreased during the fiscal year ended May, 31, 2009. Identify the cash generated (or used) by operating activities, by investing activities, and by financing activities. **Palm**

🔲 connect

An internal control system consists of all policies and procedures used to protect assets, ensure reliable accounting, promote efficient operations, and urge adherence to company policies.

1. What is the main objective of internal control procedures? How is that objective achieved?

2. Why should recordkeeping for assets be separated from custody over those assets?

3. Why should the responsibility for a transaction be divided between two or more individuals or departments?

QUICK STUDY

QS 6-1
Internal control objectives
C1 🎲

A good system of internal control for cash provides adequate procedures for protecting both cash receipts and cash disbursements.

1. What are three basic guidelines that help achieve this protection?

2. Identify two control systems or procedures for cash disbursements.

QS 6-2
Internal control for cash
P1 🎲

Good accounting systems help in managing cash and controlling who has access to it.

1. What items are included in the category of cash?

2. What items are included in the category of cash equivalents?

3. What does the term *liquidity* refer to?

QS 6-3
Cash and equivalents
C2

---

1. The petty cash fund of the Rio Agency is established at $75. At the end of the current period, the fund contained $14 and had the following receipts: film rentals, $19, refreshments for meetings, $23 (both expenditures to be classified as Entertainment Expense); postage, $6; and printing, $13. Prepare journal entries to record (a) establishment of the fund and (b) reimbursement of the fund at the end of the current period.

2. Identify the two events that cause a Petty Cash account to be credited in a journal entry.

QS 6-4
Petty cash accounting
P2

---

1. For each of the following items, indicate whether its amount (i) affects the bank or book side of a bank reconciliation and (ii) represents an addition or a subtraction in a bank reconciliation.

   a. Outstanding checks   **d.** Unrecorded deposits   **g.** Bank service charges

   b. Debit memos   **e.** Interest on cash balance

   c. NSF checks   **f.** Credit memos

2. Which of the items in part 1 require an adjusting journal entry?

QS 6-5
Bank reconciliation
P3

QS 6-6
Bank reconciliation
P3

Cruz Company deposits all cash receipts on the day when they are received and it makes all cash payments by check. At the close of business on June 30, 2011, its Cash account shows an $11,352 debit balance. Cruz's June 30 bank statement shows $10,332 on deposit in the bank. Prepare a bank reconciliation for Cruz Company using the following information.

a. Outstanding checks as of June 30 total $1,713.

b. The June 30 bank statement included a $23 debit memorandum for bank services; Cruz has not yet recorded the cost of these services.

c. In reviewing the bank statement, a $90 check written by Cruz Company was mistakenly recorded in Cruz Company's books at $99.

d. June 30 cash receipts of $2,724 were placed in the bank's night depository after banking hours and were not recorded on the June 30 bank statement.

e. The bank statement included a $5 credit for interest earned on the cash in the bank.

QS 6-7
Days' sales uncollected
A1

The following annual account balances are taken from ProTeam Sports at December 31.

	2011	2010
Accounts receivable	$ 75,692	$ 70,484
Net sales	2,591,933	2,296,673

What is the change in the number of days' sales uncollected between years 2010 and 2011? According to this analysis, is the company's collection of receivables improving? Explain.

QS 6-8^A
Documents in a voucher system
P4

Management uses a voucher system to help control and monitor cash disbursements. Identify and describe at least four key documents that are part of a voucher system of control.

QS 6-9^B
Purchase discounts   P5

An important part of cash management is knowing when, and if, to take purchase discounts.

a. Which accounting method uses a Discounts Lost account?

b. What is the advantage of this method for management?

QS 6-10
International accounting and internal controls
C1 P1

Answer each of the following related to international accounting standards.

a. Explain how the purposes and principles of internal controls are different between accounting systems reporting under IFRS versus U.S. GAAP.

b. Cash presents special internal control challenges. How do internal controls for cash differ for accounting systems reporting under IFRS versus U.S. GAAP? How do the procedures applied differ across those two accounting systems?

QS 6-11
Reviewing bank statements
P3

An entrepreneur commented that a bank reconciliation may not be necessary as she regularly reviews her online bank statement for any unusual items and errors.

a. Describe how a bank reconciliation and an online review (or reading) of the bank statement are not equivalent.

b. Identify and explain at least two frauds or errors that would be uncovered through a bank reconciliation and that would *not* be uncovered through an online review of the bank statement.

---

 connect

EXERCISES

Exercise 6-1
Internal control recommendations
C1

What internal control procedures would you recommend in each of the following situations?

1. A concession company has one employee who sells towels, coolers, and sunglasses at the beach. Each day, the employee is given enough towels, coolers, and sunglasses to last through the day and enough cash to make change. The money is kept in a box at the stand.

2. An antique store has one employee who is given cash and sent to garage sales each weekend. The employee pays cash for any merchandise acquired that the antique store resells.

Cantu Company is a rapidly growing start-up business. Its recordkeeper, who was hired nine months ago, left town after the company's manager discovered that a large sum of money had disappeared over the past three months. An audit disclosed that the recordkeeper had written and signed several checks made payable to her fiancé and then recorded the checks as salaries expense. The fiancé, who cashed the checks but never worked for the company, left town with the recordkeeper. As a result, the company incurred an uninsured loss of $84,000. Evaluate Cantu's internal control system and indicate which principles of internal control appear to have been ignored.

Exercise 6-2
Analyzing internal control
C1

Some of Chester Company's cash receipts from customers are received by the company with the regular mail. Chester's recordkeeper opens these letters and deposits the cash received each day. (*a*) Identify any internal control problem(s) in this arrangement. (*b*) What changes to its internal control system do you recommend?

Exercise 6-3
Control of cash receipts by mail
P1

Good accounting systems help with the management and control of cash and cash equivalents.
1. Define and contrast the terms *liquid asset* and *cash equivalent*.
2. Why would companies invest their idle cash in cash equivalents?
3. Identify five principles of effective cash management.

Exercise 6-4
Cash, liquidity, and return
C2

Hawk Company establishes a $400 petty cash fund on September 9. On September 30, the fund shows $166 in cash along with receipts for the following expenditures: transportation-in, $32; postage expenses, $113; and miscellaneous expenses, $87. The petty cashier could not account for a $2 shortage in the fund. Hawk uses the perpetual system in accounting for merchandise inventory. Prepare (1) the September 9 entry to establish the fund, (2) the September 30 entry to reimburse the fund, and (3) an October 1 entry to decrease the fund to $300.

Exercise 6-5
Petty cash fund with a shortage
P2

Check (2) Cr. Cash $234 and (3) Dr. Cash $100

NetPerks Co. establishes a $200 petty cash fund on January 1. On January 8, the fund shows $28 in cash along with receipts for the following expenditures: postage, $64; transportation-in, $19; delivery expenses, $36; and miscellaneous expenses, $53. NetPerks uses the perpetual system in accounting for merchandise inventory. Prepare journal entries to (1) establish the fund on January 1, (2) reimburse it on January 8, and (3) both reimburse the fund and increase it to $500 on January 8, assuming no entry in part 2. (*Hint*: Make two separate entries for part 3.)

Exercise 6-6
Petty cash fund accounting
P2

Check (3) Cr. Cash $472 (total)

Prepare a table with the following headings for a monthly bank reconciliation dated September 30.

Exercise 6-7
Bank reconciliation and adjusting entries
P3

| Bank Balance | | Book Balance | | | Not Shown on the Reconciliation |
Add	Deduct	Add	Deduct	Adjust	

For each item 1 through 12, place an *x* in the appropriate column to indicate whether the item should be added to or deducted from the book or bank balance, or whether it should not appear on the reconciliation. If the book balance is to be adjusted, place a *Dr.* or *Cr.* in the Adjust column to indicate whether the Cash balance should be debited or credited. At the left side of your table, number the items to correspond to the following list.
1. Bank service charge for September.
2. Checks written and mailed to payees on October 2.
3. Checks written by another depositor but charged against this company's account.
4. Principal and interest on a note receivable to this company is collected by the bank but not yet recorded by the company.
5. Special bank charge for collection of note in part 4 on this company's behalf.
6. Check written against the company's account and cleared by the bank; erroneously not recorded by the company's recordkeeper.
7. Interest earned on the September cash balance in the bank.
8. Night deposit made on September 30 after the bank closed.
9. Checks outstanding on August 31 that cleared the bank in September.
10. NSF check from customer is returned on September 25 but not yet recorded by this company.
11. Checks written by the company and mailed to payees on September 30.
12. Deposit made on September 5 and processed by the bank on September 6.

Exercise 6-8

Voucher system

P1

The voucher system of control is designed to control cash disbursements and the acceptance of obligations.

1. The voucher system of control establishes procedures for what two processes?
2. What types of expenditures should be overseen by a voucher system of control?
3. When is the voucher initially prepared? Explain.

Exercise 6-9

Bank reconciliation

P3

Frederick Clinic deposits all cash receipts on the day when they are received and it makes all cash payments by check. At the close of business on June 30, 2011, its Cash account shows a $15,141 debit balance. Frederick Clinic's June 30 bank statement shows $14,275 on deposit in the bank. Prepare a bank reconciliation for Frederick Clinic using the following information:

a. Outstanding checks as of June 30 total $2,500.
b. The June 30 bank statement included a $125 debit memorandum for bank services.
c. Check No. 919, listed with the canceled checks, was correctly drawn for $645 in payment of a utility bill on June 15. Frederick Clinic mistakenly recorded it with a debit to Utilities Expense and a credit to Cash in the amount of $654.

Check   Reconciled bal., $15,025

d. The June 30 cash receipts of $3,250 were placed in the bank's night depository after banking hours and were not recorded on the June 30 bank statement.

Exercise 6-10

Adjusting entries from bank reconciliation   P3

Prepare the adjusting journal entries that Frederick Clinic must record as a result of preparing the bank reconciliation in Exercise 6-9.

Exercise 6-11

Bank reconciliation

P3

Chung Company deposits all cash receipts on the day when they are received and it makes all cash payments by check. At the close of business on May 31, 2011, its Cash account shows a $15,500 debit balance. Chung's May 31 bank statement shows $13,800 on deposit in the bank. Prepare a bank reconciliation for Chung Company using the following information.

a. May 31 cash receipts of $2,200 were placed in the bank's night depository after banking hours and were not recorded on the May 31 bank statement.
b. Outstanding checks as of May 31 total $1,600.
c. The May 31 bank statement included a $100 debit memorandum for bank services; Chung has not yet recorded the cost of these services.
d. In reviewing the bank statement, a $400 check written by Wald Company was mistakenly drawn against Chung's account.

Check   Reconciled bal., $14,800

e. A debit memorandum for $600 refers to a $600 NSF check from a customer; Chung has not yet recorded this NSF check.

Exercise 6-12

Liquid assets and accounts receivable

A1

Deacon Co. reported annual net sales for 2010 and 2011 of $565,000 and $647,000, respectively. Its year-end balances of accounts receivable follow: December 31, 2010, $51,000; and December 31, 2011, $83,000. (*a*) Calculate its days' sales uncollected at the end of each year. (*b*) Evaluate and comment on any changes in the amount of liquid assets tied up in receivables.

Exercise 6-13ᴬ

Documents in a voucher system

P4

Match each document in a voucher system in column one with its description in column two.

Document
1. Voucher
2. Invoice approval
3. Receiving report
4. Invoice
5. Purchase order
6. Purchase requisition

Description

A. A document used to notify the appropriate persons that ordered goods have arrived, including a description of the quantities and condition of goods.

B. An internal file used to store documents and information to control cash disbursements and to ensure that a transaction is properly authorized and recorded.

C. A document used to place an order with a vendor that authorizes the vendor to ship ordered merchandise at the stated price and terms.

D. A checklist of steps necessary for the approval of an invoice for recording and payment; also known as a check authorization.

E. A document used by department managers to inform the purchasing department to place an order with a vendor.

F. An itemized statement of goods prepared by the vendor listing the customer's name, items sold, sales prices, and terms of sale.

USA Imports uses the perpetual system in accounting for merchandise inventory and had the following transactions during the month of October. Prepare entries to record these transactions assuming that USA Imports records invoices (*a*) at gross amounts and (*b*) at net amounts.

Oct. 2   Purchased merchandise at a $4,000 price, invoice dated October 2, terms 2/10, n/30.
10   Received a $400 credit memorandum (at full invoice price) for the return of merchandise that it purchased on October 2.
17   Purchased merchandise at a $4,400 price, invoice dated October 16, terms 2/10, n/30.
26   Paid for the merchandise purchased on October 17, less the discount.
31   Paid for the merchandise purchased on October 2. Payment was delayed because the invoice was mistakenly filed for payment today. This error caused the discount to be lost.

Exercise 6-14ᴮ

Record invoices at gross or net amounts

P5

⊞ connect

For each of these five separate cases, identify the principle(s) of internal control that is violated. Recommend what the business should do to ensure adherence to principles of internal control.

1. Heather Flat records all incoming customer cash receipts for her employer and posts the customer payments to their respective accounts.
2. At Netco Company, Jeff and Jose alternate lunch hours. Jeff is the petty cash custodian, but if someone needs petty cash when he is at lunch, Jose fills in as custodian.
3. Nadine Cox posts all patient charges and payments at the Dole Medical Clinic. Each night Nadine backs up the computerized accounting system to a tape and stores the tape in a locked file at her desk.
4. Barto Sayles prides himself on hiring quality workers who require little supervision. As office manager, Barto gives his employees full discretion over their tasks and for years has seen no reason to perform independent reviews of their work.
5. Desi West's manager has told her to reduce costs. Desi decides to raise the deductible on the plant's property insurance from $5,000 to $10,000. This cuts the property insurance premium in half. In a related move, she decides that bonding the plant's employees is a waste of money since the company has not experienced any losses due to employee theft. Desi saves the entire amount of the bonding insurance premium by dropping the bonding insurance.

PROBLEM SET A

Problem 6-1A
Analyzing internal control

C1

Shawnee Co. set up a petty cash fund for payments of small amounts. The following transactions involving the petty cash fund occurred in May (the last month of the company's fiscal year).

May 1   Prepared a company check for $250 to establish the petty cash fund.
15   Prepared a company check to replenish the fund for the following expenditures made since May 1.
   a.   Paid $78 for janitorial services.
   b.   Paid $63.68 for miscellaneous expenses.
   c.   Paid postage expenses of $43.50.
   d.   Paid $57.15 to *The County Gazette* (the local newspaper) for an advertisement.
   e.   Counted $11.15 remaining in the petty cash box.
16   Prepared a company check for $200 to increase the fund to $450.
31   The petty cashier reports that $293.39 cash remains in the fund. A company check is drawn to replenish the fund for the following expenditures made since May 15.
   f.   Paid postage expenses of $48.36.
   g.   Reimbursed the office manager for business mileage, $38.50.
   h.   Paid $39.75 to deliver merchandise to a customer, terms FOB destination.
31   The company decides that the May 16 increase in the fund was too large. It reduces the fund by $50, leaving a total of $400.

Problem 6-2A
Establish, reimburse, and adjust petty cash

P2

Required

1. Prepare journal entries to establish the fund on May 1, to replenish it on May 15 and on May 31, and to reflect any increase or decrease in the fund balance on May 16 and May 31.

Check   (1) Cr. to Cash: May 15, $238.85; May 16, $200.00

Analysis Component

2. Explain how the company's financial statements are affected if the petty cash fund is not replenished and no entry is made on May 31.

Problem 6-3A

Establish, reimburse, and increase petty cash

P2

Shelton Gallery had the following petty cash transactions in February of the current year.

Feb. 2   Wrote a $300 check, cashed it, and gave the proceeds and the petty cashbox to Bo Brown, the petty cashier.
5   Purchased bond paper for the copier for $10.13 that is immediately used.
9   Paid $22.50 COD shipping charges on merchandise purchased for resale, terms FOB shipping point. Shelton uses the perpetual system to account for merchandise inventory.
12   Paid $9.95 postage to express mail a contract to a client.
14   Reimbursed Alli Buck, the manager, $58 for business mileage on her car.
20   Purchased stationery for $77.76 that is immediately used.
23   Paid a courier $18 to deliver merchandise sold to a customer, terms FOB destination.
25   Paid $15.10 COD shipping charges on merchandise purchased for resale, terms FOB shipping point.
27   Paid $64 for postage expenses.
28   The fund had $21.23 remaining in the petty cash box. Sorted the petty cash receipts by accounts affected and exchanged them for a check to reimburse the fund for expenditures.
28   The petty cash fund amount is increased by $100 to a total of $400.

Required

1. Prepare the journal entry to establish the petty cash fund.

2. Prepare a petty cash payments report for February with these categories: delivery expense, mileage expense, postage expense, merchandise inventory (for transportation-in), and office supplies expense. Sort the payments into the appropriate categories and total the expenditures in each category.

Check   (3a & 3b) Total Cr. to Cash $378.77

3. Prepare the journal entries for part 2 to both (*a*) reimburse and (*b*) increase the fund amount.

Problem 6-4A

Prepare a bank reconciliation and record adjustments

P3

mhhe.com/wildFA6e

The following information is available to reconcile Clark Company's book balance of cash with its bank statement cash balance as of July 31, 2011.

a. On July 31, the company's Cash account has a $26,193 debit balance, but its July bank statement shows a $28,020 cash balance.

b. Check No. 3031 for $1,380 and Check No. 3040 for $552 were outstanding on the June 30 bank reconciliation. Check No. 3040 is listed with the July canceled checks, but Check No. 3031 is not. Also, Check No. 3065 for $336 and Check No. 3069 for $2,148, both written in July, are not among the canceled checks on the July 31 statement.

c. In comparing the canceled checks on the bank statement with the entries in the accounting records, it is found that Check No. 3056 for July rent was correctly written and drawn for $1,250 but was erroneously entered in the accounting records as $1,230.

d. A credit memorandum enclosed with the July bank statement indicates the bank collected $9,000 cash on a non-interest-bearing note for Clark, deducted a $45 collection fee, and credited the remainder to its account. Clark had not recorded this event before receiving the statement.

e. A debit memorandum for $805 lists a $795 NSF check plus a $10 NSF charge. The check had been received from a customer, Jim Shaw. Clark has not yet recorded this check as NSF.

f. Enclosed with the July statement is a $15 debit memorandum for bank services. It has not yet been recorded because no previous notification had been received.

g. Clark's July 31 daily cash receipts of $10,152 were placed in the bank's night depository on that date, but do not appear on the July 31 bank statement.

Required

Check   (1) Reconciled balance, $34,308; (2) Cr. Note Receivable $9,000

1. Prepare the bank reconciliation for this company as of July 31, 2011.

2. Prepare the journal entries necessary to bring the company's book balance of cash into conformity with the reconciled cash balance as of July 31, 2011.

Analysis Component

3. Assume that the July 31, 2011, bank reconciliation for this company is prepared and some items are treated incorrectly. For each of the following errors, explain the effect of the error on (i) the adjusted bank statement cash balance and (ii) the adjusted cash account book balance.

   a. The company's unadjusted cash account balance of $26,193 is listed on the reconciliation as $26,139.

   b. The bank's collection of the $9,000 note less the $45 collection fee is added to the bank statement cash balance on the reconciliation.

Els Company most recently reconciled its bank statement and book balances of cash on August 31 and it reported two checks outstanding, No. 5888 for $1,038.05 and No. 5893 for $484.25. The following information is available for its September 30, 2011, reconciliation.

Problem 6-5A
Prepare a bank reconciliation and record adjustments
P3

mhhe.com/wildFA6e

From the September 30 Bank Statement

PREVIOUS BALANCE	TOTAL CHECKS AND DEBITS	TOTAL DEPOSITS AND CREDITS	CURRENT BALANCE
16,800.45	9,620.05	11,182.85	18,363.25

CHECKS AND DEBITS			DEPOSITS AND CREDITS		DAILY BALANCE	
Date	No.	Amount	Date	Amount	Date	Amount
09/03	5888	1,038.05	09/05	1,103.75	08/31	16,800.45
09/04	5902	731.90	09/12	2,226.90	09/03	15,762.40
09/07	5901	1,824.25	09/21	4,093.00	09/04	15,030.50
09/17		588.25 NSF	09/25	2,351.70	09/05	16,134.25
09/20	5905	937.00	09/30	22.50 IN	09/07	14,310.00
09/22	5903	399.10	09/30	1,385.00 CM	09/12	16,536.90
09/22	5904	2,080.00			09/17	15,948.65
09/28	5907	213.85			09/20	15,011.65
09/29	5909	1,807.65			09/21	19,104.65
					09/22	16,625.55
					09/25	18,977.25
					09/28	18,763.40
					09/29	16,955.75
					09/30	18,363.25

From Els Company's Accounting Records

Cash Receipts Deposited			
Date			Cash Debit
Sept.	5		1,103.75
	12		2,226.90
	21		4,093.00
	25		2,351.70
	30		1,582.75
			11,358.10

Cash Disbursements		
Check No.		Cash Credit
5901		1,824.25
5902		731.90
5903		399.10
5904		2,050.00
5905		937.00
5906		859.30
5907		213.85
5908		276.00
5909		1,807.65
		9,099.05

Cash						Acct. No. 101
Date		Explanation	PR	Debit	Credit	Balance
Aug.	31	Balance				15,278.15
Sept.	30	Total receipts	R12	11,358.10		26,636.25
	30	Total disbursements	D23		9,099.05	17,537.20

Additional Information

Check No. 5904 is correctly drawn for $2,080 to pay for computer equipment; however, the recordkeeper misread the amount and entered it in the accounting records with a debit to Computer Equipment and a credit to Cash of $2,050. The NSF check shown in the statement was originally received from a customer, S. Nilson, in payment of her account. Its return has not yet been recorded by the company. The credit memorandum is from the collection of a $1,400 note for Els Company by the bank. The bank deducted a $15 collection fee. The collection and fee are not yet recorded.

Required

Check (1) Reconciled balance, $18,326.45 (2) Cr. Note Receivable $1,400

1. Prepare the September 30, 2011, bank reconciliation for this company.
2. Prepare the journal entries to adjust the book balance of cash to the reconciled balance.

Analysis Component

3. The bank statement reveals that some of the prenumbered checks in the sequence are missing. Describe three situations that could explain this.

PROBLEM SET B

Problem 6-1B

Analyzing internal control

C1

For each of these five separate cases, identify the principle(s) of internal control that is violated. Recommend what the business should do to ensure adherence to principles of internal control.

1. Latoya Tally is the company's computer specialist and oversees its computerized payroll system. Her boss recently asked her to put password protection on all office computers. Latoya has put a password in place that allows only the boss access to the file where pay rates are changed and personnel are added or deleted from the payroll.
2. Lake Theater has a computerized order-taking system for its tickets. The system is active all week and backed up every Friday night.
3. X2U Company has two employees handling acquisitions of inventory. One employee places purchase orders and pays vendors. The second employee receives the merchandise.
4. The owner of Super-Aid Pharmacy uses a check protector to perforate checks, making it difficult for anyone to alter the amount of the check. The check protector is on the owner's desk in an office that contains company checks and is normally unlocked.
5. LeAnn Company is a small business that has separated the duties of cash receipts and cash disbursements. The employee responsible for cash disbursements reconciles the bank account monthly.

Problem 6-2B

Establishing, reimbursing, and adjusting petty cash

P2

Pepco Co. establishes a petty cash fund for payments of small amounts. The following transactions involving the petty cash fund occurred in January (the last month of the company's fiscal year).

Jan. 3   A company check for $150 is written and made payable to the petty cashier to establish the petty cash fund.

     14   A company check is written to replenish the fund for the following expenditures made since January 3.

       a.   Purchased office supplies for $16.29 that are immediately used up.

       b.   Paid $17.60 COD shipping charges on merchandise purchased for resale, terms FOB shipping point. Pepco uses the perpetual system to account for inventory.

       c.   Paid $36.57 to All-Tech for minor repairs to a computer.

       d.   Paid $14.82 for items classified as miscellaneous expenses.

       e.   Counted $62.28 remaining in the petty cash box.

     15   Prepared a company check for $25 to increase the fund to $175.

     31   The petty cashier reports that $17.35 remains in the fund. A company check is written to replenish the fund for the following expenditures made since January 14.

       f.   Paid $40 to *The Smart Shopper* for an advertisement in January's newsletter.

       g.   Paid $38.19 for postage expenses.

       h.   Paid $58 to Take-You-There for delivery of merchandise, terms FOB destination.

     31   The company decides that the January 15 increase in the fund was too little. It increases the fund by another $75, leaving a total of $250.

Required

Check (1) Cr. to Cash: Jan. 14, $87.72; Jan. 31 (total), $232.65

1. Prepare journal entries to establish the fund on January 3, to replenish it on January 14 and January 31, and to reflect any increase or decrease in the fund balance on January 15 and 31.

Analysis Component

2. Explain how the company's financial statements are affected if the petty cash fund is not replenished and no entry is made on January 31.

RPM Music Center had the following petty cash transactions in March of the current year.

Problem 6-3B
Establish, reimburse, and increase petty cash
P2

March 5   Wrote a $200 check, cashed it, and gave the proceeds and the petty cashbox to Liz Buck, the petty cashier.
       6   Paid $14.50 COD shipping charges on merchandise purchased for resale, terms FOB shipping point. RPM uses the perpetual system to account for merchandise inventory.
      11   Paid $8.75 delivery charges on merchandise sold to a customer, terms FOB destination.
      12   Purchased file folders for $12.13 that are immediately used.
      14   Reimbursed Will Nelson, the manager, $9.65 for office supplies purchased and used.
      18   Purchased printer paper for $22.54 that is immediately used.
      27   Paid $47.10 COD shipping charges on merchandise purchased for resale, terms FOB shipping point.
      28   Paid postage expenses of $16.
      30   Reimbursed Nelson $58.80 for business car mileage.
      31   Cash of $11.53 remained in the fund. Sorted the petty cash receipts by accounts affected and exchanged them for a check to reimburse the fund for expenditures.
      31   The petty cash fund amount is increased by $50 to a total of $250.

Required

1. Prepare the journal entry to establish the petty cash fund.
2. Prepare a petty cash payments report for March with these categories: delivery expense, mileage expense, postage expense, merchandise inventory (for transportation-in), and office supplies expense. Sort the payments into the appropriate categories and total the expenses in each category.
3. Prepare the journal entries for part 2 to both (*a*) reimburse and (*b*) increase the fund amount.

Check   (2) Total expenses $189.47

(3a & 3b) Total Cr. to Cash $238.47

The following information is available to reconcile Style Co.'s book balance of cash with its bank statement cash balance as of December 31, 2011.

Problem 6-4B
Prepare a bank reconciliation and record adjustments
P3

a. The December 31 cash balance according to the accounting records is $31,743.70, and the bank statement cash balance for that date is $45,091.80.

b. Check No. 1273 for $1,084.20 and Check No. 1282 for $390, both written and entered in the accounting records in December, are not among the canceled checks. Two checks, No. 1231 for $2,289 and No. 1242 for $370.50, were outstanding on the most recent November 30 reconciliation. Check No. 1231 is listed with the December canceled checks, but Check No. 1242 is not.

c. When the December checks are compared with entries in the accounting records, it is found that Check No. 1267 had been correctly drawn for $2,435 to pay for office supplies but was erroneously entered in the accounting records as $2,453.

d. Two debit memoranda are enclosed with the statement and are unrecorded at the time of the reconciliation. One debit memorandum is for $749.50 and dealt with an NSF check for $732 received from a customer, Titus Industries, in payment of its account. The bank assessed a $17.50 fee for processing it. The second debit memorandum is a $79 charge for check printing. Style did not record these transactions before receiving the statement.

e. A credit memorandum indicates that the bank collected $20,000 cash on a note receivable for the company, deducted a $20 collection fee, and credited the balance to the company's Cash account. Style did not record this transaction before receiving the statement.

f. Style's December 31 daily cash receipts of $7,666.10 were placed in the bank's night depository on that date, but do not appear on the December 31 bank statement.

Required

1. Prepare the bank reconciliation for this company as of December 31, 2011.
2. Prepare the journal entries necessary to bring the company's book balance of cash into conformity with the reconciled cash balance as of December 31, 2011.

Check   (1) Reconciled balance, $50,913.20; (2) Cr. Note Receivable $20,000

Analysis Component

3. Explain the nature of the communications conveyed by a bank when the bank sends the depositor (*a*) a debit memorandum and (*b*) a credit memorandum.

Problem 6-5B
Prepare a bank reconciliation and record adjustments

P3

Safe Systems most recently reconciled its bank balance on April 30 and reported two checks outstanding at that time, No. 1771 for $781 and No. 1780 for $1,325.90. The following information is available for its May 31, 2011, reconciliation.

From the May 31 Bank Statement

PREVIOUS BALANCE	TOTAL CHECKS AND DEBITS	TOTAL DEPOSITS AND CREDITS	CURRENT BALANCE
18,290.70	12,898.90	16,416.80	21,808.60

CHECKS AND DEBITS			DEPOSITS AND CREDITS		DAILY BALANCE	
Date	No.	Amount	Date	Amount	Date	Amount
05/01	1771	781.00	05/04	2,438.00	04/30	18,290.70
05/02	1783	195.30	05/14	2,898.00	05/01	17,509.70
05/04	1782	1,285.50	05/22	1,801.80	05/02	17,314.40
05/11	1784	1,449.60	05/25	7,200.00 CM	05/04	18,466.90
05/18		431.80 NSF	05/26	2,079.00	05/11	17,017.30
05/25	1787	8,032.50			05/14	19,915.30
05/26	1785	157.20			05/18	19,483.50
05/29	1788	554.00			05/22	21,285.30
05/31		12.00 SC			05/25	20,452.80
					05/26	22,374.60
					05/29	21,820.60
					05/31	21,808.60

From Safe Systems' Accounting Records

Cash Receipts Deposited				Cash Disbursements		
Date			Cash Debit	Check No.		Cash Credit
May	4		2,438.00	1782		1,285.50
	14		2,898.00	1783		195.30
	22		1,801.80	1784		1,449.60
	26		2,079.00	1785		157.20
	31		2,526.30	1786		353.10
			11,743.10	1787		8,032.50
				1788		544.00
				1789		639.50
						12,656.70

Cash						Acct. No. 101
Date		Explanation	PR	Debit	Credit	Balance
Apr.	30	Balance				16,183.80
May	31	Total receipts	R7	11,743.10		27,926.90
	31	Total disbursements	D8		12,656.70	15,270.20

Additional Information

Check No. 1788 is correctly drawn for $554 to pay for May utilities; however, the recordkeeper misread the amount and entered it in the accounting records with a debit to Utilities Expense and a credit to Cash for $544. The bank paid and deducted the correct amount. The NSF check shown in the statement was originally received from a customer, S. Bax, in payment of her account. The company has not yet recorded its return. The credit memorandum is from a $7,300 note that the bank collected for the company. The bank deducted a $100 collection fee and deposited the remainder in the company's account. The collection and fee have not yet been recorded.

Required

1. Prepare the May 31, 2011, bank reconciliation for Safe Systems.
2. Prepare the journal entries to adjust the book balance of cash to the reconciled balance.

Check   (1) Reconciled balance, $22,016.40; (2) Cr. Note Receivable $7,300

Analysis Component

3. The bank statement reveals that some of the prenumbered checks in the sequence are missing. Describe three possible situations to explain this.

(This serial problem began in Chapter 1 and continues through most of the book. If previous chapter segments were not completed, the serial problem can begin at this point. It is helpful, but not necessary, to use the Working Papers that accompany the book.)

SERIAL PROBLEM
Business Solutions
P3

SP 6   Santana Rey receives the March bank statement for Business Solutions on April 11, 2012. The March 31 bank statement shows an ending cash balance of $67,566. A comparison of the bank statement with the general ledger Cash account, No. 101, reveals the following.

a. S. Rey notices that the bank erroneously cleared a $500 check against her account in March that she did not issue. The check documentation included with the bank statement shows that this check was actually issued by a company named Business Systems.

b. On March 25, the bank issued a $50 debit memorandum for the safety deposit box that Business Solutions agreed to rent from the bank beginning March 25.

c. On March 26, the bank issued a $102 debit memorandum for printed checks that Business Solutions ordered from the bank.

d. On March 31, the bank issued a credit memorandum for $33 interest earned on Business Solutions' checking account for the month of March.

e. S. Rey notices that the check she issued for $128 on March 31, 2012, has not yet cleared the bank.

f. S. Rey verifies that all deposits made in March do appear on the March bank statement.

g. The general ledger Cash account, No. 101, shows an ending cash balance per books of $68,057 as of March 31 (prior to any reconciliation).

Required

1. Prepare a bank reconciliation for Business Solutions for the month ended March 31, 2012.
2. Prepare any necessary adjusting entries. Use Miscellaneous Expenses, No. 677, for any bank charges. Use Interest Revenue, No. 404, for any interest earned on the checking account for the month of March.

Check   (1) Adj. bank bal. $67,938

Beyond the Numbers

BTN 6-1   Refer to **Research In Motion**'s financial statements in Appendix A to answer the following.

1. For both fiscal year-ends February 27, 2010, and February 28, 2009, identify the total amount of cash and cash equivalents. Determine the percent this amount represents of total current assets, total current liabilities, total shareholders' equity, and total assets for both years. Comment on any trends.

2. For fiscal years ended February 27, 2010, and February 28, 2009, use the information in the statement of cash flows to determine the percent change between the beginning and ending year amounts of cash and cash equivalents.

3. Compute the days' sales uncollected as of February 27, 2010, and February 28, 2009. Has the collection of receivables improved? Are accounts receivable an important asset for Research In Motion? Explain.

REPORTING IN ACTION

C2 A1

RIM

Fast Forward

4. Access Research In Motion's financial statements for fiscal years ending after February 27, 2010, from its Website (**RIM.com**) or the SEC's EDGAR database (**www.sec.gov**). Recompute its days' sales uncollected for fiscal years ending after February 27, 2010. Compare this to the days' sales uncollected for 2010 and 2009.

COMPARATIVE ANALYSIS

A1

RIM

Apple

BTN 6-2 Key comparative figures for **Research In Motion** and **Apple** follow.

($ millions)	Research In Motion		Apple	
	Current Year	**Prior Year**	**Current Year**	**Prior Year**
Accounts receivable	$ 2,594	$ 2,112	$ 3,361	$ 2,422
Net sales	14,953	11,065	42,905	37,491

Required

Compute days' sales uncollected for these companies for each of the two years shown. Comment on any trends for the companies. Which company has the largest percent change in days' sales uncollected?

ETHICS CHALLENGE

C1

BTN 6-3 Carol Benton, Sue Knox, and Marcia Diamond work for a family physician, Dr. Gwen Conrad, who is in private practice. Dr. Conrad is knowledgeable about office management practices and has segregated the cash receipt duties as follows. Benton opens the mail and prepares a triplicate list of money received. She sends one copy of the list to Knox, the cashier, who deposits the receipts daily in the bank. Diamond, the recordkeeper, receives a copy of the list and posts payments to patients' accounts. About once a month the office clerks have an expensive lunch they pay for as follows. First, Knox endorses a patient's check in Dr. Conrad's name and cashes it at the bank. Benton then destroys the remittance advice accompanying the check. Finally, Diamond posts payment to the customer's account as a miscellaneous credit. The three justify their actions by their relatively low pay and knowledge that Dr. Conrad will likely never miss the money.

Required

1. Who is the best person in Dr. Conrad's office to reconcile the bank statement?
2. Would a bank reconciliation uncover this office fraud?
3. What are some procedures to detect this type of fraud?
4. Suggest additional internal controls that Dr. Conrad could implement.

COMMUNICATING IN PRACTICE

P5

BTN 6-4[B] Assume you are a business consultant. The owner of a company sends you an e-mail expressing concern that the company is not taking advantage of its discounts offered by vendors. The company currently uses the gross method of recording purchases. The owner is considering a review of all invoices and payments from the previous period. Due to the volume of purchases, however, the owner recognizes that this is time-consuming and costly. The owner seeks your advice about monitoring purchase discounts in the future. Provide a response in memorandum form.

TAKING IT TO THE NET

C1 P1

BTN 6-5 Visit the Association of Certified Fraud Examiners Website at **cfenet.com**. Find and open the file "2008 Report to the Nation." Read the two-page Executive Summary and fill in the following blanks. (The report is under its *Fraud Resources* tab or under its *About the ACFE* tab [under Press Room]; we can also use the *Search* tab.)

1. The median loss caused by occupational frauds was $_____.
2. More than _____ of fraud cases caused at least $1 million in losses.
3. Companies lose ___% of their annual revenues to fraud; this figure translates to $_____ billion in fraud losses.
4. The typical length of fraud schemes was ____ years from the time the fraud began until it was detected.
5. Companies that conducted surprise audits suffered a median loss of $_____, whereas those without surprise audits had a median loss of $_____.
6. The median loss suffered by companies with fewer than 100 employees was $_____ per scheme.
7. _____ and _____ were the most common small business fraud schemes.
8. ___% of respondents cited inadequate internal controls as the primary contributing factor in the frauds investigated.
9. Only ___% of the perpetrators had convictions prior to committing their frauds.

BTN 6-6   Organize the class into teams. Each team must prepare a list of 10 internal controls a consumer could observe in a typical retail department store. When called upon, the team's spokesperson must be prepared to share controls identified by the team that have not been shared by another team's spokesperson.

TEAMWORK IN ACTION
C1

BTN 6-7   Review the opening feature of this chapter that highlights Kim Jordan and her company New Belgium Brewing Company.

ENTREPRENEURIAL DECISION
C1 P1

Required

1. List the seven principles of internal control and explain how Kim could implement each of them in one of her retail brewing pubs.
2. Do you believe that Kim will need to add controls as her business expands? Explain.

BTN 6-8   Visit an area of your college that serves the student community with either products or services. Some examples are food services, libraries, and bookstores. Identify and describe between four and eight internal controls being implemented.

HITTING THE ROAD
C1

BTN 6-9   The following information is from Nokia (www.Nokia.com), which is a leading global manufacturer of mobile devices and services.

GLOBAL DECISION
C2 A1

NOKIA

EUR millions	Current Year	Prior Year
Cash	1,142	1,706
Accounts receivable	7,981	9,444
Current assets	23,613	24,470
Total assets	35,738	39,582
Current liabilities	15,188	20,355
Shareholders' equity	14,749	16,510
Net sales	40,984	50,710

Required

1. For each year, compute the percentage that cash represents of current assets, total assets, current liabilities, and shareholders' equity. Comment on any trends in these percentages.
2. Determine the percentage change between the current and prior year cash balances.
3. Compute the days' sales uncollected at the end of both the current year and the prior year. Has the collection of receivables improved? Explain.

ANSWERS TO MULTIPLE CHOICE QUIZ

1. e; The entry follows.

Debits to expenses (or assets)	420	
Cash Over and Short	5	
Cash		425

2. a; recognizes cash collection of note by bank.
3. a; the bank reconciliation follows.

4. d; ($6,720/$84,000) × 365 = 29.2 days
5. b; The entry follows.

| Merchandise Inventory* | 5,880 | |
| Accounts Payable | | 5,880 |

*$6,000 × 98%

Bank Reconciliation November 30			
Balance per bank statement	$1,895	Balance per books	$1,742
Add: Deposit in transit	795	Add: Note collected less fee	320
Deduct: Outstanding checks	(638)	Deduct: Service charge	(10)
Reconciled balance	$2,052	Reconciled balance	$2,052

A Look Back

Chapter 6 focused on internal control and reporting for cash. We described internal control procedures and the accounting for and management of cash.

A Look at This Chapter

This chapter emphasizes receivables. We explain that they are liquid assets and describe how companies account for and report them. We also discuss the importance of estimating uncollectibles.

A Look Ahead

Chapter 8 focuses on plant assets, natural resources, and intangible assets. We explain how to account for, report, and analyze these long-term assets.

7

Reporting and Analyzing Receivables

Learning Objectives

CAP

CONCEPTUAL

C1 Describe accounts receivable and how they occur and are recorded. (p. 294)

C2 Describe a note receivable, the computation of its maturity date, and the recording of its existence. (p. 304)

C3 Explain how receivables can be converted to cash before maturity. (p. 307)

ANALYTICAL

A1 Compute accounts receivable turnover and use it to help assess financial condition. (p. 309)

LP7

PROCEDURAL

P1 Apply the direct write-off method to account for accounts receivable. (p. 297)

P2 Apply the allowance method and estimate uncollectibles based on sales and accounts receivable. (p. 300)

P3 Record the honoring and dishonoring of a note and adjustments for interest. (p. 306)

Heeeere's Johnny!

"I'll sit down with my customers, take them out to eat, hang out. . . with them."
— **JOHN EARLE**

BOSTON, MS—Working at a music store, John Earle's co-workers coined new nicknames for him on an almost daily basis: Johnny Appleseed, Johnny Pancakes, Johnny Cupcakes. As a joke, John printed up a few t-shirts with the Johnny Cupcakes nickname for the heavy-metal band he played in. The shirts, based on a skull and crossbones design with a cupcake replacing the skull, drew attention, and John dropped his heavy-metal dreams to start his company, **Johnny Cupcakes, Inc. (JohnnyCupcakes.com).**

John was always a small-scale serial entrepreneur, operating lemonade stands, peddling glow sticks on the beach near his home, and selling packs of pranks and magic tricks. Like his itching powder prank that went awry at his school, "the Johnny Cupcakes brand started as a complete joke," admits John. One day John's mother Lorraine interrupted his band's tour to tell him he had a real business on his hands. Now, the company's designs—like a Statue of Liberty holding a cupcake, Marilyn Monroe with a tiny cupcake-shaped mole, and the cupcakes and crossbones motif—attract a cult following. By the time John opened his first store, over 500 people had lined up to get in (see photo above).

Sales quickly soared, and John had to contend with receivables and day-to-day recordkeeping. Special attention was focused on monitoring receivables, including decisions on credit sales and policies for extending credit. John explains that he understands his customers, including cash payment patterns that allow him to estimate uncollectibles and minimize bad debts. Both accounts and notes receivables receive John's attention, along with regular reviews of the allowance for doubtful accounts.

Though still a prankster, John knows that successful entrepreneurs must understand receivables to succeed. Identifying nonpaying customers and cultivating relationships with credit customers are as crucial as his new limited edition T-shirts. With an expanding product line, an understanding of receivables and how uncollectibles relate to income become even more important.

From a handful of gag T-shirts made as a joke, Johnny Cupcakes now boasts sales of nearly $4 million per year. "I never expected it to get this big," John says, encouraging potential entrepreneurs to get out and make it happen. "I work very hard," he says, "and I enjoy every minute of it."

[Sources: *Johnny Cupcakes Website,* January 2012; *Boston Globe,* October 2007; *Businessweek.com,* August 2008; *Inc magazine,* May 2010; *NPR.org,* August 2006; *Quick Sprout,* February 2011] its maturity date. Many notes mature in less than a full year, and the period they cover is often expressed in days. When the time of a note is expressed in days, its maturity date is the specified number of days after the note's date. As an example, a five-day note dated June 15 matures and is due on June 20. A 90-day note dated July 10 matures on October 8. This October 8 due date is computed as shown in Exhibit 7.15. The period of a note is sometimes expressed in months or years. When months are used, the note matures and is payable in the month of its maturity on the *same day of the month* as its original date. A nine-month note dated July 10, for instance, is payable on April 10. The same analysis applies when years are used.

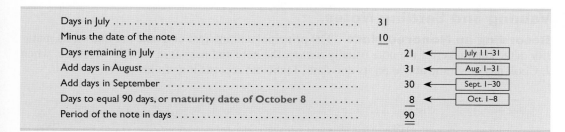

Days in July	31	
Minus the date of the note	10	
Days remaining in July	21	July 11–31
Add days in August	31	Aug. 1–31
Add days in September	30	Sept. 1–30
Days to equal 90 days, or **maturity date of October 8**	8	Oct. 1–8
Period of the note in days	90	

EXHIBIT 7.15

Maturity Date Computation

Interest Computation   *Interest* is the cost of borrowing money for the borrower or, alternatively, the profit from lending money for the lender. Unless otherwise stated, the rate of interest on a note is the rate charged for the use of the principal for one year. The formula for computing interest on a note is shown in Exhibit 7.16.

$$\frac{\textbf{Principal}}{\textbf{of the note}} \times \frac{\textbf{Annual}}{\textbf{interest rate}} \times \frac{\textbf{Time expressed}}{\textbf{in fraction of year}} = \textbf{Interest}$$

EXHIBIT 7.16

Computation of Interest Formula

To simplify interest computations, a year is commonly treated as having 360 days (called the *banker's rule* in the business world and widely used in commercial transactions). **We treat a year as having 360 days for interest computations in the examples and assignments.** Using the promissory note in Exhibit 7.14 where we have a 90-day, 12%, $1,000 note, the total interest is computed as follows.

$$\$1,000 \times 12\% \times \frac{90}{360} = \$1,000 \times 0.12 \times 0.25 = \$30$$

Recognizing Notes Receivable

Notes receivable are usually recorded in a single Notes Receivable account to simplify recordkeeping. The original notes are kept on file, including information on the maker, rate of interest, and due date. (When a company holds a large number of notes, it sometimes sets up a controlling account and a subsidiary ledger for notes. This is similar to the handling of accounts receivable.) To illustrate the recording for the receipt of a note, we use the $1,000, 90-day, 12% promissory note in Exhibit 7.14. TechCom received this note at the time of a product sale to Julia Browne. This transaction is recorded as follows.

July 10*	Notes Receivable	1,000	
	Sales		1,000
	Sold goods in exchange for a 90-day, 12% note.		

Assets = Liabilities + Equity
+1,000   +1,000

* We omit the entry to Dr. Cost of Sales and Cr. Merchandise Inventory to focus on sales and receivables.

When a seller accepts a note from an overdue customer as a way to grant a time extension on a past-due account receivable, it will often collect part of the past-due balance in cash. This partial payment forces a concession from the customer, reduces the customer's debt (and the seller's risk), and produces a note for a smaller amount. To illustrate, assume that TechCom agreed to accept $232 in cash along with a $600, 60-day, 15% note from Jo Cook to

Point: Notes receivable often are a major part of a company's assets. Likewise, notes payable often are a large part of a company's liabilities.

settle her $832 past-due account. TechCom made the following entry to record receipt of this cash and note.

Assets = Liabilities + Equity
+232
+600
−832

Oct. 5	Cash	232	
	Notes Receivable	600	
	Accounts Receivable—J. Cook		832
	Received cash and note to settle account.		

Valuing and Settling Notes

P3 Record the honoring and dishonoring of a note and adjustments for interest.

Recording an Honored Note   The principal and interest of a note are due on its maturity date. The maker of the note usually *honors* the note and pays it in full. To illustrate, when J. Cook pays the note above on its due date, TechCom records it as follows.

Assets = Liabilities + Equity
+615   +15
−600

Dec. 4	Cash	615	
	Notes Receivable		600
	Interest Revenue		15
	Collect note with interest of $600 × 15% × 60/360.		

Interest Revenue, also called *Interest Earned,* is reported on the income statement.

Recording a Dishonored Note   When a note's maker is unable or refuses to pay at maturity, the note is *dishonored.* The act of dishonoring a note does not relieve the maker of the obligation to pay. The payee should use every legitimate means to collect. How do companies report this event? The balance of the Notes Receivable account should include only those notes that have not matured. Thus, when a note is dishonored, we remove the amount of this note from the Notes Receivable account and charge it back to an account receivable from its maker. To illustrate, TechCom holds an $800, 12%, 60-day note of Greg Hart. At maturity, Hart dishonors the note. TechCom records this dishonoring of the note as follows.

Point: When posting a dishonored note to a customer's account, an explanation is included so as not to misinterpret the debit as a sale on account.

Assets = Liabilities + Equity
+816   +16
−800

Oct. 14	Accounts Receivable—G. Hart	816	
	Interest Revenue		16
	Notes Receivable		800
	To charge account of G. Hart for a dishonored note and interest of $800 × 12% × 60/360.		

Point: Reporting the details of notes is consistent with the **full disclosure principle,** which requires financial statements (including footnotes) to report all relevant information.

Charging a dishonored note back to the account of its maker serves two purposes. First, it removes the amount of the note from the Notes Receivable account and records the dishonored note in the maker's account. Second, and more important, if the maker of the dishonored note applies for credit in the future, his or her account will reveal all past dealings, including the dishonored note. Restoring the account also reminds the company to continue collection efforts from Hart for both principal and interest. The entry records the full amount, including interest, to ensure that it is included in collection efforts.

Recording End-of-Period Interest Adjustment   When notes receivable are outstanding at the end of a period, any accrued interest earned is computed and recorded. To illustrate, on December 16, TechCom accepts a $3,000, 60-day, 12% note from a customer in granting an extension on a past-due account. When TechCom's accounting period ends on December 31, $15 of interest has accrued on this note ($3,000 × 12% × 15/360). The following adjusting entry records this revenue.

Assets = Liabilities + Equity
+15   +15

Dec. 31	Interest Receivable	15	
	Interest Revenue		15
	To record accrued interest earned.		

Interest Revenue appears on the income statement, and Interest Receivable appears on the balance sheet as a current asset. When the December 16 note is collected on February 14, TechCom's entry to record the cash receipt is

Feb. 14	Cash	3,060	
	Interest Revenue		45
	Interest Receivable		15
	Notes Receivable		3,000
	Received payment of note and its interest.		

Assets = Liabilities + Equity
+3,060   +45
−15
−3,000

Total interest earned on the 60-day note is $60. The $15 credit to Interest Receivable on February 14 reflects the collection of the interest accrued from the December 31 adjusting entry. The $45 interest earned reflects TechCom's revenue from holding the note from January 1 to February 14 of the current period.

Fraud

Skimming. *Skimming* refers to stealing money from a cash register, a customer's payment, or refunds received. A point-of-sale employee who operates a cash register is especially at risk for skimming. For example, a cash register employee might receive $900 cash but only ring up $600 on the register (or nothing), which enables the employee to steal $300 cash (or the entire amount). A crucial control is to require that each sale is entered into the register. Skimming is then revealed when the record on the register differs from the cash in the register. To ensure that *all* sales are recorded on the register, we use customer help by hanging a sign: "Sales without a receipt are free!"

Quick Check

Answers — p. 313 ✅

8. Irwin purchases $7,000 of merchandise from Stamford on December 16, 2011. Stamford accepts Irwin's $7,000, 90-day, 12% note as payment. Stamford's accounting period ends on December 31, and it does not make reversing entries. Prepare entries for Stamford on December 16, 2011, and December 31, 2011.

9. Using the information in Quick Check 8, prepare Stamford's March 16, 2012, entry if Irwin dishonors the note.

DISPOSAL OF RECEIVABLES

Companies can convert receivables to cash before they are due. Reasons for this include the need for cash or the desire not to be involved in collection activities. Converting receivables is usually done either by (1) selling them or (2) using them as security for a loan. A recent survey shows that about 20% of companies obtain cash from either selling receivables or pledging them as security. In some industries such as textiles, apparel and furniture, this is common practice.

C3 Explain how receivables can be converted to cash before maturity.

Selling Receivables

A company can sell all or a portion of its receivables to a finance company or bank. The buyer, called a *factor*, charges the seller a *factoring fee* and then the buyer takes ownership of the receivables and receives cash when they come due. By incurring a factoring fee, the seller receives cash earlier and can pass the risk of bad debts to the factor. The seller can also choose to avoid costs of billing and accounting for the receivables. To illustrate, if TechCom sells $20,000 of its accounts receivable and is charged a 4% factoring fee, it records this sale as follows.

Global: Firms in export sales increasingly sell their receivables to factors.

Aug. 15	Cash	19,200	
	Factoring Fee Expense	800	
	Accounts Receivable		20,000
	Sold accounts receivable for cash, less 4% fee.		

Assets = Liabilities + Equity
+19,200   −800
−20,000

The accounting for sales of notes receivable is similar to that for accounts receivable. The detailed entries are covered in advanced courses.

Pledging Receivables

A company can raise cash by borrowing money and *pledging* its receivables as security for the loan. Pledging receivables does not transfer the risk of bad debts to the lender because the borrower retains ownership of the receivables. If the borrower defaults on the loan, the lender has a right to be paid from the cash receipts of the receivable when collected. To illustrate, when TechCom borrows $35,000 and pledges its receivables as security, it records this transaction as follows.

Assets = Liabilities + Equity
+35,000   +35,000

Aug. 20	Cash	35,000	
	Notes Payable		35,000
	Borrowed money with a note secured by pledging receivables.		

Since pledged receivables are committed as security for a specific loan, the borrower's financial statements disclose the pledging of them. TechCom, for instance, includes the following note with its statements: Accounts receivable of $40,000 are pledged as security for a $35,000 note payable.

Decision Insight

What's the Proper Allowance?   How can we assess whether a company has properly estimated its allowance for uncollectibles? One way is to compute the ratio of the allowance account to the gross accounts receivable. When this ratio is analyzed over several consecutive periods, trends often emerge that reflect on the adequacy of the allowance amount. ■

GLOBAL VIEW

This section discusses similarities and differences between U.S. GAAP and IFRS regarding the recognition, measurement, and disposition of receivables.

Recognition of Receivables   Both U.S. GAAP and IFRS have similar asset criteria that apply to recognition of receivables. Further, receivables that arise from revenue-generating activities are subject to broadly similar criteria for U.S. GAAP and IFRS. Specifically, both refer to the realization principle and an earnings process. The realization principle under U.S. GAAP implies an *arm's-length transaction* occurs, whereas under IFRS this notion is applied in terms of reliable measurement and likelihood of economic benefits. Regarding U.S. GAAP's reference to an earnings process, IFRS instead refers to risk transfer and ownership reward. While these criteria are broadly similar, differences do exist, and they arise mainly from industry-specific guidance under U.S. GAAP, which is very limited under IFRS.

Valuation of Receivables   Both U.S. GAAP and IFRS require that receivables be reported net of estimated uncollectibles. Further, both systems require that the expense for estimated uncollectibles be recorded in the same period when any revenues from those receivables are recorded. This means that for accounts receivable, both U.S. GAAP and IFRS require the allowance method for uncollectibles (unless uncollectibles are immaterial). The allowance method using percent of sales, percent of receivables, and aging was explained in this chapter. Nokia reports the following for its allowance for uncollectibles:

NOKIA

Management specifically analyzes accounts receivables and historical bad debt, customer concentrations, customer creditworthiness, current economic trends and changes in our customer payment terms when evaluating the adequacy of the allowance.

Disposition of Receivables   Both U.S. GAAP and IFRS apply broadly similar rules in recording dispositions of receivables. Those rules are discussed in this chapter. We should be aware of an important difference in terminology. Companies reporting under U.S. GAAP disclose Bad Debts Expense, which is also referred to as Provision for Bad Debts or the Provision for Uncollectible Accounts. For U.S. GAAP, *provision* here refers to expense. Under IFRS, the term *provision* usually refers to a liability whose amount or timing (or both) is uncertain.

Accounts Receivable Turnover		**Decision Analysis**

For a company selling on credit, we want to assess both the quality and liquidity of its accounts receivable. *Quality* of receivables refers to the likelihood of collection without loss. Experience shows that the longer receivables are outstanding beyond their due date, the lower the likelihood of collection. *Liquidity* of receivables refers to the speed of collection. **Accounts receivable turnover** is a measure of both the quality and liquidity of accounts receivable. It indicates how often, on average, receivables are received and collected during the period. The formula for this ratio is shown in Exhibit 7.17.

A1 Compute accounts receivable turnover and use it to help assess financial condition.

$$\text{Accounts receivable turnover} = \frac{\text{Net sales}}{\text{Average accounts receivable, net}}$$

EXHIBIT 7.17

Accounts Receivable Turnover

We prefer to use net *credit* sales in the numerator because cash sales do not create receivables. However, since financial statements rarely report net credit sales, our analysis uses net sales. The denominator is the *average* accounts receivable balance, computed as (Beginning balance + Ending balance) ÷ 2. TechCom has an accounts receivable turnover of 5.1. This indicates its average accounts receivable balance is converted into cash 5.1 times during the period. Exhibit 7.18 shows graphically this turnover activity for TechCom.

5.1 times per year

Jan. Feb. March Apr. May June July Aug. Sept. Oct. Nov. Dec.

EXHIBIT 7.18

Rate of Accounts Receivable Turnover for TechCom

Accounts receivable turnover also reflects how well management is doing in granting credit to customers in a desire to increase sales. A high turnover in comparison with competitors suggests that management should consider using more liberal credit terms to increase sales. A low turnover suggests management should consider stricter credit terms and more aggressive collection efforts to avoid having its resources tied up in accounts receivable.

Point: Credit risk ratio is computed by dividing the Allowance for Doubtful Accounts by Accounts Receivable. The higher this ratio, the higher is credit risk.

To illustrate, we take fiscal year data from two competitors: Dell and Apple. Exhibit 7.19 shows accounts receivable turnover for both companies.

Company	Figure ($ millions)	2008	2007	2006	2005
Dell	Net sales	$61,101	$61,133	$57,420	$55,788
	Average accounts receivable, net	$ 5,346	$ 5,292	$ 4,352	$ 3,826
	Accounts receivable turnover	11.4	11.6	13.2	14.6
Apple	Net sales	$32,479	$24,006	$19,315	$13,931
	Average accounts receivable, net	$ 2,030	$ 1,445	$ 1,074	$ 835
	Accounts receivable turnover	16.0	16.6	18.0	16.7

EXHIBIT 7.19

Analysis Using Accounts Receivable Turnover

Dell's 2008 turnover is 11.4, computed as $61,101/$5,346 ($ millions). This means that Dell's average accounts receivable balance was converted into cash 11.4 times in 2008. Its turnover declined in 2008, as it has for each of the past 3 years. Apple's turnover exceeds that for Dell in each of the past 4 years. Is either company's turnover too high? Since sales are stable or markedly growing over this time period, each company's turnover rate does not appear to be too high. Instead, both Dell and Apple seem to be doing well in managing receivables. This is especially true given the recessionary period of 2008 and 2009. Turnover for competitors is generally in the range of 7 to 12 for this same period.[1]

■ **Decision Maker**   Answer — p. 312

Family Physician   Your medical practice is barely profitable, so you hire a health care analyst. The analyst highlights several points including the following: *"Accounts receivable turnover is too low. Tighter credit policies are recommended along with discontinuing service to those most delayed in payments."* How do you interpret these recommendations? What actions do you take? ■

DEMONSTRATION PROBLEM

Clayco Company completes the following selected transactions during year 2011.

July 14   Writes off a $750 account receivable arising from a sale to Briggs Company that dates to 10 months ago. (Clayco Company uses the allowance method.)

      30   Clayco Company receives a $1,000, 90-day, 10% note in exchange for merchandise sold to Sumrell Company (the merchandise cost $600).

Aug. 15   Receives $2,000 cash plus a $10,000 note from JT Co. in exchange for merchandise that sells for $12,000 (its cost is $8,000). The note is dated August 15, bears 12% interest, and matures in 120 days.

Nov. 1   Completed a $200 credit card sale with a 4% fee (the cost of sales is $150). The cash is received immediately from the credit card company.

       3   Sumrell Company refuses to pay the note that was due to Clayco Company on October 28. Prepare the journal entry to charge the dishonored note plus accrued interest to Sumrell Company's accounts receivable.

       5   Completed a $500 credit card sale with a 5% fee (the cost of sales is $300). The payment from the credit card company is received on Nov. 9.

      15   Received the full amount of $750 from Briggs Company that was previously written off on July 14. Record the bad debts recovery.

Dec. 13   Received payment of principal plus interest from JT for the August 15 note.

Required

1. Prepare journal entries to record these transactions on Clayco Company's books.

2. Prepare an adjusting journal entry as of December 31, 2011, assuming the following:

   a. Bad debts are estimated to be $20,400 by aging accounts receivable. The unadjusted balance of the Allowance for Doubtful Accounts is $1,000 debit.

   b. Alternatively, assume that bad debts are estimated using the percent of sales method. The Allowance for Doubtful Accounts had a $1,000 debit balance before adjustment, and the company estimates bad debts to be 1% of its credit sales of $2,000,000.

PLANNING THE SOLUTION

● Examine each transaction to determine the accounts affected, and then record the entries.

● For the year-end adjustment, record the bad debts expense for the two approaches.

---

[1] As an estimate of *average days' sales uncollected,* we compute how many days (*on average*) it takes to collect receivables as follows: 365 days ÷ accounts receivable turnover. An increase in this *average collection period* can signal a decline in customers' financial condition.

SOLUTION TO DEMONSTRATION PROBLEM

1.

Date	Account	Debit	Credit
July 14	Allowance for Doubtful Accounts	750	
	Accounts Receivable—Briggs Co.		750
	Wrote off an uncollectible account.		
July 30	Notes Receivable—Sumrell Co.	1,000	
	Sales		1,000
	Sold merchandise for a 90-day, 10% note.		
July 30	Cost of Goods Sold	600	
	Merchandise Inventory		600
	To record the cost of July 30 sale.		
Aug. 15	Cash	2,000	
	Notes Receivable—JT Co.	10,000	
	Sales		12,000
	Sold merchandise to customer for $2,000 cash and $10,000 note.		
Aug. 15	Cost of Goods Sold	8,000	
	Merchandise Inventory		8,000
	To record the cost of Aug. 15 sale.		
Nov. 1	Cash	192	
	Credit Card Expense	8	
	Sales		200
	To record credit card sale less a 4% credit card expense.		
Nov. 1	Cost of Goods Sold	150	
	Merchandise Inventory		150
	To record the cost of Nov. 1 sale.		
Nov. 3	Accounts Receivable—Sumrell Co.	1,025	
	Interest Revenue		25
	Notes Receivable—Sumrell Co.		1,000
	To charge account of Sumrell Company for a $1,000 dishonored note and interest of $1,000 × 10% × 90/360.		
Nov. 5	Accounts Receivable—Credit Card Co.	475	
	Credit Card Expense	25	
	Sales		500
	To record credit card sale less a 5% credit card expense.		
Nov. 5	Cost of Goods Sold	300	
	Merchandise Inventory		300
	To record the cost of Nov. 5 sale.		
Nov. 9	Cash	475	
	Accounts Receivable—Credit Card Co.		475
	To record cash receipt from Nov. 5 sale.		
Nov. 15	Accounts Receivable—Briggs Co.	750	
	Allowance for Doubtful Accounts		750
	To reinstate the account of Briggs Company previously written off.		
Nov. 15	Cash	750	
	Accounts Receivable—Briggs Co.		750
	Cash received in full payment of account.		
Dec. 13	Cash	10,400	
	Interest Revenue		400
	Note Receivable—JT Co.		10,000
	Collect note with interest of $10,000 × 12% × 120/360.		

2a. Aging of accounts receivable method.

Dec. 31	Bad Debts Expense	21,400	
	Allowance for Doubtful Accounts		21,400
	To adjust allowance account from a $1,000		
	debit balance to a $20,400 credit balance.		

2b. Percent of sales method.*

Dec. 31	Bad Debts Expense	20,000	
	Allowance for Doubtful Accounts		20,000
	To provide for bad debts as 1% × $2,000,000		
	in credit sales.		

* For the income statement approach, which requires estimating bad debts as a percent of sales or credit sales, the Allowance account balance is *not* considered when making the adjusting entry.

Summary

C1 **Describe accounts receivable and how they occur and are recorded.** Accounts receivable are amounts due from customers for credit sales. A subsidiary ledger lists amounts owed by each customer. Credit sales arise from at least two sources: (1) sales on credit and (2) credit card sales. *Sales on credit* refers to a company's granting credit directly to customers. Credit card sales involve customers' use of third-party credit cards.

C2 **Describe a note receivable, the computation of its maturity date, and the recording of its existence.** A note receivable is a written promise to pay a specified amount of money at a definite future date. The maturity date is the day the note (principal and interest) must be repaid. Interest rates are normally stated in annual terms. The amount of interest on the note is computed by expressing time as a fraction of one year and multiplying the note's principal by this fraction and the annual interest rate. A note received is recorded at its principal amount by debiting the Notes Receivable account. The credit amount is to the asset, product, or service provided in return for the note.

C3 **Explain how receivables can be converted to cash before maturity.** Receivables can be converted to cash before maturity in three ways. First, a company can sell accounts receivable to a factor, who charges a factoring fee. Second, a company can borrow money by signing a note payable that is secured by pledging the accounts receivable. Third, notes receivable can be discounted at (sold to) a financial institution.

A1 **Compute accounts receivable turnover and use it to help assess financial condition.** Accounts receivable turnover is a measure of both the quality and liquidity of accounts receivable.

The accounts receivable turnover measure indicates how often, on average, receivables are received and collected during the period. Accounts receivable turnover is computed as net sales divided by average accounts receivable.

P1 **Apply the direct write-off method to account for accounts receivable.** The direct write-off method charges Bad Debts Expense when accounts are written off as uncollectible. This method is acceptable only when the amount of bad debts expense is immaterial.

P2 **Apply the allowance method and estimate uncollectibles based on sales and accounts receivable.** Under the allowance method, bad debts expense is recorded with an adjustment at the end of each accounting period that debits the Bad Debts Expense account and credits the Allowance for Doubtful Accounts. The uncollectible accounts are later written off with a debit to the Allowance for Doubtful Accounts. Uncollectibles are estimated by focusing on either (1) the income statement relation between bad debts expense and credit sales or (2) the balance sheet relation between accounts receivable and the allowance for doubtful accounts. The first approach emphasizes the matching principle using the income statement. The second approach emphasizes realizable value of accounts receivable using the balance sheet.

P3 **Record the honoring and dishonoring of a note and adjustments for interest.** When a note is honored, the payee debits the money received and credits both Notes Receivable and Interest Revenue. Dishonored notes are credited to Notes Receivable and debited to Accounts Receivable (to the account of the maker in an attempt to collect), and Interest Revenue is recorded for interest earned for the time the note is held.

Guidance Answers to Decision Maker and Decision Ethics

Entrepreneur Analysis of credit card sales should weigh the benefits against the costs. The primary benefit is the potential to increase sales by attracting customers who prefer the convenience of credit cards. The primary cost is the fee charged by the credit card company for providing this service. Analysis should therefore estimate the expected increase in dollar sales from allowing credit card sales and then subtract (1) the normal costs and expenses and (2) the credit card fees associated with this expected increase in dollar sales. If your analysis shows an increase in profit from allowing credit card sales, your store should probably accept them.

Labor Union Chief   Yes, this information is likely to impact your negotiations. The obvious question is why the company markedly increased this allowance. The large increase in this allowance means a substantial increase in bad debts expense *and* a decrease in earnings. This change (coming immediately prior to labor contract discussions) also raises concerns since it reduces the union's bargaining power for increased compensation. You want to ask management for supporting documentation justifying this increase. You also want data for two or three prior years and similar data from competitors.

These data should give you some sense of whether the change in the allowance for uncollectibles is justified.

Family Physician   The recommendations are twofold. First, the analyst suggests more stringent screening of patients' credit standing. Second, the analyst suggests dropping patients who are most overdue in payments. You are likely bothered by both suggestions. They are probably financially wise recommendations, but you are troubled by eliminating services to those less able to pay. One alternative is to follow the recommendations while implementing a care program directed at patients less able to pay for services. This allows you to continue services to patients less able to pay and lets you discontinue services to patients able but unwilling to pay.

Guidance Answers to Quick Checks

1. If cash is immediately received when credit card sales receipts are deposited, the company debits Cash at the time of sale. If the company does not receive payment until after it submits receipts to the credit card company, it debits Accounts Receivable at the time of sale. (Cash is later debited when payment is received from the credit card company.)

2. Credit card expenses are usually *recorded* and *incurred* at the time of their related sales, not when cash is received from the credit card company.

3. If possible, bad debts expense must be matched with the sales that gave rise to the accounts receivable. This requires that companies estimate future bad debts at the end of each period before they learn which accounts are uncollectible.

4. Realizable value (also called *net realizable value*).

5. The estimated amount of bad debts expense cannot be credited to the Accounts Receivable account because the specific customer accounts that will prove uncollectible cannot yet be identified and removed from the accounts receivable subsidiary ledger. Moreover, if only the Accounts Receivable account is credited, its balance would not equal the sum of its subsidiary account balances.

6.

Dec. 31	Bad Debts Expense	5,702	
	Allowance for Doubtful Accounts		5,702

7.

Jan. 10	Allowance for Doubtful Accounts	300	
	Accounts Receivable—Cool Jam		300
Apr. 12	Accounts Receivable—Cool Jam	300	
	Allowance for Doubtful Accounts		300
Apr. 12	Cash	300	
	Accounts Receivable—Cool Jam		300

8.

Dec. 16	Note Receivable—Irwin	7,000	
	Sales		7,000
Dec. 31	Interest Receivable	35	
	Interest Revenue		35
	($7,000 × 12% × 15/360)		

9.

Mar. 16	Accounts Receivable—Irwin	7,210	
	Interest Revenue		175
	Interest Receivable		35
	Notes Receivable—Irwin		7,000

Key Terms

Accounts receivable (p. 294)
Accounts receivable turnover (p. 309)
Aging of accounts receivable (p. 302)
Allowance for Doubtful Accounts (p. 299)
Allowance method (p. 298)
Bad debts (p. 297)
Credit risk ratio (p. 309)

Direct write-off method (p. 297)
Full disclosure principle (p. 306)
Interest (p. 304)
Maker of the note (p. 304)
Matching (expense recognition) principle (p. 298)
Materiality constraint (p. 298)

Maturity date of a note (p. 304)
Payee of the note (p. 304)
Principal of a note (p. 304)
Promissory note (or note) (p. 304)
Realizable value (p. 299)

Additional quiz questions are available at the book's Website.

1. A company's Accounts Receivable balance at its December 31 year-end is $125,650, and its Allowance for Doubtful Accounts has a credit balance of $328 before year-end adjustment. Its net sales are $572,300. It estimates that 4% of outstanding accounts receivable are uncollectible. What amount of Bad Debts Expense is recorded at December 31?
- **a.** $5,354
- **b.** $328
- **c.** $5,026
- **d.** $4,698
- **e.** $34,338

2. A company's Accounts Receivable balance at its December 31 year-end is $489,300, and its Allowance for Doubtful Accounts has a debit balance of $554 before year-end adjustment. Its net sales are $1,300,000. It estimates that 6% of outstanding accounts receivable are uncollectible. What amount of Bad Debts Expense is recorded at December 31?
- **a.** $29,912
- **b.** $28,804
- **c.** $78,000
- **d.** $29,358
- **e.** $554

3. Total interest to be earned on a $7,500, 5%, 90-day note is
- **a.** $93.75
- **b.** $375.00
- **c.** $1,125.00
- **d.** $31.25
- **e.** $125.00

4. A company receives a $9,000, 8%, 60-day note. The maturity value of the note is
- **a.** $120
- **b.** $9,000
- **c.** $9,120
- **d.** $720
- **e.** $9,720

5. A company has net sales of $489,600 and average accounts receivable of $40,800. What is its accounts receivable turnover?
- **a.** 0.08
- **b.** 30.41
- **c.** 1,341.00
- **d.** 12.00
- **e.** 111.78

Icon denotes assignments that involve decision making.

Discussion Questions

1. How do sellers benefit from allowing their customers to use credit cards?

2. Why does the direct write-off method of accounting for bad debts usually fail to match revenues and expenses?

3. Explain the accounting constraint of materiality.

4. Explain why writing off a bad debt against the Allowance for Doubtful Accounts does not reduce the estimated realizable value of a company's accounts receivable.

5. Why does the Bad Debts Expense account usually not have the same adjusted balance as the Allowance for Doubtful Accounts?

6. Why might a business prefer a note receivable to an account receivable?

7. Refer to the financial statements and notes of **Research In Motion** in Appendix A. In its presentation of accounts receivable on the balance sheet, how does it   *RIM*

title accounts receivable? What does it report for its allowance as of February 27, 2010?

8. Refer to the balance sheet of **Apple** in Appendix A. Does it use the direct write-off method or allowance method in accounting for its Accounts Receivable? What is the realizable value of its receivable's balance as of September 26, 2009?   *Apple*

9. Refer to the financial statements of **Palm** in Appendix A. What are Palm's gross accounts receivable at May 31, 2009? What percentage of its accounts receivable does it believe to be uncollectible at this date?   *Palm*

10. Refer to the December 31, 2009, financial statements of **Nokia** in Appendix A. What does it title its accounts receivable on its statement of financial position? What percent of its accounts receivable does it believe to be uncollectible?   *NOKIA*

connect

QUICK STUDY

QS 7-1
Credit card sales

C1

Prepare journal entries for the following credit card sales transactions (the company uses the perpetual inventory system).

1. Sold $10,000 of merchandise, that cost $7,500, on MasterCard credit cards. The net cash receipts from sales are immediately deposited in the seller's bank account. MasterCard charges a 5% fee.

2. Sold $3,000 of merchandise, that cost $1,500, on an assortment of credit cards. Net cash receipts are received 7 days later, and a 4% fee is charged.

Milner Corp. uses the allowance method to account for uncollectibles. On October 31, it wrote off a $1,000 account of a customer, C. Schaub. On December 9, it receives a $200 payment from Schaub.

QS 7-2
Allowance method for bad debts
P2

1. Prepare the journal entry or entries for October 31.
2. Prepare the journal entry or entries for December 9; assume no additional money is expected from Schaub.

Wecker Company's year-end unadjusted trial balance shows accounts receivable of $89,000, allowance for doubtful accounts of $500 (credit), and sales of $270,000. Uncollectibles are estimated to be 1.5% of accounts receivable.

QS 7-3
Percent of accounts receivable method
P2

1. Prepare the December 31 year-end adjusting entry for uncollectibles.
2. What amount would have been used in the year-end adjusting entry if the allowance account had a year-end unadjusted debit balance of $200?

Assume the same facts as in QS 7-3, except that Wecker estimates uncollectibles as 1.0% of sales. Prepare the December 31 year-end adjusting entry for uncollectibles.

QS 7-4
Percent of sales method   P2

On August 2, 2011, JLK Co. receives a $5,500, 90-day, 12% note from customer Tom Menke as payment on his $9,000 account. (1) Compute the maturity date for this note. (2) Prepare JLK's journal entry for August 2.

QS 7-5
Note receivable   C2

Refer to the information in QS 7-5 and prepare the journal entry assuming the note is honored by the customer on October 31, 2011.

QS 7-6
Note receivable   P3

Dekon Company's December 31 year-end unadjusted trial balance shows a $8,000 balance in Notes Receivable. This balance is from one 6% note dated December 1, with a period of 45 days. Prepare any necessary journal entries for December 31 and for the note's maturity date assuming it is honored.

QS 7-7
Note receivable   P3

Record the sale by Kroll Company of $1,000 in accounts receivable on May 1. Kroll is charged a 3% factoring fee.

QS 7-8
Disposing receivables   C3

Krugg Company determines on May 1 that it cannot collect $1,000 of its accounts receivable from its customer P. Carroll. Apply the direct write-off method to record this loss as of May 1.

QS 7-9
Direct write-off method   P1

Refer to the information in QS 7-9. On May 30, P. Carroll unexpectedly paid his account in full to Krugg Company. Record Krugg's entry(ies) to reflect this recovery of this bad debt.

QS 7-10
Recovering a bad debt   P1

The following data are taken from the comparative balance sheets of Fulton Company. Compute and interpret its accounts receivable turnover for year 2011 (competitors average a turnover of 7.5).

QS 7-11
Accounts receivable turnover

A1

	2011	2010
Accounts receivable, net	$152,900	$133,700
Net sales	754,200	810,600

Answer each of the following related to international accounting standards.

QS 7-12
International accounting standards

C1

a. Explain (in general terms) how the accounting for recognition of receivables is different between IFRS and U.S. GAAP.
b. Explain (in general terms) how the accounting for valuation of receivables is different between IFRS and U.S. GAAP.

EXERCISES

Exercise 7-1
Accounting for credit card sales
C1

Petri Company uses the perpetual inventory system and allows customers to use two credit cards in charging purchases. With the Omni Bank Card, Petri receives an immediate credit to its account when it deposits sales receipts. Omni assesses a 4% service charge for credit card sales. The second credit card that Petri accepts is the Continental Card. Petri sends its accumulated receipts to Continental on a weekly basis and is paid by Continental about a week later. Continental assesses a 2.5% charge on sales for using its card. Prepare journal entries to record the following selected credit card transactions of Petri Company.

Apr. 8   Sold merchandise for $9,200 (that had cost $6,800) and accepted the customer's Omni Bank Card. The Omni receipts are immediately deposited in Petri's bank account.
     12   Sold merchandise for $5,400 (that had cost $3,500) and accepted the customer's Continental Card. Transferred $5,400 of credit card receipts to Continental, requesting payment.
     20   Received Continental's check for the April 12 billing, less the service charge.

Exercise 7-2
Accounts receivable subsidiary ledger; schedule of accounts receivable
C1

Sami Company recorded the following selected transactions during November 2011.

Nov. 5	Accounts Receivable—Surf Shop	4,417	
	Sales		4,417
10	Accounts Receivable—Yum Enterprises	1,250	
	Sales		1,250
13	Accounts Receivable—Matt Albin.................	733	
	Sales		733
21	Sales Returns and Allowances	189	
	Accounts Receivable—Matt Albin		189
30	Accounts Receivable—Surf Shop	2,606	
	Sales		2,606

1. Open a general ledger having T-accounts for Accounts Receivable, Sales, and Sales Returns and Allowances. Also open an accounts receivable subsidiary ledger having a T-account for each customer. Post these entries to both the general ledger and the accounts receivable ledger.

Check Accounts Receivable ending balance, $8,817

2. Prepare a schedule of accounts receivable (see Exhibit 7.4) and compare its total with the balance of the Accounts Receivable controlling account as of November 30.

Exercise 7-3
Direct write-off method
P1

Diablo Company applies the direct write-off method in accounting for uncollectible accounts. Prepare journal entries to record the following selected transactions of Diablo.

June 11   Diablo determines that it cannot collect $9,000 of its accounts receivable from its customer Chaffey Company.
      29   Chaffey Company unexpectedly pays its account in full to Diablo Company. Diablo records its recovery of this bad debt.

Exercise 7-4
Percent of sales method; write-off
P2

At year-end (December 31), Alvare Company estimates its bad debts as 0.5% of its annual credit sales of $875,000. Alvare records its Bad Debts Expense for that estimate. On the following February 1, Alvare decides that the $420 account of P. Coble is uncollectible and writes it off as a bad debt. On June 5, Coble unexpectedly pays the amount previously written off. Prepare the journal entries of Alvare to record these transactions and events of December 31, February 1, and June 5.

Exercise 7-5
Percent of accounts receivable method
P2

At each calendar year-end, Cabool Supply Co. uses the percent of accounts receivable method to estimate bad debts. On December 31, 2011, it has outstanding accounts receivable of $53,000, and it estimates that 4% will be uncollectible. Prepare the adjusting entry to record bad debts expense for year 2011 under the assumption that the Allowance for Doubtful Accounts has (*a*) a $915 credit balance before the adjustment and (*b*) a $1,332 debit balance before the adjustment.

Exercise 7-6
Aging of receivables method
P2

Hecter Company estimates uncollectible accounts using the allowance method at December 31. It prepared the following aging of receivables analysis.

			Days Past Due			
	Total	0	1 to 30	31 to 60	61 to 90	Over 90
Accounts receivable	$190,000	$132,000	$30,000	$12,000	$6,000	$10,000
Percent uncollectible		1%	2%	4%	7%	12%

a. Estimate the balance of the Allowance for Doubtful Accounts using the aging of accounts receivable method.

b. Prepare the adjusting entry to record Bad Debts Expense using the estimate from part *a*. Assume the unadjusted balance in the Allowance for Doubtful Accounts is a $600 credit.

c. Prepare the adjusting entry to record Bad Debts Expense using the estimate from part *a*. Assume the unadjusted balance in the Allowance for Doubtful Accounts is a $400 debit.

Refer to the information in Exercise 7-6 to complete the following requirements.

a. Estimate the balance of the Allowance for Doubtful Accounts assuming the company uses 3.5% of total accounts receivable to estimate uncollectibles, instead of the aging of receivables method.

b. Prepare the adjusting entry to record Bad Debts Expense using the estimate from part *a*. Assume the unadjusted balance in the Allowance for Doubtful Accounts is a $300 credit.

c. Prepare the adjusting entry to record Bad Debts Expense using the estimate from part *a*. Assume the unadjusted balance in the Allowance for Doubtful Accounts is a $200 debit.

Exercise 7-7
Percent of receivables method
P2

Refer to the information in Exercise 7-6 to complete the following requirements.

a. On February 1 of the next period, the company determined that $1,900 in customer accounts is uncollectible; specifically, $400 for Oxford Co. and $1,500 for Brookes Co. Prepare the journal entry to write off those accounts.

b. On June 5 of that next period, the company unexpectedly received a $400 payment on a customer account, Oxford Company, that had previously been written off in part *a*. Prepare the entries necessary to reinstate the account and to record the cash received.

Exercise 7-8
Writing off receivables
P2

At December 31, GreenTea Company reports the following results for its calendar-year.

Cash sales	$1,200,000
Credit sales	900,000

Its year-end unadjusted trial balance includes the following items.

Accounts receivable	$195,000 debit
Allowance for doubtful accounts	3,000 debit

a. Prepare the adjusting entry to record Bad Debts Expense assuming uncollectibles are estimated to be 1.5% of credit sales.

b. Prepare the adjusting entry to record Bad Debts Expense assuming uncollectibles are estimated to be 0.5% of total sales.

c. Prepare the adjusting entry to record Bad Debts Expense assuming uncollectibles are estimated to be 6% of year-end accounts receivable.

Exercise 7-9
Estimating bad debts
P2

Check Dr. Bad Debts Expense: (*a*) $13,500

(*c*) $14,700

On June 30, Roman Co. has $125,900 of accounts receivable. Prepare journal entries to record the following selected July transactions. Also prepare any footnotes to the July 31 financial statements that result from these transactions. (The company uses the perpetual inventory system.)

July	4	Sold $6,295 of merchandise (that had cost $4,000) to customers on credit.
	9	Sold $18,000 of accounts receivable to Center Bank. Center charges a 4% factoring fee.
	17	Received $3,436 cash from customers in payment on their accounts.
	27	Borrowed $10,000 cash from Center Bank, pledging $13,000 of accounts receivable as security for the loan.

Exercise 7-10
Selling and pledging accounts receivable
C3

Prepare journal entries to record these selected transactions for Eduardo Company.

Nov.	1	Accepted a $5,000, 180-day, 6% note dated November 1 from Melosa Allen in granting a time extension on her past-due account receivable.
Dec.	31	Adjusted the year-end accounts for the accrued interest earned on the Allen note.
Apr.	30	Allen honors her note when presented for payment; February has 28 days for the current year.

Exercise 7-11
Honoring a note
P3

Exercise 7-12

Dishonoring a note

P3

Prepare journal entries to record the following selected transactions of Paloma Company.

Mar. 21   Accepted a $3,100, 180-day, 10% note dated March 21 from Salma Hernandez in granting a time extension on her past-due account receivable.

Sept. 17 Hernandez dishonors her note when it is presented for payment.

Dec. 31   After exhausting all legal means of collection, Paloma Company writes off Hernandez's account against the Allowance for Doubtful Accounts.

Exercise 7-13

Notes receivable transactions

C2

Check   Dec. 31, Cr. Interest
Revenue $40

Prepare journal entries for the following selected transactions of Deshawn Company for 2010.

2010

Dec. 13   Accepted a $10,000, 45-day, 8% note dated December 13 in granting Latisha Clark a time extension on her past-due account receivable.

  31   Prepared an adjusting entry to record the accrued interest on the Clark note.

Exercise 7-14

Notes receivable transactions

P3

Check   Jan. 27, Dr. Cash $10,100

June 1, Dr. Cash $4,100

Refer to the information in Exercise 7-13 and prepare the journal entries for the following selected transactions of Deshawn Company for 2011.

2011

Jan. 27   Received Clark's payment for principal and interest on the note dated December 13.

Mar. 3   Accepted a $4,000, 10%, 90-day note dated March 3 in granting a time extension on the past-due account receivable of Shandi Company.

  17   Accepted a $2,000, 30-day, 9% note dated March 17 in granting Juan Torres a time extension on his past-due account receivable.

Apr. 16   Torres dishonors his note when presented for payment.

May 1   Wrote off the Torres account against the Allowance for Doubtful Accounts.

June 1   Received the Shandi payment for principal and interest on the note dated March 3.

Exercise 7-15

Accounts receivable turnover

A1

The following information is from the annual financial statements of Waseem Company. Compute its accounts receivable turnover for 2010 and 2011. Compare the two years results and give a possible explanation for any change (competitors average a turnover of 11).

	2011	2010	2009
Net sales	$305,000	$236,000	$288,000
Accounts receivable, net (year-end)	22,900	20,700	17,400

Exercise 7-16

Accounting for bad debts following IFRS

P2

Hitachi, Ltd., reports total revenues of ¥10,000,369 million for its fiscal year ending March 31, 2009, and its March 31, 2009, unadjusted trial balance reports a debit balance for trade receivables (gross) of ¥2,179,764 million.

a. Prepare the adjusting entry to record its Bad Debts Expense assuming uncollectibles are estimated to be 0.4% of total revenues and its unadjusted trial balance reports a credit balance of ¥10,000 million.

b. Prepare the adjusting entry to record Bad Debts Expense assuming uncollectibles are estimated to be 2.1% of year-end trade receivables (gross) and its unadjusted trial balance reports a credit balance of ¥10,000 million.

connect

PROBLEM SET A

Problem 7-1A

Sales on account and credit card sales

C1

Atlas Co. allows select customers to make purchases on credit. Its other customers can use either of two credit cards: Zisa or Access. Zisa deducts a 3% service charge for sales on its credit card and credits the bank account of Atlas immediately when credit card receipts are deposited. Atlas deposits the Zisa credit card receipts each business day. When customers use Access credit cards, Atlas accumulates the receipts for several days before submitting them to Access for payment. Access deducts a 2% service charge and usually pays within one week of being billed. Atlas completes the following transactions in June. (The terms of all credit sales are 2/15, n/30, and all sales are recorded at the gross price.)

June 4   Sold $750 of merchandise (that had cost $500) on credit to Anne Cianci.

  5   Sold $5,900 of merchandise (that had cost $3,200) to customers who used their Zisa cards.

6   Sold $4,800 of merchandise (that had cost $2,800) to customers who used their Access cards.
8   Sold $3,200 of merchandise (that had cost $1,900) to customers who used their Access cards.
10 Submitted Access card receipts accumulated since June 6 to the credit card company for payment.
13 Wrote off the account of Nakia Wells against the Allowance for Doubtful Accounts. The $329 balance in Wells's account stemmed from a credit sale in October of last year.
17 Received the amount due from Access.
18 Received Cianci's check in full payment for the purchase of June 4.

Check   June 17, Dr. Cash $7,840

Required

Prepare journal entries to record the preceding transactions and events. (The company uses the perpetual inventory system. Round amounts to the nearest dollar.)

Lopez Company began operations on January 1, 2010, and it estimates uncollectible accounts using the allowance method. During its first two years, the company completed a number of transactions involving sales on credit, accounts receivable collections, and bad debts. These transactions are summarized as follows.

Problem 7-2A
Accounts receivable transactions and bad debts adjustments

C1 P2

2010

a. Sold $1,803,750 of merchandise (that had cost $1,475,000) on credit, terms n/30.
b. Wrote off $20,300 of uncollectible accounts receivable.
c. Received $789,200 cash in payment of accounts receivable.
d. In adjusting the accounts on December 31, the company estimated that 1.5% of accounts receivable will be uncollectible.

Check   (d) Dr. Bad Debts Expense $35,214

2011

e. Sold $1,825,700 of merchandise (that had cost $1,450,000) on credit, terms n/30.
f. Wrote off $28,800 of uncollectible accounts receivable.
g. Received $1,304,800 cash in payment of accounts receivable.
h. In adjusting the accounts on December 31, the company estimated that 1.5% of accounts receivable will be uncollectible.

(h) Dr. Bad Debts Expense $36,181

Required

Prepare journal entries to record Lopez's 2010 and 2011 summarized transactions and its year-end adjustments to record bad debts expense. (The company uses the perpetual inventory system. Round amounts to the nearest dollar.)

At December 31, 2011, Ethan Company reports the following results for its calendar-year.

Cash sales	$1,803,750
Credit sales	3,534,000

In addition, its unadjusted trial balance includes the following items.

Accounts receivable	$1,070,100 debit
Allowance for doubtful accounts	15,750 debit

Problem 7-3A
Estimating and reporting bad debts

P2

Required

1. Prepare the adjusting entry for this company to recognize bad debts under each of the following independent assumptions.
   a. Bad debts are estimated to be 2% of credit sales.
   b. Bad debts are estimated to be 1% of total sales.
   c. An aging analysis estimates that 5% of year-end accounts receivable are uncollectible.
2. Show how Accounts Receivable and the Allowance for Doubtful Accounts appear on its December 31, 2011, balance sheet given the facts in part 1a.
3. Show how Accounts Receivable and the Allowance for Doubtful Accounts appear on its December 31, 2011, balance sheet given the facts in part 1c.

Check   Bad Debts Expense: (1a) $70,680, (1c) $69,255

Problem 7-4A

Aging accounts receivable and accounting for bad debts

P2

Carmack Company has credit sales of $2.6 million for year 2011. On December 31, 2011, the company's Allowance for Doubtful Accounts has an unadjusted credit balance of $13,400. Carmack prepares a schedule of its December 31, 2011, accounts receivable by age. On the basis of past experience, it estimates the percent of receivables in each age category that will become uncollectible. This information is summarized here.

File Edit View Insert Format Tools Data Accounting Window Help		
December 31, 2011 Accounts Receivable	Age of Accounts Receivable	Expected Percent Uncollectible
$730,000	Not yet due	1.25%
354,000	1 to 30 days past due	2.00
76,000	31 to 60 days past due	6.50
48,000	61 to 90 days past due	32.75
12,000	Over 90 days past due	68.00

Required

1. Estimate the required balance of the Allowance for Doubtful Accounts at December 31, 2011, using the aging of accounts receivable method.

Check (2) Dr. Bad Debts Expense $31,625

2. Prepare the adjusting entry to record bad debts expense at December 31, 2011.

Analysis Component

3. On June 30, 2012, Carmack Company concludes that a customer's $3,750 receivable (created in 2011) is uncollectible and that the account should be written off. What effect will this action have on Carmack's 2012 net income? Explain.

Problem 7-5A

Analyzing and journalizing notes receivable transactions

C2 C3 P3

The following selected transactions are from Ohlde Company.

2010

Dec. 16   Accepted a $9,600, 60-day, 9% note dated this day in granting Todd Duke a time extension on his past-due account receivable.

    31   Made an adjusting entry to record the accrued interest on the Duke note.

2011

Check Feb. 14, Cr. Interest Revenue $108

Feb. 14   Received Duke's payment of principal and interest on the note dated December 16.

Mar. 2   Accepted an $4,120, 8%, 90-day note dated this day in granting a time extension on the past-due account receivable from Mare Co.

    17   Accepted a $2,400, 30-day, 7% note dated this day in granting Jolene Halaam a time extension on her past-due account receivable.

Apr. 16   Halaam dishonored her note when presented for payment.

June 2, Cr. Interest Revenue $82

June 2   Mare Co. refuses to pay the note that was due to Ohlde Co. on May 31. Prepare the journal entry to charge the dishonored note plus accrued interest to Mare Co.'s accounts receivable.

July 17   Received payment from Mare Co. for the maturity value of its dishonored note plus interest for 46 days beyond maturity at 8%.

Aug. 7   Accepted an $5,440, 90-day, 10% note dated this day in granting a time extension on the past-due account receivable of Birch and Byer Co.

Sept. 3   Accepted a $2,080, 60-day, 10% note dated this day in granting Kevin York a time extension on his past-due account receivable.

Nov. 2, Cr. Interest Revenue $35

Nov. 2   Received payment of principal plus interest from York for the September 3 note.

Nov. 5   Received payment of principal plus interest from Birch and Byer for the August 7 note.

Dec. 1   Wrote off the Jolene Halaam account against Allowance for Doubtful Accounts.

Required

1. Prepare journal entries to record these transactions and events. (Round amounts to the nearest dollar.)

Analysis Component

2. What reporting is necessary when a business pledges receivables as security for a loan and the loan is still outstanding at the end of the period? Explain the reason for this requirement and the accounting principle being satisfied.

Able Co. allows select customers to make purchases on credit. Its other customers can use either of two credit cards: Commerce Bank or Aztec. Commerce Bank deducts a 3% service charge for sales on its credit card and immediately credits the bank account of Able when credit card receipts are deposited. Able deposits the Commerce Bank credit card receipts each business day. When customers use the Aztec card, Able accumulates the receipts for several days and then submits them to Aztec for payment. Aztec deducts a 2% service charge and usually pays within one week of being billed. Able completed the following transactions in August (terms of all credit sales are 2/10, n/30; and all sales are recorded at the gross price).

Aug. 4 Sold $2,780 of merchandise (that had cost $1,750) on credit to Stacy Dalton.
10 Sold $3,248 of merchandise (that had cost $2,456) to customers who used their Commerce Bank credit cards.
11 Sold $1,575 of merchandise (that had cost $1,150) to customers who used their Aztec cards.
14 Received Dalton's check in full payment for the purchase of August 4.
15 Sold $2,960 of merchandise (that had cost $1,758) to customers who used their Aztec cards.
18 Submitted Aztec card receipts accumulated since August 11 to the credit card company for payment.
22 Wrote off the account of Ness City against the Allowance for Doubtful Accounts. The $398 balance in Ness City's account stemmed from a credit sale in November of last year.
25 Received the amount due from Aztec.

PROBLEM SET B

Problem 7-1B
Sales on account and credit card sales

C1

Check Aug. 25, Dr. Cash $4,444

Required

Prepare journal entries to record the preceding transactions and events. (The company uses the perpetual inventory system. Round amounts to the nearest dollar.)

Crist Co. began operations on January 1, 2010, and it estimates uncollectible accounts using the allowance method. It completed several transactions during 2010 and 2011 that involved sales on credit, accounts receivable collections, and bad debts. These transactions are summarized as follows.

Problem 7-2B
Accounts receivable transactions and bad debts adjustments

C1 P2

2010

a. Sold $673,490 of merchandise (that had cost $500,000) on credit, terms n/30.
b. Received $437,250 cash in payment of accounts receivable.
c. Wrote off $8,330 of uncollectible accounts receivable.
d. In adjusting the accounts on December 31, the company estimated that 1% of accounts receivable will be uncollectible.

Check (d) Dr. Bad Debts Expense
$10,609

2011

e. Sold $930,100 of merchandise (that had cost $650,000) on credit, terms n/30.
f. Received $890,220 cash in payment of accounts receivable.
g. Wrote off $10,090 of uncollectible accounts receivable.
h. In adjusting the accounts on December 31, the company estimated that 1% of accounts receivable will be uncollectible.

(h) Dr. Bad Debts Expense
$10,388

Required

Prepare journal entries to record Crist's 2010 and 2011 summarized transactions and its year-end adjusting entry to record bad debts expense. (The company uses the perpetual inventory system. Round amounts to the nearest dollar.)

At December 31, 2011, Klimek Company reports the following results for the year.

Problem 7-3B
Estimating and reporting bad debts

P2

Cash sales	....	$1,015,000
Credit sales	....	1,241,000

In addition, its unadjusted trial balance includes the following items.

Accounts receivable	....	$475,000 debit
Allowance for doubtful accounts	....	5,200 credit

Required

1. Prepare the adjusting entry for Klimek Co. to recognize bad debts under each of the following independent assumptions.

   a. Bad debts are estimated to be 2.5% of credit sales.

   b. Bad debts are estimated to be 1.5% of total sales.

   c. An aging analysis estimates that 6% of year-end accounts receivable are uncollectible.

2. Show how Accounts Receivable and the Allowance for Doubtful Accounts appear on its December 31, 2011, balance sheet given the facts in part 1*a*.

3. Show how Accounts Receivable and the Allowance for Doubtful Accounts appear on its December 31, 2011, balance sheet given the facts in part 1*c*.

Check Bad debts expense: (1*b*) $33,840, (1*c*) $23,300

Problem 7-4B

Aging accounts receivable and accounting for bad debts

P2

Quisp Company has credit sales of $3.5 million for year 2011. At December 31, 2011, the company's Allowance for Doubtful Accounts has an unadjusted debit balance of $4,100. Quisp prepares a schedule of its December 31, 2011, accounts receivable by age. On the basis of past experience, it estimates the percent of receivables in each age category that will become uncollectible. This information is summarized here.

December 31, 2011 Accounts Receivable	Age of Accounts Receivable	Expected Percent Uncollectible
$296,400	Not yet due	2.0%
177,800	1 to 30 days past due	4.0
58,000	31 to 60 days past due	8.5
7,600	61 to 90 days past due	39.0
3,700	Over 90 days past due	82.0

Required

1. Compute the required balance of the Allowance for Doubtful Accounts at December 31, 2011, using the aging of accounts receivable method.

2. Prepare the adjusting entry to record bad debts expense at December 31, 2011.

Check (2) Dr. Bad Debts Expense $28,068

Analysis Component

3. On July 31, 2012, Quisp concludes that a customer's $2,345 receivable (created in 2011) is uncollectible and that the account should be written off. What effect will this action have on Quisp's 2012 net income? Explain.

Problem 7-5B

Analyzing and journalizing notes receivable transactions

C2 C3 P3

The following selected transactions are from Seeker Company.

2010

Nov. 1 Accepted a $4,800, 90-day, 8% note dated this day in granting Julie Stephens a time extension on her past-due account receivable.

Dec. 31 Made an adjusting entry to record the accrued interest on the Stephens note.

2011

Jan. 30 Received Stephens's payment for principal and interest on the note dated November 1.

Feb. 28 Accepted a $12,600, 6%, 30-day note dated this day in granting a time extension on the past-due account receivable from Kramer Co.

Mar. 1 Accepted a $6,200, 60-day, 8% note dated this day in granting Shelly Myers a time extension on her past-due account receivable.

      30 The Kramer Co. dishonored its note when presented for payment.

April 30 Received payment of principal plus interest from Myers for the March 1 note.

June 15 Accepted a $2,000, 60-day, 10% note dated this day in granting a time extension on the past-due account receivable of Rhonda Rye.

      21 Accepted a $9,500, 90-day, 12% note dated this day in granting J. Striker a time extension on his past-due account receivable.

Aug. 14 Received payment of principal plus interest from R. Rye for the note of June 15.

Sep. 19 Received payment of principal plus interest from J. Striker for the June 21 note.

Nov. 30 Wrote off Kramer's account against Allowance for Doubtful Accounts.

Check Jan. 30, Cr. Interest Revenue $32

April 30, Cr. Interest Revenue $83

Sep. 19, Cr. Interest Revenue $285

Required

1. Prepare journal entries to record these transactions and events. (Round amounts to the nearest dollar.)

Analysis Component

2. What reporting is necessary when a business pledges receivables as security for a loan and the loan is still outstanding at the end of the period? Explain the reason for this requirement and the accounting principle being satisfied.

(This serial problem began in Chapter 1 and continues through most of the book. If previous chapter segments were not completed, the serial problem can begin at this point. It is helpful, but not necessary, to use the Working Papers that accompany the book.)

SP 7   Santana Rey, owner of Business Solutions, realizes that she needs to begin accounting for bad debts expense. Assume that Business Solutions has total revenues of $44,000 during the first three months of 2012, and that the Accounts Receivable balance on March 31, 2012, is $22,867.

SERIAL PROBLEM
Business Solutions
P1   P2

Required

1. Prepare the adjusting entry needed for Business Solutions to recognize bad debts expense on March 31, 2012, under each of the following independent assumptions (assume a zero unadjusted balance in the Allowance for Doubtful Accounts at March 31).

  a. Bad debts are estimated to be 1% of total revenues. (Round amounts to the dollar.)

  b. Bad debts are estimated to be 2% of accounts receivable. (Round amounts to the dollar.)

2. Assume that Business Solutions' Accounts Receivable balance at June 30, 2012, is $20,250 and that one account of $100 has been written off against the Allowance for Doubtful Accounts since March 31, 2012. If S. Rey uses the method prescribed in Part 1*b*, what adjusting journal entry must be made to recognize bad debts expense on June 30, 2012?

3. Should S. Rey consider adopting the direct write-off method of accounting for bad debts expense rather than one of the allowance methods considered in part 1? Explain.

Check   (2) Bad Debts Expense, $48

Beyond the Numbers

BTN 7-1   Refer to **Research In Motion**'s financial statements in Appendix A to answer the following.

1. What is the amount of Research In Motion's accounts receivable as of February 27, 2010?

2. Compute Research In Motion's accounts receivable turnover as of February 27, 2010.

3. How long does it take, *on average*, for the company to collect receivables? Do you believe that customers actually pay the amounts due within this short period? Explain.

4. Research In Motion's most liquid assets include (*a*) cash and cash equivalents, (*b*) short-term investments, and (*c*) receivables. Compute the percentage that these liquid assets make up of current liabilities as of February 27, 2010. Do the same computations for February 28, 2009. Comment on the company's ability to satisfy its current liabilities as of its 2010 fiscal year-end compared to its 2009 fiscal year-end.

5. What criteria did Research In Motion use to classify items as cash equivalents?

REPORTING IN ACTION

A1

RIM

Fast Forward

6. Access Research In Motion's financial statements for fiscal years after February 27, 2010, at its Website (www.RIM.com) or the SEC's EDGAR database (www.SEC.gov). Recompute parts 2 and 4 and comment on any changes since February 27, 2010.

BTN 7-2   Comparative figures for **Research In Motion** and **Apple** follow.

COMPARATIVE ANALYSIS

A1   P2

RIM
Apple

($ millions)	Research In Motion			Apple		
	Current Year	One Year Prior	Two Years Prior	Current Year	One Year Prior	Two Years Prior
Accounts receivable, net	$ 2,594	$ 2,112	$1,175	$ 3,361	$ 2,422	$ 1,637
Net sales	14,953	11,065	6,009	42,905	37,491	24,578

Hint: Average collection period equals 365 divided by the accounts receivable turnover.

Required

1. Compute the accounts receivable turnover for Research In Motion and Apple for each of the two most recent years using the data shown.
2. Using results from part 1, compute how many days it takes each company, *on average,* to collect receivables. Compare the collection periods for RIM and Apple, and suggest at least one explanation for the difference.
3. Which company is more efficient in collecting its accounts receivable? Explain.

ETHICS CHALLENGE

P2

BTN 7-3   Kelly Steinman is the manager of a medium-size company. A few years ago, Steinman persuaded the owner to base a part of her compensation on the net income the company earns each year. Each December she estimates year-end financial figures in anticipation of the bonus she will receive. If the bonus is not as high as she would like, she offers several recommendations to the accountant for year-end adjustments. One of her favorite recommendations is for the controller to reduce the estimate of doubtful accounts.

Required

1. What effect does lowering the estimate for doubtful accounts have on the income statement and balance sheet?
2. Do you believe Steinman's recommendation to adjust the allowance for doubtful accounts is within her right as manager, or do you believe this action is an ethics violation? Justify your response.
3. What type of internal control(s) might be useful for this company in overseeing the manager's recommendations for accounting changes?

COMMUNICATING IN PRACTICE

P2

BTN 7-4   As the accountant for Pure-Air Distributing, you attend a sales managers' meeting devoted to a discussion of credit policies. At the meeting, you report that bad debts expense is estimated to be $59,000 and accounts receivable at year-end amount to $1,750,000 less a $43,000 allowance for doubtful accounts. Sid Omar, a sales manager, expresses confusion over why bad debts expense and the allowance for doubtful accounts are different amounts. Write a one-page memorandum to him explaining why a difference in bad debts expense and the allowance for doubtful accounts is not unusual. The company estimates bad debts expense as 2% of sales.

TAKING IT TO THE NET

C1

BTN 7-5   Access eBay's February 17, 2010, filing of its 10-K report for the year ended December 31, 2009, at www.sec.gov.

Required

1. What is the amount of eBay's net accounts receivable at December 31, 2009, and at December 31, 2008?
2. "Financial Statement Schedule II" to its financial statements lists eBay's allowance for doubtful accounts (including authorized credits). For the two years ended December 31, 2009 and 2008, compute its allowance for doubtful accounts (including authorized credits) as a percent of gross accounts receivable.
3. Do you believe that these percentages are reasonable based on what you know about eBay? Explain.

TEAMWORK IN ACTION

P2

BTN 7-6   Each member of a team is to participate in estimating uncollectibles using the aging schedule and percents shown in Problem 7-4A. The division of labor is up to the team. Your goal is to accurately complete this task as soon as possible. After estimating uncollectibles, check your estimate with the instructor. If the estimate is correct, the team then should prepare the adjusting entry and the presentation of accounts receivable (net) for the December 31, 2011, balance sheet.

ENTREPRENEURIAL DECISION

C1

BTN 7-7   John Earle of Johnny Cupcakes is introduced in the chapter's opening feature. John currently sells his products through multiple outlets. Assume that he is considering two new selling options.

Plan A. Johnny Cupcakes would begin selling additional products online directly to customers, which are only currently sold directly to outlet stores. These new online customers would use their credit cards. It currently has the capability of selling through its Website with no additional investment in hardware or software. Credit sales are expected to increase by $250,000 per year. Costs associated with this plan are: cost of these sales will be $135,500, credit card fees will be 4.75% of sales, and additional recordkeeping and shipping costs will be 6% of sales. These online sales will reduce the sales to stores by $35,000 because some customers will now purchase items online. Sales to stores have a 25% gross margin percentage.

Plan B. Johnny Cupcakes would expand its market to more outlet stores. It would make additional credit sales of $500,000 to those stores. Costs associated with those sales are: cost of sales will be $375,000, additional recordkeeping and shipping will be 4% of sales, and uncollectible accounts will be 6.2% of sales.

Required

1. Compute the additional annual net income or loss expected under (a) Plan A and (b) Plan B.
2. Should Johnny Cupcakes pursue either plan? Discuss both the financial and nonfinancial factors relevant to this decision.

Check (1*b*) Net income, $74,000

HITTING THE ROAD
C1

BTN 7-8 Many commercials include comments similar to the following: "We accept **VISA**" or "We do not accept **American Express**." Conduct your own research by contacting at least five companies via interviews, phone calls, or the Internet to determine the reason(s) companies discriminate in their use of credit cards. Collect information on the fees charged by the different cards for the companies contacted. (The instructor can assign this as a team activity.)

GLOBAL DECISION
C1 P2

NOKIA
RIM
Apple

BTN 7-9 Key information from Nokia (www.Nokia.com), which is a leading global manufacturer of mobile devices and services, follows.

EUR millions	Current Year	Prior Year
Accounts receivable, net*	7,981	9,444
Sales	40,984	50,710

*Nokia refers to it as "Accounts receivable, net of allowance for doubtful accounts."

1. Compute the accounts receivable turnover for the current year.
2. How long does it take on average for Nokia to collect receivables?
3. Refer to BTN 7-2. How does Nokia compare to Research In Motion and Apple in terms of its accounts receivable turnover and its collection period?
4. Nokia reports an aging analysis of its receivables, based on due dates, as follows (in EUR millions) as of December 31, 2009. Compute the percent of receivables in each category.

EUR millions	Total Receivables
Current	7,302
Past due 1–30 days	393
Past due 31–180 days	170
More than 180 days	116

ANSWERS TO MULTIPLE CHOICE QUIZ

1. d; Desired balance in Allowance for Doubtful Accounts = $ 5,026 cr.
   ($125,650 × 0.04)
   Current balance in Allowance for Doubtful Accounts = (328) cr.
   Bad Debts Expense to be recorded = $ 4,698
2. a; Desired balance in Allowance for Doubtful Accounts = $29,358 cr.
   ($489,300 × 0.06)
   Current balance in Allowance for Doubtful Accounts = 554 dr.
   Bad Debts Expense to be recorded = $29,912
3. a; $7,500 × 0.05 × 90/360 = $93.75

4. c; Principal amount $9,000
   Interest accrued .... 120 ($9,000 × 0.08 × 60/360)
   Maturity value $9,120
5. d; $489,600/$40,800 = 12

Chapters 6 and 7 focused on short-term assets: cash, cash equivalents, and receivables. We explained why they are known as liquid assets and described how companies account and report for them.

This chapter introduces us to long-term assets. We explain how to account for a long-term asset's cost, the allocation of an asset's cost to periods benefiting from it, the recording of additional costs after an asset is purchased, and the disposal of an asset.

Chapter 9 focuses on current liabilities. We explain how they are computed, recorded, and reported in financial statements. We also explain the accounting for company payroll and contingencies.

8
Reporting and Analyzing Long-Term Assets

Learning Objectives

CAP

CONCEPTUAL

C1 Explain the cost principle for computing the cost of plant assets. (p. 329)

C2 Explain depreciation for partial years and changes in estimates. (p. 336)

C3 Distinguish between revenue and capital expenditures, and account for them. (p. 338)

ANALYTICAL

A1 Compute total asset turnover and apply it to analyze a company's use of assets. (p. 347)

LP8

PROCEDURAL

P1 Compute and record depreciation using the straight-line, units-of-production, and declining-balance methods. (p. 332)

P2 Account for asset disposal through discarding or selling an asset. (p. 340)

P3 Account for natural resource assets and their depletion. (p. 342)

P4 Account for intangible assets. (p. 343)

P5 *Appendix 8A*—Account for asset exchanges. (p. 350)

Gaming Assets

"We want the average kid to have a party like a rock star."
—**DAVID PIKOFF**

AUSTIN, TX—Fun and games are the common bond for brothers Stuart and David Pikoff. That bond was also the driving force for an excursion into business. "We're both fun guys, we love kids, and we love games," explains David. "So we thought, 'Why not create our own game franchise?'" What they did was create **Games2U (Games2U.com),** a business focused on bringing fun and games to children and adults, using vans and trailers outfitted with state-of-the-art games and activities.

The brothers started operations by scraping up just enough money. However, long-term assets such as mobile vehicles outfitted with video games, large flat-screen displays, high-quality sound systems, and laser-light and fog machines for effects, are very expensive. David explains that financing such equipment, machinery, and similar assets is a struggle. "We would be much bigger, much quicker, if we didn't have that challenge." The owners had to work out depreciation schedules and estimate payback for different games and accessories.

Games2U is now rocking—employing nearly 20 workers, offering franchise agreements to others interested in mimicking their fun and games business, and generating several million in annual sales. Still, a constant challenge for the brothers is maintaining the right kind and amount of assets to meet people's demands and be profitable. "That made us hone in on product development," explains David. "How do we provide unique entertainment at your doorstep?" Games2U's success depends on monitoring and controlling those asset costs, which range from a mobile 4-D movie theater to decked-out trailers to a patented seven-foot tall kid-controlled robot.

Each of these tangible and intangible assets commands Stuart and David's attention. The brothers account for, manage, and focus on recovering all costs of these long-term assets. "We're never done," says David. "We're always challenging ourselves." Their success in asset management permits them to pursue further expansion and new ideas for gaming experiences. They have expanded into outdoor laser tag, human gyros, air cannons, and a version of capture-the-flag called "Booger Wars." "We have a unique concept, a solid infrastructure," explains David. "We provide unique entertainment."

[Sources: *Games2U Website,* January 2012; *Entrepreneur,* June 2009; *The Wall Street Journal,* March 2010; *Inc.com* October 2009; *The Monitor,* September 2009; *Franchise Update,* August 2009; *AOL,* January 2011] not extend an asset's useful life beyond its original estimate or increase its productivity beyond original expectations. Examples are normal costs of cleaning, lubricating, adjusting, and replacing small parts of a machine. Ordinary repairs are treated as *revenue expenditures.* This means their costs are reported as expenses on the current period income statement. Following this rule, Brunswick reports that "maintenance and repair costs are expensed as incurred." If Brunswick's current year repair costs are $9,500, it makes the following entry.

Point: Many companies apply the *materiality constraint* to treat *low-cost plant assets* (say, less than $500) as revenue expenditures. This practice is referred to as a "capitalization policy."

Dec. 31	Repairs Expense	9,500	
	Cash		9,500
	To record ordinary repairs of equipment.		

Assets = Liabilities + Equity
−9,500   −9,500

Betterments and Extraordinary Repairs

Accounting for betterments and extraordinary repairs is similar—both are treated as *capital expenditures.*

Betterments (Improvements)   **Betterments,** also called *improvements,* are expenditures that make a plant asset more efficient or productive. A betterment often involves adding a component to an asset or replacing one of its old components with a better one, and does not always increase an asset's useful life. An example is replacing manual controls on a machine with automatic controls. One special type of betterment is an *addition,* such as adding a new wing or dock to a warehouse. Since a betterment benefits future periods, it is debited to the asset account as a capital expenditure. The new book value (less salvage value) is then depreciated over the asset's remaining useful life. To illustrate, suppose a company pays $8,000 for a machine with an eight-year useful life and no salvage value. After three years and $3,000 of depreciation, it adds an automated control system to the machine at a cost of $1,800. This results in reduced labor costs in future periods. The cost of the betterment is added to the Machinery account with this entry.

Example: Assume a firm owns a Web server. Identify each cost as a revenue or capital expenditure: (1) purchase price, (2) necessary wiring, (3) platform for operation, (4) circuits to increase capacity, (5) cleaning after each month of use, (6) repair of a faulty switch, and (7) replaced a worn fan. *Answer:* Capital expenditures: 1, 2, 3, 4; revenue expenditures: 5, 6, 7.

Jan. 2	Machinery	1,800	
	Cash		1,800
	To record installation of automated system.		

Assets = Liabilities + Equity
+1,800
−1,800

After the betterment is recorded, the remaining cost to be depreciated is $6,800, computed as $8,000 − $3,000 + $1,800. Depreciation expense for the remaining five years is $1,360 per year, computed as $6,800/5 years.

Point: Both extraordinary repairs and betterments require revising future depreciation.

Extraordinary Repairs (Replacements)   **Extraordinary repairs** are expenditures extending the asset's useful life beyond its original estimate. Extraordinary repairs are *capital expenditures* because they benefit future periods. Their costs are debited to the asset account (or to accumulated depreciation). For example, Delta Air Lines reports, "modifications that ... extend the useful lives of airframes or engines are capitalized and amortized [depreciated] over the remaining estimated useful life of the asset."

 Decision Maker   Answer — p. 352

Entrepreneur   Your start-up Internet services company needs cash, and you are preparing financial statements to apply for a short-term loan. A friend suggests that you treat as many expenses as possible as capital expenditures. What are the impacts on financial statements of this suggestion? What do you think is the aim of this suggestion? ■

DISPOSALS OF PLANT ASSETS

Plant assets are disposed of for several reasons. Some are discarded because they wear out or become obsolete. Others are sold because of changing business plans. Regardless of the reason, disposals of plant assets occur in one of three basic ways: discarding, sale, or exchange. The general steps in accounting for a disposal of plant assets are described in Exhibit 8.15.

EXHIBIT 8.15

Accounting for Disposals of Plant Assets

1. Record depreciation up to the date of disposal—this also updates Accumulated Depreciation.
2. Record the removal of the disposed asset's account balances—including its Accumulated Depreciation.
3. Record any cash (and/or other assets) received or paid in the disposal.
4. Record any gain or loss—computed by comparing the disposed asset's book value with the market value of any assets received.*

* An exception to step 4 is the case of an exchange that lacks *commercial substance*—see Appendix 8A.

Discarding Plant Assets

P2 Account for asset disposal through discarding or selling an asset.

A plant asset is *discarded* when it is no longer useful to the company and it has no market value. To illustrate, assume that a machine costing $9,000 with accumulated depreciation of $9,000 is discarded. When accumulated depreciation equals the asset's cost, it is said to be *fully depreciated* (zero book value). The entry to record the discarding of this asset is

Assets = Liabilities + Equity
+9,000
−9,000

June 5	Accumulated Depreciation—Machinery	9,000	
	Machinery		9,000
	To discard fully depreciated machinery.		

This entry reflects all four steps of Exhibit 8.15. Step 1 is unnecessary since the machine is fully depreciated. Step 2 is reflected in the debit to Accumulated Depreciation and credit to Machinery. Since no other asset is involved, step 3 is irrelevant. Finally, since book value is zero and no other asset is involved, no gain or loss is recorded in step 4.

Point: Recording depreciation expense up-to-date gives an up-to-date book value for determining gain or loss.

How do we account for discarding an asset that is not fully depreciated or one whose depreciation is not up-to-date? To answer this, consider equipment costing $8,000 with accumulated depreciation of $6,000 on December 31 of the prior fiscal year-end. This equipment is being depreciated using the straight-line method over eight years with zero salvage. On July 1 of the current year it is discarded. Step 1 is to bring depreciation up-to-date.

Assets = Liabilities + Equity
−500   −500

July 1	Depreciation Expense	500	
	Accumulated Depreciation—Equipment		500
	To record 6 months' depreciation ($1,000 × 6/12).		

Steps 2 through 4 of Exhibit 8.15 are reflected in the second (and final) entry.

Assets = Liabilities + Equity
+6,500   −1,500
−8,000

July 1	Accumulated Depreciation—Equipment	6,500	
	Loss on Disposal of Equipment	1,500	
	Equipment		8,000
	To discard equipment with a $1,500 book value.		

Point: Gain or loss is determined by comparing "value given" (book value) to "value received."

This loss is computed by comparing the equipment's $1,500 book value ($8,000 − $6,000 − $500) with the zero net cash proceeds. The loss is reported in the Other Expenses and Losses section of the income statement. Discarding an asset can sometimes require a cash payment that would increase the loss.

Selling Plant Assets

Companies often sell plant assets when they restructure or downsize operations. To illustrate the accounting for selling plant assets, we consider BTO's March 31 sale of equipment that cost $16,000 and has accumulated depreciation of $12,000 at December 31 of the prior calendar year-end. Annual depreciation on this equipment is $4,000 computed using straight-line depreciation. Step 1 of this sale is to record depreciation expense and update accumulated depreciation to March 31 of the current year.

March 31	Depreciation Expense	1,000	
	Accumulated Depreciation—Equipment		1,000
	To record 3 months' depreciation ($4,000 × 3/12).		

Assets = Liabilities + Equity
−1,000   −1,000

Steps 2 through 4 of Exhibit 8.15 can be reflected in one final entry that depends on the amount received from the asset's sale. We consider three different possibilities.

Sale at Book Value   If BTO receives $3,000 cash, an amount equal to the equipment's book value as of March 31 (book value = $16,000 − $12,000 − $1,000), no gain or loss occurs on disposal. The entry is

Sale price = Book value → No gain or loss

March 31	Cash	3,000	
	Accumulated Depreciation—Equipment	13,000	
	Equipment		16,000
	To record sale of equipment for no gain or loss.		

Assets = Liabilities + Equity
+3,000
+13,000
−16,000

Sale above Book Value   If BTO receives $7,000, an amount that is $4,000 above the equipment's $3,000 book value as of March 31, a gain on disposal occurs. The entry is

Sale price > Book value → Gain

March 31	Cash	7,000	
	Accumulated Depreciation—Equipment	13,000	
	Gain on Disposal of Equipment		4,000
	Equipment		16,000
	To record sale of equipment for a $4,000 gain.		

Assets = Liabilities + Equity
+7,000   +4,000
+13,000
−16,000

Sale below Book Value   If BTO receives $2,500, an amount that is $500 below the equipment's $3,000 book value as of March 31, a loss on disposal occurs. The entry is

Sale price < Book value → Loss

March 31	Cash	2,500	
	Loss on Disposal of Equipment	500	
	Accumulated Depreciation—Equipment	13,000	
	Equipment		16,000
	To record sale of equipment for a $500 loss.		

Assets = Liabilities + Equity
+2,500   −500
+13,000
−16,000

IFRS

Unlike U.S. GAAP, IFRS requires an annual review of useful life and salvage value estimates. IFRS also permits revaluation of plant assets to market value if market value is reliably determined. ●

Quick Check   Answers – p. 353

8. Early in the fifth year of a machine's six-year useful life, it is overhauled, and its useful life is extended to nine years. This machine originally cost $108,000 and the overhaul cost is $12,000. Prepare the entry to record the overhaul cost.

9. Explain the difference between revenue expenditures and capital expenditures and how both are recorded.

10. What is a betterment? How is a betterment recorded?

11. A company acquires equipment on January 10, 2011, at a cost of $42,000. Straight-line depreciation is used with a five-year life and $7,000 salvage value. On June 27, 2012, the company sells this equipment for $32,000. Prepare the entry(ies) for June 27, 2012.

Section 2—Natural Resources

P3	Account for natural resource assets and their depletion.

Natural resources are assets that are physically consumed when used. Examples are standing timber, mineral deposits, and oil and gas fields. Since they are consumed when used, they are often called *wasting assets*. These assets represent soon-to-be inventories of raw materials that will be converted into one or more products by cutting, mining, or pumping. Until that conversion takes place, they are noncurrent assets and are shown in a balance sheet using titles such as timberlands, mineral deposits, or oil reserves. Natural resources are reported under either plant assets or their own separate category. Alcoa, for instance, reports its natural resources under the balance sheet title *Properties, plants and equipment.* In a note to its financial statements, Alcoa reports a separate amount for *Land and land rights, including mines.* Weyerhaeuser, on the other hand, reports its timber holdings in a separate balance sheet category titled *Timber and timberlands.*

Cost Determination and Depletion

Natural resources are recorded at cost, which includes all expenditures necessary to acquire the resource and prepare it for its intended use. **Depletion** is the process of allocating the cost of a natural resource to the period when it is consumed. Natural resources are reported on the balance sheet at cost less *accumulated depletion.* The depletion expense per period is usually based on units extracted from cutting, mining, or pumping. This is similar to units-of-production depreciation. Exxon Mobil uses this approach to amortize the costs of discovering and operating its oil wells.

To illustrate depletion of natural resources, let's consider a mineral deposit with an estimated 250,000 tons of available ore. It is purchased for $500,000, and we expect zero salvage value. The depletion charge per ton of ore mined is $2, computed as $500,000 ÷ 250,000 tons. If 85,000 tons are mined and sold in the first year, the depletion charge for that year is $170,000. These computations are detailed in Exhibit 8.16.

EXHIBIT 8.16

Depletion Formula and Example

Step 1

$$\text{Depletion per unit} = \frac{\text{Cost} - \text{Salvage value}}{\text{Total units of capacity}} = \frac{\$500,000 - \$0}{250,000 \text{ tons}} = \$2 \text{ per ton}$$

Step 2

$$\text{Depletion expense} = \text{Depletion per unit} \times \text{Units extracted and sold in period}$$
$$= \$2 \times 85,000 = \$170,000$$

Depletion expense for the first year is recorded as follows.

Assets	= Liabilities +	Equity
−170,000		−170,000

Dec. 31	Depletion Expense—Mineral Deposit	170,000	
	Accumulated Depletion—Mineral Deposit		170,000
	To record depletion of the mineral deposit.		

The period-end balance sheet reports the mineral deposit as shown in Exhibit 8.17.

EXHIBIT 8.17

Balance Sheet Presentation of Natural Resources

Mineral deposit	$500,000	
Less accumulated depletion	170,000	$330,000

Since all 85,000 tons of the mined ore are sold during the year, the entire $170,000 of depletion is reported on the income statement. If some of the ore remains unsold at year-end, however, the depletion related to the unsold ore is carried forward on the balance sheet and reported as

Ore Inventory, a current asset. To illustrate, and continuing with our example, assume that 40,000 tons are mined in the second year, but only 34,000 tons are sold. We record depletion of $68,000 (34,000 tons × $2 depletion per unit) and the remaining Ore Inventory of $12,000 (6,000 tons × $2 depletion per unit) as follows.

Dec. 31	Depletion Expense—Mineral Deposit	68,000	
	Ore Inventory	12,000	
	Accumulated Depletion—Mineral Deposit		80,000
	To record depletion and inventory of mineral deposit.		

Assets = Liabilities + Equity
−80,000   −68,000
+12,000

Plant Assets Used in Extracting

The conversion of natural resources by mining, cutting, or pumping usually requires machinery, equipment, and buildings. When the usefulness of these plant assets is directly related to the depletion of a natural resource, their costs are depreciated using the units-of-production method in proportion to the depletion of the natural resource. For example, if a machine is permanently installed in a mine and 10% of the ore is mined and sold in the period, then 10% of the machine's cost (less any salvage value) is allocated to depreciation expense. The same procedure is used when a machine is abandoned once resources have been extracted. If, however, a machine will be moved to and used at another site when extraction is complete, the machine is depreciated over its own useful life.

▲ **Fraud** ▬▬▬▬▬▬▬▬▬▬▬▬▬▬▬▬

Asset Control. Long-term assets must be safeguarded against theft, misuse, and other damages. Controls take many forms depending on the asset, including use of security tags, the legal monitoring of rights infringements, and approvals of all asset disposals. A study reports that 44% of employees in operations and service areas witnessed the wasting, mismanaging, or abusing of assets in the past year (KPMG 2009). Another 21% in general management and administration observed stealing or misappropriation of assets.

Section 3—Intangible Assets

Intangible assets are nonphysical assets (used in operations) that confer on their owners long-term rights, privileges, or competitive advantages. Examples are patents, copyrights, licenses, leaseholds, franchises, goodwill, and trademarks. Lack of physical substance does not necessarily imply an intangible asset. Notes and accounts receivable, for instance, lack physical substance, but they are not intangibles. This section identifies the more common types of intangible assets and explains the accounting for them.

P4 Account for intangible assets.

Cost Determination and Amortization

An intangible asset is recorded at cost when purchased. Intangibles are then separated into those with limited lives or indefinite lives. If an intangible has a **limited life,** its cost is systematically allocated to expense over its estimated useful life through the process of **amortization.** If an intangible asset has an **indefinite life**—meaning that no legal, regulatory, contractual, competitive, economic, or other factors limit its useful life—it should not be amortized. (If an intangible with an indefinite life is later judged to have a limited life, it is amortized over that limited life.) Amortization of intangible assets is similar to depreciation of plant assets and the depletion of natural resources in that it is a process of cost allocation. However, only the straight-line method is used for amortizing intangibles *unless* the company can show that another method is preferred. The effects of amortization are recorded in a contra account (Accumulated Amortization). The gross acquisition cost of intangible assets is disclosed in the balance sheet along with their accumulated amortization (these disclosures are new). The eventual disposal of an intangible asset involves removing its book value, recording any other asset(s) received or given up, and recognizing any gain or loss for the difference.

7. [i] What accounting concept justifies charging low-cost plant asset purchases immediately to an expense account?

8. What is the difference between ordinary repairs and extra-ordinary repairs? How should each be recorded?

9. [i] Identify events that might lead to disposal of a plant asset.

10. What is the process of allocating the cost of natural resources to expense as they are used?

11. Is the declining-balance method an acceptable way to compute depletion of natural resources? Explain.

12. What are the characteristics of an intangible asset?

13. What general procedures are applied in accounting for the acquisition and potential cost allocation of intangible assets?

14. [i] When do we know that a company has goodwill? When can goodwill appear in a company's balance sheet?

15. [i] Assume that a company buys another business and pays for its goodwill. If the company plans to incur costs each year to maintain the value of the goodwill, must it also amortize this goodwill?

16. [i] How is total asset turnover computed? Why would a financial statement user be interested in total asset turnover?

17. Refer to **Research In Motion**'s balance sheet in Appendix A. What property, plant and equipment **RIM** assets does RIM list on its balance sheet? What is the book value of its total net property, plant and equipment assets at February 27, 2010?

18. **Apple** lists its plant assets as "Property, plant and equipment, net." What does "net" mean in this title? Apple

19. [i] Refer to **Nokia**'s balance sheet in Appendix A. What does it title its plant assets? What is the book value of its plant assets at December 31, 2009? **NOKIA**

20. Refer to the May 31, 2009, balance sheet of **Palm** in Appendix A. What long-term assets discussed in this chapter are reported by the company? **Palm**

connect

Strike Bowling installs automatic scorekeeping equipment with an invoice cost of $180,000. The electrical work required for the installation costs $8,000. Additional costs are $3,000 for delivery and $12,600 for sales tax. During the installation, a component of the equipment is carelessly left on a lane and hit by the automatic lane-cleaning machine. The cost of repairing the component is $2,250. What is the total recorded cost of the automatic scorekeeping equipment?

QUICK STUDY

QS 8-1

Cost of plant assets C1

Identify the main difference between (1) plant assets and inventory, (2) plant assets and current assets, and (3) plant assets and long-term investments.

QS 8-2

Defining assets C1

On January 2, 2011, the Crossover Band acquires sound equipment for concert performances at a cost of $55,900. The band estimates it will use this equipment for four years, during which time it anticipates performing about 120 concerts. It estimates that after four years it can sell the equipment for $1,900. During year 2011, the band performs 40 concerts. Compute the year 2011 depreciation using the straight-line method.

QS 8-3

Straight-line depreciation

P1

Refer to the information in QS 8-3. Compute the year 2011 depreciation using the units-of-production method.

QS 8-4

Units-of-production depreciation

P1

Refer to the facts in QS 8-3. Assume that the Crossover Band uses straight-line depreciation but realizes at the start of the second year that due to concert bookings beyond expectations, this equipment will last only a total of three years. The salvage value remains unchanged. Compute the revised depreciation for both the second and third years.

QS 8-5

Computing revised depreciation

C2

A fleet of refrigerated delivery trucks is acquired on January 5, 2011, at a cost of $930,000 with an estimated useful life of eight years and an estimated salvage value of $150,000. Compute the depreciation expense for the first three years using the double-declining-balance method.

QS 8-6

Double-declining-balance method P1

Assume a company's equipment carries a book value of $4,000 ($4,500 cost less $500 accumulated depreciation) and a fair value of $3,750, *and* that the $250 decline in fair value in comparison to the book value meets the 2-step impairment test. Prepare the entry to record this $250 impairment.

QS 8-7

Recording plant asset impairment C2

QS 8-8
Revenue and capital expenditures
C3

1. Classify the following as either revenue or capital expenditures.
   a. Completed an addition to an office building for $250,000 cash.
   b. Paid $160 for the monthly cost of replacement filters on an air-conditioning system.
   c. Paid $300 cash per truck for the cost of their annual tune-ups.
   d. Paid $50,000 cash to replace a compressor on a refrigeration system that extends its useful life by four years.
2. Prepare the journal entries to record transactions *a* and *d* of part 1.

QS 8-9
Disposal of assets   P2

Horizon Co. owns equipment that cost $138,750, with accumulated depreciation of $81,000. Horizon sells the equipment for cash. Record the sale of the equipment assuming Horizon sells the equipment for (1) $63,000 cash, (2) $57,750 cash, and (3) $46,500 cash.

QS 8-10
Natural resources and depletion
P3

Diamond Company acquires an ore mine at a cost of $1,300,000. It incurs additional costs of $200,000 to access the mine, which is estimated to hold 500,000 tons of ore. The estimated value of the land after the ore is removed is $150,000.

1. Prepare the entry(ies) to record the cost of the ore mine.
2. Prepare the year-end adjusting entry if 90,000 tons of ore are mined and sold the first year.

QS 8-11
Classify assets
P3   P4

Which of the following assets are reported on the balance sheet as intangible assets? Which are reported as natural resources? (*a*) timberland, (*b*) patent, (*c*) leasehold, (*d*) Oil well, (*e*) equipment, (*f*) copyright, (*g*) franchise, (*h*) gold mine.

QS 8-12
Intangible assets and amortization   P4

On January 4 of this year, Larsen Boutique incurs a $95,000 cost to modernize its store. Improvements include new floors, ceilings, wiring, and wall coverings. These improvements are estimated to yield benefits for 10 years. Larsen leases its store and has eight years remaining on the lease. Prepare the entry to record (1) the cost of modernization and (2) amortization at the end of this current year.

QS 8-13
Computing total asset turnover
A1

Eastman Company reports the following (dollar amounts are in thousands): net sales of $13,557 for 2011 and $12,670 for 2010; end-of-year total assets of $14,968 for 2011 and $18,810 for 2010. Compute its total asset turnover for 2011, and assess its level if competitors average a total asset turnover of 2.0 times.

QS 8-14^A
Asset exchange
P5

Esteban Co. owns a machine that costs $38,400 with accumulated depreciation of $20,400. Esteban exchanges the machine for a newer model that has a market value of $48,000. (1) Record the exchange assuming Esteban paid $32,000 cash and the exchange has commercial substance. (2) Record the exchange assuming Esteban pays $24,000 cash and the exchange lacks commercial substance.

QS 8-15
International accounting standards
C1   C3

Answer each of the following related to international accounting standards.

a. Accounting for plant assets involves cost determination, depreciation, additional expenditures, and disposals. Is plant asset accounting broadly similar or dissimilar between IFRS and U.S. GAAP? Identify one notable difference between IFRS and U.S. GAAP in accounting for plant assets.
b. Describe how IFRS and U.S. GAAP treat increases in the value of plant assets subsequent to their acquisition (but before their disposition).

 connect™

EXERCISES

Exercise 8-1
Cost of plant assets
C1

Farha Co. purchases a machine for $11,500, terms 2/10, n/60, FOB shipping point. The seller prepaid the $260 freight charges, adding the amount to the invoice and bringing its total to $11,760. The machine requires special steel mounting and power connections costing $795. Another $375 is paid to assemble the machine and get it into operation. In moving the machine to its steel mounting, $190 in damages occurred. Materials costing $30 are used in adjusting the machine to produce a satisfactory product. The adjustments are normal for this machine and are not the result of the damages. Compute the cost recorded for this machine. (Farha pays for this machine within the cash discount period.)

Cerner Manufacturing purchases a large lot on which an old building is located as part of its plans to build a new plant. The negotiated purchase price is $225,000 for the lot plus $120,000 for the old building. The company pays $34,500 to tear down the old building and $51,000 to fill and level the lot. It also pays a total of $1,440,000 in construction costs—this amount consists of $1,354,500 for the new building and $85,500 for lighting and paving a parking area next to the building. Prepare a single journal entry to record these costs incurred by Cerner, all of which are paid in cash.

Exercise 8-2
Recording costs of assets
C1

Ming Yue Company pays $368,250 for real estate plus $19,600 in closing costs. The real estate consists of land appraised at $166,320; land improvements appraised at $55,440; and a building appraised at $174,240. Allocate the total cost among the three purchased assets and prepare the journal entry to record the purchase.

Exercise 8-3
Lump-sum purchase of plant assets C1

In early January 2011, LabTech purchases computer equipment for $147,000 to use in operating activities for the next four years. It estimates the equipment's salvage value at $30,000. Prepare a table showing depreciation and book value for each of the four years assuming straight-line depreciation.

Exercise 8-4
Straight-line depreciation P1

Refer to the information in Exercise 8-4. Prepare a table showing depreciation and book value for each of the four years assuming double-declining-balance depreciation.

Exercise 8-5
Double-declining-balance depreciation P1

Feng Company installs a computerized manufacturing machine in its factory at the beginning of the year at a cost of $42,300. The machine's useful life is estimated at 10 years, or 363,000 units of product, with a $6,000 salvage value. During its second year, the machine produces 35,000 units of product. Determine the machine's second-year depreciation under the straight-line method.

Exercise 8-6
Straight-line depreciation
P1

Refer to the information in Exercise 8-6. Determine the machine's second-year depreciation using the units-of-production method.

Exercise 8-7
Units-of-production depreciation
P1

Refer to the information in Exercise 8-6. Determine the machine's second-year depreciation using the double-declining-balance method.

Exercise 8-8
Double-declining-balance depreciation P1

On April 1, 2010, Stone's Backhoe Co. purchases a trencher for $250,000. The machine is expected to last five years and have a salvage value of $25,000. Compute depreciation expense for both 2010 and 2011 assuming the company uses the straight-line method.

Exercise 8-9
Straight-line, partial-year depreciation C2

Refer to the information in Exercise 8-9. Compute depreciation expense for both 2010 and 2011 assuming the company uses the double-declining-balance method.

Exercise 8-10
Double-declining-balance, partial-year depreciation C2

Supreme Fitness Club uses straight-line depreciation for a machine costing $21,750, with an estimated four-year life and a $2,250 salvage value. At the beginning of the third year, Supreme determines that the machine has three more years of remaining useful life, after which it will have an estimated $1,800 salvage value. Compute (1) the machine's book value at the end of its second year and (2) the amount of depreciation for each of the final three years given the revised estimates.

Exercise 8-11
Revising depreciation
C2

Check   (2) $3,400

Mulan Enterprises pays $235,200 for equipment that will last five years and have a $52,500 salvage value. By using the equipment in its operations for five years, the company expects to earn $85,500 annually, after deducting all expenses except depreciation. Prepare a table showing income before depreciation, depreciation expense, and net (pretax) income for each year and for the total five-year period, assuming straight-line depreciation.

Exercise 8-12
Straight-line depreciation and income effects P1

Refer to the information in Exercise 8-12. Prepare a table showing income before depreciation, depreciation expense, and net (pretax) income for each year and for the total five-year period, assuming double-declining-balance depreciation is used.

Exercise 8-13
Double-declining-balance depreciation P1

Check   Year 3 NI, $53,328

Exercise 8-14

Extraordinary repairs; plant asset age

C3

Passat Company owns a building that appears on its prior year-end balance sheet at its original $561,000 cost less $420,750 accumulated depreciation. The building is depreciated on a straight-line basis assuming a 20-year life and no salvage value. During the first week in January of the current calendar year, major structural repairs are completed on the building at a $67,200 cost. The repairs extend its useful life for 7 years beyond the 20 years originally estimated.

1. Determine the building's age (plant asset age) as of the prior year-end balance sheet date.
2. Prepare the entry to record the cost of the structural repairs that are paid in cash.
3. Determine the book value of the building immediately after the repairs are recorded.
4. Prepare the entry to record the current calendar year's depreciation.

Exercise 8-15

Ordinary repairs, extraordinary repairs and betterments

C3

Patterson Company pays $262,500 for equipment expected to last four years and have a $30,000 salvage value. Prepare journal entries to record the following costs related to the equipment.

1. During the second year of the equipment's life, $21,000 cash is paid for a new component expected to increase the equipment's productivity by 10% a year.
2. During the third year, $5,250 cash is paid for normal repairs necessary to keep the equipment in good working order.
3. During the fourth year, $13,950 is paid for repairs expected to increase the useful life of the equipment from four to five years.

Exercise 8-16

Disposal of assets

P2

Millworks Company owns a milling machine that cost $125,000 and has accumulated depreciation of $91,000. Prepare the entry to record the disposal of the milling machine on January 5 under each of the following independent situations.

1. The machine needed extensive repairs, and it was not worth repairing. Millworks disposed of the machine, receiving nothing in return.
2. Millworks sold the machine for $17,500 cash.
3. Millworks sold the machine for $34,000 cash.
4. Millworks sold the machine for $40,000 cash.

Exercise 8-17

Partial-year depreciation; disposal of plant asset

P2

Finesse Co. purchases and installs a machine on January 1, 2011, at a total cost of $92,750. Straight-line depreciation is taken each year for four years assuming a seven-year life and no salvage value. The machine is disposed of on July 1, 2015, during its fifth year of service. Prepare entries to record the partial year's depreciation on July 1, 2015, and to record the disposal under the following separate assumptions: (1) the machine is sold for $35,000 cash and (2) Finesse receives an insurance settlement of $30,000 resulting from the total destruction of the machine in a fire.

Exercise 8-18

Depletion of natural resources

P1 P3

On April 2, 2011, Idaho Mining Co. pays $3,633,750 for an ore deposit containing 1,425,000 tons. The company installs machinery in the mine costing $171,000, with an estimated seven-year life and no salvage value. The machinery will be abandoned when the ore is completely mined. Idaho begins mining on May 1, 2011, and mines and sells 156,200 tons of ore during the remaining eight months of 2011. Prepare the December 31, 2011, entries to record both the ore deposit depletion and the mining machinery depreciation. Mining machinery depreciation should be in proportion to the mine's depletion.

Exercise 8-19

Amortization of intangible assets

P4

Busch Gallery purchases the copyright on an oil painting for $236,700 on January 1, 2011. The copyright legally protects its owner for 12 more years. The company plans to market and sell prints of the original for 15 years. Prepare entries to record the purchase of the copyright on January 1, 2011, and its annual amortization on December 31, 2011.

Exercise 8-20

Goodwill

P4

On January 1, 2011, Timothy Company purchased Macys Company at a price of $3,750,000. The fair market value of the net assets purchased equals $2,700,000.

1. What is the amount of goodwill that Timothy records at the purchase date?
2. Explain how Timothy would determine the amount of goodwill amortization for the year ended December 31, 2011.
3. Timothy Company believes that its employees provide superior customer service, and through their efforts, Timothy Company believes it has created $1,350,000 of goodwill. How would Timothy Company record this goodwill?

Refer to the statement of cash flows for **Apple** in Appendix A for the fiscal year ended September 26, 2009, to answer the following.

1. What amount of cash is used to purchase property, plant, and equipment?

2. How much depreciation, amortization, and accretion are recorded?

3. What total amount of net cash is used in investing activities?

Exercise 8-21
Cash flows related to assets
C1

Apple

Joy Co. reports net sales of $4,862,000 for 2010 and $7,542,000 for 2011. End-of-year balances for total assets are 2009, $1,586,000; 2010, $1,700,000; and 2011, $1,882,000. (*a*) Compute Joy's total asset turnover for 2010 and 2011. (*b*) Comment on Joy's efficiency in using its assets if its competitors average a total asset turnover of 3.0.

Exercise 8-22
Evaluating efficient use of assets
A1

Ramond Construction trades in an old tractor for a new tractor, receiving a $31,850 trade-in allowance and paying the remaining $93,275 in cash. The old tractor had cost $107,900, and straight-line accumulated depreciation of $58,500 had been recorded to date under the assumption that it would last eight years and have a $14,300 salvage value. Answer the following questions assuming the exchange has commercial substance.

1. What is the book value of the old tractor at the time of exchange?

2. What is the loss on this asset exchange?

3. What amount should be recorded (debited) in the asset account for the new tractor?

Exercise 8-23ᴬ
Exchanging assets
P5

Check (2) $17,550

On January 5, 2011, Holstrom Co. disposes of a machine costing $65,500 with accumulated depreciation of $35,284. Prepare the entries to record the disposal under each of the following separate assumptions.

1. The machine is sold for $25,343 cash.

2. The machine is traded in for a newer machine having an $86,125 cash price. A $31,912 trade-in allowance is received, and the balance is paid in cash. Assume the asset exchange lacks commercial substance.

3. The machine is traded in for a newer machine having an $86,125 cash price. A $23,393 trade-in allowance is received, and the balance is paid in cash. Assume the asset exchange has commercial substance.

Exercise 8-24ᴬ
Recording plant asset disposals
P2 P5
Check (2) Dr. Machinery (new), $84,429

Volkswagen Group reports the following information for property, plant and equipment as of December 31, 2008, along with additions, disposals, depreciation, and impairments for the year ended December 31, 2008 (euros in millions):

Exercise 8-25
Accounting for plant assets under IFRS
C2 P1 P2

Property, plant and equipment, net	€23,121
Additions to property, plant and equipment	6,651
Disposals of property, plant and equipment	2,322
Depreciation on property, plant and equipment	4,625
Impairments to property, plant and equipment	184

1. Prepare Volkswagen's journal entry to record its depreciation for 2008.

2. Prepare Volkswagen's journal entry to record its additions for 2008 assuming they are paid in cash and are treated as "betterments (improvements)" to the assets.

3. Prepare Volkswagen's journal entry to record its €2,322 in disposals for 2008 assuming it receives €700 cash in return and the accumulated depreciation on the disposed assets totals €1,322.

4. Volkswagen reports €184 of impairments. Do these impairments increase or decrease the property, plant and equipment account? And, by what amount?

■ connect _____

Xavier Construction negotiates a lump-sum purchase of several assets from a company that is going out of business. The purchase is completed on January 1, 2011, at a total cash price of $787,500 for a building, land, land improvements, and four vehicles. The estimated market values of the assets are building, $408,000; land, $289,000; land improvements, $42,500; and four vehicles, $110,500. The company's fiscal year ends on December 31.

PROBLEM SET A

Problem 8-1A
Plant asset costs; depreciation methods C1 P1

Required

1. Prepare a table to allocate the lump-sum purchase price to the separate assets purchased (round percents to the nearest 1%). Prepare the journal entry to record the purchase.

mhhe.com/wildFA6e

2. Compute the depreciation expense for year 2011 on the building using the straight-line method, assuming a 15-year life and a $25,650 salvage value.

3. Compute the depreciation expense for year 2011 on the land improvements assuming a five-year life and double-declining-balance depreciation.

Analysis Component

4. Defend or refute this statement: Accelerated depreciation results in payment of less taxes over the asset's life.

Problem 8-2A
Asset cost allocation;
straight-line depreciation

C1 P1

mhhe.com/wildFA6e

In January 2011, Keona Co. pays $2,800,000 for a tract of land with two buildings on it. It plans to demolish Building 1 and build a new store in its place. Building 2 will be a company office; it is appraised at $641,300, with a useful life of 20 years and an $80,000 salvage value. A lighted parking lot near Building 1 has improvements (Land Improvements 1) valued at $408,100 that are expected to last another 14 years with no salvage value. Without the buildings and improvements, the tract of land is valued at $1,865,600. The company also incurs the following additional costs:

Cost to demolish Building 1	$ 422,600
Cost of additional land grading	167,200
Cost to construct new building (Building 3), having a useful life of 25 years and a $390,100 salvage value	2,019,000
Cost of new land improvements (Land Improvements 2) near Building 2 having a 20-year useful life and no salvage value	158,000

Required

1. Prepare a table with the following column headings: Land, Building 2, Building 3, Land Improvements 1, and Land Improvements 2. Allocate the costs incurred by Keona to the appropriate columns and total each column (round percents to the nearest 1%).

2. Prepare a single journal entry to record all the incurred costs assuming they are paid in cash on January 1, 2011.

3. Using the straight-line method, prepare the December 31 adjusting entries to record depreciation for the 12 months of 2011 when these assets were in use.

Problem 8-3A
Computing and revising
depreciation; revenue and
capital expenditures

C1 C2 C3

Clarion Contractors completed the following transactions and events involving the purchase and operation of equipment in its business.

2010

Jan. 1 Paid $255,440 cash plus $15,200 in sales tax and $2,500 in transportation (FOB shipping point) for a new loader. The loader is estimated to have a four-year life and a $34,740 salvage value. Loader costs are recorded in the Equipment account.

Jan. 3 Paid $3,660 to enclose the cab and install air conditioning in the loader to enable operations under harsher conditions. This increased the estimated salvage value of the loader by another $1,110.

Dec. 31 Recorded annual straight-line depreciation on the loader.

2011

Jan. 1 Paid $4,500 to overhaul the loader's engine, which increased the loader's estimated useful life by two years.

Feb. 17 Paid $920 to repair the loader after the operator backed it into a tree.

Dec. 31 Recorded annual straight-line depreciation on the loader.

Required

Prepare journal entries to record these transactions and events.

Problem 8-4A
Computing and revising
depreciation; selling plant assets

C2 P1 P2

Chen Company completed the following transactions and events involving its delivery trucks.

2010

Jan. 1 Paid $19,415 cash plus $1,165 in sales tax for a new delivery truck estimated to have a five-year life and a $3,000 salvage value. Delivery truck costs are recorded in the Trucks account.

Dec. 31 Recorded annual straight-line depreciation on the truck.

2011

Dec. 31 Due to new information obtained earlier in the year, the truck's estimated useful life was changed from five to four years, and the estimated salvage value was increased to $3,500. Recorded annual straight-line depreciation on the truck.

Check Dec. 31, 2011, Dr. Depr. Expense—Trucks, $4,521

2012

Dec. 31 Recorded annual straight-line depreciation on the truck.
Dec. 31 Sold the truck for $6,200 cash.

Dec. 31, 2012, Dr. Loss on Disposal of Trucks, $1,822

Required

Prepare journal entries to record these transactions and events.

A machine costing $210,000 with a four-year life and an estimated $20,000 salvage value is installed in Calhoon Company's factory on January 1. The factory manager estimates the machine will produce 475,000 units of product during its life. It actually produces the following units: year 1, 121,400; year 2, 122,400; year 3, 119,600; and year 4, 118,200. The total number of units produced by the end of year 4 exceeds the original estimate—this difference was not predicted. (The machine must not be depreciated below its estimated salvage value.)

Problem 8-5A
Depreciation methods
P1

Required

Prepare a table with the following column headings and compute depreciation for each year (and total depreciation of all years combined) for the machine under each depreciation method.

Year	Straight-Line	Units-of-Production	Double-Declining-Balance

Check Year 4: units-of-production depreciation, $44,640; DDB depreciation, $6,250

Saturn Co. purchases a used machine for $167,000 cash on January 2 and readies it for use the next day at an $3,420 cost. On January 3, it is installed on a required operating platform costing $1,080, and it is further readied for operations. The company predicts the machine will be used for six years and have a $14,600 salvage value. Depreciation is to be charged on a straight-line basis. On December 31, at the end of its fifth year in operations, it is disposed of.

Problem 8-6A
Disposal of plant assets
C1 P1 P2

Required

1. Prepare journal entries to record the machine's purchase and the costs to ready and install it. Cash is paid for all costs incurred.
2. Prepare journal entries to record depreciation of the machine at December 31 of (*a*) its first year in operations and (*b*) the year of its disposal.
3. Prepare journal entries to record the machine's disposal under each of the following separate assumptions: (*a*) it is sold for $13,500 cash; (*b*) it is sold for $45,000 cash; and (*c*) it is destroyed in a fire and the insurance company pays $24,000 cash to settle the loss claim.

Check (2*b*) Depr. Exp., $26,150

(3*c*) Dr. Loss from Fire, $16,750

On July 23 of the current year, Dakota Mining Co. pays $4,836,000 for land estimated to contain 7,800,000 tons of recoverable ore. It installs machinery costing $390,000 that has a 10-year life and no salvage value and is capable of mining the ore deposit in eight years. The machinery is paid for on July 25, seven days before mining operations begin. The company removes and sells 400,000 tons of ore during its first five months of operations ending on December 31. Depreciation of the machinery is in proportion to the mine's depletion as the machinery will be abandoned after the ore is mined.

Problem 8-7A
Natural resources
P3

Required

Prepare entries to record (*a*) the purchase of the land, (*b*) the cost and installation of machinery, (*c*) the first five months' depletion assuming the land has a net salvage value of zero after the ore is mined, and (*d*) the first five months' depreciation on the machinery.

Check (*c*) Depletion, $248,000
(*d*) Depreciation, $20,000

Analysis Component

Describe both the similarities and differences in amortization, depletion, and depreciation.

Problem 8-8A
Intangible assets

P4

On July 1, 2006, Sweetman Company signed a contract to lease space in a building for 15 years. The lease contract calls for annual (prepaid) rental payments of $70,000 on each July 1 throughout the life of the lease and for the lessee to pay for all additions and improvements to the leased property. On June 25, 2011, Sweetman decides to sublease the space to Kirk & Associates for the remaining 10 years of the lease—Kirk pays $185,000 to Sweetman for the right to sublease and it agrees to assume the obligation to pay the $70,000 annual rent to the building owner beginning July 1, 2011. After taking possession of the leased space, Kirk pays for improving the office portion of the leased space at a $129,840 cost. The improvements are paid for by Kirk on July 5, 2011, and are estimated to have a useful life equal to the 16 years remaining in the life of the building.

Required

1. Prepare entries for Kirk to record (*a*) its payment to Sweetman for the right to sublease the building space, (*b*) its payment of the 2011 annual rent to the building owner, and (*c*) its payment for the office improvements.

Check Dr. Rent Expense for (2*a*) $9,250, (2*c*) $35,000

2. Prepare Kirk's year-end adjusting entries required at December 31, 2011, to (*a*) amortize the $185,000 cost of the sublease, (*b*) amortize the office improvements, and (*c*) record rent expense.

PROBLEM SET B

Problem 8-1B
Plant asset costs; depreciation methods

C1 P1

Racerback Company negotiates a lump-sum purchase of several assets from a contractor who is relocating. The purchase is completed on January 1, 2011, at a total cash price of $1,610,000 for a building, land, land improvements, and six trucks. The estimated market values of the assets are building, $784,800; land, $540,640; land improvements, $226,720; and six trucks, $191,840. The company's fiscal year ends on December 31.

Required

1. Prepare a table to allocate the lump-sum purchase price to the separate assets purchased (round percents to the nearest 1%). Prepare the journal entry to record the purchase.

Check (2) $52,000

2. Compute the depreciation expense for year 2011 on the building using the straight-line method, assuming a 12-year life and a $100,500 salvage value.

(3) $41,860

3. Compute the depreciation expense for year 2011 on the land improvements assuming a 10-year life and double-declining-balance depreciation.

Analysis Component

4. Defend or refute this statement: Accelerated depreciation results in payment of more taxes over the asset's life.

Problem 8-2B
Asset cost allocation; straight-line depreciation

C1 P1

In January 2011, InTech Co. pays $1,350,000 for a tract of land with two buildings. It plans to demolish Building A and build a new shop in its place. Building B will be a company office; it is appraised at $472,770, with a useful life of 15 years and a $90,000 salvage value. A lighted parking lot near Building B has improvements (Land Improvements B) valued at $125,145 that are expected to last another six years with no salvage value. Without the buildings and improvements, the tract of land is valued at $792,585. The company also incurs the following additional costs.

Cost to demolish Building A	$ 117,000
Cost of additional land grading	172,500
Cost to construct new building (Building C), having a useful life of 20 years and a $295,500 salvage value	1,356,000
Cost of new land improvements (Land Improvements C) near Building C, having a 10-year useful life and no salvage value	101,250

Required

Check (1) Land costs, $1,059,000; Building B costs, $459,000

1. Prepare a table with the following column headings: Land, Building B, Building C, Land Improvements B, and Land Improvements C. Allocate the costs incurred by InTech to the appropriate columns and total each column (round percents to the nearest 1%).

2. Prepare a single journal entry to record all incurred costs assuming they are paid in cash on January 1, 2011.

(3) Depr.—Land Improv. B and C, $20,250 and $10,125

3. Using the straight-line method, prepare the December 31 adjusting entries to record depreciation for the 12 months of 2011 when these assets were in use.

Xpress Delivery Service completed the following transactions and events involving the purchase and operation of equipment for its business.

2010

Jan. 1   Paid $24,950 cash plus $1,950 in sales tax for a new delivery van that was estimated to have a five-year life and a $3,400 salvage value. Van costs are recorded in the Equipment account.
Jan. 3   Paid $1,550 to install sorting racks in the van for more accurate and quicker delivery of packages. This increases the estimated salvage value of the van by another $200.
Dec. 31   Recorded annual straight-line depreciation on the van.

2011

Jan. 1   Paid $1,970 to overhaul the van's engine, which increased the van's estimated useful life by two years.
May 10   Paid $600 to repair the van after the driver backed it into a loading dock.
Dec. 31   Record annual straight-line depreciation on the van. (Round to the nearest dollar.)

Required

Prepare journal entries to record these transactions and events.

Field Instruments completed the following transactions and events involving its machinery.

2010

Jan. 1   Paid $106,600 cash plus $6,400 in sales tax for a new machine. The machine is estimated to have a six-year life and a $9,800 salvage value.
Dec. 31   Recorded annual straight-line depreciation on the machinery.

2011

Dec. 31   Due to new information obtained earlier in the year, the machine's estimated useful life was changed from six to four years, and the estimated salvage value was increased to $13,050. Recorded annual straight-line depreciation on the machinery.

2012

Dec. 31   Recorded annual straight-line depreciation on the machinery.
Dec. 31   Sold the machine for $25,240 cash.

Required

Prepare journal entries to record these transactions and events.

On January 2, Gannon Co. purchases and installs a new machine costing $312,000 with a five-year life and an estimated $28,000 salvage value. Management estimates the machine will produce 1,136,000 units of product during its life. Actual production of units is as follows: year 1, 245,600; year 2, 230,400; year 3, 227,000; year 4, 232,600; and year 5, 211,200. The total number of units produced by the end of year 5 exceeds the original estimate—this difference was not predicted. (The machine must not be depreciated below its estimated salvage value.)

Required

Prepare a table with the following column headings and compute depreciation for each year (and total depreciation of all years combined) for the machine under each depreciation method.

Year	Straight-Line	Units-of-Production	Double-Declining-Balance

---

On January 1, Jefferson purchases a used machine for $130,000 and readies it for use the next day at a cost of $3,390. On January 4, it is mounted on a required operating platform costing $4,800, and it is further readied for operations. Management estimates the machine will be used for seven years and have an $18,000 salvage value. Depreciation is to be charged on a straight-line basis. On December 31, at the end of its sixth year of use, the machine is disposed of.

Required

1. Prepare journal entries to record the machine's purchase and the costs to ready and install it. Cash is paid for all costs incurred.

Check   (2*b*) Depr. Exp., $17,170

2. Prepare journal entries to record depreciation of the machine at December 31 of (*a*) its first year in operations and (*b*) the year of its disposal.

(3*c*) Dr. Loss from Fire, $15,170

3. Prepare journal entries to record the machine's disposal under each of the following separate assumptions: (*a*) it is sold for $30,000 cash; (*b*) it is sold for $50,000 cash; and (*c*) it is destroyed in a fire and the insurance company pays $20,000 cash to settle the loss claim.

Problem 8-7B
Natural resources
P3

On February 19 of the current year, Rock Chalk Co. pays $4,450,000 for land estimated to contain 5 million tons of recoverable ore. It installs machinery costing $200,000 that has a 16-year life and no salvage value and is capable of mining the ore deposit in 12 years. The machinery is paid for on March 21, eleven days before mining operations begin. The company removes and sells 352,000 tons of ore during its first nine months of operations ending on December 31. Depreciation of the machinery is in proportion to the mine's depletion as the machinery will be abandoned after the ore is mined.

Required

Check   (*c*) Depletion, $313,280;
(*d*) Depreciation, $14,080

Prepare entries to record (*a*) the purchase of the land, (*b*) the cost and installation of the machinery, (*c*) the first nine months' depletion assuming the land has a net salvage value of zero after the ore is mined, and (*d*) the first nine months' depreciation on the machinery.

Analysis Component

Describe both the similarities and differences in amortization, depletion, and depreciation.

Problem 8-8B
Intangible assets
P4

On January 1, 2004, Liberty Co. entered into a 12-year lease on a building. The lease contract requires (1) annual (prepaid) rental payments of $26,400 each January 1 throughout the life of the lease and (2) for the lessee to pay for all additions and improvements to the leased property. On January 1, 2011, Liberty decides to sublease the space to Moberly Co. for the remaining five years of the lease—Moberly pays $30,000 to Liberty for the right to sublease and agrees to assume the obligation to pay the $26,400 annual rent to the building owner beginning January 1, 2011. After taking possession of the leased space, Moberly pays for improving the office portion of the leased space at an $18,000 cost. The improvements are paid for by Moberly on January 3, 2011, and are estimated to have a useful life equal to the 13 years remaining in the life of the building.

Required

1. Prepare entries for Moberly to record (*a*) its payment to Liberty for the right to sublease the building space, (*b*) its payment of the 2011 annual rent to the building owner, and (*c*) its payment for the office improvements.

Check   Dr. Rent Expense:
(2*a*) $6,000, (2*c*) $26,400

2. Prepare Moberly's year-end adjusting entries required on December 31, 2011, to (*a*) amortize the $30,000 cost of the sublease, (*b*) amortize the office improvements, and (*c*) record rent expense.

SERIAL PROBLEM
Business Solutions
P1   A1

(This serial problem began in Chapter 1 and continues through most of the book. If previous chapter segments were not completed, the serial problem can begin at this point. It is helpful, but not necessary, to use the Working Papers that accompany the book.)

SP 8   Selected ledger account balances for Business Solutions follow.

	For Three Months Ended December 31, 2011	For Three Months Ended March 31, 2012
Office equipment	$ 8,000	$ 8,000
Accumulated depreciation— Office equipment	400	800
Computer equipment	20,000	20,000
Accumulated depreciation— Computer equipment	1,250	2,500
Total revenue	31,284	44,000
Total assets	83,460	120,268

Required

1. Assume that Business Solutions does not acquire additional office equipment or computer equipment in 2012. Compute amounts for *the year ended* December 31, 2012, for Depreciation Expense—Office Equipment and for Depreciation Expense—Computer Equipment (assume use of the straight-line method).

2. Given the assumptions in part 1, what is the book value of both the office equipment and the computer equipment as of December 31, 2012?

3. Compute the three-month total asset turnover for Business Solutions as of March 31, 2012. Use total revenue for the numerator and average the December 31, 2011, total assets and the March 31, 2012, total assets for the denominator. Interpret its total asset turnover if competitors average 2.5 for annual periods. (Round turnover to two decimals.)

Check (3) Three-month (annual) turnover = 0.43 (1.73 annual)

Beyond the Numbers

BTN 8-1   Refer to the financial statements of **Research In Motion** in Appendix A to answer the following.

1. What percent of the original cost of RIM's property, plant and equipment remains to be depreciated as of February 27, 2010, and at February 28, 2009? Assume these assets have no salvage value.

2. Over what length(s) of time is RIM depreciating its major categories of property, plant and equipment?

3. What is the change in total property, plant and equipment (before accumulated depreciation) for the year ended February 27, 2010? What is the amount of cash provided (used) by investing activities for property, plant and equipment for the year ended February 27, 2010? What is one possible explanation for the difference between these two amounts?

4. Compute its total asset turnover for the year ended February 27, 2010, and the year ended February 28, 2009. Assume total assets at March 1, 2008, are $5,511 ($ millions).

Fast Forward

5. Access RIM's financial statements for fiscal years ending after February 27, 2010, at its Website (**RIM.com**) or the SEC's EDGAR database (**www.sec.gov**). Recompute RIM's total asset turnover for the additional years' data you collect. Comment on any differences relative to the turnover computed in part 4.

REPORTING IN ACTION

A1 ♟

RIM

BTN 8-2   Comparative figures for **Research In Motion** and **Apple** follow.

($ millions)	Research In Motion			Apple		
	Current Year	One Year Prior	Two Years Prior	Current Year	One Year Prior	Two Years Prior
Total assets	$10,204	$ 8,101	$5,511	$47,501	$36,171	$25,347
Net sales	14,953	11,065	6,009	42,905	37,491	24,578

COMPARATIVE ANALYSIS

A1

RIM

Apple

Required

1. Compute total asset turnover for the most recent two years for Research In Motion and Apple using the data shown.

2. Which company is more efficient in generating net sales given the total assets it employs? Assume an industry average of 1.0 for asset turnover.

BTN 8-3   Flo Choi owns a small business and manages its accounting. Her company just finished a year in which a large amount of borrowed funds was invested in a new building addition as well as in equipment and fixture additions. Choi's banker requires her to submit semiannual financial statements so he can monitor the financial health of her business. He has warned her that if profit margins erode, he might raise the interest rate on the borrowed funds to reflect the increased loan risk from the bank's point of view. Choi knows profit margin is likely to decline this year. As she prepares year-end adjusting entries, she decides to apply the following depreciation rule: All asset additions are considered to be in use on the first day of the following month. (The previous rule assumed assets are in use on the first day of the month nearest to the purchase date.)

ETHICS CHALLENGE

C1

Required

1. Identify decisions that managers like Choi must make in applying depreciation methods.
2. Is Choi's rule an ethical violation, or is it a legitimate decision in computing depreciation?
3. How will Choi's new depreciation rule affect the profit margin of her business?

COMMUNICATING IN PRACTICE

A1

BTN 8-4   Teams are to select an industry, and each team member is to select a different company in that industry. Each team member is to acquire the financial statements (Form 10-K) of the company selected—see the company's Website or the SEC's EDGAR database (www.SEC.gov). Use the financial statements to compute total asset turnover. Communicate with teammates via a meeting, e-mail, or telephone to discuss the meaning of this ratio, how different companies compare to each other, and the industry norm. The team must prepare a one-page report that describes the ratios for each company and identifies the conclusions reached during the team's discussion.

TAKING IT TO THE NET

P4

BTN 8-5   Access the Yahoo! (ticker: YHOO) 10-K report for the year ended December 31, 2009, filed on February 26, 2010, at www.SEC.gov.

Required

1. What amount of goodwill is reported on Yahoo!'s balance sheet? What percentage of total assets does its goodwill represent? Is goodwill a major asset for Yahoo!? Explain.
2. Locate Note 5 to its financial statements. Identify the change in goodwill from December 31, 2008, to December 31, 2009. Comment on the change in goodwill over this period.
3. Locate Note 6 to its financial statements. What are the three categories of intangible assets that Yahoo! reports at December 31, 2009? What proportion of total assets do the intangibles represent?
4. What does Yahoo! indicate is the life of "Trade names, trademarks, and domain names" according to its Note 6? Comment on the difference between the estimated useful life and the legal life of Yahoo!'s trademark.

TEAMWORK IN ACTION

P1

BTN 8-6   Each team member is to become an expert on one depreciation method to facilitate teammates' understanding of that method. Follow these procedures:

a. Each team member is to select an area for expertise from one of the following depreciation methods: straight-line, units-of-production, or double-declining-balance.
b. Expert teams are to be formed from those who have selected the same area of expertise. The instructor will identify the location where each expert team meets.
c. Using the following data, expert teams are to collaborate and develop a presentation answering the requirements. Expert team members must write the presentation in a format they can show to their learning teams.

Data and Requirements   On January 8, 2009, Waverly Riders purchases a van to transport rafters back to the point of departure at the conclusion of the rafting adventures they operate. The cost of the van is $44,000. It has an estimated salvage value of $2,000 and is expected to be used for four years and driven 60,000 miles. The van is driven 12,000 miles in 2009, 18,000 miles in 2010, 21,000 in 2011, and 10,000 in 2012.

1. Compute the annual depreciation expense for each year of the van's estimated useful life.
2. Explain when and how annual depreciation is recorded.
3. Explain the impact on income of this depreciation method versus others over the van's life.
4. Identify the van's book value for each year of its life and illustrate the reporting of this amount for any one year.

d. Re-form original learning teams. In rotation, experts are to present to their teams the results from part *c*. Experts are to encourage and respond to questions.

Point: This activity can follow an overview of each method. Step 1 allows for three areas of expertise. Larger teams will have some duplication of areas, but the straight-line choice should not be duplicated. Expert teams can use the book and consult with the instructor.

ENTREPRENEURIAL DECISION

A1

BTN 8-7   Review the chapter's opening feature involving Games2U. Assume that the company currently has net sales of $8,000,000, and that it is planning an expansion that will increase net sales by $4,000,000. To accomplish this expansion, Games2U must increase its average total assets from $2,500,000 to $3,000,000.

Required

1. Compute the company's total asset turnover under (*a*) current conditions and (*b*) proposed conditions.
2. Evaluate and comment on the merits of the proposal given your analysis in part 1. Identify any concerns you would express about the proposal.

BTN 8-8   Team up with one or more classmates for this activity. Identify companies in your community or area that must account for at least one of the following assets: natural resource; patent; lease; leasehold improvement; copyright; trademark; or goodwill. You might find a company having more than one type of asset. Once you identify a company with a specific asset, describe the accounting this company uses to allocate the cost of that asset to the periods benefited from its use.

HITTING THE ROAD

P3   P4

BTN 8-9   Nokia (www.Nokia.com), Research In Motion, and Apple are all competitors in the global marketplace. Comparative figures for these companies' recent annual accounting periods follow.

GLOBAL DECISION

A1

NOKIA

RIM

Apple

(in millions, except turnover)	Nokia (EUR millions)			Research In Motion		Apple	
	Current Year	Prior Year	Two Years Prior	Current Year	Prior Year	Current Year	Prior Year
Total assets	35,738	39,582	37,599	$10,204	$ 8,101	$47,501	$36,171
Net sales	40,984	50,710	51,058	14,953	11,065	42,905	37,491
Total asset turnover	?	?	—	1.63	1.63	1.03	1.22

Required

1. Compute total asset turnover for the most recent two years for Nokia using the data shown.
2. Which company is most efficient in generating net sales given the total assets it employs?

ANSWERS TO MULTIPLE CHOICE QUIZ

1. b;

	Appraisal Value	%	Total Cost	Allocated
Land	$175,000	50%	$326,000	$163,000
Land improvements	70,000	20	326,000	65,200
Building	105,000	30	326,000	97,800
Totals	$350,000			$326,000

2. c; ($35,000 − $1,000)/4 years = $8,500 per year.

3. c; 2011: $10,800,000 × (2 × 10%) = $2,160,000
      2012: ($10,800,000 − $2,160,000) × (2 × 10%) = $1,728,000

4. c;

Cost of machine	$250,000
Accumulated depreciation	100,000
Book value	150,000
Cash received	120,000
Loss on sale	$ 30,000

5. b; $550,000/$500,000 = 1.10

A Look Back

Chapter 8 focused on long-term assets including plant assets, natural resources, and intangibles. We showed how to account for and analyze those assets.

A Look at This Chapter

This chapter explains how to identify, compute, record, and report current liabilities in financial statements. We also analyze and interpret these liabilities, including those related to employee costs.

A Look Ahead

Chapter 10 focuses on long-term liabilities. We explain how to value, record, amortize, and report these liabilities in financial statements.

9
Reporting and Analyzing Current Liabilities

Learning Objectives

CAP

CONCEPTUAL

C1 Describe current and long-term liabilities and their characteristics. (p. 370)

C2 Identify and describe known current liabilities. (p. 372)

C3 Explain how to account for contingent liabilities. (p. 382)

ANALYTICAL

A1 Compute the times interest earned ratio and use it to analyze liabilities. (p. 384)

LP9

PROCEDURAL

P1 Prepare entries to account for short-term notes payable. (p. 373)

P2 Compute and record *employee* payroll deductions and liabilities. (p. 376)

P3 Compute and record *employer* payroll expenses and liabilities. (p. 377)

P4 Account for estimated liabilities, including warranties and bonuses. (p. 379)

P5 *Appendix 9A*—Identify and describe the details of payroll reports, records, and procedures. (p. 387) expense averages about 4% of a car's selling price, or $640 in this case ($16,000 × 4%). The dealer records the estimated expense and liability related to this sale with this entry:

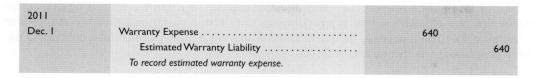

2011			
Dec. 1	Warranty Expense	640	
	Estimated Warranty Liability		640
	To record estimated warranty expense.		

Assets = Liabilities + Equity
+640   −640

This entry alternatively could be made as part of end-of-period adjustments. Either way, the estimated warranty expense is reported on the 2011 income statement and the warranty liability on the 2011 balance sheet. To further extend this example, suppose the customer returns the car for warranty repairs on January 9, 2012. The dealer performs this work by replacing parts costing $200. The entry to record partial settlement of the estimated warranty liability is

Point: Recognition of warranty liabilities is necessary to comply with the matching and full disclosure principles.

2012			
Jan. 9	Estimated Warranty Liability	200	
	Auto Parts Inventory		200
	To record costs of warranty repairs.		

Assets = Liabilities + Equity
−200   −200

This entry reduces the balance of the estimated warranty liability. Warranty expense was previously recorded in 2011, the year the car was sold with the warranty. Finally, what happens if total warranty expenses are more or less than the estimated 4%, or $640? The answer is that management should monitor actual warranty expenses to see whether the 4% rate is accurate. If experience reveals a large difference from the estimate, the rate for current and future sales should be changed. Differences are expected, but they should be small.

Point: Both U.S. GAAP and IFRS account for restructuring costs in a manner similar to accounting for warranties.

Decision Insight

Guaranteed Profits   Best Buy earns a 60% profit margin on its warranty contracts, and those contracts are a large part of its profit—see table to the side [*BusinessWeek*]. ■

Warranty contracts as a percentage of sales	4%
Warranty contracts as a percentage of operating profit	45%
Profit margin on warranty contracts	60%

Multi-Period Estimated Liabilities

Estimated liabilities can be both current and long term. For example, pension liabilities to employees are long term to workers who will not retire within the next period. For employees who are retired or will retire within the next period, a portion of pension liabilities is current. Other examples include employee health benefits and warranties. Specifically, many warranties are for 30 or 60 days in length. Estimated costs under these warranties are properly reported in current liabilities. Many other automobile warranties are for three years or 36,000 miles. A portion of these warranties is reported as long term.

Quick Check   Answers — p. 395

7. Estimated liabilities involve an obligation to pay which of these? (*a*) An uncertain but reasonably estimated amount owed on a known obligation or (*b*) A known amount to a specific entity on an uncertain due date.

8. A car is sold for $15,000 on June 1, 2011, with a one-year warranty on parts. Warranty expense is estimated at 1.5% of selling price at each calendar year-end. On March 1, 2012, the car is returned for warranty repairs costing $135. The amount recorded as warranty expense on March 1 is (*a*) $0; (*b*) $60; (*c*) $75; (*d*) $135; (*e*) $225.

CONTINGENT LIABILITIES

C3   Explain how to account for contingent liabilities.

A **contingent liability** is a potential obligation that depends on a future event arising from a past transaction or event. An example is a pending lawsuit. Here, a past transaction or event leads to a lawsuit whose result depends on the outcome of the suit. Future payment of a contingent liability depends on whether an uncertain future event occurs.

Accounting for Contingent Liabilities

Accounting for contingent liabilities depends on the likelihood that a future event will occur and the ability to estimate the future amount owed if this event occurs. Three different possibilities are identified in the following chart: record liability, disclose in notes, or no disclosure.

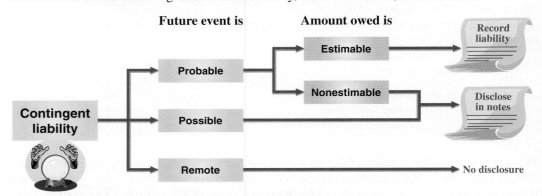

The conditions that determine each of these three possibilities follow:

1. The future event is *probable* (likely) and the amount owed can be *reasonably estimated*. We then record this amount as a liability. Examples are the estimated liabilities described earlier such as warranties, vacation pay, and income taxes.
2. The future event is *reasonably possible* (could occur). We disclose information about this type of contingent liability in notes to the financial statements.
3. The future event is *remote* (unlikely). We do not record or disclose information on remote contingent liabilities.

Point: A contingency is an *if*. Namely, if a future event occurs, then financial consequences are likely for the entity.

Reasonably Possible Contingent Liabilities

This section identifies and discusses contingent liabilities that commonly fall in the second category—when the future event is reasonably possible. Disclosing information about contingencies in this category is motivated by the *full-disclosure principle,* which requires information relevant to decision makers be reported and not ignored.

Point: A sale of a note receivable is often a contingent liability. It becomes a liability if the original signer of the note fails to pay it at maturity.

Potential Legal Claims   Many companies are sued or at risk of being sued. The accounting issue is whether the defendant should recognize a liability on its balance sheet or disclose a contingent liability in its notes while a lawsuit is outstanding and not yet settled. The answer is that a potential claim is recorded in the accounts *only* if payment for damages is probable and the amount can be reasonably estimated. If the potential claim cannot be reasonably estimated or is less than probable but reasonably possible, it is disclosed. **Ford Motor Company**, for example, includes the following note in its annual report: "Various legal actions, governmental investigations and proceedings and claims are pending . . . arising out of alleged defects in our products."

Debt Guarantees   Sometimes a company guarantees the payment of debt owed by a supplier, customer, or another company. The guarantor usually discloses the guarantee in its financial statement notes as a contingent liability. If it is probable that the debtor will default, the guarantor needs to record and report the guarantee in its financial statements as a liability. The **Boston Celtics** report a unique guarantee when it comes to coaches and players: "Certain of the contracts provide for guaranteed payments which must be paid even if the employee [player] is injured or terminated."

Other Contingencies   Other examples of contingencies include environmental damages, possible tax assessments, insurance losses, and government investigations. **Sunoco**, for instance, reports that "federal, state and local laws . . . result in liabilities and loss contingencies. Sunoco accrues . . . cleanup costs [that] are probable and reasonably estimable. Management believes it is reasonably possible (i.e., less than probable but greater than remote) that additional . . . losses will be incurred." Many of Sunoco's contingencies are revealed only in notes.

Point: Auditors and managers often have different views about whether a contingency is recorded, disclosed, or omitted.

Decision Insight

Pricing Priceless What's it worth to see from one side of the Grand Canyon to the other? What's the cost when gulf coast beaches are closed due to an oil well disaster? A method to measure environmental liabilities is *contingent valuation,* by which people answer such questions. Regulators use their answers to levy fines and assess punitive damages. ∎

Uncertainties That Are Not Contingencies

All organizations face uncertainties from future events such as natural disasters and the development of new competing products or services. These uncertainties are not contingent liabilities because they are future events *not* arising from past transactions. Accordingly, they are not disclosed.

 Fraud

Risky Payables. Following are some warning signs of potential fraud involving payables:

- **Duplicate** payments in the same or similar amount to the same vendor (or invoices to the same vendor with the same or similar date).
- **Invoices** at amounts just below the limit requiring managerial approval.
- **Irregular vendor information** such as the absence of a business/home phone number or phone numbers that always go to an answering system; multiple vendors with the same phone number; vendors with PO box billing addresses; vendors with similar-sounding or similar-spelled names.
- **Unusual invoice activity** such as increases or decreases in invoice activity, or above-average invoice amounts, or activity at abnormal dates.

Quick Check
Answers — p. 395

9. A future payment is reported as a liability on the balance sheet if payment is contingent on a future event that (*a*) is reasonably possible but the payment cannot be reasonably estimated; (*b*) is probable and the payment can be reasonably estimated; or (*c*) is not probable but the payment is known.

10. Under what circumstances is a future payment reported in the notes to the financial statements as a contingent liability?

GLOBAL VIEW

This section discusses similarities and differences between U.S. GAAP and IFRS in accounting and reporting for current liabilities.

Characteristics of Liabilities The definitions and characteristics of current liabilities are broadly similar for both U.S. GAAP and IFRS. Although differences exist, the similarities vastly outweigh any differences. Remembering that "provision" is typically used under IFRS to refer to what is titled "liability" under U.S. GAAP, Nokia describes its recognition of liabilities as follows:

NOKIA

> Provisions are recognized when the Group has a present legal or constructive obligation as a result of past events, it is probable that an outflow of resources will be required to settle the obligation and a reliable estimate of the amount can be made.

Known (Determinable) Liabilities　When there is little uncertainty surrounding current liabilities, both U.S. GAAP and IFRS require companies to record them in a similar manner. This correspondence in accounting applies to accounts payable, sales taxes payable, unearned revenues, short-term notes, and payroll liabilities. Of course, tax regulatory systems of countries are different, which implies use of different rates and levels. Still, the basic approach is the same.

Estimated Liabilities　When there is a known current obligation that involves an uncertain amount, but one that can be reasonably estimated, both U.S. GAAP and IFRS require similar treatment. This treatment extends to many obligations such as those arising from vacations, warranties, restructurings, pensions, and health care. Both accounting systems require that companies record estimated expenses related to these obligations when they can reasonably estimate the amounts. **Nokia** reports wages, salaries and bonuses of €5,658 million. It also reports pension expenses of €427 million.

 Decision Analysis ■ ■ ■   **Times Interest Earned Ratio**

A1   Compute the times interest earned ratio and use it to analyze liabilities.

A company incurs interest expense on many of its current and long-term liabilities. Examples extend from its short-term notes and the current portion of long-term liabilities to its long-term notes and bonds. Interest expense is often viewed as a *fixed expense* because the amount of these liabilities is likely to remain in one form or another for a substantial period of time. This means that the amount of interest is unlikely to vary due to changes in sales or other operating activities. While fixed expenses can be advantageous when a company is growing, they create risk. This risk stems from the possibility that a company might be unable to pay fixed expenses if sales decline. To illustrate, consider Diego Co.'s results for 2011 and two possible outcomes for year 2012 in Exhibit 9.5.

EXHIBIT 9.5

Actual and Projected Results

($ thousands)	2011	2012 Projections	
		Sales Increase	Sales Decrease
Sales	$600	$900	$300
Expenses (75% of sales)	450	675	225
Income before interest	150	225	75
Interest expense (fixed)	60	60	60
Net income	$ 90	$165	$ 15

Expenses excluding interest are at, and expected to remain at, 75% of sales. Expenses such as these that change with sales volume are called *variable expenses*. However, interest expense is at, and expected to remain at, $60,000 per year due to its fixed nature.

The middle numerical column of Exhibit 9.5 shows that Diego's income increases by 83% to $165,000 if sales increase by 50% to $900,000. In contrast, the far right column shows that income decreases by 83% if sales decline by 50%. These results reveal that the amount of fixed interest expense affects a company's risk of its ability to pay interest, which is numerically reflected in the **times interest earned** ratio in Exhibit 9.6.

EXHIBIT 9.6

Times Interest Earned

$$\text{Times interest earned} = \frac{\text{Income before interest expense and income taxes}}{\text{Interest expense}}$$

For 2011, Diego's times interest earned is computed as $150,000/$60,000, or 2.5 times. This ratio suggests that Diego faces low to moderate risk because its sales must decline sharply before it would be unable to cover its interest expenses. (Diego is an LLC and does not pay income taxes.)

Experience shows that when times interest earned falls below 1.5 to 2.0 and remains at that level or lower for several periods, the default rate on liabilities increases sharply. This reflects increased risk for companies and their creditors. We also must interpret the times interest earned ratio in light of information about the variability of a company's income before interest. If income is stable from year to year or if it is growing, the company can afford to take on added risk by borrowing. If its income greatly varies from year to year, fixed interest expense can increase the risk that it will not earn enough income to pay interest.

☐ Decision Maker   Answer — p. 394

Entrepreneur   You wish to invest in a franchise for either one of two national chains. Each franchise has an expected annual net income *after* interest and taxes of $100,000. Net income for the first franchise includes a regular fixed interest charge of $200,000. The fixed interest charge for the second franchise is $40,000. Which franchise is riskier to you if sales forecasts are not met? Does your decision change if the first franchise has more variability in its income stream? ■

DEMONSTRATION PROBLEM

The following transactions and events took place at Kern Company during its recent calendar-year reporting period (Kern does not use reversing entries).

a. In September 2011, Kern sold $140,000 of merchandise covered by a 180-day warranty. Prior experience shows that costs of the warranty equal 5% of sales. Compute September's warranty expense and prepare the adjusting journal entry for the warranty liability as recorded at September 30. Also prepare the journal entry on October 8 to record a $300 cash expenditure to provide warranty service on an item sold in September.

b. On October 12, 2011, Kern arranged with a supplier to replace Kern's overdue $10,000 account payable by paying $2,500 cash and signing a note for the remainder. The note matures in 90 days and has a 12% interest rate. Prepare the entries recorded on October 12, December 31, and January 10, 2012, related to this transaction.

c. In late December, Kern learns it is facing a product liability suit filed by an unhappy customer. Kern's lawyer advises that although it will probably suffer a loss from the lawsuit, it is not possible to estimate the amount of damages at this time.

d. Sally Bline works for Kern. For the pay period ended November 30, her gross earnings are $3,000. Bline has $800 deducted for federal income taxes and $200 for state income taxes from each paycheck. Additionally, a $35 premium for her health care insurance and a $10 donation for the United Way are deducted. Bline pays FICA Social Security taxes at a rate of 6.2% and FICA Medicare taxes at a rate of 1.45%. She has not earned enough this year to be exempt from any FICA taxes. Journalize the accrual of salaries expense of Bline's wages by Kern.

e. On November 1, Kern borrows $5,000 cash from a bank in return for a 60-day, 12%, $5,000 note. Record the note's issuance on November 1 and its repayment with interest on December 31.

f.[B] Kern has estimated and recorded its quarterly income tax payments. In reviewing its year-end tax adjustments, it identifies an additional $5,000 of income tax expense that should be recorded. A portion of this additional expense, $1,000, is deferrable to future years. Record this year-end income taxes expense adjusting entry.

g. For this calendar-year, Kern's net income is $1,000,000, its interest expense is $275,000, and its income taxes expense is $225,000. Calculate Kern's times interest earned ratio.

PLANNING THE SOLUTION

● For *a,* compute the warranty expense for September and record it with an estimated liability. Record the October expenditure as a decrease in the liability.

● For *b,* eliminate the liability for the account payable and create the liability for the note payable. Compute interest expense for the 80 days that the note is outstanding in 2011 and record it as an additional liability. Record the payment of the note, being sure to include the interest for the 10 days in 2012.

● For *c,* decide whether the company's contingent liability needs to be disclosed or accrued (recorded) according to the two necessary criteria: probable loss and reasonably estimable.

● For *d,* set up payable accounts for all items in Bline's paycheck that require deductions. After deducting all necessary items, credit the remaining amount to Salaries Payable.

● For *e,* record the issuance of the note. Calculate 60 days' interest due using the 360-day convention in the interest formula.

● For *f,* determine how much of the income taxes expense is payable in the current year and how much needs to be deferred.

● For *g,* apply and compute times interest earned.

SOLUTION TO DEMONSTRATION PROBLEM

a. Warranty expense = 5% × $140,000 = $7,000

Sept. 30	Warranty Expense	7,000	
	Estimated Warranty Liability		7,000
	To record warranty expense for the month.		
Oct. 8	Estimated Warranty Liability	300	
	Cash		300
	To record the cost of the warranty service.		

b. Interest expense for 2011 = 12% × $7,500 × 80/360 = $200
Interest expense for 2012 = 12% × $7,500 × 10/360 = $25

Oct. 12	Accounts Payable	10,000	
	Notes Payable		7,500
	Cash		2,500
	Paid $2,500 cash and gave a 90-day, 12% note to extend the due date on the account.		
Dec. 31	Interest Expense	200	
	Interest Payable		200
	To accrue interest on note payable.		
Jan. 10	Interest Expense	25	
	Interest Payable	200	
	Notes Payable	7,500	
	Cash		7,725
	Paid note with interest, including the accrued interest payable.		

c. Disclose the pending lawsuit in the financial statement notes. Although the loss is probable, no liability can be accrued since the loss cannot be reasonably estimated.

d.

Nov. 30	Salaries Expense	3,000.00	
	FICA—Social Security Taxes Payable (6.2%)		186.00
	FICA—Medicare Taxes Payable (1.45%)		43.50
	Employee Federal Income Taxes Payable		800.00
	Employee State Income Taxes Payable		200.00
	Employee Medical Insurance Payable		35.00
	Employee United Way Payable		10.00
	Salaries Payable		1,725.50
	To record Bline's accrued payroll.		

e.

Nov. 1	Cash	5,000	
	Notes Payable		5,000
	Borrowed cash with a 60-day, 12% note.		

When the note and interest are paid 60 days later, Kern Company records this entry:

Dec. 31	Notes Payable	5,000	
	Interest Expense	100	
	Cash		5,100
	Paid note with interest ($5,000 × 12% × 60/360).		

f.

Dec. 31	Income Taxes Expense	5,000	
	Income Taxes Payable		4,000
	Deferred Income Tax Liability		1,000
	To record added income taxes expense and the deferred tax liability.		

g. Times interest earned $= \dfrac{\$1,000,000 + \$275,000 + \$225,000}{\$275,000} = \underline{\underline{5.45 \text{ times}}}$

APPENDIX

Payroll Reports, Records, and Procedures

9A

Understanding payroll procedures and keeping adequate payroll reports and records are essential to a company's success. This appendix focuses on payroll accounting and its reports, records, and procedures.

Payroll Reports   Most employees and employers are required to pay local, state, and federal payroll taxes. Payroll expenses involve liabilities to individual employees, to federal and state governments, and to other organizations such as insurance companies. Beyond paying these liabilities, employers are required to prepare and submit reports explaining how they computed these payments.

> **P5** Identify and describe the details of payroll reports, records, and procedures.

Reporting FICA Taxes and Income Taxes   The Federal Insurance Contributions Act (FICA) requires each employer to file an Internal Revenue Service (IRS) **Form 941,** the *Employer's Quarterly Federal Tax Return,* within one month after the end of each calendar quarter. A sample Form 941 is shown in Exhibit 9A.1 for Phoenix Sales & Service, a landscape design company. Accounting information and software are helpful in tracking payroll transactions and reporting the accumulated information on Form 941. Specifically, the employer reports total wages subject to income tax withholding on line 2 of Form 941. (For simplicity, this appendix uses *wages* to refer to both wages and salaries.) The income tax withheld is reported on line 3. The combined amount of employee and employer FICA (Social Security) taxes for Phoenix Sales & Service is reported on line 5a (taxable Social Security wages, $36,599 \times 12.4\% = \$4,538.28$). The 12.4% is the sum of the Social Security tax withheld, computed as 6.2% tax withheld from the employee wages for the quarter plus the 6.2% tax levied on the employer. The combined amount of employee Medicare wages is reported on line 5c. The 2.9% is the sum of 1.45% withheld from employee wages for the quarter plus 1.45% tax levied on the employer. Total FICA taxes are reported on line 5d and are added to the total income taxes withheld of $3,056.47 to yield a total of $8,656.12. For this year, assume that income up to $110,100 is subject to Social Security tax. There is no income limit on amounts subject to Medicare tax. Congress sets annual limits on the amount owed for Social Security tax.

Federal depository banks are authorized to accept deposits of amounts payable to the federal government. Deposit requirements depend on the amount of tax owed. For example, when the sum of FICA taxes plus the employee income taxes is less than $2,500 for a quarter, the taxes can be paid when Form 941 is filed. Companies with large payrolls are often required to pay monthly or even semiweekly.

Reporting FUTA Taxes and SUTA Taxes   An employer's federal unemployment taxes (FUTA) are reported on an annual basis by filing an *Annual Federal Unemployment Tax Return,* IRS **Form 940.** It must be mailed on or before January 31 following the end of each tax year. Ten more days are allowed if all required tax deposits are filed on a timely basis and the full amount of tax is paid on or before January 31. FUTA payments are made quarterly to a federal depository bank if the total amount due exceeds $500. If $500 or less is due, the taxes are remitted annually. Requirements for paying and reporting state unemployment taxes (SUTA) vary depending on the laws of each state. Most states require quarterly payments and reports.

Form **941**

Employer's QUARTERLY Federal Tax Return

Department of the Treasury — Internal Revenue Service

(EIN)
Employer identification number 8 6 – 3 2 1 4 5 8 7

Name (not your trade name) Phoenix Sales & Service

Trade name (if any)

Address 1214 Mill Road
Number Street Suite or room number

Phoenix AZ 85621
City State ZIP code

Report for this Quarter ...
(Check one.)

☐ 1: January, February, March

☐ 2: April, May, June

☐ 3: July, August, September

☒ 4: October, November, December

Part 1: Answer these questions for this quarter.

1	Number of employees who received wages, tips, or other compensation for the pay period including: *Mar. 12* (Quarter 1), *June 12* (Quarter 2), *Sept. 12* (Quarter 3), *Dec. 12* (Quarter 4)	1	1
2	Wages, tips, and other compensation	2	36,599.00
3	Total income tax withheld from wages, tips, and other compensation	3	3,056.47
4	If no wages, tips, and other compensation are subject to social security or Medicare tax .	☐ Check and go to line 6.	
5	Taxable social security and Medicare wages and tips:		

		Column 1		Column 2
5a	Taxable social security wages . .	36,599.00	× .124 =	4,538.28
5b	Taxable social security tips . . .	.	× .124 =	.
5c	Taxable Medicare wages & tips . .	36,599.00	× .029 =	1,061.37

5d	Total social security and Medicare taxes (*Column 2*, lines 5a + 5b + 5c = line 5d) . **5d**		5,599.65
6	Total taxes before adjustments (lines 3 + 5d = line 6)	6	8,656.12
7	TAX ADJUSTMENTS (Read the instructions for line 7 before completing lines 7a through 7h.):		
7a	Current quarter's fractions of cents		
7b	Current quarter's sick pay		
7c	Current quarter's adjustments for tips and group-term life insurance		
7d	Current year's income tax withholding (attach Form 941c) . .		
7e	Prior quarters' social security and Medicare taxes (attach Form 941c)		
7f	Special additions to federal income tax (attach Form 941c) . .		
7g	Special additions to social security and Medicare (attach Form 941c)		
7h	TOTAL ADJUSTMENTS (Combine all amounts: lines 7a through 7g.) **7h**		0.00
8	Total taxes after adjustments (Combine lines 6 and 7h.) **8**		8,656.12
9	Advance earned income credit (EIC) payments made to employees **9**		.
10	Total taxes after adjustment for advance EIC (lines 8 – line 9 = line 10) **10**		8,656.12
11	Total deposits for this quarter, including overpayment applied from a prior quarter . **11**		8,656.12
12	Balance due (If line 10 is more than line 11, write the difference here.) **12**		0.00
	Make checks payable to *United States Treasury.*		
13	Overpayment (If line 11 is more than line 10, write the difference here.)	0.00	Check one ☐ Apply to next return. ☐ Send a refund.

Part 2: Tell us about your deposit schedule and tax liability for this quarter.

If you are unsure about whether you are a monthly schedule depositor or a semiweekly schedule depositor, see *Pub. 15 (Circular E),* section 11.

14 A Z Write the state abbreviation for the state where you made your deposits OR write "MU" if you made your deposits in *multiple* states.

15 Check one: ☐ Line 10 is less than $2,500. Go to Part 3.

☒ You were a monthly schedule depositor for the entire quarter. Fill out your tax liability for each month. Then go to Part 3.

Tax liability:	Month 1	3,079.11
	Month 2	2,049.77
	Month 3	3,527.24
	Total liability for quarter	8,656.12	Total must equal line 10.

☐ You were a semiweekly schedule depositor for any part of this quarter. Fill out *Schedule B (Form 941): Report of Tax Liability for Semiweekly Schedule Depositors,* and attach it to this form.

Part 3: Tell us about your business. If a question does NOT apply to your business, leave it blank.

16 If your business has closed or you stopped paying wages . . . . ☐ Check here, and

enter the final date you paid wages / / .

17 If you are a seasonal employer and you do not have to file a return for every quarter of the year . ☐ Check here.

Part 4: May we speak with your third-party designee?

Do you want to allow an employee, a paid tax preparer, or another person to discuss this return with the IRS? See the instructions for details.

☐ Yes. Designee's name

Phone (   )   –   Personal Identification Number (PIN)

☒ No.

Part 5: Sign here. You MUST fill out both sides of this form and SIGN it.

Under penalties of perjury, I declare that I have examined this return, including accompanying schedules and statements, and to the best of my knowledge and belief, it is true, correct, and complete.

X Sign your name here

Print name and title

Date / / Phone (   )   –

Reporting Wages and Salaries Employers are required to give each employee an annual report of his or her wages subject to FICA and federal income taxes along with the amounts of these taxes withheld. This report is called a *Wage and Tax Statement,* or **Form W-2.** It must be given to employees before January 31 following the year covered by the report. Exhibit 9A.2 shows Form W-2 for one of the employees at Phoenix Sales & Service. Copies of the W-2 Form must be sent to the Social Security Administration, where the amount of the employee's wages subject to FICA taxes and FICA taxes withheld are posted to each employee's Social Security account. These posted amounts become the basis for determining an employee's retirement and survivors' benefits. The Social Security Administration also transmits to the IRS the amount of each employee's wages subject to federal income taxes and the amount of taxes withheld.

EXHIBIT 9A.2

Form W-2

Form **W-2** Wage and Tax Statement		Department of Treasury—Internal Revenue Service	
Copy 1–For State, City, or Local Tax Department			

a Control number AR101	22222	OMB No. 1545-0006	
b Employer identification number (EIN) 86-3214587		**1** Wages, tips, other compensation 4,910.00	**2** Federal income tax withheld 333.37
c Employer's name, address and ZIP code Phoenix Sales & Service 1214 Mill Road Phoenix, AZ 85621		**3** Social security wages 4,910.00	**4** Social security tax withheld 304.42
		5 Medicare wages and tips 4,910.00	**6** Medicare tax withheld 71.20
		7 Social security tips	**8** Allocated tips
d Employee's social security number 333-22-9999		**9** Advance EIC payment	**10** Dependent care benefits
e Employee's first name and initial Robert J. Last name Austin		**11** Nonqualified plans	**12a** Code
f Employee's address and ZIP code 18 Roosevelt Blvd., Apt. C Tempe, AZ 86322		**13** Statutory employee / Retirement plan / Third-party sick pay	**12b** Code
		14 Other	**12c** Code
			12d Code
15 State AZ Employer's state ID number 13-902319	**16** State wages, tips, etc. 4,910.00	**17** State income tax 26.68	**18** Local wages, tips, etc. **19** Local income tax **20** Locality name

Payroll Records Employers must keep payroll records in addition to reporting and paying taxes. These records usually include a payroll register and an individual earnings report for each employee.

Payroll Register A **payroll register** usually shows the pay period dates, hours worked, gross pay, deductions, and net pay of each employee for each pay period. Exhibit 9A.3 shows a payroll register for Phoenix Sales & Service. It is organized into nine columns:

Col. 1 Employee identification (ID); Employee name; Social Security number (SS No.); Reference (check number); and Date (date check issued)
Col. 2 Pay Type (regular and overtime)
Col. 3 Pay Hours (number of hours worked as regular and overtime)
Col. 4 Gross Pay (amount of gross pay)[2]
Col. 5 FIT (federal income taxes withheld); FUTA (federal unemployment taxes)
Col. 6 SIT (state income taxes withheld); SUTA (state unemployment taxes)
Col. 7 FICA-SS_EE (social security taxes withheld, employee); FICA-SS_ER (social security taxes, employer)
Col. 8 FICA-Med_EE (medicare tax withheld, employee); FICA-Med_ER (medicare tax, employer)
Col. 9 Net pay (Gross pay less amounts withheld from employees)

---

[2] The Gross Pay column shows regular hours worked on the first line multiplied by the regular pay rate—this equals regular pay. Overtime hours multiplied by the overtime premium rate equals overtime premium pay reported on the second line. If employers are engaged in interstate commerce, federal law sets a minimum overtime rate of pay to employees. For this company, workers earn 150% of their regular rate for hours in excess of 40 per week.

EXHIBIT 9A.3

Payroll Register

Net pay for each employee is computed as gross pay minus the items on the first line of columns 5–8. The employer's payroll tax for each employee is computed as the sum of items on the third line of columns 5–8. A payroll register includes all data necessary to record payroll. In some software programs the entries to record payroll are made in a special *payroll journal.*

Payroll Check   Payment of payroll is usually done by check or electronic funds transfer. Exhibit 9A.4 shows a *payroll check* for a Phoenix employee. This check is accompanied with a detachable *statement of earnings* (at top) showing gross pay, deductions, and net pay.

Employee Earnings Report   An **employee earnings report** is a cumulative record of an employee's hours worked, gross earnings, deductions, and net pay. Payroll information on this report is taken from the payroll register. The employee earnings report for R. Austin at Phoenix Sales & Service is shown in Exhibit 9A.5. An employee earnings report accumulates information that can show when an employee's earnings reach the tax-exempt points for FICA, FUTA, and SUTA taxes. It also gives data an employer needs to prepare Form W-2.

Payroll Procedures   Employers must be able to compute federal income tax for payroll purposes. This section explains how we compute this tax and how to use a payroll bank account.

Computing Federal Income Taxes   To compute the amount of taxes withheld from each employee's wages, we need to determine both the employee's wages earned and the employee's number of *withholding*

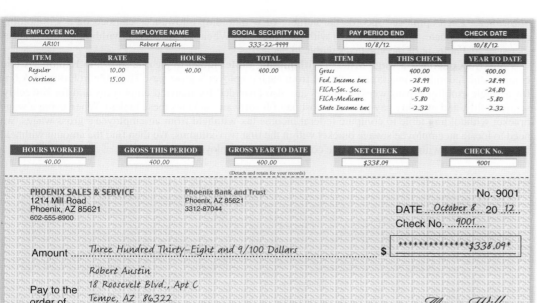

EXHIBIT 9A.4
Check and Statement of Earnings

EMPLOYEE NO.	EMPLOYEE NAME	SOCIAL SECURITY NO.	PAY PERIOD END	CHECK DATE
AR101	Robert Austin	333-22-9999	10/8/12	10/8/12

ITEM	RATE	HOURS	TOTAL	ITEM	THIS CHECK	YEAR TO DATE
Regular	10.00	40.00	400.00	Gross	400.00	400.00
Overtime	15.00			Fed. Income tax	-28.99	-28.99
				FICA-Soc. Sec.	-24.80	-24.80
				FICA-Medicare	-5.80	-5.80
				State Income tax	-2.32	-2.32

HOURS WORKED	GROSS THIS PERIOD	GROSS YEAR TO DATE	NET CHECK	CHECK No.
40.00	400.00	400.00	$338.09	9001

(Detach and retain for your records)

PHOENIX SALES & SERVICE
1214 Mill Road
Phoenix, AZ 85621
602-555-8900

Phoenix Bank and Trust
Phoenix, AZ 85621
3312-87044

No. 9001

DATE *October 8* 20 *12*

Check No. *9001*

Amount *Three Hundred Thirty-Eight and 9/100 Dollars* $ **************$338.09*

Pay to the order of *Robert Austin*
18 Roosevelt Blvd., Apt C
Tempe, AZ 86322

Mary Wills
AUTHORIZED SIGNATURE

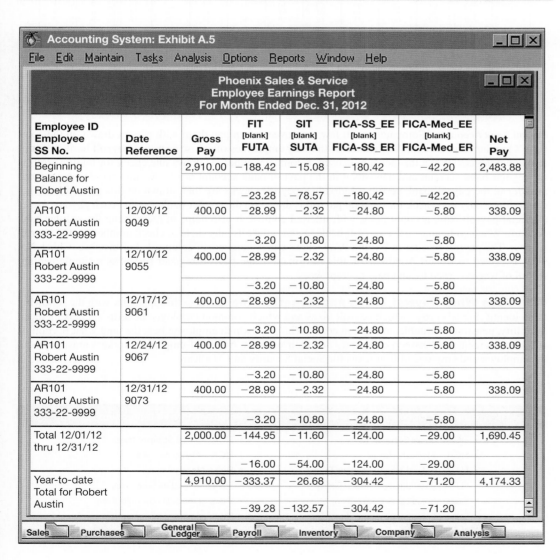

EXHIBIT 9A.5
Employee Earnings Report

Accounting System: Exhibit A.5

File Edit Maintain Tasks Analysis Options Reports Window Help

Phoenix Sales & Service
Employee Earnings Report
For Month Ended Dec. 31, 2012

Employee ID Employee SS No.	Date Reference	Gross Pay	FIT [blank] FUTA	SIT [blank] SUTA	FICA-SS_EE [blank] FICA-SS_ER	FICA-Med_EE [blank] FICA-Med_ER	Net Pay
Beginning Balance for Robert Austin		2,910.00	-188.42	-15.08	-180.42	-42.20	2,483.88
			-23.28	-78.57	-180.42	-42.20	
AR101 Robert Austin 333-22-9999	12/03/12 9049	400.00	-28.99	-2.32	-24.80	-5.80	338.09
			-3.20	-10.80	-24.80	-5.80	
AR101 Robert Austin 333-22-9999	12/10/12 9055	400.00	-28.99	-2.32	-24.80	-5.80	338.09
			-3.20	-10.80	-24.80	-5.80	
AR101 Robert Austin 333-22-9999	12/17/12 9061	400.00	-28.99	-2.32	-24.80	-5.80	338.09
			-3.20	-10.80	-24.80	-5.80	
AR101 Robert Austin 333-22-9999	12/24/12 9067	400.00	-28.99	-2.32	-24.80	-5.80	338.09
			-3.20	-10.80	-24.80	-5.80	
AR101 Robert Austin 333-22-9999	12/31/12 9073	400.00	-28.99	-2.32	-24.80	-5.80	338.09
			-3.20	-10.80	-24.80	-5.80	
Total 12/01/12 thru 12/31/12		2,000.00	-144.95	-11.60	-124.00	-29.00	1,690.45
			-16.00	-54.00	-124.00	-29.00	
Year-to-date Total for Robert Austin		4,910.00	-333.37	-26.68	-304.42	-71.20	4,174.33
			-39.28	-132.57	-304.42	-71.20	

Sales   Purchases   General Ledger   Payroll   Inventory   Company   Analysis *allowances.* Each employee records the number of withholding allowances claimed on a withholding allowance certificate, **Form W-4,** filed with the employer. When the number of withholding allowances increases, the amount of income taxes withheld decreases.

Employers often use a **wage bracket withholding table** similar to the one shown in Exhibit 9A.6 to compute the federal income taxes withheld from each employee's gross pay. The table in Exhibit 9A.6 is for a single employee paid weekly. Tables are also provided for married employees and for biweekly, semimonthly, and monthly pay periods (most payroll software includes these tables). When using a wage bracket withholding table to compute federal income tax withheld from an employee's gross wages, we need to locate an employee's wage bracket within the first two columns. We then find the amount withheld by looking in the withholding allowance column for that employee.

EXHIBIT 9A.6

Wage Bracket Withholding Table

SINGLE Persons—WEEKLY Payroll Period

At least	But less than	0	1	2	3	4	5	6	7	8	9	10
$600	$610	$76	$67	$58	$49	$39	$30	$21	$12	$6	$0	$0
610	620	79	69	59	50	41	32	22	13	7	1	0
620	630	81	70	61	52	42	33	24	15	8	2	0
630	640	84	72	62	53	44	35	25	16	9	3	0
640	650	86	73	64	55	45	36	27	18	10	4	0
650	660	89	75	65	56	47	38	28	19	11	5	0
660	670	91	76	67	58	48	39	30	21	12	6	0
670	680	94	78	68	59	50	41	31	22	13	7	1
680	690	96	81	70	61	51	42	33	24	14	8	2
690	700	99	83	71	62	53	44	34	25	16	9	3
700	710	101	86	73	64	54	45	35	27	17	10	4
710	720	104	88	74	65	56	47	37	28	19	11	5
720	730	106	91	76	67	57	48	39	30	20	12	6
730	740	109	93	78	68	59	50	40	31	22	13	7
740	750	111	96	80	70	60	51	42	33	23	14	8

Payroll Bank Account Companies with few employees often pay them with checks drawn on the company's regular bank account. Companies with many employees often use a special **payroll bank account** to pay employees. When this account is used, a company either (1) draws one check for total payroll on the regular bank account and deposits it in the payroll bank account or (2) executes an *electronic funds transfer* to the payroll bank account. Individual payroll checks are then drawn on this payroll bank account. Since only one check for the total payroll is drawn on the regular bank account each payday, use of a special payroll bank account helps with internal control. It also helps in reconciling the regular bank account. When companies use a payroll bank account, they usually include check numbers in the payroll register. The payroll register in Exhibit 9A.3 shows check numbers in column 1. For instance, Check No. 9001 is issued to Robert Austin. With this information, the payroll register serves as a supplementary record of wages earned by and paid to employees.

Who Pays What Payroll Taxes and Benefits We conclude this appendix with the following table identifying who pays which payroll taxes and which common employee benefits such as medical, disability, pension, charitable, and union costs. Who pays which employee benefits, and what portion, is subject to agreements between companies and their workers. Also, self-employed workers must pay both the employer and employee FICA taxes for Social Security and Medicare.

Employer Payroll Taxes and Costs	Employee Payroll Deductions
• FICA—Social Security Taxes	• FICA—Social Security taxes
• FICA—Medicare Taxes	• FICA—Medicare taxes
• FUTA (Federal Unemployment Taxes)	• Federal Income taxes
• SUTA (State Unemployment Taxes)	• State and local income taxes
• Share of medical coverage, if any	• Share of medical coverage, if any
• Share of pension coverage, if any	• Share of pension coverage, if any
• Share of other benefits, if any	• Share of other benefits, if any

11. What three items determine the amount deducted from an employee's wages for federal income taxes?

12. What amount of income tax is withheld from the salary of an employee who is single with three withholding allowances and earnings of $675 in a week? (*Hint:* Use the wage bracket withholding table in Exhibit 9A.6.)

13. Which of the following steps are executed when a company draws one check for total payroll and deposits it in a special payroll bank account? (*a*) Write a check to the payroll bank account for the total payroll and record it with a debit to Salaries Payable and a credit to Cash. (*b*) Deposit a check (or transfer funds) for the total payroll in the payroll bank account. (*c*) Issue individual payroll checks drawn on the payroll bank account. (*d*) All of the above.

APPENDIX

Corporate Income Taxes

9B

This appendix explains current liabilities involving income taxes for corporations.

Income Tax Liabilities   Corporations are subject to income taxes and must estimate their income tax liability when preparing financial statements. Since income tax expense is created by earning income, a liability is incurred when income is earned. This tax must be paid quarterly under federal regulations. To illustrate, consider a corporation that prepares monthly financial statements. Based on its income in January 2011, this corporation estimates that it owes income taxes of $12,100. The following adjusting entry records this estimate:

Jan. 31	Income Taxes Expense	12,100	
	Income Taxes Payable		12,100
	To accrue January income taxes.		

Assets = Liabilities + Equity
      +12,100 −12,100

The tax liability is recorded each month until the first quarterly payment is made. If the company's estimated taxes for this first quarter total $30,000, the entry to record its payment is

Apr. 10	Income Taxes Payable	30,000	
	Cash		30,000
	Paid estimated quarterly income taxes based on		
	first quarter income.		

Assets = Liabilities + Equity
−30,000 −30,000

This process of accruing and then paying estimated income taxes continues through the year. When annual financial statements are prepared at year-end, the corporation knows its actual total income and the actual amount of income taxes it must pay. This information allows it to properly record income taxes expense for the fourth quarter so that the total of the four quarters' expense amounts equals the actual taxes paid to the government.

Deferred Income Tax Liabilities   An income tax liability for corporations can arise when the amount of income before taxes that the corporation reports on its income statement is not the same as the amount of income reported on its income tax return. This difference occurs because income tax laws and GAAP measure income differently. (Differences between tax laws and GAAP arise because Congress uses tax laws to generate receipts, stimulate the economy, and influence behavior, whereas GAAP are intended to provide financial information useful for business decisions. Also, tax accounting often follows the cash basis, whereas GAAP follows the accrual basis.)

Some differences between tax laws and GAAP are temporary. *Temporary differences* arise when the tax return and the income statement report a revenue or expense in different years. As an example, companies are often able to deduct higher amounts of depreciation in the early years of an asset's life and smaller amounts in later years for tax reporting in comparison to GAAP. This means that in the early years, depreciation for tax reporting is often more than depreciation on the income statement. In later years, depreciation for tax reporting is often less than depreciation on the income statement. When temporary differences exist between taxable income on the tax return and the income before taxes on the income statement, corporations compute income taxes expense based on the income reported on the income statement. The result is that income taxes expense reported in the income statement is often different from the amount of income taxes payable to the government. This difference is the **deferred income tax liability.**

To illustrate, assume that in recording its usual quarterly income tax payments, a corporation computes $25,000 of income taxes expense. It also determines that only $21,000 is currently due and $4,000 is deferred to future years (a timing difference). The entry to record this end-of-period adjustment is

Assets = Liabilities + Equity
+21,000　　　　 −25,000
+4,000

Dec. 31	Income Taxes Expense	25,000	
	Income Taxes Payable		21,000
	Deferred Income Tax Liability		4,000
	To record tax expense and deferred tax liability.		

The credit to Income Taxes Payable reflects the amount currently due to be paid. The credit to Deferred Income Tax Liability reflects tax payments deferred until future years when the temporary difference reverses.

Temporary differences also can cause a company to pay income taxes *before* they are reported on the income statement as expense. If so, the company reports a *Deferred Income Tax Asset* on its balance sheet.

Summary

C1　Describe current and long-term liabilities and their characteristics. Liabilities are probable future payments of assets or services that past transactions or events obligate an entity to make. Current liabilities are due within one year or the operating cycle, whichever is longer. All other liabilities are long term.

C2　Identify and describe known current liabilities. Known (determinable) current liabilities are set by agreements or laws and are measurable with little uncertainty. They include accounts payable, sales taxes payable, unearned revenues, notes payable, payroll liabilities, and the current portion of long-term debt.

C3　Explain how to account for contingent liabilities. If an uncertain future payment depends on a probable future event and the amount can be reasonably estimated, the payment is recorded as a liability. The uncertain future payment is reported as a contingent liability (in the notes) if (*a*) the future event is reasonably possible but not probable or (*b*) the event is probable but the payment amount cannot be reasonably estimated.

A1　Compute the times interest earned ratio and use it to analyze liabilities. Times interest earned is computed by dividing a company's net income before interest expense and income taxes by the amount of interest expense. The times interest earned ratio reflects a company's ability to pay interest obligations.

P1　Prepare entries to account for short-term notes payable. Short-term notes payable are current liabilities; most bear interest. When a short-term note's face value equals the amount borrowed, it identifies a rate of interest to be paid at maturity.

P2　Compute and record *employee* payroll deductions and liabilities. Employee payroll deductions include FICA taxes, income taxes, and voluntary deductions such as for pensions and charities. They make up the difference between gross and net pay.

P3　Compute and record *employer* payroll expenses and liabilities. An employer's payroll expenses include employees' gross earnings, any employee benefits, and the payroll taxes levied on the employer. Payroll liabilities include employees' net pay amounts, withholdings from employee wages, any employer-promised benefits, and the employer's payroll taxes.

P4　Account for estimated liabilities, including warranties and bonuses. Liabilities for health and pension benefits, warranties, and bonuses are recorded with estimated amounts. These items are recognized as expenses when incurred and matched with revenues generated.

P5^A　Identify and describe the details of payroll reports, records, and procedures. Employers report FICA taxes and federal income tax withholdings using Form 941. FUTA taxes are reported on Form 940. Earnings and deductions are reported to each employee and the federal government on Form W-2. An employer's payroll records often include a payroll register for each pay period, payroll checks and statements of earnings, and individual employee earnings reports.

Guidance Answers to **Decision Maker** and Decision Ethics	

Web Designer　You need to be concerned about being an accomplice to unlawful payroll activities. Not paying federal and state taxes on wages earned is illegal and unethical. Such payments also will not provide the employee with Social Security and some Medicare credits. The best course of action is to request payment by check. If this fails to change the owner's payment practices, you must consider quitting this job.

Entrepreneur　Risk is partly reflected by the times interest earned ratio. This ratio for the first franchise is 1.5 [($100,000 +

$200,000)/$200,000], whereas the ratio for the second franchise is 3.5 [($100,000 + $40,000)/$40,000]. This analysis shows that the first franchise is more at risk of incurring a loss if its sales decline. The second question asks about variability of income. If income greatly varies, this increases the risk an owner will not earn sufficient income to cover interest. Since the first franchise has the greater variability, it is a riskier investment.

Guidance Answers to Quick Checks

1. A liability involves a probable future payment of assets or services that an entity is presently obligated to make as a result of past transactions or events.

2. No, an expected future payment is not a liability unless an existing obligation was created by a past event or transaction.

3. In most cases, a liability due in 15 months is classified as long term. It is classified as a current liability if the company's operating cycle is 15 months or longer.

4. A creditor prefers a note payable instead of a past-due account payable so as to (*a*) charge interest and/or (*b*) have evidence of the debt and its terms for potential litigation or disputes.

5. $1,000* × (.008) + $1,000* × (.04) + $3,000 × (.062) + $3,000 × (.0145) = $277.50

_____

* $1,000 of the $3,000 March pay is subject to FUTA and SUTA—the entire $6,000 pay from January and February was subject to them.

6. (*a*) FICA taxes are incurred by both employee and employer. (*b*) FUTA taxes are incurred by the employer. (*c*) SUTA taxes are incurred by the employer. (*d*) Withheld income taxes are incurred by the employee.

7. (*a*)

8. (*a*) Warranty expense was previously estimated and recorded.

9. (*b*)

10. A future payment is reported in the notes as a contingent liability if (*a*) the uncertain future event is probable but the amount of payment cannot be reasonably estimated or (*b*) the uncertain future event is not probable but has a reasonable possibility of occurring.

11. An employee's marital status, gross earnings and number of withholding allowances determine the deduction for federal income taxes.

12. $59

13. (*d*)

Key Terms

Contingent liability (p. 382)
Current liabilities (p. 371)
Current portion of long-term debt (p. 379)
Deferred income tax liability (p. 394)
Employee benefits (p. 379)
Employee earnings report (p. 390)
Estimated liability (p. 379)
Federal depository bank (p. 387)
Federal Insurance Contributions Act (FICA) taxes (p. 376)

Federal Unemployment Taxes (FUTA) (p. 378)
Form 940 (p. 387)
Form 941 (p. 387)
Form W-2 (p. 389)
Form W-4 (p. 392)
Gross pay (p. 376)
Known liabilities (p. 372)
Long-term liabilities (p. 371)
Merit rating (p. 378)

Net pay (p. 376)
Payroll bank account (p. 392)
Payroll deductions (p. 376)
Payroll register (p. 389)
Short-term note payable (p. 373)
State Unemployment Taxes (SUTA) (p. 378)
Times interest earned (p. 384)
Wage bracket withholding table (p. 392)
Warranty (p. 380)

Multiple Choice Quiz   Answers on p. 411   mhhe.com/wildFA6e

Additional quiz questions are available at the book's Website.

1. On December 1, a company signed a $6,000, 90-day, 5% note payable, with principal plus interest due on March 1 of the following year. What amount of interest expense should be accrued at December 31 on the note?
  a. $300
  b. $25
  c. $100
  d. $75
  e. $0

2. An employee earned $50,000 during the year. FICA tax for social security is 6.2% and FICA tax for Medicare is 1.45%. The employer's share of FICA taxes is
  a. Zero, since the employee's pay exceeds the FICA limit.
  b. Zero, since FICA is not an employer tax.
  c. $3,100
  d. $725
  e. $3,825

3. Assume the FUTA tax rate is 0.8% and the SUTA tax rate is 5.4%. Both taxes are applied to the first $7,000 of an employee's pay. What is the total unemployment tax an employer must pay on an employee's annual wages of $40,000?
  a. $2,480
  b. $434
  c. $56
  d. $378
  e. Zero; the employee's wages exceed the $7,000 maximum.

4. A company sells big screen televisions for $3,000 each. Each television has a two-year warranty that covers the replacement of defective parts. It is estimated that 1% of all televisions sold will be returned under warranty at an average cost of $250 each. During July, the company sold 10,000 big screen televisions, and 80 were serviced under the warranty during July at a total cost of $18,000. The credit balance in the Estimated

Warranty Liability account at July 1 was $26,000. What is the company's warranty expense for the month of July?

a. $51,000
b. $1,000
c. $25,000
d. $33,000
e. $18,000

5. Employees earn vacation pay at the rate of 1 day per month. During October, 150 employees qualify for one vacation day

each. Their average daily wage is $175 per day. What is the amount of vacation benefit expense for October?

a. $26,250
b. $175
c. $2,100
d. $63,875
e. $150

A(B) *Superscript letter A (B) denotes assignments based on Appendix 9A (9B).*

Icon denotes assignments that involve decision making.

Discussion Questions

1. What are the three important questions concerning the uncertainty of liabilities?

2. What is the difference between a current and a long-term liability?

3. What is an estimated liability?

4. If $988 is the total of a sale that includes its sales tax of 4%, what is the selling price of the item only?

5. What is the combined amount (in percent) of the employee and employer Social Security tax rate?

6. What is the current Medicare tax rate? This rate is applied to what maximum level of salary and wages?

7. What determines the amount deducted from an employee's wages for federal income taxes?

8. Which payroll taxes are the employee's responsibility and which are the employer's responsibility?

9. What is an employer's unemployment merit rating? How are these ratings assigned to employers?

10. Why are warranty liabilities usually recognized on the balance sheet as liabilities even when they are uncertain?

11. Suppose that a company has a facility located where disastrous weather conditions often occur. Should it report a probable loss from a future disaster as a liability on its balance sheet? Explain.

12.A What is a wage bracket withholding table?

13.A What amount of income tax is withheld from the salary of an employee who is single with two withholding allowances and earning $725 per week? What if the employee earned $625 and has no withholding allowances? (Use Exhibit 9A.6.)

14. Refer to **Research In Motion**'s balance sheet in Appendix A. What revenue-related liability does Research In Motion report at February 27, 2010?   **RIM**

15. Refer to **Apple**'s balance sheet in Appendix A. What is the amount of Apple's accounts payable as of September 26, 2009?   Apple

16. Refer to **Nokia**'s balance sheet in Appendix A. List Nokia's current liabilities as of December 31, 2009.   **NOKIA**

17. Refer to **Palm**'s balance sheet in Appendix A. What current liabilities related to income taxes are on its balance sheet? Explain the meaning of each income tax account identified.   **Palm**

≣ connect

QUICK STUDY

QS 9-1

Classifying liabilities   C1

Which of the following items are normally classified as a current liability for a company that has a 15-month operating cycle?

1. Salaries payable.
2. Note payable due in 19 months.
3. FICA taxes payable.
4. Note payable maturing in 3 years.
5. Note payable due in 10 months.
6. Portion of long-term note due in 15 months.

QS 9-2

Accounting for sales taxes

C2

Wrecker Computing sells merchandise for $5,000 cash on September 30 (cost of merchandise is $2,900). The sales tax law requires Wrecker to collect 4% sales tax on every dollar of merchandise sold. Record the entry for the $5,000 sale and its applicable sales tax. Also record the entry that shows the remittance of the 4% tax on this sale to the state government on October 15.

QS 9-3

Unearned revenue   C2

Tickets, Inc., receives $5,500,000 cash in advance ticket sales for a four-date tour of Bruce Springsteen. Record the advance ticket sales on October 31. Record the revenue earned for the first concert date of November 8, assuming it represents one-fourth of the advance ticket sales.

The following legal claims exist for Kalamazoo Co. Identify the accounting treatment for each claim as either (*a*) a liability that is recorded or (*b*) an item described in notes to its financial statements.

1. Kalamazoo (defendant) estimates that a pending lawsuit could result in damages of $1,000,000; it is reasonably possible that the plaintiff will win the case.

2. Kalamazoo faces a probable loss on a pending lawsuit; the amount is not reasonably estimable.

3. Kalamazoo estimates damages in a case at $2,500,000 with a high probability of losing the case.

QS 9-4
Accounting for contingent liabilities
C3

On November 7, 2011, Ortez Company borrows $150,000 cash by signing a 90-day, 8% note payable with a face value of $150,000. (1) Compute the accrued interest payable on December 31, 2011, (2) prepare the journal entry to record the accrued interest expense at December 31, 2011, and (3) prepare the journal entry to record payment of the note at maturity.

QS 9-5
Interest-bearing note transactions **P1**

On January 14, the end of the first bi-weekly pay period of the year, Rockin Company's payroll register showed that its employees earned $14,000 of sales salaries. Withholdings from the employees' salaries include FICA Social Security taxes at the rate of 6.2%, FICA Medicare taxes at the rate of 1.45%, $2,600 of federal income taxes, $309 of medical insurance deductions, and $120 of union dues. No employee earned more than $7,000 in this first period. Prepare the journal entry to record Rockin Company's January 14 (employee) payroll expenses and liabilities.

QS 9-6
Record employee payroll taxes
P2

Merger Co. has ten employees, each of whom earns $2,000 per month and has been employed since January 1. FICA Social Security taxes are 6.2% of the first $110,100 paid to each employee, and FICA Medicare taxes are 1.45% of gross pay. FUTA taxes are 0.8% and SUTA taxes are 5.4% of the first $7,000 paid to each employee. Prepare the March 31 journal entry to record the March payroll taxes expense.

QS 9-7
Record employer payroll taxes
P3

On September 11, 2010, Home Store sells a mower for $400 with a one-year warranty that covers parts. Warranty expense is estimated at 5% of sales. On July 24, 2011, the mower is brought in for repairs covered under the warranty requiring $35 in materials taken from the Repair Parts Inventory. Prepare the July 24, 2011, entry to record the warranty repairs.

QS 9-8
Recording warranty repairs
P4

Paris Company offers an annual bonus to employees if the company meets certain net income goals. Prepare the journal entry to record a $10,000 bonus owed to its workers (to be shared equally) at calendar year-end.

QS 9-9
Accounting for bonuses **P4**

Chester Co.'s salaried employees earn four weeks vacation per year. It pays $192,000.12 in total employee salaries for 52 weeks but its employees work only 48 weeks. This means Chester's total weekly expense is $4,000 ($192,000/48 weeks) instead of the $3,692.31 cash paid weekly to the employees ($192,000/52 weeks). Record Chester's weekly vacation benefits expense.

QS 9-10
Accounting for vacations
P4

Compute the times interest earned for Weltin Company, which reports income before interest expense and income taxes of $2,044,000, and interest expense of $350,000. Interpret its times interest earned (assume that its competitors average a times interest earned of 4.0).

QS 9-11
Times interest earned **A1**

The payroll records of Clix Software show the following information about Trish Farqua, an employee, for the weekly pay period ending September 30, 2012. Farqua is single and claims one allowance. Compute her Social Security tax (6.2%), Medicare tax (1.45%), federal income tax withholding, state income tax (1.0%), and net pay for the current pay period. (Use the withholding table in Exhibit 9A.6 and round tax amounts to the nearest cent.)

Total (gross) earnings for current pay period	$ 735
Cumulative earnings of previous pay periods	9,700

QS 9-12ᴬ
Net pay and tax computations
P5

Check Net pay, $578.42

Cather Corporation has made and recorded its quarterly income tax payments. After a final review of taxes for the year, the company identifies an additional $30,000 of income tax expense that should be recorded. A portion of this additional expense, $8,000, is deferred for payment in future years. Record Cather's year-end adjusting entry for income tax expense.

QS 9-13ᴮ
Record deferred income tax liability **P4**

Answer each of the following related to international accounting standards.

a. In general, how similar or different are the definitions and characteristics of current liabilities between IFRS and U.S. GAAP?

b. Companies reporting under IFRS often reference a set of current liabilities with the title *financial liabilities*. Identify two current liabilities that would be classified under financial liabilities per IFRS. (*Hint:* **Nokia** provides examples in this chapter and in Appendix A.)

QS 9-14
International accounting standards

C1 C2

EXERCISES

Exercise 9-1

Classifying liabilities

C1

The following items appear on the balance sheet of a company with a two-month operating cycle. Identify the proper classification of each item as follows: *C* if it is a current liability, *L* if it is a long-term liability, or *N* if it is not a liability.

_____ **1.** Sales taxes payable.
_____ **2.** FUTA taxes payable.
_____ **3.** Accounts receivable.
_____ **4.** Wages payable.
_____ **5.** Salaries payable.
_____ **6.** Notes payable (due in 6 to 12 months).
_____ **7.** Notes payable (due in 120 days).
_____ **8.** Current portion of long-term debt.
_____ **9.** Notes payable (mature in five years).
_____**10.** Notes payable (due in 13 to 24 months).

Exercise 9-2

Recording known current liabilities

C2

Prepare any necessary adjusting entries at December 31, 2011, for Yacht Company's year-end financial statements for each of the following separate transactions and events.

1. Yacht Company records an adjusting entry for $2,000,000 of previously unrecorded cash sales (costing $1,000,000) and its sales taxes at a rate of 5%.

2. The company earned $40,000 of $100,000 previously received in advance for services.

Exercise 9-3

Accounting for contingent liabilities

C3

Prepare any necessary adjusting entries at December 31, 2011, for Moor Company's year-end financial statements for each of the following separate transactions and events.

1. A disgruntled employee is suing Moor Company. Legal advisers believe that the company will probably need to pay damages, but the amount cannot be reasonably estimated.

2. Moor Company guarantees the $5,000 debt of a supplier. The supplier will probably not default on the debt.

Exercise 9-4

Accounting for note payable

P1

Check (2b) Interest expense, $1,880

Perfect Systems borrows $94,000 cash on May 15, 2011, by signing a 60-day, 12% note.

1. On what date does this note mature?

2. Suppose the face value of the note equals $94,000, the principal of the loan. Prepare the journal entries to record (*a*) issuance of the note and (*b*) payment of the note at maturity.

Exercise 9-5

Interest-bearing notes payable with year-end adjustments

P1

Check (2) $2,250
(3) $1,125

Kwon Co. borrows $150,000 cash on November 1, 2011, by signing a 90-day, 9% note with a face value of $150,000.

1. On what date does this note mature? (Assume that February of 2011 has 28 days.)

2. How much interest expense results from this note in 2011? (Assume a 360-day year.)

3. How much interest expense results from this note in 2012? (Assume a 360-day year.)

4. Prepare journal entries to record (*a*) issuance of the note, (*b*) accrual of interest at the end of 2011, and (*c*) payment of the note at maturity.

Exercise 9-6

Computing payroll taxes

P2 P3

Check (*a*) FUTA, $4.80; SUTA, $17.40

MRI Company has one employee. FICA Social Security taxes are 6.2% of the first $110,100 paid to its employee, and FICA Medicare taxes are 1.45% of gross pay. For MRI, its FUTA taxes are 0.8% and SUTA taxes are 2.9% of the first $7,000 paid to its employee. Compute MRI's amounts for each of these four taxes as applied to the employee's gross earnings for September under each of three separate situations (*a*), (*b*), and (*c*).

	Gross Pay through August	Gross Pay for September
a.	$ 6,400	$ 800
b.	18,200	2,100
c.	103,800	8,000

Exercise 9-7

Payroll-related journal entries P2

Using the data in situation *a* of Exercise 9-6, prepare the employer's September 30 journal entries to record salary expense and its related payroll liabilities for this employee. The employee's federal income taxes withheld by the employer are $135 for this pay period.

Exercise 9-8

Payroll-related journal entries P3

Using the data in situation *a* of Exercise 9-6, prepare the employer's September 30 journal entries to record the *employer's* payroll taxes expense and its related liabilities.

For the year ended December 31, 2011, Winter Company has implemented an employee bonus program equal to 3% of Winter's net income, which employees will share equally. Winter's net income (prebonus) is expected to be $1,000,000, and bonus expense is deducted in computing net income.

1. Compute the amount of the bonus payable to the employees at year-end (use the method described in the chapter and round to the nearest dollar).

2. Prepare the journal entry at December 31, 2011, to record the bonus due the employees.

3. Prepare the journal entry at January 19, 2012, to record payment of the bonus to employees.

Exercise 9-9
Computing and recording bonuses P4

Check (1) $29,126

Prepare any necessary adjusting entries at December 31, 2011, for Jester Company's year-end financial statements for each of the following separate transactions and events.

1. During December, Jester Company sold 3,000 units of a product that carries a 60-day warranty. December sales for this product total $120,000. The company expects 8% of the units to need warranty repairs, and it estimates the average repair cost per unit will be $15.

2. Employees earn vacation pay at a rate of one day per month. During December, 20 employees qualify for one vacation day each. Their average daily wage is $120 per employee.

Exercise 9-10
Accounting for estimated liabilities
P4

Chang Co. sold a copier costing $3,800 with a two-year parts warranty to a customer on August 16, 2011, for $5,500 cash. Chang uses the perpetual inventory system. On November 22, 2012, the copier requires on-site repairs that are completed the same day. The repairs cost $199 for materials taken from the Repair Parts Inventory. These are the only repairs required in 2012 for this copier. Based on experience, Chang expects to incur warranty costs equal to 4% of dollar sales. It records warranty expense with an adjusting entry at the end of each year.

1. How much warranty expense does the company report in 2011 for this copier?

2. How much is the estimated warranty liability for this copier as of December 31, 2011?

3. How much warranty expense does the company report in 2012 for this copier?

4. How much is the estimated warranty liability for this copier as of December 31, 2012?

5. Prepare journal entries to record (*a*) the copier's sale; (*b*) the adjustment on December 31, 2011, to recognize the warranty expense; and (*c*) the repairs that occur in November 2012.

Exercise 9-11
Warranty expense and liability computations and entries
P4

Check (1) $220

(4) $21

Use the following information from separate companies *a* through *f* to compute times interest earned. Which company indicates the strongest ability to pay interest expense as it comes due?

	Net Income (Loss)	Interest Expense	Income Taxes
a.	$140,000	$48,000	$ 35,000
b.	140,000	15,000	50,000
c.	140,000	8,000	70,000
d.	265,000	12,000	130,000
e.	79,000	12,000	30,000
f.	(4,000)	12,000	0

Exercise 9-12
Computing and interpreting times interest earned
A1

Check (b) 13.67

Tony Newbern, an unmarried employee, works 48 hours in the week ended January 12. His pay rate is $12 per hour, and his wages are subject to no deductions other than FICA—Social Security, FICA—Medicare, and federal income taxes. He claims two withholding allowances. Compute his regular pay, overtime pay (for this company, workers earn 150% of their regular rate for hours in excess of 40 per week), and gross pay. Then compute his FICA tax deduction (use 6.2% for the Social Security portion and 1.45% for the Medicare portion), income tax deduction (use the wage bracket withholding table of Exhibit 9A.6), total deductions, and net pay. (Round tax amounts to the nearest cent.)

Exercise 9-13ᴬ
Gross and net pay computation
P5

Check Net pay, $515.26

Ming Corporation prepares financial statements for each month-end. As part of its accounting process, estimated income taxes are accrued each month for 30% of the current month's net income. The income taxes are paid in the first month of each quarter for the amount accrued for the prior quarter. The following information is available for the fourth quarter of year 2011. When tax computations are completed on January 20, 2012, Ming determines that the quarter's Income Taxes Payable account balance should be $29,100 on December 31, 2011 (its unadjusted balance is $23,640).

Exercise 9-14ᴮ
Accounting for income taxes
P4

October 2011 net income	$27,900
November 2011 net income	18,200
December 2011 net income	32,700

Check   (1) $5,460

1. Determine the amount of the accounting adjustment (dated as of December 31, 2011) to produce the proper ending balance in the Income Taxes Payable account.

2. Prepare journal entries to record (*a*) the December 31, 2011, adjustment to the Income Taxes Payable account and (*b*) the January 20, 2012, payment of the fourth-quarter taxes.

Exercise 9-15
Accounting for current liabilities under IFRS

P4

Volvo Group reports the following information for its product warranty costs as of December 31, 2008, along with provisions and utilizations of warranty liabilities for the year ended December 31, 2008 (SEK in millions).

Product warranty costs

Estimated costs for product warranties are charged to cost of sales when the products are sold. Estimated warranty costs include contractual warranty and goodwill warranty. Warranty provisions are estimated with consideration of historical claims statistics, the warranty period, the average time-lag between faults occurring and claims to the company, and anticipated changes in quality indexes. Differences between actual warranty claims and the estimated claims generally affect the recognized expense and provisions in future periods. At December 31, 2008, warranty cost provisions amounted to 10,354.

Product warranty liabilities, December 31, 2007	SEK 9,373
Additional provisions to product warranty liabilities	6,201
Utilizations and reductions of product warranty liabilities	(5,220)
Product warranty liabilities, December 31, 2008	10,354

1. Prepare Volvo's journal entry to record its estimated warranty liabilities (provisions) for 2008.

2. Prepare Volvo's journal entry to record its costs (utilizations) related to its warranty program for 2008. Assume those costs involve replacements taken out of Inventory, with no cash involved.

3. How much warranty expense does Volvo report for 2008?

Exercise 9-16
Recording payroll

P2   P3

The following monthly data are taken from Nunez Company at July 31: Sales salaries, $120,000; Office salaries, $60,000; Federal income taxes withheld, $45,000; State income taxes withheld, $10,000; Social security taxes withheld, $11,160; Medicare taxes withheld, $2,610; Medical insurance premiums, $7,000; Life insurance premiums, $4,000; Union dues deducted, $1,000; and Salaries subject to unemployment taxes, $50,000. The employee pays forty percent of medical and life insurance premiums.

Prepare journal entries to record: (1) accrued payroll, including employee deductions, for July; (2) cash payment of the net payroll (salaries payable) for July; (3) accrued employer payroll taxes, and other related employment expenses, for July—assume that FICA taxes are identical to those on employees and that SUTA taxes are 5.4% and FUTA taxes are 0.8%; and (4) cash payment of all liabilities related to the July payroll.

Exercise 9-17
Computing payroll taxes

P2   P3

Madison Company has nine employees. FICA Social Security taxes are 6.2% of the first $110,100 paid to each employee, and FICA Medicare taxes are 1.45% of gross pay. FUTA taxes are 0.8% and SUTA taxes are 5.4% of the first $7,000 paid to each employee. Cumulative pay for the current year for each of its employees follows.

Employee	Cumulative Pay	Employee	Cumulative Pay	Employee	Cumulative Pay
Steve S.	$ 6,000	Christina S.	$156,600	Dana W.	$116,600
Tim V.	60,000	Michelle H.	106,900	Stewart M.	36,800
Brent G.	87,000	Kathleen K.	110,100	Sankha B.	4,000

a. Prepare a table with the following column headings: Employee; Cumulative Pay; Pay Subject to FICA Social Security Taxes; Pay Subject to FICA Medicare Taxes; Pay Subject to FUTA Taxes; Pay Subject to SUTA Taxes. Compute the amounts in this table for each employee and total the columns.

b. For the company, compute each total for: FICA Social Security taxes, FICA Medicare taxes, FUTA taxes, and SUTA taxes. (*Hint:* Remember to include in those totals any employee share of taxes that the company must collect.)

Exercise 9-18
Preparing payroll register and related entries   P5

SP Company has five employees. Employees paid by the hour receive a $10 per hour pay rate for the regular 40-hour work week plus one and one-half times the hourly rate for each overtime hour beyond the 40-hours per week. Hourly employees are paid every two weeks, but salaried employees are paid monthly on the last biweekly payday of each month. FICA Social Security taxes are 6.2% of the first $110,100 paid to each employee, and FICA Medicare taxes are 1.45% of gross pay. FUTA taxes are 0.8% and SUTA taxes are 5.4% of the first $7,000 paid to each employee. The company has a benefits plan that includes medical insurance, life insurance, and retirement funding for employees. Under this plan, employees must contribute 5 percent of their gross income as a payroll withholding, which the company matches with double the amount. Following is the partially completed payroll register for the biweekly period ending August 31, which is the last payday of August.

Employee	Cumulative Pay (Excludes Current Period)	Pay Type	Pay Hours	Gross Pay	FIT / SIT	FUTA / SUTA	FICA-SS_EE / FICA-SS_ER	FICA-Med_EE / FICA-Med_ER	EE-Ben_Plan Withholding / ER-Ben_Plan Withholding	Employee Net Pay
Kathleen	$108,300.00	Salary	---	$7,000.00	$2,000.00 / 300.00					
Nichole	6,800.00	Salary	---	500.00	80.00 / 20.00					
Anthony	15,000.00	Regular / Overtime	80 / 8		110.00 / 25.00					
Zoey	6,500.00	Regular / Overtime	80 / 4		100.00 / 22.00					
Gracie	5,000.00	Regular / Overtime	74 / 0	740.00 / 0.00	90.00 / 21.00					
Totals	141,600.00				2,380.00 / 388.00					

Note: Table abbreviations follow those in Exhibit 9A.3 (see pages 389–390); and, "Ben_Plan" refers to employee (EE) or employer (ER) withholding for the benefits plan.

a. Complete this payroll register by filling in all cells for the pay period ended August 31. *Hint:* See Exhibit 9A.3 for guidance. (Round amounts to cents.)

b. Prepare the August 31 journal entry to record the accrued biweekly payroll and related liabilities for deductions.

c. Prepare the August 31 journal entry to record the employer's cash payment of the net payroll of part *b.*

d. Prepare the August 31 journal entry to record the employer's payroll taxes including the contribution to the benefits plan.

e. Prepare the August 31 journal entry to pay all liabilities (expect net payroll in part *c*) for this biweekly period.

⊞ connect

Tytus Co. entered into the following transactions involving short-term liabilities in 2010 and 2011.

2010

Apr. 20 Purchased $38,500 of merchandise on credit from Frier, terms are 1/10, n/30. Tytus uses the perpetual inventory system.

May 19 Replaced the April 20 account payable to Frier with a 90-day, $30,000 note bearing 9% annual interest along with paying $8,500 in cash.

July 8 Borrowed $60,000 cash from Community Bank by signing a 120-day, 10% interest-bearing note with a face value of $60,000.

___?___ Paid the amount due on the note to Frier at the maturity date.

___?___ Paid the amount due on the note to Community Bank at the maturity date.

Nov. 28 Borrowed $21,000 cash from UMB Bank by signing a 60-day, 8% interest-bearing note with a face value of $21,000.

Dec. 31 Recorded an adjusting entry for accrued interest on the note to UMB Bank.

2011

___?___ Paid the amount due on the note to UMB Bank at the maturity date.

Required

1. Determine the maturity date for each of the three notes described.

2. Determine the interest due at maturity for each of the three notes. (Assume a 360-day year.)

3. Determine the interest expense to be recorded in the adjusting entry at the end of 2010.

4. Determine the interest expense to be recorded in 2011.

5. Prepare journal entries for all the preceding transactions and events for years 2010 and 2011.

PROBLEM SET A

Problem 9-1A
Short-term notes payable transactions and entries

P1

mhhe.com/wildFA6e

Check (2) Frier, $675
(3) $154
(4) $126

Problem 9-2A
Warranty expense and liability estimation

P4

On October 29, 2010, Lue Co. began operations by purchasing razors for resale. Lue uses the perpetual inventory method. The razors have a 90-day warranty that requires the company to replace any nonworking razor. When a razor is returned, the company discards it and mails a new one from Merchandise Inventory to the customer. The company's cost per new razor is $18 and its retail selling price is $80 in both 2010 and 2011. The manufacturer has advised the company to expect warranty costs to equal 7% of dollar sales. The following transactions and events occurred.

2010

Nov. 11 Sold 75 razors for $6,000 cash.
    30 Recognized warranty expense related to November sales with an adjusting entry.
Dec. 9 Replaced 15 razors that were returned under the warranty.
    16 Sold 210 razors for $16,800 cash.
    29 Replaced 30 razors that were returned under the warranty.
    31 Recognized warranty expense related to December sales with an adjusting entry.

2011

Jan. 5 Sold 130 razors for $10,400 cash.
    17 Replaced 50 razors that were returned under the warranty.
    31 Recognized warranty expense related to January sales with an adjusting entry.

Required

1. Prepare journal entries to record these transactions and adjustments for 2010 and 2011.
2. How much warranty expense is reported for November 2010 and for December 2010?
3. How much warranty expense is reported for January 2011?
4. What is the balance of the Estimated Warranty Liability account as of December 31, 2010?
5. What is the balance of the Estimated Warranty Liability account as of January 31, 2011?

Check (3) $728
     (4) $786 Cr.
     (5) $614 Cr.

Problem 9-3A
Computing and analyzing times interest earned

A1

Shown here are condensed income statements for two different companies (both are organized as LLCs and pay no income taxes).

Ace Company	
Sales	$500,000
Variable expenses (80%)	400,000
Income before interest	100,000
Interest expense (fixed)	30,000
Net income	$ 70,000

Deuce Company	
Sales	$500,000
Variable expenses (60%)	300,000
Income before interest	200,000
Interest expense (fixed)	130,000
Net income	$ 70,000

Required

1. Compute times interest earned for Ace Company.
2. Compute times interest earned for Deuce Company.
3. What happens to each company's net income if sales increase by 30%?
4. What happens to each company's net income if sales increase by 50%?
5. What happens to each company's net income if sales increase by 80%?
6. What happens to each company's net income if sales decrease by 10%?
7. What happens to each company's net income if sales decrease by 20%?
8. What happens to each company's net income if sales decrease by 40%?

Check (3) Ace net income, $100,000 (43% increase)

(6) Deuce net income, $50,000 (29% decrease)

Analysis Component

9. Comment on the results from parts 3 through 8 in relation to the fixed-cost strategies of the two companies and the ratio values you computed in parts 1 and 2.

Problem 9-4A
Payroll expenses, withholdings, and taxes

P2 P3

Legal Stars has four employees. FICA Social Security taxes are 6.2% of the first $110,100 paid to each employee, and FICA Medicare taxes are 1.45% of gross pay. Also, for the first $7,000 paid to each employee, the company's FUTA taxes are 0.8% and SUTA taxes are 2.15%. The company is preparing its payroll calculations for the week ended August 25. Payroll records show the following information for the company's four employees.

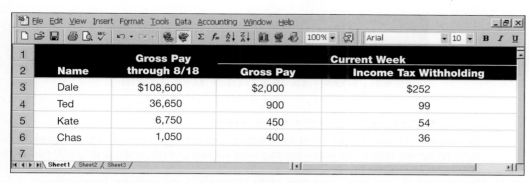

Name	Gross Pay through 8/18	Current Week	
		Gross Pay	Income Tax Withholding
Dale	$108,600	$2,000	$252
Ted	36,650	900	99
Kate	6,750	450	54
Chas	1,050	400	36

In addition to gross pay, the company must pay one-half of the $32 per employee weekly health insurance; each employee pays the remaining one-half. The company also contributes an extra 8% of each employee's gross pay (at no cost to employees) to a pension fund.

Required

Compute the following for the week ended August 25 (round amounts to the nearest cent):

1. Each employee's FICA withholdings for Social Security.
2. Each employee's FICA withholdings for Medicare.
3. Employer's FICA taxes for Social Security.
4. Employer's FICA taxes for Medicare.
5. Employer's FUTA taxes.
6. Employer's SUTA taxes.
7. Each employee's net (take-home) pay.
8. Employer's total payroll-related expense for each employee.

Check (3) $201.50
(4) $54.38
(5) $5.20

(7) Total net pay, $2,989.12

On January 8, the end of the first weekly pay period of the year, Royal Company's payroll register showed that its employees earned $11,380 of office salaries and $32,920 of sales salaries. Withholdings from the employees' salaries include FICA Social Security taxes at the rate of 6.2%, FICA Medicare taxes at the rate of 1.45%, $6,340 of federal income taxes, $670 of medical insurance deductions, and $420 of union dues. No employee earned more than $7,000 in this first period.

Problem 9-5A
Entries for payroll transactions
P2 P3

Required

1. Calculate FICA Social Security taxes payable and FICA Medicare taxes payable. Prepare the journal entry to record Royal Company's January 8 (employee) payroll expenses and liabilities.
2. Prepare the journal entry to record Royal's (employer) payroll taxes resulting from the January 8 payroll. Royal's merit rating reduces its state unemployment tax rate to 4% of the first $7,000 paid each employee. The federal unemployment tax rate is 0.8%.

Check (1) Cr. Salaries Payable, $33,481.05

(2) Dr. Payroll Taxes Expense, $5,515.35

Polo Company has 10 employees, each of whom earns $2,600 per month and is paid on the last day of each month. All 10 have been employed continuously at this amount since January 1. Polo uses a payroll bank account and special payroll checks to pay its employees. On March 1, the following accounts and balances exist in its general ledger:

Problem 9-6A[A]
Entries for payroll transactions
P2 P3 P5

a. FICA—Social Security Taxes Payable, $3,224; FICA—Medicare Taxes Payable, $754. (The balances of these accounts represent total liabilities for *both* the employer's and employees' FICA taxes for the February payroll only.)
b. Employees' Federal Income Taxes Payable, $3,900 (liability for February only).
c. Federal Unemployment Taxes Payable, $416 (liability for January and February together).
d. State Unemployment Taxes Payable, $2,080 (liability for January and February together).

During March and April, the company had the following payroll transactions.

Mar. 15 Issued check payable to Fleet Bank, a federal depository bank authorized to accept employers' payments of FICA taxes and employee income tax withholdings. The $7,878 check is in payment of the February FICA and employee income taxes.
31 Recorded the March payroll and transferred funds from the regular bank account to the payroll bank account. Issued checks payable to each employee in payment of the March payroll. The payroll register shows the following summary totals for the March pay period.

Check March 31: Cr. Salaries Payable, $20,111

Salaries and Wages					
Office Salaries	Shop Wages	Gross Pay	FICA Taxes*	Federal Income Taxes	Net Pay
$10,400	$15,600	$26,000	$1,612	$3,900	$20,111
			$ 377		

* FICA taxes are Social Security and Medicare, respectively.

March 31: Dr. Payroll Taxes
Expenses, $2,853

April 15: Cr. Cash, $7,878
(Fleet Bank)

31 Recorded the employer's payroll taxes resulting from the March payroll. The company has a merit rating that reduces its state unemployment tax rate to 4.0% of the first $7,000 paid each employee. The federal rate is 0.8%.

Apr. 15 Issued check to Fleet Bank in payment of the March FICA and employee income taxes.

15 Issued check to the State Tax Commission for the January, February, and March state unemployment taxes. Mailed the check and the first quarter tax return to the Commission.

30 Issued check payable to Fleet Bank in payment of the employer's FUTA taxes for the first quarter of the year.

30 Mailed Form 941 to the IRS, reporting the FICA taxes and the employees' federal income tax withholdings for the first quarter.

Required

Prepare journal entries to record the transactions and events for both March and April.

PROBLEM SET B

Problem 9-1B
Short-term notes payable transactions and entries

P1

Bargen Co. entered into the following transactions involving short-term liabilities in 2010 and 2011.

2010

Apr. 22 Purchased $4,000 of merchandise on credit from Quinn Products, terms are 1/10, n/30. Bargen uses the perpetual inventory system.

May 23 Replaced the April 22 account payable to Quinn Products with a 60-day, $3,600 note bearing 15% annual interest along with paying $400 in cash.

July 15 Borrowed $9,000 cash from Blackhawk Bank by signing a 120-day, 10% interest-bearing note with a face value of $9,000.

___?___ Paid the amount due on the note to Quinn Products at maturity.

___?___ Paid the amount due on the note to Blackhawk Bank at maturity.

Dec. 6 Borrowed $16,000 cash from City Bank by signing a 45-day, 9% interest-bearing note with a face value of $16,000.

31 Recorded an adjusting entry for accrued interest on the note to City Bank.

2011

___?___ Paid the amount due on the note to City Bank at maturity.

Required

Check (2) Quinn, $90
(3) $100
(4) $80

1. Determine the maturity date for each of the three notes described.

2. Determine the interest due at maturity for each of the three notes. (Assume a 360-day year.)

3. Determine the interest expense to be recorded in the adjusting entry at the end of 2010.

4. Determine the interest expense to be recorded in 2011.

5. Prepare journal entries for all the preceding transactions and events for years 2010 and 2011.

Problem 9-2B
Warranty expense and liability estimation

P4

On November 10, 2011, Byung Co. began operations by purchasing coffee grinders for resale. Byung uses the perpetual inventory method. The grinders have a 60-day warranty that requires the company to replace any nonworking grinder. When a grinder is returned, the company discards it and mails a new one from Merchandise Inventory to the customer. The company's cost per new grinder is $14 and its retail selling price is $35 in both 2011 and 2012. The manufacturer has advised the company to expect warranty costs to equal 10% of dollar sales. The following transactions and events occurred.

2011

Nov. 16 Sold 50 grinders for $1,750 cash.

30 Recognized warranty expense related to November sales with an adjusting entry.

Dec. 12 Replaced six grinders that were returned under the warranty.

18 Sold 150 grinders for $5,250 cash.

28 Replaced 17 grinders that were returned under the warranty.

31 Recognized warranty expense related to December sales with an adjusting entry.

2012

Jan. 7 Sold 60 grinders for $2,100 cash.
    21 Replaced 38 grinders that were returned under the warranty.
    31 Recognized warranty expense related to January sales with an adjusting entry.

Required

1. Prepare journal entries to record these transactions and adjustments for 2011 and 2012.
2. How much warranty expense is reported for November 2011 and for December 2011?
3. How much warranty expense is reported for January 2012?
4. What is the balance of the Estimated Warranty Liability account as of December 31, 2011?
5. What is the balance of the Estimated Warranty Liability account as of January 31, 2012?

Check (3) $210
        (4) $378 Cr.
        (5) $56 Cr.

Shown here are condensed income statements for two different companies (both are organized as LLCs and pay no income taxes).

Problem 9-3B
Computing and analyzing times interest earned

A1

Virgo Company	
Sales	$120,000
Variable expenses (50%)	60,000
Income before interest	60,000
Interest expense (fixed)	45,000
Net income	$ 15,000

Zodiac Company	
Sales	$120,000
Variable expenses (75%)	90,000
Income before interest	30,000
Interest expense (fixed)	15,000
Net income	$ 15,000

Required

1. Compute times interest earned for Virgo Company.
2. Compute times interest earned for Zodiac Company.
3. What happens to each company's net income if sales increase by 10%?
4. What happens to each company's net income if sales increase by 40%?
5. What happens to each company's net income if sales increase by 90%?
6. What happens to each company's net income if sales decrease by 20%?
7. What happens to each company's net income if sales decrease by 50%?
8. What happens to each company's net income if sales decrease by 80%?

Check (4) Virgo net income,
$39,000 (160% increase)

(6) Zodiac net income,
$9,000 (40% decrease)

Analysis Component

9. Comment on the results from parts 3 through 8 in relation to the fixed-cost strategies of the two companies and the ratio values you computed in parts 1 and 2.

Sea Biz Co. has four employees. FICA Social Security taxes are 6.2% of the first $110,100 paid to each employee, and FICA Medicare taxes are 1.45% of gross pay. Also, for the first $7,000 paid to each employee, the company's FUTA taxes are 0.8% and SUTA taxes are 1.75%. The company is preparing its payroll calculations for the week ended September 30. Payroll records show the following information for the company's four employees.

Problem 9-4B
Payroll expenses, withholdings, and taxes

P2 P3

File Edit View Insert Format Tools Data Accounting Window Help			|_|8|×|
		Current Week	
Name	Gross Pay through 9/23	Gross Pay	Income Tax Withholding
Alli	$107,600	$2,500	$198
Eve	36,650	1,515	182
Hong	6,650	475	52
Juan	22,200	600	48

In addition to gross pay, the company must pay one-half of the $44 per employee weekly health insurance; each employee pays the remaining one-half. The company also contributes an extra 5% of each employee's gross pay (at no cost to employees) to a pension fund.

Required

Compute the following for the week ended September 30 (round amounts to the nearest cent):

1. Each employee's FICA withholdings for Social Security.
2. Each employee's FICA withholdings for Medicare.
3. Employer's FICA taxes for Social Security.
4. Employer's FICA taxes for Medicare.
5. Employer's FUTA taxes.
6. Employer's SUTA taxes.
7. Each employee's net (take-home) pay.
8. Employer's total payroll-related expense for each employee.

Check (3) $315.58
(4) $73.81
(5) $2.80
(7) Total net pay, $4,132.61

Problem 9-5B
Entries for payroll transactions
P2 P3

Palmer Company's first weekly pay period of the year ends on January 8. On that date, the column totals in Palmer's payroll register indicate its sales employees earned $69,490, its office employees earned $42,450, and its delivery employees earned $2,060. The employees are to have withheld from their wages FICA Social Security taxes at the rate of 6.2%, FICA Medicare taxes at the rate of 1.45%, $17,250 of federal income taxes, $2,320 of medical insurance deductions, and $275 of union dues. No employee earned more than $7,000 in the first pay period.

Required

Check (1) Cr. Salaries Payable, $85,434

(2) Dr. Payroll Taxes Expense, $13,509

1. Calculate FICA Social Security taxes payable and FICA Medicare taxes payable. Prepare the journal entry to record Palmer Company's January 8 (employee) payroll expenses and liabilities.
2. Prepare the journal entry to record Palmer's (employer) payroll taxes resulting from the January 8 payroll. Palmer's merit rating reduces its state unemployment tax rate to 3.4% of the first $7,000 paid each employee. The federal unemployment tax rate is 0.8%.

Problem 9-6B[A]
Entries for payroll transactions
P2 P3 P5

JLK Company has five employees, each of whom earns $1,200 per month and is paid on the last day of each month. All five have been employed continuously at this amount since January 1. JLK uses a payroll bank account and special payroll checks to pay its employees. On June 1, the following accounts and balances exist in its general ledger:

a. FICA—Social Security Taxes Payable, $744; FICA—Medicare Taxes Payable, $174. (The balances of these accounts represent total liabilities for *both* the employer's and employees' FICA taxes for the May payroll only.)
b. Employees' Federal Income Taxes Payable, $900 (liability for May only).
c. Federal Unemployment Taxes Payable, $96 (liability for April and May together).
d. State Unemployment Taxes Payable, $480 (liability for April and May together).

During June and July, the company had the following payroll transactions.

June 15   Issued check payable to Security Bank, a federal depository bank authorized to accept employers' payments of FICA taxes and employee income tax withholdings. The $1,818 check is in payment of the May FICA and employee income taxes.

30   Recorded the June payroll and transferred funds from the regular bank account to the payroll bank account. Issued checks payable to each employee in payment of the June payroll. The payroll register shows the following summary totals for the June pay period.

Check June 30: Cr. Salaries Payable, $4,641

Salaries and Wages					
Office Salaries	Shop Wages	Gross Pay	FICA Taxes*	Federal Income Taxes	Net Pay
$2,000	$4,000	$6,000	$372	$900	$4,641
			$ 87		

* FICA taxes are Social Security and Medicare, respectively.

Check June 30: Dr. Payroll Taxes Expenses, $699

30   Recorded the employer's payroll taxes resulting from the June payroll. The company has a merit rating that reduces its state unemployment tax rate to 4.0% of the first $7,000 paid each employee. The federal rate is 0.8%.

July 15   Issued check payable to Security Bank in payment of the June FICA and employee income taxes.

15   Issued check to the State Tax Commission for the April, May and June state unemployment taxes. Mailed the check and the second quarter tax return to the State Tax Commission.

Check July 15: Cr. Cash $1,818 (Security Bank)

31   Issued check payable to Security Bank in payment of the employer's FUTA taxes for the first quarter of the year.

31   Mailed Form 941 to the IRS, reporting the FICA taxes and the employees' federal income tax withholdings for the second quarter.

Required

Prepare journal entries to record the transactions and events for both June and July.

SERIAL PROBLEM
Business Solutions
P2 P3 C2

(This serial problem began in Chapter 1 and continues through most of the book. If previous chapter segments were not completed, the serial problem can begin at this point. It is helpful, but not necessary, to use the Working Papers that accompany the book.)

SP 9 Review the February 26 and March 25 transactions for Business Solutions (SP 4) from Chapter 4.

Required

1. Assume that Lyn Addie is an unmarried employee. Her $1,000 of wages are subject to no deductions other than FICA Social Security taxes, FICA Medicare taxes, and federal income taxes. Her federal income taxes for this pay period total $159. Compute her net pay for the eight days' work paid on February 26. (Round amounts to the nearest cent.)
2. Record the journal entry to reflect the payroll payment to Lyn Addie as computed in part 1.
3. Record the journal entry to reflect the (employer) payroll tax expenses for the February 26 payroll payment. Assume Lyn Addie has not met earnings limits for FUTA and SUTA—the FUTA rate is 0.8% and the SUTA rate is 4% for Business Solutions. (Round amounts to the nearest cent.)
4. Record the entry(ies) for the merchandise sold on March 25 if a 4% sales tax rate applies.

COMPREHENSIVE PROBLEM
Bug-Off Exterminators
(Review of Chapters 1–9)

CP 9 Bug-Off Exterminators provides pest control services and sells extermination products manufactured by other companies. The following six-column table contains the company's unadjusted trial balance as of December 31, 2011.

BUG-OFF EXTERMINATORS
December 31, 2011

	Unadjusted Trial Balance		Adjustments		Adjusted Trial Balance	
Cash	$ 17,000					
Accounts receivable	4,000					
Allowance for doubtful accounts		$ 828				
Merchandise inventory	11,700					
Trucks	32,000					
Accum. depreciation—Trucks		0				
Equipment	45,000					
Accum. depreciation—Equipment		12,200				
Accounts payable		5,000				
Estimated warranty liability		1,400				
Unearned services revenue		0				
Interest payable		0				
Long-term notes payable		15,000				
Common stock		10,000				
Retained earnings		49,700				
Dividends	10,000					
Extermination services revenue		60,000				
Interest revenue		872				
Sales (of merchandise)		71,026				
Cost of goods sold	46,300					
Depreciation expense—Trucks	0					
Depreciation expense—Equipment	0					
Wages expense	35,000					
Interest expense	0					
Rent expense	9,000					
Bad debts expense	0					
Miscellaneous expense	1,226					
Repairs expense	8,000					
Utilities expense	6,800					
Warranty expense	0					
Totals	$226,026	$226,026				

The following information in *a* through *h* applies to the company at the end of the current year.

a. The bank reconciliation as of December 31, 2011, includes the following facts.

Cash balance per bank	$15,100
Cash balance per books	17,000
Outstanding checks	1,800
Deposit in transit	2,450
Interest earned (on bank account)	52
Bank service charges (miscellaneous expense)	15

Reported on the bank statement is a canceled check that the company failed to record. (Information from the bank reconciliation allows you to determine the amount of this check, which is a payment on an account payable.)

b. An examination of customers' accounts shows that accounts totaling $679 should be written off as uncollectible. Using an aging of receivables, the company determines that the ending balance of the Allowance for Doubtful Accounts should be $700.

c. A truck is purchased and placed in service on January 1, 2011. Its cost is being depreciated with the straight-line method using the following facts and estimates.

Original cost	$32,000
Expected salvage value	8,000
Useful life (years)	4

d. Two items of equipment (a sprayer and an injector) were purchased and put into service in early January 2009. They are being depreciated with the straight-line method using these facts and estimates.

	Sprayer	Injector
Original cost	$27,000	$18,000
Expected salvage value	3,000	2,500
Useful life (years)	8	5

e. On August 1, 2011, the company is paid $3,840 cash in advance to provide monthly service for an apartment complex for one year. The company began providing the services in August. When the cash was received, the full amount was credited to the Extermination Services Revenue account.

f. The company offers a warranty for the services it sells. The expected cost of providing warranty service is 2.5% of the extermination services revenue of $57,760 for 2011. No warranty expense has been recorded for 2011. All costs of servicing warranties in 2011 were properly debited to the Estimated Warranty Liability account.

g. The $15,000 long-term note is an 8%, five-year, interest-bearing note with interest payable annually on December 31. The note was signed with First National Bank on December 31, 2011.

h. The ending inventory of merchandise is counted and determined to have a cost of $11,700. Bug-Off uses a perpetual inventory system.

Required

1. Use the preceding information to determine amounts for the following items.

    a. Correct (reconciled) ending balance of Cash, and the amount of the omitted check.

    b. Adjustment needed to obtain the correct ending balance of the Allowance for Doubtful Accounts.

    c. Depreciation expense for the truck used during year 2011.

    d. Depreciation expense for the two items of equipment used during year 2011.

    e. The adjusted 2011 ending balances of the Extermination Services Revenue and Unearned Services Revenue accounts.

    f. The adjusted 2011 ending balances of the accounts for Warranty Expense and Estimated Warranty Liability.

    g. The adjusted 2011 ending balances of the accounts for Interest Expense and Interest Payable. (Round amounts to nearest whole dollar.)

Check (1*a*) Cash bal. $15,750
(1*b*) $551 credit

(1*f*) Estim. warranty liability, $2,844 Cr.

2. Use the results of part 1 to complete the six-column table by first entering the appropriate adjustments for items *a* through *g* and then completing the adjusted trial balance columns. (*Hint:* Item *b* requires two adjustments.)

3. Prepare journal entries to record the adjustments entered on the six-column table. Assume Bug-Off's adjusted balance for Merchandise Inventory matches the year-end physical count.

4. Prepare a single-step income statement, a statement of retained earnings (cash dividends declared during 2011 were $10,000), and a classified balance sheet.

(2) Adjusted trial balance totals, $238,207

(4) Net income, $9,274; Total assets, $82,771

Beyond the Numbers

BTN 9-1 Refer to the financial statements of **Research In Motion** in Appendix A to answer the following.

1. Compute times interest earned for the fiscal years ended 2010, 2009, and 2008. Comment on RIM's ability to cover its interest expense for this period. Assume interest expense of $1, $502, and $31 for fiscal years ended 2010, 2009, and 2008 ($ thousands); and, assume an industry average of 18.1 for times interest earned.

2. RIM's current liabilities include "deferred revenue"; assume that this account reflects "Unredeemed gift card liabilities." Explain how this liability is created and how RIM satisfies this liability.

3. Does RIM have any commitments or contingencies? Briefly explain them.

Fast Forward

4. Access RIM's financial statements for fiscal years ending after February 27, 2010, at its Website (**RIM.com**) or the SEC's EDGAR database (**www.sec.gov**). Compute its times interest earned for years ending after February 27, 2010, and compare your results to those in part 1.

REPORTING IN ACTION
A1 P4

RIM

BTN 9-2 Key figures for **Research In Motion** and **Apple** follow. (Interest expense figures for Apple are assumed as it has no interest expense for these years.)

| ($ millions) | Research In Motion | | | Apple | | |
	Current Year	One Year Prior	Two Years Prior	Current Year	One Year Prior	Two Years Prior
Net income	$2,457.144	$1,892.616	$1,293.867	$8,235	$6,119	$3,495
Income taxes	809.366	907.747	516.653	3,831	2,828	1,511
Interest expense	.001	.502	.031	3	2	1

COMPARATIVE ANALYSIS
A1

RIM
Apple

Required

1. Compute times interest earned for the three years' data shown for each company.

2. Comment on which company appears stronger in its ability to pay interest obligations if income should decline. Assume an industry average of 18.1.

BTN 9-3 Connor Bly is a sales manager for an automobile dealership. He earns a bonus each year based on revenue from the number of autos sold in the year less related warranty expenses. Actual warranty expenses have varied over the prior 10 years from a low of 3% of an automobile's selling price to a high of 10%. In the past, Bly has tended to estimate warranty expenses on the high end to be conservative. He must work with the dealership's accountant at year-end to arrive at the warranty expense accrual for cars sold each year.

1. Does the warranty accrual decision create any ethical dilemma for Bly?

2. Since warranty expenses vary, what percent do you think Bly should choose for the current year? Justify your response.

ETHICS CHALLENGE
P4

BTN 9-4 Dustin Clemens is the accounting and finance manager for a manufacturer. At year-end, he must determine how to account for the company's contingencies. His manager, Madeline Pretti, objects to Clemens's proposal to recognize an expense and a liability for warranty service on units of a new product introduced in the fourth quarter. Pretti comments, "There's no way we can estimate this warranty cost. We don't owe anyone anything until a product fails and it is returned. Let's report an expense if and when we do any warranty work."

COMMUNICATING IN PRACTICE
C3

Required

Prepare a one-page memorandum for Clemens to send to Pretti defending his proposal.

TAKING IT TO THE NET

C1 A1

BTN 9-5 Access the February 26, 2010, filing of the December 31, 2009, annual 10-K report of McDonald's Corporation (Ticker: MCD), which is available from www.SEC.gov.

Required

1. Identify the current liabilities on McDonald's balance sheet as of December 31, 2009.
2. What portion (in percent) of McDonald's long-term debt matures within the next 12 months?
3. Use the consolidated statement of income for the year ended December 31, 2009, to compute McDonald's times interest earned ratio. Comment on the result. Assume an industry average of 12.0.

TEAMWORK IN ACTION

C2 P1

BTN 9-6 Assume that your team is in business and you must borrow $6,000 cash for short-term needs. You have been shopping banks for a loan, and you have the following two options.

A. Sign a $6,000, 90-day, 10% interest-bearing note dated June 1.
B. Sign a $6,000, 120-day, 8% interest-bearing note dated June 1.

Required

1. Discuss these two options and determine the best choice. Ensure that all teammates concur with the decision and understand the rationale.
2. Each member of the team is to prepare *one* of the following journal entries.
    a. Option A—at date of issuance.
    b. Option B—at date of issuance.
    c. Option A—at maturity date.
    d. Option B—at maturity date.
3. In rotation, each member is to explain the entry he or she prepared in part 2 to the team. Ensure that all team members concur with and understand the entries.
4. Assume that the funds are borrowed on December 1 (instead of June 1) and your business operates on a calendar-year reporting period. Each member of the team is to prepare *one* of the following entries.
    a. Option A—the year-end adjustment.
    b. Option B—the year-end adjustment.
    c. Option A—at maturity date.
    d. Option B—at maturity date.
5. In rotation, each member is to explain the entry he or she prepared in part 4 to the team. Ensure that all team members concur with and understand the entries.

ENTREPRENEURIAL DECISION

A1

BTN 9-7 Review the chapter's opening feature about Matt and Bryan Walls, and their start-up company, SnorgTees. Assume that these young entrepreneurs are considering expanding their business to open an outlet in Europe. Assume their current income statement is as follows.

SNORGTEES	
Income Statement	
For Year Ended December 31, 2011	
Sales............................	$1,000,000
Cost of goods sold (30%)..........	300,000
Gross profit....................	700,000
Operating expenses (25%)........	250,000
Net income....................	$ 450,000

SnorgTees currently has no interest-bearing debt. If it expands to open a European location, it will require a $300,000 loan. SnorgTees has found a bank that will loan it the money on a 7% note payable. The company believes that, at least for the first few years, sales at its European location will be $250,000, and that all expenses (including cost of goods sold) will follow the same patterns as its current locations.

Required

1. Prepare an income statement (showing three separate columns for current operations, European, and total) for SnorgTees assuming that it borrows the funds and expands to Europe. Annual revenues for current operations are expected to remain at $1,000,000.
2. Compute SnorgTees' times interest earned under the expansion assumptions in part 1.
3. Assume sales at its European location are $400,000. Prepare an income statement (with columns for current operations, European, and total) for the company and compute times interest earned.
4. Assume sales at its European location are $100,000. Prepare an income statement (with columns for current operations, European, and total) for the company and compute times interest earned.
5. Comment on your results from parts 1 through 4.

BTN 9-8 Check your phone book or the Social Security Administration Website (www.ssa.gov) to locate the Social Security office near you. Visit the office to request a personal earnings and estimate form. Fill out the form and mail according to the instructions. You will receive a statement from the Social Security Administration regarding your earnings history and future Social Security benefits you can receive. (Formerly the request could be made online. The online service has been discontinued and is now under review by the Social Security Administration due to security concerns.) It is good to request an earnings and benefit statement every 5 to 10 years to make sure you have received credit for all wages earned and for which you and your employer have paid taxes into the system.

HITTING THE ROAD

P2

BTN 9-9 Nokia, Research In Motion, and Apple are all competitors in the global marketplace. Comparative figures for Nokia (www.Nokia.com), along with selected figures from Research In Motion and Apple, follow.

GLOBAL DECISION

A1

NOKIA

RIM

Apple

Key Figures	Nokia (EUR millions) Current Year	Prior Year	Research In Motion Current Year	Prior Year	Apple Current Year	Prior Year
Net income	260	3,889	—	—	—	—
Income taxes	702	1,081	—	—	—	—
Interest expense	243	185	—	—	—	—
Times interest earned	?	?	3,267	5,579	4,023	4,475

Required

1. Compute the times interest earned ratio for the most recent two years for Nokia using the data shown.
2. Which company of the three presented provides the best coverage of interest expense? Explain.

ANSWERS TO MULTIPLE CHOICE QUIZ

1. b; $6,000 × 0.05 × 30/360 = $25
2. e; $50,000 × (.062 + .0145) = $3,825
3. b; $7,000 × (.008 + .054) = $434
4. c; 10,000 television sets × .01 × $250 = $25,000
5. a; 150 employees × $175 per day × 1 vacation day earned = $26,250

◄◄ A Look Back

Chapter 9 focused on how current liabilities are identified, computed, recorded, and reported. Attention was directed at notes, payroll, sales taxes, warranties, employee benefits, and contingencies.

A Look at This Chapter ▶

This chapter describes the accounting for and analysis of bonds and notes. We explain their characteristics, payment patterns, interest computations, retirement, and reporting requirements. An appendix to this chapter introduces leases and pensions.

A Look Ahead ▶▶▶

Chapter 11 focuses on corporate equity transactions, including stock issuances and dividends. We also explain how to report and analyze income, earnings per share, and retained earnings.

10
Reporting and Analyzing Long-Term Liabilities

Learning Objectives

CAP

CONCEPTUAL

C1 Explain the types and payment patterns of notes. (p. 424)

C2 *Appendix 10A*—Explain and compute the present value of an amount(s) to be paid at a future date(s). (p. 432)

C3 *Appendix 10C*—Describe interest accrual when bond payment periods differ from accounting periods. (p. 436)

C4 *Appendix 10D*—Describe accounting for leases and pensions. (p. 438)

ANALYTICAL

A1 Compare bond financing with stock financing. (p. 414)

A2 Assess debt features and their implications. (p. 428)

A3 Compute the debt-to-equity ratio and explain its use. (p. 428)

LP10

PROCEDURAL

P1 Prepare entries to record bond issuance and interest expense. (p. 416)

P2 Compute and record amortization of bond discount. (p. 417)

P3 Compute and record amortization of bond premium. (p. 420)

P4 Record the retirement of bonds. (p. 423)

P5 Prepare entries to account for notes. (p. 426)

notes and bonds is similar to that for unsecured notes and bonds, except that the mortgage agreement must be disclosed. For example, **TIBCO Software** reports that its "mortgage note payable ... is collateralized by the commercial real property acquired [corporate headquarters]."

Fraud

Hidden Liabilities. Some companies arguably "hide" debt from their balance sheets by pursuing joint ventures, R&D partnerships, operating leases, and the like. While there are many sound economic reasons to pursue these activities, they also present the "less-principled" company with an opportunity to deceive readers of its balance sheet. Specifically, under certain conditions, companies can hide liabilities from such transactions when the economics suggest they should not. Notes to financial statements can often reveal this risk, but not always.

Global: Countries vary in the preference given to debtholders vs. stockholders when a company is in financial distress. Some countries such as Germany, France, and Japan give preference to stockholders over debtholders.

Quick Check

Answers — p. 441

11. Which of the following is true for an installment note requiring a series of equal total cash payments? (*a*) Payments consist of increasing interest and decreasing principal; (*b*) payments consist of changing amounts of principal but constant interest; or (*c*) payments consist of decreasing interest and increasing principal.

12. How is the interest portion of an installment note payment computed?

13. When a borrower records an interest payment on an installment note, how are the balance sheet and income statement affected?

GLOBAL VIEW

This section discusses similarities and differences between U.S. GAAP and IFRS in accounting and reporting for long-term liabilities such as bonds and notes.

Accounting for Bonds and Notes   The definitions and characteristics of bonds and notes are broadly similar for both U.S. GAAP and IFRS. Although slight differences exist, accounting for bonds and notes under U.S. GAAP and IFRS is similar. Specifically, the accounting for issuances (including recording discounts and premiums), market pricing, and retirement of both bonds and notes follows the procedures in this chapter. **Nokia** describes its accounting for bonds, which follows the amortized cost approach explained in this chapter (and in Appendix 10B), as follows: Loans payable [bonds] are recognized initially at fair value, net of transaction costs incurred. In the subsequent periods, they are stated at amortized cost.

Both U.S. GAAP and IFRS allow companies to account for bonds and notes using fair value (different from the amortized value described in this chapter). This method is referred to as the **fair value option.** This method is similar to that applied in measuring and accounting for debt and equity securities. *Fair value* is the amount a company would receive if it settled a liability (or sold an asset) in an orderly transaction as of the balance sheet date. Companies can use several sources of inputs to determine fair value, and those inputs fall into three classes (ranked in order of preference):

Level 1: Observable quoted market prices in active markets for identical items.
Level 2: Observable inputs other than those in Level 1 such as prices from inactive markets or from similar, but not identical, items.
Level 3: Unobservable inputs reflecting a company's assumptions about value.

The exact procedures for marking liabilities to fair value at each balance sheet date are in advanced courses.

Accounting for Leases and Pensions   Both U.S. GAAP and IFRS require companies to distinguish between operating leases and capital leases; the latter is referred to as *finance leases* under IFRS. The accounting and reporting for leases are broadly similar for both U.S. GAAP and IFRS. The main difference is the criteria for identifying a lease as a capital lease are more general under IFRS. However, the basic approach applies. **Nokia** describes its accounting for operating leases as follows: the payments ... are treated as rentals and recognized in the profit and loss account.

For pensions, both U.S. GAAP and IFRS require companies to record costs of retirement benefits as employees work and earn them. The basic methods are similar in accounting and reporting for pensions.

Decision Analysis □ □ □ Debt Features and the Debt-to-Equity Ratio

Collateral agreements can reduce the risk of loss for both bonds and notes. Unsecured bonds and notes are riskier because the issuer's obligation to pay interest and principal has the same priority as all other unsecured liabilities in the event of bankruptcy. If a company is unable to pay its debts in full, the unsecured creditors (including the holders of debentures) lose all or a portion of their balances. These types of legal agreements and other characteristics of long-term liabilities are crucial for effective business decisions. The first part of this section describes the different types of features sometimes included with bonds and notes. The second part explains and applies the debt-to-equity ratio.

Features of Bonds and Notes

| A2 | Assess debt features and their implications. |

This section describes common features of debt securities.

Secured Debt

Unsecured Debt

Secured or Unsecured   **Secured bonds** (and notes) have specific assets of the issuer pledged (or *mortgaged*) as collateral. This arrangement gives holders added protection against the issuer's default. If the issuer fails to pay interest or par value, the secured holders can demand that the collateral be sold and the proceeds used to pay the obligation. **Unsecured bonds** (and notes), also called *debentures,* are backed by the issuer's general credit standing. Unsecured debt is riskier than secured debt. *Subordinated debentures* are liabilities that are not repaid until the claims of the more senior, unsecured (and secured) liabilities are settled.

Term or Serial   **Term bonds** (and notes) are scheduled for maturity on one specified date. **Serial bonds** (and notes) mature at more than one date (often in series) and thus are usually repaid over a number of periods. For instance, $100,000 of serial bonds might mature at the rate of $10,000 each year from 6 to 15 years after they are issued. Many bonds are **sinking fund bonds,** which to reduce the holder's risk require the issuer to create a *sinking fund* of assets set aside at specified amounts and dates to repay the bonds.

Registered or Bearer   Bonds issued in the names and addresses of their holders are **registered bonds.** The issuer makes bond payments by sending checks (or cash transfers) to registered holders. A registered holder must notify the issuer of any ownership change. Registered bonds offer the issuer the practical advantage of not having to actually issue bond certificates. Bonds payable to whoever holds them (the *bearer*) are called **bearer bonds** or *unregistered bonds.* Sales or exchanges might not be recorded, so the holder of a bearer bond is presumed to be its rightful owner. As a result, lost bearer bonds are difficult to replace. Many bearer bonds are also **coupon bonds.** This term reflects interest coupons that are attached to the bonds. When each coupon matures, the holder presents it to a bank or broker for collection. At maturity, the holder follows the same process and presents the bond certificate for collection. Issuers of coupon bonds cannot deduct the related interest expense for taxable income. This is to prevent abuse by taxpayers who own coupon bonds but fail to report interest income on their tax returns.

Convertible Debt

Callable Debt

Convertible and/or Callable   **Convertible bonds** (and notes) can be exchanged for a fixed number of shares of the issuing corporation's common stock. Convertible debt offers holders the potential to participate in future increases in stock price. Holders still receive periodic interest while the debt is held and the par value if they hold the debt to maturity. In most cases, the holders decide whether and when to convert debt to stock. **Callable bonds** (and notes) have an option exercisable by the issuer to retire them at a stated dollar amount before maturity.

> ○ **Decision Insight**
>
> **Munis**   More than a million municipal bonds, or "munis," exist, and many are tax exempt. Munis are issued by state, city, town, and county governments to pay for public projects including schools, libraries, roads, bridges, and stadiums. ■

| A3 | Compute the debt-to-equity ratio and explain its use. |

Debt-to-Equity Ratio

Beyond assessing different characteristics of debt as just described, we want to know the level of debt, especially in relation to total equity. Such knowledge helps us assess the risk of a company's financing structure. A company financed mainly with debt is more risky because liabilities must be repaid—usually with periodic interest—whereas equity financing does not. A measure to assess the risk of a company's financing structure is the **debt-to-equity ratio** (see Exhibit 10.15).

$$\text{Debt-to-equity} = \frac{\text{Total liabilities}}{\text{Total equity}}$$

EXHIBIT 10.15

Debt-to-Equity Ratio

The debt-to-equity ratio varies across companies and industries. Industries that are more variable and less stable tend to have lower ratios, while more stable industries tend to have higher ratios. To apply the debt-to-equity ratio, let's look at this measure for **Cedar Fair** in Exhibit 10.16.

EXHIBIT 10.16

Cedar Fair's Debt-to-Equity Ratio

($ millions)	2009	2008	2007	2006	2005
Total liabilities	$2,017.577	$2,079.297	$2,133.576	$2,100.306	$590.560
Total equity	$ 127.862	$ 106.786	$ 285.092	$ 410.615	$434.234
Debt-to-equity	15.8	19.5	7.5	5.1	1.4
Industry debt-to-equity	11.4	10.3	5.7	3.2	1.2

Cedar Fair's 2009 debt-to-equity ratio is 15.8, meaning that debtholders contributed $15.8 for each $1 contributed by equityholders. This implies a fairly risky financing structure for Cedar Fair. A similar concern is drawn from a comparison of Cedar Fair with its competitors, where the 2009 industry ratio is 11.4. Analysis across the years shows that Cedar Fair's financing structure has grown increasingly risky in recent years. Given its sluggish revenues and increasing operating expenses in recent years (see its annual report), Cedar Fair is increasingly at risk of financial distress.

☐ **Decision Maker**   Answer — p. 441

Bond Investor   You plan to purchase debenture bonds from one of two companies in the same industry that are similar in size and performance. The first company has $350,000 in total liabilities, and $1,750,000 in equity. The second company has $1,200,000 in total liabilities, and $1,000,000 in equity. Which company's debenture bonds are less risky based on the debt-to-equity ratio? ■

DEMONSTRATION PROBLEM

Water Sports Company (WSC) patented and successfully test-marketed a new product. To expand its ability to produce and market the new product, WSC needs to raise $800,000 of financing. On January 1, 2011, the company obtained the money in two ways:

a. WSC signed a $400,000, 10% installment note to be repaid with five equal annual installments to be made on December 31 of 2011 through 2015.

b. WSC issued five-year bonds with a par value of $400,000. The bonds have a 12% annual contract rate and pay interest on June 30 and December 31. The bonds' annual market rate is 10% as of January 1, 2011.

Required

1. For the installment note, (a) compute the size of each annual payment, (b) prepare an amortization table such as Exhibit 10.14, and (c) prepare the journal entry for the first payment.

2. For the bonds, (a) compute their issue price; (b) prepare the January 1, 2011, journal entry to record their issuance; (c) prepare an amortization table using the straight-line method; (d) prepare the June 30, 2011, journal entry to record the first interest payment; and (e) prepare a journal entry to record retiring the bonds at a $416,000 call price on January 1, 2013.

3.[B] Redo parts 2(c), 2(d), and 2(e) assuming the bonds are amortized using the effective interest method.

PLANNING THE SOLUTION

● For the installment note, divide the borrowed amount by the annuity factor (from Table B.3) using the 10% rate and five payments to compute the amount of each payment. Prepare a table similar to Exhibit 10.14 and use the numbers in the table's first line for the journal entry.

● Compute the bonds' issue price by using the market rate to find the present value of their cash flows (use tables found in Appendix B). Then use this result to record the bonds' issuance. Next, prepare an amortization table like Exhibit 10.11 (and Exhibit 10B.2) and use it to get the numbers needed for the journal entry. Also use the table to find the carrying value as of the date of the bonds' retirement that you need for the journal entry.

SOLUTION TO DEMONSTRATION PROBLEM

Part 1: Installment Note

a. Annual payment = Note balance/Annuity factor = $400,000/3.7908 = $105,519 (The annuity factor is for five payments and a rate of 10%.)

b. An amortization table follows.

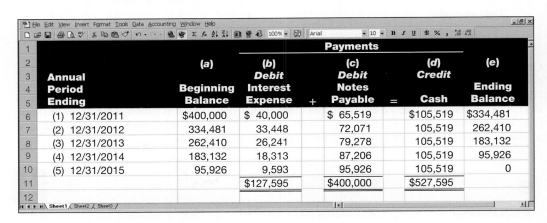

		Payments			
Annual Period Ending	**(a)** Beginning Balance	**(b)** Debit Interest Expense +	**(c)** Debit Notes Payable =	**(d)** Credit Cash	**(e)** Ending Balance
(1) 12/31/2011	$400,000	$ 40,000	$ 65,519	$105,519	$334,481
(2) 12/31/2012	334,481	33,448	72,071	105,519	262,410
(3) 12/31/2013	262,410	26,241	79,278	105,519	183,132
(4) 12/31/2014	183,132	18,313	87,206	105,519	95,926
(5) 12/31/2015	95,926	9,593	95,926	105,519	0
		$127,595	$400,000	$527,595	

c. Journal entry for December 31, 2011, payment.

Dec. 31	Interest Expense	40,000	
	Notes Payable	65,519	
	Cash		105,519
	To record first installment payment.		

Part 2: Bonds (Straight-Line Amortization)

a. Compute the bonds' issue price.

Cash Flow	Table	Present Value Factor*	Amount	Present Value
Par (maturity) value	B.1 in App. B (PV of 1)	0.6139	× 400,000	= $245,560
Interest payments	B.3 in App. B (PV of annuity)	7.7217	× 24,000	= 185,321
Price of bond				$430,881

* Present value factors are for 10 payments using a semiannual market rate of 5%.

b. Journal entry for January 1, 2011, issuance.

Jan. 1	Cash	430,881	
	Premium on Bonds Payable		30,881
	Bonds Payable		400,000
	Sold bonds at a premium.		

c. Straight-line amortization table for premium bonds.

Semiannual Period-End	Unamortized Premium	Carrying Value
(0) 1/1/2011	$30,881	$430,881
(1) 6/30/2011	27,793	427,793
(2) 12/31/2011	24,705	424,705
(3) 6/30/2012	21,617	421,617
(4) 12/31/2012	18,529	418,529
(5) 6/30/2013	15,441	415,441
(6) 12/31/2013	12,353	412,353
(7) 6/30/2014	9,265	409,265
(8) 12/31/2014	6,177	406,177
(9) 6/30/2015	3,089	403,089
(10) 12/31/2015	0*	400,000

* Adjusted for rounding.

d. Journal entry for June 30, 2011, bond payment.

June 30	Bond Interest Expense	20,912	
	Premium on Bonds Payable	3,088	
	Cash		24,000
	Paid semiannual interest on bonds.		

e. Journal entry for January 1, 2013, bond retirement.

Jan. 1	Bonds Payable	400,000	
	Premium on Bonds Payable	18,529	
	Cash		416,000
	Gain on Retirement of Bonds		2,529
	To record bond retirement (carrying value as of Dec. 31, 2012).		

Part 3: Bonds (Effective Interest Amortization)[B]

c. The effective interest amortization table for premium bonds.

Semiannual Interest Period	(A) Cash Interest Paid 6% × $400,000	(B) Interest Expense 5% × Prior (E)	(C) Premium Amortization (A) − (B)	(D) Unamortized Premium Prior (D) − (C)	(E) Carrying Value $400,000 + (D)
(0) 1/1/2011				$30,881	$430,881
(1) 6/30/2011	$ 24,000	$ 21,544	$ 2,456	28,425	428,425
(2) 12/31/2011	24,000	21,421	2,579	25,846	425,846
(3) 6/30/2012	24,000	21,292	2,708	23,138	423,138
(4) 12/31/2012	24,000	21,157	2,843	20,295	420,295
(5) 6/30/2013	24,000	21,015	2,985	17,310	417,310
(6) 12/31/2013	24,000	20,866	3,134	14,176	414,176
(7) 6/30/2014	24,000	20,709	3,291	10,885	410,885
(8) 12/31/2014	24,000	20,544	3,456	7,429	407,429
(9) 6/30/2015	24,000	20,371	3,629	3,800	403,800
(10) 12/31/2015	24,000	20,200*	3,800	0	400,000
	$240,000	$209,119	$30,881		

* Adjusted for rounding

option or purchasing them in the market. Bondholders can also retire bonds early by exercising a conversion feature on convertible bonds. The issuer recognizes a gain or loss for the difference between the amount paid and the bond carrying value.

P5 **Prepare entries to account for notes.** Interest is allocated to each period in a note's life by multiplying its beginning-period carrying value by its market rate at issuance. If a note is repaid with equal payments, the payment amount is computed by dividing the borrowed amount by the present value of an annuity factor (taken from a present value table) using the market rate and the number of payments.

Guidance Answers to Decision Maker

Entrepreneur This is a "present value" question. The market interest rate (10%) and present value ($3,000) are known, but the payment required two years later is unknown. This amount ($3,630) can be computed as $3,000 \times 1.10 \times 1.10$. Thus, the sale price is $3,630 when no payments are received for two years. The $3,630 received two years from today is equivalent to $3,000 cash today.

Bond Investor The debt-to-equity ratio for the first company is 0.2 ($350,000/$1,750,000) and for the second company is 1.2 ($1,200,000/$1,000,000), suggesting that the financing structure of the second company is more risky than that of the first company. Consequently, as a buyer of unsecured debenture bonds, you prefer the first company (all else equal).

Bond Rater Bonds with longer repayment periods (life) have higher risk. Also, bonds issued by companies in financial difficulties or facing higher than normal uncertainties have higher risk. Moreover, companies with higher than normal debt and large fluctuations in earnings are considered of higher risk. Discount bonds are more risky on one or more of these factors.

Guidance Answers to Quick Checks

1.

2011			
Jan. 1	Cash	10,000	
	Bonds Payable		10,000
June 30	Bond Interest Expense	450	
	Cash		450

2. Multiply the bond's par value by its contract rate of interest.
3. Bonds sell at a premium when the contract rate exceeds the market rate and the purchasers pay more than their par value.
4. The bonds are issued at a discount, meaning that issue price is less than par value. A discount occurs because the bond contract rate (6%) is less than the market rate (8%).
5.

Cash	91,893	
Discount on Bonds Payable	8,107	
Bonds Payable		100,000

6. $3,811 (total bond interest expense of $38,107 divided by 10 periods; or the $3,000 semiannual cash payment plus the $8,107 discount divided by 10 periods).
7. The bonds are issued at a premium, meaning issue price is higher than par value. A premium occurs because the bonds' contract rate (16%) is higher than the market rate (14%).
8. (*b*) For each semiannual period: $10,592/20 periods = $530 premium amortization.

9.

Bonds payable, 16%, due 12/31/2020	$100,000	
Plus premium on bonds payable	9,532*	$109,532

* Original premium balance of $10,592 less $530 and $530 amortized on 6/30/2011 and 12/31/2011, respectively.

10. $9,375 loss, computed as the difference between the repurchase price of $256,250 [50% of ($500,000 × 102.5%)] and the carrying value of $246,875 (50% of $493,750).
11. (*c*)
12. The interest portion of an installment payment equals the period's beginning loan balance multiplied by the market interest rate at the time of the note's issuance.
13. On the balance sheet, the account balances of the related liability (note payable) and asset (cash) accounts are decreased. On the income statement, interest expense is recorded.
14. (*c*), computed as 3.3121 × $1,000 = $3,312.
15. The option of paying $10,000 after one year has a lower present value. It postpones paying the first $5,000 by six months. More generally, the present value of a further delayed payment is always lower than a less delayed payment.
16. (*a*) Reflects payment of accrued interest recorded back on May 1; $500,000 × 9% × ¹⁄₁₂ = $15,000.

Key Terms

Annuity (p. 433)
Bearer bonds (p. 428)
Bond (p. 414)

Bond certificate (p. 416)
Bond indenture (p. 416)
Callable bonds (p. 428)

Capital leases (p. 439)
Carrying (book) value of bonds (p. 418)
Contract rate (p. 417)

Convertible bonds (p. 428)
Coupon bonds (p. 428)
Debt-to-equity ratio (p. 429)
Discount on bonds payable (p. 417)
Effective interest method (p. 434)
Fair value option (p. 427)
Installment note (p. 425)
Lease (p. 438)

Market rate (p. 417)
Mortgage (p. 426)
Off-balance-sheet financing (p. 439)
Operating leases (p. 438)
Par value of a bond (p. 414)
Pension plan (p. 440)
Premium on bonds (p. 420)
Registered bonds (p. 428)

Secured bonds (p. 428)
Serial bonds (p. 428)
Sinking fund bonds (p. 428)
Straight-line bond amortization (p. 418)
Term bonds (p. 428)
Unsecured bonds (p. 428)

Multiple Choice Quiz   Answers on p. 455   mhhe.com/wildFA6e

Additional quiz questions are available at the book's Website.

1. A bond traded at 97½ means that
 a. The bond pays 97½% interest.
 b. The bond trades at $975 per $1,000 bond.
 c. The market rate of interest is below the contract rate of interest for the bond.
 d. The bonds can be retired at $975 each.
 e. The bond's interest rate is 2½%.

2. A bondholder that owns a $1,000, 6%, 15-year bond has
 a. The right to receive $1,000 at maturity.
 b. Ownership rights in the bond issuing entity.
 c. The right to receive $60 per month until maturity.
 d. The right to receive $1,900 at maturity.
 e. The right to receive $600 per year until maturity.

3. A company issues 8%, 20-year bonds with a par value of $500,000. The current market rate for the bonds is 8%. The amount of interest owed to the bondholders for each semiannual interest payment is
 a. $40,000.
 b. $0.
 c. $20,000.

 d. $800,000.
 e. $400,000.

4. A company issued 5-year, 5% bonds with a par value of $100,000. The company received $95,735 for the bonds. Using the straight-line method, the company's interest expense for the first semiannual interest period is
 a. $2,926.50.
 b. $5,853.00.
 c. $2,500.00.
 d. $5,000.00.
 e. $9,573.50.

5. A company issued 8-year, 5% bonds with a par value of $350,000. The company received proceeds of $373,745. Interest is payable semiannually. The amount of premium amortized for the first semiannual interest period, assuming straight-line bond amortization, is
 a. $2,698.
 b. $23,745.
 c. $8,750.
 d. $9,344.
 e. $1,484.

^{B(C,D)} *Superscript letter B(C, D) denotes assignments based on Appendix 10B (10C, 10D).*
🎲 Icon denotes assignments that involve decision making.

Discussion Questions

1. What is the main difference between a bond and a share of stock?
2. What is the main difference between notes payable and bonds payable?
3. 🎲 What is the advantage of issuing bonds instead of obtaining financing from the company's owners?
4. What are the duties of a trustee for bondholders?
5. What is a bond indenture? What provisions are usually included in it?
6. What are the *contract* rate and the *market* rate for bonds?
7. 🎲 What factors affect the market rates for bonds?

8.^B 🎲 Does the straight-line or effective interest method produce an interest expense allocation that yields a constant rate of interest over a bond's life? Explain.
9.^C Why does a company that issues bonds between interest dates collect accrued interest from the bonds' purchasers?
10. 🎲 If you know the par value of bonds, the contract rate, and the market rate, how do you compute the bonds' price?
11. What is the issue price of a $2,000 bond sold at 98¼? What is the issue price of a $6,000 bond sold at 101½?
12. Describe the debt-to-equity ratio and explain how creditors and owners would use this ratio to evaluate a company's risk.

13. What obligation does an entrepreneur (owner) have to investors that purchase bonds to finance the business?

14. Refer to **Research In Motion**'s annual report in Appendix A. Is there any indication that RIM has issued bonds? **RIM**

15. By what amount did **Palm**'s long-term debt increase or decrease in 2009? **Palm**

16. Refer to the statement of cash flows for **Nokia** in Appendix A. For the year ended December 31, 2009, what was the amount for repayment of bank loans? **NOKIA**

17. Refer to the annual report for **Apple** in Appendix A. For the year ended September 26, 2009, what is its debt-to-equity ratio? What does this ratio tell us? Apple

18.^D When can a lease create both an asset and a liability for the lessee?

19.^D Compare and contrast an operating lease with a capital lease.

20.^D Describe the two basic types of pension plans.

---

connect

| Round dollar amounts to the nearest whole dollar. |

Enter the letter of the description *A* through *H* that best fits each term or phrase 1 through 8.

A. Records and tracks the bondholders' names.

B. Is unsecured; backed only by the issuer's credit standing.

C. Has varying maturity dates for amounts owed.

D. Identifies rights and responsibilities of the issuer and the bondholders.

E. Can be exchanged for shares of the issuer's stock.

F. Is unregistered; interest is paid to whoever possesses them.

G. Maintains a separate asset account from which bondholders are paid at maturity.

H. Pledges specific assets of the issuer as collateral.

1. _____ Debenture

2. _____ Bond indenture

3. _____ Bearer bond

4. _____ Registered bond

5. _____ Sinking fund bond

6. _____ Convertible bond

7. _____ Secured bond

8. _____ Serial bond

QUICK STUDY

QS 10-1
Bond features and terminology
A2

Alberto Company issues 8%, 10-year bonds with a par value of $350,000 and semiannual interest payments. On the issue date, the annual market rate for these bonds is 10%, which implies a selling price of 87½. The straight-line method is used to allocate interest expense.

1. What are the issuer's cash proceeds from issuance of these bonds?

2. What total amount of bond interest expense will be recognized over the life of these bonds?

3. What is the amount of bond interest expense recorded on the first interest payment date?

QS 10-2
Bond computations—
straight-line
P1 P2

Sanchez Company issues 10%, 15-year bonds with a par value of $120,000 and semiannual interest payments. On the issue date, the annual market rate for these bonds is 8%, which implies a selling price of 117¼. The effective interest method is used to allocate interest expense.

1. What are the issuer's cash proceeds from issuance of these bonds?

2. What total amount of bond interest expense will be recognized over the life of these bonds?

3. What amount of bond interest expense is recorded on the first interest payment date?

QS 10-3^B
Bond computations—
effective interest
P1 P3

Prepare the journal entries for the issuance of the bonds in both QS 10-2 and QS 10-3. Assume that both bonds are issued for cash on January 1, 2011.

QS 10-4
Journalize bond issuance   P1

Using the bond details in both QS 10-2 and QS 10-3, confirm that the bonds' selling prices given in each problem are approximately correct. Use the present value tables B.1 and B.3 in Appendix B.

QS 10-5
Computing bond price   P2 P3

QS 10-6
Recording bond issuance and discount amortization   **P1 P2**

Bellvue Company issues 10%, five-year bonds, on December 31, 2010, with a par value of $100,000 and semiannual interest payments. Use the following straight-line bond amortization table and prepare journal entries to record (*a*) the issuance of bonds on December 31, 2010; (*b*) the first interest payment on June 30, 2011; and (*c*) the second interest payment on December 31, 2011.

Semiannual Period-End		Unamortized Discount	Carrying Value
(0)	12/31/2010	$7,360	$92,640
(1)	6/30/2011	6,624	93,376
(2)	12/31/2011	5,888	94,112

QS 10-7
Bond retirement by call option
P4

On July 1, 2011, Jackson Company exercises a $5,000 call option (plus par value) on its outstanding bonds that have a carrying value of $208,000 and par value of $200,000. The company exercises the call option after the semiannual interest is paid on June 30, 2011. Record the entry to retire the bonds.

QS 10-8
Bond retirement by stock conversion   **P4**

On January 1, 2011, the $1,000,000 par value bonds of Gruden Company with a carrying value of $1,000,000 are converted to 500,000 shares of $0.50 par value common stock. Record the entry for the conversion of the bonds.

QS 10-9
Computing payments for an installment note   **C1**

Valdez Company borrows $170,000 cash from a bank and in return signs an installment note for five annual payments of equal amount, with the first payment due one year after the note is signed. Use Table B.3 in Appendix B to compute the amount of the annual payment for each of the following annual market rates: (*a*) 4%, (*b*) 8%, and (*c*) 12%.

QS 10-10
Debt-to-equity ratio

A2

Compute the debt-to-equity ratio for each of the following companies. Which company appears to have a riskier financing structure? Explain.

	Canal Company	Sears Company
Total liabilities	$492,000	$ 384,000
Total equity	656,000	1,200,000

QS 10-11ᶜ
Issuing bonds between interest dates   **P1**

Kemper Company plans to issue 6% bonds on January 1, 2011, with a par value of $1,000,000. The company sells $900,000 of the bonds on January 1, 2011. The remaining $100,000 sells at par on March 1, 2011. The bonds pay interest semiannually as of June 30 and December 31. Record the entry for the March 1 cash sale of bonds.

QS 10-12ᴰ
Recording operating leases   **C4**

Lauren Wright, an employee of ETrain.com, leases a car at O'Hare airport for a three-day business trip. The rental cost is $350. Prepare the entry by ETrain.com to record Lauren's short-term car lease cost.

QS 10-13ᴰ
Recording capital leases   **C4**

Juicyfruit, Inc., signs a five-year lease for office equipment with Office Solutions. The present value of the lease payments is $20,859. Prepare the journal entry that Juicyfruit records at the inception of this capital lease.

QS 10-14
International liabilities disclosures

P1 P2

Vodafone Group Plc reports the following information among its bonds payable as of March 31, 2009 (pounds in millions).

Financial Long-Term Liabilities Measured at Amortised Cost			
(£ millions)	Nominal (par) Value	Carrying Value	Fair Value
4.625% (US dollar 500 million) bond due July 2018	£350	£392	£315

a. What is the par value of the 4.625% bond issuance? What is its book (carrying) value?

b. Was the 4.625% bond sold at a discount or a premium? Explain.

Refer to the information in QS 10-14 for **Vodafone Group Plc**. The following price quotes (from Yahoo! Finance Bond Center) relate to its bonds payable as of late 2009. For example, the price quote indicates that the 4.625% bonds have a market price of 98.0 (98.0% of par value), resulting in a yield to maturity of 4.899%.

QS 10-15
International liabilities disclosures and interpretations

P1   P2

Price	Contract Rate (coupon)	Maturity Date	Market Rate (YTM)
98.0	4.625%	15-Jul-2018	4.899%

a. Assuming that the 4.625% bonds were originally issued at par value, what does the market price reveal about interest rate changes since bond issuance? (Assume that Vodafone's credit rating has remained the same.)

b. Does the change in market rates since the issuance of these bonds affect the amount of interest expense reported on Vodafone's income statement? Explain.

c. How much cash would Vodafone need to pay to repurchase the 4.625% bonds at the quoted market price of 98.0? (Assume no interest is owed when the bonds are repurchased.)

d. Assuming that the 4.625% bonds remain outstanding until maturity, at what market price will the bonds sell on the due date in 2018?

connect

Round dollar amounts to the nearest whole dollar. Assume no reversing entries are used.

EXERCISES

On January 1, 2011, Kidman Enterprises issues bonds that have a $1,700,000 par value, mature in 20 years, and pay 9% interest semiannually on June 30 and December 31. The bonds are sold at par.

1. How much interest will Kidman pay (in cash) to the bondholders every six months?

2. Prepare journal entries to record (*a*) the issuance of bonds on January 1, 2011; (*b*) the first interest payment on June 30, 2011; and (*c*) the second interest payment on December 31, 2011.

3. Prepare the journal entry for issuance assuming the bonds are issued at (*a*) 98 and (*b*) 102.

Exercise 10-1
Recording bond issuance and interest
P1

Moss issues bonds with a par value of $90,000 on January 1, 2011. The bonds' annual contract rate is 8%, and interest is paid semiannually on June 30 and December 31. The bonds mature in three years. The annual market rate at the date of issuance is 10%, and the bonds are sold for $85,431.

1. What is the amount of the discount on these bonds at issuance?

2. How much total bond interest expense will be recognized over the life of these bonds?

3. Prepare an amortization table like the one in Exhibit 10.7 for these bonds; use the straight-line method to amortize the discount.

Exercise 10-2
Straight-line amortization of bond discount
P2

Welch issues bonds dated January 1, 2011, with a par value of $250,000. The bonds' annual contract rate is 9%, and interest is paid semiannually on June 30 and December 31. The bonds mature in three years. The annual market rate at the date of issuance is 12%, and the bonds are sold for $231,570.

1. What is the amount of the discount on these bonds at issuance?

2. How much total bond interest expense will be recognized over the life of these bonds?

3. Prepare an amortization table like the one in Exhibit 10B.1 for these bonds; use the effective interest method to amortize the discount.

Exercise 10-3[B]
Effective interest amortization of bond discount
P2

Prairie Dunes Co. issues bonds dated January 1, 2011, with a par value of $800,000. The bonds' annual contract rate is 13%, and interest is paid semiannually on June 30 and December 31. The bonds mature in three years. The annual market rate at the date of issuance is 12%, and the bonds are sold for $819,700.

1. What is the amount of the premium on these bonds at issuance?

2. How much total bond interest expense will be recognized over the life of these bonds?

3. Prepare an amortization table like the one in Exhibit 10.11 for these bonds; use the straight-line method to amortize the premium.

Exercise 10-4
Straight-line amortization of bond premium
P3

Exercise 10-5ᴮ
Effective interest amortization of bond premium   P3

Refer to the bond details in Exercise 10-4 and prepare an amortization table like the one in Exhibit 10B.2 for these bonds using the effective interest method to amortize the premium.

Exercise 10-6
Recording bond issuance and premium amortization

P1   P3

Jobbs Company issues 10%, five-year bonds, on December 31, 2010, with a par value of $100,000 and semiannual interest payments. Use the following straight-line bond amortization table and prepare journal entries to record (*a*) the issuance of bonds on December 31, 2010; (*b*) the first interest payment on June 30, 2011; and (*c*) the second interest payment on December 31, 2011.

Semiannual Period-End	Unamortized Premium	Carrying Value
(0) 12/31/2010	$8,111	$108,111
(1) 6/30/2011	7,300	107,300
(2) 12/31/2011	6,489	106,489

Exercise 10-7
Recording bond issuance and discount amortization

P1   P2

Matchbox Company issues 6%, four-year bonds, on December 31, 2011, with a par value of $100,000 and semiannual interest payments. Use the following straight-line bond amortization table and prepare journal entries to record (*a*) the issuance of bonds on December 31, 2011; (*b*) the first interest payment on June 30, 2012; and (*c*) the second interest payment on December 31, 2012.

Semiannual Period-End	Unamortized Discount	Carrying Value
(0) 12/31/2011	$6,733	$93,267
(1) 6/30/2012	5,891	94,109
(2) 12/31/2012	5,049	94,951

Exercise 10-8
Recording bond issuance and discount amortization

P1   P2

Oneil Company issues 5%, two-year bonds, on December 31, 2011, with a par value of $100,000 and semiannual interest payments. Use the following straight-line bond amortization table and prepare journal entries to record (*a*) the issuance of bonds on December 31, 2011; (*b*) the first through fourth interest payments on each June 30 and December 31; and (*c*) the maturity of the bond on December 31, 2013.

Semiannual Period-End	Unamortized Discount	Carrying Value
(0) 12/31/2011	$6,000	$ 94,000
(1) 6/30/2012	4,500	95,500
(2) 12/31/2012	3,000	97,000
(3) 6/30/2013	1,500	98,500
(4) 12/31/2013	0	100,000

Exercise 10-9
Computing bond interest and price; recording bond issuance

P2

Jester Company issues bonds with a par value of $600,000 on their stated issue date. The bonds mature in 10 years and pay 6% annual interest in semiannual payments. On the issue date, the annual market rate for the bonds is 8%.

1. What is the amount of each semiannual interest payment for these bonds?
2. How many semiannual interest payments will be made on these bonds over their life?
3. Use the interest rates given to determine whether the bonds are issued at par, at a discount, or at a premium.
4. Compute the price of the bonds as of their issue date.
5. Prepare the journal entry to record the bonds' issuance.

Check (4) $518,465

Exercise 10-10
Computing bond interest and price; recording bond issuance

P3

Metro Company issues bonds with a par value of $75,000 on their stated issue date. The bonds mature in five years and pay 10% annual interest in semiannual payments. On the issue date, the annual market rate for the bonds is 8%.

1. What is the amount of each semiannual interest payment for these bonds?
2. How many semiannual interest payments will be made on these bonds over their life?
3. Use the interest rates given to determine whether the bonds are issued at par, at a discount, or at a premium.

4. Compute the price of the bonds as of their issue date.

5. Prepare the journal entry to record the bonds' issuance.

Check   (4) $81,086

On January 1, 2011, Steadman issues $350,000 of 10%, 15-year bonds at a price of 97¾. Six years later, on January 1, 2017, Steadman retires 20% of these bonds by buying them on the open market at 104½. All interest is accounted for and paid through December 31, 2016, the day before the purchase. The straight-line method is used to amortize any bond discount.

1. How much does the company receive when it issues the bonds on January 1, 2011?

2. What is the amount of the discount on the bonds at January 1, 2011?

3. How much amortization of the discount is recorded on the bonds for the entire period from January 1, 2011, through December 31, 2016?

4. What is the carrying (book) value of the bonds as of the close of business on December 31, 2016? What is the carrying value of the 20% soon-to-be-retired bonds on this same date?

5. How much did the company pay on January 1, 2017, to purchase the bonds that it retired?

6. What is the amount of the recorded gain or loss from retiring the bonds?

7. Prepare the journal entry to record the bond retirement at January 1, 2017.

Exercise 10-11
Bond computations, straight-line amortization, and bond retirement
P2 P4

Check   (6) $4,095 loss

On May 1, 2011, Fellenger Enterprises issues bonds dated January 1, 2011, that have a $1,700,000 par value, mature in 20 years, and pay 9% interest semiannually on June 30 and December 31. The bonds are sold at par plus four months' accrued interest.

1. How much accrued interest do the bond purchasers pay Fellenger on May 1, 2011?

2. Prepare Fellenger's journal entries to record (a) the issuance of bonds on May 1, 2011; (b) the first interest payment on June 30, 2011; and (c) the second interest payment on December 31, 2011.

Exercise 10-12ᶜ
Recording bond issuance with accrued interest
C4 P1

Check   (1) $51,000

Simon issues four-year bonds with a $50,000 par value on June 1, 2011, at a price of $47,974. The annual contract rate is 7%, and interest is paid semiannually on November 30 and May 31.

1. Prepare an amortization table like the one in Exhibit 10.7 for these bonds. Use the straight-line method of interest amortization.

2. Prepare journal entries to record the first two interest payments and to accrue interest as of December 31, 2011.

Exercise 10-13
Straight-line amortization and accrued bond interest expense
P1 P2

On January 1, 2011, Randa borrows $25,000 cash by signing a four-year, 7% installment note. The note requires four equal total payments of accrued interest and principal on December 31 of each year from 2011 through 2014.

1. Compute the amount of each of the four equal total payments.

2. Prepare an amortization table for this installment note like the one in Exhibit 10.14.

Exercise 10-14
Installment note with equal total payments C1 P5

Check   (1) $7,381

Use the information in Exercise 10-14 to prepare the journal entries for Randa to record the loan on January 1, 2011, and the four payments from December 31, 2011, through December 31, 2014.

Exercise 10-15
Installment note entries P5

Ramirez Company is considering a project that will require a $500,000 loan. It presently has total liabilities of $220,000, and total assets of $620,000.

1. Compute Ramirez's (a) present debt-to-equity ratio and (b) the debt-to-equity ratio assuming it borrows $500,000 to fund the project.

2. Evaluate and discuss the level of risk involved if Ramirez borrows the funds to pursue the project.

Exercise 10-16
Applying debt-to-equity ratio
A3

Indicate whether the company in each separate case 1 through 3 has entered into an operating lease or a capital lease.

1. The present value of the lease payments is 95% of the leased asset's market value, and the lease term is 70% of the leased asset's useful life.

2. The title is transferred to the lessee, the lessee can purchase the asset for $1 at the end of the lease, and the lease term is five years. The leased asset has an expected useful life of six years.

3. The lessor retains title to the asset, and the lease term is three years on an asset that has a five-year useful life.

Exercise 10-17ᴰ
Identifying capital and operating leases
C4

Exercise 10-18^D

Accounting for capital lease

C4

Flyer (lessee) signs a five-year capital lease for office equipment with a $20,000 annual lease payment. The present value of the five annual lease payments is $82,000, based on a 7% interest rate.

1. Prepare the journal entry Flyer will record at inception of the lease.

2. If the leased asset has a five-year useful life with no salvage value, prepare the journal entry Flyer will record each year to recognize depreciation expense related to the leased asset.

Exercise 10-19^D

Analyzing lease options

C2 C3 C4

General Motors advertised three alternatives for a 25-month lease on a new Chevrolet Volt: (1) zero dollars down and a lease payment of $1,750 per month for 25 months, (2) $5,000 down and $1,500 per month for 25 months, or (3) $38,500 down and no payments for 25 months. Use the present value Table B.3 in Appendix B to determine which is the best alternative (assume you have enough cash to accept any alternative and the annual interest rate is 12% compounded monthly).

Exercise 10-20

Accounting for long-term liabilities under IFRS

P1 P2 P3

Heineken N.V. reports the following information for its Loans and Borrowings as of December 31, 2008, including proceeds and repayments for the year ended December 31, 2008 (euros in millions).

Loans and borrowings (noncurrent liabilities)	
Loans and borrowings, December 31, 2008	€ 9,084
Proceeds (cash) from issuances of loans and borrowings	6,361
Repayments (in cash) of loans and borrowings	(2,532)

1. Prepare Heineken's journal entry to record its cash proceeds from issuances of its loans and borrowings for 2008. Assume that the par value of these issuances is €6,000.

2. Prepare Heineken's journal entry to record its cash repayments of its loans and borrowings for 2008. Assume that the par value of these issuances is €2,400, and the premium on them is €32.

3. Compute the discount or premium on its loans and borrowings as of December 31, 2008, assuming that the par value of these liabilities is €9,000.

4. Given the facts in part 3 and viewing the entirety of loans and borrowings as one issuance, was the contract rate on these loans and borrowings higher or lower than the market rate at the time of issuance? Explain. (Assume that Heineken's credit rating has remained the same.)

■ connect

PROBLEM SET A

> *Round dollar amounts to the nearest whole dollar. Assume no reversing entries are used.*

Problem 10-1A

Computing bond price and recording issuance

P1 P2 P3

Check (1) Premium, $2,718

(3) Discount, $2,294

Stowers Research issues bonds dated January 1, 2011, that pay interest semiannually on June 30 and December 31. The bonds have a $20,000 par value and an annual contract rate of 10%, and they mature in 10 years.

Required

For each of the following three separate situations, (*a*) determine the bonds' issue price on January 1, 2011, and (*b*) prepare the journal entry to record their issuance.

1. The market rate at the date of issuance is 8%.

2. The market rate at the date of issuance is 10%.

3. The market rate at the date of issuance is 12%.

Problem 10-2A

Straight-line amortization of bond discount

P1 P2

X

mhhe.com/wildFA6e

Check (3) $2,071,776

(4) 12/31/2012 carrying value, $1,764,460

Heathrow issues $2,000,000 of 6%, 15-year bonds dated January 1, 2011, that pay interest semiannually on June 30 and December 31. The bonds are issued at a price of $1,728,224.

Required

1. Prepare the January 1, 2011, journal entry to record the bonds' issuance.

2. For each semiannual period, compute (*a*) the cash payment, (*b*) the straight-line discount amortization, and (*c*) the bond interest expense.

3. Determine the total bond interest expense to be recognized over the bonds' life.

4. Prepare the first two years of an amortization table like Exhibit 10.7 using the straight-line method.

5. Prepare the journal entries to record the first two interest payments.

Refer to the bond details in Problem 10-2A, *except* assume that the bonds are issued at a price of $2,447,990.

Required

1. Prepare the January 1, 2011, journal entry to record the bonds' issuance.
2. For each semiannual period, compute (*a*) the cash payment, (*b*) the straight-line premium amortization, and (*c*) the bond interest expense.
3. Determine the total bond interest expense to be recognized over the bonds' life.
4. Prepare the first two years of an amortization table like Exhibit 10.7 using the straight-line method.
5. Prepare the journal entries to record the first two interest payments.

Problem 10-3A
Straight-line amortization of bond premium
P1   P3

Check   (3) $1,352,010
(4) 12/31/2012 carrying value, $2,388,258

Saturn issues 6.5%, five-year bonds dated January 1, 2011, with a $500,000 par value. The bonds pay interest on June 30 and December 31 and are issued at a price of $510,666. The annual market rate is 6% on the issue date.

Required

1. Calculate the total bond interest expense over the bonds' life.
2. Prepare a straight-line amortization table like Exhibit 10.11 for the bonds' life.
3. Prepare the journal entries to record the first two interest payments.

Problem 10-4A
Straight-line amortization of bond premium
P1   P3

mhhe.com/wildFA6e

Check   (2) 6/30/2013 carrying value, $505,331

Refer to the bond details in Problem 10-4A.

Required

1. Compute the total bond interest expense over the bonds' life.
2. Prepare an effective interest amortization table like the one in Exhibit 10B.2 for the bonds' life.
3. Prepare the journal entries to record the first two interest payments.
4. Use the market rate at issuance to compute the present value of the remaining cash flows for these bonds as of December 31, 2013. Compare your answer with the amount shown on the amortization table as the balance for that date (from part 2) and explain your findings.

Problem 10-5A[B]
Effective interest amortization of bond premium; computing bond price   P1   P3

Check   (2) 6/30/2013 carrying value, $505,728

(4) $504,653

Patton issues $650,000 of 5%, four-year bonds dated January 1, 2011, that pay interest semiannually on June 30 and December 31. They are issued at $584,361 and their market rate is 8% at the issue date.

Required

1. Prepare the January 1, 2011, journal entry to record the bonds' issuance.
2. Determine the total bond interest expense to be recognized over the bonds' life.
3. Prepare a straight-line amortization table like the one in Exhibit 10.7 for the bonds' first two years.
4. Prepare the journal entries to record the first two interest payments.

Analysis Component

5. Assume the market rate on January 1, 2011, is 4% instead of 8%. Without providing numbers, describe how this change affects the amounts reported on Patton's financial statements.

Problem 10-6A
Straight-line amortization of bond discount
P1   P2

Check   (2) $195,639
(3) 12/31/2012 carrying value, $617,181

Refer to the bond details in Problem 10-6A.

Required

1. Prepare the January 1, 2011, journal entry to record the bonds' issuance.
2. Determine the total bond interest expense to be recognized over the bonds' life.
3. Prepare an effective interest amortization table like the one in Exhibit 10B.1 for the bonds' first two years.
4. Prepare the journal entries to record the first two interest payments.

Problem 10-7A[B]
Effective interest amortization of bond discount   P1   P2

Check   (2) $195,639
(3) 12/31/2012 carrying value, $614,614

mhhe.com/wildFA6e

Problem 10-8A[B]

Effective interest amortization of bond premium; retiring bonds

P1 P3 P4

Check (3) 6/30/2012 carrying value, $91,224

(5) $2,635 gain

McFad issues $90,000 of 11%, three-year bonds dated January 1, 2011, that pay interest semiannually on June 30 and December 31. They are issued at $92,283. Their market rate is 10% at the issue date.

Required

1. Prepare the January 1, 2011, journal entry to record the bonds' issuance.
2. Determine the total bond interest expense to be recognized over the bonds' life.
3. Prepare an effective interest amortization table like Exhibit 10B.2 for the bonds' first two years.
4. Prepare the journal entries to record the first two interest payments.
5. Prepare the journal entry to record the bonds' retirement on January 1, 2013, at 98.

Analysis Component

6. Assume that the market rate on January 1, 2011, is 12% instead of 10%. Without presenting numbers, describe how this change affects the amounts reported on McFad's financial statements.

Problem 10-9A

Installment notes

C1 P5

Check (2) 10/31/2015 ending balance, $92,759

On November 1, 2011, Leetch Ltd. borrows $400,000 cash from a bank by signing a five-year installment note bearing 8% interest. The note requires equal total payments each year on October 31.

Required

1. Compute the total amount of each installment payment.
2. Complete an amortization table for this installment note similar to the one in Exhibit 10.14.
3. Prepare the journal entries in which Leetch records (*a*) accrued interest as of December 31, 2011 (the end of its annual reporting period), and (*b*) the first annual payment on the note.

Problem 10-10A

Applying the debt-to-equity ratio

A3

At the end of the current year, the following information is available for both Kumar Company and Asher Company.

	Kumar Company	Asher Company
Total assets	$2,254,500	$1,123,500
Total liabilities	904,500	598,500
Total equity	1,350,000	525,000

Required

1. Compute the debt-to-equity ratios for both companies.
2. Comment on your results and discuss the riskiness of each company's financing structure.

Problem 10-11A[D]

Capital lease accounting

C4

Check (1) $79,854

(3) Year 3 ending balance, $35,664

Montana Company signs a five-year capital lease with Elway Company for office equipment. The annual lease payment is $20,000, and the interest rate is 8%.

Required

1. Compute the present value of Montana's five-year lease payments.
2. Prepare the journal entry to record Montana's capital lease at its inception.
3. Complete a lease payment schedule for the five years of the lease with the following headings. Assume that the beginning balance of the lease liability (present value of lease payments) is $79,854. (*Hint:* To find the amount allocated to interest in year 1, multiply the interest rate by the beginning-of-year lease liability. The amount of the annual lease payment not allocated to interest is allocated to principal. Reduce the lease liability by the amount allocated to principal to update the lease liability at each year-end.)

Period Ending Date	Beginning Balance of Lease Liability	Interest on Lease Liability	Reduction of Lease Liability	Cash Lease Payment	Ending Balance of Lease Liability

4. Use straight-line depreciation and prepare the journal entry to depreciate the leased asset at the end of year 1. Assume zero salvage value and a five-year life for the office equipment.

Round dollar amounts to the nearest whole dollar. Assume no reversing entries are used.

PROBLEM SET B

Sedona Systems issues bonds dated January 1, 2011, that pay interest semiannually on June 30 and December 31. The bonds have a $45,000 par value and an annual contract rate of 12%, and they mature in five years.

Problem 10-1B
Computing bond price and recording issuance
P1 P2 P3

Required

For each of the following three separate situations, (*a*) determine the bonds' issue price on January 1, 2011, and (*b*) prepare the journal entry to record their issuance.

1. The market rate at the date of issuance is 10%.
2. The market rate at the date of issuance is 12%.
3. The market rate at the date of issuance is 14%.

Check (1) Premium, $3,475

(3) Discount, $3,162

ParFour issues $1,700,000 of 10%, 10-year bonds dated January 1, 2011, that pay interest semiannually on June 30 and December 31. The bonds are issued at a price of $1,505,001.

Problem 10-2B
Straight-line amortization of bond discount
P1 P2

Required

1. Prepare the January 1, 2011, journal entry to record the bonds' issuance.
2. For each semiannual period, compute (*a*) the cash payment, (*b*) the straight-line discount amortization, and (*c*) the bond interest expense.
3. Determine the total bond interest expense to be recognized over the bonds' life.
4. Prepare the first two years of an amortization table like Exhibit 10.7 using the straight-line method.
5. Prepare the journal entries to record the first two interest payments.

Check (3) $1,894,999

(4) 6/30/2012 carrying value, $1,534,251

Refer to the bond details in Problem 10-2B, *except* assume that the bonds are issued at a price of $2,096,466.

Problem 10-3B
Straight-line amortization of bond premium
P1 P3

Required

1. Prepare the January 1, 2011, journal entry to record the bonds' issuance.
2. For each semiannual period, compute (*a*) the cash payment, (*b*) the straight-line premium amortization, and (*c*) the bond interest expense.
3. Determine the total bond interest expense to be recognized over the bonds' life.
4. Prepare the first two years of an amortization table like Exhibit 10.7 using the straight-line method.
5. Prepare the journal entries to record the first two interest payments.

Check (3) $1,303,534

(4) 6/30/2012 carrying value, $2,036,997

Zooba Company issues 9%, five-year bonds dated January 1, 2011, with a $160,000 par value. The bonds pay interest on June 30 and December 31 and are issued at a price of $166,494. Their annual market rate is 8% on the issue date.

Problem 10-4B
Straight-line amortization of bond premium
P1 P3

Required

1. Calculate the total bond interest expense over the bonds' life.
2. Prepare a straight-line amortization table like Exhibit 10.11 for the bonds' life.
3. Prepare the journal entries to record the first two interest payments.

Check (2) 6/30/2013 carrying value, $163,249

Refer to the bond details in Problem 10-4B.

Problem 10-5B[B]
Effective interest amortization of bond premium; computing bond price P1 P3

Required

1. Compute the total bond interest expense over the bonds' life.
2. Prepare an effective interest amortization table like the one in Exhibit 10B.2 for the bonds' life.
3. Prepare the journal entries to record the first two interest payments.
4. Use the market rate at issuance to compute the present value of the remaining cash flows for these bonds as of December 31, 2013. Compare your answer with the amount shown on the amortization table as the balance for that date (from part 2) and explain your findings.

Check (2) 6/30/2013 carrying value, $163,568

(4) $162,903

certificates as necessary. Registrars and transfer agents are usually large banks or trust companies with computer facilities and staff to do this work.

> ### ◯ Decision **Insight**
>
> **Pricing Stock** A prospectus accompanies a stock's initial public offering (IPO), giving financial information about the company issuing the stock. A prospectus should help answer these questions to price an IPO: (1) Is the underwriter reliable? (2) Is there growth in revenues, profits, and cash flows? (3) What is management's view of operations? (4) Are current owners selling? (5) What are the risks? ■

Basics of Capital Stock

Capital stock is a general term that refers to any shares issued to obtain capital (owner financing). This section introduces terminology and accounting for capital stock.

Authorized Stock **Authorized stock** is the number of shares that a corporation's charter allows it to sell. The number of authorized shares usually exceeds the number of shares issued (and outstanding), often by a large amount. (*Outstanding stock* refers to issued stock held by stockholders.) No formal journal entry is required for stock authorization. A corporation must apply to the state for a change in its charter if it wishes to issue more shares than previously authorized. A corporation discloses the number of shares authorized in the equity section of its balance sheet or notes. **Apple**'s balance sheet in Appendix A reports 1.8 billion common shares authorized as of the start of its 2010 fiscal year.

Subcategories of Authorized Stock

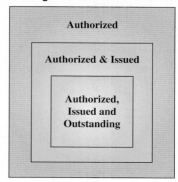

Selling (Issuing) Stock A corporation can sell stock directly or indirectly. To *sell directly,* it advertises its stock issuance to potential buyers. This type of issuance is most common with privately held corporations. To *sell indirectly,* a corporation pays a brokerage house (investment banker) to issue its stock. Some brokerage houses *underwrite* an indirect issuance of stock; that is, they buy the stock from the corporation and take all gains or losses from its resale.

Market Value of Stock **Market value per share** is the price at which a stock is bought and sold. Expected future earnings, dividends, growth, and other company and economic factors influence market value. Traded stocks' market values are available daily in newspapers such as *The Wall Street Journal* and online. The current market value of previously issued shares (for example, the price of stock in trades between investors) does not impact the issuing corporation's stockholders' equity.

Classes of Stock When all authorized shares have the same rights and characteristics, the stock is called *common stock*. A corporation is sometimes authorized to issue more than one class of stock, including preferred stock and different classes of common stock. **American Greetings**, for instance, has two types of common stock: Class A stock has 1 vote per share and Class B stock has 10 votes per share.

Par Value Stock **Par value stock** is stock that is assigned a **par value,** which is an amount assigned per share by the corporation in its charter. For example, **Palm**'s common stock has a par value of $0.001. Other commonly assigned par values are $10, $5, $1 and $0.01. There is no restriction on the assigned par value. In many states, the par value of a stock establishes **minimum legal capital,** which refers to the least amount that the buyers of stock must contribute to the corporation or be subject to paying at a future date. For example, if a corporation issues 1,000 shares of $10 par value stock, the corporation's minimum legal capital in these states would be $10,000. Minimum legal capital is intended to protect a corporation's creditors. Since creditors cannot demand payment from stockholders' personal assets, their claims are limited to the corporation's assets and any minimum legal capital. At liquidation, creditor claims are paid before any amounts are distributed to stockholders.

No-Par Value Stock **No-par value stock,** or simply *no-par stock,* is stock *not* assigned a value per share by the corporate charter. Its advantage is that it can be issued at any price without the possibility of a minimum legal capital deficiency.

Point: Managers are motivated to set a low par value when minimum legal capital or state issuance taxes are based on par value.

Point: Minimum legal capital was intended to protect creditors by requiring a minimum level of net assets.

Point: Par, no-par, and stated value do *not* set the stock's market value.

EXHIBIT 11.3

Equity Composition

Corporation

Common Stock

Normal bal.

Paid-In Capital in Excess of Par

Normal bal.

Retained Earnings

Normal bal.

Total Paid-In Capital

Point: Paid-in capital comes from stock-related transactions, whereas retained earnings comes from operations.

Stated Value Stock Stated value stock is no-par stock to which the directors assign a "stated" value per share. Stated value per share becomes the minimum legal capital per share in this case.

Stockholders' Equity A corporation's equity is known as **stockholders' equity,** also called *shareholders' equity* or *corporate capital.* Stockholders' equity consists of (1) paid-in (or contributed) capital and (2) retained earnings; see Exhibit 11.3. **Paid-in capital** is the total amount of cash and other assets the corporation receives from its stockholders in exchange for its stock. **Retained earnings** is the cumulative net income (and loss) not distributed as dividends to its stockholders.

Decision Insight

Stock Quote The **Best Buy** stock quote is interpreted as (left to right):
Hi, highest price in past 52 weeks;
Lo, lowest price in past 52 weeks;

52 Weeks				Yld		Vol				Net
Hi	Lo	Sym	Div	%	PE	mil.	Hi	Lo	Close	Chg
54.15	41.85	BBY	0.13	0.98	19	7.2	53.14	52.36	52.91	+0.20

Sym, company exchange symbol; **Div,** dividends paid per share in past year; **Yld %,** dividend divided by closing price; **PE,** stock price per share divided by earnings per share; **Vol mil.,** number (in millions) of shares traded; **Hi,** highest price for the day; **Lo,** lowest price for the day; **Close,** closing price for the day; **Net Chg,** change in closing price from prior day. ■

Quick Check

Answers — p. 483

1. Which of the following is *not* a characteristic of the corporate form of business? (*a*) Ease of capital accumulation, (*b*) Stockholder responsibility for corporate debts, (*c*) Ease in transferability of ownership rights, or (*d*) Double taxation.
2. Why is a corporation's income said to be taxed twice?
3. What is a proxy?

COMMON STOCK

 P1 Record the issuance of corporate stock.

Accounting for the issuance of common stock affects only paid-in (contributed) capital accounts; no retained earnings accounts are affected.

Issuing Par Value Stock

Par value stock can be issued at par, at a premium (above par), or at a discount (below par). In each case, stock can be exchanged for either cash or noncash assets.

Issuing Par Value Stock at Par When common stock is issued at par value, we record amounts for both the asset(s) received and the par value stock issued. To illustrate, the entry to record Dillon Snowboards' issuance of 30,000 shares of $10 par value stock for $300,000 cash on June 5, 2011, follows.

Assets = Liabilities + Equity
+300,000   +300,000

$10 par value × 30,000 shares

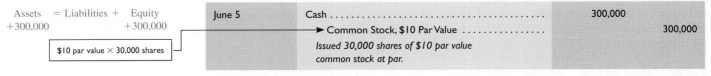

June 5	Cash	300,000	
	➤ Common Stock, $10 Par Value		300,000
	Issued 30,000 shares of $10 par value		
	common stock at par.		

Exhibit 11.4 shows the stockholders' equity of Dillon Snowboards at year-end 2011 (its first year of operations) after income of $65,000 and no dividend payments.

Stockholders' Equity	
Common Stock—$10 par value; 50,000 shares authorized;	
30,000 shares issued and outstanding	$300,000
Retained earnings	65,000
Total stockholders' equity	$365,000

EXHIBIT 11.4

Stockholders' Equity for Stock Issued at Par

Issuing Par Value Stock at a Premium

A premium on stock occurs when a corporation sells its stock for more than par (or stated) value. To illustrate, if Dillon Snowboards issues its $10 par value common stock at $12 per share, its stock is sold at a $2 per share premium. The premium, known as **paid-in capital in excess of par value,** is reported as part of equity; it is not revenue and is not listed on the income statement. The entry to record Dillon Snowboards' issuance of 30,000 shares of $10 par value stock for $12 per share on June 5, 2011, follows

Point: A *premium* is the amount by which issue price exceeds par (or stated) value. It is recorded in the "Paid-In Capital in Excess of Par Value, Common Stock" account; also called "Additional Paid-In Capital, Common Stock."

June 5	Cash	360,000	
	Common Stock, $10 Par Value		300,000
	Paid-In Capital in Excess of Par Value, Common Stock		60,000
	Sold and issued 30,000 shares of $10 par value common stock at $12 per share.		

Assets = Liabilities + Equity
+360,000 +300,000
+60,000

$10 par value × 30,000 shares

[$12 issue price − $10 par value] × 30,000 shares

The Paid-In Capital in Excess of Par Value account is added to the par value of the stock in the equity section of the balance sheet as shown in Exhibit 11.5.

Point: The *Paid-In Capital* terminology is interchangeable with *Contributed Capital.*

Stockholders' Equity	
Common Stock—$10 par value; 50,000 shares authorized;	
30,000 shares issued and outstanding	$300,000
Paid-in capital in excess of par value, common stock	60,000
Retained earnings	65,000
Total stockholders' equity	$425,000

EXHIBIT 11.5

Stockholders' Equity for Stock Issued at a Premium

Issuing Par Value Stock at a Discount

A discount on stock occurs when a corporation sells its stock for less than par (or stated) value. Most states prohibit the issuance of stock at a discount. In states that allow stock to be issued at a discount, its buyers usually become contingently liable to creditors for the discount. If stock is issued at a discount, the amount by which issue price is less than par is debited to a *Discount on Common Stock* account, a contra to the common stock account, and its balance is subtracted from the par value of stock in the equity section of the balance sheet. This discount is not an expense and does not appear on the income statement.

Point: Retained earnings can be negative, reflecting accumulated losses. Amazon.com had an accumulated deficit of $730 million at the start of 2009.

Issuing No-Par Value Stock

When no-par stock is issued and is not assigned a stated value, the amount the corporation receives becomes legal capital and is recorded as Common Stock. This means that the entire proceeds are credited to a no-par stock account. To illustrate, a corporation records its October 20 issuance of 1,000 shares of no-par stock for $40 cash per share as follows.

Oct. 20	Cash	40,000	
	Common Stock, No-Par Value		40,000
	Issued 1,000 shares of no-par value common stock at $40 per share.		

Assets = Liabilities + Equity
+40,000 +40,000

$40 issue price × 1,000 no-par shares

Frequency of Stock Types

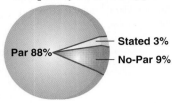

Par 88%
Stated 3%
No-Par 9%

Issuing Stated Value Stock

When no-par stock is issued and assigned a stated value, its stated value becomes legal capital and is credited to a stated value stock account. Assuming that stated value stock is issued at an amount in excess of stated value (the usual case), the excess is credited to Paid-In Capital in Excess of Stated Value, Common Stock, which is reported in the stockholders' equity section. To illustrate, a corporation that issues 1,000 shares of no-par common stock having a stated value of $40 per share in return for $50 cash per share records this as follows.

Assets = Liabilities + Equity
+50,000   +40,000
                      +10,000

$40 stated value × 1,000 shares

[$50 issue price − $40 stated value] × 1,000 shares

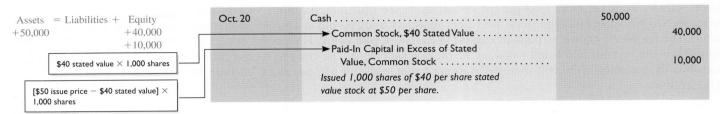

Oct. 20	Cash	50,000	
	▶ Common Stock, $40 Stated Value		40,000
	▶ Paid-In Capital in Excess of Stated Value, Common Stock		10,000
	Issued 1,000 shares of $40 per share stated value stock at $50 per share.		

Issuing Stock for Noncash Assets

Point: Stock issued for noncash assets should be recorded at the market value of either the stock or the noncash asset, whichever is more clearly determinable.

A corporation can receive assets other than cash in exchange for its stock. (It can also assume liabilities on the assets received such as a mortgage on property received.) The corporation records the assets received at their market values as of the date of the transaction. The stock given in exchange is recorded at its par (or stated) value with any excess recorded in the Paid-In Capital in Excess of Par (or Stated) Value account. (If no-par stock is issued, the stock is recorded at the assets' market value.) To illustrate, the entry to record receipt of land valued at $105,000 in return for issuance of 4,000 shares of $20 par value common stock on June 10 is

Assets = Liabilities + Equity
+105,000   +80,000
                     +25,000

$20 par value × 4,000 shares

$105,000 asset value − $80,000 stock value

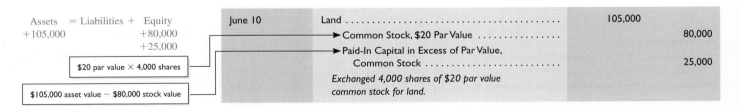

June 10	Land	105,000	
	▶ Common Stock, $20 Par Value		80,000
	▶ Paid-In Capital in Excess of Par Value, Common Stock		25,000
	Exchanged 4,000 shares of $20 par value common stock for land.		

Point: Any type of stock can be issued for noncash assets.

A corporation sometimes gives shares of its stock to promoters in exchange for their services in organizing the corporation, which the corporation records as **Organization Expenses.** The entry to record receipt of services valued at $12,000 in organizing the corporation in return for 600 shares of $15 par value common stock on June 5 is

Assets = Liabilities + Equity
                     −12,000
                     +9,000
                     +3,000

$15 par value × 600 shares

$12,000 services value − $9,000 stock value

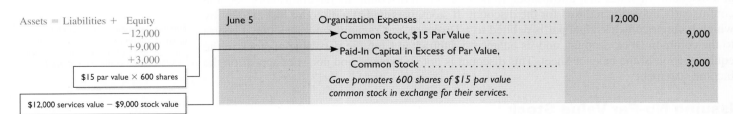

June 5	Organization Expenses	12,000	
	▶ Common Stock, $15 Par Value		9,000
	▶ Paid-In Capital in Excess of Par Value, Common Stock		3,000
	Gave promoters 600 shares of $15 par value common stock in exchange for their services.		

Quick Check
Answers — p. 483

4. A company issues 7,000 shares of its $10 par value common stock in exchange for equipment valued at $105,000. The entry to record this transaction includes a credit to (a) Paid-In Capital in Excess of Par Value, Common Stock, for $35,000. (b) Retained Earnings for $35,000. (c) Common Stock, $10 Par Value, for $105,000.
5. What is a premium on stock issuance?
6. Who is intended to be protected by minimum legal capital?

DIVIDENDS

This section describes both cash and stock dividend transactions.

Cash Dividends

The decision to pay cash dividends rests with the board of directors and involves more than evaluating the amounts of retained earnings and cash. The directors, for instance, may decide to keep the cash to invest in the corporation's growth, to meet emergencies, to take advantage of unexpected opportunities, or to pay off debt. Alternatively, many corporations pay cash dividends to their stockholders at regular dates. These cash flows provide a return to investors and almost always affect the stock's market value.

> **P2** Record transactions involving cash dividends, stock dividends, and stock splits.

Accounting for Cash Dividends Dividend payment involves three important dates: declaration, record, and payment. **Date of declaration** is the date the directors vote to declare and pay a dividend. This creates a legal liability of the corporation to its stockholders. **Date of record** is the future date specified by the directors for identifying those stockholders listed in the corporation's records to receive dividends. The date of record usually follows the date of declaration by at least two weeks. Persons who own stock on the date of record receive dividends. **Date of payment** is the date when the corporation makes payment; it follows the date of record by enough time to allow the corporation to arrange checks, money transfers, or other means to pay dividends.

Percent of Corporations Paying Dividends

Cash Dividend to Common — 75%

Cash Dividend to Preferred — 22%

0% 20% 40% 60% 80% 100%

To illustrate, the entry to record a January 9 declaration of a $1 per share cash dividend by the directors of Z-Tech, Inc., with 5,000 outstanding shares is

Date of Declaration

Jan. 9	Retained Earnings	5,000	
	Common Dividend Payable		5,000
	Declared $1 per common share cash dividend.[1]		

Assets = Liabilities + Equity
+5,000   −5,000

$1 per share declared dividend × 5,000 shares

Common Dividend Payable is a current liability. The date of record for the Z-Tech dividend is January 22. *No formal journal entry is needed on the date of record.* The February 1 date of payment requires an entry to record both the settlement of the liability and the reduction of the cash balance, as follows:

Date of Payment

Feb. 1	Common Dividend Payable	5,000	
	Cash		5,000
	Paid $1 per common share cash dividend.		

Assets = Liabilities + Equity
−5,000   −5,000

Deficits and Cash Dividends A corporation with a debit (abnormal) balance for retained earnings is said to have a **retained earnings deficit**, which arises when a company incurs cumulative losses and/or pays more dividends than total earnings from current and prior years. A deficit is reported as a deduction on the balance sheet, as shown in Exhibit 11.6. Most states prohibit a corporation with a deficit from paying a cash dividend to its stockholders. This legal restriction is designed to protect creditors by preventing distribution of assets to stockholders when the company may be in financial difficulty.

> **Point:** It is often said a dividend is a distribution of retained earnings, but it is more precise to describe a dividend as a distribution of assets to satisfy stockholder claims.

> **Point:** The Retained Earnings Deficit account is also called *Accumulated Deficit.*

---

[1] An alternative entry is to debit Dividends instead of Retained Earnings. The balance in Dividends is then closed to Retained Earnings at the end of the reporting period. The effect is the same: Retained Earnings is decreased and a Dividend Payable is increased. For simplicity, all assignments in this chapter use the Retained Earnings account to record dividend declarations.

Prior Period Adjustments   **Prior period adjustments** are corrections of material errors in prior period financial statements. These errors include arithmetic mistakes, unacceptable accounting, and missed facts. Prior period adjustments are reported in the *statement of retained earnings* (or the statement of stockholders' equity), net of any income tax effects. Prior period adjustments result in changing the beginning balance of retained earnings for events occurring prior to the earliest period reported in the current set of financial statements. To illustrate, assume that ComUS makes an error in a 2009 journal entry for the purchase of land by incorrectly debiting an expense account. When this is discovered in 2011, the statement of retained earnings includes a prior period adjustment, as shown in Exhibit 11.15. This exhibit also shows the usual format of the statement of retained earnings.

Point: If a year 2009 error is discovered in 2010, the company records the adjustment in 2010. But if the financial statements include 2009 and 2010 figures, the statements report the correct amounts for 2009, and a note describes the correction.

EXHIBIT 11.15

Statement of Retained Earnings with a Prior Period Adjustment

ComUS Statement of Retained Earnings For Year Ended December 31, 2011	
Retained earnings, Dec. 31, 2010, as previously reported	$4,745,000
Prior period adjustment	
Cost of land incorrectly expensed (net of $63,000 income taxes)	**147,000**
Retained earnings, Dec. 31, 2010, as adjusted	4,892,000
Plus net income	1,224,300
Less cash dividends declared	(301,800)
Retained earnings, Dec. 31, 2011	$5,814,500

Many items reported in financial statements are based on estimates. Future events are certain to reveal that some of these estimates were inaccurate even when based on the best data available at the time. These inaccuracies are *not* considered errors and are *not* reported as prior period adjustments. Instead, they are identified as **changes in accounting estimates** and are accounted for in current and future periods. To illustrate, we know that depreciation is based on estimated useful lives and salvage values. As time passes and new information becomes available, managers may need to change these estimates and the resulting depreciation expense for current and future periods.

Point: Accounting for changes in estimates is sometimes criticized as two wrongs to make a right. Consider a change in an asset's life. Depreciation neither before nor after the change is the amount computed if the revised estimate were originally selected. Regulators chose this approach to avoid restating prior period numbers.

Closing Process   The closing process was explained earlier in the book as: (1) Close credit balances in revenue accounts to Income Summary, (2) Close debit balances in expense accounts to Income Summary, and (3) Close Income Summary to Retained Earnings. If dividends are recorded in a Dividends account, and not as an immediate reduction to Retained Earnings (as shown in this chapter), a fourth step is necessary to close the Dividends account to Retained Earnings.

Statement of Stockholders' Equity

Instead of a separate statement of retained earnings, companies commonly report a statement of stockholders' equity that includes changes in retained earnings. A **statement of stockholders' equity** lists the beginning and ending balances of key equity accounts and describes the changes that occur during the period. The companies in Appendix A report such a statement. The usual format is to provide a column for each component of equity and use the rows to describe events occurring in the period. Exhibit 11.16 shows a condensed statement for **Apple**.

EXHIBIT 11.16

Statement of Stockholders' Equity

Apple

APPLE Statement of Stockholders' Equity					
($ millions, shares in thousands)	Common Stock Shares	Common Stock Amount	Retained Earnings	Other	Total Equity
Balance, Sept. 27, 2008	888,326	$7,177	$15,129	$(9)	$22,297
Net income	—	—	8,235	—	8,235
Issuance of Common Stock	11,480	404	(11)	—	393
Other	—	629	—	86	715
Cash Dividends ($0.00 per share)	—	—	—	—	—
Balance, Sept. 26, 2009	899,806	$8,210	$23,353	$77	$31,640

Reporting Stock Options

The majority of corporations whose shares are publicly traded issue **stock options,** which are rights to purchase common stock at a fixed price over a specified period. As the stock's price rises, the option's value increases. **Starbucks** and **Home Depot** offer stock options to both full- and part-time employees. Stock options are said to motivate managers and employees to (1) focus on company performance, (2) take a long-run perspective, and (3) remain with the company. A stock option is like having an investment with no risk ("a carrot with no stick").

To illustrate, Quantum grants each of its employees the option to purchase 100 shares of its $1 par value common stock at its current market price of $50 per share anytime within the next 10 years. If the stock price rises to $70 per share, an employee can exercise the option at a gain of $20 per share (acquire a $70 stock at the $50 option price). With 100 shares, a single employee would have a total gain of $2,000, computed as $20 × 100 shares. Companies report the cost of stock options in the income statement. Measurement of this cost is explained in advanced courses.

Fraud

Pump 'n Dump. Fraudulent information can be used by the owners of a company's stock to pump it up and claim it is undervalued, which causes naïve investors to seek to acquire the stock and drive up its price. After that, those behind the release of fraudulent information dump the stock at an inflated price. When later information reveals that the stock is overvalued, its price declines and investors still holding the stock lose value. This scheme is called *pump 'n dump.* Jonathan Lebed, at 15 years old, is one of the most infamous cases of pump 'n dump, in which he allegedly made about $1 million.

GLOBAL VIEW

This section discusses similarities and differences between U.S. GAAP and IFRS in accounting and reporting for equity.

Accounting for Common Stock   The accounting for and reporting of common stock under U.S. GAAP and IFRS are similar. Specifically, procedures for issuing common stock at par, at a premium, at a discount, and for noncash assets are similar across the two systems. However, we must be aware of legal and cultural differences across the world that can impact the rights and responsibilities of common share-holders. **Nokia**'s terminology is a bit different as it uses the phrase "share capital" in reference to what U.S. GAAP would title "common shares" (see Appendix A). It also discloses that it has issued (and out-standing) shares of 3,744,956,052.

Accounting for Dividends   Accounting for and reporting of dividends under U.S. GAAP and IFRS are consistent. This applies to cash dividends, stock dividends, and stock splits. For **Nokia**, a "divi-dend of EUR 0.40 per share is to be paid out on the shares of the Company." Nokia, like many other companies, follows a dividend policy set by management and its board.

Accounting for Preferred Stock   Accounting and reporting for preferred stock are similar for U.S. GAAP and IFRS, but there are some important differences. First, preferred stock that is redeemable at the option of the preferred stockholders is reported *between* liabilities and equity in U.S. GAAP balance sheets. However, that same stock is reported as a liability in IFRS balance sheets. Second, the issue price of convertible preferred stock (and bonds) is recorded entirely under preferred stock (or bonds) *and none is assigned to the conversion feature* under U.S. GAAP. However, IFRS requires that a portion of the issue price be allocated to the conversion feature when it exists. Nokia has no preferred stock.

Accounting for Treasury Stock   Both U.S. GAAP and IFRS apply the principle that companies do not record gains or losses on transactions involving their own stock. This applies to purchases, reissu-ances, and retirements of treasury stock. Consequently, the accounting for treasury stock explained in this chapter is consistent with that under IFRS. However, IFRS in this area is less detailed than that of U.S. GAAP. **Nokia**'s policy regarding treasury stock follows: "[It] recognizes acquired treasury shares as a deduction from equity at their acquisition cost."

Earnings per Share, Price-Earnings Ratio, Dividend Yield, and
Book Value per Share

□■□   **Decision Analysis**

Earnings per Share

The income statement reports **earnings per share,** also called *EPS* or *net income per share,* which is the amount of income earned per each share of a company's outstanding common stock. The **basic earnings per share** formula is shown in Exhibit 11.17. When a company has no preferred stock, then preferred dividends are zero. The weighted-average common shares outstanding is measured over the income reporting period; its computation is explained in advanced courses.

A1 Compute earnings per share and describe its use.

$$\text{Basic earnings per share} = \frac{\text{Net income} - \text{Preferred dividends}}{\text{Weighted-average common shares outstanding}}$$

EXHIBIT 11.17

Basic Earnings per Share

To illustrate, assume that Quantum Co. earns $40,000 net income in 2011 and declares dividends of $7,500 on its noncumulative preferred stock. (If preferred stock is *non*cumulative, the income available [numerator] is the current period net income less any preferred dividends *declared* in that same period. If preferred stock is cumulative, the income available [numerator] is the current period net income less the preferred dividends whether declared or not.) Quantum has 5,000 weighted-average common shares outstanding during 2011. Its basic EPS[3] is

$$\text{Basic earnings per share} = \frac{\$40,000 - \$7,500}{5,000 \text{ shares}} = \$6.50$$

Price-Earnings Ratio

A stock's market value is determined by its *expected* future cash flows. A comparison of a company's EPS and its market value per share reveals information about market expectations. This comparison is traditionally made using a **price-earnings (or PE) ratio,** expressed also as *price earnings, price to earnings,* or *PE.* Some analysts interpret this ratio as what price the market is willing to pay for a company's current earnings stream. Price-earnings ratios can differ across companies that have similar earnings because of either higher or lower expectations of future earnings. The price-earnings ratio is defined in Exhibit 11.18.

A2 Compute price-earnings ratio and describe its use in analysis.

Point: The average PE ratio of stocks in the 1950–2010 period is about 14.

$$\text{Price-earnings ratio} = \frac{\text{Market value (price) per share}}{\text{Earnings per share}}$$

EXHIBIT 11.18

Price-Earnings Ratio

This ratio is often computed using EPS from the most recent period (for Amazon, its PE is 52; for Altria, its PE is 13). However, many users compute this ratio using *expected* EPS for the next period.

Some analysts view stocks with high PE ratios (higher than 20 to 25) as more likely to be overpriced and stocks with low PE ratios (less than 5 to 8) as more likely to be underpriced. These investors prefer to sell or avoid buying stocks with high PE ratios and to buy or hold stocks with low PE ratios. However, investment decision making is rarely so simple as to rely on a single ratio. For instance, a stock with a high PE ratio can prove to be a good investment if its earnings continue to increase beyond current expectations. Similarly, a stock with a low PE ratio can prove to be a poor investment if its earnings decline below expectations.

Point: Average PE ratios for U.S. stocks increased over the past two decades. Some analysts interpret this as a signal the market is overpriced. But higher ratios can at least partly reflect accounting changes that have reduced reported earnings.

---

[3] A corporation can be classified as having either a simple or complex capital structure. The term **simple capital structure** refers to a company with only common stock and nonconvertible preferred stock outstanding. The term **complex capital structure** refers to companies with dilutive securities. **Dilutive securities** include options, rights to purchase common stock, and any bonds or preferred stock that are convertible into common stock. A company with a complex capital structure must often report two EPS figures: basic and diluted. **Diluted earnings per share** is computed by adding all dilutive securities to the denominator of the basic EPS computation. It reflects the decrease in basic EPS *assuming* that all dilutive securities are converted into common shares.

Decision Maker Answer — p. 483

Money Manager You plan to invest in one of two companies identified as having identical future prospects. One has a PE of 19 and the other a PE of 25. Which do you invest in? Does it matter if your *estimate* of PE for these two companies is 29 as opposed to 22? ∎

Dividend Yield

A3 Compute dividend yield and explain its use in analysis.

Investors buy shares of a company's stock in anticipation of receiving a return from either or both cash dividends and stock price increases. Stocks that pay large dividends on a regular basis, called *income stocks,* are attractive to investors who want recurring cash flows from their investments. In contrast, some stocks pay little or no dividends but are still attractive to investors because of their expected stock price increases. The stocks of companies that distribute little or no cash but use their cash to finance expansion are called *growth stocks*. One way to help identify whether a stock is an income stock or a growth stock is to analyze its dividend yield. **Dividend yield,** defined in Exhibit 11.19, shows the annual amount of cash dividends distributed to common shares relative to their market value.

EXHIBIT 11.19

Dividend Yield

$$\text{Dividend yield} = \frac{\text{Annual cash dividends per share}}{\text{Market value per share}}$$

Dividend yield can be computed for current and prior periods using actual dividends and stock prices and for future periods using expected values. Exhibit 11.20 shows recent dividend and stock price data for **Amazon** and **Altria Group** to compute dividend yield.

EXHIBIT 11.20

Dividend and Stock Price Information

Company	Cash Dividends per Share	Market Value per Share	Dividend Yield
Amazon	$0.00	$80	0.0%
Altria Group.	1.68	20	8.4

Point: The *payout ratio* equals cash dividends declared on common stock divided by net income. A low payout ratio suggests that a company is retaining earnings for future growth.

Dividend yield is zero for Amazon, implying it is a growth stock. An investor in Amazon would look for increases in stock prices (and eventual cash from the sale of stock). Altria has a dividend yield of 8.4%, implying it is an income stock for which dividends are important in assessing its value.

Book Value per Share

A4 Compute book value and explain its use in analysis.

Case 1: Common Stock (Only) Outstanding. **Book value per common share,** defined in Exhibit 11.21, reflects the amount of equity applicable to *common* shares on a per share basis. To illustrate, we use Dillon Snowboards' data from Exhibit 11.4. Dillon has 30,000 outstanding common shares, and the stockholders' equity applicable to common shares is $365,000. Dillon's book value per common share is $12.17, computed as $365,000 divided by 30,000 shares.

EXHIBIT 11.21

Book Value per Common Share

$$\text{Book value per common share} = \frac{\text{Stockholders' equity applicable to common shares}}{\text{Number of common shares outstanding}}$$

Point: Book value per share is also referred to as *stockholders' claim to assets on a per share basis.*

Case 2: Common and Preferred Stock Outstanding. To compute book value when both common and preferred shares are outstanding, we allocate total equity between the two types of shares. The **book value per preferred share** is computed first; its computation is shown in Exhibit 11.22.

EXHIBIT 11.22

Book Value per Preferred Share

$$\text{Book value per preferred share} = \frac{\text{Stockholders' equity applicable to preferred shares}}{\text{Number of preferred shares outstanding}}$$

The equity applicable to preferred shares equals the preferred share's call price (or par value if the preferred is not callable) plus any cumulative dividends in arrears. The remaining equity is the portion applicable to common shares. To illustrate, consider LTD's equity in Exhibit 11.23. Its preferred stock is callable at $108 per share, and two years of cumulative preferred dividends are in arrears.

Stockholders' Equity

Preferred stock—$100 par value, 7% cumulative, 2,000 shares authorized, 1,000 shares issued and outstanding	$100,000
Common stock—$25 par value, 12,000 shares authorized, 10,000 shares issued and outstanding	250,000
Paid-in capital in excess of par value, common stock	15,000
Retained earnings	82,000
Total stockholders' equity	$447,000

EXHIBIT 11.23

Stockholders' Equity with Preferred and Common Stock

The book value computations are in Exhibit 11.24. Equity is first allocated to preferred shares before the book value of common shares is computed.

Total stockholders' equity		$447,000
Less equity applicable to preferred shares		
Call price (1,000 shares × $108)	$108,000	
Dividends in arrears ($100,000 × 7% × 2 years)	14,000	(122,000)
Equity applicable to common shares		$325,000
Book value per preferred share ($122,000/1,000 shares)		$122.00
Book value per common share ($325,000/10,000 shares)		$ 32.50

EXHIBIT 11.24

Computing Book Value per Preferred and Common Share

Book value per share reflects the value per share if a company is liquidated at balance sheet amounts. Book value is also the starting point in many stock valuation models, merger negotiations, price setting for public utilities, and loan contracts. The main limitation in using book value is the potential difference between recorded value and market value for assets and liabilities. Investors often adjust their analysis for estimates of these differences.

 Decision Maker Answer — p. 483

Investor You are considering investing in **BMX**, whose book value per common share is $4 and price per common share on the stock exchange is $7. From this information, are BMX's net assets priced higher or lower than its recorded values? ■

DEMONSTRATION PROBLEM 1

Barton Corporation began operations on January 1, 2010. The following transactions relating to stockholders' equity occurred in the first two years of the company's operations.

2010

Jan. 1 Authorized the issuance of 2 million shares of $5 par value common stock and 100,000 shares of $100 par value, 10% cumulative, preferred stock.
Jan. 2 Issued 200,000 shares of common stock for $12 cash per share.
Jan. 3 Issued 100,000 shares of common stock in exchange for a building valued at $820,000 and merchandise inventory valued at $380,000.
Jan. 4 Paid $10,000 cash to the company's founders for organization activities.
Jan. 5 Issued 12,000 shares of preferred stock for $110 cash per share.

2011

June 4 Issued 100,000 shares of common stock for $15 cash per share.

Required

1. Prepare journal entries to record these transactions.

2. Prepare the stockholders' equity section of the balance sheet as of December 31, 2010, and December 31, 2011, based on these transactions.

3. Prepare a table showing dividend allocations and dividends per share for 2010 and 2011 assuming Barton declares the following cash dividends: 2010, $50,000, and 2011, $300,000.

4. Prepare the January 2, 2010, journal entry for Barton's issuance of 200,000 shares of common stock for $12 cash per share assuming

    a. Common stock is no-par stock without a stated value.

    b. Common stock is no-par stock with a stated value of $10 per share.

PLANNING THE SOLUTION

- Record journal entries for the transactions for 2010 and 2011.
- Determine the balances for the 2010 and 2011 equity accounts for the balance sheet.
- Prepare the contributed capital portion of the 2010 and 2011 balance sheets.
- Prepare a table similar to Exhibit 11.11 showing dividend allocations for 2010 and 2011.
- Record the issuance of common stock under both specifications of no-par stock.

SOLUTION TO DEMONSTRATION PROBLEM 1

1. Journal entries.

2010			
Jan. 2	Cash	2,400,000	
	Common Stock, $5 Par Value		1,000,000
	Paid-In Capital in Excess of Par Value,		
	Common Stock		1,400,000
	Issued 200,000 shares of common stock.		
Jan. 3	Building	820,000	
	Merchandise Inventory	380,000	
	Common Stock, $5 Par Value		500,000
	Paid-In Capital in Excess of Par Value,		
	Common Stock		700,000
	Issued 100,000 shares of common stock.		
Jan. 4	Organization Expenses	10,000	
	Cash		10,000
	Paid founders for organization costs.		
Jan. 5	Cash	1,320,000	
	Preferred Stock, $100 Par Value		1,200,000
	Paid-In Capital in Excess of Par Value,		
	Preferred Stock		120,000
	Issued 12,000 shares of preferred stock.		
2011			
June 4	Cash	1,500,000	
	Common Stock, $5 Par Value		500,000
	Paid-In Capital in Excess of Par Value,		
	Common Stock		1,000,000
	Issued 100,000 shares of common stock.		

2. Balance sheet presentations (at December 31 year-end).

	2011	2010
Stockholders' Equity		
Preferred stock—$100 par value, 10% cumulative, 100,000 shares authorized, 12,000 shares issued and outstanding	$1,200,000	$1,200,000
Paid-in capital in excess of par value, preferred stock	120,000	120,000
Total paid-in capital by preferred stockholders	1,320,000	1,320,000
Common stock—$5 par value, 2,000,000 shares authorized, 300,000 shares issued and outstanding in 2010, and 400,000 shares issued and outstanding in 2011	2,000,000	1,500,000
Paid-in capital in excess of par value, common stock	3,100,000	2,100,000
Total paid-in capital by common stockholders	5,100,000	3,600,000
Total paid-in capital	$6,420,000	$4,920,000

3. Dividend allocation table.

	Common	Preferred
2010 ($50,000)		
Preferred—current year (12,000 shares × $10 = $120,000)	$ 0	$ 50,000
Common—remainder (300,000 shares outstanding)	0	0
Total for the year	$ 0	$ 50,000
2011 ($300,000)		
Preferred—dividend in arrears from 2010 ($120,000 − $50,000)	$ 0	$ 70,000
Preferred—current year	0	120,000
Common—remainder (400,000 shares outstanding)	110,000	0
Total for the year	$110,000	$190,000
Dividends per share		
2010	$ 0.00	$ 4.17
2011	$ 0.28	$ 15.83

4. Journal entries.

a. For 2010 (no-par stock without a stated value):

Jan. 2	Cash	2,400,000	
	Common Stock, No-Par Value		2,400,000
	Issued 200,000 shares of no-par common stock at $12 per share.		

b. For 2010 (no-par stock with a stated value):

Jan. 2	Cash	2,400,000	
	Common Stock, $10 Stated Value		2,000,000
	Paid-In Capital in Excess of Stated Value, Common Stock		400,000
	Issued 200,000 shares of $10 stated value common stock at $12 per share.		

DEMONSTRATION PROBLEM 2

Precision Company began year 2011 with the following balances in its stockholders' equity accounts.

Common stock—$10 par, 500,000 shares authorized, 200,000 shares issued and outstanding	$2,000,000
Paid-in capital in excess of par, common stock	1,000,000
Retained earnings	5,000,000
Total	$8,000,000

All outstanding common stock was issued for $15 per share when the company was created. Prepare journal entries to account for the following transactions during year 2011.

Jan. 10 The board declared a $0.10 cash dividend per share to shareholders of record Jan. 28.
Feb. 15 Paid the cash dividend declared on January 10.
Mar. 31 Declared a 20% stock dividend. The market value of the stock is $18 per share.
May 1 Distributed the stock dividend declared on March 31.
July 1 Purchased 30,000 shares of treasury stock at $20 per share.
Sept. 1 Sold 20,000 treasury shares at $26 cash per share.
Dec. 1 Sold the remaining 10,000 shares of treasury stock at $7 cash per share.

PLANNING THE SOLUTION

- Calculate the total cash dividend to record by multiplying the cash dividend declared by the number of shares as of the date of record.
- Decide whether the stock dividend is a small or large dividend. Then analyze each event to determine the accounts affected and the appropriate amounts to be recorded.

SOLUTION TO DEMONSTRATION PROBLEM 2

Jan. 10	Retained Earnings	20,000	
	Common Dividend Payable		20,000
	Declared a $0.10 per share cash dividend.		
Feb. 15	Common Dividend Payable	20,000	
	Cash		20,000
	Paid $0.10 per share cash dividend.		
Mar. 31	Retained Earnings	720,000	
	Common Stock Dividend Distributable		400,000
	Paid-In Capital in Excess of		
	Par Value, Common Stock		320,000
	Declared a small stock dividend of 20% or		
	40,000 shares; market value is $18 per share.		
May 1	Common Stock Dividend Distributable	400,000	
	Common Stock		400,000
	Distributed 40,000 shares of common stock.		
July 1	Treasury Stock, Common	600,000	
	Cash		600,000
	Purchased 30,000 common shares at $20 per share.		
Sept. 1	Cash	520,000	
	Treasury Stock, Common		400,000
	Paid-In Capital, Treasury Stock		120,000
	Sold 20,000 treasury shares at $26 per share.		
Dec. 1	Cash	70,000	
	Paid-In Capital, Treasury Stock	120,000	
	Retained Earnings	10,000	
	Treasury Stock, Common		200,000
	Sold 10,000 treasury shares at $7 per share.		

Summary

C1 **Identify characteristics of corporations and their organization.** Corporations are legal entities whose stockholders are not liable for its debts. Stock is easily transferred, and the life of a corporation does not end with the incapacity of a stockholder. A corporation acts through its agents, who are its officers and managers. Corporations are regulated and subject to income taxes. Authorized stock is the stock that a corporation's charter authorizes it to sell. Issued stock is the portion of authorized shares sold. Par value stock is a value per share assigned by the charter. No-par value stock is stock *not* assigned a value per share by the charter. Stated value stock is no-par stock to which the directors assign a value per share.

C2 **Explain characteristics of, and distribute dividends between, common and preferred stock.** Preferred stock has a priority (or senior status) relative to common stock in one or more areas, usually (1) dividends and (2) assets in case of liquidation. Preferred stock usually does not carry voting rights and can be convertible or callable. Convertibility permits the holder to convert preferred to common. Callability permits the issuer to buy back preferred stock under specified conditions. Preferred stockholders usually hold the right to dividend distributions before common stockholders. When preferred stock is cumulative and in arrears, the amount in arrears must be distributed to preferred before any dividends are distributed to common.

C3 **Explain the items reported in retained earnings.** Stockholders' equity is made up of (1) paid-in capital and (2) retained earnings. Paid-in capital consists of funds raised by stock issuances. Retained earnings consists of cumulative net income (losses) not distributed. Many companies face statutory and contractual restrictions on retained earnings. Corporations can voluntarily appropriate retained earnings to inform others about their disposition. Prior period adjustments are corrections of errors in prior financial statements.

A1 **Compute earnings per share and describe its use.** A company with a simple capital structure computes basic EPS by dividing net income less any preferred dividends by the weighted-average number of outstanding common shares. A company with a complex capital structure must usually report both basic and diluted EPS.

A2 **Compute price-earnings ratio and describe its use in analysis.** A common stock's price-earnings (PE) ratio is computed by dividing the stock's market value (price) per share by its EPS. A stock's PE is based on expectations that can prove to be better or worse than eventual performance.

A3 **Compute dividend yield and explain its use in analysis.** Dividend yield is the ratio of a stock's annual cash dividends per share to its market value (price) per share. Dividend yield can be compared with the yield of other companies to determine whether the stock is expected to be an income or growth stock.

A4 **Compute book value and explain its use in analysis.** Book value per common share is equity applicable to common shares divided by the number of outstanding common shares. Book value per preferred share is equity applicable to preferred shares divided by the number of outstanding preferred shares.

P1 **Record the issuance of corporate stock.** When stock is issued, its par or stated value is credited to the stock account and any excess is credited to a separate contributed capital account. If a stock has neither par nor stated value, the entire proceeds are credited to the stock account. Stockholders must contribute assets equal to minimum legal capital or be potentially liable for the deficiency.

P2 **Record transactions involving cash dividends, stock dividends, and stock splits.** Cash dividends involve three events. On the date of declaration, the directors bind the company to pay the dividend. A dividend declaration reduces retained earnings and creates a current liability. On the date of record, recipients of the dividend are identified. On the date of payment, cash is paid to stockholders and the current liability is removed. Neither a stock dividend nor a stock split alters the value of the company. However, the value of each share is less due to the distribution of additional shares. The distribution of additional shares is according to individual stockholders' ownership percent. Small stock dividends (≤25%) are recorded by capitalizing retained earnings equal to the market value of distributed shares. Large stock dividends (>25%) are recorded by capitalizing retained earnings equal to the par or stated value of distributed shares. Stock splits do not necessitate journal entries but do necessitate changes in the description of stock.

P3 **Record purchases and sales of treasury stock and the retirement of stock.** When a corporation purchases its own previously issued stock, it debits the cost of these shares to Treasury Stock. Treasury stock is subtracted from equity in the balance sheet. If treasury stock is reissued, any proceeds in excess of cost are credited to Paid-In Capital, Treasury Stock. If the proceeds are less than cost, they are debited to Paid-In Capital, Treasury Stock to the extent a credit balance exists. Any remaining amount is debited to Retained Earnings. When stock is retired, all accounts related to the stock are removed.

Guidance Answers to Decision Maker and Decision Ethics

Entrepreneur The 50% stock dividend provides you no direct income. A stock dividend often reveals management's optimistic expectations about the future and can improve a stock's marketability by making it affordable to more investors. Accordingly, a stock dividend usually reveals "good news" and because of this, it likely increases (slightly) the market value for your stock. The same conclusions apply to the 3-for-2 stock split.

Concert Organizer You have two basic options: (1) different classes of common stock or (2) common and preferred stock. Your objective is to issue to yourself stock that has all or a majority of the voting power. The other class of stock would carry limited or no voting rights. In this way, you maintain control and are able to raise the necessary funds.

Money Manager Since one company requires a payment of $19 for each $1 of earnings, and the other requires $25, you would prefer the stock with the PE of 19; it is a better deal given identical prospects. You should make sure these companies' earnings computations are roughly the same, for example, no extraordinary items, unusual events, and so forth. Also, your PE estimates for these companies do matter. If you are willing to pay $29 for each $1 of earnings for these companies, you obviously expect both to exceed current market expectations.

Investor Book value reflects recorded values. BMX's book value is $4 per common share. Stock price reflects the market's expectation of net asset value (both tangible and intangible items). BMX's market value is $7 per common share. Comparing these figures suggests BMX's market value of net assets is higher than its recorded values (by an amount of $7 versus $4 per share).

Guidance Answers to Quick Checks

1. (b)

2. A corporation pays taxes on its income, and its stockholders normally pay personal income taxes (at the 15% rate or lower) on any cash dividends received from the corporation.

3. A proxy is a legal document used to transfer a stockholder's right to vote to another person.

4. (a)

5. A stock premium is an amount in excess of par (or stated) value paid by purchasers of newly issued stock.

6. Minimum legal capital intends to protect creditors of a corporation by obligating stockholders to some minimum level of equity financing and by constraining a corporation from excessive payments to stockholders.

7. Common Dividend Payable is a current liability account.

8. The date of declaration, date of record, and date of payment.

9. A dividend is a legal liability at the date of declaration, on which date it is recorded as a liability.

10. A stock dividend does not transfer assets to stockholders, but it does require an amount of retained earnings to be transferred to a contributed capital account(s).

11. A small stock dividend is 25% or less of the previous outstanding shares. A large stock dividend is more than 25%.

12. Retained earnings equal to the distributable shares' market value should be capitalized for a small stock dividend.

13. Typically, preferred stock has a preference in receipt of dividends and in distribution of assets.

14. (*a*)

15. (*b*)

Total cash dividend	$288,000
To preferred shareholders	135,000*
Remainder to common shareholders	$153,000

* 9,000 × $50 × 10% × 3 years = $135,000.

16. (*b*)

17. No. The shares are an investment for Southern Co. and are issued and outstanding shares for Northern Corp.

18. Treasury stock does not affect the number of authorized or issued shares, but it reduces the outstanding shares.

19. (*a*)

Key Terms

Appropriated retained earnings (p. 474)
Authorized stock (p. 461)
Basic earnings per share (p. 477)
Book value per common share (p. 478)
Book value per preferred share (p. 478)
Call price (p. 471)
Callable preferred stock (p. 471)
Capital stock (p. 461)
Changes in accounting estimates (p. 475)
Common stock (p. 460)
Complex capital structure (p. 477)
Convertible preferred stock (p. 470)
Corporation (p. 458)
Cumulative preferred stock (p. 469)
Date of declaration (p. 465)
Date of payment (p. 465)
Date of record (p. 465)
Diluted earnings per share (p. 477)
Dilutive securities (p. 477)

Discount on stock (p. 463)
Dividend in arrears (p. 469)
Dividend yield (p. 478)
Earnings per share (EPS) (p. 477)
Financial leverage (p. 471)
Large stock dividend (p. 466)
Liquidating cash dividend (p. 466)
Market value per share (p. 461)
Minimum legal capital (p. 461)
Noncumulative preferred stock (p. 469)
Nonparticipating preferred stock (p. 470)
No-par value stock (p. 461)
Organization expenses (p. 459)
Paid-in capital (p. 462)
Paid-in capital in excess of par value (p. 463)
Participating preferred stock (p. 470)
Par value (p. 461)
Par value stock (p. 461)

Preemptive right (p. 460)
Preferred stock (p. 468)
Premium on stock (p. 463)
Price-earnings (PE) ratio (p. 477)
Prior period adjustments (p. 475)
Proxy (p. 459)
Restricted retained earnings (p. 474)
Retained earnings (p. 462)
Retained earnings deficit (p. 465)
Reverse stock split (p. 468)
Simple capital structure (p. 477)
Small stock dividend (p. 466)
Stated value stock (p. 462)
Statement of stockholders' equity (p. 475)
Stock dividend (p. 466)
Stock options (p. 476)
Stock split (p. 468)
Stockholders' equity (p. 462)
Treasury stock (p. 472)

Multiple Choice Quiz   Answers on p. 499   mhhe.com/wildFA6e

Additional quiz questions are available at the book's Website.

1. A corporation issues 6,000 shares of $5 par value common stock for $8 cash per share. The entry to record this transaction includes:
   a. A debit to Paid-In Capital in Excess of Par Value for $18,000.
   b. A credit to Common Stock for $48,000.
   c. A credit to Paid-In Capital in Excess of Par Value for $30,000.
   d. A credit to Cash for $48,000.
   e. A credit to Common Stock for $30,000.

2. A company reports net income of $75,000. Its weighted-average common shares outstanding is 19,000. It has no other stock outstanding. Its earnings per share is:
   a. $4.69
   b. $3.95
   c. $3.75
   d. $2.08
   e. $4.41

3. A company has 5,000 shares of $100 par preferred stock and 50,000 shares of $10 par common stock outstanding. Its total stockholders' equity is $2,000,000. Its book value per common share is:
 a. $100.00
 b. $ 10.00
 c. $ 40.00
 d. $ 30.00
 e. $ 36.36

4. A company paid cash dividends of $0.81 per share. Its earnings per share is $6.95 and its market price per share is $45.00. Its dividend yield is:
 a. 1.8%
 b. 11.7%

 c. 15.4%
 d. 55.6%
 e. 8.6%

5. A company's shares have a market value of $85 per share. Its net income is $3,500,000, and its weighted-average common shares outstanding is 700,000. Its price-earnings ratio is:
 a. 5.9
 b. 425.0
 c. 17.0
 d. 10.4
 e. 41.2

[I] Icon denotes assignments that involve decision making.

Discussion Questions

1. What are organization expenses? Provide examples.
2. How are organization expenses reported?
3. [I] Who is responsible for directing a corporation's affairs?
4. What is the preemptive right of common stockholders?
5. List the general rights of common stockholders.
6. What is the difference between authorized shares and outstanding shares?
7. [I] Why would an investor find convertible preferred stock attractive?
8. What is the difference between the market value per share and the par value per share?
9. What is the difference between the par value and the call price of a share of preferred stock?
10. Identify and explain the importance of the three dates relevant to corporate dividends.
11. Why is the term *liquidating dividend* used to describe cash dividends debited against paid-in capital accounts?
12. [I] How does declaring a stock dividend affect the corporation's assets, liabilities, and total equity? What are the effects of the eventual distribution of that stock?
13. [I] What is the difference between a stock dividend and a stock split?
14. [I] Courts have ruled that a stock dividend is not taxable income to stockholders. What justifies this decision?

15. How does the purchase of treasury stock affect the purchaser's assets and total equity?
16. [I] Why do laws place limits on treasury stock purchases?
17. How are EPS results computed for a corporation with a simple capital structure?
18. What is a stock option?
19. How is book value per share computed for a corporation with no preferred stock? What is the main limitation of using book value per share to value a corporation?
20. Review the 2009 balance sheet for Nokia in Appendix A and list the amounts for treasury shares and retained earnings. **NOKIA**
21. Refer to Research In Motion's 2010 balance sheet in Appendix A. How many shares of common stock are authorized? How many shares of voting common stock are issued? **RIM**
22. [I] Refer to the 2009 balance sheet for Palm in Appendix A. What is the par value per share of its common stock? Suggest a rationale for the amount of par value it assigned. **Palm**
23. [I] Refer to the financial statements for Apple in Appendix A. What are its cash proceeds from issuance of common stock *and* its cash repurchases of common stock for the year ended September 26, 2009? Explain. **Apple**

connect

Of the following statements, which are true for the corporate form of organization?
1. Owners are not agents of the corporation.
2. It is a separate legal entity.
3. It has a limited life.
4. Capital is more easily accumulated than with most other forms of organization.
5. Corporate income that is distributed to shareholders is usually taxed twice.
6. Owners have unlimited liability for corporate debts.
7. Ownership rights cannot be easily transferred.

QUICK STUDY

QS 11-1
Characteristics of corporations
C1

QS 11-2
Issuance of common stock
P1

Prepare the journal entry to record Channel One Company's issuance of 100,000 shares of $0.50 par value common stock assuming the shares sell for:

a. $0.50 cash per share.

b. $2 cash per share.

QS 11-3
Issuance of no-par
common stock
P1

Prepare the journal entry to record Selectist Company's issuance of 104,000 shares of no-par value common stock assuming the shares:

a. Sell for $15 cash per share.

b. Are exchanged for land valued at $1,560,000.

QS 11-4
Issuance of par and stated
value common stock
P1

Prepare the journal entry to record Typist Company's issuance of 250,000 shares of its common stock assuming the shares have a:

a. $1 par value and sell for $10 cash per share.

b. $1 stated value and sell for $10 cash per share.

QS 11-5
Issuance of common stock
P1

Prepare the issuer's journal entry for each separate transaction. (*a*) On March 1, Edgar Co. issues 44,500 shares of $4 par value common stock for $255,000 cash. (*b*) On April 1, GT Co. issues no-par value common stock for $50,000 cash. (*c*) On April 6, MTV issues 2,000 shares of $20 par value common stock for $35,000 of inventory, $135,000 of machinery, and acceptance of an $84,000 note payable.

QS 11-6
Issuance of preferred stock
P1 P2

a. Prepare the journal entry to record Stefan Company's issuance of 12,000 shares of $50 par value 6% cumulative preferred stock for $75 cash per share.

b. Assuming the facts in part 1, if Stefan declares a year-end cash dividend, what is the amount of dividend paid to preferred shareholders? (Assume no dividends in arrears.)

QS 11-7
Accounting for cash dividends
P2

Prepare journal entries to record the following transactions for Emerson Corporation.

April 15　Declared a cash dividend payable to common stockholders of $40,000.
May 15　Date of record is May 15 for the cash dividend declared on April 15.
May 31　Paid the dividend declared on April 15.

QS 11-8
Dividend allocation between
classes of shareholders
C2

Stockholders' equity of STIX Company consists of 75,000 shares of $5 par value, 8% cumulative preferred stock and 200,000 shares of $1 par value common stock. Both classes of stock have been outstanding since the company's inception. STIX did not declare any dividends in the prior year, but it now declares and pays a $108,000 cash dividend at the current year-end. Determine the amount distributed to each class of stockholders for this two-year-old company.

QS 11-9
Accounting for small
stock dividend
P2

The stockholders' equity section of Zacman Company's balance sheet as of April 1 follows. On April 2, Zacman declares and distributes a 10% stock dividend. The stock's per share market value on April 2 is $25 (prior to the dividend). Prepare the stockholders' equity section immediately after the stock dividend.

Common stock—$5 par value, 375,000 shares authorized, 150,000 shares issued and outstanding	$ 750,000
Paid-in capital in excess of par value, common stock	352,500
Retained earnings	633,000
Total stockholders' equity	$1,735,500

QS 11-10
Accounting for changes in
estimates; error adjustments
C3

Answer the following questions related to a company's activities for the current year:

1. After using an expected useful life of 20 years and no salvage value to depreciate its office equipment over the preceding 15 years, the company decided early this year that the equipment will last only two more years. How should the effects of this decision be reported in the current year financial statements?

2. A review of the notes payable files discovers that two years ago the company reported the entire amount of a payment (principal and interest) on an installment note payable as interest expense. This mistake had a material effect on the amount of income in that year. How should the correction be reported in the current year financial statements?

On May 3, Lassman Corporation purchased 3,000 shares of its own stock for $27,000 cash. On November 4, Lassman reissued 750 shares of this treasury stock for $7,080. Prepare the May 3 and November 4 journal entries to record Lassman's purchase and reissuance of treasury stock.

QS 11-11
Purchase and sale of treasury stock P3

Barnes Company earned net income of $450,000 this year. The number of common shares outstanding during the entire year was 200,000, and preferred shareholders received a $10,000 cash dividend. Compute Barnes Company's basic earnings per share.

QS 11-12
Basic earnings per share A1

Campbell Company reports net income of $1,200,000 for the year. It has no preferred stock, and its weighted-average common shares outstanding is 300,000 shares. Compute its basic earnings per share.

QS 11-13
Basic earnings per share A1

Compute Fox Company's price-earnings ratio if its common stock has a market value of $30.75 per share and its EPS is $4.10. Would an analyst likely consider this stock potentially over- or underpriced? Explain.

QS 11-14
Price-earnings ratio A2

Fiona Company expects to pay a $2.10 per share cash dividend this year on its common stock. The current market value of Fiona stock is $28.50 per share. Compute the expected dividend yield on the Fiona stock. Would you classify the Fiona stock as a growth or an income stock? Explain.

QS 11-15
Dividend yield A3

The stockholders' equity section of Axel Company's balance sheet follows. The preferred stock's call price is $30. Determine the book value per share of the common stock.

QS 11-16
Book value per common share
A4

Preferred stock—5% cumulative, $10 par value, 10,000 shares authorized, issued and outstanding	$100,000
Common stock—$5 par value, 100,000 shares authorized, 75,000 shares issued and outstanding	375,000
Retained earnings	445,000
Total stockholders' equity	$920,000

Air France-KLM reports the following equity information for its fiscal year ended March 31, 2009 (euros in millions). Prepare its journal entry, using its account titles, to record the issuance of capital stock assuming that its entire par value stock was issued on March 31, 2009, for cash.

QS 11-17
International equity disclosures
P1

March 31	2009
Issued capital	€2,552
Additional paid-in capital	765

connect

Describe how each of the following characteristics of organizations applies to corporations.

EXERCISES

Exercise 11-1
Characteristics of corporations
C1

1. Duration of life
2. Owner liability
3. Legal status
4. Tax status of income
5. Owner authority and control
6. Ease of formation
7. Transferability of ownership
8. Ability to raise large capital amounts

Aloha Corporation issues 6,000 shares of its common stock for $144,000 cash on February 20. Prepare journal entries to record this event under each of the following separate situations.
1. The stock has neither par nor stated value.
2. The stock has a $20 par value.
3. The stock has an $8 stated value.

Exercise 11-2
Accounting for par, stated, and no-par stock issuances
P1

Exercise 11-3

Recording stock issuances

P1

Prepare journal entries to record the following four separate issuances of stock.

1. A corporation issued 2,000 shares of no-par common stock to its promoters in exchange for their efforts, estimated to be worth $30,000. The stock has no stated value.

2. A corporation issued 2,000 shares of no-par common stock to its promoters in exchange for their efforts, estimated to be worth $30,000. The stock has a $1 per share stated value.

3. A corporation issued 4,000 shares of $10 par value common stock for $70,000 cash.

4. A corporation issued 1,000 shares of $100 par value preferred stock for $120,000 cash.

Exercise 11-4

Stock issuance for noncash assets

P1

Soku Company issues 36,000 shares of $9 par value common stock in exchange for land and a building. The land is valued at $225,000 and the building at $360,000. Prepare the journal entry to record issuance of the stock in exchange for the land and building.

Exercise 11-5

Identifying characteristics of preferred stock

C2

Match each description 1 through 6 with the characteristic of preferred stock that it best describes by writing the letter of that characteristic in the blank next to each description.

A. Cumulative   **B.** Noncumulative   **C.** Convertible

D. Callable   **E.** Nonparticipating   **F.** Participating

_____ **1.** Holders of the stock lose any dividends that are not declared in the current year.

_____ **2.** The issuing corporation can retire the stock by paying a prespecified price.

_____ **3.** Holders of the stock can receive dividends exceeding the stated rate under certain conditions.

_____ **4.** Holders of the stock are not entitled to receive dividends in excess of the stated rate.

_____ **5.** Holders of this stock can exchange it for shares of common stock.

_____ **6.** Holders of the stock are entitled to receive current and all past dividends before common stockholders receive any dividends.

Exercise 11-6

Stock dividends and splits

P2

On June 30, 2011, Quinn Corporation's common stock is priced at $31 per share before any stock dividend or split, and the stockholders' equity section of its balance sheet appears as follows.

Common stock—$10 par value, 60,000 shares	
authorized, 25,000 shares issued and outstanding	$250,000
Paid-in capital in excess of par value, common stock	100,000
Retained earnings	330,000
Total stockholders' equity	$680,000

1. Assume that the company declares and immediately distributes a 100% stock dividend. This event is recorded by capitalizing retained earnings equal to the stock's par value. Answer these questions about stockholders' equity as it exists *after* issuing the new shares.

   a. What is the retained earnings balance?

Check (1*b*) $680,000

   b. What is the amount of total stockholders' equity?

   c. How many shares are outstanding?

2. Assume that the company implements a 2-for-1 stock split instead of the stock dividend in part 1. Answer these questions about stockholders' equity as it exists *after* issuing the new shares.

   (2*a*) $330,000

   a. What is the retained earnings balance?

   b. What is the amount of total stockholders' equity?

   c. How many shares are outstanding?

3. Explain the difference, if any, to a stockholder from receiving new shares distributed under a large stock dividend versus a stock split.

Exercise 11-7

Stock dividends and per share book values

P2

The stockholders' equity of Whiz.com Company at the beginning of the day on February 5 follows.

Common stock—$25 par value, 150,000 shares	
authorized, 60,000 shares issued and outstanding	$1,500,000
Paid-in capital in excess of par value, common stock	525,000
Retained earnings	675,000
Total stockholders' equity	$2,700,000

On February 5, the directors declare a 20% stock dividend distributable on February 28 to the February 15 stockholders of record. The stock's market value is $40 per share on February 5 before the stock dividend. The stock's market value is $34 per share on February 28.

1. Prepare entries to record both the dividend declaration and its distribution.
2. One stockholder owned 750 shares on February 5 before the dividend. Compute the book value per share and total book value of this stockholder's shares immediately before *and* after the stock dividend of February 5.
3. Compute the total market value of the investor's shares in part 2 as of February 5 and February 28.

Check (2) Book value per share: before, $45; after, $37.50

Wade's outstanding stock consists of 40,000 shares of *noncumulative* 7.5% preferred stock with a $10 par value and also 100,000 shares of common stock with a $1 par value. During its first four years of operation, the corporation declared and paid the following total cash dividends.

Exercise 11-8
Dividends on common and noncumulative preferred stock
C2

2011	$ 10,000
2012	24,000
2013	100,000
2014	196,000

Determine the amount of dividends paid each year to each of the two classes of stockholders: preferred and common. Also compute the total dividends paid to each class for the four years combined.

Check 4-year total paid to preferred, $94,000

Use the data in Exercise 11-8 to determine the amount of dividends paid each year to each of the two classes of stockholders assuming that the preferred stock is *cumulative*. Also determine the total dividends paid to each class for the four years combined.

Exercise 11-9
Dividends on common and cumulative preferred stock C2

On October 10, the stockholders' equity of Noble Systems appears as follows.

Exercise 11-10
Recording and reporting treasury stock transactions
P3

Common stock—$10 par value, 36,000 shares authorized, issued, and outstanding	$360,000
Paid-in capital in excess of par value, common stock	108,000
Retained earnings	432,000
Total stockholders' equity	$900,000

1. Prepare journal entries to record the following transactions for Noble Systems.
   a. Purchased 4,500 shares of its own common stock at $30 per share on October 11.
   b. Sold 1,200 treasury shares on November 1 for $36 cash per share.
   c. Sold all remaining treasury shares on November 25 for $25 cash per share.
2. Explain how the company's equity section changes after the October 11 treasury stock purchase, and prepare the revised equity section of its balance sheet at that date.

Check (1c) Dr. Retained Earnings, $9,300

The following information is available for Ballard Company for the year ended December 31, 2011.
a. Balance of retained earnings, December 31, 2010, prior to discovery of error, $850,000.
b. Cash dividends declared and paid during 2011, $15,000.
c. It neglected to record 2009 depreciation expense of $55,600, which is net of $5,500 in income taxes.
d. The company earned $205,000 in 2011 net income.
Prepare a 2011 statement of retained earnings for Ballard Company.

Exercise 11-11
Preparing a statement of retained earnings
C3

Guess Company reports $648,500 of net income for 2011 and declares $102,500 of cash dividends on its preferred stock for 2011. At the end of 2011, the company had 260,000 weighted-average shares of common stock.

1. What amount of net income is available to common stockholders for 2011?
2. What is the company's basic EPS for 2011?

Exercise 11-12
Earnings per share
A1

Check (2) $2.10

Exercise 11-13

Earnings per share

A1

Check   (2) $3.56

Franklin Company reports $698,000 of net income for 2011 and declares $75,500 of cash dividends on its preferred stock for 2011. At the end of 2011, the company had 175,000 weighted-average shares of common stock.

1. What amount of net income is available to common stockholders for 2011?

2. What is the company's basic EPS for 2011? Round your answer to the nearest whole cent.

Exercise 11-14

Dividend yield computation and interpretation

A3

Compute the dividend yield for each of these four separate companies. Which company's stock would probably *not* be classified as an income stock? Explain.

Company	Annual Cash Dividend per Share	Market Value per Share
1	$15.00	$216.00
2	12.00	128.00
3	6.00	61.00
4	1.20	86.00

Exercise 11-15

Price-earnings ratio computation and interpretation

A2

Compute the price-earnings ratio for each of these four separate companies. Which stock might an analyst likely investigate as being potentially undervalued by the market? Explain.

Company	Earnings per Share	Market Value per Share
1	$10.00	$166.00
2	9.00	90.00
3	6.50	84.50
4	40.00	240.00

Exercise 11-16

Book value per share

A4

The equity section of Webster Corporation's balance sheet shows the following.

Preferred stock—5% cumulative, $10 par value, $15 call price, 10,000 shares issued and outstanding	$100,000
Common stock—$10 par value, 55,000 shares issued and outstanding	550,000
Retained earnings	267,500
Total stockholders' equity	$917,500

Determine the book value per share of the preferred and common stock under two separate situations.

1. No preferred dividends are in arrears.

2. Three years of preferred dividends are in arrears.

Check   (1) Book value of common, $13.95

Exercise 11-17

Accounting for equity under IFRS

C3 P1

Unilever Group reports the following equity information for the years ended December 31, 2007 and 2008 (euros in millions).

December 31	2008	2007
Share capital	€ 484	€ 484
Share premium	121	153
Other reserves	(6,469)	(3,412)
Retained profit	15,812	15,162
Shareholders' equity	€ 9,948	€12,387

1. For each of the three account titles *share capital, share premium,* and *retained profit,* match it with the usual account title applied under U.S. GAAP from the following options:

  a. Paid-in capital in excess of par value, common stock

  b. Retained earnings

  c. Common stock, par value

2. Prepare Unilever's journal entry, using its account titles, to record the issuance of capital stock assuming that its entire par value stock was issued on December 31, 2007, for cash.

3. What were Unilever's 2008 dividends assuming that only dividends and income impacted retained profit for 2008 and that its 2008 income totaled €2,692?

Kroll Corporation reports the following components of stockholders' equity on December 31, 2011.

Common stock—$25 par value, 40,000 shares authorized, 30,000 shares issued and outstanding	$ 750,000
Paid-in capital in excess of par value, common stock	50,000
Retained earnings	260,000
Total stockholders' equity	$1,060,000

Exercise 11-18
Cash dividends, treasury stock, and statement of retained earnings

C3 P2 P3

In year 2012, the following transactions affected its stockholders' equity accounts.

Jan.   2   Purchased 2,000 shares of its own stock at $25 cash per share.
Jan.   7   Directors declared a $2 per share cash dividend payable on Feb. 28 to the Feb. 9 stockholders of record.
Feb. 28   Paid the dividend declared on January 7.
July   9   Sold 500 of its treasury shares at $30 cash per share.
Aug. 27   Sold 1,500 of its treasury shares at $23 cash per share.
Sept. 9   Directors declared a $2 per share cash dividend payable on October 22 to the September 23 stockholders of record.
Oct. 22   Paid the dividend declared on September 9.
Dec. 31   Closed the $8,000 credit balance (from net income) in the Income Summary account to Retained Earnings.

Required

1. Prepare journal entries to record each of these transactions for 2012.

2. Prepare a statement of retained earnings for the year ended December 31, 2012.

3. Prepare the stockholders' equity section of the company's balance sheet as of December 31, 2012.

connect

Oxygen Co. is incorporated at the beginning of this year and engages in a number of transactions. The following journal entries impacted its stockholders' equity during its first year of operations.

a.	Cash	150,000	
	Common Stock, $25 Par Value		125,000
	Paid-In Capital in Excess of Par Value, Common Stock		25,000
b.	Organization Expenses	75,000	
	Common Stock, $25 Par Value		62,500
	Paid-In Capital in Excess of Par Value, Common Stock		12,500
c.	Cash	21,500	
	Accounts Receivable	7,500	
	Building	30,000	
	Notes Payable		19,000
	Common Stock, $25 Par Value		25,000
	Paid-In Capital in Excess of Par Value, Common Stock		15,000

PROBLEM SET A

Problem 11-1A
Stockholders' equity transactions and analysis

C2 P1

[continued on next page]

[continued from previous page]

d.	Cash	60,000	
	Common Stock, $25 Par Value		37,500
	Paid-In Capital in Excess of		
	Par Value, Common Stock		22,500

Required

1. Explain the transaction(s) underlying each journal entry (*a*) through (*d*).
2. How many shares of common stock are outstanding at year-end?
3. What is the amount of minimum legal capital (based on par value) at year-end?
4. What is the total paid-in capital at year-end?
5. What is the book value per share of the common stock at year-end if total paid-in capital plus retained earnings equals $347,500?

Check   (2) 10,000 shares
(3) $250,000
(4) $325,000

Problem 11-2A
Cash dividends, treasury stock, and statement of retained earnings
C3 P2 P3

Context Corporation reports the following components of stockholders' equity on December 31, 2011.

Common stock—$10 par value, 50,000 shares authorized,	
20,000 shares issued and outstanding	$200,000
Paid-in capital in excess of par value, common stock	30,000
Retained earnings	135,000
Total stockholders' equity	$365,000

In year 2012, the following transactions affected its stockholders' equity accounts.

Jan.   1   Purchased 2,000 shares of its own stock at $20 cash per share.
Jan.   5   Directors declared a $2 per share cash dividend payable on Feb. 28 to the Feb. 5 stockholders of record.
Feb. 28   Paid the dividend declared on January 5.
July   6   Sold 750 of its treasury shares at $24 cash per share.
Aug. 22   Sold 1,250 of its treasury shares at $17 cash per share.
Sept. 5   Directors declared a $2 per share cash dividend payable on October 28 to the September 25 stockholders of record.
Oct. 28   Paid the dividend declared on September 5.
Dec. 31   Closed the $194,000 credit balance (from net income) in the Income Summary account to Retained Earnings.

Required

1. Prepare journal entries to record each of these transactions for 2012.
2. Prepare a statement of retained earnings for the year ended December 31, 2012.
3. Prepare the stockholders' equity section of the company's balance sheet as of December 31, 2012.

Check   (2) Retained earnings, Dec. 31, 2012, $252,250

Problem 11-3A
Equity analysis—journal entries and account balances
P2

At September 30, the end of Excel Company's third quarter, the following stockholders' equity accounts are reported.

Common stock, $12 par value	$720,000
Paid-in capital in excess of par value, common stock	180,000
Retained earnings	640,000

In the fourth quarter, the following entries related to its equity are recorded.

Oct. 2	Retained Earnings	120,000	
	Common Dividend Payable		120,000
Oct. 25	Common Dividend Payable	120,000	
	Cash		120,000
Oct. 31	Retained Earnings	150,000	
	Common Stock Dividend Distributable		72,000
	Paid-In Capital in Excess of		
	Par Value, Common Stock		78,000

[continued on next page]

[continued from previous page]

Nov. 5	Common Stock Dividend Distributable	72,000	
	Common Stock, $12 Par Value		72,000
Dec. 1	Memo—Change the title of the common stock account to reflect the new par value of $4.		
Dec. 31	Income Summary	420,000	
	Retained Earnings		420,000

Required

1. Explain the transaction(s) underlying each journal entry.
2. Complete the following table showing the equity account balances at each indicated date (include the balances from September 30).

	Oct. 2	Oct. 25	Oct. 31	Nov. 5	Dec. 1	Dec. 31
Common stock	$____	$____	$____	$____	$____	$____
Common stock dividend distributable	____	____	____	____	____	____
Paid-in capital in excess of par, common stock	____	____	____	____	____	____
Retained earnings	____	____	____	____	____	____
Total equity	$____	$____	$____	$____	$____	$____

Check Total equity: Oct. 2, $1,420,000; Dec. 31, $1,840,000

The equity sections from Salazar Group's 2011 and 2012 year-end balance sheets follow.

Problem 11-4A
Analysis of changes in stockholders' equity accounts

C3 P2 P3

Stockholders' Equity (December 31, 2011)

Common stock—$4 par value, 50,000 shares authorized, 20,000 shares issued and outstanding	$ 80,000
Paid-in capital in excess of par value, common stock	60,000
Retained earnings	160,000
Total stockholders' equity	$300,000

Stockholders' Equity (December 31, 2012)

Common stock—$4 par value, 50,000 shares authorized, 23,700 shares issued, 1,500 shares in treasury	$ 94,800
Paid-in capital in excess of par value, common stock	89,600
Retained earnings ($15,000 restricted by treasury stock)	200,000
	384,400
Less cost of treasury stock	(15,000)
Total stockholders' equity	$369,400

The following transactions and events affected its equity during year 2012.

Jan. 5   Declared a $0.50 per share cash dividend, date of record January 10.
Mar. 20   Purchased treasury stock for cash.
Apr. 5   Declared a $0.50 per share cash dividend, date of record April 10.
July 5   Declared a $0.50 per share cash dividend, date of record July 10.
July 31   Declared a 20% stock dividend when the stock's market value is $12 per share.
Aug. 14   Issued the stock dividend that was declared on July 31.
Oct. 5   Declared a $0.50 per share cash dividend, date of record October 10.

Required

1. How many common shares are outstanding on each cash dividend date?
2. What is the total dollar amount for each of the four cash dividends?
3. What is the amount of the capitalization of retained earnings for the stock dividend?
4. What is the per share cost of the treasury stock purchased?
5. How much net income did the company earn during year 2012?

Check (3) $44,400

(4) $10

(5) $124,000

Problem 11-5A
Computation of book values and dividend allocations

C2　A4

Razz Corporation's common stock is currently selling on a stock exchange at $170 per share, and its current balance sheet shows the following stockholders' equity section.

Preferred stock—5% cumulative, $___ par value, 1,000 shares authorized, issued, and outstanding	$100,000
Common stock—$___ par value, 4,000 shares authorized, issued, and outstanding	160,000
Retained earnings	300,000
Total stockholders' equity	$560,000

Required (Round per share amounts to cents.)

1. What is the current market value (price) of this corporation's common stock?
2. What are the par values of the corporation's preferred stock and its common stock?
3. If no dividends are in arrears, what are the book values per share of the preferred stock and the common stock?
4. If two years' preferred dividends are in arrears, what are the book values per share of the preferred stock and the common stock?
5. If two years' preferred dividends are in arrears and the preferred stock is callable at $110 per share, what are the book values per share of the preferred stock and the common stock?
6. If two years' preferred dividends are in arrears and the board of directors declares cash dividends of $20,000, what total amount will be paid to the preferred and to the common shareholders? What is the amount of dividends per share for the common stock?

Check (4) Book value of common, $112.50

(5) Book value of common, $110

(6) Dividends per common share, $1.25

Analysis Component

7. What are some factors that can contribute to a difference between the book value of common stock and its market value (price)?

PROBLEM SET B

Problem 11-1B
Stockholders' equity transactions and analysis

C2　P1

Nilson Company is incorporated at the beginning of this year and engages in a number of transactions. The following journal entries impacted its stockholders' equity during its first year of operations.

a.	Cash	60,000	
	Common Stock, $1 Par Value		1,500
	Paid-In Capital in Excess of Par Value, Common Stock		58,500
b.	Organization Expenses	20,000	
	Common Stock, $1 Par Value		500
	Paid-In Capital in Excess of Par Value, Common Stock		19,500
c.	Cash	6,650	
	Accounts Receivable	4,000	
	Building	12,500	
	Notes Payable		3,150
	Common Stock, $1 Par Value		400
	Paid-In Capital in Excess of Par Value, Common Stock		19,600
d.	Cash	30,000	
	Common Stock, $1 Par Value		600
	Paid-In Capital in Excess of Par Value, Common Stock		29,400

Required

1. Explain the transaction(s) underlying each journal entry (a) through (d).
2. How many shares of common stock are outstanding at year-end?
3. What is the amount of minimum legal capital (based on par value) at year-end?

Check (2) 3,000 shares

(3) $3,000

4. What is the total paid-in capital at year-end?

5. What is the book value per share of the common stock at year-end if total paid-in capital plus retained earnings equals $141,500?

(4) $130,000

Baycore Corp. reports the following components of stockholders' equity on December 31, 2011.

Problem 11-2B
Cash dividends, treasury stock, and statement of retained earnings
C3 P2 P3

Common stock—$1 par value, 160,000 shares authorized, 100,000 shares issued and outstanding	$ 100,000
Paid-in capital in excess of par value, common stock	700,000
Retained earnings	1,080,000
Total stockholders' equity	$1,880,000

It completed the following transactions related to stockholders' equity in year 2012.

Jan. 10 Purchased 20,000 shares of its own stock at $12 cash per share.
Mar. 2 Directors declared a $1.50 per share cash dividend payable on March 31 to the March 15 stockholders of record.
Mar. 31 Paid the dividend declared on March 2.
Nov. 11 Sold 12,000 of its treasury shares at $13 cash per share.
Nov. 25 Sold 8,000 of its treasury shares at $9.50 cash per share.
Dec. 1 Directors declared a $2.50 per share cash dividend payable on January 2 to the December 10 stockholders of record.
Dec. 31 Closed the $536,000 credit balance (from net income) in the Income Summary account to Retained Earnings.

Required

1. Prepare journal entries to record each of these transactions for 2012.
2. Prepare a statement of retained earnings for the year ended December 31, 2012.
3. Prepare the stockholders' equity section of the company's balance sheet as of December 31, 2012.

Check (2) Retained earnings, Dec. 31, 2012, $1,238,000

At December 31, the end of Intertec Communication's third quarter, the following stockholders' equity accounts are reported.

Problem 11-3B
Equity analysis—journal entries and account balances
P2

Common stock, $10 par value	$480,000
Paid-in capital in excess of par value, common stock	192,000
Retained earnings	800,000

In the fourth quarter, the following entries related to its equity are recorded.

Jan. 17	Retained Earnings	48,000	
	Common Dividend Payable		48,000
Feb. 5	Common Dividend Payable	48,000	
	Cash		48,000
Feb. 28	Retained Earnings	126,000	
	Common Stock Dividend Distributable		60,000
	Paid-In Capital in Excess of Par Value, Common Stock		66,000
Mar. 14	Common Stock Dividend Distributable	60,000	
	Common Stock, $10 Par Value		60,000
Mar. 25	Memo—Change the title of the common stock account to reflect the new par value of $5.		
Mar. 31	Income Summary	360,000	
	Retained Earnings		360,000

Required

1. Explain the transaction(s) underlying each journal entry.
2. Complete the following table showing the equity account balances at each indicated date (include the balances from December 31).

	Jan. 17	Feb. 5	Feb. 28	Mar. 14	Mar. 25	Mar. 31
Common stock	$_____	$_____	$_____	$_____	$_____	$_____
Common stock dividend distributable	_____	_____	_____	_____	_____	_____
Paid-in capital in excess of par, common stock	_____	_____	_____	_____	_____	_____
Retained earnings	_____	_____	_____	_____	_____	_____
Total equity	$_____	$_____	$_____	$_____	$_____	$_____

Check Total equity: Jan. 17, $1,424,000; Mar. 31, $1,784,000

Problem 11-4B
Analysis of changes in stockholders' equity accounts

C3 P2 P3

The equity sections from Jetta Corporation's 2011 and 2012 balance sheets follow.

Stockholders' Equity (December 31, 2011)	
Common stock—$20 par value, 15,000 shares authorized, 8,500 shares issued and outstanding	$170,000
Paid-in capital in excess of par value, common stock	30,000
Retained earnings	135,000
Total stockholders' equity	$335,000

Stockholders' Equity (December 31, 2012)	
Common stock—$20 par value, 15,000 shares authorized, 9,500 shares issued, 500 shares in treasury	$190,000
Paid-in capital in excess of par value, common stock	52,000
Retained earnings ($20,000 restricted by treasury stock)	147,600
	389,600
Less cost of treasury stock	(20,000)
Total stockholders' equity	$369,600

The following transactions and events affected its equity during year 2012.

Feb. 15 Declared a $0.40 per share cash dividend, date of record five days later.
Mar. 2 Purchased treasury stock for cash.
May 15 Declared a $0.40 per share cash dividend, date of record five days later.
Aug. 15 Declared a $0.40 per share cash dividend, date of record five days later.
Oct. 4 Declared a 12.5% stock dividend when the stock's market value is $42 per share.
Oct. 20 Issued the stock dividend that was declared on October 4.
Nov. 15 Declared a $0.40 per share cash dividend, date of record five days later.

Required

1. How many common shares are outstanding on each cash dividend date?
2. What is the total dollar amount for each of the four cash dividends?
3. What is the amount of the capitalization of retained earnings for the stock dividend?
4. What is the per share cost of the treasury stock purchased?
5. How much net income did the company earn during year 2012?

Check (3) $42,000
(4) $40
(5) $68,000

Problem 11-5B
Computation of book values and dividend allocations

C2 A4

Scotch Company's common stock is currently selling on a stock exchange at $45 per share, and its current balance sheet shows the following stockholders' equity section.

Preferred stock—8% cumulative, $___ par value, 1,500 shares authorized, issued, and outstanding	$ 187,500
Common stock—$___ par value, 18,000 shares authorized, issued, and outstanding	450,000
Retained earnings	562,500
Total stockholders' equity	$1,200,000

Required (Round per share amounts to cents.)

1. What is the current market value (price) of this corporation's common stock?
2. What are the par values of the corporation's preferred stock and its common stock?
3. If no dividends are in arrears, what are the book values per share of the preferred stock and the common stock? (Round per share values to the nearest cent.)
4. If two years' preferred dividends are in arrears, what are the book values per share of the preferred stock and the common stock? (Round per share values to the nearest cent.)
5. If two years' preferred dividends are in arrears and the preferred stock is callable at $140 per share, what are the book values per share of the preferred stock and the common stock? (Round per share values to the nearest cent.)
6. If two years' preferred dividends are in arrears and the board of directors declares cash dividends of $50,000, what total amount will be paid to the preferred and to the common shareholders? What is the amount of dividends per share for the common stock? (Round per share values to the nearest cent.)

Check (4) Book value of common, $54.58

(5) Book value of common, $53.33

(6) Dividends per common share, $0.28

Analysis Component

7. Discuss why the book value of common stock is not always a good estimate of its market value.

(This serial problem began in Chapter 1 and continues through most of the book. If previous chapter segments were not completed, the serial problem can begin at this point. It is helpful, but not necessary, to use the Working Papers that accompany the book.)

SERIAL PROBLEM
Business Solutions
P1 C1 C2

SP 11   Santana Rey created Business Solutions on October 1, 2011. The company has been successful, and Santana plans to expand her business. She believes that an additional $86,000 is needed and is investigating three funding sources.

a. Santana's sister Cicely is willing to invest $86,000 in the business as a common shareholder. Since Santana currently has about $129,000 invested in the business, Cicely's investment will mean that Santana will maintain about 60% ownership, and Cicely will have 40% ownership of Business Solutions.
b. Santana's uncle Marcello is willing to invest $86,000 in the business as a preferred shareholder. Marcello would purchase 860 shares of $100 par value, 7% preferred stock.
c. Santana's banker is willing to lend her $86,000 on a 7%, 10-year note payable. She would make monthly payments of $1,000 per month for 10 years.

Required

1. Prepare the journal entry to reflect the initial $86,000 investment under each of the options (a), (b), and (c).
2. Evaluate the three proposals for expansion, providing the pros and cons of each option.
3. Which option do you recommend Santana adopt? Explain.

Beyond the Numbers

BTN 11-1   Refer to **Research In Motion**'s financial statements in Appendix A to answer the following.

1. How many shares of common stock are issued and outstanding at February 27, 2010, and February 28, 2009? How do these numbers compare with the basic weighted-average common shares outstanding at February 27, 2010, and February 28, 2009?
2. What is the book value of its entire common stock at February 27, 2010?
3. What is the total amount of cash dividends paid to common stockholders for the years ended February 27, 2010, and February 28, 2009?
4. Identify and compare basic EPS amounts across fiscal years 2010, 2009, and 2008. Identify and comment on any notable changes.
5. How many shares does Research In Motion hold in treasury stock, if any, as of February 27, 2010? As of February 28, 2009?

REPORTING IN ACTION

C2 A1 A4

RIM

Fast Forward

6. Access Research In Motion's financial statements for fiscal years ending after February 27, 2010, from its Website (**RIM.com**) or the SEC's EDGAR database (**www.sec.gov**). Has the number of common shares outstanding increased since that date? Has the company increased the total amount of cash dividends paid compared to the total amount for fiscal year 2010?

COMPARATIVE ANALYSIS

A1 A2 A3 A4

RIM
Palm
Apple

BTN 11-2 Key comparative figures for **Research In Motion**, **Palm**, and **Apple** follow.

Key Figures	Research In Motion	Palm	Apple
Net income (in millions)	$2,457	$ (753)	$8,235
Cash dividends declared per common share	$ —	$ —	$ —
Common shares outstanding (in millions)	557	140	900
Weighted-average common shares outstanding (in mil.)	564	116	893
Market value (price) per share	$69.76	$12.19	$184.40
Equity applicable to common shares (in millions)	$7,603	$ (414)	$31,640

Required

1. Compute the book value per common share for each company using these data.
2. Compute the basic EPS for each company using these data.
3. Compute the dividend yield for each company using these data. Does the dividend yield of any of the companies characterize it as an income or growth stock? Explain.
4. Compute, compare, and interpret the price-earnings ratio for each company using these data.

ETHICS CHALLENGE

C3

BTN 11-3 Gianna Tuck is an accountant for Post Pharmaceuticals. Her duties include tracking research and development spending in the new product development division. Over the course of the past six months, Gianna notices that a great deal of funds have been spent on a particular project for a new drug. She hears "through the grapevine" that the company is about to patent the drug and expects it to be a major advance in antibiotics. Gianna believes that this new drug will greatly improve company performance and will cause the company's stock to increase in value. Gianna decides to purchase shares of Post in order to benefit from this expected increase.

Required

What are Gianna's ethical responsibilities, if any, with respect to the information she has learned through her duties as an accountant for Post Pharmaceuticals? What are the implications to her planned purchase of Post shares?

COMMUNICATING IN PRACTICE

A1 A2

Hint: Make a transparency of each team's memo for a class discussion.

BTN 11-4 Teams are to select an industry, and each team member is to select a different company in that industry. Each team member then is to acquire the selected company's financial statements (or Form 10-K) from the SEC site (www.SEC.gov). Use these data to identify basic EPS. Use the financial press (or finance.yahoo.com) to determine the market price of this stock, and then compute the price-earnings ratio. Communicate with teammates via a meeting, e-mail, or telephone to discuss the meaning of this ratio, how companies compare, and the industry norm. The team must prepare a single memorandum reporting the ratio for each company and identifying the team conclusions or consensus of opinion. The memorandum is to be duplicated and distributed to the instructor and teammates.

TAKING IT TO THE NET

C1 C3

BTN 11-5 Access the February 26, 2010, filing of the 2009 calendar-year 10-K report of **McDonald's**, (ticker MCD) from www.SEC.gov.

Required

1. Review McDonald's balance sheet and identify how many classes of stock it has issued.
2. What are the par values, number of authorized shares, and issued shares of the classes of stock you identified in part 1?
3. Review its statement of cash flows and identify what total amount of cash it paid in 2009 to purchase treasury stock.
4. What amount did McDonald's pay out in common stock cash dividends for 2009?

TEAMWORK IN ACTION

P3

Hint: Instructor should be sure each team accurately completes part 1 before proceeding.

BTN 11-6 This activity requires teamwork to reinforce understanding of accounting for treasury stock.

1. Write a brief team statement (*a*) generalizing what happens to a corporation's financial position when it engages in a stock "buyback" and (*b*) identifying reasons why a corporation would engage in this activity.
2. Assume that an entity acquires 100 shares of its $100 par value common stock at a cost of $134 cash per share. Discuss the entry to record this acquisition. Next, assign *each* team member to prepare *one* of the following entries (assume each entry applies to all shares):
   a. Reissue treasury shares at cost.
   b. Reissue treasury shares at $150 per share.

c. Reissue treasury shares at $120 per share; assume the paid-in capital account from treasury shares has a $1,500 balance.

d. Reissue treasury shares at $120 per share; assume the paid-in capital account from treasury shares has a $1,000 balance.

e. Reissue treasury shares at $120 per share; assume the paid-in capital account from treasury shares has a zero balance.

3. In sequence, each member is to present his/her entry to the team and explain the *similarities* and *differences* between that entry and the previous entry.

BTN 11-7 Assume that Kelly Giard of **Clean Air Lawn Care** decides to launch a new retail chain to market electrical mowers. This chain, named Mow Green, requires $500,000 of start-up capital. Kelly contributes $375,000 of personal assets in return for 15,000 shares of common stock, but he must raise another $125,000 in cash. There are two alternative plans for raising the additional cash. *Plan A* is to sell 3,750 shares of common stock to one or more investors for $125,000 cash. *Plan B* is to sell 1,250 shares of cumulative preferred stock to one or more investors for $125,000 cash (this preferred stock would have a $100 par value, an annual 8% dividend rate, and be issued at par).

ENTREPRENEURIAL DECISION
C2 P2

1. If the new business is expected to earn $72,000 of after-tax net income in the first year, what rate of return on beginning equity will Kelly earn under each alternative plan? Which plan will provide the higher expected return?

2. If the new business is expected to earn $16,800 of after-tax net income in the first year, what rate of return on beginning equity will Kelly earn under each alternative plan? Which plan will provide the higher expected return?

3. Analyze and interpret the differences between the results for parts 1 and 2.

BTN 11-8 Review 30 to 60 minutes of financial news programming on television. Take notes on companies that are catching analysts' attention. You might hear reference to over- and undervaluation of firms and to reports about PE ratios, dividend yields, and earnings per share. Be prepared to give a brief description to the class of your observations.

HITTING THE ROAD
A1 A2 A3

BTN 11-9 Financial information for **Nokia Corporation** (www.nokia.com) follows.

GLOBAL DECISION
A1 C3

NOKIA

Net income (in millions)	€ 260
Cash dividends declared (in millions)	€ 1,481
Cash dividends declared per share	€ 0.40
Number of shares outstanding (in millions)*	3,708
Equity applicable to shares (in millions)	€14,749

* Assume that for Nokia the year-end number of shares outstanding approximates the weighted-average shares outstanding.

Required

1. Compute book value per share for Nokia.
2. Compute earnings per share (EPS) for Nokia.
3. Compare Nokia's dividends per share with its EPS. Is Nokia paying out a large or small amount of its income as dividends? Explain.

ANSWERS TO MULTIPLE CHOICE QUIZ

1. e; Entry to record this stock issuance is:

Cash (6,000 × $8)	48,000	
Common Stock (6,000 × $5)		30,000
Paid-In Capital in Excess of Par Value, Common Stock		18,000

2. b; $75,000/19,000 shares = $3.95 per share

3. d; Preferred stock = 5,000 × $100 = $500,000
Book value per share = ($2,000,000 − $500,000)/50,000 shares = $30 per common share

4. a; $0.81/$45.00 = 1.8%

5. c; Earnings per share = $3,500,000/700,000 shares = $5 per share
PE ratio = $85/$5 = 17.0

A Look Back	A Look at This Chapter	A Look Ahead
Chapter 11 focused on corporate equity transactions, including stock issuances and dividends. We also explained how to report and analyze income, earnings per share, and retained earnings.	This chapter focuses on reporting and analyzing cash inflows and cash outflows. We emphasize how to prepare and interpret the statement of cash flows.	Chapter 13 focuses on tools to help us analyze financial statements. We also describe comparative analysis and the application of ratios for financial analysis.

Reporting and Analyzing Cash Flows

Learning Objectives

CAP

CONCEPTUAL

C1 Distinguish between operating, investing, and financing activities, and describe how noncash investing and financing activities are disclosed. (p. 503)

ANALYTICAL

A1 Analyze the statement of cash flows and apply the cash flow on total assets ratio. (p. 520)

LP12

PROCEDURAL

P1 Prepare a statement of cash flows. (p. 506)

P2 Compute cash flows from operating activities using the indirect method. (p. 509)

P3 Determine cash flows from both investing and financing activities. (p. 515)

P4 *Appendix 12A*—Illustrate use of a spreadsheet to prepare a statement of cash flows. (p. 524)

P5 *Appendix 12B*—Compute cash flows from operating activities using the direct method. (p. 527)

The amount by which cash paid exceeds recorded expense—as reflected in the $1,000 decrease in Interest Payable—is subtracted from net income (see Exhibit 12.11).

Income taxes payable. Income taxes payable *increase* $10,000, from a $12,000 beginning balance to a $22,000 ending balance. This increase implies that reported income taxes exceed the cash paid for taxes, which is reflected in the Income Taxes Payable T-account:

Income Taxes Payable			
		Bal., Dec. 31, 2010	12,000
Cash paid for taxes =	5,000	Income taxes expense	15,000
		Bal., Dec. 31, 2011	22,000

The amount by which cash paid falls short of the reported taxes expense—as reflected in the $10,000 increase in Income Taxes Payable—is added to net income when computing cash provided by operating activities (see Exhibit 12.11).

② **Adjustments for Operating Items Not Providing or Using Cash**   The income statement usually includes some expenses that do not reflect cash outflows in the period. Examples are depreciation, amortization, depletion, and bad debts expense. The indirect method for reporting operating cash flows requires that

> **Expenses with no cash outflows are added back to net income.**

To see the logic of this adjustment, recall that items such as depreciation, amortization, depletion, and bad debts originate from debits to expense accounts and credits to noncash accounts. These entries have *no* cash effect, and we add them back to net income when computing net cash flows from operations. Adding them back cancels their deductions.

Similarly, when net income includes revenues that do not reflect cash inflows in the period, the indirect method for reporting operating cash flows requires that

> **Revenues with no cash inflows are subtracted from net income.**

We apply these adjustments to the Genesis operating items that do not provide or use cash.

Depreciation.   Depreciation expense is the only Genesis operating item that has no effect on cash flows in the period. We must add back the $24,000 depreciation expense to net income when computing cash provided by operating activities. (We later explain that any cash outflow to acquire a plant asset is reported as an investing activity.)

③ **Adjustments for Nonoperating Items**   Net income often includes losses that are not part of operating activities but are part of either investing or financing activities. Examples are a loss from the sale of a plant asset and a loss from retirement of notes payable. The indirect method for reporting operating cash flows requires that

> **Nonoperating losses are added back to net income.**

To see the logic, consider that items such as a plant asset sale and a notes retirement are normally recorded by recognizing the cash, removing all plant asset or notes accounts, and recognizing any loss or gain. The cash received or paid is not part of operating activities but is part of either investing or financing activities. *No* operating cash flow effect occurs. However, because the nonoperating loss is a deduction in computing net income, we need to add it back to net income when computing cash flow from operations. Adding it back cancels the deduction.

Similarly, when net income includes gains not part of operating activities, the indirect method for reporting operating cash flows requires that

> **Nonoperating gains are subtracted from net income.**

To illustrate these adjustments, we consider the nonoperating items of Genesis.

Summary Adjustments for Changes in Current Assets and Current Liabilities		
Account	**Increases**	**Decreases**
Noncash current assets	Deduct from NI	Add to NI
Current liabilities.	Add to NI	Deduct from NI

Point: An income statement reports revenues, gains, expenses, and losses on an accrual basis. The statement of cash flows reports cash received and cash paid for operating, financing, and investing activities.

Loss on sale of plant assets. Genesis reports a $6,000 loss on sale of plant assets as part of net income. This loss is a proper deduction in computing income, but it is *not part of operating activities*. Instead, a sale of plant assets is part of investing activities. Thus, the $6,000 nonoperating loss is added back to net income (see Exhibit 12.11). Adding it back cancels the loss. We later explain how to report the cash inflow from the asset sale in investing activities.

Gain on retirement of debt. A $16,000 gain on retirement of debt is properly included in net income, but it is *not part of operating activities*. This means the $16,000 nonoperating gain must be subtracted from net income to obtain net cash provided by operating activities (see Exhibit 12.11). Subtracting it cancels the recorded gain. We later describe how to report the cash outflow to retire debt.

Summary of Adjustments for Indirect Method

Exhibit 12.12 summarizes the most common adjustments to net income when computing net cash provided or used by operating activities under the indirect method.

EXHIBIT 12.12

Summary of Selected Adjustments for Indirect Method

Net Income

+ Decrease in noncash current asset
− Increase in noncash current asset
+ Increase in current liability*
− Decrease in current liability* } ① Adjustments for changes in current assets and current liabilities

+ Depreciation, depletion, and amortization } ② Adjustments for operating items not providing or using cash

+ Losses from disposal of long-term assets and retirement of debt
− Gains from disposal of long-term assets and retirement of debt } ③ Adjustments for nonoperating items

Net cash provided (used) by operating activities

* Excludes current portion of long-term debt and any (nonsales-related) short-term notes payable—both are financing activities.

The computations in determining cash provided or used by operating activities are different for the indirect and direct methods, but the result is identical. Both methods yield the same $20,000 figure for cash from operating activities for Genesis; see Exhibits 12.7 and 12.11.

Decision Insight

Cash or Income The difference between net income and operating cash flows can be large and sometimes reflects on the quality of earnings. This bar chart shows the net income and operating cash flows of three companies. Operating cash flows can be either higher or lower than net income. ■

	Net Income	Operating Cash Flows
Gap	$778	$1,250
Harley	$1,043	$762
Starbucks	$673	$1,331

$0 $300 $600 $900 $1,200 $1,500
$ Millions

Quick Check   Answers — p. 532

4. Determine the net cash provided or used by operating activities using the following data: net income, $74,900; decrease in accounts receivable, $4,600; increase in inventory, $11,700; decrease in accounts payable, $1,000; loss on sale of equipment, $3,400; payment of cash dividends, $21,500.

5. Why are expenses such as depreciation and amortization added to net income when cash flow from operating activities is computed by the indirect method?

6. A company reports net income of $15,000 that includes a $3,000 gain on the sale of plant assets. Why is this gain subtracted from net income in computing cash flow from operating activities using the indirect method?

CASH FLOWS FROM INVESTING

The third major step in preparing the statement of cash flows is to compute and report cash flows from investing activities. We normally do this by identifying changes in (1) all noncurrent asset accounts and (2) the current accounts for both notes receivable and investments in securities (excluding trading securities). We then analyze changes in these accounts to determine their effect, if any, on cash and report the cash flow effects in the investing activities section of the statement of cash flows. **Reporting of investing activities is identical under the direct method and indirect method.**

Three-Stage Process of Analysis

Information to compute cash flows from investing activities is usually taken from beginning and ending balance sheets and the income statement. We use a three-stage process to determine cash provided or used by investing activities: (1) identify changes in investing-related accounts, (2) explain these changes using reconstruction analysis, and (3) report their cash flow effects.

P3   Determine cash flows from both investing and financing activities.

Analysis of Noncurrent Assets

Information about the Genesis transactions provided earlier reveals that the company both purchased and sold plant assets during the period. Both transactions are investing activities and are analyzed for their cash flow effects in this section.

Plant Asset Transactions   The first stage in analyzing the Plant Assets account and its related Accumulated Depreciation is to identify any changes in these accounts from comparative balance sheets in Exhibit 12.10. This analysis reveals a $40,000 increase in plant assets from $210,000 to $250,000 and a $12,000 increase in accumulated depreciation from $48,000 to $60,000.

The second stage is to explain these changes. Items *b* and *c* of the additional information for Genesis (page 509) are relevant in this case. Recall that the Plant Assets account is affected by both asset purchases and sales, while its Accumulated Depreciation account is normally increased from depreciation and decreased from the removal of accumulated depreciation in asset sales. To explain changes in these accounts and to identify their cash flow effects, we prepare *reconstructed entries* from prior transactions; *they are not the actual entries by the preparer.*

To illustrate, item *b* reports that Genesis purchased plant assets of $70,000 by issuing $60,000 in notes payable to the seller and paying $10,000 in cash. The reconstructed entry for analysis of item *b* follows:

Point: Investing activities include (1) purchasing and selling long-term assets, (2) lending and collecting on notes receivable, and (3) purchasing and selling short-term investments other than cash equivalents and trading securities.

Point: Financing and investing info is available in ledger accounts to help explain changes in comparative balance sheets. Post references lead to relevant entries and explanations.

Reconstruction	Plant Assets	70,000	
	Notes Payable		60,000
	Cash		**10,000**

This entry reveals a $10,000 cash outflow for plant assets and a $60,000 noncash investing and financing transaction involving notes exchanged for plant assets.

Next, item *c* reports that Genesis sold plant assets costing $30,000 (with $12,000 of accumulated depreciation) for $12,000 cash, resulting in a $6,000 loss. The reconstructed entry for analysis of item *c* follows:

Reconstruction	**Cash**	12,000	
	Accumulated Depreciation	12,000	
	Loss on Sale of Plant Assets	6,000	
	Plant Assets		30,000

This entry reveals a $12,000 cash inflow from assets sold. The $6,000 loss is computed by comparing the asset book value to the cash received and does not reflect any cash inflow or outflow. We also reconstruct the entry for Depreciation Expense using information from the income statement.

Reconstruction	Depreciation Expense	24,000	
	Accumulated Depreciation		24,000

This entry shows that Depreciation Expense results in no cash flow effect. These three reconstructed entries are reflected in the following plant asset and related T-accounts.

Plant Assets			
Bal., Dec. 31, 2010	210,000		
Purchase	**70,000**	Sale	30,000
Bal., Dec. 31, 2011	250,000		

Accumulated Depreciation—Plant Assets			
		Bal., Dec. 31, 2010	48,000
Sale	12,000	**Depr. expense**	**24,000**
		Bal., Dec. 31, 2011	60,000

This reconstruction analysis is complete in that the change in plant assets from $210,000 to $250,000 is fully explained by the $70,000 purchase and the $30,000 sale. Also, the change in accumulated depreciation from $48,000 to $60,000 is fully explained by depreciation expense of $24,000 and the removal of $12,000 in accumulated depreciation from an asset sale. (Preparers of the statement of cash flows have the entire ledger and additional information at their disposal, but for brevity reasons only the information needed for reconstructing accounts is given.)

The third stage looks at the reconstructed entries for identification of cash flows. The two identified cash flow effects are reported in the investing section of the statement as follows (also see Exhibit 12.7 or 12.11):

Cash flows from investing activities
Cash received from sale of plant assets $12,000
Cash paid for purchase of plant assets . . . .   (10,000)

The $60,000 portion of the purchase described in item *b* and financed by issuing notes is a noncash investing and financing activity. It is reported in a note or in a separate schedule to the statement as follows:

Noncash investing and financing activity
Purchased plant assets with issuance of notes $60,000

Analysis of Other Assets

Many other asset transactions (including those involving current notes receivable and investments in certain securities) are considered investing activities and can affect a company's cash flows. Since Genesis did not enter into other investing activities impacting assets, we do not need to extend our analysis to these other assets. If such transactions did exist, we would analyze them using the same three-stage process illustrated for plant assets.

Example: If a plant asset costing $40,000 with $37,000 of accumulated depreciation is sold at a $1,000 loss, what is the cash flow? What is the cash flow if this asset is sold at a gain of $3,000? *Answers:* +$2,000; +$6,000.

Fraud ▬▬▬▬▬▬

Cash Control. For frauds involving misappropriation of assets, cash is the target over 90% of the time. Further, frauds involving cash theft are not restricted to employees stealing currency but include bank deposits, checks, bank drafts, and money orders. Following are common types of cash schemes.

- *Fraudulent disbursements* of cash include falsification of invoices to nonexistent parties and recording extra hours not really worked.
- *Skimming* of cash is most frequent in the retail industry at the point of sale when an employee receives cash from a customer but does not record it.
- *Lapping/hiking* of cash occurs when customer payments are stolen and then concealed by recording later customer payments to those accounts, and so forth; to avoid lapping, one must separate cash recordkeeping from cash custody.

Quick Check   Answer — p. 532

7. Equipment costing $80,000 with accumulated depreciation of $30,000 is sold at a loss of $10,000. What is the cash receipt from this sale? In what section of the statement of cash flows is this transaction reported?

CASH FLOWS FROM FINANCING

The fourth major step in preparing the statement of cash flows is to compute and report cash flows from financing activities. We normally do this by identifying changes in all noncurrent liability accounts (including the current portion of any notes and bonds) and the equity accounts. These accounts include long-term debt, notes payable, bonds payable, common stock, and retained earnings. Changes in these accounts are then analyzed using available information to determine their effect, if any, on cash. Results are reported in the financing activities section of the statement. **Reporting of financing activities is identical under the direct method and indirect method.**

Three-Stage Process of Analysis

We again use a three-stage process to determine cash provided or used by financing activities: (1) identify changes in financing-related accounts, (2) explain these changes using reconstruction analysis, and (3) report their cash flow effects.

Analysis of Noncurrent Liabilities

Information about Genesis provided earlier reveals two transactions involving noncurrent liabilities. We analyzed one of those, the $60,000 issuance of notes payable to purchase plant assets. This transaction is reported as a significant noncash investing and financing activity in a footnote or a separate schedule to the statement of cash flows. The other remaining transaction involving noncurrent liabilities is the cash retirement of notes payable.

Point: Financing activities generally refer to changes in the noncurrent liability and the equity accounts. Examples are (1) receiving cash from issuing debt or repaying amounts borrowed and (2) receiving cash from or distributing cash to owners.

Notes Payable Transactions   The first stage in analysis of notes is to review the comparative balance sheets from Exhibit 12.10. This analysis reveals an increase in notes payable from $64,000 to $90,000.

The second stage explains this change. Item *e* of the additional information for Genesis (page 509) reports that notes with a carrying value of $34,000 are retired for $18,000 cash, resulting in a $16,000 gain. The reconstructed entry for analysis of item *e* follows:

Reconstruction	Notes Payable	34,000	
	Gain on retirement of debt		16,000
	Cash		**18,000**

This entry reveals an $18,000 cash outflow for retirement of notes and a $16,000 gain from comparing the notes payable carrying value to the cash received. This gain does not reflect any cash inflow or outflow. Also, item *b* of the additional information reports that Genesis purchased plant assets costing $70,000 by issuing $60,000 in notes payable to the seller and paying $10,000 in cash. We reconstructed this entry when analyzing investing activities: It showed a $60,000 increase to notes payable that is reported as a noncash investing and financing transaction. The Notes Payable account reflects (and is fully explained by) these reconstructed entries as follows:

Notes Payable			
		Bal., Dec. 31, 2010	64,000
Retired notes	**34,000**	**Issued notes**	**60,000**
		Bal., Dec. 31, 2011	90,000

The third stage is to report the cash flow effect of the notes retirement in the financing section of the statement as follows (also see Exhibit 12.7 or 12.11):

Cash flows from financing activities	
Cash paid to retire notes	$(18,000)

Direct Method of Reporting Operating Cash Flows

12B

We compute cash flows from operating activities under the direct method by adjusting accrual-based income statement items to the cash basis. The usual approach is to adjust income statement accounts related to operating activities for changes in their related balance sheet accounts as follows:

P5 Compute cash flows from operating activities using the direct method.

| Revenue or expense | + or − | Adjustments for changes in related balance sheet accounts | = | Cash receipts or cash payments |

The framework for reporting cash receipts and cash payments for the operating section of the cash flow statement under the direct method is shown in Exhibit 12B.1. We consider cash receipts first and then cash payments.

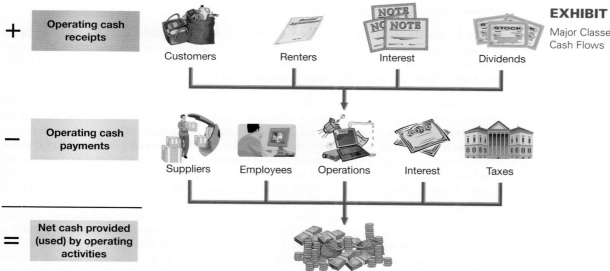

+ Operating cash receipts
Customers   Renters   Interest   Dividends

− Operating cash payments
Suppliers   Employees   Operations   Interest   Taxes

= Net cash provided (used) by operating activities

EXHIBIT 12B.1

Major Classes of Operating Cash Flows

Operating Cash Receipts   A review of Exhibit 12.10 and the additional information reported by Genesis suggests only one potential cash receipt: sales to customers. This section, therefore, starts with sales to customers as reported on the income statement and then adjusts it as necessary to obtain cash received from customers to report on the statement of cash flows.

Cash Received from Customers   If all sales are for cash, the amount received from customers equals the sales reported on the income statement. When some or all sales are on account, however, we must adjust the amount of sales for the change in Accounts Receivable. It is often helpful to use *account analysis* to do this. This usually involves setting up a T-account and reconstructing its major entries, with emphasis on cash receipts and payments. To illustrate, we use a T-account that includes accounts receivable balances for Genesis on December 31, 2010 and 2011. The beginning balance is $40,000 and the ending balance is $60,000. Next, the income statement shows sales of $590,000, which we enter on the debit side of this account. We now can reconstruct the Accounts Receivable account to determine the amount of cash received from customers as follows:

Point: An accounts receivable increase implies that cash received from customers is less than sales (the converse is also true).

Accounts Receivable			
Bal., Dec. 31, 2010	40,000		
Sales	590,000	Cash receipts =	570,000
Bal., Dec. 31, 2011	60,000		

Example: If the ending balance of accounts receivable is $20,000 (instead of $60,000), what is cash received from customers? *Answer:* $610,000

This T-account shows that the Accounts Receivable balance begins at $40,000 and increases to $630,000 from sales of $590,000, yet its ending balance is only $60,000. This implies that cash receipts from customers are $570,000, computed as $40,000 + $590,000 − [?] = $60,000. This computation can be rearranged to express cash received as equal to sales of $590,000 minus a $20,000 increase in accounts receivable. This computation is summarized as a general rule in Exhibit 12B.2. The statement of cash flows in Exhibit 12.7 reports the $570,000 cash received from customers as a cash inflow from operating activities.

EXHIBIT 12B.2

Formula to Compute Cash Received from Customers—Direct Method

$$\text{Cash received from customers} = \text{Sales} \begin{cases} + \text{ Decrease in accounts receivable} \\ \quad\quad\quad\quad\quad\quad\text{or} \\ - \text{ Increase in accounts receivable} \end{cases}$$

Other Cash Receipts   While Genesis's cash receipts are limited to collections from customers, we often see other types of cash receipts, most commonly cash receipts involving rent, interest, and dividends. We compute cash received from these items by subtracting an increase in their respective receivable or adding a decrease. For instance, if rent receivable increases in the period, cash received from renters is less than rent revenue reported on the income statement. If rent receivable decreases, cash received is more than reported rent revenue. The same logic applies to interest and dividends. The formulas for these computations are summarized later in this appendix.

Point: Net income is measured using accrual accounting. Cash flows from operations are measured using cash basis accounting.

Operating Cash Payments   A review of Exhibit 12.10 and the additional Genesis information shows four operating expenses: cost of goods sold; wages and other operating expenses; interest expense; and taxes expense. We analyze each expense to compute its cash amounts for the statement of cash flows. (We then examine depreciation and the other losses and gains.)

Cash Paid for Merchandise   We compute cash paid for merchandise by analyzing both cost of goods sold and merchandise inventory. If all merchandise purchases are for cash and the ending balance of Merchandise Inventory is unchanged from the beginning balance, the amount of cash paid for merchandise equals cost of goods sold—an uncommon situation. Instead, there normally is some change in the Merchandise Inventory balance. Also, some or all merchandise purchases are often made on credit, and this yields changes in the Accounts Payable balance. When the balances of both Merchandise Inventory and Accounts Payable change, we must adjust the cost of goods sold for changes in both accounts to compute cash paid for merchandise. This is a two-step adjustment.

First, we use the change in the account balance of Merchandise Inventory, along with the cost of goods sold amount, to compute cost of purchases for the period. An increase in merchandise inventory implies that we bought more than we sold, and we add this inventory increase to cost of goods sold to compute cost of purchases. A decrease in merchandise inventory implies that we bought less than we sold, and we subtract the inventory decrease from cost of goods sold to compute purchases. We illustrate the *first step* by reconstructing the Merchandise Inventory account of Genesis:

Merchandise Inventory			
Bal., Dec. 31, 2010	70,000		
Purchases =	314,000	Cost of goods sold	300,000
Bal., Dec. 31, 2011	84,000		

The beginning balance is $70,000, and the ending balance is $84,000. The income statement shows that cost of goods sold is $300,000, which we enter on the credit side of this account. With this information, we determine the amount for cost of purchases to be $314,000. This computation can be rearranged to express cost of purchases as equal to cost of goods sold of $300,000 plus the $14,000 increase in inventory.

The second step uses the change in the balance of Accounts Payable, and the amount of cost of purchases, to compute cash paid for merchandise. A decrease in accounts payable implies that we paid for more goods than we acquired this period, and we would then add the accounts payable decrease to cost of purchases to compute cash paid for merchandise. An increase in accounts payable implies that we paid for less than the amount of goods acquired, and we would subtract the accounts payable increase from purchases to compute cash paid for merchandise. The *second step* is applied to Genesis by reconstructing its Accounts Payable account:

Accounts Payable		
	Bal., Dec. 31, 2010	40,000
Cash payments = 319,000	Purchases	314,000
	Bal., Dec. 31, 2011	35,000

Its beginning balance of $40,000 plus purchases of $314,000 minus an ending balance of $35,000 yields cash paid of $319,000 (or $40,000 + $314,000 − [?] = $35,000). Alternatively, we can express cash paid for merchandise as equal to purchases of $314,000 plus the $5,000 decrease in accounts payable. The $319,000 cash paid for merchandise is reported on the statement of cash flows in Exhibit 12.7 as a cash outflow under operating activities.

We summarize this two-step adjustment to cost of goods sold to compute cash paid for merchandise inventory in Exhibit 12B.3.

Example: If the ending balances of Inventory and Accounts Payable are $60,000 and $50,000, respectively (instead of $84,000 and $35,000), what is cash paid for merchandise? *Answer:* $280,000

EXHIBIT 12B.3

Two Steps to Compute Cash Paid for Merchandise—Direct Method

Cash Paid for Wages and Operating Expenses (Excluding Depreciation)   The income statement of Genesis shows wages and other operating expenses of $216,000 (see Exhibit 12.10). To compute cash paid for wages and other operating expenses, we adjust this amount for any changes in their related balance sheet accounts. We begin by looking for any prepaid expenses and accrued liabilities related to wages and other operating expenses in the balance sheets of Genesis in Exhibit 12.10. The balance sheets show prepaid expenses but no accrued liabilities. Thus, the adjustment is limited to the change in prepaid expenses. The amount of adjustment is computed by assuming that all cash paid for wages and other operating expenses is initially debited to Prepaid Expenses. This assumption allows us to reconstruct the Prepaid Expenses account:

Prepaid Expenses		
Bal., Dec. 31, 2010	4,000	
Cash payments = 218,000		Wages and other operating exp. 216,000
Bal., Dec. 31, 2011	6,000	

Prepaid Expenses increase by $2,000 in the period, meaning that cash paid for wages and other operating expenses exceeds the reported expense by $2,000. Alternatively, we can express cash paid for wages and other operating expenses as equal to its reported expenses of $216,000 plus the $2,000 increase in prepaid expenses.[1]

Exhibit 12B.4 summarizes the adjustments to wages (including salaries) and other operating expenses. The Genesis balance sheet did not report accrued liabilities, but we include them in the formula to explain the adjustment to cash when they do exist. A decrease in accrued liabilities implies that we paid cash for more goods or services than received this period, so we add the decrease in accrued liabilities to the expense amount to obtain cash paid for these goods or services. An increase in accrued liabilities implies that we paid cash for less than what was acquired, so we subtract this increase in accrued liabilities from the expense amount to get cash paid.

Point: A decrease in prepaid expenses implies that reported expenses include an amount(s) that did not require a cash outflow in the period.

---

[1] The assumption that all cash payments for wages and operating expenses are initially debited to Prepaid Expenses is not necessary for our analysis to hold. If cash payments are debited directly to the expense account, the total amount of cash paid for wages and other operating expenses still equals the $216,000 expense plus the $2,000 increase in Prepaid Expenses (which arise from end-of-period adjusting entries).

EXHIBIT 12B.4

Formula to Compute Cash Paid for Wages and Operating Expenses—Direct Method

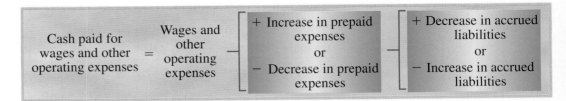

Cash paid for interest and income taxes   Computing operating cash flows for interest and taxes is similar to that for operating expenses. Both require adjustments to their amounts reported on the income statement for changes in their related balance sheet accounts. We begin with the Genesis income statement showing interest expense of $7,000 and income taxes expense of $15,000. To compute the cash paid, we adjust interest expense for the change in interest payable and then the income taxes expense for the change in income taxes payable. These computations involve reconstructing both liability accounts:

Interest Payable		
	Bal., Dec. 31, 2010	4,000
Cash paid for interest =　8,000	Interest expense	7,000
	Bal., Dec. 31, 2011	3,000

Income Taxes Payable		
	Bal., Dec. 31, 2010	12,000
Cash paid for taxes =　5,000	Income taxes expense	15,000
	Bal., Dec. 31, 2011	22,000

These accounts reveal cash paid for interest of $8,000 and cash paid for income taxes of $5,000. The formulas to compute these amounts are in Exhibit 12B.5. Both of these cash payments are reported as operating cash outflows on the statement of cash flows in Exhibit 12.7.

EXHIBIT 12B.5

Formulas to Compute Cash Paid for Both Interest and Taxes—Direct Method

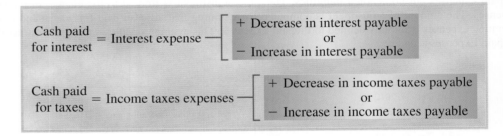

Analysis of Additional Expenses, Gains, and Losses   Genesis has three additional items reported on its income statement: depreciation, loss on sale of assets, and gain on retirement of debt. We must consider each for its potential cash effects.

Depreciation Expense   Depreciation expense is $24,000. It is often called a *noncash expense* because depreciation has no cash flows. Depreciation expense is an allocation of an asset's depreciable cost. The cash outflow with a plant asset is reported as part of investing activities when it is paid for. Thus, depreciation expense is *never* reported on a statement of cash flows using the direct method; nor is depletion or amortization expense.

Loss on Sale of Assets   Sales of assets frequently result in gains and losses reported as part of net income, but the amount of recorded gain or loss does *not* reflect any cash flows in these transactions. Asset sales result in cash inflow equal to the cash amount received, regardless of whether the asset was sold at a gain or a loss. This cash inflow is reported under investing activities. Thus, the loss or gain on a sale of assets is *never* reported on a statement of cash flows using the direct method.

Gain on Retirement of Debt   Retirement of debt usually yields a gain or loss reported as part of net income, but that gain or loss does *not* reflect cash flow in this transaction. Debt retirement results in cash outflow equal to the cash paid to settle the debt, regardless of whether the debt is retired at a gain or a loss.

Point: The direct method is usually viewed as *user friendly* because less accounting knowledge is required to understand and use it.

This cash outflow is reported under financing activities; the loss or gain from retirement of debt is *never* reported on a statement of cash flows using the direct method.

Summary of Adjustments for Direct Method   Exhibit 12B.6 summarizes common adjustments for net income to yield net cash provided (used) by operating activities under the direct method.

Item	From Income Statement	Adjustments to Obtain Cash Flow Numbers	
Receipts			
From sales	Sales Revenue	⎡ + Decrease in Accounts Receivable ⎣ − Increase in Accounts Receivable	
From rent	Rent Revenue	⎡ + Decrease in Rent Receivable ⎣ − Increase in Rent Receivable	
From interest	Interest Revenue	⎡ + Decrease in Interest Receivable ⎣ − Increase in Interest Receivable	
From dividends	Dividend Revenue	⎡ + Decrease in Dividends Receivable ⎣ − Increase in Dividends Receivable	
Payments			
To suppliers	Cost of Goods Sold	⎡ + Increase in Inventory ⎣ − Decrease in Inventory	⎡ + Decrease in Accounts Payable ⎣ − Increase in Accounts Payable
For operations	Operating Expense	⎡ + Increase in Prepaids ⎣ − Decrease in Prepaids	⎡ + Decrease in Accrued Liabilities ⎣ − Increase in Accrued Liabilities
To employees	Wages (Salaries) Expense	⎡ + Decrease in Wages (Salaries) Payable ⎣ − Increase in Wages (Salaries) Payable	
For interest	Interest Expense	⎡ + Decrease in Interest Payable ⎣ − Increase in Interest Payable	
For taxes	Income Tax Expense	⎡ + Decrease in Income Tax Payable ⎣ − Increase in Income Tax Payable	

EXHIBIT 12B.6

Summary of Selected Adjustments for Direct Method

Direct Method Format of Operating Activities Section   Exhibit 12.7 shows the Genesis statement of cash flows using the direct method. Major items of cash inflows and cash outflows are listed separately in the operating activities section. The format requires that operating cash outflows be subtracted from operating cash inflows to get net cash provided (used) by operating activities. The FASB recommends that the operating activities section of the statement of cash flows be reported using the direct method, which is considered more useful to financial statement users. *However, the FASB requires a reconciliation of net income to net cash provided (used) by operating activities when the direct method is used* (which can be reported in the notes). This reconciliation is similar to preparation of the operating activities section of the statement of cash flows using the indirect method.

Point: Some preparers argue that it is easier to prepare a statement of cash flows using the indirect method. This likely explains its greater frequency in financial statements.

 IFRS _____

Like U.S. GAAP, IFRS allows cash flows from operating activities to be reported using either the indirect method or the direct method. ●

Quick Check   Answers — p. 532

8. Net sales in a period are $590,000, beginning accounts receivable are $120,000, and ending accounts receivable are $90,000. What cash amount is collected from customers in the period?

9. The Merchandise Inventory account balance decreases in the period from a beginning balance of $32,000 to an ending balance of $28,000. Cost of goods sold for the period is $168,000. If the Accounts Payable balance increases $2,400 in the period, what is the cash amount paid for merchandise inventory?

10. This period's wages and other operating expenses total $112,000. Beginning-of-period prepaid expenses totaled $1,200, and its ending balance is $4,200. There were no beginning-of-period accrued liabilities, but end-of-period wages payable equal $5,600. How much cash is paid for wages and other operating expenses?

Refer to the data in Exercise 12-10.
Using the *direct method,* prepare the statement of cash flows for the year ended June 30, 2011.

Exercise 12-11B
Preparation of statement of cash flows (direct)
P1

Use the following information about the cash flows of Kansas Company to prepare a complete statement of cash flows (*direct method*) for the year ended December 31, 2011. Use a note disclosure for any noncash investing and financing activities.

Exercise 12-12B
Preparation of statement of cash flows (direct) and supporting note
P1

Cash and cash equivalents balance, December 31, 2010	$ 25,000
Cash and cash equivalents balance, December 31, 2011	70,000
Cash received as interest	2,500
Cash paid for salaries	72,500
Bonds payable retired by issuing common stock (no gain or loss on retirement)	187,500
Cash paid to retire long-term notes payable	125,000
Cash received from sale of equipment	61,250
Cash received in exchange for six-month note payable	25,000
Land purchased by issuing long-term note payable	106,250
Cash paid for store equipment	23,750
Cash dividends paid	15,000
Cash paid for other expenses	40,000
Cash received from customers	485,000
Cash paid for merchandise	252,500

The following summarized Cash T-account reflects the total debits and total credits to the Cash account of Texas Corporation for calendar year 2011.

(1) Use this information to prepare a complete statement of cash flows for year 2011. The cash provided or used by operating activities should be reported using the *direct method.*

(2) Refer to the statement of cash flows prepared for part 1 to answer the following questions *a* through *d*:
(*a*) Which section—operating, investing, or financing—shows the largest cash (i) inflow and (ii) outflow?
(*b*) What is the largest individual item among the investing cash outflows? (*c*) Are the cash proceeds larger from issuing notes or issuing stock? (*d*) Does the company have a net cash inflow or outflow from borrowing activities?

Exercise 12-13B
Preparation of statement of cash flows (direct) from Cash T-account
P1

```
Accounting System:                                                        _ □ ×
File  Edit  Maintain  Tasks  Analysis  Options  Reports  Window  Help

                                   Cash                                   _ □ ×
Balance, Dec. 31, 2010 .................    135,200
Receipts from customers .............. 6,000,000  Payments for merchandise ................   1,590,000
Receipts from dividends ...............   208,400  Payments for wages .............................    550,000
Receipts from land sale .................  220,000  Payments for rent ...................................    320,000
Receipts from machinery sale .......   710,000  Payments for interest .............................    218,000
Receipts from issuing stock .......... 1,540,000  Payments for taxes ................................    450,000
Receipts from borrowing .............. 2,600,000  Payments for machinery .........................  2,236,000
                                                  Payments for long-term investments ........  2,260,000
                                                  Payments for note payable .......................    386,000
                                                  Payments for dividends .........................    500,000
                                                  Payments for treasury stock ...................    218,000
Balance, Dec. 31, 2011 .................   $    ?

Sales    Purchases    General/    Payroll    Inventory    Company    Analysis
                      Ledger
```

Exercise 12-14
Reporting cash flows from
operations (indirect)
P2

Harold Company reports the following information for its recent calendar year.

Sales	$70,000
Expenses	
Cost of goods sold	40,000
Salaries expense	12,000
Depreciation expense	6,000
Net income	$12,000
Accounts receivable increase	$ 9,000
Inventory decrease	3,000
Salaries payable increase	800

Required
Prepare the operating activities section of the statement of cash flows for Harold Company using the indirect method.

Exercise 12-15
Reporting and interpreting cash
flows from operations (indirect)
P2

Oregon Company disclosed the following information for its recent calendar year.

Revenues	$100,000
Expenses	
Salaries expense	68,000
Utilities expense	28,000
Depreciation expense	29,200
Other expenses	6,800
Net loss	$ (32,000)
Accounts receivable decrease	$ 28,000
Purchased a machine	20,000
Salaries payable increase	26,000
Other accrued liabilities decrease	16,000

Required
1. Prepare the operating activities section of the statement of cash flows using the indirect method.
2. What were the major reasons that this company was able to report a net loss but positive cash flow from operations?
3. Of the potential causes of differences between cash flow from operations and net income, which are the most important to investors?

Exercise 12-16
Analyses of cash flow on
total assets A1

A company reported average total assets of $248,000 in 2010 and $302,000 in 2011. Its net operating cash flow in 2010 was $20,575 and $27,750 in 2011. Calculate its cash flow on total assets ratio for both years. Comment on the results and any change in performance.

Exercise 12-17
Cash flows spreadsheet
(indirect method)
P4

Complete the following spreadsheet in preparation of the statement of cash flows. (The statement of cash flows is not required.) Prepare the spreadsheet as in Exhibit 12A.1; report operating activities under the indirect method. Identify the debits and credits in the Analysis of Changes columns with letters that correspond to the following transactions and events *a* through *h*.
a. Net income for the year was $30,000.
b. Dividends of $10,000 cash were declared and paid.
c. Stylish's only noncash expense was $50,000 of depreciation.
d. The company purchased plant assets for $70,000 cash.
e. Notes payable of $40,000 were issued for $40,000 cash.
f. Change in accounts receivable.
g. Change in merchandise inventory.
h. Change in accounts payable.

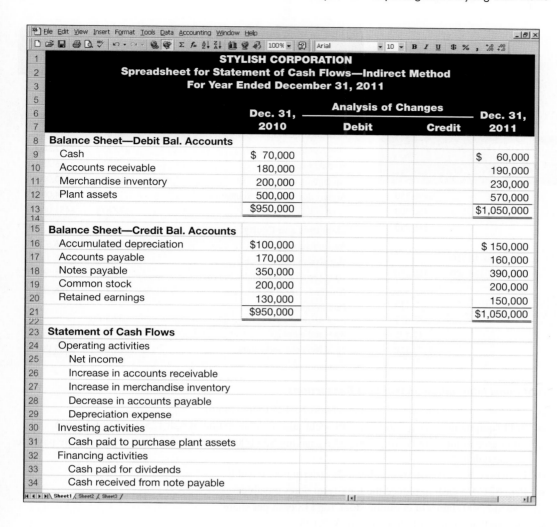

File Edit View Insert Format Tools Data Accounting Window Help

	Dec. 31, 2010	Analysis of Changes Debit	Analysis of Changes Credit	Dec. 31, 2011
Balance Sheet—Debit Bal. Accounts				
Cash	$ 70,000			$ 60,000
Accounts receivable	180,000			190,000
Merchandise inventory	200,000			230,000
Plant assets	500,000			570,000
	$950,000			$1,050,000
Balance Sheet—Credit Bal. Accounts				
Accumulated depreciation	$100,000			$ 150,000
Accounts payable	170,000			160,000
Notes payable	350,000			390,000
Common stock	200,000			200,000
Retained earnings	130,000			150,000
	$950,000			$1,050,000

STYLISH CORPORATION — Spreadsheet for Statement of Cash Flows—Indirect Method — For Year Ended December 31, 2011

Statement of Cash Flows
- Operating activities
  - Net income
  - Increase in accounts receivable
  - Increase in merchandise inventory
  - Decrease in accounts payable
  - Depreciation expense
- Investing activities
  - Cash paid to purchase plant assets
- Financing activities
  - Cash paid for dividends
  - Cash received from note payable

Peugeot S.A. reports the following financial information for the year ended December 31, 2008 (euros in millions). Prepare its statement of cash flows under the indirect method.

Exercise 12-18
Statement of cash flows under IFRS (indirect)

P1

Net loss	€ 500	Cash from sales of treasury stock and other	€	812
Depreciation and amortization	3,679	Cash paid for dividends		361
Gains on disposals and other	(362)	Cash from disposal of plant assets and intangibles		88
Net increase in current assets	(417)	Cash paid for plant assets and intangibles		(3,331)
Net decrease in current liabilities ...	(2,338)	Cash and cash equivalents, December 31, 2007		5,937

█ connect

Kazaam Company, a merchandiser, recently completed its calendar-year 2011 operations. For the year, (1) all sales are credit sales, (2) all credits to Accounts Receivable reflect cash receipts from customers, (3) all purchases of inventory are on credit, (4) all debits to Accounts Payable reflect cash payments for inventory, and (5) Other Expenses are paid in advance and are initially debited to Prepaid Expenses. The company's balance sheets and income statement follow.

PROBLEM SET A

Problem 12-1A
Statement of cash flows (indirect method)

A1 P1 P2 P3

KAZAAM COMPANY
Income Statement
For Year Ended December 31, 2011

Sales		$496,250
Cost of goods sold		250,000
Gross profit		246,250
Operating expenses		
Depreciation expense	$ 18,750	
Other expenses	136,500	155,250
Other gains (losses)		
Loss on sale of equipment		5,125
Income before taxes		85,875
Income taxes expense		12,125
Net income		$ 73,750

KAZAAM COMPANY
Comparative Balance Sheets
December 31, 2011 and 2010

	2011	2010
Assets		
Cash	$ 53,875	$ 76,625
Accounts receivable	65,000	49,625
Merchandise inventory	273,750	252,500
Prepaid expenses	5,375	6,250
Equipment	159,500	110,000
Accum. depreciation—Equipment	(34,625)	(44,000)
Total assets	$522,875	$451,000
Liabilities and Equity		
Accounts payable	$ 88,125	$116,625
Short-term notes payable	10,000	6,250
Long-term notes payable	93,750	53,750
Common stock, $5 par value	168,750	156,250
Paid-in capital in excess of par, common stock	32,500	0
Retained earnings	129,750	118,125
Total liabilities and equity	$522,875	$451,000

Additional Information on Year 2011 Transactions

a. The loss on the cash sale of equipment was $5,125 (details in b).
b. Sold equipment costing $46,875, with accumulated depreciation of $28,125, for $13,625 cash.
c. Purchased equipment costing $96,375 by paying $25,000 cash and signing a long-term note payable for the balance.
d. Borrowed $3,750 cash by signing a short-term note payable.
e. Paid $31,375 cash to reduce the long-term notes payable.
f. Issued 2,500 shares of common stock for $18 cash per share.
g. Declared and paid cash dividends of $62,125.

Required

Check Cash from operating activities, $33,375

1. Prepare a complete statement of cash flows; report its operating activities using the *indirect method*. Disclose any noncash investing and financing activities in a note.

Analysis Component

2. Analyze and discuss the statement of cash flows prepared in part 1, giving special attention to the wisdom of the cash dividend payment.

Problem 12-2A[B]
Statement of cash flows (direct method) P1 P3 P5

Check Cash used in financing activities, $(44,750)

Refer to Kazaam Company's financial statements and related information in Problem 12-1A.

Required

Prepare a complete statement of cash flows; report its operating activities according to the *direct method*. Disclose any noncash investing and financing activities in a note.

Problem 12-3A[A]
Cash flows spreadsheet (indirect method)
P1 P2 P3 P4

Refer to the information reported about Kazaam Company in Problem 12-1A.

Required

Prepare a complete statement of cash flows using a spreadsheet as in Exhibit 12A.1; report its operating activities using the indirect method. Identify the debits and credits in the Analysis of Changes columns with letters that correspond to the following list of transactions and events.

a. Net income was $73,750.
b. Accounts receivable increased.
c. Merchandise inventory increased.

d. Prepaid expenses decreased.

e. Accounts payable decreased.

f. Depreciation expense was $18,750.

g. Sold equipment costing $46,875, with accumulated depreciation of $28,125, for $13,625 cash. This yielded a loss of $5,125.

h. Purchased equipment costing $96,375 by paying $25,000 cash and **(i.)** by signing a long-term note payable for the balance.

j. Borrowed $3,750 cash by signing a short-term note payable.

k. Paid $31,375 cash to reduce the long-term notes payable.

l. Issued 2,500 shares of common stock for $18 cash per share.

m. Declared and paid cash dividends of $62,125.

Check Analysis of Changes column totals, $515,375

Galley Corp., a merchandiser, recently completed its 2011 operations. For the year, (1) all sales are credit sales, (2) all credits to Accounts Receivable reflect cash receipts from customers, (3) all purchases of inventory are on credit, (4) all debits to Accounts Payable reflect cash payments for inventory, (5) Other Expenses are all cash expenses, and (6) any change in Income Taxes Payable reflects the accrual and cash payment of taxes. The company's balance sheets and income statement follow.

Problem 12-4A

Statement of cash flows (indirect method)

P1 P2 P3

mhhe.com/wildFA6e

GALLEY CORPORATION
Comparative Balance Sheets
December 31, 2011 and 2010

Assets	2011	2010
Cash	$ 174,000	$117,000
Accounts receivable	93,000	81,000
Merchandise inventory	609,000	534,000
Equipment	333,000	297,000
Accum. depreciation—Equipment	(156,000)	(102,000)
Total assets	$1,053,000	$927,000
Liabilities and Equity		
Accounts payable	$ 69,000	$ 96,000
Income taxes payable	27,000	24,000
Common stock, $2 par value	582,000	558,000
Paid-in capital in excess of par value, common stock	198,000	162,000
Retained earnings	177,000	87,000
Total liabilities and equity	$1,053,000	$927,000

GALLEY CORPORATION
Income Statement
For Year Ended December 31, 2011

Sales		$1,992,000
Cost of goods sold		1,194,000
Gross profit		798,000
Operating expenses		
Depreciation expense	$ 54,000	
Other expenses	501,000	555,000
Income before taxes		243,000
Income taxes expense		42,000
Net income		$ 201,000

Additional Information on Year 2011 Transactions

a. Purchased equipment for $36,000 cash.

b. Issued 12,000 shares of common stock for $5 cash per share.

c. Declared and paid $111,000 in cash dividends.

Required

Prepare a complete statement of cash flows; report its cash inflows and cash outflows from operating activities according to the *indirect method*.

Check Cash from operating activities, $144,000

Refer to Galley Corporation's financial statements and related information in Problem 12-4A.

Required

Prepare a complete statement of cash flows; report its cash flows from operating activities according to the *direct method*.

Problem 12-5A[B]

Statement of cash flows (direct method) P1 P3 P5

mhhe.com/wildFA6e

Check Cash used in financing activities, $(51,000)

Problem 12-6A^A

Cash flows spreadsheet
(indirect method)

P1 P2 P3 P4

mhhe.com/wildFA6e

Refer to the information reported about Galley Corporation in Problem 12-4A.

Required

Prepare a complete statement of cash flows using a spreadsheet as in Exhibit 12A.1; report operating activities under the indirect method. Identify the debits and credits in the Analysis of Changes columns with letters that correspond to the following list of transactions and events.

  a. Net income was $201,000.

  b. Accounts receivable increased.

  c. Merchandise inventory increased.

  d. Accounts payable decreased.

  e. Income taxes payable increased.

  f. Depreciation expense was $54,000.

  g. Purchased equipment for $36,000 cash.

  h. Issued 12,000 shares at $5 cash per share.

  i. Declared and paid $111,000 of cash dividends.

Check Analysis of Changes column totals, $579,000

Problem 12-7A

Computing cash flows from operations (indirect)

P2

Rapture Company's 2011 income statement and selected balance sheet data at December 31, 2010 and 2011, follow ($ thousands).

RAPTURE COMPANY
Selected Balance Sheet Accounts

At December 31	2011	2010
Accounts receivable	$380	$390
Inventory	99	77
Accounts payable...........	120	130
Salaries payable	44	35
Utilities payable	11	8
Prepaid insurance	13	14
Prepaid rent	11	9

RAPTURE COMPANY
Income Statement
For Year Ended December 31, 2011

Sales revenue	$58,600
Expenses	
Cost of goods sold	21,000
Depreciation expense	6,000
Salaries expense	11,000
Rent expense	2,500
Insurance expense	1,900
Interest expense	1,800
Utilities expense	1,400
Net income	$13,000

Required

Prepare the cash flows from operating activities section only of the company's 2011 statement of cash flows using the indirect method.

Check Cash from operating activities, $18,989

Problem 12-8A^B

Computing cash flows from operations (direct)

P5

Refer to the information in Problem 12-7A.

Required

Prepare the cash flows from operating activities section only of the company's 2011 statement of cash flows using the direct method.

PROBLEM SET B

Problem 12-1B

Statement of cash flows
(indirect method)

A1 P1 P2 P3

Kite Corporation, a merchandiser, recently completed its calendar-year 2011 operations. For the year, (1) all sales are credit sales, (2) all credits to Accounts Receivable reflect cash receipts from customers, (3) all purchases of inventory are on credit, (4) all debits to Accounts Payable reflect cash payments for inventory, and (5) Other Expenses are paid in advance and are initially debited to Prepaid Expenses. The company's balance sheets and income statement follow.

KITE CORPORATION
Comparative Balance Sheets
December 31, 2011 and 2010

	2011	2010
Assets		
Cash	$136,500	$ 71,550
Accounts receivable	74,100	90,750
Merchandise inventory	454,500	490,200
Prepaid expenses	17,100	19,200
Equipment	278,250	216,000
Accum. depreciation—Equipment	(108,750)	(93,000)
Total assets	$851,700	$794,700
Liabilities and Equity		
Accounts payable	$117,450	$123,450
Short-term notes payable	17,250	11,250
Long-term notes payable	112,500	82,500
Common stock, $5 par	465,000	450,000
Paid-in capital in excess of par, common stock	18,000	0
Retained earnings	121,500	127,500
Total liabilities and equity	$851,700	$794,700

KITE CORPORATION
Income Statement
For Year Ended December 31, 2011

Sales		$1,083,000
Cost of goods sold		585,000
Gross profit		498,000
Operating expenses		
Depreciation expense	$ 36,600	
Other expenses	392,850	
Total operating expenses		429,450
		68,550
Other gains (losses)		
Loss on sale of equipment		2,100
Income before taxes		66,450
Income taxes expense		9,450
Net income		$ 57,000

Additional Information on Year 2011 Transactions

a. The loss on the cash sale of equipment was $2,100 (details in *b*).

b. Sold equipment costing $51,000, with accumulated depreciation of $20,850, for $28,050 cash.

c. Purchased equipment costing $113,250 by paying $38,250 cash and signing a long-term note payable for the balance.

d. Borrowed $6,000 cash by signing a short-term note payable.

e. Paid $45,000 cash to reduce the long-term notes payable.

f. Issued 3,000 shares of common stock for $11 cash per share.

g. Declared and paid cash dividends of $63,000.

Required

1. Prepare a complete statement of cash flows; report its operating activities using the *indirect method.* Disclose any noncash investing and financing activities in a note.

Check Cash from operating activities, $144,150

Analysis Component

2. Analyze and discuss the statement of cash flows prepared in part 1, giving special attention to the wisdom of the cash dividend payment.

Refer to Kite Corporation's financial statements and related information in Problem 12-1B.

Required

Prepare a complete statement of cash flows; report its operating activities according to the *direct method.* Disclose any noncash investing and financing activities in a note.

Problem 12-2B[B]
Statement of cash flows (direct method)   P1 P3 P5

Check Cash used in financing activities, $(69,000)

Refer to the information reported about Kite Corporation in Problem 12-1B.

Required

Prepare a complete statement of cash flows using a spreadsheet as in Exhibit 12A.1; report its operating activities using the *indirect method.* Identify the debits and credits in the Analysis of Changes columns with letters that correspond to the following list of transactions and events.

Problem 12-3B[A]
Cash flows spreadsheet (indirect method)

P1 P2 P3 P4

a. Net income was $57,000.

b. Accounts receivable decreased.

c. Merchandise inventory decreased.

d. Prepaid expenses decreased.

e. Accounts payable decreased.

f. Depreciation expense was $36,600.

g. Sold equipment costing $51,000, with accumulated depreciation of $20,850, for $28,050 cash. This yielded a loss of $2,100.

h. Purchased equipment costing $113,250 by paying $38,250 cash and **(i.)** by signing a long-term note payable for the balance.

j. Borrowed $6,000 cash by signing a short-term note payable.

k. Paid $45,000 cash to reduce the long-term notes payable.

l. Issued 3,000 shares of common stock for $11 cash per share.

Check Analysis of Changes column totals, $540,300

m. Declared and paid cash dividends of $63,000.

Problem 12-4B
Statement of cash flows (indirect method)
P1 P2 P3

Taurasi Company, a merchandiser, recently completed its 2011 operations. For the year, (1) all sales are credit sales, (2) all credits to Accounts Receivable reflect cash receipts from customers, (3) all purchases of inventory are on credit, (4) all debits to Accounts Payable reflect cash payments for inventory, (5) Other Expenses are cash expenses, and (6) any change in Income Taxes Payable reflects the accrual and cash payment of taxes. The company's balance sheets and income statement follow.

TAURASI COMPANY
Comparative Balance Sheets
December 31, 2011 and 2010

	2011	2010
Assets		
Cash	$ 53,925	$ 31,800
Accounts receivable	19,425	23,250
Merchandise inventory	175,350	139,875
Equipment	105,450	76,500
Accum. depreciation—Equipment	(48,300)	(30,600)
Total assets	$305,850	$240,825
Liabilities and Equity		
Accounts payable	$ 38,475	$ 35,625
Income taxes payable	4,500	6,750
Common stock, $2 par value	165,000	150,000
Paid-in capital in excess of par, common stock	42,000	15,000
Retained earnings	55,875	33,450
Total liabilities and equity	$305,850	$240,825

TAURASI COMPANY
Income Statement
For Year Ended December 31, 2011

Sales		$609,750
Cost of goods sold		279,000
Gross profit		330,750
Operating expenses		
Depreciation expense	$ 17,700	
Other expenses	179,775	197,475
Income before taxes		133,275
Income taxes expense		44,850
Net income		$ 88,425

Additional Information on Year 2011 Transactions

a. Purchased equipment for $28,950 cash.

b. Issued 3,000 shares of common stock for $14 cash per share.

c. Declared and paid $66,000 of cash dividends.

Required

Check Cash from operating activities, $75,075

Prepare a complete statement of cash flows; report its cash inflows and cash outflows from operating activities according to the *indirect method*.

Problem 12-5Bᴮ
Statement of cash flows (direct method) P1 P3 P5

Refer to Taurasi Company's financial statements and related information in Problem 12-4B.

Required

Check Cash used by financing activities, $(24,000)

Prepare a complete statement of cash flows; report its cash flows from operating activities according to the *direct method*.

Refer to the information reported about Taurasi Company in Problem 12-4B.

Problem 12-6B[A]
Cash flows spreadsheet
(indirect method)
P1 P2 P3 P4

Required

Prepare a complete statement of cash flows using a spreadsheet as in Exhibit 12A.1; report operating activities under the *indirect method*. Identify the debits and credits in the Analysis of Changes columns with letters that correspond to the following list of transactions and events.

a. Net income was $88,425.

b. Accounts receivable decreased.

c. Merchandise inventory increased.

d. Accounts payable increased.

e. Income taxes payable decreased.

f. Depreciation expense was $17,700.

g. Purchased equipment for $28,950 cash.

h. Issued 3,000 shares at $14 cash per share.

i. Declared and paid $66,000 of cash dividends.

Check Analysis of Changes column totals, $287,475

Tyra Company's 2011 income statement and selected balance sheet data at December 31, 2010 and 2011, follow ($ thousands).

Problem 12-7B
Computing cash flows from operations (indirect)
P2

TYRA COMPANY Income Statement For Year Ended December 31, 2011	
Sales revenue	$412,000
Expenses	
Cost of goods sold	244,000
Depreciation expense	64,000
Salaries expense	30,000
Rent expense	20,000
Insurance expense	5,200
Interest expense	4,800
Utilities expense	4,000
Net income	$ 40,000

TYRA COMPANY Selected Balance Sheet Accounts		
At December 31	2011	2010
Accounts receivable	$820	$700
Inventory	272	296
Accounts payable	480	520
Salaries payable	280	220
Utilities payable	40	0
Prepaid insurance	28	36
Prepaid rent	40	60

Required

Prepare the cash flows from operating activities section only of the company's 2011 statement of cash flows using the indirect method.

Check Cash from operating activities, $103,992

Refer to the information in Problem 12-7B.

Problem 12-8B[B]
Computing cash flows from operations (direct)
P5

Required

Prepare the cash flows from operating activities section only of the company's 2011 statement of cash flows using the direct method.

(This serial problem began in Chapter 1 and continues through most of the book. If previous chapter segments were not completed, the serial problem can begin at this point. It is helpful, but not necessary, to use the Working Papers that accompany the book.)

SERIAL PROBLEM
Business Solutions
P1 P2 P3

SP 12   Santana Rey, owner of Business Solutions, decides to prepare a statement of cash flows for her business. (Although the serial problem allowed for various ownership changes in earlier chapters, we will prepare the statement of cash flows using the following financial data.)

BUSINESS SOLUTIONS
Income Statement
For Three Months Ended March 31, 2012

Computer services revenue		$25,307
Net sales		18,693
Total revenue		44,000
Cost of goods sold	$14,052	
Depreciation expense— Office equipment	400	
Depreciation expense— Computer equipment	1,250	
Wages expense	3,250	
Insurance expense	555	
Rent expense	2,475	
Computer supplies expense	1,305	
Advertising expense	600	
Mileage expense	320	
Repairs expense—Computer	960	
Total expenses		25,167
Net income		$18,833

BUSINESS SOLUTIONS
Comparative Balance Sheets
December 31, 2011, and March 31, 2012

	2012	2011
Assets		
Cash	$ 68,057	$48,372
Accounts receivable	22,867	5,668
Merchandise inventory	704	0
Computer supplies	2,005	580
Prepaid insurance	1,110	1,665
Prepaid rent	825	825
Office equipment	8,000	8,000
Accumulated depreciation—Office equipment	(800)	(400)
Computer equipment	20,000	20,000
Accumulated depreciation—Computer equipment	(2,500)	(1,250)
Total assets	$120,268	$83,460
Liabilities and Equity		
Accounts payable	$ 0	$ 1,100
Wages payable	875	500
Unearned computer service revenue	0	1,500
Common stock	98,000	73,000
Retained earnings	21,393	7,360
Total liabilities and equity	$120,268	$83,460

Required

Prepare a statement of cash flows for Business Solutions using the *indirect method* for the three months ended March 31, 2012. Recall that the owner Santana Rey contributed $25,000 to the business in exchange for additional stock in the first quarter of 2012 and has received $4,800 in cash dividends.

Check Cash flows used by operations: $(515)

Beyond the Numbers

REPORTING IN ACTION

A1

 RIM

BTN 12-1 Refer to Research In Motion's financial statements in Appendix A to answer the following.

1. Is Research In Motion's statement of cash flows prepared under the direct method or the indirect method? How do you know?
2. For each fiscal year 2010, 2009, and 2008, is the amount of cash provided by operating activities more or less than the cash paid for dividends?
3. What is the largest amount in reconciling the difference between net income and cash flow from operating activities in 2010? In 2009? In 2008?
4. Identify the largest cash inflow and outflow for investing *and* for financing activities in 2010 and in 2009.

Fast Forward

5. Obtain Research In Motion's financial statements for a fiscal year ending after February 27, 2010, from either its Website (RIM.com) or the SEC's database (www.sec.gov). Since February 27, 2010, what are Research In Motion's largest cash outflows and cash inflows in the investing and in the financing sections of its statement of cash flows?

BTN 12-2 Key figures for Research In Motion and Apple follow.

($ millions)	Research In Motion			Apple		
	Current Year	1 Year Prior	2 Years Prior	Current Year	1 Year Prior	2 Years Prior
Operating cash flows	$ 3,035	$1,452	$1,577	$10,159	$ 9,596	$ 5,470
Total assets	10,204	8,101	5,511	47,501	36,171	25,347

COMPARATIVE ANALYSIS

A1

RIM

Apple

Required

1. Compute the recent two years' cash flow on total assets ratios for Research In Motion and Apple.
2. What does the cash flow on total assets ratio measure?
3. Which company has the highest cash flow on total assets ratio for the periods shown?
4. Does the cash flow on total assets ratio reflect on the quality of earnings? Explain.

BTN 12-3 Lisa Gish is preparing for a meeting with her banker. Her business is finishing its fourth year of operations. In the first year, it had negative cash flows from operations. In the second and third years, cash flows from operations were positive. However, inventory costs rose significantly in year 4, and cash flows from operations will probably be down 25%. Gish wants to secure a line of credit from her banker as a financing buffer. From experience, she knows the banker will scrutinize operating cash flows for years 1 through 4 and will want a projected number for year 5. Gish knows that a steady progression upward in operating cash flows for years 1 through 4 will help her case. She decides to use her discretion as owner and considers several business actions that will turn her operating cash flow in year 4 from a decrease to an increase.

ETHICS CHALLENGE

C1 A1

Required

1. Identify two business actions Gish might take to improve cash flows from operations.
2. Comment on the ethics and possible consequences of Gish's decision to pursue these actions.

BTN 12-4 Your friend, Jessica Willard, recently completed the second year of her business and just received annual financial statements from her accountant. Willard finds the income statement and balance sheet informative but does not understand the statement of cash flows. She says the first section is especially confusing because it contains a lot of additions and subtractions that do not make sense to her. Willard adds, "The income statement tells me the business is more profitable than last year and that's most important. If I want to know how cash changes, I can look at comparative balance sheets."

COMMUNICATING IN PRACTICE

C1

Required

Write a half-page memorandum to your friend explaining the purpose of the statement of cash flows. Speculate as to why the first section is so confusing and how it might be rectified.

BTN 12-5 Access the March 19, 2010, filing of the 10-K report (for fiscal year ending January 30, 2010) of J. Crew Group, Inc. (ticker JCG), at www.sec.gov.

TAKING IT TO THE NET

A1

Required

1. Does J. Crew use the direct or indirect method to construct its consolidated statement of cash flows?
2. For the fiscal year ended January 30, 2010, what is the largest item in reconciling the net income to net cash provided by operating activities?
3. In the recent three years, has the company been more successful in generating operating cash flows or in generating net income? Identify the figures to support the answer.
4. In the year ended January 30, 2010, what was the largest cash outflow for investing activities *and* for financing activities?
5. What item(s) does J. Crew report as supplementary cash flow information?
6. Does J. Crew report any noncash financing activities for fiscal year 2010? Identify them, if any.

TEAMWORK IN ACTION

C1 A1 P2 P5

BTN 12-6   Team members are to coordinate and independently answer one question within each of the following three sections. Team members should then report to the team and confirm or correct teammates' answers.

1. Answer *one* of the following questions about the statement of cash flows.
    a. What are this statement's reporting objectives?
    b. What two methods are used to prepare it? Identify similarities and differences between them.
    c. What steps are followed to prepare the statement?
    d. What types of analyses are often made from this statement's information?
2. Identify and explain the adjustment from net income to obtain cash flows from operating activities using the indirect method for *one* of the following items.
    a. Noncash operating revenues and expenses.
    b. Nonoperating gains and losses.
    c. Increases and decreases in noncash current assets.
    d. Increases and decreases in current liabilities.
3.ᴮIdentify and explain the formula for computing cash flows from operating activities using the direct method for *one* of the following items.
    a. Cash receipts from sales to customers.
    b. Cash paid for merchandise inventory.
    c. Cash paid for wages and operating expenses.
    d. Cash paid for interest and taxes.

Note: For teams of more than four, some pairing within teams is necessary. Use as an in-class activity or as an assignment. If used in class, specify a time limit on each part. Conclude with reports to the entire class, using team rotation. Each team can prepare responses on a transparency.

ENTREPRENEURIAL DECISION

C1 A1

BTN 12-7   Review the chapter's opener involving **Animoto** and its four young entrepreneurial owners.

Required

1. In a business such as Animoto, monitoring cash flow is always a priority. Even though Animoto now has thousands in annual sales and earns a positive net income, explain how cash flow can lag behind earnings.
2. Animoto is a closely held corporation. What are potential sources of financing for its future expansion?

C1 A1

BTN 12-8   Jenna and Matt Wilder are completing their second year operating Mountain High, a downhill ski area and resort. Mountain High reports a net loss of $(10,000) for its second year, which includes an $85,000 extraordinary loss from fire. This past year also involved major purchases of plant assets for renovation and expansion, yielding a year-end total asset amount of $800,000. Mountain High's net cash outflow for its second year is $(5,000); a summarized version of its statement of cash flows follows:

Net cash flow provided by operating activities	$295,000
Net cash flow used by investing activities	(310,000)
Net cash flow provided by financing activities	10,000

Required

Write a one-page memorandum to the Wilders evaluating Mountain High's current performance and assessing its future. Give special emphasis to cash flow data and their interpretation.

HITTING THE ROAD

C1

BTN 12-9   Visit **The Motley Fool**'s Website (Fool.com). Enter the *Fool's School* (at *Fool.com/School*). Identify and select the link *How to Value Stocks*.

Required

1. Click on *Introduction to Valuation Methods,* and then *Cash-Flow-Based Valuations.* How does the Fool's school define cash flow? What is the school's reasoning for this definition?
2. Per the school's instruction, why do analysts focus on earnings before interest and taxes (EBIT)?
3. Visit other links at this Website that interest you such as "How to Read a Balance Sheet," or find out what the "Fool's Ratio" is. Write a half-page report on what you find.

BTN 12-10   Key comparative information for Nokia (www.Nokia.com), which is a leading global manufacturer of mobile devices and services, follows (in EUR).

GLOBAL DECISION

C1

NOKIA

RIM

Apple

(Euro millions)	Current Year	1 Year Prior	2 Years Prior
Operating cash flows	3,247	3,197	7,882
Total assets	35,738	39,582	37,599

Required

1. Compute the recent two years' cash flow on total assets ratio for Nokia.

2. How does Nokia's ratio compare to Research In Motion's and Apple's ratios from BTN 12-2?

ANSWERS TO MULTIPLE CHOICE QUIZ

1. b;

Net income	$15,200
Depreciation expense	10,000
Gain on sale of land	(3,000)
Increase in inventory	(1,500)
Increase in accounts payable	2,850
Net cash provided by operations	$23,550

2. c; cash received from sale of machine is reported as an investing activity.

3. d; FASB requires cash interest paid to be reported under operating.

4. a; Cash paid for salaries and wages = $255,000 + $8,200 − $10,900 = $252,300

5. e; Increase in inventory = $112,000 − $105,000 = $7,000
Increase in accounts payable = $101,300 − $98,500 = $2,800
Cash paid for merchandise = $545,000 + $7,000 − $2,800 = $549,200

EXHIBIT 13.9

Common-Size Comparative Income Statements

RIM

RESEARCH IN MOTION
Common-Size Comparative Income Statements
For Years Ended February 27, 2010 and February 28, 2009

($ thousands)	2010	2009	Common-Size Percents* 2010	Common-Size Percents* 2009
Revenue	$14,953,224	$11,065,186	100.0%	100.0%
Cost of sales	8,368,958	5,967,888	56.0	53.9
Gross margin	6,584,266	5,097,298	44.0	46.1
Research and development	964,841	684,702	6.5	6.2
Selling, marketing, and administration	1,907,398	1,495,697	12.8	13.5
Amortization	310,357	194,803	2.1	1.8
Litigation	163,800	—	1.1	0.0
Income from operations	3,237,870	2,722,096	21.7	24.6
Investment income	28,640	78,267	0.2	0.7
Income before income taxes	3,266,510	2,800,363	21.8	25.3
Provision for income taxes	809,366	907,747	5.4	8.2
Net income	$ 2,457,144	$ 1,892,616	16.4%	17.1%

* Percents are rounded to tenths and thus may not exactly sum to totals and subtotals.

Common-Size Graphics

Two of the most common tools of common-size analysis are trend analysis of common-size statements and graphical analysis. The trend analysis of common-size statements is similar to that of comparative statements discussed under vertical analysis. It is not illustrated here because the only difference is the substitution of common-size percents for trend percents. Instead, this section discusses graphical analysis of common-size statements.

An income statement readily lends itself to common-size graphical analysis. This is so because revenues affect nearly every item in an income statement. Exhibit 13.10 shows **RIM**'s 2010 common-size income statement in graphical form. This pie chart highlights the contribution of each cost component of revenue for net income, excluding investment income.

EXHIBIT 13.10

Common-Size Graphic of Income Statement

Exhibit 13.11 previews more complex graphical analyses available and the insights they provide. The data for this exhibit are taken from **RIM**'s *Segments* footnote. RIM has at least two reportable segments: (1) United States, and (2) outside the United States (titled Non-U.S.).

EXHIBIT 13.11

Revenue and Total Asset Breakdown by Segment

EXHIBIT 13.12

Common-Size Graphic of
Asset Components

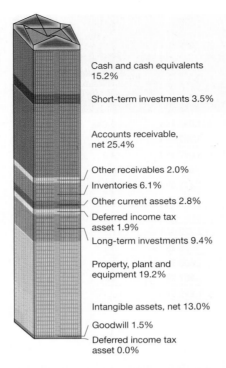

Cash and cash equivalents
15.2%

Short-term investments 3.5%

Accounts receivable,
net 25.4%

Other receivables 2.0%

Inventories 6.1%

Other current assets 2.8%

Deferred income tax
asset 1.9%

Long-term investments 9.4%

Property, plant and
equipment 19.2%

Intangible assets, net 13.0%

Goodwill 1.5%

Deferred income tax
asset 0.0%

The upper set of bars in Exhibit 13.11 shows the percent of revenues from, and the assets invested in, its U.S. segment. Its U.S. segment generates 57.7% of its revenue, while only 39.8% of its assets are in the United States. The lower set of bars shows that 42.3% of its revenue is generated outside the United States, while 60.2% of its assets are outside the United States. This can lead to questions about the revenue generated per assets invested across different countries. This type of information can help users in determining strategic analyses and actions.

Graphical analysis is also useful in identifying (1) sources of financing including the distribution among current liabilities, noncurrent liabilities, and equity capital and (2) focuses of investing activities, including the distribution among current and noncurrent assets. To illustrate, Exhibit 13.12 shows a common-size graphical display of RIM's assets. Common-size balance sheet analysis can be extended to examine the composition of these subgroups. For instance, in assessing liquidity of current assets, knowing what proportion of *current* assets consists of inventories is usually important, and not simply what proportion inventories are of *total* assets.

Common-size financial statements are also useful in comparing different companies. Exhibit 13.13 shows common-size graphics of **RIM**, **Apple** and **Nokia** on financing sources. This graphic highlights the larger percent of equity financing for RIM and Apple than for Nokia. It also highlights the much larger noncurrent (debt) financing of Nokia and Apple versus RIM. Comparison of a company's common-size statements with competitors' or industry common-size statistics alerts us to differences in the structure or distribution of its financial statements but not to their dollar magnitude.

EXHIBIT 13.13

Common-Size Graphic of Financing
Sources—Competitor Analysis

RIM

Apple

NOKIA

	RIM	Apple	Nokia
Current liabilities	23.8%	24.2%	42.5%
1.7%		9.2%	
Noncurrent liabilities			16.2%
Equity	74.5%	66.6%	41.3%

Quick Check

Answers — p. 583

5. Which of the following is true for common-size comparative statements? (*a*) Each item is expressed as a percent of a base amount. (*b*) Total assets often are assigned a value of 100%. (*c*) Amounts from successive periods are placed side by side. (*d*) All are true. (*e*) None is true.

6. What is the difference between the percents shown on a comparative income statement and those shown on a common-size comparative income statement?

7. Trend percents are (*a*) shown on comparative income statements and balance sheets, (*b*) shown on common-size comparative statements, or (*c*) also called *index numbers*.

RATIO ANALYSIS

P3 Define and apply ratio analysis.

Ratios are among the more widely used tools of financial analysis because they provide clues to and symptoms of underlying conditions. A ratio can help us uncover conditions and trends difficult to detect by inspecting individual components making up the ratio. Ratios, like other analysis tools, are usually future oriented; that is, they are often adjusted for their probable future trend and magnitude, and their usefulness depends on skillful interpretation.

A ratio expresses a mathematical relation between two quantities. It can be expressed as a percent, rate, or proportion. For instance, a change in an account balance from $100 to $250 can be expressed as (1) 150% increase, (2) 2.5 times, or (3) 2.5 to 1 (or 2.5:1). Computation of a ratio is a simple arithmetic operation, but its interpretation is not. To be meaningful, a ratio must refer to an economically important relation. For example, a direct and crucial relation exists between an item's sales price and its cost. Accordingly, the ratio of cost of goods sold to sales is meaningful. In contrast, no obvious relation exists between freight costs and the balance of long-term investments.

This section describes an important set of financial ratios and its application. The selected ratios are organized into the four building blocks of financial statement analysis: (1) liquidity and efficiency, (2) solvency, (3) profitability, and (4) market prospects. All of these ratios were explained at relevant points in prior chapters. The purpose here is to organize and apply them under a summary framework. We use four common standards, in varying degrees, for comparisons: intracompany, competitor, industry, and guidelines.

Point: Some sources for industry norms are *Annual Statement Studies* by Robert Morris Associates, *Industry Norms & Key Business Ratios* by Dun & Bradstreet, *Standard & Poor's Industry Surveys,* and Reuters.com/finance.

Liquidity and Efficiency

Liquidity refers to the availability of resources to meet short-term cash requirements. It is affected by the timing of cash inflows and outflows along with prospects for future performance. Analysis of liquidity is aimed at a company's funding requirements. *Efficiency* refers to how productive a company is in using its assets. Efficiency is usually measured relative to how much revenue is generated from a certain level of assets.

Both liquidity and efficiency are important and complementary. If a company fails to meet its current obligations, its continued existence is doubtful. Viewed in this light, all other measures of analysis are of secondary importance. Although accounting measurements assume the company's continued existence, our analysis must always assess the validity of this assumption using liquidity measures. Moreover, inefficient use of assets can cause liquidity problems. A lack of liquidity often precedes lower profitability and fewer opportunities. It can foretell a loss of owner control. To a company's creditors, lack of liquidity can yield delays in collecting interest and principal payments or the loss of amounts due them. A company's customers and suppliers of goods and services also are affected by short-term liquidity problems. Implications include a company's inability to execute contracts and potential damage to important customer and supplier relationships. This section describes and illustrates key ratios relevant to assessing liquidity and efficiency.

Working Capital and Current Ratio   The amount of current assets less current liabilities is called **working capital,** or *net working capital.* A company needs adequate working capital to meet current debts, to carry sufficient inventories, and to take advantage of cash discounts. A company that runs low on working capital is less likely to meet current obligations or to continue operating. When evaluating a company's working capital, we must not only look at the dollar amount of current assets less current liabilities, but also at their ratio. The *current ratio* is defined as follows (see Chapter 3 for additional explanation):

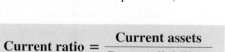

$$\text{Current ratio} = \frac{\text{Current assets}}{\text{Current liabilities}}$$

Drawing on information in Exhibit 13.1, **RIM**'s working capital and current ratio for both 2010 and 2009 are shown in Exhibit 13.14. Also, **Apple** (2.74), **Palm** (1.03), and the industry's current ratio (2.4) are shown in the margin. RIM's 2010 ratio (2.39) is between the competitors' ratios, and it does not appear in danger of defaulting on loan payments. A high current ratio suggests a strong liquidity position and an ability to meet current obligations. A company can, however, have a current ratio that is too high. An excessively high current ratio means that the company has invested too much in current assets compared to its current obligations.

($ thousands)	2010	2009
Current assets	$ 5,812,656	$ 4,841,586
Current liabilities	2,431,777	2,115,351
Working capital	$3,380,879	$2,726,235
Current ratio		
$5,812,656/$2,431,777 =	2.39 to 1	
$4,841,586/$2,115,351 =		2.29 to 1

EXHIBIT 13.14

RIM's Working Capital and Current Ratio

Current ratio
Apple = 2.74
Palm = 1.03
Industry = 2.4

An excessive investment in current assets is not an efficient use of funds because current assets normally generate a low return on investment (compared with long-term assets).

Many users apply a guideline of 2:1 (or 1.5:1) for the current ratio in helping evaluate a company's debt-paying ability. A company with a 2:1 or higher current ratio is generally thought to be a good credit risk in the short run. Such a guideline or any analysis of the current ratio must recognize at least three additional factors: (1) type of business, (2) composition of current assets, and (3) turnover rate of current asset components.

Type of business. A service company that grants little or no credit and carries few inventories can probably operate on a current ratio of less than 1:1 if its revenues generate enough cash to pay its current liabilities. On the other hand, a company selling high-priced clothing or furniture requires a higher ratio because of difficulties in judging customer demand and cash receipts. For instance, if demand falls, inventory may not generate as much cash as expected. Accordingly, analysis of the current ratio should include a comparison with ratios from successful companies in the same industry and from prior periods. We must also recognize that a company's accounting methods, especially choice of inventory method, affect the current ratio. For instance, when costs are rising, a company using LIFO tends to report a smaller amount of current assets than when using FIFO.

Composition of current assets. The composition of a company's current assets is important to an evaluation of short-term liquidity. For instance, cash, cash equivalents, and short-term investments are more liquid than accounts and notes receivable. Also, short-term receivables normally are more liquid than inventory. Cash, of course, can be used to immediately pay current debts. Items such as accounts receivable and inventory, however, normally must be converted into cash before payment is made. An excessive amount of receivables and inventory weakens a company's ability to pay current liabilities. The acid-test ratio (see below) can help with this assessment.

Turnover rate of assets. Asset turnover measures a company's efficiency in using its assets. One relevant measure of asset efficiency is the revenue generated. A measure of total asset turnover is revenues divided by total assets, but evaluation of turnover for individual assets is also useful. We discuss both receivables turnover and inventory turnover on the next page.

> **Point:** When a firm uses LIFO in a period of rising costs, the standard for an adequate current ratio usually is lower than if it used FIFO.

☐ **Decision Maker**   Answer — p. 582

Banker A company requests a one-year, $200,000 loan for expansion. This company's current ratio is 4:1, with current assets of $160,000. Key competitors carry a current ratio of about 1.9:1. Using this information, do you approve the loan application? Does your decision change if the application is for a 10-year loan? ■

Acid-Test Ratio Quick assets are cash, short-term investments, and current receivables. These are the most liquid types of current assets. The *acid-test ratio,* also called *quick ratio,* and introduced in Chapter 4, reflects on a company's short-term liquidity.

$$\text{Acid-test ratio} = \frac{\text{Cash + Short-term investments + Current receivables}}{\text{Current liabilities}}$$

RIM's acid-test ratio is computed in Exhibit 13.15. RIM's 2010 acid-test ratio (1.94) is between that for Apple (2.33) and Palm (0.94), and greater than the 1:1 common guideline for an

EXHIBIT 13.15

Acid-Test Ratio

($ thousands)	2010	2009
Cash and equivalents	$1,550,861	$ 835,546
Short-term investments	360,614	682,666
Current receivables	2,800,115	2,269,845
Total quick assets	$4,711,590	$3,788,057
Current liabilities	$2,431,777	$2,115,351
Acid-test ratio		
$4,711,590/$2,431,777	1.94 to 1	
$3,788,057/$2,115,351		1.79 to 1

Acid-test ratio
Apple = 2.33
Palm = 0.94
Industry = 1.5

acceptable acid-test ratio. The ratios for both RIM and Apple exceed the 1.5 industry norm. As with analysis of the current ratio, we need to consider other factors. For instance, the frequency with which a company converts its current assets into cash affects its working capital requirements. This implies that analysis of short-term liquidity should also include an analysis of receivables and inventories, which we consider next.

Accounts Receivable Turnover   We can measure how frequently a company converts its receivables into cash by computing the *accounts receivable turnover*. This ratio is defined as follows (see Chapter 7 for additional explanation):

$$\text{Accounts receivable turnover} = \frac{\text{Net sales}}{\text{Average accounts receivable, net}}$$

Short-term receivables from customers are often included in the denominator along with accounts receivable. Also, accounts receivable turnover is more precise if credit sales are used for the numerator, but external users generally use net sales (or net revenues) because information about credit sales is typically not reported. RIM's 2010 accounts receivable turnover is computed as follows ($ millions).

$$\frac{14{,}953{,}224}{(\$2{,}593{,}742 + \$2{,}112{,}117)/2} = 6.4 \text{ times}$$

RIM's value of 6.4 is less than that of Apple's 14.8 and Palm's 8.0. Accounts receivable turnover is high when accounts receivable are quickly collected. A high turnover is favorable because it means the company need not commit large amounts of funds to accounts receivable. However, an accounts receivable turnover can be too high; this can occur when credit terms are so restrictive that they negatively affect sales volume.

Inventory Turnover   How long a company holds inventory before selling it will affect working capital requirements. One measure of this effect is *inventory turnover*, also called *merchandise turnover* or *merchandise inventory turnover*, which is defined as follows (see Chapter 5 for additional explanation):

$$\text{Inventory turnover} = \frac{\text{Cost of goods sold}}{\text{Average inventory}}$$

Using RIM's cost of goods sold and inventories information, we compute its inventory turnover for 2010 as follows (if the beginning and ending inventories for the year do not represent the usual inventory amount, an average of quarterly or monthly inventories can be used).

$$\frac{\$8{,}368{,}958}{(\$621{,}611 + \$682{,}400)/2} = 12.84 \text{ times}$$

RIM's inventory turnover of 12.84 is less than Apple's 53.28, but similar to Palm's 13.22, and the industry's 10.1. A company with a high turnover requires a smaller investment in inventory than one producing the same sales with a lower turnover. Inventory turnover can be too high, however, if the inventory a company keeps is so small that it restricts sales volume.

Days' Sales Uncollected   Accounts receivable turnover provides insight into how frequently a company collects its accounts. Days' sales uncollected is one measure of this activity, which is defined as follows (Chapter 6 provides additional explanation):

$$\text{Days' sales uncollected} = \frac{\text{Accounts receivable, net}}{\text{Net sales}} \times 365$$

Any short-term notes receivable from customers are normally included in the numerator.

Global: Ratio analysis helps overcome currency translation problems, but it does *not* overcome differences in accounting principles.

Point: Some users prefer using gross accounts receivable (before subtracting the allowance for doubtful accounts) to avoid the influence of a manager's bad debts estimate.

Accounts receivable turnover
Apple = 14.8
Palm = 8.0
Industry = 6.6

Point: Ending accounts receivable can be substituted for the average balance in computing accounts receivable turnover if the difference between ending and average receivables is small.

Inventory turnover
Apple = 53.28
Palm = 13.22
Industry = 10.1

year—yielding a 129% increase in profit margin! This is what concerns the partner, and it suggests expanding audit tests to verify or refute the client's figures.

Banker   Your decision on the loan application is positive for at least two reasons. First, the current ratio suggests a strong ability to meet short-term obligations. Second, current assets of $160,000 and a current ratio of 4:1 imply current liabilities of $40,000 (one-fourth of current assets) and a working capital excess of $120,000. This working capital excess is 60% of the loan amount. However, if the application is for a 10-year loan, our decision is less optimistic. The

current ratio and working capital suggest a good safety margin, but indications of inefficiency in operations exist. In particular, a 4:1 current ratio is more than double its key competitors' ratio. This is characteristic of inefficient asset use.

Small Business Owner   The frost loss is probably not extraordinary. Jacksonville experiences enough recurring frost damage to make it difficult to argue this event is both unusual and infrequent. Still, you want to highlight the frost loss and hope the bank views this uncommon event separately from continuing operations.

Guidance Answers to Quick Checks

1. General-purpose financial statements are intended for a variety of users interested in a company's financial condition and performance—users without the power to require specialized financial reports to meet their specific needs.

2. General-purpose financial statements include the income statement, balance sheet, statement of stockholders' (owners') equity, and statement of cash flows plus the notes related to these statements.

3. *a*

4. Data from one or more direct competitors are usually preferred for comparative purposes.

5. *d*

6. Percents on comparative income statements show the increase or decrease in each item from one period to the next. On common-size comparative income statements, each item is shown as a percent of net sales for that period.

7. *c*

8. (*a*) ($820,000 + $240,000 + $470,000)/
    ($350,000 + $180,000) = 2.9 to 1.

(*b*) ($820,000 + $240,000)/($350,000 + $180,000) = 2:1.

9. (*a*) $2,500,000/[($290,000 + $240,000)/2] = 9.43 times.

(*b*) ($290,000/$2,500,000) × 365 = 42 days.

(*c*) $750,000/[($530,000 + $470,000)/2] = 1.5 times.

(*d*) ($530,000/$750,000) × 365 = 258 days.

10. *c*

11. *b*

12. $\text{Profit margin} \times \dfrac{\text{Total asset}}{\text{turnover}} = \dfrac{\text{Return on}}{\text{total assets}}$

    $\dfrac{\$945,000}{\$8,500,000} \quad \times \quad 1.8 \quad = \quad 20\%$

13. (*b*)

14. The four (potentially reportable) major sections are income from continuing operations, discontinued segments, extraordinary items, and earnings per share.

15. (*a*); known as retrospective application.

Key Terms

Business segment (p. 580)

Common-size financial statement (p. 563)

Comparative financial statements (p. 559)

Efficiency (p. 557)

Equity ratio (p. 571)

Extraordinary gains and losses (p. 580)

Financial reporting (p. 557)

Financial statement analysis (p. 556)

General-purpose financial statements (p. 557)

Horizontal analysis (p. 558)

Infrequent gain or loss (p. 580)

Liquidity (p. 557)

Market prospects (p. 557)

Profitability (p. 557)

Ratio analysis (p. 558)

Solvency (p. 557)

Unusual gain or loss (p. 580)

Vertical analysis (p. 558)

Working capital (p. 567)

Multiple Choice Quiz   Answers on p. 599   mhhe.com/wildFA6e

Additional quiz questions are available at the book's Website.

1. A company's sales in 2010 were $300,000 and in 2011 were $351,000. Using 2010 as the base year, the sales trend percent for 2011 is:

   a. 17%

   b. 85%

   c. 100%

   d. 117%

   e. 48%

Use the following information for questions 2 through 5.

GALLOWAY COMPANY
Balance Sheet
December 31, 2011

Assets

Cash	$ 86,000
Accounts receivable	76,000
Merchandise inventory	122,000
Prepaid insurance	12,000
Long-term investments	98,000
Plant assets, net	436,000
Total assets	$830,000

Liabilities and Equity

Current liabilities	$124,000
Long-term liabilities	90,000
Common stock	300,000
Retained earnings	316,000
Total liabilities and equity	$830,000

2. What is Galloway Company's current ratio?
   a. 0.69
   b. 1.31

   c. 3.88
   d. 6.69
   e. 2.39

3. What is Galloway Company's acid-test ratio?
   a. 2.39
   b. 0.69
   c. 1.31
   d. 6.69
   e. 3.88

4. What is Galloway Company's debt ratio?
   a. 25.78%
   b. 100.00%
   c. 74.22%
   d. 137.78%
   e. 34.74%

5. What is Galloway Company's equity ratio?
   a. 25.78%
   b. 100.00%
   c. 34.74%
   d. 74.22%
   e. 137.78%

---

^A *Superscript letter A denotes assignments based on Appendix 13A.*

🔲 Icon denotes assignments that involve decision making.

Discussion Questions

1. What is the difference between comparative financial statements and common-size comparative statements?

2. Which items are usually assigned a 100% value on (*a*) a common-size balance sheet and (*b*) a common-size income statement?

3. Explain the difference between financial reporting and financial statements.

4. 🔲 What three factors would influence your evaluation as to whether a company's current ratio is good or bad?

5. 🔲 Suggest several reasons why a 2:1 current ratio might not be adequate for a particular company.

6. 🔲 Why is working capital given special attention in the process of analyzing balance sheets?

7. 🔲 What does the number of days' sales uncollected indicate?

8. 🔲 What does a relatively high accounts receivable turnover indicate about a company's short-term liquidity?

9. 🔲 Why is a company's capital structure, as measured by debt and equity ratios, important to financial statement analysts?

10. 🔲 How does inventory turnover provide information about a company's short-term liquidity?

11. 🔲 What ratios would you compute to evaluate management performance?

12. 🔲 Why would a company's return on total assets be different from its return on common stockholders' equity?

13. Where on the income statement does a company report an unusual gain not expected to occur more often than once every two years or so?

14. Use **Research In Motion**'s financial statements in Appendix A to compute its return on total assets for fiscal years ended February 27, 2010, and February 28, 2009. Total assets at March 1, 2008, were $5,511,187 (in thousands). **RIM**

15. Refer to **Palm**'s financial statements in Appendix A to compute its equity ratio as of May 31, 2009 and May 31, 2008. **Palm**

16. Refer to **Nokia**'s financial statements in Appendix A. Compute its debt ratio as of December 31, 2009, and December 31, 2008. **NOKIA**

17. Refer to **Apple**'s financial statements in Appendix A. Compute its profit margin for the fiscal year ended September 26, 2009. Apple

■ connect

Which of the following items (1) through (9) are part of financial reporting but are *not* included as part of general-purpose financial statements? (1) stock price information and analysis, (2) statement of cash flows, (3) management discussion and analysis of financial performance, (4) income statement, (5) company news releases, (6) balance sheet, (7) financial statement notes, (8) statement of shareholders' equity, (9) prospectus.

What are four possible standards of comparison used to analyze financial statement ratios? Which of these is generally considered to be the most useful? Which one is least likely to provide a good basis for comparison?

QS 13-2
Standard of comparison   **C2**

Use the following information for Tipster Corporation to determine the 2010 and 2011 trend percents for net sales using 2010 as the base year.

QS 13-3
Trend percents
P1

($ thousands)	2011	2010
Net sales	$201,600	$114,800
Cost of goods sold	109,200	60,200

Refer to the information in QS 13-3. Use that information for Tipster Corporation to determine the 2010 and 2011 common-size percents for cost of goods sold using net sales as the base.

QS 13-4
Common-size analysis   **P2**

Compute the annual dollar changes and percent changes for each of the following accounts.

QS 13-5
Horizontal analysis
P1

	2011	2010
Short-term investments	$217,800	$165,000
Accounts receivable	42,120	48,000
Notes payable	57,000	0

For each ratio listed, identify whether the change in ratio value from 2010 to 2011 is usually regarded as favorable or unfavorable.

QS 13-6
Ratio interpretation
P3

Ratio	2011	2010	Ratio	2011	2010
1. Profit margin	8%	6%	5. Accounts receivable turnover	5.4	6.6
2. Debt ratio	45%	40%	6. Basic earnings per share	$1.24	$1.20
3. Gross margin	33%	45%	7. Inventory turnover	3.5	3.3
4. Acid-test ratio	0.99	1.10	8. Dividend yield	1%	0.8%

The following information is available for Silverado Company and Titan Company, similar firms operating in the same industry. Write a half-page report comparing Silverado and Titan using the available information. Your discussion should include their ability to meet current obligations and to use current assets efficiently.

QS 13-7
Analysis of short-term financial condition
A1

X Microsoft Excel - Book1

File Edit View Insert Format Tools Data Accounting Window Help

	Silverado			Titan		
	2012	**2011**	**2010**	**2012**	**2011**	**2010**
3 Current ratio	1.6	1.7	2.0	3.1	2.6	1.8
4 Acid-test ratio	0.9	1.0	1.1	2.7	2.4	1.5
5 Accounts receivable turnover	29.5	24.2	28.2	15.4	14.2	15.0
6 Merchandise inventory turnover	23.2	20.9	16.1	13.5	12.0	11.6
7 Working capital	$60,000	$48,000	$42,000	$121,000	$93,000	$68,000

Sheet1 / Sheet2 / Sheet3 /

Team Project: Assume that the two companies apply for a one-year loan from the team. Identify additional information the companies must provide before the team can make a loan decision.

QS 13-8ᴬ
Error adjustments
A2

A review of the notes payable files discovers that three years ago the company reported the entire amount of a payment (principal and interest) on an installment note payable as interest expense. This mistake had a material effect on the amount of income in that year. How should the correction be reported in the current year financial statements?

QS 13-9
International ratio analysis
C2

Answer each of the following related to international accounting and analysis.
a. Identify an advantage to using horizontal and vertical analyses when examining companies reporting under different currencies.
b. Identify a limitation to using ratio analysis when examining companies reporting under different accounting systems such as IFRS versus U.S. GAAP.

EXERCISES

Exercise 13-1
Building blocks of analysis
C1

Match the ratio to the building block of financial statement analysis to which it best relates.

A. Liquidity and efficiency   **C.** Profitability
B. Solvency   **D.** Market prospects

1. _____ Book value per common share
2. _____ Days' sales in inventory
3. _____ Accounts receivable turnover
4. _____ Debt-to-equity
5. _____ Times interest earned

6. _____ Gross margin ratio
7. _____ Acid-test ratio
8. _____ Equity ratio
9. _____ Return on total assets
10. _____ Dividend yield

Exercise 13-2
Identifying financial ratios
C2

1. Which two short-term liquidity ratios measure how frequently a company collects its accounts?
2. What measure reflects the difference between current assets and current liabilities?
3. Which two ratios are key components in measuring a company's operating efficiency? Which ratio summarizes these two components?

Exercise 13-3
Computation and analysis of trend percents
P1

Compute trend percents for the following accounts, using 2009 as the base year. State whether the situation as revealed by the trends appears to be favorable or unfavorable for each account.

	2013	2012	2011	2010	2009
Sales	$283,880	$271,800	$253,680	$235,560	$151,000
Cost of goods sold	129,200	123,080	116,280	107,440	68,000
Accounts receivable	19,100	18,300	17,400	16,200	10,000

Exercise 13-4
Determination of income effects from common-size and trend percents
P1 P2

Common-size and trend percents for Aziz Company's sales, cost of goods sold, and expenses follow. Determine whether net income increased, decreased, or remained unchanged in this three-year period.

	Common-Size Percents			Trend Percents		
	2012	2011	2010	2012	2011	2010
Sales	100.0%	100.0%	100.0%	104.4%	103.2%	100.0%
Cost of goods sold	62.4	60.9	58.1	102.0	108.1	100.0
Total expenses	14.3	13.8	14.1	105.9	101.0	100.0

Express the following comparative income statements in common-size percents and assess whether or not this company's situation has improved in the most recent year.

Exercise 13-5
Common-size percent computation and interpretation
P2 ♟

GERALDO CORPORATION Comparative Income Statements For Years Ended December 31, 2011 and 2010		
	2011	**2010**
Sales	$720,000	$535,000
Cost of goods sold	475,200	280,340
Gross profit	244,800	254,660
Operating expenses	151,200	103,790
Net income	$ 93,600	$150,870

Rolf Company and Kent Company are similar firms that operate in the same industry. Kent began operations in 2011 and Rolf in 2008. In 2013, both companies pay 7% interest on their debt to creditors. The following additional information is available.

Exercise 13-6
Analysis of efficiency and financial leverage
A1 ♟

	Rolf Company			Kent Company		
	2013	**2012**	**2011**	**2013**	**2012**	**2011**
Total asset turnover	3.0	2.7	2.9	1.6	1.4	1.1
Return on total assets	6.9%	6.5%	6.4%	4.3%	4.1%	3.1%
Profit margin ratio	2.3%	2.4%	2.2%	2.7%	2.9%	2.8%
Sales	$400,000	$370,000	$386,000	$200,000	$160,000	$100,000

Write a half-page report comparing Rolf and Kent using the available information. Your analysis should include their ability to use assets efficiently to produce profits. Also comment on their success in employing financial leverage in 2013.

Sanderson Company's year-end balance sheets follow. Express the balance sheets in common-size percents. Round amounts to the nearest one-tenth of a percent. Analyze and comment on the results.

Exercise 13-7
Common-size percents
P2 ♟

At December 31	2012	2011	2010
Assets			
Cash	$ 30,800	$ 35,625	$ 36,800
Accounts receivable, net	88,500	62,500	49,200
Merchandise inventory	111,500	82,500	53,000
Prepaid expenses	9,700	9,375	4,000
Plant assets, net	277,500	255,000	229,500
Total assets	$518,000	$445,000	$372,500
Liabilities and Equity			
Accounts payable	$128,900	$ 75,250	$ 49,250
Long-term notes payable secured by mortgages on plant assets	97,500	102,500	82,500
Common stock, $10 par value	162,500	162,500	162,500
Retained earnings	129,100	104,750	78,250
Total liabilities and equity	$518,000	$445,000	$372,500

Refer to Sanderson Company's balance sheets in Exercise 13-7. Analyze its year-end short-term liquidity position at the end of 2012, 2011, and 2010 by computing (1) the current ratio and (2) the acid-test ratio. Comment on the ratio results. (Round ratio amounts to two decimals.)

Exercise 13-8
Liquidity analysis
P3

Exercise 13-9
Liquidity analysis and interpretation

P3

Refer to the Sanderson Company information in Exercise 13-7. The company's income statements for the years ended December 31, 2012 and 2011, follow. Assume that all sales are on credit and then compute: (1) days' sales uncollected, (2) accounts receivable turnover, (3) inventory turnover, and (4) days' sales in inventory. Comment on the changes in the ratios from 2011 to 2012. (Round amounts to one decimal.)

For Year Ended December 31	2012		2011	
Sales		$672,500		$530,000
Cost of goods sold	$410,225		$344,500	
Other operating expenses	208,550		133,980	
Interest expense	11,100		12,300	
Income taxes	8,525		7,845	
Total costs and expenses		638,400		498,625
Net income		$ 34,100		$ 31,375
Earnings per share		$ 2.10		$ 1.93

Exercise 13-10
Risk and capital structure analysis P3

Refer to the Sanderson Company information in Exercises 13-7 and 13-9. Compare the company's long-term risk and capital structure positions at the end of 2012 and 2011 by computing these ratios: (1) debt and equity ratios, (2) debt-to-equity ratio, and (3) times interest earned. Comment on these ratio results.

Exercise 13-11
Efficiency and profitability analysis P3

Refer to Sanderson Company's financial information in Exercises 13-7 and 13-9. Evaluate the company's efficiency and profitability by computing the following for 2012 and 2011: (1) profit margin ratio, (2) total asset turnover, and (3) return on total assets. Comment on these ratio results.

Exercise 13-12
Profitability analysis

P3

Refer to Sanderson Company's financial information in Exercises 13-7 and 13-9. Additional information about the company follows. To help evaluate the company's profitability, compute and interpret the following ratios for 2012 and 2011: (1) return on common stockholders' equity, (2) price-earnings ratio on December 31, and (3) dividend yield.

Common stock market price, December 31, 2012	$15.00
Common stock market price, December 31, 2011	14.00
Annual cash dividends per share in 2012	0.30
Annual cash dividends per share in 2011	0.15

Exercise 13-13^A
Income statement categories

A2

In 2011, Jin Merchandising, Inc., sold its interest in a chain of retail outlets, taking the company completely out of the retailing business. The company still operates its wholesale outlets. A listing of the major sections of an income statement follows:

A. Income (loss) from continuing operations

B. Income (loss) from operating, or gain (loss) from disposing, a discontinued segment

C. Extraordinary gain (loss)

Indicate where each of the following income-related items for this company appears on its 2011 income statement by writing the letter of the appropriate section in the blank beside each item.

Section	Item	Debit	Credit
_____	1. Net sales		$3,000,000
_____	2. Gain on state's condemnation of company property (net of tax)		330,000
_____	3. Salaries expense	$ 640,000	
_____	4. Income taxes expense	117,000	
_____	5. Depreciation expense	432,500	
_____	6. Gain on sale of retail business segment (net of tax)		875,000
_____	7. Loss from operating retail business segment (net of tax)	544,000	
_____	8. Cost of goods sold	1,580,000	

Use the financial data for Jin Merchandising, Inc., in Exercise 13-13 to prepare its income statement for calendar year 2011. (Ignore the earnings per share section.)

Exercise 13-14ᴬ
Income statement presentation
A2

Nintendo Company, Ltd., reports the following financial information as of, or for the year ended, March 31, 2008. Nintendo reports its financial statements in both Japanese yen and U.S. dollars as shown (amounts in millions).

Exercise 13-15
Ratio analysis under different currencies

P3

Current assets	¥1,646,834	$16,468.348
Total assets	1,802,490	18,024.903
Current liabilities	567,222	5,672.229
Net sales	1,672,423	16,724.230
Net income	257,342	2,573.426

1. Compute Nintendo's current ratio, net profit margin, and sales-to-total-assets using the financial information reported in (a) yen and (b) dollars.
2. What can we conclude from a review of the results for part 1?

connect

Selected comparative financial statements of Bennington Company follow.

PROBLEM SET A

Problem 13-1A
Ratios, common-size statements, and trend percents
P1 P2 P3

mhhe.com/wildFA6e

BENNINGTON COMPANY Comparative Income Statements For Years Ended December 31, 2012, 2011, and 2010			
	2012	**2011**	**2010**
Sales	$444,000	$340,000	$236,000
Cost of goods sold	267,288	212,500	151,040
Gross profit	176,712	127,500	84,960
Selling expenses	62,694	46,920	31,152
Administrative expenses	40,137	29,920	19,470
Total expenses	102,831	76,840	50,622
Income before taxes	73,881	50,660	34,338
Income taxes	13,764	10,370	6,962
Net income	$ 60,117	$ 40,290	$ 27,376

BENNINGTON COMPANY Comparative Balance Sheets December 31, 2012, 2011, and 2010			
	2012	**2011**	**2010**
Assets			
Current assets	$ 48,480	$ 37,924	$ 50,648
Long-term investments	0	500	3,720
Plant assets, net	90,000	96,000	57,000
Total assets	$138,480	$134,424	$111,368
Liabilities and Equity			
Current liabilities	$ 20,200	$ 19,960	$ 19,480
Common stock	72,000	72,000	54,000
Other paid-in capital	9,000	9,000	6,000
Retained earnings	37,280	33,464	31,888
Total liabilities and equity	$138,480	$134,424	$111,368

Required

1. Compute each year's current ratio. (Round ratio amounts to one decimal.)
2. Express the income statement data in common-size percents. (Round percents to two decimals.)

3. Express the balance sheet data in trend percents with 2010 as the base year. (Round percents to two decimals.)

Analysis Component

4. Comment on any significant relations revealed by the ratios and percents computed.

Problem 13-2A

Calculation and analysis of trend percents

A1 P1

Selected comparative financial statements of Sugo Company follow.

SUGO COMPANY							
Comparative Income Statements							
For Years Ended December 31, 2012–2006							
($ thousands)	2012	2011	2010	2009	2008	2007	2006
Sales	$1,594	$1,396	$1,270	$1,164	$1,086	$1,010	$828
Cost of goods sold	1,146	932	802	702	652	610	486
Gross profit	448	464	468	462	434	400	342
Operating expenses	340	266	244	180	156	154	128
Net income	$ 108	$ 198	$ 224	$ 282	$ 278	$ 246	$214

SUGO COMPANY							
Comparative Balance Sheets							
December 31, 2012–2006							
($ thousands)	2012	2011	2010	2009	2008	2007	2006
Assets							
Cash	$ 68	$ 88	$ 92	$ 94	$ 98	$ 96	$ 99
Accounts receivable, net	480	504	456	350	308	292	206
Merchandise inventory	1,738	1,264	1,104	932	836	710	515
Other current assets	46	42	24	44	38	38	19
Long-term investments	0	0	0	136	136	136	136
Plant assets, net	2,120	2,114	1,852	1,044	1,078	960	825
Total assets	$4,452	$4,012	$3,528	$2,600	$2,494	$2,232	$1,800
Liabilities and Equity							
Current liabilities	$1,120	$ 942	$ 618	$ 514	$ 446	$ 422	$ 272
Long-term liabilities	1,194	1,040	1,012	470	480	520	390
Common stock	1,000	1,000	1,000	840	840	640	640
Other paid-in capital	250	250	250	180	180	160	160
Retained earnings	888	780	648	596	548	490	338
Total liabilities and equity	$4,452	$4,012	$3,528	$2,600	$2,494	$2,232	$1,800

Required

1. Compute trend percents for all components of both statements using 2006 as the base year. (Round percents to one decimal.)

Analysis Component

2. Analyze and comment on the financial statements and trend percents from part 1.

Problem 13-3A

Transactions, working capital, and liquidity ratios

P3

mhhe.com/wildFA6e

Park Corporation began the month of May with $650,000 of current assets, a current ratio of 2.50:1, and an acid-test ratio of 1.10:1. During the month, it completed the following transactions (the company uses a perpetual inventory system).

May 2   Purchased $75,000 of merchandise inventory on credit.
     8   Sold merchandise inventory that cost $58,000 for $103,000 cash.
     10 Collected $19,000 cash on an account receivable.
     15 Paid $21,000 cash to settle an account payable.

17 Wrote off a $3,000 bad debt against the Allowance for Doubtful Accounts account.
22 Declared a $1 per share cash dividend on its 40,000 shares of outstanding common stock.
26 Paid the dividend declared on May 22.
27 Borrowed $75,000 cash by giving the bank a 30-day, 10% note.
28 Borrowed $90,000 cash by signing a long-term secured note.
29 Used the $165,000 cash proceeds from the notes to buy new machinery.

Check May 22: Current ratio, 2.12; Acid-test ratio, 1.04

May 29: Current ratio, 1.82; Working capital, $320,000

Required

Prepare a table showing Park's (1) current ratio, (2) acid-test ratio, and (3) working capital, after each transaction. Round ratios to two decimals.

Selected year-end financial statements of McCord Corporation follow. (All sales were on credit; selected balance sheet amounts at December 31, 2010, were inventory, $32,400; total assets, $182,400; common stock, $90,000; and retained earnings, $31,300.)

Problem 13-4A
Calculation of financial statement ratios
P3

mhhe.com/wildFA6e

McCORD CORPORATION Income Statement For Year Ended December 31, 2011	
Sales	$348,600
Cost of goods sold	229,150
Gross profit	119,450
Operating expenses	52,500
Interest expense	3,100
Income before taxes	63,850
Income taxes	15,800
Net income	$ 48,050

McCORD CORPORATION
Balance Sheet
December 31, 2011

Assets		Liabilities and Equity	
Cash	$ 9,000	Accounts payable	$ 16,500
Short-term investments	7,400	Accrued wages payable	2,200
Accounts receivable, net	28,200	Income taxes payable	2,300
Notes receivable (trade)*	3,500	Long-term note payable, secured	
Merchandise inventory	31,150	by mortgage on plant assets	62,400
Prepaid expenses	1,650	Common stock	90,000
Plant assets, net	152,300	Retained earnings	59,800
Total assets	$233,200	Total liabilities and equity	$233,200

* These are short-term notes receivable arising from customer (trade) sales.

Required

Compute the following: (1) current ratio, (2) acid-test ratio, (3) days' sales uncollected, (4) inventory turnover, (5) days' sales in inventory, (6) debt-to-equity ratio, (7) times interest earned, (8) profit margin ratio, (9) total asset turnover, (10) return on total assets, and (11) return on common stockholders' equity.

Check Acid-test ratio, 2.3 to 1; Inventory turnover, 7.2

Summary information from the financial statements of two companies competing in the same industry follows.

Problem 13-5A
Comparative ratio analysis

A1 P3

	Ryan Company	Priest Company		Ryan Company	Priest Company
Data from the current year-end balance sheets			**Data from the current year's income statement**		
Assets			Sales	$660,000	$780,200
Cash	$ 18,500	$ 33,000	Cost of goods sold	485,100	532,500
Accounts receivable, net	36,400	56,400	Interest expense	6,900	11,000
Current notes receivable (trade)	8,100	6,200	Income tax expense	12,800	19,300
Merchandise inventory	83,440	131,500	Net income	67,770	105,000
Prepaid expenses	4,000	5,950	Basic earnings per share	1.94	2.56
Plant assets, net	284,000	303,400			
Total assets	$434,440	$536,450			
			Beginning-of-year balance sheet data		
Liabilities and Equity			Accounts receivable, net	$ 28,800	$ 53,200
Current liabilities	$ 60,340	$ 92,300	Current notes receivable (trade)	0	0
Long-term notes payable	79,800	100,000	Merchandise inventory	54,600	106,400
Common stock, $5 par value	175,000	205,000	Total assets	388,000	372,500
Retained earnings	119,300	139,150	Common stock, $5 par value	175,000	205,000
Total liabilities and equity	$434,440	$536,450	Retained earnings	94,300	90,600

Required

Check   (1) Priest: Accounts receivable turnover, 13.5; Inventory turnover, 4.5

(2) Ryan: Profit margin, 10.3%; PE, 12.9

1. For both companies compute the (*a*) current ratio, (*b*) acid-test ratio, (*c*) accounts (including notes) receivable turnover, (*d*) inventory turnover, (*e*) days' sales in inventory, and (*f*) days' sales uncollected. Identify the company you consider to be the better short-term credit risk and explain why.

2. For both companies compute the (*a*) profit margin ratio, (*b*) total asset turnover, (*c*) return on total assets, and (*d*) return on common stockholders' equity. Assuming that each company paid cash dividends of $1.50 per share and each company's stock can be purchased at $25 per share, compute their (*e*) price-earnings ratios and (*f*) dividend yields. Identify which company's stock you would recommend as the better investment and explain why.

Problem 13-6A[A]
Income statement computations and format

A2

Selected account balances from the adjusted trial balance for Zen Corporation as of its calendar year-end December 31, 2011, follow.

	Debit	Credit
a. Income taxes expense	$?	
b. Correction of overstatement of prior year's sales (pretax)	17,000	
c. Loss on sale of machinery	26,850	
d. Loss from settlement of lawsuit	24,750	
e. Other operating expenses	107,400	
f. Accumulated depreciation—Machinery		$ 72,600
g. Gain from settlement of lawsuit		45,000
h. Accumulated depreciation—Buildings		175,500
i. Loss from operating a discontinued segment (pretax)	19,250	
j. Gain on insurance recovery of tornado damage (pretax and extraordinary)		30,120
k. Net sales		999,500
l. Depreciation expense—Buildings	53,000	
m. Depreciation expense—Machinery	35,000	
n. Gain on sale of discontinued segment's assets (pretax)		35,000
o. Accounts payable		45,000
p. Interest revenue		15,000
q. Cost of goods sold	483,500	

Required

Answer each of the following questions by providing supporting computations.

1. Assume that the company's income tax rate is 30% for all items. Identify the tax effects and after-tax amounts of the four items labeled pretax.
2. What is the amount of income from continuing operations before income taxes? What is the amount of the income taxes expense? What is the amount of income from continuing operations?
3. What is the total amount of after-tax income (loss) associated with the discontinued segment?
4. What is the amount of income (loss) before the extraordinary items?
5. What is the amount of net income for the year?

Check (3) $11,025

(4) $241,325

(5) $262,409

Selected comparative financial statement information of Sawgrass Corporation follows.

PROBLEM SET B

Problem 13-1B
Ratios, common-size statements, and trend percents

P1 P2 P3

SAWGRASS CORPORATION Comparative Income Statements For Years Ended December 31, 2012, 2011, and 2010			
	2012	**2011**	**2010**
Sales	$199,800	$167,000	$144,800
Cost of goods sold	109,890	87,175	67,200
Gross profit	89,910	79,825	77,600
Selling expenses	23,680	20,790	19,000
Administrative expenses	17,760	15,610	16,700
Total expenses	41,440	36,400	35,700
Income before taxes	48,470	43,425	41,900
Income taxes	5,050	4,910	4,300
Net income	$ 43,420	$ 38,515	$ 37,600

SAWGRASS CORPORATION Comparative Balance Sheets December 31, 2012, 2011, and 2010			
	2012	**2011**	**2010**
Assets			
Current assets	$ 55,860	$ 33,660	$ 37,300
Long-term investments	0	2,700	11,600
Plant assets, net	113,810	114,660	80,000
Total assets	$169,670	$151,020	$128,900
Liabilities and Equity			
Current liabilities	$ 23,370	$ 20,180	$ 17,500
Common stock	47,500	47,500	38,000
Other paid-in capital	14,850	14,850	12,300
Retained earnings	83,950	68,490	61,100
Total liabilities and equity	$169,670	$151,020	$128,900

Required

1. Compute each year's current ratio. (Round ratio amounts to one decimal.)
2. Express the income statement data in common-size percents. (Round percents to two decimals.)
3. Express the balance sheet data in trend percents with 2010 as the base year. (Round percents to two decimals.)

Check (3) 2012, Total assets trend, 131.63%

Analysis Component

4. Comment on any significant relations revealed by the ratios and percents computed.

Problem 13-2B
Calculation and analysis of trend percents

A1 P1

Selected comparative financial statements of Deuce Company follow.

DEUCE COMPANY Comparative Income Statements For Years Ended December 31, 2012–2006							
($ thousands)	2012	2011	2010	2009	2008	2007	2006
Sales	$660	$710	$730	$780	$840	$870	$960
Cost of goods sold	376	390	394	414	440	450	480
Gross profit	284	320	336	366	400	420	480
Operating expenses	184	204	212	226	240	244	250
Net income	$100	$116	$124	$140	$160	$176	$230

DEUCE COMPANY Comparative Balance Sheets December 31, 2012–2006							
($ thousands)	2012	2011	2010	2009	2008	2007	2006
Assets							
Cash	$ 34	$ 36	$ 42	$ 44	$ 50	$ 52	$ 58
Accounts receivable, net	120	126	130	134	140	144	150
Merchandise inventory	156	162	168	170	176	180	198
Other current assets	24	24	26	28	28	30	30
Long-term investments	26	20	16	100	100	100	100
Plant assets, net	410	414	420	312	320	328	354
Total assets	$770	$782	$802	$788	$814	$834	$890
Liabilities and Equity							
Current liabilities	$138	$146	$176	$180	$200	$250	$270
Long-term liabilities	82	110	132	138	184	204	250
Common stock	150	150	150	150	150	150	150
Other paid-in capital	60	60	60	60	60	60	60
Retained earnings	340	316	284	260	220	170	160
Total liabilities and equity	$770	$782	$802	$788	$814	$834	$890

Required

Check (1) 2012, Total assets trend, 86.5%

1. Compute trend percents for all components of both statements using 2006 as the base year. (Round percents to one decimal.)

Analysis Component

2. Analyze and comment on the financial statements and trend percents from part 1.

Problem 13-3B
Transactions, working capital, and liquidity ratios P3

Check June 1: Current ratio, 3.19; Acid-test ratio, 2.21

Ready Corporation began the month of June with $280,000 of current assets, a current ratio of 2.8:1, and an acid-test ratio of 1.2:1. During the month, it completed the following transactions (the company uses a perpetual inventory system).

June 1 Sold merchandise inventory that cost $62,000 for $101,000 cash.
    3 Collected $78,000 cash on an account receivable.
    5 Purchased $130,000 of merchandise inventory on credit.
    7 Borrowed $90,000 cash by giving the bank a 60-day, 10% note.
    10 Borrowed $180,000 cash by signing a long-term secured note.
    12 Purchased machinery for $280,000 cash.
    15 Declared a $1 per share cash dividend on its 60,000 shares of outstanding common stock.
    19 Wrote off a $7,000 bad debt against the Allowance for Doubtful Accounts account.
    22 Paid $11,000 cash to settle an account payable.
    30 Paid the dividend declared on June 15.

June 30: Working capital, $59,000; Current ratio, 1.19

Required

Prepare a table showing the company's (1) current ratio, (2) acid-test ratio, and (3) working capital after each transaction. Round ratios to two decimals.

Selected year-end financial statements of Overland Corporation follow. (All sales were on credit; selected balance sheet amounts at December 31, 2010, were inventory, $16,400; total assets, $95,900; common stock, $41,500; and retained earnings, $19,800.)

Problem 13-4B
Calculation of financial statement ratios

P3

OVERLAND CORPORATION
Income Statement
For Year Ended December 31, 2011

Sales	$215,500
Cost of goods sold	136,100
Gross profit	79,400
Operating expenses	50,200
Interest expense	1,200
Income before taxes	28,000
Income taxes	2,200
Net income	$ 25,800

OVERLAND CORPORATION
Balance Sheet
December 31, 2011

Assets		Liabilities and Equity	
Cash	$ 5,100	Accounts payable	$ 10,500
Short-term investments	5,900	Accrued wages payable	2,300
Accounts receivable, net	11,100	Income taxes payable	1,600
Notes receivable (trade)*	2,000	Long-term note payable, secured	
Merchandise inventory	12,500	by mortgage on plant assets	25,000
Prepaid expenses	1,000	Common stock, $5 par value	41,000
Plant assets, net	72,900	Retained earnings	30,100
Total assets	$110,500	Total liabilities and equity	$110,500

* These are short-term notes receivable arising from customer (trade) sales.

Required

Compute the following: (1) current ratio, (2) acid-test ratio, (3) days' sales uncollected, (4) inventory turnover, (5) days' sales in inventory, (6) debt-to-equity ratio, (7) times interest earned, (8) profit margin ratio, (9) total asset turnover, (10) return on total assets, and (11) return on common stockholders' equity.

Check   Acid-test ratio, 1.7 to 1; Inventory turnover, 9.4

Summary information from the financial statements of two companies competing in the same industry follows.

Problem 13-5B
Comparative ratio analysis

A1 P3

	Loud Company	Clear Company		Loud Company	Clear Company
Data from the current year-end balance sheets			**Data from the current year's income statement**		
Assets			Sales	$395,600	$669,500
Cash	$ 22,000	$ 38,500	Cost of goods sold	292,600	482,000
Accounts receivable, net	79,100	72,500	Interest expense	7,900	12,400
Current notes receivable (trade)	13,600	11,000	Income tax expense	7,700	14,300
Merchandise inventory	88,800	84,000	Net income	35,850	63,700
Prepaid expenses	11,700	12,100	Basic earnings per share	1.33	2.23
Plant assets, net	178,900	254,300			
Total assets	$394,100	$472,400			
			Beginning-of-year balance sheet data		
Liabilities and Equity			Accounts receivable, net	$ 74,200	$ 75,300
Current liabilities	$ 92,500	$ 99,000	Current notes receivable (trade)	0	0
Long-term notes payable	95,000	95,300	Merchandise inventory	107,100	82,500
Common stock, $5 par value	135,000	143,000	Total assets	385,400	445,000
Retained earnings	71,600	135,100	Common stock, $5 par value	135,000	143,000
Total liabilities and equity	$394,100	$472,400	Retained earnings	51,100	111,700

Required

1. For both companies compute the (*a*) current ratio, (*b*) acid-test ratio, (*c*) accounts (including notes) receivable turnover, (*d*) inventory turnover, (*e*) days' sales in inventory, and (*f*) days' sales uncollected. Identify the company you consider to be the better short-term credit risk and explain why.

2. For both companies compute the (*a*) profit margin ratio, (*b*) total asset turnover, (*c*) return on total assets, and (*d*) return on common stockholders' equity. Assuming that each company paid cash dividends of $3.00 per share and each company's stock can be purchased at $25 per share, compute their (*e*) price-earnings ratios and (*f*) dividend yields. Identify which company's stock you would recommend as the better investment and explain why.

Problem 13-6B[A]

Income statement computations and format

A2

Selected account balances from the adjusted trial balance for Halogen Corp. as of its calendar year-end December 31, 2011, follow.

	Debit	Credit
a. Other operating expenses	$ 338,000	
b. Depreciation expense—Buildings	110,000	
c. Loss from settlement of lawsuit	46,000	
d. Income taxes expense	?	
e. Loss on hurricane damage (pretax and extraordinary)	74,000	
f. Accumulated depreciation—Buildings		$ 230,000
g. Accumulated depreciation—Equipment		410,000
h. Interest revenue		30,000
i. Net sales		2,650,000
j. Gain from settlement of lawsuit		78,000
k. Loss on sale of building	34,000	
l. Loss from operating a discontinued segment (pretax)	130,000	
m. Accounts payable		142,000
n. Correction of overstatement of prior year's expense (pretax)		58,000
o. Cost of goods sold	1,050,000	
p. Loss on sale of discontinued segment's assets (pretax)	190,000	
q. Depreciation expense—Equipment	166,000	

Required

Answer each of the following questions by providing supporting computations.

1. Assume that the company's income tax rate is 25% for all items. Identify the tax effects and after-tax amounts of the four items labeled pretax.

2. What is the amount of income from continuing operations before income taxes? What is the amount of income taxes expense? What is the amount of income from continuing operations?

3. What is the total amount of after-tax income (loss) associated with the discontinued segment?

4. What is the amount of income (loss) before the extraordinary items?

5. What is the amount of net income for the year?

SERIAL PROBLEM

Business Solutions

P3

(This serial problem began in Chapter 1 and continues through most of the book. If previous chapter segments were not completed, the serial problem can begin at this point. It is helpful, but not necessary, to use the Working Papers that accompany the book.)

SP 13   Use the following selected data from Business Solutions' income statement for the three months ended March 31, 2012, and from its March 31, 2012, balance sheet to complete the requirements below: computer services revenue, $25,307; net sales (of goods), $18,693; total sales and revenue, $44,000; cost of goods sold, $14,052; net income, $18,833; quick assets, $90,924; current assets, $95,568; total assets, $120,268; current liabilities, $875; total liabilities, $875; and total equity, $119,393.

Required

1. Compute the gross margin ratio (both with and without services revenue) and net profit margin ratio.

2. Compute the current ratio and acid-test ratio.

3. Compute the debt ratio and equity ratio.

4. What percent of its assets are current? What percent are long term?

Beyond the Numbers

BTN 13-1 Refer to **Research In Motion** financial statements in Appendix A to answer the following.

1. Using fiscal 2008 as the base year, compute trend percents for fiscal years 2008, 2009, and 2010 for revenues, cost of sales, operating expenses, income taxes, and net income. (Round percents to one decimal.)

2. Compute common-size percents for fiscal years 2009 and 2010 for the following categories of assets: (*a*) total current assets, (*b*) property and equipment, net, and (*c*) intangible assets. (Round to the nearest tenth of a percent.)

3. Comment on any notable changes across the years for the income statement trends computed in part 1 and the balance sheet percents computed in part 2.

Fast Forward

4. Access Research In Motion's financial statements for fiscal years ending after February 27, 2010, from its Website (**RIM.com**) or the SEC database (**www.sec.gov**). Update your work for parts 1, 2, and 3 using the new information accessed.

REPORTING IN ACTION
A1 P1 P2

RIM

BTN 13-2 Key figures for **Research In Motion** and **Apple** follow.

($ millions)	Research In Motion	Apple
Cash and equivalents	$ 1,551	$ 5,263
Accounts receivable, net	2,594	3,361
Inventories	622	455
Retained earnings	5,274	23,353
Cost of sales	8,369	25,683
Revenues	14,953	42,905
Total assets	10,204	47,501

COMPARATIVE ANALYSIS
C2 P2
RIM
Apple

Required

1. Compute common-size percents for each of the companies using the data provided. (Round percents to one decimal.)
2. Which company retains a higher portion of cumulative net income in the company?
3. Which company has a higher gross margin ratio on sales?
4. Which company holds a higher percent of its total assets as inventory?

BTN 13-3 As Baldwin Company controller, you are responsible for informing the board of directors about its financial activities. At the board meeting, you present the following information.

ETHICS CHALLENGE
A1

	2011	2010	2009
Sales trend percent	147.0%	135.0%	100.0%
Selling expenses to sales	10.1%	14.0%	15.6%
Sales to plant assets ratio	3.8 to 1	3.6 to 1	3.3 to 1
Current ratio	2.9 to 1	2.7 to 1	2.4 to 1
Acid-test ratio	1.1 to 1	1.4 to 1	1.5 to 1
Inventory turnover	7.8 times	9.0 times	10.2 times
Accounts receivable turnover	7.0 times	7.7 times	8.5 times
Total asset turnover	2.9 times	2.9 times	3.3 times
Return on total assets	10.4%	11.0%	13.2%
Return on stockholders' equity.........	10.7%	11.5%	14.1%
Profit margin ratio	3.6%	3.8%	4.0%

RIM—<u>SELECTED</u> Notes to the Consolidated Financial Statements

$US in thousands, except share and per share data, and where otherwise indicated

1. RESEARCH IN MOTION LIMITED AND SUMMARY OF SIGNIFICANT ACCOUNTING POLICIES

Research In Motion Limited ("RIM" or the "Company") is a leading designer, manufacturer and marketer of innovative wireless solutions for the worldwide mobile communications market. Through the development of integrated hardware, software and services that support multiple wireless network standards, RIM provides platforms and solutions for seamless access to time-sensitive information including email, phone, short messaging service (SMS), Internet and intranet-based applications. RIM technology also enables a broad array of third party developers and manufacturers to enhance their products and services with wireless connectivity to data. RIM's portfolio of award-winning products, services and embedded technologies are used by thousands of organizations and millions of consumers around the world and include the BlackBerry wireless solution, and other software and hardware. The Company's sales and marketing efforts include collaboration with strategic partners and distribution channels, as well as its own supporting sales and marketing teams, to promote the sale of its products and services.

Basis of presentation and preparation

The consolidated financial statements include the accounts of all subsidiaries of the Company with intercompany transactions and balances eliminated on consolidation. All of the Company's subsidiaries are wholly-owned. These consolidated financial statements have been prepared by management in accordance with United States generally accepted accounting principles ("U.S. GAAP") on a basis consistent for all periods presented except as described in note 2. Certain of the comparative figures have been reclassified to conform to the current year presentation. The Company's fiscal year end date is the 52 or 53 weeks ending on the last Saturday of February, or the first Saturday of March. The fiscal years ended February 27, 2010, February 28, 2009, and March 1, 2008 comprise 52 weeks.

The significant accounting policies used in these U.S. GAAP consolidated financial statements are as follows:

Use of estimates

The preparation of the consolidated financial statements requires management to make estimates and assumptions with respect to the reported amounts of assets, liabilities, revenues and expenses and the disclosure of contingent assets and liabilities. Significant areas requiring the use of management estimates relate to the determination of reserves for various litigation claims, provisions for excess and obsolete inventories and liabilities for purchase commitments with contract manufacturers and suppliers, fair values of assets acquired and liabilities assumed in business combinations, royalties, amortization expense, implied fair value of goodwill, provision for income taxes, realization of deferred income tax assets and the related components of the valuation allowance, provisions for warranty and the fair values of financial instruments. Actual results could differ from these estimates.

Foreign currency translation

The U.S. dollar is the functional and reporting currency of the Company. Foreign currency denominated assets and liabilities of the Company and all of its subsidiaries are translated into U.S. dollars. Accordingly, monetary assets and liabilities are translated using the exchange rates in effect at the consolidated balance sheet date and revenues and expenses at the rates of exchange prevailing when the transactions occurred. Remeasurement adjustments are included in income. Non-monetary assets and liabilities are translated at historical exchange rates.

Cash and cash equivalents

Cash and cash equivalents consist of balances with banks and liquid investments with maturities of three months or less at the date of acquisition.

Accounts receivable, net

The accounts receivable balance which reflects invoiced and accrued revenue is presented net of an allowance for doubtful accounts. The allowance for doubtful accounts reflects estimates of probable losses in accounts receivables. The Company is dependent on a number of significant customers and on large complex contracts with respect to sales of the majority of its products, software and services. The Company expects the majority of its accounts receivable balances to continue to come from large customers as it sells the majority of its devices and software products and service relay access through network carriers and resellers rather than directly.

The Company evaluates the collectability of its accounts receivables based upon a combination of factors on a periodic basis such as specific credit risk of its customers, historical trends and economic circumstances. The Company, in the normal course of business, monitors the financial condition of its customers and reviews the credit history of each new

$US in thousands, except share and per share data, and where otherwise indicated

Intangible assets, net

Intangible assets are stated at cost less accumulated amortization and are comprised of acquired technology, licenses, and patents. Acquired technology consists of purchased developed technology arising from the Company's business acquisitions. Licenses include licenses or agreements that the Company has negotiated with third parties upon use of third parties' technology. Patents comprise trademarks, internally developed patents, as well as individual patents or portfolios of patents acquired from third parties. Costs capitalized and subsequently amortized include all costs necessary to acquire intellectual property, such as patents and trademarks, as well as legal defense costs arising out of the assertion of any Company-owned patents.

Intangible assets are amortized as follows:

Acquired technology	Straight-line over 2 to 5 years
Licenses	Straight-line over terms of the license agreements or on a per unit basis based upon the anticipated number of units sold during the terms, subject to a maximum of 5 years
Patents	Straight-line over 17 years or over estimated useful life

Goodwill

Goodwill represents the excess of the purchase price of business acquisitions over the fair value of identifiable net assets acquired. Goodwill is allocated as at the date of the business combination. Goodwill is not amortized, but is tested for impairment annually, or more frequently if events or changes in circumstances indicate the asset may be impaired.

Impairment of long-lived assets

The Company reviews long-lived assets such as property, plant and equipment and intangible assets with finite useful lives for impairment whenever events or changes in circumstances indicate that the carrying amount may not be recoverable. If the total of the expected undiscounted future cash flows is less than the carrying amount of the asset, a loss is recognized for the excess of the carrying amount over the fair value of the asset.

Income taxes

The Company uses the liability method of tax allocation to account for income taxes. Deferred income tax assets and liabilities are recognized based upon temporary differences between the financial reporting and tax bases of assets and liabilities, and measured using enacted tax rates and laws that will be in effect when the differences are expected to reverse. The Company records a valuation allowance to reduce deferred income tax assets to the amount that is more likely than not to be realized. The Company considers both positive evidence and negative evidence, to determine whether, based upon the weight of that evidence, a valuation allowance is required. Judgment is required in considering the relative impact of negative and positive evidence.

Revenue recognition

The Company recognizes revenue when it is realized or realizable and earned. The Company considers revenue realized or realizable and earned when it has persuasive evidence of an arrangement, the product has been delivered or the services have been provided to the customer, the sales price is fixed or determinable and collectability is reasonably assured. In addition to this general policy, the following paragraphs describe the specific revenue recognition policies for each major category of revenue.

Devices

Revenue from the sales of BlackBerry devices is recognized when title is transferred to the customer and all significant contractual obligations that affect the customer's final acceptance have been fulfilled. For hardware products for which software is deemed not to be incidental, the Company recognizes revenue in accordance with industry specific software revenue recognition guidance. The Company records reductions to revenue for estimated commitments related to price protection and for customer incentive programs, including reseller and end-user rebates. The estimated cost of the incentive programs are accrued based on historical experience, as a reduction to revenue in the period the Company has sold the product and committed to a plan. Price protection is accrued as a reduction to revenue based on estimates of future price reductions and certain agreed customer inventories at the date of the price adjustment. In addition, provisions are made at the time of sale for warranties and royalties.

Service

Revenue from service is recognized rateably on a monthly basis when the service is provided. In instances where the Company bills the customer prior to performing the service, the prebilling is recorded as deferred revenue.

Software

Revenue from licensed software is recognized at the inception of the license term and in accordance with industry

$US in thousands, except share and per share data, and where otherwise indicated

specific software revenue recognition guidance. When the fair value of a delivered element has not been established, the Company uses the residual method to recognize revenue if the fair value of undelivered elements is determinable. Revenue from software maintenance, unspecified upgrades and technical support contracts is recognized over the period that such items are delivered or that services are provided.

Other

Revenue from the sale of accessories is recognized when title is transferred to the customer and all significant contractual obligations that affect the customer's final acceptance have been fulfilled. Technical support ("T-Support") contracts extending beyond the current period are recorded as deferred revenue. Revenue from repair and maintenance programs is recognized when the service is delivered which is when the title is transferred to the customer and all significant contractual obligations that affect the customer's final acceptance have been fulfilled. Revenue for non-recurring engineering contracts is recognized as specific contract milestones are met. The attainment of milestones approximates actual performance.

Shipping and handling costs

Shipping and handling costs charged to income are included in cost of sales where they can be reasonably attributed to certain revenue; otherwise they are included in selling, marketing and administration.

Multiple-element arrangements

The Company enters into transactions that represent multiple-element arrangements which may include any combination of hardware and/or service or software and T-Support. These multiple-element arrangements are assessed to determine whether they can be separated into more than one unit of accounting or element for the purpose of revenue recognition. When the appropriate criteria for separating revenue into more than one unit of accounting is met and there is vendor specific objective evidence of fair value for all units of accounting or elements in an arrangement, the arrangement consideration is allocated to the separate units of accounting or elements based on each unit's relative fair value. When the fair value of a delivered element has not been established, the Company uses the residual method to recognize revenue if the fair value of undelivered elements is determinable. This vendor specific objective evidence of fair value is established through prices charged for each revenue element when that element is sold separately. The revenue recognition policies described above are then applied to each unit of accounting.

Research and development

Research costs are expensed as incurred. Development costs for BlackBerry devices and licensed software to be sold, leased or otherwise marketed are subject to capitalization beginning when a product's technological feasibility has been established and ending when a product is available for general release to customers. The Company's products are generally released soon after technological feasibility has been established and therefore costs incurred subsequent to achievement of technological feasibility are not significant and have been expensed as incurred.

Comprehensive income (loss)

Comprehensive income (loss) is defined as the change in net assets of a business enterprise during a period from transactions and other events and circumstances from non-owner sources and includes all changes in equity during a period except those resulting from investments by owners and distributions to owners. The Company's reportable items of comprehensive income are cash flow hedges and changes in the fair value of available-for-sale investments. Realized gains or losses on available-for-sale investments are reclassified into investment income using the specific identification basis.

Earnings per share

Earnings per share is calculated based on the weighted-average number of shares outstanding during the year. The treasury stock method is used for the calculation of the dilutive effect of stock options.

Stock-based compensation plans

The Company has stock-based compensation plans.

Warranty

The Company provides for the estimated costs of product warranties at the time revenue is recognized. BlackBerry devices are generally covered by a time-limited warranty for varying periods of time. The Company's warranty obligation is affected by product failure rates, differences in warranty periods, regulatory developments with respect to warranty obligations in the countries in which the Company carries on business, freight expense, and material usage and other related repair costs. The Company's estimates of costs are based upon historical experience and expectations of future return rates and unit warranty repair cost. If the Company experiences increased or decreased warranty activity, or increased or decreased costs associated with servicing those obligations, revisions to the estimated warranty liability would be recognized in the reporting period when such revisions are made.

Advertising costs

The Company expenses all advertising costs as incurred. These costs are included in selling, marketing, and administration.

$US in thousands, except share and per share data, and where otherwise indicated

4.   CASH, CASH EQUIVALENTS AND INVESTMENTS
The components of cash, cash equivalents and investments were as follows:

	Cost Basis	Unrealized Gains	Unrealized Losses	Recorded Basis	Cash and Cash Equivalents	Short-term Investments	Long-term Investments
As at February 27, 2010							
Bank balances	$ 535,445	$ —	$ —	$ 535,445	$ 535,445	$ —	$ —
Money market fund	3,278	—	—	3,278	3,278	—	—
Bankers acceptances and term deposits/certificates	377,596	—	—	377,596	377,596	—	—
Commercial paper and corporate notes/bonds	855,145	6,528	(49)	861,624	472,312	187,369	201,943
Treasury bills/notes	203,514	129	(12)	203,631	92,272	50,786	60,573
Government sponsored enterprise notes	447,131	2,590	(13)	449,708	69,958	111,977	267,773
Asset-backed securities	393,751	5,280	(50)	398,981	—	10,482	388,499
Auction-rate securities	40,527	—	(7,688)	32,839	—	—	32,839
Other investments	6,621	—	—	6,621	—	—	6,621
	$2,863,008	$14,527	$ (7,812)	$2,869,723	$1,550,861	$360,614	$958,248

Realized gains and losses on available-for-sale securities comprise the following:

For the year ended	February 27, 2010	February 28, 2009	March 1, 2008
Realized gains	$439	$ 158	$ 10
Realized losses	(17)	(1,801)	(410)
Net realized gains (losses)	$422	$(1,643)	$(400)

The contractual maturities of available-for-sale investments at February 27, 2010 were as follows:

	Cost Basis	Fair Value
Due in one year or less	$1,371,047	$1,372,752
Due in one to five years	773,471	783,451
Due after five years	173,146	168,176
No fixed maturity date	3,278	3,278
	$2,320,942	$2,327,657

5.   FAIR VALUE MEASUREMENTS

The Company defines fair value as the price that would be received to sell an asset or paid to transfer a liability in an orderly transaction between market participants at the measurement date. When determining the fair value measurements for assets and liabilities required to be recorded at fair value, the Company considers the principal or most advantageous market in which it would transact and considers assumptions that market participants would use in pricing the asset or liability such as inherent risk, non-performance risk, and credit risk. The Company applies the following fair value hierarchy, which prioritizes the inputs used in the valuation methodologies in measuring fair value into three levels:

- Level 1 — Unadjusted quoted prices at the measurement date for identical assets or liabilities in active markets.

- Level 2 — Observable inputs other than quoted prices included in Level 1, such as quoted prices for similar assets and liabilities in active markets; quoted prices for identical or similar assets and liabilities in markets that are not active; or other inputs that are observable or can be corroborated by observable market data.

- Level 3 — Significant unobservable inputs which are supported by little or no market activity.

The fair value hierarchy also requires the Company to maximize the use of observable inputs and minimize the use of unobservable inputs when measuring fair value. The carrying amounts of the Company's cash and cash equivalents, accounts receivable, other receivables, accounts payable and accrued liabilities, approximate fair value due to their short maturities. When determining the fair value of its investments held, the Company primarily relies on an independent third party valuator for the fair valuation of securities.

$US in thousands, except share and per share data, and where otherwise indicated

6. INVENTORIES

Inventories were comprised as follows:

	February 27, 2010	February 28, 2009
Raw materials	$ 490,063	$464,497
Work in process	231,939	250,728
Finished goods	17,068	35,264
Provision for excess and obsolete inventories	(117,459)	(68,089)
	$ 621,611	$682,400

7. PROPERTY, PLANT AND EQUIPMENT, NET

Property, plant and equipment were comprised of the following:

February 27, 2010	Cost	Accumulated amortization	Net book value
Land	$ 104,254	$ —	$ 104,254
Buildings, leaseholds and other	926,747	115,216	811,531
BlackBerry operations and other information technology	1,152,637	484,180	668,457
Manufacturing equipment, research and development equipment, and tooling	347,692	182,228	165,464
Furniture and fixtures	346,641	139,766	206,875
	$2,877,971	$921,390	$1,956,581

As at February 27, 2010, the carrying amount of assets under construction was $254.3 million (February 28, 2009 — $88.9 million). Of this amount, $110.9 million (February 28, 2009 — $50.0 million) was included in buildings, leaseholds and other; $102.5 million (February 28, 2009 - $35.8 million) was included in BlackBerry operations and other information technology; and $40.9 million (February 28, 2009 — $3.2 million) was included in manufacturing equipment, research and development equipment, and tooling. As at February 27, 2010, $31.7 million has been classified as an asset held for sale and accordingly has been reclassified from property, plant and equipment to other current assets. For the year ended February 27, 2010, amortization expense related to property, plant and equipment was $344.5 million (February 28, 2009 — $203.4 million; March 1, 2008 — $133.1 million).

8. INTANGIBLE ASSETS, NET

Intangible assets were comprised of the following:

February 27, 2010	Cost	Accumulated amortization	Net book value
Acquired technology	$ 165,791	$ 70,777	$ 95,014
Licenses	711,969	196,618	515,351
Patents	889,467	173,469	715,998
	$1,767,227	$440,864	$1,326,363

For the year ended February 27, 2010, amortization expense related to intangible assets was $271.1 million (February 28, 2009 — $124.5 million; March 1, 2008 — $44.3 million). Total additions to intangible assets in fiscal 2010 were $531.0 million (2009 — $721.1 million). Based on the carrying value of the identified intangible assets as at February 27, 2010 and assuming no subsequent impairment of the underlying assets, the annual amortization expense for the next five fiscal years is expected to be as follows: 2011 — $324 million; 2012 — $275 million; 2013 — $227 million; 2014 — $139 million; and 2015 — $61 million. The weighted-average remaining useful life of the acquired technology is 3.4 years (2009 – 3.7 years).

$US in thousands, except share and per share data, and where otherwise indicated

10. INCOME TAXES

The difference between the amount of the provision for income taxes and the amount computed by multiplying income before income taxes by the statutory Canadian tax rate is reconciled as follows:

For the year ended	February 27, 2010	February 28, 2009
Statutory Canadian tax rate	32.8%	33.4%
Expected income tax provision	$1,072,395	$935,881
Differences in income taxes resulting from:		
Impact of Canadian U.S. dollar functional currency election	(145,000)	—
Investment tax credits	(101,214)	(81,173)
Manufacturing and processing activities	(52,053)	(49,808)
Foreign exchange	2,837	99,575
Foreign tax rate differences	5,291	(16,273)
Non-deductible stock compensation	9,600	10,500
Adjustments to deferred tax balances for enacted changes in tax laws and rates	7,927	1,260
Other differences	9,583	7,785
	$ 809,366	$907,747

11. CAPITAL STOCK

(a) Capital stock

The Company is authorized to issue an unlimited number of non-voting, redeemable, retractable Class A common shares, an unlimited number of voting common shares and an unlimited number of non-voting, cumulative, redeemable, retractable preferred shares. At February 27, 2010 and February 28, 2009, there were no Class A common shares or preferred shares outstanding. The Company declared a 3-for-1 stock split of the Company's outstanding common shares on June 28, 2007. The stock split was implemented by way of a stock dividend. Shareholders received an additional two common shares of the Company for each common share held. The stock dividend was paid on August 20, 2007 to common shareholders of record at the close of business on August 17, 2007. All share, earnings per share and stock option data have been adjusted to reflect this stock dividend.

The following details the changes in issued and outstanding common shares for the year ended February 27, 2010:

	Capital Stock		Treasury Stock	
	Stock Outstanding (000's)	Amount	Stock Outstanding (000's)	Amount
Common shares outstanding as at February 28, 2009	566,219	2,208,235	—	—
Exercise of stock options	3,408	30,246	—	—
Conversion of restricted share units	2	—	—	—
Transfers to capital stock resulting from stock option exercises	—	15,647	—	—
Restricted share unit plan purchase of shares	—	—	1,459	(94,463)
Common shares repurchased	(12,300)	(46,519)	—	—
Common shares outstanding as at February 27, 2010	557,329	$2,207,609	1,459	$(94,463)

On November 4, 2009, the Company's Board of Directors authorized a Common Share Repurchase Program for the repurchase and cancellation, through the facilities of the NASDAQ Stock Market, common shares having an aggregate purchase price of up to $1.2 billion, or approximately 21 million common shares based on trading prices at the time of the authorization. This represents approximately 3.6% of the outstanding common shares of the Company at the time of the authorization. All common shares repurchased by the Company pursuant to the Common Share Repurchase Program have been cancelled. The Common Share Repurchase Program will remain in place for up to 12 months from November 4, 2009 or until the purchases are completed or the program is terminated by the Company.

(b) Stock-based compensation

Stock Option Plan

The Company recorded a charge to income and a credit to paid-in-capital of $37.0 million in fiscal 2010 (fiscal 2009 — $38.1 million; fiscal 2008 — $33.7 million) in relation to stock-based compensation expense.

The Company has not paid a dividend in the previous twelve fiscal years and has no current expectation of paying cash dividends on its common shares.

Restricted Share Unit Plan

During fiscal 2010, the trustee purchased 1,458,950 common shares for total consideration of approximately $94.5 million

$US in thousands, except share and per share data, and where otherwise indicated

to comply with its obligations to deliver shares upon vesting. These purchased shares are classified as treasury stock for accounting purposes and included in the shareholders' equity section of the Company's consolidated balance sheet. The Company recorded compensation expense with respect to RSUs of $21.0 million in the year ended February 27, 2010 (February 28, 2009 — $196; March 1, 2008 — $33).

Deferred Share Unit Plan

The Company issued 14,593 DSUs in the year ended February 27, 2010. There are 34,801 DSUs outstanding as at February 27, 2010 (February 28, 2009 — 20,208). The Company had a liability of $2.5 million in relation to the DSU plan as at February 27, 2010 (February 28, 2009 — $834).

12.   COMMITMENTS AND CONTINGENCIES

(a) Credit Facility

The Company has $150.0 million in unsecured demand credit facilities (the "Facilities") to support and secure operating and financing requirements. As at February 27, 2010, the Company has utilized $6.9 million of the Facilities for outstanding letters of credit, and $143.1 million of the Facilities are unused.

(b) Lease commitments

The Company is committed to future minimum annual lease payments under operating leases as follows:

	Real Estate	Equipment and other	Total
For the years ending			
2011	$ 35,088	$1,917	$ 37,005
2012	30,611	1,202	31,813
2013	27,841	163	28,004
2014	26,178	—	26,178
2015	21,755	—	21,755
Thereafter	63,631	—	63,631
	$205,104	$3,282	$208,386

For the year ended February 27, 2010, the Company incurred rental expense of $39.6 million (February 28, 2009 — $22.7 million; March 1, 2008 — $15.5 million).

(c) Litigation

The Company is involved in litigation in the normal course of its business, both as a defendant and as a plaintiff. The Company may be subject to claims (including claims related to patent infringement, purported class actions and derivative actions) either directly or through indemnities against these claims that it provides to certain of its partners.

13.   PRODUCT WARRANTY

The Company estimates its warranty costs at the time of revenue recognition based on historical warranty claims experience and records the expense in cost of sales. The warranty accrual balance is reviewed quarterly to establish that it materially reflects the remaining obligation based on the anticipated future expenditures over the balance of the obligation period. Adjustments are made when the actual warranty claim experience differs from estimates. The change in the Company's warranty expense and actual warranty experience from March 3, 2007 to February 27, 2010 as well as the accrued warranty obligations as at February 27, 2010 are set forth in the following table:

Accrued warranty obligations as at March 3, 2007	$ 36,669
Actual warranty experience during fiscal 2008	(68,166)
Fiscal 2008 warranty provision	116,045
Accrued warranty obligations as at March 1, 2008	84,548
Actual warranty experience during fiscal 2009	(146,434)
Fiscal 2009 warranty provision	258,757
Adjustments for changes in estimate	(12,536)
Accrued warranty obligations as at February 28, 2009	184,335
Actual warranty experience during fiscal 2010	(416,393)
Fiscal 2010 warranty provision	462,834
Adjustments for changes in estimate	21,541
Accrued warranty obligations as at February 27, 2010	$ 252,317

$US in thousands, except share and per share data, and where otherwise indicated

14. EARNINGS PER SHARE

The following table sets forth the computation of basic and diluted earnings per share:

For the year ended	February 27, 2010	February 28, 2009	March 1, 2008
Net income for basic and diluted earnings per share available to common shareholders	$2,457,144	$1,892,616	$1,293,867
Weighted-average number of shares outstanding (000's) — basic	564,492	565,059	559,778
Effect of dilutive securities (000's) — stock-based compensation	5,267	9,097	13,052
Weighted-average number of shares and assumed conversions (000's) — diluted	569,759	574,156	572,830
Earnings per share — reported			
Basic	$ 4.35	$ 3.35	$ 2.31
Diluted	$ 4.31	$ 3.30	$ 2.26

15. COMPREHENSIVE INCOME (LOSS)

The components of comprehensive income (loss) are shown in the following table:

For the year ended	February 27, 2010	February 28, 2009	March 1, 2008
Net income	$2,457,144	$1,892,616	$1,293,867
Net change in unrealized gains (losses) on available-for-sale investments	6,803	(7,161)	13,467
Net change in fair value of derivatives designated as cash flow hedges during the year, net of income taxes of $13,190 (February 28, 2009 - tax recovery of $8,641; March 1, 2008 - income taxes of $19,238)	28,324	(6,168)	37,564
Amounts reclassified to earnings during the year, net of income tax recovery of $6,079 (February 28, 2009 - income taxes of $4,644; March 1, 2008 - income taxes of $5,142)	15,508	(16,497)	(9,232)
Comprehensive income	$2,507,779	$1,862,790	$1,335,666

The components of accumulated other comprehensive income (loss) are as follows:

	February 27, 2010	February 28, 2009	March 1, 2008
Accumulated net unrealized gains (losses) on available-for-sale investments	$ 6,715	$ (88)	$ 7,073
Accumulated net unrealized gains on derivative instruments designated as cash flow hedges	44,377	545	23,210
Total accumulated other comprehensive income	$51,092	$457	$30,283

16. SUPPLEMENTAL INFORMATION

(a) Cash flows resulting from net changes in working capital items are as follows:

For the year ended	February 27, 2010	February 28, 2009	March 1, 2008
Accounts receivable	$(480,610)	$(936,514)	$(602,055)
Other receivables	(44,719)	(83,039)	(34,515)
Inventories	60,789	(286,133)	(140,360)
Other current assets	(52,737)	(50,280)	(26,161)
Accounts payable	167,281	177,263	140,806
Accrued liabilities	442,065	506,859	383,020
Income taxes payable	(266,517)	(113,868)	401,270
Deferred revenue	13,739	16,598	8,789
	$(160,709)	$(769,114)	$ 130,794

(b) Certain statement of cash flow information related to interest and income taxes paid is summarized as follows:

For the year ended	February 27, 2010	February 28, 2009	March 1, 2008
Interest paid during the year	$ —	$ 502	$ 518
Income taxes paid during the year	$1,081,720	$946,237	$216,095

Palm, Inc.
Consolidated Statements of Stockholders' Equity (Deficit) and Comprehensive Income (Loss)
(In thousands)

	Common Stock	Additional Paid-In Capital	Unamortized Deferred Stock-Based Compensation	Accumulated Deficit	Accumulated Other Comprehensive Income (Loss)	Total
Balances, May 31, 2006	$ 103	$1,475,319	$ (2,752)	$ (488,081)	$ (684)	$ 983,905
Components of comprehensive income:						
Net income	—	—	—	56,383	—	56,383
Net unrealized gains on available-for-sale investments	—	—	—	—	1,522	1,522
Recognized gains included in results of operations	—	—	—	—	(110)	(110)
Accumulated translation adjustments	—	—	—	—	915	915
Total comprehensive income	—	—	—	—	—	58,710
Common stock issued under stock plans, net	3	21,923			—	21,926
Stock-based compensation expense	—	21,503	2,752	—	—	24,255
Tax benefit from employee stock options	—	4,578	—	—	—	4,578
Shares repurchased and retired	(2)	(30,961)				(30,963)
Balances, May 31, 2007	104	1,492,362	—	(431,698)	1,643	1,062,411
Components of comprehensive loss:						
Net loss	—	—	—	(105,419)	—	(105,419)
Net unrealized losses on available-for-sale investments	—	—	—	—	(1,261)	(1,261)
Net unrealized losses in value of non-current auction rate securities	—	—	—	—	(44,706)	(44,706)
Net recognized losses on non-current auction rate securities included in results of operations	—	—	—	—	32,175	32,175
Net recognized gains on available-for-sale investments included in results of operations	—	—	—	—	(68)	(68)
Accumulated translation adjustments	—	—	—	—	1,472	1,472
Total comprehensive loss	—	—	—	—	—	(117,807)
Common stock issued under stock plans, net	4	28,433	—	—	—	28,437
Stock-based compensation expense	—	32,181	—	—	—	32,181
Tax deficiency from employee stock options	—	(3,663)	—	—	—	(3,663)
Cash distribution to stockholders	—	(949,691)	—	—	—	(949,691)
Discount recognized on issuance of series B redeemable convertible preferred stock	—	65,035	—	—	—	65,035
Accretion of series B redeemable convertible preferred stock	—	(5,516)	—	—	—	(5,516)
Adjustment to accumulated deficit due to adoption of FIN No. 48 (see Note 16)	—	—	—	(367)	—	(367)
Balances, May 31, 2008	108	659,141	—	(537,484)	(10,745)	111,020
Components of comprehensive loss:						
Net loss	—	—	—	(732,188)	—	(732,188)
Net unrealized losses on available-for-sale investments	—	—	—	—	(1,649)	(1,649)
Net unrealized losses in value of non-current auction rate securities	—	—	—	—	(23,354)	(23,354)
Net recognized losses on non-current auction rate securities included in results of operations	—	—	—	—	35,885	35,885
Net recognized losses on available-for-sale investments included in results of operations	—	—	—	—	3,594	3,594
Accumulated translation adjustments	—	—	—	—	(2,713)	(2,713)
Total comprehensive loss	—	—	—	—	—	(720,425)
Common stock issued under stock plans, net	5	15,531	—	—	—	15,536
Stock-based compensation expense	—	23,853	—	—	—	23,853
Tax benefit from employee stock options	—	1,924	—	—	—	1,924
Contribution liability related to canceled shares of restricted stock	—	34	—	—	—	34
Accretion of series B and series C redeemable convertible preferred stock	—	(21,285)	—	—	—	(21,285)
Warrants recorded in connection with issuance of series C units	—	21,966	—	—	—	21,966
Conversion of series C units and issuance of additional common stock, net	27	101,544	—	—	—	101,571
Discount recognized on issuance of series C redeemable convertible preferred stock	—	51,941	—	—	—	51,941
Balances, May 31, 2009	$ 140	$ 854,649	$ —	$ (1,269,672)	$ 1,018	$ (413,865)

PALM

Palm, Inc.

Consolidated Statements of Cash Flows

(In thousands)

Years Ended May 31	2009	2008	2007
Cash flows from operating activities			
Net income (loss)	$(732,188)	$(105,419)	$ 56,383
Adjustments to reconcile net income (loss) to net cash flows from operating activities			
Depreciation	19,677	19,699	13,316
Stock-based compensation	23,853	32,181	24,255
Amortization of intangible assets	12,134	16,510	8,315
Amortization of debt issuance costs	3,139	1,834	—
In-process research and development	—	—	3,700
Deferred income taxes	401,670	(58,227)	11,313
Realized (gain) loss on short-term investments	3,594	(68)	(110)
Excess tax benefit related to stock-based compensation	(142)	(40)	(5,241)
Realized loss (gain) on disposition of property and equipment and sale of land	619	(4,446)	—
Impairment of non-current auction rate securities	35,885	32,175	—
Loss on series C derivative	2,515	—	—
Changes in assets and liabilities			
Accounts receivable	48,425	89,312	2
Inventories	47,571	(28,147)	18,842
Prepaids and other	4,542	736	1,790
Accounts payable	(54,883)	(35,840)	11,654
Income taxes payable	(346)	3,033	16,421
Accrued restructuring	(361)	6,303	(1,803)
Deferred revenues/costs, net	12,530	—	—
Other accrued liabilities	(16,746)	12,866	9,354
Net cash provided by (used in) operating activities	(188,512)	(17,538)	168,191
Cash flows from investing activities			
Purchase of brand name intangible asset	—	(1,500)	(44,000)
Purchase of property and equipment	(13,452)	(22,999)	(24,651)
Proceeds from sale of land	—	64,446	—
Cash paid for business acquisitions	—	(495)	(19,000)
Purchase of short-term investments	(112,385)	(517,104)	(682,882)
Sales/maturities of short-term investments	88,109	777,917	671,623
Purchase of restricted investments	(2,000)	(8,951)	—
Sale of restricted investments	1,124	331	—
Proceeds related to investments in non-current auction rate securities	485	250	—
Net cash provided by (used in) investing activities	(38,119)	291,895	(98,910)
Cash flows from financing activities			
Proceeds from issuance of common stock, net	104,049	—	—
Proceeds from issuance of common stock, employee stock plans	15,536	28,437	21,926
Purchase and subsequent retirement of common stock	—	—	(30,963)
Excess tax benefit related to stock-based compensation	142	40	5,241
Proceeds from issuance of redeemable convertible preferred stock and series C units, net	99,173	315,190	—
Proceeds from issuance of debt, net	—	381,107	—
Repayment of debt	(14,446)	(3,089)	(50,816)
Cash distribution to stockholders	(439)	(948,949)	—
Net cash provided by (used in) financing activities	204,015	(227,264)	(54,612)
Effects of exchange rate changes on cash and cash equivalents	(1,902)	1,695	—
Change in cash and cash equivalents	(24,518)	48,788	14,669
Cash and cash equivalents, beginning of period	176,918	128,130	113,461
Cash and cash equivalents, end of period	$ 152,400	$ 176,918	$ 128,130
Supplemental cash flow information:			
Cash paid for income taxes	$ 3,402	$ 3,391	$ 8,900
Cash paid for interest	$ 21,828	$ 18,042	$ 1,741
Non-cash investing and financing activities:			
Liability for property and equipment acquired	$ —	$ 3,334	$ 2,309

Nokia Financial Report

Nokia Corporation and Subsidiaries
Consolidated Statements of Financial Position

December 31	2009 EURm	2008 EURm
ASSETS		
Non-current assets		
Capitalized development costs	143	244
Goodwill	5 171	6 257
Other intangible assets	2 762	3 913
Property, plant and equipment	1 867	2 090
Investments in associated companies	69	96
Available-for-sale investments	554	512
Deferred tax assets	1 507	1 963
Long-term loans receivable	46	27
Other non-current assets	6	10
	12 125	15 112
Current assets		
Inventories	1 865	2 533
Accounts receivable, net of allowances for doubtful accounts (2009: EUR 391 million, 2008: EUR 415 million)	7 981	9 444
Prepaid expenses and accrued income	4 551	4 538
Current portion of long-term loans receivable	14	101
Other financial assets	329	1 034
Investments at fair value through profit and loss, liquid assets	580	—
Available-for-sale investments, liquid assets	2 367	1 272
Available-for-sale investments, cash equivalents	4 784	3 842
Bank and cash	1 142	1 706
	23 613	24 470
Total assets	35 738	39 582
SHAREHOLDERS' EQUITY AND LIABILITIES		
Capital and reserves attributable to equity holders of the parent		
Share capital	246	246
Share issue premium	279	442
Treasury shares, at cost	(681)	(1 881)
Translation differences	(127)	341
Fair value and other reserves	69	62
Reserve for invested non-restricted equity	3 170	3 306
Retained earnings	10 132	11 692
	13 088	14 208
Minority interests	1 661	2 302
Total equity	14 749	16 510
Non-current liabilities		
Long-term interest-bearing liabilities	4 432	861
Deferred tax liabilities	1 303	1 787
Other long-term liabilities	66	69
	5 801	2 717
Current liabilities		
Current portion of long-term loans	44	13
Short-term borrowings	727	3 578
Other financial liabilities	245	924
Accounts payable	4 950	5 225
Accrued expenses	6 504	7 023
Provisions	2 718	3 592
	15 188	20 355
Total shareholders' equity and liabilities	35 738	39 582

NOKIA

because a future value table defines *p* equal to 1 and *f* as a multiple of 1. We look for a value nearest to 1.9990 (*f*), which we find in the column for 8% interest (*i*). This means that $2,001 invested for nine periods at 8% interest accumulates to $4,000.

Quick Check   Answer — p. B-7

2. Assume that you win a $150,000 cash sweepstakes. You decide to deposit this cash in an account earning 8% annual interest, and you plan to quit your job when the account equals $555,000. How many years will it be before you can quit working?

PRESENT VALUE OF AN ANNUITY

An *annuity* is a series of equal payments occurring at equal intervals. One example is a series of three annual payments of $100 each. An *ordinary annuity* is defined as equal end-of-period payments at equal intervals. An ordinary annuity of $100 for three periods and its present value (*p*) are illustrated in Exhibit B.6.

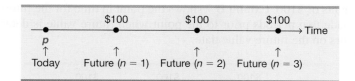

EXHIBIT B.6

Present Value of an Ordinary Annuity Diagram

One way to compute the present value of an ordinary annuity is to find the present value of each payment using our present value formula from Exhibit B.3. We then add each of the three present values. To illustrate, let's look at three $100 payments at the end of each of the next three periods with an interest rate of 15%. Our present value computations are

P3 Apply present value concepts to an annuity by using interest tables.

$$p = \frac{\$100}{(1 + 0.15)^1} + \frac{\$100}{(1 + 0.15)^2} + \frac{\$100}{(1 + 0.15)^3} = \$228.32$$

This computation is identical to computing the present value of each payment (from Table B.1) and taking their sum or, alternatively, adding the values from Table B.1 for each of the three payments and multiplying their sum by the $100 annuity payment.

A more direct way is to use a present value of annuity table. Table B.3 at the end of this appendix is one such table. This table is called a **present value of an annuity of 1 table**. If we look at Table B.3 where *n* = 3 and *i* = 15%, we see the present value is 2.2832. This means that the present value of an annuity of 1 for three periods, with a 15% interest rate, equals 2.2832.

A present value of an annuity formula is used to construct Table B.3. It can also be constructed by adding the amounts in a present value of 1 table. To illustrate, we use Tables B.1 and B.3 to confirm this relation for the prior example:

From Table B.1		From Table B.3	
i = 15%, *n* = 1	0.8696		
i = 15%, *n* = 2	0.7561		
i = 15%, *n* = 3	0.6575		
Total	2.2832	*i* = 15%, *n* = 3	2.2832

We can also use business calculators or spreadsheet programs to find the present value of an annuity.

Decision Insight

Better Lucky Than Good   "I don't have good luck—I'm blessed," proclaimed Andrew "Jack" Whittaker, 55, a sewage treatment contractor, after winning the largest ever undivided jackpot in a U.S. lottery. Whittaker had to choose between $315 million in 30 annual installments or $170 million in one lump sum ($112 million after-tax). ■

Quick Check   Answer — p. B-7

3. A company is considering an investment paying $10,000 every six months for three years. The first payment would be received in six months. If this company requires an 8% annual return, what is the maximum amount it is willing to pay for this investment?

FUTURE VALUE OF AN ANNUITY

The future value of an *ordinary annuity* is the accumulated value of each annuity payment with interest as of the date of the final payment. To illustrate, let's consider the earlier annuity of three annual payments of $100. Exhibit B.7 shows the point in time for the future value (f). The first payment is made two periods prior to the point when future value is determined, and the final payment occurs on the future value date.

EXHIBIT B.7

Future Value of an Ordinary Annuity Diagram

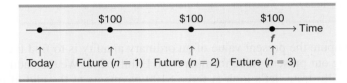

One way to compute the future value of an annuity is to use the formula to find the future value of *each* payment and add them. If we assume an interest rate of 15%, our calculation is

$$f = \$100 \times (1 + 0.15)^2 + \$100 \times (1 + 0.15)^1 + \$100 \times (1 + 0.15)^0 = \$347.25$$

This is identical to using Table B.2 and summing the future values of each payment, or adding the future values of the three payments of 1 and multiplying the sum by $100.

A more direct way is to use a table showing future values of annuities. Such a table is called a **future value of an annuity of 1 table**. Table B.4 at the end of this appendix is one such table. Note that in Table B.4 when $n = 1$, the future values equal 1 ($f = 1$) for all rates of interest. This is so because such an annuity consists of only one payment and the future value is determined on the date of that payment—no time passes between the payment and its future value. The future value of an annuity formula is used to construct Table B.4. We can also construct it by adding the amounts from a future value of 1 table. To illustrate, we use Tables B.2 and B.4 to confirm this relation for the prior example:

P4   Apply future value concepts to an annuity by using interest tables.

From Table B.2		From Table B.4	
$i = 15\%, n = 0$	1.0000		
$i = 15\%, n = 1$	1.1500		
$i = 15\%, n = 2$	1.3225		
Total	3.4725	$i = 15\%, n = 3$	3.4725

Note that the future value in Table B.2 is 1.0000 when $n = 0$, but the future value in Table B.4 is 1.0000 when $n = 1$. Is this a contradiction? No. When $n = 0$ in Table B.2, the future value is determined on the date when a single payment occurs. This means that no interest is earned because no time has passed, and the future value equals the payment. Table B.4 describes annuities with equal payments occurring at the end of each period. When $n = 1$, the annuity has one payment, and its future value equals 1 on the date of its final and only payment. Again, no time passes between the payment and its future value date.

Quick Check   Answer — p. B-7

4. A company invests $45,000 per year for five years at 12% annual interest. Compute the value of this annuity investment at the end of five years.

Summary

C1 **Describe the earning of interest and the concepts of present and future values.** Interest is payment by a borrower to the owner of an asset for its use. Present and future value computations are a way for us to estimate the interest component of holding assets or liabilities over a period of time.

P1 **Apply present value concepts to a single amount by using interest tables.** The present value of a single amount received at a future date is the amount that can be invested now at the specified interest rate to yield that future value.

P2 **Apply future value concepts to a single amount by using interest tables.** The future value of a single amount invested

at a specified rate of interest is the amount that would accumulate by the future date.

P3 **Apply present value concepts to an annuity by using interest tables.** The present value of an annuity is the amount that can be invested now at the specified interest rate to yield that series of equal periodic payments.

P4 **Apply future value concepts to an annuity by using interest tables.** The future value of an annuity invested at a specific rate of interest is the amount that would accumulate by the date of the final payment.

Guidance Answers to Quick Checks

1. $70,000 × 0.6302 = $44,114 (use Table B.1, $i = 8\%$, $n = 6$).

2. $555,000/$150,000 = 3.7000; Table B.2 shows this value is not achieved until after 17 years at 8% interest.

3. $10,000 × 5.2421 = $52,421 (use Table B.3, $i = 4\%$, $n = 6$).

4. $45,000 × 6.3528 = $285,876 (use Table B.4, $i = 12\%$, $n = 5$).

connect

Assume that you must make future value estimates using the *future value of 1 table* (Table B.2). Which interest rate column do you use when working with the following rates?
1. 8% compounded quarterly
2. 12% compounded annually
3. 6% compounded semiannually
4. 12% compounded monthly

QUICK STUDY

QS B-1
Identifying interest rates in tables
C1

Ken Francis is offered the possibility of investing $2,745 today and in return to receive $10,000 after 15 years. What is the annual rate of interest for this investment? (Use Table B.1.)

QS B-2
Interest rate on an investment P1

Megan Brink is offered the possibility of investing $6,651 today at 6% interest per year in a desire to accumulate $10,000. How many years must Brink wait to accumulate $10,000? (Use Table B.1.)

QS B-3
Number of periods of an investment P1

Flaherty is considering an investment that, if paid for immediately, is expected to return $140,000 five years from now. If Flaherty demands a 9% return, how much is she willing to pay for this investment?

QS B-4
Present value of an amount P1

CII, Inc., invests $630,000 in a project expected to earn a 12% annual rate of return. The earnings will be reinvested in the project each year until the entire investment is liquidated 10 years later. What will the cash proceeds be when the project is liquidated?

QS B-5
Future value of an amount P2

QS B-6
Present value
of an annuity P3

Beene Distributing is considering a project that will return $150,000 annually at the end of each year for six years. If Beene demands an annual return of 7% and pays for the project immediately, how much is it willing to pay for the project?

QS B-7
Future value
of an annuity P4

Claire Fitch is planning to begin an individual retirement program in which she will invest $1,500 at the end of each year. Fitch plans to retire after making 30 annual investments in the program earning a return of 10%. What is the value of the program on the date of the last payment?

■ connect

EXERCISES

Exercise B-1
Number of periods
of an investment P2

Bill Thompson expects to invest $10,000 at 12% and, at the end of a certain period, receive $96,463. How many years will it be before Thompson receives the payment? (Use Table B.2.)

Exercise B-2
Interest rate on
an investment P2

Ed Summers expects to invest $10,000 for 25 years, after which he wants to receive $108,347. What rate of interest must Summers earn? (Use Table B.2.)

Exercise B-3
Interest rate on
an investment P3

Jones expects an immediate investment of $57,466 to return $10,000 annually for eight years, with the first payment to be received one year from now. What rate of interest must Jones earn? (Use Table B.3.)

Exercise B-4
Number of periods
of an investment P3

Keith Riggins expects an investment of $82,014 to return $10,000 annually for several years. If Riggins earns a return of 10%, how many annual payments will he receive? (Use Table B.3.)

Exercise B-5
Interest rate on
an investment P4

Algoe expects to invest $1,000 annually for 40 years to yield an accumulated value of $154,762 on the date of the last investment. For this to occur, what rate of interest must Algoe earn? (Use Table B.4.)

Exercise B-6
Number of periods
of an investment P4

Kate Beckwith expects to invest $10,000 annually that will earn 8%. How many annual investments must Beckwith make to accumulate $303,243 on the date of the last investment? (Use Table B.4.)

Exercise B-7
Present value
of an annuity P3

Sam Weber finances a new automobile by paying $6,500 cash and agreeing to make 40 monthly payments of $500 each, the first payment to be made one month after the purchase. The loan bears interest at an annual rate of 12%. What is the cost of the automobile?

Exercise B-8
Present value of bonds
P1 P3

Spiller Corp. plans to issue 10%, 15-year, $500,000 par value bonds payable that pay interest semiannually on June 30 and December 31. The bonds are dated December 31, 2011, and are issued on that date. If the market rate of interest for the bonds is 8% on the date of issue, what will be the total cash proceeds from the bond issue?

Exercise B-9
Present value
of an amount P1

McAdams Company expects to earn 10% per year on an investment that will pay $606,773 six years from now. Use Table B.1 to compute the present value of this investment. (Round the amount to the nearest dollar.)

Exercise B-10
Present value of
an amount and
of an annuity P1 P3

Compute the amount that can be borrowed under each of the following circumstances:
1. A promise to repay $90,000 seven years from now at an interest rate of 6%.
2. An agreement made on February 1, 2011, to make three separate payments of $20,000 on February 1 of 2012, 2013, and 2014. The annual interest rate is 10%.

Exercise B-11
Present value
of an amount P1

On January 1, 2011, a company agrees to pay $20,000 in three years. If the annual interest rate is 10%, determine how much cash the company can borrow with this agreement.

Find the amount of money that can be borrowed today with each of the following separate debt agreements *a* through *f.* (Round amounts to the nearest dollar.)

Exercise B-12
Present value
of an amount P1

Case	Single Future Payment	Number of Periods	Interest Rate
a.	$40,000	3	4%
b.	75,000	7	8
c.	52,000	9	10
d.	18,000	2	4
e.	63,000	8	6
f.	89,000	5	2

C&H Ski Club recently borrowed money and agrees to pay it back with a series of six annual payments of $5,000 each. C&H subsequently borrows more money and agrees to pay it back with a series of four annual payments of $7,500 each. The annual interest rate for both loans is 6%.

1. Use Table B.1 to find the present value of these two separate annuities. (Round amounts to the nearest dollar.)

2. Use Table B.3 to find the present value of these two separate annuities. (Round amounts to the nearest dollar.)

Exercise B-13
Present values of annuities
P3

Otto Co. borrows money on April 30, 2011, by promising to make four payments of $13,000 each on November 1, 2011; May 1, 2012; November 1, 2012; and May 1, 2013.

1. How much money is Otto able to borrow if the interest rate is 8%, compounded semiannually?

2. How much money is Otto able to borrow if the interest rate is 12%, compounded semiannually?

3. How much money is Otto able to borrow if the interest rate is 16%, compounded semiannually?

Exercise B-14
Present value with semiannual
compounding
C1 P3

Mark Welsch deposits $7,200 in an account that earns interest at an annual rate of 8%, compounded quarterly. The $7,200 plus earned interest must remain in the account 10 years before it can be withdrawn. How much money will be in the account at the end of 10 years?

Exercise B-15
Future value
of an amount P2

Kelly Malone plans to have $50 withheld from her monthly paycheck and deposited in a savings account that earns 12% annually, compounded monthly. If Malone continues with her plan for two and one-half years, how much will be accumulated in the account on the date of the last deposit?

Exercise B-16
Future value
of an annuity P4

Starr Company decides to establish a fund that it will use 10 years from now to replace an aging production facility. The company will make a $100,000 initial contribution to the fund and plans to make quarterly contributions of $50,000 beginning in three months. The fund earns 12%, compounded quarterly. What will be the value of the fund 10 years from now?

Exercise B-17
Future value of
an amount plus
an annuity P2 P4

Catten, Inc., invests $163,170 today earning 7% per year for nine years. Use Table B.2 to compute the future value of the investment nine years from now. (Round the amount to the nearest dollar.)

Exercise B-18
Future value of
an amount P2

For each of the following situations, identify (1) the case as either (*a*) a present or a future value and (*b*) a single amount or an annuity, (2) the table you would use in your computations (but do not solve the problem), and (3) the interest rate and time periods you would use.

a. You need to accumulate $10,000 for a trip you wish to take in four years. You are able to earn 8% compounded semiannually on your savings. You plan to make only one deposit and let the money accumulate for four years. How would you determine the amount of the one-time deposit?

b. Assume the same facts as in part (*a*) except that you will make semiannual deposits to your savings account.

c. You want to retire after working 40 years with savings in excess of $1,000,000. You expect to save $4,000 a year for 40 years and earn an annual rate of interest of 8%. Will you be able to retire with more than $1,000,000 in 40 years? Explain.

d. A sweepstakes agency names you a grand prize winner. You can take $225,000 immediately or elect to receive annual installments of $30,000 for 20 years. You can earn 10% annually on any investments you make. Which prize do you choose to receive?

Exercise B-19
Using present and future
value tables
C1 P1 P2 P3 P4

TABLE B.1

Present Value of 1

$$p = 1/(1 + i)^n$$

Periods	1%	2%	3%	4%	5%	6%	7%	8%	9%	10%	12%	15%
1	0.9901	0.9804	0.9709	0.9615	0.9524	0.9434	0.9346	0.9259	0.9174	0.9091	0.8929	0.8696
2	0.9803	0.9612	0.9426	0.9246	0.9070	0.8900	0.8734	0.8573	0.8417	0.8264	0.7972	0.7561
3	0.9706	0.9423	0.9151	0.8890	0.8638	0.8396	0.8163	0.7938	0.7722	0.7513	0.7118	0.6575
4	0.9610	0.9238	0.8885	0.8548	0.8227	0.7921	0.7629	0.7350	0.7084	0.6830	0.6355	0.5718
5	0.9515	0.9057	0.8626	0.8219	0.7835	0.7473	0.7130	0.6806	0.6499	0.6209	0.5674	0.4972
6	0.9420	0.8880	0.8375	0.7903	0.7462	0.7050	0.6663	0.6302	0.5963	0.5645	0.5066	0.4323
7	0.9327	0.8706	0.8131	0.7599	0.7107	0.6651	0.6227	0.5835	0.5470	0.5132	0.4523	0.3759
8	0.9235	0.8535	0.7894	0.7307	0.6768	0.6274	0.5820	0.5403	0.5019	0.4665	0.4039	0.3269
9	0.9143	0.8368	0.7664	0.7026	0.6446	0.5919	0.5439	0.5002	0.4604	0.4241	0.3606	0.2843
10	0.9053	0.8203	0.7441	0.6756	0.6139	0.5584	0.5083	0.4632	0.4224	0.3855	0.3220	0.2472
11	0.8963	0.8043	0.7224	0.6496	0.5847	0.5268	0.4751	0.4289	0.3875	0.3505	0.2875	0.2149
12	0.8874	0.7885	0.7014	0.6246	0.5568	0.4970	0.4440	0.3971	0.3555	0.3186	0.2567	0.1869
13	0.8787	0.7730	0.6810	0.6006	0.5303	0.4688	0.4150	0.3677	0.3262	0.2897	0.2292	0.1625
14	0.8700	0.7579	0.6611	0.5775	0.5051	0.4423	0.3878	0.3405	0.2992	0.2633	0.2046	0.1413
15	0.8613	0.7430	0.6419	0.5553	0.4810	0.4173	0.3624	0.3152	0.2745	0.2394	0.1827	0.1229
16	0.8528	0.7284	0.6232	0.5339	0.4581	0.3936	0.3387	0.2919	0.2519	0.2176	0.1631	0.1069
17	0.8444	0.7142	0.6050	0.5134	0.4363	0.3714	0.3166	0.2703	0.2311	0.1978	0.1456	0.0929
18	0.8360	0.7002	0.5874	0.4936	0.4155	0.3503	0.2959	0.2502	0.2120	0.1799	0.1300	0.0808
19	0.8277	0.6864	0.5703	0.4746	0.3957	0.3305	0.2765	0.2317	0.1945	0.1635	0.1161	0.0703
20	0.8195	0.6730	0.5537	0.4564	0.3769	0.3118	0.2584	0.2145	0.1784	0.1486	0.1037	0.0611
25	0.7798	0.6095	0.4776	0.3751	0.2953	0.2330	0.1842	0.1460	0.1160	0.0923	0.0588	0.0304
30	0.7419	0.5521	0.4120	0.3083	0.2314	0.1741	0.1314	0.0994	0.0754	0.0573	0.0334	0.0151
35	0.7059	0.5000	0.3554	0.2534	0.1813	0.1301	0.0937	0.0676	0.0490	0.0356	0.0189	0.0075
40	0.6717	0.4529	0.3066	0.2083	0.1420	0.0972	0.0668	0.0460	0.0318	0.0221	0.0107	0.0037

TABLE B.2

Future Value of 1

$$f = (1 + i)^n$$

Periods	1%	2%	3%	4%	5%	6%	7%	8%	9%	10%	12%	15%
0	1.0000	1.0000	1.0000	1.0000	1.0000	1.0000	1.0000	1.0000	1.0000	1.0000	1.0000	1.0000
1	1.0100	1.0200	1.0300	1.0400	1.0500	1.0600	1.0700	1.0800	1.0900	1.1000	1.1200	1.1500
2	1.0201	1.0404	1.0609	1.0816	1.1025	1.1236	1.1449	1.1664	1.1881	1.2100	1.2544	1.3225
3	1.0303	1.0612	1.0927	1.1249	1.1576	1.1910	1.2250	1.2597	1.2950	1.3310	1.4049	1.5209
4	1.0406	1.0824	1.1255	1.1699	1.2155	1.2625	1.3108	1.3605	1.4116	1.4641	1.5735	1.7490
5	1.0510	1.1041	1.1593	1.2167	1.2763	1.3382	1.4026	1.4693	1.5386	1.6105	1.7623	2.0114
6	1.0615	1.1262	1.1941	1.2653	1.3401	1.4185	1.5007	1.5869	1.6771	1.7716	1.9738	2.3131
7	1.0721	1.1487	1.2299	1.3159	1.4071	1.5036	1.6058	1.7138	1.8280	1.9487	2.2107	2.6600
8	1.0829	1.1717	1.2668	1.3686	1.4775	1.5938	1.7182	1.8509	1.9926	2.1436	2.4760	3.0590
9	1.0937	1.1951	1.3048	1.4233	1.5513	1.6895	1.8385	1.9990	2.1719	2.3579	2.7731	3.5179
10	1.1046	1.2190	1.3439	1.4802	1.6289	1.7908	1.9672	2.1589	2.3674	2.5937	3.1058	4.0456
11	1.1157	1.2434	1.3842	1.5395	1.7103	1.8983	2.1049	2.3316	2.5804	2.8531	3.4785	4.6524
12	1.1268	1.2682	1.4258	1.6010	1.7959	2.0122	2.2522	2.5182	2.8127	3.1384	3.8960	5.3503
13	1.1381	1.2936	1.4685	1.6651	1.8856	2.1329	2.4098	2.7196	3.0658	3.4523	4.3635	6.1528
14	1.1495	1.3195	1.5126	1.7317	1.9799	2.2609	2.5785	2.9372	3.3417	3.7975	4.8871	7.0757
15	1.1610	1.3459	1.5580	1.8009	2.0789	2.3966	2.7590	3.1722	3.6425	4.1772	5.4736	8.1371
16	1.1726	1.3728	1.6047	1.8730	2.1829	2.5404	2.9522	3.4259	3.9703	4.5950	6.1304	9.3576
17	1.1843	1.4002	1.6528	1.9479	2.2920	2.6928	3.1588	3.7000	4.3276	5.0545	6.8660	10.7613
18	1.1961	1.4282	1.7024	2.0258	2.4066	2.8543	3.3799	3.9960	4.7171	5.5599	7.6900	12.3755
19	1.2081	1.4568	1.7535	2.1068	2.5270	3.0256	3.6165	4.3157	5.1417	6.1159	8.6128	14.2318
20	1.2202	1.4859	1.8061	2.1911	2.6533	3.2071	3.8697	4.6610	5.6044	6.7275	9.6463	16.3665
25	1.2824	1.6406	2.0938	2.6658	3.3864	4.2919	5.4274	6.8485	8.6231	10.8347	17.0001	32.9190
30	1.3478	1.8114	2.4273	3.2434	4.3219	5.7435	7.6123	10.0627	13.2677	17.4494	29.9599	66.2118
35	1.4166	1.9999	2.8139	3.9461	5.5160	7.6861	10.6766	14.7853	20.4140	28.1024	52.7996	133.1755
40	1.4889	2.2080	3.2620	4.8010	7.0400	10.2857	14.9745	21.7245	31.4094	45.2593	93.0510	267.8635

$$p = \left[1 - \frac{1}{(1 + i)^n}\right]/i$$

TABLE B.3

Present Value of an Annuity of 1

Periods	Rate											
	1%	2%	3%	4%	5%	6%	7%	8%	9%	10%	12%	15%
1	0.9901	0.9804	0.9709	0.9615	0.9524	0.9434	0.9346	0.9259	0.9174	0.9091	0.8929	0.8696
2	1.9704	1.9416	1.9135	1.8861	1.8594	1.8334	1.8080	1.7833	1.7591	1.7355	1.6901	1.6257
3	2.9410	2.8839	2.8286	2.7751	2.7232	2.6730	2.6243	2.5771	2.5313	2.4869	2.4018	2.2832
4	3.9020	3.8077	3.7171	3.6299	3.5460	3.4651	3.3872	3.3121	3.2397	3.1699	3.0373	2.8550
5	4.8534	4.7135	4.5797	4.4518	4.3295	4.2124	4.1002	3.9927	3.8897	3.7908	3.6048	3.3522
6	5.7955	5.6014	5.4172	5.2421	5.0757	4.9173	4.7665	4.6229	4.4859	4.3553	4.1114	3.7845
7	6.7282	6.4720	6.2303	6.0021	5.7864	5.5824	5.3893	5.2064	5.0330	4.8684	4.5638	4.1604
8	7.6517	7.3255	7.0197	6.7327	6.4632	6.2098	5.9713	5.7466	5.5348	5.3349	4.9676	4.4873
9	8.5660	8.1622	7.7861	7.4353	7.1078	6.8017	6.5152	6.2469	5.9952	5.7590	5.3282	4.7716
10	9.4713	8.9826	8.5302	8.1109	7.7217	7.3601	7.0236	6.7101	6.4177	6.1446	5.6502	5.0188
11	10.3676	9.7868	9.2526	8.7605	8.3064	7.8869	7.4987	7.1390	6.8052	6.4951	5.9377	5.2337
12	11.2551	10.5753	9.9540	9.3851	8.8633	8.3838	7.9427	7.5361	7.1607	6.8137	6.1944	5.4206
13	12.1337	11.3484	10.6350	9.9856	9.3936	8.8527	8.3577	7.9038	7.4869	7.1034	6.4235	5.5831
14	13.0037	12.1062	11.2961	10.5631	9.8986	9.2950	8.7455	8.2442	7.7862	7.3667	6.6282	5.7245
15	13.8651	12.8493	11.9379	11.1184	10.3797	9.7122	9.1079	8.5595	8.0607	7.6061	6.8109	5.8474
16	14.7179	13.5777	12.5611	11.6523	10.8378	10.1059	9.4466	8.8514	8.3126	7.8237	6.9740	5.9542
17	15.5623	14.2919	13.1661	12.1657	11.2741	10.4773	9.7632	9.1216	8.5436	8.0216	7.1196	6.0472
18	16.3983	14.9920	13.7535	12.6593	11.6896	10.8276	10.0591	9.3719	8.7556	8.2014	7.2497	6.1280
19	17.2260	15.6785	14.3238	13.1339	12.0853	11.1581	10.3356	9.6036	8.9501	8.3649	7.3658	6.1982
20	18.0456	16.3514	14.8775	13.5903	12.4622	11.4699	10.5940	9.8181	9.1285	8.5136	7.4694	6.2593
25	22.0232	19.5235	17.4131	15.6221	14.0939	12.7834	11.6536	10.6748	9.8226	9.0770	7.8431	6.4641
30	25.8077	22.3965	19.6004	17.2920	15.3725	13.7648	12.4090	11.2578	10.2737	9.4269	8.0552	6.5660
35	29.4086	24.9986	21.4872	18.6646	16.3742	14.4982	12.9477	11.6546	10.5668	9.6442	8.1755	6.6166
40	32.8347	27.3555	23.1148	19.7928	17.1591	15.0463	13.3317	11.9246	10.7574	9.7791	8.2438	6.6418

$$f = [(1 + i)^n - 1]/i$$

TABLE B.4

Future Value of an Annuity of 1

Periods	Rate											
	1%	2%	3%	4%	5%	6%	7%	8%	9%	10%	12%	15%
1	1.0000	1.0000	1.0000	1.0000	1.0000	1.0000	1.0000	1.0000	1.0000	1.0000	1.0000	1.0000
2	2.0100	2.0200	2.0300	2.0400	2.0500	2.0600	2.0700	2.0800	2.0900	2.1000	2.1200	2.1500
3	3.0301	3.0604	3.0909	3.1216	3.1525	3.1836	3.2149	3.2464	3.2781	3.3100	3.3744	3.4725
4	4.0604	4.1216	4.1836	4.2465	4.3101	4.3746	4.4399	4.5061	4.5731	4.6410	4.7793	4.9934
5	5.1010	5.2040	5.3091	5.4163	5.5256	5.6371	5.7507	5.8666	5.9847	6.1051	6.3528	6.7424
6	6.1520	6.3081	6.4684	6.6330	6.8019	6.9753	7.1533	7.3359	7.5233	7.7156	8.1152	8.7537
7	7.2135	7.4343	7.6625	7.8983	8.1420	8.3938	8.6540	8.9228	9.2004	9.4872	10.0890	11.0668
8	8.2857	8.5830	8.8923	9.2142	9.5491	9.8975	10.2598	10.6366	11.0285	11.4359	12.2997	13.7268
9	9.3685	9.7546	10.1591	10.5828	11.0266	11.4913	11.9780	12.4876	13.0210	13.5795	14.7757	16.7858
10	10.4622	10.9497	11.4639	12.0061	12.5779	13.1808	13.8164	14.4866	15.1929	15.9374	17.5487	20.3037
11	11.5668	12.1687	12.8078	13.4864	14.2068	14.9716	15.7836	16.6455	17.5603	18.5312	20.6546	24.3493
12	12.6825	13.4121	14.1920	15.0258	15.9171	16.8699	17.8885	18.9771	20.1407	21.3843	24.1331	29.0017
13	13.8093	14.6803	15.6178	16.6268	17.7130	18.8821	20.1406	21.4953	22.9534	24.5227	28.0291	34.3519
14	14.9474	15.9739	17.0863	18.2919	19.5986	21.0151	22.5505	24.2149	26.0192	27.9750	32.3926	40.5047
15	16.0969	17.2934	18.5989	20.0236	21.5786	23.2760	25.1290	27.1521	29.3609	31.7725	37.2797	47.5804
16	17.2579	18.6393	20.1569	21.8245	23.6575	25.6725	27.8881	30.3243	33.0034	35.9497	42.7533	55.7175
17	18.4304	20.0121	21.7616	23.6975	25.8404	28.2129	30.8402	33.7502	36.9737	40.5447	48.8837	65.0751
18	19.6147	21.4123	23.4144	25.6454	28.1324	30.9057	33.9990	37.4502	41.3013	45.5992	55.7497	75.8364
19	20.8109	22.8406	25.1169	27.6712	30.5390	33.7600	37.3790	41.4463	46.0185	51.1591	63.4397	88.2118
20	22.0190	24.2974	26.8704	29.7781	33.0660	36.7856	40.9955	45.7620	51.1601	57.2750	72.0524	102.4436
25	28.2432	32.0303	36.4593	41.6459	47.7271	54.8645	63.2490	73.1059	84.7009	98.3471	133.3339	212.7930
30	34.7849	40.5681	47.5754	56.0849	66.4388	79.0582	94.4608	113.2832	136.3075	164.4940	241.3327	434.7451
35	41.6603	49.9945	60.4621	73.6522	90.3203	111.4348	138.2369	172.3168	215.7108	271.0244	431.6635	881.1702
40	48.8864	60.4020	75.4013	95.0255	120.7998	154.7620	199.6351	259.0565	337.8824	442.5926	767.0914	1,779.0903

To illustrate, consider return on total assets and its components for **Gap Inc.** in Exhibit C.10.

Fiscal Year	Return on Total Assets	=	Profit Margin	×	Total Asset Turnover
2009	12.6%	=	6.66%	×	1.89
2008	10.2*	=	5.28	×	1.92
2007	9.0	=	4.9	×	1.84
2006	11.8*	=	6.9	×	1.70
2005	11.1	=	7.1	×	1.57

EXHIBIT C.10

Gap's Components of Return on Total Assets

* Differences due to rounding.

At least three findings emerge. First, Gap's return on total assets improved from 9.0% in 2007 to 12.6% in 2009. Second, total asset turnover has slightly improved over this period, from 1.84 to 1.89. Third, Gap's profit margin steadily increased over this period, from 4.9% in 2007 to 6.66% in 2009. These components reveal the dual role of profit margin and total asset turnover in determining return on total assets. They also reveal that the driver of Gap's recent improvement in return on total assets is not total asset turnover but profit margin.

Generally, if a company is to maintain or improve its return on total assets, it must meet any decline in either profit margin or total asset turnover with an increase in the other. If not, return on assets will decline. Companies consider these components in planning strategies. A component analysis can also reveal where a company is weak and where changes are needed, especially in a competitor analysis. If asset turnover is lower than the industry norm, for instance, a company should focus on raising asset turnover at least to the norm. The same applies to profit margin.

Decision Maker   Answer — p. C-18

Retailer   You are an entrepreneur and owner of a retail sporting goods store. The store's recent annual performance reveals (industry norms in parentheses): return on total assets = 11% (11.2%); profit margin = 4.4% (3.5%); and total asset turnover = 2.5 (3.2). What does your analysis of these figures reveal? ■

DEMONSTRATION PROBLEM—1

Garden Company completes the following selected transactions related to its short-term investments during 2011.

May 8   Purchased 300 shares of FedEx stock as a short-term investment in available-for-sale securities at $40 per share plus $975 in broker fees.

Sept. 2   Sold 100 shares of its investment in FedEx stock at $47 per share and held the remaining 200 shares; broker's commission was $225.

Oct. 2   Purchased 400 shares of Ajay stock for $60 per share plus $1,600 in commissions. The stock is held as a short-term investment in available-for-sale securities.

Required

1. Prepare journal entries for the above transactions of Garden Company for 2011.

2. Prepare an adjusting journal entry as of December 31, 2011, if the fair values of the equity securities held by Garden Company are $48 per share for FedEx and $55 per share for Ajay. (Year 2011 is the first year Garden Company acquired short-term investments.)

SOLUTION TO DEMONSTRATION PROBLEM—1

1.

May 8	Short-Term Investments—AFS (FedEx)	12,975	
	Cash		12,975
	Purchased 300 shares of FedEx stock *(300 × $40) + $975.*		

[continued on next page]

[continued from previous page]

Sept. 2	Cash	4,475	
	Gain on Sale of Short-Term Investment		150
	Short-Term Investments—AFS (FedEx)		4,325
	Sold 100 shares of FedEx for $47 per share less a $225 commission. The original cost is ($12,975 × 100/300).		
Oct. 2	Short-Term Investments—AFS (Ajay)	25,600	
	Cash		25,600
	Purchased 400 shares of Ajay for $60 per share plus $1,600 in commissions.		

2. Computation of unrealized gain or loss follows.

Short-Term Investments in Available-for-Sale Securities	Shares	Cost per Share	Total Cost	Fair Value per Share	Total Fair Value	Unrealized Gain (Loss)
FedEx	200	$43.25	$ 8,650	$48.00	$ 9,600	
Ajay	400	64.00	25,600	55.00	22,000	
Totals			$34,250		$31,600	$(2,650)

The adjusting entry follows.

Dec. 31	Unrealized Loss—Equity	2,650	
	Fair Value Adjustment—Available-for-Sale (ST)		2,650
	To reflect an unrealized loss in fair values of available-for-sale securities.		

DEMONSTRATION PROBLEM—2

The following transactions relate to Brown Company's long-term investments during 2010 and 2011. Brown did not own any long-term investments prior to 2010. Show (1) the appropriate journal entries and (2) the relevant portions of each year's balance sheet and income statement that reflect these transactions for both 2010 and 2011.

2010

Sept. 9 Purchased 1,000 shares of Packard, Inc., common stock for $80,000 cash. These shares represent 30% of Packard's outstanding shares.

Oct. 2 Purchased 2,000 shares of AT&T common stock for $60,000 cash as a long-term investment. These shares represent less than a 1% ownership in AT&T.

17 Purchased as a long-term investment 1,000 shares of Apple Computer common stock for $40,000 cash. These shares are less than 1% of Apple's outstanding shares.

Nov. 1 Received $5,000 cash dividend from Packard.

30 Received $3,000 cash dividend from AT&T.

Dec. 15 Received $1,400 cash dividend from Apple.

31 Packard's net income for this year is $70,000.

31 Fair values for the investments in equity securities are Packard, $84,000; AT&T, $48,000; and Apple Computer, $45,000.

31 For preparing financial statements, note the following post-closing account balances: Common Stock, $500,000, and Retained Earnings, $350,000.

2011

Jan. 1 Sold Packard, Inc., shares for $108,000 cash.

May 30 Received $3,100 cash dividend from AT&T.

June 15 Received $1,600 cash dividend from Apple.

Aug. 17 Sold the AT&T stock for $52,000 cash.

   19 Purchased 2,000 shares of Coca-Cola common stock for $50,000 cash as a long-term invest-
        ment. The stock represents less than a 5% ownership in Coca-Cola.

Dec. 15 Received $1,800 cash dividend from Apple.

   31 Fair values of the investments in equity securities are Apple, $39,000, and Coca-Cola,
        $48,000.

   31 For preparing financial statements, note the following post-closing account balances: Common
        Stock, $500,000, and Retained Earnings, $410,000.

PLANNING THE SOLUTION

- Account for the investment in Packard under the equity method.
- Account for the investments in AT&T, Apple, and Coca-Cola as long-term investments in available-for-
  sale securities.
- Prepare the information for the two years' balance sheets by including the relevant asset and equity
  accounts, and the two years' income statements by identifying the relevant revenues, earnings, gains,
  and losses.

SOLUTION TO DEMONSTRATION PROBLEM—2

1. Journal entries for 2010.

Date	Account	Debit	Credit
Sept. 9	Long-Term Investments—Packard	80,000	
	Cash		80,000
	Acquired 1,000 shares, representing a 30% equity in Packard.		
Oct. 2	Long-Term Investments—AFS (AT&T)	60,000	
	Cash		60,000
	Acquired 2,000 shares as a long-term investment in available-for-sale securities.		
Oct. 17	Long-Term Investments—AFS (Apple)	40,000	
	Cash		40,000
	Acquired 1,000 shares as a long-term investment in available-for-sale securities.		
Nov. 1	Cash	5,000	
	Long-Term Investments—Packard		5,000
	Received dividend from Packard.		
Nov. 30	Cash	3,000	
	Dividend Revenue		3,000
	Received dividend from AT&T.		
Dec. 15	Cash	1,400	
	Dividend Revenue		1,400
	Received dividend from Apple.		
Dec. 31	Long-Term Investments—Packard	21,000	
	Earnings from Investment (Packard)		21,000
	To record 30% share of Packard's annual earnings of $70,000.		
Dec. 31	Unrealized Loss—Equity	7,000	
	Fair Value Adjustment—Available-for-Sale (LT)*		7,000
	To record change in fair value of long-term available-for-sale securities.		

* Fair value adjustment computations:

	Cost	Fair Value	Unrealized Gain (Loss)
AT&T	$ 60,000	$48,000	$(12,000)
Apple	40,000	45,000	5,000
Total	$100,000	$93,000	$ (7,000)

Required balance of the Fair Value
Adjustment—Available-for-Sale
(LT) account (credit) . . . . $(7,000)
Existing balance 0
Necessary adjustment (credit) . . . . . . $(7,000)

2. The December 31, 2010, selected balance sheet items appear as follows.

Assets	
Long-term investments	
Available-for-sale securities (at fair value; cost is $100,000)	$ 93,000
Investment in equity securities	96,000
Total long-term investments	189,000
Stockholders' Equity	
Common stock	500,000
Retained earnings	350,000
Unrealized loss—Equity	(7,000)

The relevant income statement items for the year ended December 31, 2010, follow.

Dividend revenue	$ 4,400
Earnings from investment	21,000

1. Journal entries for 2011.

Jan. 1	Cash	108,000	
	Long-Term Investments—Packard		96,000
	Gain on Sale of Long-Term Investments		12,000
	Sold 1,000 shares for cash.		
May 30	Cash	3,100	
	Dividend Revenue		3,100
	Received dividend from AT&T.		
June 15	Cash	1,600	
	Dividend Revenue		1,600
	Received dividend from Apple.		
Aug. 17	Cash	52,000	
	Loss on Sale of Long-Term Investments	8,000	
	Long-Term Investments—AFS (AT&T)		60,000
	Sold 2,000 shares for cash.		
Aug. 19	Long-Term Investments—AFS (Coca-Cola)	50,000	
	Cash		50,000
	Acquired 2,000 shares as a long-term		
	investment in available-for-sale securities.		
Dec. 15	Cash	1,800	
	Dividend Revenue		1,800
	Received dividend from Apple.		
Dec. 31	Fair Value Adjustment—Available-for-Sale (LT)*	4,000	
	Unrealized Loss—Equity		4,000
	To record change in fair value of long-term		
	available-for-sale securities.		

* Fair value adjustment computations:

	Cost	Fair Value	Unrealized Gain (Loss)
Apple	$40,000	$39,000	$(1,000)
Coca-Cola	50,000	48,000	(2,000)
Total	$90,000	$87,000	$(3,000)

Required balance of the Fair Value Adjustment—Available-for-Sale (LT) account (credit)	$(3,000)
Existing balance (credit)	(7,000)
Necessary adjustment (debit)	$ 4,000

2. The December 31, 2011, balance sheet items appear as follows.

Assets	
Long-term investments	
Available-for-sale securities (at fair value; cost is $90,000)	$ 87,000
Stockholders' Equity	
Common stock	500,000
Retained earnings	410,000
Unrealized loss—Equity	(3,000)

The relevant income statement items for the year ended December 31, 2011, follow.

Dividend revenue	$ 6,500
Gain on sale of long-term investments..........	12,000
Loss on sale of long-term investments..........	(8,000)

Investments in International Operations

C-A

Many entities from small entrepreneurs to large corporations conduct business internationally. Some entities' operations occur in so many different countries that the companies are called **multinationals.** Many of us think of **Coca-Cola** and **McDonald's,** for example, as primarily U.S. companies, but most of their sales occur outside the United States. Exhibit C-A.1 shows the percent of international sales and income for selected U.S. companies. Managing and accounting for multinationals present challenges. This section describes some of these challenges and how to account for and report these activities.

Two major accounting challenges that arise when companies have international operations relate to transactions that involve more than one currency. The first is to account for sales and purchases listed in a foreign currency. The second is to prepare consolidated financial statements with international subsidiaries. For ease in this discussion, we use companies with a U.S. base of operations and assume the need to prepare financial statements in U.S. dollars. This means the *reporting currency* of these companies is the U.S. dollar.

EXHIBIT C-A.1

International Sales and Income as a Percent of Their Totals

Point: Transactions *listed* or *stated* in a foreign currency are said to be *denominated* in that currency.

Exchange Rates between Currencies   Markets for the purchase and sale of foreign currencies exist all over the world. In these markets, U.S. dollars can be exchanged for Canadian dollars, British pounds, Japanese yen, Euros, or any other legal currencies. The price of one currency stated in terms of another currency is called a **foreign exchange rate.** Exhibit C-A.2 lists recent exchange rates for selected currencies. The exchange rate for British pounds and U.S. dollars is $1.8980, meaning 1 British pound could be purchased for $1.8980. On that same day, the exchange rate between Mexican pesos and U.S. dollars is $0.0925, or 1 Mexican peso can be purchased for $0.0925. Exchange rates fluctuate due to changing economic and political conditions, including the supply and demand for currencies and expectations about future events.

C3 Explain foreign exchange rates and record transactions listed in a foreign currency.

Point: To convert currency, see XE.com

Decision Insight

Rush to Russia   Investors are still eager to buy Russian equities even in the face of rampant crime, corruption, and slow economic growth. Why? Many argue Russia remains a bargain-priced, if risky, bet on future growth. Some analysts argue that natural-resource-rich Russia is one of the least expensive emerging markets. ■

EXHIBIT C-A.2

Foreign Exchange Rates for Selected Currencies*

Source (unit)	Price in $U.S.	Source (unit)	Price in $U.S.
Britain (pound)	$1.8980	Canada (dollar)	$0.9793
Mexico (peso)	0.0925	Japan (yen)	0.0090
Taiwan (dollar)	0.0305	Europe (Euro)	1.2920

* Rates will vary over time based on economic, political, and other changes.

Sales and Purchases Listed in a Foreign Currency   When a U.S. company makes a credit sale to an international customer, accounting for the sale and the account receivable is straightforward if sales terms require the international customer's payment in U.S. dollars. If sale terms require (or allow) payment in a foreign currency, however, the U.S. company must account for the sale and the account receivable in a different manner.

Sales in a Foreign Currency   To illustrate, consider the case of the U.S.-based manufacturer Boston Company, which makes credit sales to London Outfitters, a British retail company. A sale occurs on December 12, 2010, for a price of £10,000 with payment due on February 10, 2011. Boston Company keeps its accounting records in U.S. dollars. To record the sale, Boston Company must translate the sales price from pounds to dollars. This is done using the exchange rate on the date of the sale. Assuming the exchange rate on December 12, 2010, is $1.80, Boston records this sale as follows.

Assets = Liabilities + Equity
+18,000   +18,000

Dec. 12	Accounts Receivable—London Outfitters	18,000	
	Sales*		18,000
	To record a sale at £10,000, when the exchange rate equals $1.80. * (£10,000 × $1.80/£)		

When Boston Company prepares its annual financial statements on December 31, 2010, the current exchange rate is $1.84. Thus, the current dollar value of Boston Company's receivable is $18,400 (£10,000 × $1.84/£). This amount is $400 higher than the amount recorded on December 12. Accounting principles require a receivable to be reported in the balance sheet at its current dollar value. Thus, Boston Company must make the following entry to record the increase in the dollar value of this receivable at year-end.

Assets = Liabilities + Equity
+400   +400

Dec. 31	Accounts Receivable—London Outfitters	400	
	Foreign Exchange Gain		400
	To record the increased value of the British pound for the receivable.		

Point: Foreign exchange gains are credits, and foreign exchange losses are debits.

On February 10, 2011, Boston Company receives London Outfitters' payment of £10,000. It immediately exchanges the pounds for U.S. dollars. On this date, the exchange rate for pounds is $1.78. Thus, Boston Company receives only $17,800 (£10,000 × $1.78/£). It records the cash receipt and the loss associated with the decline in the exchange rate as follows.

Assets = Liabilities + Equity
+17,800   −600
−18,400

Feb. 10	Cash	17,800	
	Foreign Exchange Loss	600	
	Accounts Receivable—London Outfitters		18,400
	Received foreign currency payment of an account and converted it into dollars.		

Gains and losses from foreign exchange transactions are accumulated in the Foreign Exchange Gain (or Loss) account. After year-end adjustments, the balance in the Foreign Exchange Gain (or Loss) account is reported on the income statement and closed to the Income Summary account.

Example: Assume that a U.S. company makes a credit purchase from a British company for £10,000 when the exchange rate is $1.62. At the balance sheet date, this rate is $1.72. Does this imply a gain or loss for the U.S. company? *Answer:* A loss.

Purchases in a Foreign Currency   Accounting for credit purchases from an international seller is similar to the case of a credit sale to an international customer. In particular, if the U.S. company is required to make payment in a foreign currency, the account payable must be translated into dollars before the U.S. company can record it. If the exchange rate is different when preparing financial statements and when paying for the purchase, the U.S. company must recognize a foreign exchange gain or loss at those dates. To illustrate, assume NC Imports, a U.S. company, purchases products costing €20,000 (euros) from

Hamburg Brewing on January 15, when the exchange rate is $1.20 per euro. NC records this transaction as follows.

Jan. 15	Inventory	24,000	
	Accounts Payable—Hamburg Brewing		24,000
	To record a €20,000 purchase when exchange rate is $1.20 (€20,000 × $1.20/€)		

Assets = Liabilities + Equity
+24,000   +24,000

NC Imports makes payment in full on February 14 when the exchange rate is $1.25 per euro, which is recorded as follows.

Feb. 14	Accounts Payable—Hamburg Brewing	24,000	
	Foreign Exchange Loss	1,000	
	Cash		25,000
	To record cash payment towards €20,000 account when exchange rate is $1.25 (€20,000 × $1.25/€).		

Assets = Liabilities + Equity
−25,000   −24,000   −1,000

Decision Insight

Global Greenback   What do changes in foreign exchange rates mean? A decline in the price of the U.S. dollar against other currencies usually yields increased international sales for U.S. companies, without hiking prices or cutting costs, and puts them on a stronger competitive footing abroad. At home, they can raise prices without fear that foreign rivals will undercut them. ■

Consolidated Statements with International Subsidiaries   A second challenge in accounting for international operations involves preparing consolidated financial statements when the parent company has one or more international subsidiaries. Consider a U.S.-based company that owns a controlling interest in a French subsidiary. The reporting currency of the U.S. parent is the dollar. The French subsidiary maintains its financial records in euros. Before preparing consolidated statements, the parent must translate financial statements of the French company into U.S. dollars. After this translation is complete (including that for accounting differences), it prepares consolidated statements the same as for domestic subsidiaries. Procedures for translating an international subsidiary's account balances depend on the nature of the subsidiary's operations. The process requires the parent company to select appropriate foreign exchange rates and to apply those rates to the foreign subsidiary's account balances. This is described in advanced courses.

Global: A weaker U.S. dollar often increases global sales for U.S. companies.

Decision Maker

Answer — p. C-18

Entrepreneur   You are a U.S. home builder that purchases lumber from mills in both the U.S. and Canada. The price of the Canadian dollar in terms of the U.S. dollar jumps from US$0.70 to US$0.80. Are you now more or less likely to buy lumber from Canadian or U.S. mills? ■

Summary

C1 Distinguish between debt and equity securities and between short-term and long-term investments. *Debt securities* reflect a creditor relationship and include investments in notes, bonds, and certificates of deposit. *Equity securities* reflect an owner relationship and include shares of stock issued by other companies. Short-term investments in securities are current assets that meet two criteria: (1) They are expected to be converted into cash within one year or the current operating cycle of the business, whichever is longer and (2) they are readily convertible to cash, or *marketable*. All other investments in securities are long-term. Long-term investments also include assets not used in operations and those held for special purposes, such as land for expansion.

Investments in securities are classified into one of five groups: (1) trading securities, which are always short-term, (2) debt securities held-to-maturity, (3) debt and equity securities available-for-sale, (4) equity securities in which an investor has a significant influence over the investee, and (5) equity securities in which an investor has a controlling influence over the investee.

C2 Describe how to report equity securities with controlling influence. If an investor owns more than 50% of another company's voting stock and controls the investee, the investor's financial reports are prepared on a consolidated basis. These reports are prepared as if the company were organized as one entity.

C3^A **Explain foreign exchange rates and record transactions listed in a foreign currency.** A foreign exchange rate is the price of one currency stated in terms of another. An entity with transactions in a foreign currency when the exchange rate changes between the transaction dates and their settlement will experience exchange gains or losses. When a company makes a credit sale to a foreign customer and sales terms call for payment in a foreign currency, the company must translate the foreign currency into dollars to record the receivable. If the exchange rate changes before payment is received, exchange gains or losses are recognized in the year they occur. The same treatment is used when a company makes a credit purchase from a foreign supplier and is required to make payment in a foreign currency.

A1 **Compute and analyze the components of return on total assets.** Return on total assets has two components: profit margin and total asset turnover. A decline in one component must be met with an increase in another if return on assets is to be maintained. Component analysis is helpful in assessing company performance compared to that of competitors and its own past.

P1 **Account for trading securities.** Investments are initially recorded at cost, and any dividend or interest from these investments is recorded in the income statement. Investments classified as trading securities are reported at fair value. Unrealized gains and losses on trading securities are reported in income. When investments are sold, the difference between the net proceeds from the sale and the cost of the securities is recognized as a gain or loss.

P2 **Account for held-to-maturity securities.** Debt securities held-to-maturity are reported at cost when purchased. Interest revenue is recorded as it accrues. The cost of long-term held-to-maturity securities is adjusted for the amortization of any difference between cost and maturity value.

P3 **Account for available-for-sale securities.** Debt and equity securities available-for-sale are recorded at cost when purchased. Available-for-sale securities are reported at their fair values on the balance sheet with unrealized gains or losses shown in the equity section. Gains and losses realized on the sale of these investments are reported in the income statement.

P4 **Account for equity securities with significant influence.** The equity method is used when an investor has a significant influence over an investee. This usually exists when an investor owns 20% or more of the investee's voting stock but not more than 50%. The equity method means an investor records its share of investee earnings with a debit to the investment account and a credit to a revenue account. Dividends received reduce the investment account balance.

Guidance Answers to Decision Maker

Money Manager If you have investments in fixed-rate bonds and notes when interest rates fall, the value of your investments increases. This is so because the bonds and notes you hold continue to pay the same (high) rate while the market is demanding a new lower interest rate. Your strategy is to continue holding your investments in bonds and notes, and, potentially, to increase these holdings through additional purchases.

Retailer Your store's return on assets is 11%, which is similar to the industry norm of 11.2%. However, disaggregation of return on assets reveals that your store's profit margin of 4.4% is much higher than the norm of 3.5%, but your total asset turnover of 2.5 is much lower than the norm of 3.2. These results suggest that, as compared with competitors, you are less efficient in using assets. You need to focus on increasing sales or reducing assets. You might consider reducing prices to increase sales, provided such a strategy does not reduce your return on assets. For instance, you could reduce your profit margin to 4% to increase sales. If total asset turnover increases to more than 2.75 when profit margin is lowered to 4%, your overall return on assets is improved.

Entrepreneur You are now less likely to buy Canadian lumber because it takes more U.S. money to buy a Canadian dollar (and lumber). For instance, the purchase of lumber from a Canadian mill with a $1,000 (Canadian dollars) price would have cost the U.S. builder $700 (U.S. dollars, computed as C$1,000 × US$0.70) before the rate change, and $800 (US dollars, computed as C$1,000 × US$0.80) after the rate change.

Guidance Answers to Quick Checks

1. Short-term held-to-maturity securities are reported at cost.
2. Trading securities are reported at fair value.
3. The equity section of the balance sheet (and in comprehensive income).
4. The income statement.
5. Long-term investments include (1) long-term funds earmarked for a special purpose, (2) debt and equity securities that do not meet current asset requirements, and (3) long-term assets not used in the regular operations of the business.
6. An equity investment is classified as long term if it is not marketable or, if marketable, it is not held as an available source of cash to meet the needs of current operations.
7. Debt securities held-to-maturity and debt securities available-for-sale are both recorded at cost. Also, interest on both is accrued as earned. However, only long-term securities held-to-maturity require amortization of the difference between cost and maturity value. In addition, only securities available-for-sale require a period-end adjustment to fair value.
8. Long-term equity investments are placed in one of three categories and accounted for as follows: (a) **available-for-sale** (noninfluential, less than 20% of outstanding stock)—fair value; (b) **significant influence** (20% to 50% of outstanding stock)—equity method; and (c) **controlling influence** (holding more than 50% of outstanding stock)—equity method with consolidation.

Key Terms

Available-for-sale (AFS) securities (p. C-5)

Comprehensive income (p. C-9)

Consolidated financial statements (p. C-8)

Equity method (p. C-7)

Equity securities with controlling influence (p. C-8)

Equity securities with significant influence (p. C-7)

Foreign exchange rate (p. C-15)

Held-to-maturity (HTM) securities (p. C-5)

Long-term investments (p. C-1)

Multinational (p. C-15)

Other comprehensive income (p. C-9)

Parent (p. C-8)

Return on total assets (p. C-10)

Short-term investments (p. C-1)

Subsidiary (p. C-8)

Trading securities (p. C-4)

Unrealized gain (loss) (p. C-4)

Multiple Choice Quiz

Answers on p. C-35

mhhe.com/wildFA6e

Additional quiz questions are available at the book's Website.

1. A company purchased $30,000 of 5% bonds for investment purposes on May 1. The bonds pay interest on February 1 and August 1. The amount of interest revenue accrued at December 31 (the company's year-end) is:
   a. $1,500
   b. $1,375
   c. $1,000
   d. $625
   e. $300

2. Earlier this period, Amadeus Co. purchased its only available-for-sale investment in the stock of Bach Co. for $83,000. The period-end fair value of this stock is $84,500. Amadeus records a:
   a. Credit to Unrealized Gain—Equity for $1,500.
   b. Debit to Unrealized Loss—Equity for $1,500.
   c. Debit to Investment Revenue for $1,500.
   d. Credit to Fair Value Adjustment—Available-for-Sale for $3,500.
   e. Credit to Cash for $1,500.

3. Mozart Co. owns 35% of Melody Inc. Melody pays $50,000 in cash dividends to its shareholders for the period. Mozart's entry to record the Melody dividend includes a:
   a. Credit to Investment Revenue for $50,000.
   b. Credit to Long-Term Investments for $17,500.

   c. Credit to Cash for $17,500.
   d. Debit to Long-Term Investments for $17,500.
   e. Debit to Cash for $50,000.

4. A company has net income of $300,000, net sales of $2,500,000, and total assets of $2,000,000. Its return on total assets equals:
   a. 6.7%
   b. 12.0%
   c. 8.3%
   d. 80.0%
   e. 15.0%

5. A company had net income of $80,000, net sales of $600,000, and total assets of $400,000. Its profit margin and total asset turnover are:

	Profit Margin	Total Asset Turnover
a.	1.5%	13.3
b.	13.3%	1.5
c.	13.3%	0.7
d.	7.0%	13.3
e.	10.0%	26.7

^A Superscript A denotes assignments based on Appendix C-A.

Icon denotes assignments that involve decision making.

Discussion Questions

1. Under what two conditions should investments be classified as current assets?

2. [icon] On a balance sheet, what valuation must be reported for short-term investments in trading securities?

3. If a short-term investment in available-for-sale securities costs $6,780 and is sold for $7,500, how should the difference between these two amounts be recorded?

4. Identify the three classes of noninfluential and two classes of influential investments in securities.

5. Under what conditions should investments be classified as current assets? As long-term assets?

6. If a company purchases its only long-term investments in available-for-sale debt securities this period and their fair value is below cost at the balance sheet date, what entry is required to recognize this unrealized loss?

7. On a balance sheet, what valuation must be reported for debt securities classified as available-for-sale?

8. Under what circumstances are long-term investments in debt securities reported at cost and adjusted for amortization of any difference between cost and maturity value?

9. For investments in available-for-sale securities, how are unrealized (holding) gains and losses reported?

10. In accounting for investments in equity securities, when should the equity method be used?

11. Under what circumstances does a company prepare consolidated financial statements?

12.ᴬ What are two major challenges in accounting for international operations?

13.ᴬ Assume a U.S. company makes a credit sale to a foreign customer that is required to make payment in its foreign currency. In the current period, the exchange rate is $1.40 on the date of the sale and is $1.30 on the date the customer pays the receivable. Will the U.S. company record an exchange gain or loss?

14.ᴬ If a U.S. company makes a credit sale to a foreign customer required to make payment in U.S. dollars, can the U.S. company have an exchange gain or loss on this sale?

15. Refer to **Apple**'s statement of changes in shareholders' equity in Appendix A. What is the amount of foreign currency translation adjustment for the year ended September 26, 2009? Is this adjustment an unrealized gain or an unrealized loss?

16. Refer to **Palm**'s statement of stockholders' equity. What was the amount of its fiscal 2009 unrealized gain or loss on securities?

17. Refer to the balance sheet of **Nokia** in Appendix A. How can you tell that Nokia uses the consolidated method of accounting?

18. Refer to the financial statements of **Research In Motion** in Appendix A. Compute its return on total assets for the year ended February 27, 2010.

QUICK STUDY

QS C-1
Describing investments in securities
C1 C2

Complete the following descriptions by filling in the blanks.
1. Accrual of interest on bonds held as long-term investments requires a credit to _____ _____.
2. The controlling investor (more than 50% ownership) is called the _____, and the investee company is called the _____.
3. Trading securities are classified as _____ assets.
4. Equity securities giving an investor significant influence are accounted for using the _____ _____.
5. Available-for-sale debt securities are reported on the balance sheet at _____ _____.

QS C-2
Identifying long-term investments
C1

Which of the following statements are true of long-term investments?
a. They can include investments in trading securities.
b. They are always easily sold and therefore qualify as being marketable.
c. They can include debt and equity securities available-for-sale.
d. They are held as an investment of cash available for current operations.
e. They can include debt securities held-to-maturity.
f. They can include bonds and stocks not intended to serve as a ready source of cash.
g. They can include funds earmarked for a special purpose, such as bond sinking funds.

QS C-3
Short-term equity investments P1

On April 18, Dice Co. made a short-term investment in 500 common shares of XLT Co. The purchase price is $45 per share and the broker's fee is $150. The intent is to actively manage these shares for profit. On May 30, Dice Co. receives $1 per share from XLT in dividends. Prepare the April 18 and May 30 journal entries to record these transactions.

QS C-4
Available-for-sale securities
P3

Fender Co. purchased short-term investments in available-for-sale securities at a cost of $100,000 on November 25, 2011. At December 31, 2011, these securities had a fair value of $94,000. This is the first and only time the company has purchased such securities.
1. Prepare the December 31, 2011, year-end adjusting entry for the securities' portfolio.
2. For each account in the entry for part 1, explain how it is reported in financial statements.
3. Prepare the April 6, 2012, entry when Fender sells one-half of these securities for $52,000.

QS C-5
Available-for-sale securities
P3

Prepare Hoffman Company's journal entries to reflect the following transactions for the current year.
May 7 Purchases 100 shares of Lov stock as a short-term investment in available-for-sale securities at a cost of $25 per share plus $200 in broker fees.
June 6 Sells 100 shares of its investment in Lov stock at $28 per share. The broker's commission on this sale is $75.

Galaxy Company completes the following transactions during the current year.

May 9	Purchases 400 shares of X&O stock as a short-term investment in available-for-sale securities at a cost of $50 per share plus $400 in broker fees.
June 2	Sells 200 shares of its investment in X&O stock at $56 per share. The broker's commission on this sale is $180.
Dec. 31	The closing market price (fair value) of the X&O stock is $46 per share.

Prepare the May 9 and June 2 journal entries and the December 31 adjusting entry. This is the first and only time the company purchased such securities.

QS C-6
Available-for-sale securities
P3

On May 20, 2011, Alexis Co. paid $750,000 to acquire 25,000 common shares (10%) of TKR Corp. as a long-term investment. On August 5, 2012, Alexis sold one-half of these shares for $475,000. What valuation method should be used to account for this stock investment? Prepare entries to record both the acquisition and the sale of these shares.

QS C-7
Recording equity securities
P3

Assume the same facts as in QS C-7 except that the stock acquired represents 40% of TKR Corp.'s outstanding stock. Also assume that TKR Corp. paid a $125,000 dividend on November 1, 2011, and reported a net income of $550,000 for 2011. Prepare the entries to record (a) the receipt of the dividend and (b) the December 31, 2011, year-end adjustment required for the investment account.

QS C-8
Equity method transactions
P4

On February 1, 2011, Charo Mendez purchased 6% bonds issued by CR Utilities at a cost of $30,000, which is their par value. The bonds pay interest semiannually on July 31 and January 31. For 2011, prepare entries to record Mendez's July 31 receipt of interest and its December 31 year-end interest accrual.

QS C-9
Debt securities transactions
P2

During the current year, Patton Consulting Group acquired long-term available-for-sale securities at a $35,000 cost. At its December 31 year-end, these securities had a fair value of $29,000. This is the first and only time the company purchased such securities.

1. Prepare the necessary year-end adjusting entry related to these securities.
2. Explain how each account used in part 1 is reported in the financial statements.

QS C-10
Recording fair value adjustment for securities
P3

The return on total assets is the focus of analysts, creditors, and other users of financial statements.

1. How is the return on total assets computed?
2. What does this important ratio reflect?

QS C-11
Return on total
assets   A1

Return on total assets can be separated into two important components.

1. Write the formula to separate the return on total assets into its two basic components.
2. Explain how these components of the return on total assets are helpful to financial statement users for business decisions.

QS C-12
Component return on total
assets   A1

A U.S. company sells a product to a British company with the transaction listed in British pounds. On the date of the sale, the transaction total of $16,000 is billed as £10,000, reflecting an exchange rate of 1.60 (that is, $1.60 per pound). Prepare the entry to record (1) the sale and (2) the receipt of payment in pounds when the exchange rate is 1.50.

QS C-13[A]
Foreign currency transactions
C3

On March 1, 2011, a U.S. company made a credit sale requiring payment in 30 days from a Malaysian company, Hamac Sdn. Bhd., in 20,000 Malaysian ringgits. Assuming the exchange rate between Malaysian ringgits and U.S. dollars is $0.6811 on March 1 and $0.6985 on March 31, prepare the entries to record the sale on March 1 and the cash receipt on March 31.

QS C-14[A]
Foreign currency transactions
C3

Complete the following descriptions by filling in the blanks.

1. A long-term investment classified as equity securities with controlling influence implies that the investor can exert a _____ influence over the investee.
2. The controlling investor is called the _____, and the investee is called the _____.

QS C-15
Equity securities with controlling influence
C2

QS C-16

International accounting for investments

P1

The **Carrefour Group** reports the following description of its trading securities (titled "financial assets reported at fair value in the income statement").

> These are financial assets held by the Group in order to make a short-term profit on the sale. These assets are valued at their fair value with variations in value recognized in the income statement.

Note 10 to Carrefour's 2008 financial statements reports €117 million in unrealized gains for 2008 and €63 million in unrealized losses for 2008, both included in the fair value of those financial assets held for trading. What amount of these unrealized gains and unrealized losses, if any, are reported in its 2008 income statement? Explain.

connect

EXERCISES

Exercise C-1

Accounting for short-term held-to-maturity securities **P2**

Prepare journal entries to record the following transactions involving the short-term securities investments of Maxwell Co., all of which occurred during year 2011.

a. On February 15, paid $100,000 cash to purchase FTR's 90-day short-term debt securities ($100,000 principal), dated February 15, that pay 8% interest (categorized as held-to-maturity securities).

b. On May 16, received a check from FTR in payment of the principal and 90 days' interest on the debt securities purchased in transaction *a*.

Exercise C-2

Accounting for short-term trading securities

P1

(c) Dr. Cash $13,860

Prepare journal entries to record the following transactions involving the short-term securities investments of Smart Co., all of which occurred during year 2011.

a. On March 22, purchased 700 shares of FIX Company stock at $30 per share plus a $150 brokerage fee. These shares are categorized as trading securities.

b. On September 1, received a $1.00 per share cash dividend on the FIX Company stock purchased in transaction *a*.

c. On October 8, sold 350 shares of FIX Co. stock for $40 per share, less a $140 brokerage fee.

Exercise C-3

Accounting for short-term available-for-sale securities

P3

Prepare journal entries to record the following transactions involving the short-term securities investments of Prairie Co., all of which occurred during year 2011.

a. On August 1, paid $60,000 cash to purchase Better Buy's 10% debt securities ($60,000 principal), dated July 30, 2011, and maturing January 30, 2012 (categorized as available-for-sale securities).

b. On October 30, received a check from Better Buy for 90 days' interest on the debt securities purchased in transaction *a*.

Exercise C-4

Debt and equity securities and short- and long-term investments

C1

Complete the following descriptions by filling in the blanks.

1. Short-term investments are securities that (1) management intends to convert to cash within ___ ___ or the ___ ___ whichever is longer, and (2) are readily convertible to ___.

2. Long-term investments in securities are defined as those securities that are ___ ___ convertible to cash or are ___ ___ to be converted into cash in the short term.

3. Debt securities reflect a ___ relationship such as investments in notes, bonds, and certificates of deposit.

4. Equity securities reflect an ___ relationship such as shares of stock issued by companies.

Exercise C-5

Equity securities with controlling influence

C2

Complete the following descriptions by filling in the blanks.

1. The equity method with ___ is used to account for long-term investments in equity securities with controlling influence.

2. Consolidated ___ ___ show the financial position, results of operations, and cash flows of all entities under the parent's control, including all subsidiaries.

Exercise C-6

Accounting for trading securities

P1

Check (3) Gain, $2,000

Forex Co. purchases various investments in trading securities at a cost of $56,000 on December 27, 2011. (This is its first and only purchase of such securities.) At December 31, 2011, these securities had a fair value of $66,000.

1. Prepare the December 31, 2011, year-end adjusting entry for the trading securities' portfolio.

2. Explain how each account in the entry of part 1 is reported in financial statements.

3. Prepare the January 3, 2012, entry when Forex sells a portion of its trading securities (that had originally cost $28,000) for $30,000.

On December 31, 2011, Rollo Company held the following short-term investments in its portfolio of available-for-sale securities. Rollo had no short-term investments in its prior accounting periods. Prepare the December 31, 2011, adjusting entry to report these investments at fair value.

	Cost	Fair Value
Vicks Corporation bonds payable	$79,600	$90,600
Pace Corporation notes payable	60,600	52,900
Lake Lugano Company common stock	85,500	82,100

Exercise C-7
Adjusting available-for-sale securities to fair value

P3

Check Unrealized loss, $100

Prepare journal entries to record the following transactions involving both the short-term and long-term investments of Sophia Corp., all of which occurred during calendar year 2011. Use the account Short-Term Investments for any transactions that you determine are short term.

a. On February 15, paid $150,000 cash to purchase American General's 120-day short-term notes at par, which are dated February 15 and pay 10% interest (classified as held-to-maturity).

b. On March 22, bought 700 shares of Frain Industries common stock at $25 cash per share plus a $250 brokerage fee (classified as long-term available-for-sale securities).

c. On June 15, received a check from American General in payment of the principal and 120 days' interest on the notes purchased in transaction *a*.

d. On July 30, paid $50,000 cash to purchase MP3 Electronics' 8% notes at par, dated July 30, 2011, and maturing on January 30, 2012 (classified as trading securities).

e. On September 1, received a $0.50 per share cash dividend on the Frain Industries common stock purchased in transaction *b*.

f. On October 8, sold 350 shares of Frain Industries common stock for $32 cash per share, less a $175 brokerage fee.

g. On October 30, received a check from MP3 Electronics for three months' interest on the notes purchased in transaction *d*.

Exercise C-8
Transactions in short-term and long-term investments

P1 P2 P3

On December 31, 2011, Manhattan Co. held the following short-term available-for-sale securities.

	Cost	Fair Value
Nintendo Co. common stock	$68,900	$75,300
Atlantic bonds payable	24,500	22,800
Kellogg Co. notes payable	50,000	47,200
McDonald's Corp. common stock	91,400	86,600

Manhattan had no short-term investments prior to the current period. Prepare the December 31, 2011, year-end adjusting entry to record the fair value adjustment for these securities.

Exercise C-9
Fair value adjustment to available-for-sale securities

P3

Berroa Co. began operations in 2010. The cost and fair values for its long-term investments portfolio in available-for-sale securities are shown below. Prepare Berroa's December 31, 2011, adjusting entry to reflect any necessary fair value adjustment for these investments.

	Cost	Fair Value
December 31, 2010	$79,483	$72,556
December 31, 2011	85,120	90,271

Exercise C-10
Fair value adjustment to available-for-sale securities

P3

Ticker Services began operations in 2009 and maintains long-term investments in available-for-sale securities. The year-end cost and fair values for its portfolio of these investments follow. Prepare journal entries to record each year-end fair value adjustment for these securities.

	Cost	Fair Value
December 31, 2009	$374,000	$362,560
December 31, 2010	426,900	453,200
December 31, 2011	580,700	686,450
December 31, 2012	875,500	778,800

Exercise C-11
Multiyear fair value adjustments to available-for-sale securities

P3

Exercise C-12
Classifying investments in securities; recording fair values

C1 P2 P3 P4

Information regarding Central Company's individual investments in securities during its calendar-year 2011, along with the December 31, 2011, fair values, follows.

a. Investment in Beeman Company bonds: $418,500 cost, $455,000 fair value. Central intends to hold these bonds until they mature in 2016.

b. Investment in Baybridge common stock: 29,500 shares; $332,450 cost; $361,375 fair value. Central owns 32% of Baybridge's voting stock and has a significant influence over Baybridge.

c. Investment in Carroll common stock: 12,000 shares; $169,750 cost; $183,000 fair value. This investment amounts to 3% of Carroll's outstanding shares, and Central's goal with this investment is to earn dividends over the next few years.

d. Investment in Newtech common stock: 3,500 shares; $95,300 cost; $93,625 fair value. Central's goal with this investment is to reap an increase in fair value of the stock over the next three to five years. Newtech has 30,000 common shares outstanding.

e. Investment in Flock common stock: 16,300 shares; $102,860 cost; $109,210 fair value. This stock is marketable and is held as an investment of cash available for operations.

Required

1. Identify whether each investment should be classified as a short-term or long-term investment. For each long-term investment, indicate in which of the long-term investment classifications it should be placed.

2. Prepare a journal entry dated December 31, 2011, to record the fair value adjustment of the long-term investments in available-for-sale securities. Central had no long-term investments prior to year 2011.

Check   (2) Unrealized gain, $11,575

Exercise C-13
Securities transactions; equity method

P4

Prepare journal entries to record the following transactions and events of Kash Company.

2011

Jan. 2   Purchased 30,000 shares of Bushtex Co. common stock for $204,000 cash plus a broker's fee of $3,480 cash. Bushtex has 90,000 shares of common stock outstanding and its policies will be significantly influenced by Kash.

Sept. 1   Bushtex declared and paid a cash dividend of $3.10 per share.

Dec. 31   Bushtex announced that net income for the year is $624,900.

2012

June 1   Bushtex declared and paid a cash dividend of $3.60 per share.

Dec. 31   Bushtex announced that net income for the year is $699,750.

Dec. 31   Kash sold 10,000 shares of Bushtex for $162,500 cash.

Exercise C-14
Return on total assets

A1

The following information is available from the financial statements of Wright Industries. Compute Wright's return on total assets for 2011 and 2012. (Round returns to one-tenth of a percent.) Comment on the company's efficiency in using its assets in 2011 and 2012.

	2010	2011	2012
Total assets, December 31	$190,000	$320,000	$750,000
Net income	28,200	36,400	58,300

Exercise C-15^A
Foreign currency transactions

C3

Desi of New York sells its products to customers in the United States and the United Kingdom. On December 16, 2011, Desi sold merchandise on credit to Bronson Ltd. of London at a price of 17,000 pounds. The exchange rate on that day for £1 was $1.5238. On December 31, 2011, when Desi prepared its financial statements, the rate was £1 for $1.4990. Bronson paid its bill in full on January 15, 2012, at which time the exchange rate was £1 for $1.5156. Desi immediately exchanged the 17,000 pounds for U.S. dollars. Prepare Desi's journal entries on December 16, December 31, and January 15 (round to the nearest dollar).

On May 8, 2011, Jett Company (a U.S. company) made a credit sale to Lopez (a Mexican company). The terms of the sale required Lopez to pay 800,000 pesos on February 10, 2012. Jett prepares quarterly financial statements on March 31, June 30, September 30, and December 31. The exchange rates for pesos during the time the receivable is outstanding follow.

Exercise C-16[A]
Computing foreign exchange gains and losses on receivables
C3

May 8, 2011	$0.1984
June 30, 2011	0.2013
September 30, 2011	0.2029
December 31, 2011	0.1996
February 10, 2012	0.2047

Compute the foreign exchange gain or loss that Jett should report on each of its quarterly income statements for the last three quarters of 2011 and the first quarter of 2012. Also compute the amount reported on Jett's balance sheets at the end of each of its last three quarters of 2011.

The **Carrefour Group** reports the following description of its financial assets available-for-sale.

Exercise C-17
International accounting for investments
P3

> Assets available for sale are . . . valued at fair value. Unrealized . . . gains or losses are recorded as shareholders' equity until they are sold.

Note 10 to Carrefour's 2008 financial statements reports €6 million in *net* unrealized losses (net of unrealized gains) for 2008, which is included in the fair value of its available-for-sale securities reported on the balance sheet.

1. What amount of the €6 million net unrealized losses, if any, is reported in its 2008 income statement? Explain.

2. If the €6 million net unrealized losses are not reported in the income statement, in which statement are they reported, if any? Explain.

 connect

Ryder Company, which began operations in 2011, invests its idle cash in trading securities. The following transactions are from its short-term investments in its trading securities.

PROBLEM SET A

Problem C-1A
Recording transactions and fair value adjustments for trading securities
P1

2011

Jan. 20   Purchased 900 shares of Ford Motor Co. at $36 per share plus a $125 commission.
Feb. 9   Purchased 4,400 shares of Lucent at $10 per share plus a $200 commission.
Oct. 12   Purchased 500 shares of Z-Seven at $8 per share plus a $100 commission.

2012

Apr. 15   Sold 900 shares of Ford Motor Co. at $39 per share less a $185 commission.
July 5   Sold 500 shares of Z-Seven at $10.25 per share less a $100 commission.
July 22   Purchased 800 shares of Hunt Corp. at $30 per share plus a $225 commission.
Aug. 19   Purchased 1,000 shares of Donna Karan at $12 per share plus a $100 commission.

2013

Feb. 27   Purchased 3,400 shares of HCA at $22 per share plus a $220 commission.
Mar. 3   Sold 800 shares of Hunt at $25 per share less a $125 commission.
June 21   Sold 4,400 shares of Lucent at $8 per share less a $180 commission.
June 30   Purchased 1,000 shares of Black & Decker at $47.50 per share plus a $195 commission.
Nov. 1   Sold 1,000 shares of Donna Karan at $22 per share less a $208 commission.

Required

1. Prepare journal entries to record these short-term investment activities for the years shown. (Ignore any year-end adjusting entries.)

2. On December 31, 2013, prepare the adjusting entry to record any necessary fair value adjustment for the portfolio of trading securities when HCA's share price is $24 and Black & Decker's share price is $43.50. (Assume the Fair Value Adjustment—Trading account had an unadjusted balance of zero.)

Check   (2) Dr. Fair Value Adjustment—Trading $2,385

Problem C-2A

Recording, adjusting, and reporting short-term available-for-sale securities

P3

Perry Company had no short-term investments prior to year 2011. It had the following transactions involving short-term investments in available-for-sale securities during 2011.

Apr.	16	Purchased 8,000 shares of Gem Co. stock at $24.25 per share plus a $360 brokerage fee.
May	1	Paid $200,000 to buy 90-day U.S. Treasury bills (debt securities): $200,000 principal amount, 6% interest, securities dated May 1.
July	7	Purchased 4,000 shares of PepsiCo stock at $49.25 per share plus a $350 brokerage fee.
	20	Purchased 2,000 shares of Xerox stock at $16.75 per share plus a $410 brokerage fee.
Aug.	3	Received a check for principal and accrued interest on the U.S. Treasury bills that matured on July 29.
	15	Received an $0.85 per share cash dividend on the Gem Co. stock.
	28	Sold 4,000 shares of Gem Co. stock at $30 per share less a $450 brokerage fee.
Oct.	1	Received a $1.90 per share cash dividend on the PepsiCo shares.
Dec.	15	Received a $1.05 per share cash dividend on the remaining Gem Co. shares.
	31	Received a $1.30 per share cash dividend on the PepsiCo shares.

Required

1. Prepare journal entries to record the preceding transactions and events.

Check (2) Cost = $328,440

2. Prepare a table to compare the year-end cost and fair values of Perry's short-term investments in available-for-sale securities. The year-end fair values per share are: Gem Co., $26.50; PepsiCo, $46.50; and Xerox, $13.75.

(3) Dr. Unrealized Loss—Equity $8,940

3. Prepare an adjusting entry, if necessary, to record the year-end fair value adjustment for the portfolio of short-term investments in available-for-sale securities.

Analysis Component

4. Explain the balance sheet presentation of the fair value adjustment for Perry's short-term investments.

5. How do these short-term investments affect Perry's (a) income statement for year 2011 and (b) the equity section of its balance sheet at year-end 2011?

Problem C-3A

Recording, adjusting, and reporting long-term available-for-sale securities

P3

Shaq Security, which began operations in 2011, invests in long-term available-for-sale securities. Following is a series of transactions and events determining its long-term investment activity.

2011

Jan.	20	Purchased 900 shares of Johnson & Johnson at $18.75 per share plus a $590 commission.
Feb.	9	Purchased 2,200 shares of Sony at $46.88 per share plus a $2,578 commission.
June	12	Purchased 500 shares of Mattel at $55.50 per share plus an $832 commission.
Dec.	31	Per share fair values for stocks in the portfolio are Johnson & Johnson, $20.38; Mattel, $57.25; Sony, $39.

2012

Apr.	15	Sold 900 shares of Johnson & Johnson at $21.75 per share less a $685 commission.
July	5	Sold 500 shares of Mattel at $49.13 per share less a $491 commission.
July	22	Purchased 1,600 shares of Sara Lee at $36.25 per share plus a $1,740 commission.
Aug.	19	Purchased 1,800 shares of Eastman Kodak at $28 per share plus a $1,260 commission.
Dec.	31	Per share fair values for stocks in the portfolio are: Kodak, $31.75; Sara Lee, $30.00; Sony, $36.50.

2013

Feb.	27	Purchased 3,400 shares of Microsoft at $23.63 per share plus a $1,606 commission.
June	21	Sold 2,200 shares of Sony at $40.00 per share less a $2,640 commission.
June	30	Purchased 1,200 shares of Black & Decker at $47.50 per share plus a $1,995 commission.
Aug.	3	Sold 1,600 shares of Sara Lee at $31.25 per share less a $1,750 commission.
Nov.	1	Sold 1,800 shares of Eastman Kodak at $42.75 per share less a $2,309 commission.
Dec.	31	Per share fair values for stocks in the portfolio are: Black & Decker, $56.50; Microsoft, $28.

Required

1. Prepare journal entries to record these transactions and events and any year-end fair value adjustments to the portfolio of long-term available-for-sale securities.

2. Prepare a table that summarizes the (*a*) total cost, (*b*) total fair value adjustment, and (*c*) total fair value of the portfolio of long-term available-for-sale securities at each year-end.

3. Prepare a table that summarizes (*a*) the realized gains and losses and (*b*) the unrealized gains or losses for the portfolio of long-term available-for-sale securities at each year-end.

Check   (2b) Fair Value Adjustment bal.: 12/31/11, $(18,994); 12/31/12; $(31,664)

(3b) Unrealized Gain at 12/31/2013, $22,057

Problem C-4A
Long-term investment transactions; unrealized and realized gains and losses
C2   P3   P4

Park Co.'s long-term available-for-sale portfolio at December 31, 2010, consists of the following.

Available-for-Sale Securities	Cost	Fair Value
80,000 shares of Company A common stock	$1,070,600	$ 980,000
14,000 shares of Company B common stock	318,750	308,000
35,000 shares of Company C common stock	1,325,500	1,281,875

Park enters into the following long-term investment transactions during year 2011.

Jan. 29   Sold 7,000 shares of Company B common stock for $158,375 less a brokerage fee of $3,100.
Apr. 17   Purchased 20,000 shares of Company W common stock for $395,000 plus a brokerage fee of $3,500. The shares represent a 30% ownership in Company W.
July 6   Purchased 9,000 shares of Company X common stock for $253,125 plus a brokerage fee of $3,500. The shares represent a 10% ownership in Company X.
Aug. 22   Purchased 100,000 shares of Company Y common stock for $750,000 plus a brokerage fee of $8,200. The shares represent a 51% ownership in Company Y.
Nov. 13   Purchased 17,000 shares of Company Z common stock for $533,800 plus a brokerage fee of $6,900. The shares represent a 5% ownership in Company Z.
Dec. 9   Sold 80,000 shares of Company A common stock for $1,030,000 less a brokerage fee of $4,100.

The fair values of its investments at December 31, 2011, are: B, $162,750; C, $1,220,625; W, $382,500; X, $236,250; Y, $1,062,500; and Z, $557,600.

Required

1. Determine the amount Park should report on its December 31, 2011, balance sheet for its long-term investments in available-for-sale securities.

2. Prepare any necessary December 31, 2011, adjusting entry to record the fair value adjustment for the long-term investments in available-for-sale securities.

Check   (2) Cr. Unrealized Loss— Equity, $40,000

3. What amount of gains or losses on transactions relating to long-term investments in available-for-sale securities should Park report on its December 31, 2011, income statement?

Pillar Steel Co., which began operations on January 4, 2011, had the following subsequent transactions and events in its long-term investments.

Problem C-5A
Accounting for long-term investments in securities; with and without significant influence
P3   P4

2011

Jan. 5   Pillar purchased 30,000 shares (20% of total) of Kildaire's common stock for $780,000.
Oct. 23   Kildaire declared and paid a cash dividend of $1.60 per share.
Dec. 31   Kildaire's net income for 2011 is $582,000, and the fair value of its stock at December 31 is $27.75 per share.

2012

Oct. 15   Kildaire declared and paid a cash dividend of $1.30 per share.
Dec. 31   Kildaire's net income for 2012 is $738,000, and the fair value of its stock at December 31 is $30.45 per share.

2013

Jan. 2   Pillar sold all of its investment in Kildaire for $947,000 cash.

Part 1

Assume that Pillar has a significant influence over Kildaire with its 20% share of stock.

Required

1. Prepare journal entries to record these transactions and events for Pillar.

2. Compute the carrying (book) value per share of Pillar's investment in Kildaire common stock as reflected in the investment account on January 1, 2013.

Check   (2) Carrying value per share, $31.90

3. Compute the net increase or decrease in Pillar's equity from January 5, 2011, through January 2, 2013, resulting from its investment in Kildaire.

Part 2

Assume that although Pillar owns 20% of Kildaire's outstanding stock, circumstances indicate that it does not have a significant influence over the investee and that it is classified as an available-for-sale security investment.

Required

(1) 1/2/2013 Dr. Unrealized Gain—Equity $133,500

1. Prepare journal entries to record the preceding transactions and events for Pillar. Also prepare an entry dated January 2, 2013, to remove any balance related to the fair value adjustment.

2. Compute the cost per share of Pillar's investment in Kildaire common stock as reflected in the investment account on January 1, 2013.

(3) Net increase, $254,000

3. Compute the net increase or decrease in Pillar's equity from January 5, 2011, through January 2, 2013, resulting from its investment in Kildaire.

Problem C-6A[A]
Foreign currency transactions
C3

Roundtree Company, a U.S. corporation with customers in several foreign countries, had the following selected transactions for 2011 and 2012.

2011

Apr. 8 Sold merchandise to Salinas & Sons of Mexico for $7,938 cash. The exchange rate for pesos is $0.1323 on this day.

July 21 Sold merchandise on credit to Sumito Corp. in Japan. The price of 1.5 million yen is to be paid 120 days from the date of sale. The exchange rate for yen is $0.0096 on this day.

Oct. 14 Sold merchandise for 19,000 pounds to Smithers Ltd. of Great Britain, payment in full to be received in 90 days. The exchange rate for pounds is $1.5181 on this day.

Nov. 18 Received Sumito's payment in yen for its July 21 purchase and immediately exchanged the yen for dollars. The exchange rate for yen is $0.0091 on this day.

Dec. 20 Sold merchandise for 17,000 ringgits to Hamid Albar of Malaysia, payment in full to be received in 30 days. On this day, the exchange rate for ringgits is $0.6852.

Dec. 31 Recorded adjusting entries to recognize exchange gains or losses on Roundtree's annual financial statements. Rates for exchanging foreign currencies on this day follow.

Pesos (Mexico)	$0.1335
Yen (Japan)	0.0095
Pounds (Britain)	1.5235
Ringgits (Malaysia)	0.6807

2012

Jan. 12 Received full payment in pounds from Smithers for the October 14 sale and immediately exchanged the pounds for dollars. The exchange rate for pounds is $1.5314 on this day.

Jan. 19 Received Hamid Albar's full payment in ringgits for the December 20 sale and immediately exchanged the ringgits for dollars. The exchange rate for ringgits is $0.6771 on this day.

Required

1. Prepare journal entries for the Roundtree transactions and adjusting entries (round amounts to the nearest dollar).

2. Compute the foreign exchange gain or loss to be reported on Roundtree's 2011 income statement.

Check (2) 2011 total foreign exchange loss, $723

Analysis Component

3. What actions might Roundtree consider to reduce its risk of foreign exchange gains or losses?

PROBLEM SET B

Deal Company, which began operations in 2011, invests its idle cash in trading securities. The following transactions relate to its short-term investments in its trading securities.

Problem C-1B
Recording transactions and fair value adjustments for trading securities P1

2011

Mar. 10 Purchased 1,200 shares of AOL at $59.15 per share plus a $773 commission.
May 7 Purchased 2,500 shares of MTV at $36.25 per share plus a $1,428 commission.
Sept. 1 Purchased 600 shares of UPS at $57.25 per share plus a $625 commission.

2012

Apr. 26 Sold 2,500 shares of MTV at $34.50 per share less a $1,025 commission.
Apr. 27 Sold 600 shares of UPS at $60.50 per share less an $894 commission.

June   2   Purchased 1,800 shares of SPW at $172 per share plus a $1,625 commission.
June 14   Purchased 450 shares of Walmart at $50.25 per share plus a $541.50 commission.

2013

Jan. 28   Purchased 1,000 shares of PepsiCo at $43 per share plus a $1,445 commission.
Jan. 31   Sold 1,800 shares of SPW at $168 per share less a $1,020 commission.
Aug. 22   Sold 1,200 shares of AOL at $56.75 per share less a $1,240 commission.
Sept. 3   Purchased 750 shares of Vodaphone at $40.50 per share plus an $840 commission.
Oct.   9   Sold 450 shares of Walmart at $53.75 per share less a $610.50 commission.

Required

1. Prepare journal entries to record these short-term investment activities for the years shown. (Ignore any year-end adjusting entries.)

2. On December 31, 2013, prepare the adjusting entry to record any necessary fair value adjustment for the portfolio of trading securities when PepsiCo's share price is $41 and Vodaphone's share price is $37. (Assume the Fair Value Adjustment—Trading account had an unadjusted balance of zero.)

Check (2) Cr. Fair Value Adjustment—Trading $6,910

Day Systems had no short-term investments prior to 2011. It had the following transactions involving short-term investments in available-for-sale securities during 2011.

Feb.   6   Purchased 1,700 shares of Nokia stock at $41.25 per share plus a $1,500 brokerage fee.
      15   Paid $10,000 to buy six-month U.S. Treasury bills (debt securities): $10,000 principal amount, 6% interest, securities dated February 15.
Apr.   7   Purchased 600 shares of Dell Co. stock at $39.50 per share plus a $627 brokerage fee.
June   2   Purchased 1,250 shares of Merck stock at $72.50 per share plus a $1,945 brokerage fee.
      30   Received a $0.19 per share cash dividend on the Nokia shares.
Aug. 11   Sold 425 shares of Nokia stock at $46 per share less a $525 brokerage fee.
      16   Received a check for principal and accrued interest on the U.S. Treasury bills purchased February 15.
      24   Received a $0.10 per share cash dividend on the Dell shares.
Nov.   9   Received a $0.20 per share cash dividend on the remaining Nokia shares.
Dec. 18   Received a $0.15 per share cash dividend on the Dell shares.

Problem C-2B
Recording, adjusting, and reporting short-term available-for-sale securities

P3

Required

1. Prepare journal entries to record the preceding transactions and events.

2. Prepare a table to compare the year-end cost and fair values of the short-term investments in available-for-sale securities. The year-end fair values per share are: Nokia, $40.25; Dell, $41; and Merck, $59.

Check (2) Cost = $170,616

3. Prepare an adjusting entry, if necessary, to record the year-end fair value adjustment for the portfolio of short-term investments in available-for-sale securities.

(3) Dr. Unrealized Loss—Equity, $20,947

Analysis Component

4. Explain the balance sheet presentation of the fair value adjustment to Day's short-term investments.

5. How do these short-term investments affect (*a*) its income statement for year 2011 and (*b*) the equity section of its balance sheet at the 2011 year-end?

Venice Enterprises, which began operations in 2011, invests in long-term available-for-sale securities. Following is a series of transactions and events involving its long-term investment activity.

2011

Mar. 10   Purchased 2,400 shares of Apple at $33.25 per share plus $1,995 commission.
Apr.   7   Purchased 5,000 shares of Ford at $17.50 per share plus $2,625 commission.
Sept. 1   Purchased 1,200 shares of Polaroid at $49.00 per share plus $1,176 commission.
Dec. 31   Per share fair values for stocks in the portfolio are: Apple, $35.50; Ford, $17.00; Polaroid, $51.75.

2012

Apr. 26   Sold 5,000 shares of Ford at $16.38 per share less a $2,237 commission.
June   2   Purchased 3,600 shares of Duracell at $18.88 per share plus a $2,312 commission.
June 14   Purchased 900 shares of Sears at $24.50 per share plus a $541 commission.
Nov. 27   Sold 1,200 shares of Polaroid at $52 per share less a $1,672 commission.
Dec. 31   Per share fair values for stocks in the portfolio are: Apple, $35.50; Duracell, $18.00; Sears, $26.00.

Problem C-3B
Recording, adjusting, and reporting long-term available-for-sale securities

P3

2013

Jan. 28 Purchased 2,000 shares of Coca-Cola Co. at $41 per share plus a $3,280 commission.
Aug. 22 Sold 2,400 shares of Apple at $29.75 per share less a $2,339 commission.
Sept. 3 Purchased 1,500 shares of Motorola at $29 per share plus a $870 commission.
Oct.   9 Sold 900 shares of Sears at $27.50 per share less a $619 commission.
Oct. 31 Sold 3,600 shares of Duracell at $16.00 per share less a $1,496 commission.
Dec. 31 Per share fair values for stocks in the portfolio are: Coca-Cola, $46.00; Motorola, $22.00.

Required

1. Prepare journal entries to record these transactions and events and any year-end fair value adjustments to the portfolio of long-term available-for-sale securities.

Check (2b) Fair Value Adjustment
bal.: 12/31/11, $404; 12/31/12, $(1,266)

   (3b) Unrealized Loss at 12/31/2013, $4,650

2. Prepare a table that summarizes the (*a*) total cost, (*b*) total fair value adjustment, and (*c*) total fair value for the portfolio of long-term available-for-sale securities at each year-end.

3. Prepare a table that summarizes (*a*) the realized gains and losses and (*b*) the unrealized gains or losses for the portfolio of long-term available-for-sale securities at each year-end.

Problem C-4B

Long-term investment transactions; unrealized and realized gains and losses

C2 P3 P4

Capollo's long-term available-for-sale portfolio at December 31, 2010, consists of the following.

Available-for-Sale Securities	Cost	Fair Value
45,000 shares of Company R common stock	$1,118,250	$1,198,125
17,000 shares of Company S common stock	616,760	586,500
22,000 shares of Company T common stock	294,470	303,600

Capollo enters into the following long-term investment transactions during year 2011.

Jan. 13 Sold 4,250 shares of Company S stock for $144,500 less a brokerage fee of $2,390.
Mar. 24 Purchased 31,000 shares of Company U common stock for $565,750 plus a brokerage fee of $9,900. The shares represent a 62% ownership interest in Company U.
Apr.   5 Purchased 85,000 shares of Company V common stock for $267,750 plus a brokerage fee of $4,500. The shares represent a 10% ownership in Company V.
Sept. 2 Sold 22,000 shares of Company T common stock for $313,500 less a brokerage fee of $5,400.
Sept. 27 Purchased 5,000 shares of Company W common stock for $101,000 plus a brokerage fee of $2,100. The shares represent a 25% ownership interest in Company W.
Oct. 30 Purchased 10,000 shares of Company X common stock for $97,500 plus a brokerage fee of $2,340. The shares represent a 13% ownership interest in Company X.

The fair values of its investments at December 31, 2011, are: R, $1,136,250; S, $420,750; U, $545,600; V, $269,875; W, $109,375; and X, $91,250.

Required

1. Determine the amount Capollo should report on its December 31, 2011, balance sheet for its long-term investments in available-for-sale securities.

Check (2) Dr. Unrealized Loss—
Equity, $34,785; Cr. Fair Value
Adjustment—AFS (LT), $93,530

2. Prepare any necessary December 31, 2011, adjusting entry to record the fair value adjustment of the long-term investments in available-for-sale securities.

3. What amount of gains or losses on transactions relating to long-term investments in available-for-sale securities should Capollo report on its December 31, 2011, income statement?

Problem C-5B

Accounting for long-term investments in securities; with and without significant influence

P3 P4

Bengal Company, which began operations on January 3, 2011, had the following subsequent transactions and events in its long-term investments.

2011

Jan.   5 Bengal purchased 15,000 shares (25% of total) of Bloch's common stock for $187,500.
Aug.   1 Bloch declared and paid a cash dividend of $0.95 per share.
Dec. 31 Bloch's net income for 2011 is $92,000, and the fair value of its stock is $12.90 per share.

2012

Aug.   1 Bloch declared and paid a cash dividend of $1.25 per share.
Dec. 31 Bloch's net income for 2012 is $76,000, and the fair value of its stock is $13.55 per share.

2013

Jan.   8   Bengal sold all of its investment in Bloch for $204,750 cash.

Part 1

Assume that Bengal has a significant influence over Bloch with its 25% share.

Required

1. Prepare journal entries to record these transactions and events for Bengal.
2. Compute the carrying (book) value per share of Bengal's investment in Bloch common stock as reflected in the investment account on January 7, 2013.
3. Compute the net increase or decrease in Bengal's equity from January 5, 2011, through January 8, 2013, resulting from its investment in Bloch.

Part 2

Assume that although Bengal owns 25% of Bloch's outstanding stock, circumstances indicate that it does not have a significant influence over the investee and that it is classified as an available-for-sale security investment.

Required

1. Prepare journal entries to record these transactions and events for Bengal. Also prepare an entry dated January 8, 2013, to remove any balance related to the fair value adjustment.
2. Compute the cost per share of Bengal's investment in Bloch common stock as reflected in the investment account on January 7, 2013.
3. Compute the net increase or decrease in Bengal's equity from January 5, 2011, through January 8, 2013, resulting from its investment in Bloch.

Check (2) Carrying value per share, $13.10

(1) 1/8/2013 Dr. Unrealized Gain—Equity $15,750

(3) Net increase, $50,250

Datamix, a U.S. corporation with customers in several foreign countries, had the following selected transactions for 2011 and 2012.

Problem C-6B[A]
Foreign currency transactions
C3

2011

May 26   Sold merchandise for 6.5 million yen to Fuji Company of Japan, payment in full to be received in 60 days. On this day, the exchange rate for yen is $0.0094.

June   1   Sold merchandise to Fordham Ltd. of Great Britain for $72,613 cash. The exchange rate for pounds is $1.5277 on this day.

July 25   Received Fuji's payment in yen for its May 26 purchase and immediately exchanged the yen for dollars. The exchange rate for yen is $0.0090 on this day.

Oct. 15   Sold merchandise on credit to Martinez Brothers of Mexico. The price of 373,000 pesos is to be paid 90 days from the date of sale. On this day, the exchange rate for pesos is $0.1340.

Dec.   6   Sold merchandise for 242,000 yuans to Chi-Ying Company of China, payment in full to be received in 30 days. The exchange rate for yuans is $0.1975 on this day.

Dec. 31   Recorded adjusting entries to recognize exchange gains or losses on Datamix's annual financial statements. Rates of exchanging foreign currencies on this day follow.

Yen (Japan)	$0.0094
Pounds (Britain)	1.5318
Pesos (Mexico)	0.1560
Yuans (China)	0.2000

2012

Jan.   5   Received Chi-Ying's full payment in yuans for the December 6 sale and immediately exchanged the yuans for dollars. The exchange rate for yuans is $0.2060 on this day.

Jan. 13   Received full payment in pesos from Martinez for the October 15 sale and immediately exchanged the pesos for dollars. The exchange rate for pesos is $0.1420 on this day.

Required

1. Prepare journal entries for the Datamix transactions and adjusting entries.
2. Compute the foreign exchange gain or loss to be reported on Datamix's 2011 income statement.

Check (2) 2011 total foreign exchange gain, $6,211

Analysis Component

3. What actions might Datamix consider to reduce its risk of foreign exchange gains or losses?

SERIAL PROBLEM

Business Solutions

P1

(This serial problem began in Chapter 1 and continues through most of the book. If previous chapter segments were not completed, the serial problem can begin at this point. It is helpful, but not necessary, to use the Working Papers that accompany the book.)

SP C   While reviewing the March 31, 2012, balance sheet of Business Solutions, Santana Rey notes that the business has built a large cash balance of $68,057. Its most recent bank money market statement shows that the funds are earning an annualized return of 0.75%. S. Rey decides to make several investments with the desire to earn a higher return on the idle cash balance. Accordingly, in April 2012, Business Solutions makes the following investments in trading securities:

April 16   Purchases 400 shares of Johnson & Johnson stock at $50 per share plus $300 commission.
April 30   Purchases 200 shares of Starbucks Corporation at $22 per share plus $250 commission.

On June 30, 2012, the per share market price (fair value) of the Johnson & Johnson shares is $55 and the Starbucks shares is $19.

Required

1. Prepare journal entries to record the April purchases of trading securities by Business Solutions.
2. On June 30, 2012, prepare the adjusting entry to record any necessary fair value adjustment to its portfolio of trading securities.

Beyond the Numbers

REPORTING IN ACTION

C3 A1

RIM

BTN C-1   Refer to **Research In Motion**'s financial statements in Appendix A to answer the following.
1. Are Research In Motion's financial statements consolidated? How can you tell?
2. What is Research In Motion's *comprehensive income* for the year ended February 27, 2010?
3. Does Research In Motion have any foreign operations? How can you tell?
4. Compute Research In Motion's return on total assets for the year ended February 27, 2010.

Fast Forward

5. Access Research In Motion's annual report for a fiscal year ending after February 27, 2010, from either its Website (**RIM.com**) or the SEC's database (**www.SEC.gov**). Recompute Research In Motion's return on total assets for the years subsequent to February 27, 2010.

COMPARATIVE ANALYSIS

A1

RIM

Apple

BTN C-2   Key figures for **Research In Motion** and **Apple** follow.

($ millions)	Research In Motion			Apple		
	Current Year	1 Year Prior	2 Years Prior	Current Year	1 Year Prior	2 Years Prior
Net income	$ 2,457	$1,893	$1,294	$ 8,235	$ 6,119	$ 3,495
Net sales	12,536	9,411	4,914	42,905	37,491	24,578
Total assets	10,204	8,101	5,511	47,501	36,171	25,347

Required

1. Compute return on total assets for Research In Motion and Apple for the two most recent years.
2. Separate the return on total assets computed in part 1 into its components for both companies and both years according to the formula in Exhibit C.9.
3. Which company has the highest total return on assets? The highest profit margin? The highest total asset turnover? What does this comparative analysis reveal? (Assume an industry average of 10.0% for return on assets.)

ETHICS CHALLENGE

P2 P3

BTN C-3   Kendra Wecker is the controller for Wildcat Company, which has numerous long-term investments in debt securities. Wildcat's investments are mainly in 10-year bonds. Wecker is preparing its year-end financial statements. In accounting for long-term debt securities, she knows that each long-term investment must be designated as a held-to-maturity or an available-for-sale security. Interest rates rose sharply this past year causing the portfolio's fair value to substantially decline. The company does not intend to hold the bonds for the entire 10 years. Wecker also earns a bonus each year, which is computed as a percent of net income.

Required

1. Will Wecker's bonus depend in any way on the classification of the debt securities? Explain.
2. What criteria must Wecker use to classify the securities as held-to-maturity or available-for-sale?
3. Is there likely any company oversight of Wecker's classification of the securities? Explain.

BTN C-4 Assume that you are Jackson Company's accountant. Company owner Abel Terrio has reviewed the 2011 financial statements you prepared and questions the $6,000 loss reported on the sale of its investment in Blackhawk Co. common stock. Jackson acquired 50,000 shares of Blackhawk's common stock on December 31, 2009, at a cost of $500,000. This stock purchase represented a 40% interest in Blackhawk. The 2010 income statement reported that earnings from all investments were $126,000. On January 3, 2011, Jackson Company sold the Blackhawk stock for $575,000. Blackhawk did not pay any dividends during 2010 but reported a net income of $202,500 for that year. Terrio believes that because the Blackhawk stock purchase price was $500,000 and was sold for $575,000, the 2011 income statement should report a $75,000 gain on the sale.

COMMUNICATING IN PRACTICE

P4

Required

Draft a one-half page memorandum to Terrio explaining why the $6,000 loss on sale of Blackhawk stock is correctly reported.

BTN C-5 Access the July 30, 2009, 10-K filing (for year-end June 30, 2009) of Microsoft (MSFT) at www.sec.gov. Review its note 4, "Investments."

TAKING IT TO THE NET

C1

Required

1. How does the "cost-basis" total amount for its investments as of June 30, 2009, compare to the prior year-end amount?
2. Identify at least eight types of short-term investments held by Microsoft as of June 30, 2009.
3. What were Microsoft's unrealized gains and its unrealized losses from its investments for 2009?
4. Was the cost or fair value ("recorded basis") of the investments higher as of June 30, 2009?

BTN C-6 Each team member is to become an expert on a specific classification of long-term investments. This expertise will be used to facilitate other teammates' understanding of the concepts and procedures relevent to the classification chosen.

TEAMWORK IN ACTION

C1 C2 P1 P2 P3 P4

1. Each team member must select an area for expertise by choosing one of the following classifications of long-term investments.
  a. Held-to-maturity debt securities
  b. Available-for-sale debt and equity securities
  c. Equity securities with significant influence
  d. Equity securities with controlling influence
2. Learning teams are to disburse and expert teams are to be formed. Expert teams are made up of those who select the same area of expertise. The instructor will identify the location where each expert team will meet.
3. Expert teams will collaborate to develop a presentation based on the following requirements. Students must write the presentation in a format they can show to their learning teams in part (4).

Requirements for Expert Presentation

  a. Write a transaction for the acquisition of this type of investment security. The transaction description is to include all necessary data to reflect the chosen classification.
  b. Prepare the journal entry to record the acquisition.
  [*Note:* The expert team on equity securities with controlling influence will substitute requirements (*d*) and (*e*) with a discussion of the reporting of these investments.]

Sarbanes-Oxley Act (SOX) Created the *Public Company Accounting Oversight Board,* regulates analyst conflicts, imposes corporate governance requirements, enhances accounting and control disclosures, impacts insider transactions and executive loans, establishes new types of criminal conduct, and expands penalties for violations of federal securities laws. *(pp. 13 & 250)*

Schedule of accounts payable List of the balances of all accounts in the accounts payable ledger and their totals. *(p. E-14)*

Schedule of accounts receivable List of the balances of all accounts in the accounts receivable ledger and their totals. *(p. E-9)*

Section 404 (of SOX) Section 404 of SOX requires that company management document and assess the effectiveness of all internal control processes that can affect financial reporting; company auditors express an opinion on whether management's assessment of the effectiveness of internal controls is fairly stated. *(p. 251)*

Secured bonds Bonds that have specific assets of the issuer pledged as collateral. *(p. 428)*

Securities and Exchange Commission (SEC) Federal agency Congress has charged to set reporting rules for organizations that sell ownership shares to the public. *(p. 9)*

Segment return on assets Segment operating income divided by segment average (identifiable) assets for the period. *(p. E-18)*

Selling expenses Expenses of promoting sales, such as displaying and advertising merchandise, making sales, and delivering goods to customers. *(p. 171)*

Serial bonds Bonds consisting of separate amounts that mature at different dates. *(p. 428)*

Service company Organization that provides services instead of tangible products.

Shareholders Owners of a corporation; also called *stockholders.* *(p. 12)*

Shares Equity of a corporation divided into ownership units; also called *stock.* *(p. 12)*

Short-term investments Debt and equity securities that management expects to convert to cash within the next 3 to 12 months (or the operating cycle if longer); also called *temporary investments* or *marketable securities.* *(p. C-1)*

Short-term note payable Current obligation in the form of a written promissory note. *(p. 373)*

Shrinkage Inventory losses that occur as a result of theft or deterioration. *(p. 168)*

Signature card Includes the signatures of each person authorized to sign checks on the bank account. *(p. 262)*

Simple capital structure Capital structure that consists of only common stock and nonconvertible preferred stock; consists of no dilutive securities. *(p. 477)*

Single-step income statement Income statement format that includes cost of goods sold as an expense and shows only one subtotal for total expenses. *(p. 172)*

Sinking fund bonds Bonds that require the issuer to make deposits to a separate account; bondholders are repaid at maturity from that account. *(p. 428)*

Small stock dividend Stock dividend that is 25% or less of a corporation's previously outstanding shares. *(p. 466)*

Social responsibility Being accountable for the impact that one's actions might have on society. *(p. 8)*

Sole proprietorship Business owned by one person that is not organized as a corporation; also called *proprietorship.* *(p. 11)*

Solvency Company's long-run financial viability and its ability to cover long-term obligations. *(p. 557)*

Source documents Source of information for accounting entries that can be in either paper or electronic form; also called *business papers.* *(p. 52)*

Special journal Any journal used for recording and posting transactions of a similar type. *(p. E-6)*

Specific identification Method to assign cost to inventory when the purchase cost of each item in inventory is identified and used to compute cost of inventory. *(p. 209)*

Spreadsheet Computer program that organizes data by means of formulas and format; also called *electronic work sheet.* *(p. 524)*

State Unemployment Taxes (SUTA) State payroll taxes on employers to support its unemployment programs. *(p. 378)*

Stated value stock No-par stock assigned a stated value per share; this amount is recorded in the stock account when the stock is issued. *(p. 462)*

Statement of cash flows A financial statement that lists cash inflows (receipts) and cash outflows (payments) during a period; arranged by operating, investing, and financing. *(pp. 20 & 502)*

Statement of owner's equity Report of changes in equity over a period; adjusted for increases (owner investment and net income) and for decreases (withdrawals and net loss).

Statement of partners' equity Financial statement that shows total capital balances at the beginning of the period, any additional investment by partners, the income or loss of the period, the partners' withdrawals, and the partners' ending capital balances; also called *statement of partners' capital.* *(p. D-7)*

Statement of retained earnings Report of changes in retained earnings over a period; adjusted for increases (net income), for decreases (dividends and net loss), and for any prior period adjustment. *(p. 20)*

Statement of stockholders' equity Financial statement that lists the beginning and ending balances of each major equity account and describes all changes in those accounts. *(p. 475)*

Statements of Financial Accounting Standards (SFAS) FASB publications that establish U.S. GAAP.

Stock See *shares.* *(p. 12)*

Stock dividend Corporation's distribution of its own stock to its stockholders without the receipt of any payment. *(p. 466)*

Stock options Rights to purchase common stock at a fixed price over a specified period of time. *(p. 476)*

Stock split Occurs when a corporation calls in its stock and replaces each share with more than one new share; decreases both the market value per share and any par or stated value per share. *(p. 468)*

Stock subscription Investor's contractual commitment to purchase unissued shares at future dates and prices.

Stockholders See *shareholders.* *(p. 12)*

Stockholders' equity A corporation's equity; also called *shareholders' equity* or *corporate capital.* *(p. 462)*

Straight-line depreciation Method that allocates an equal portion of the depreciable cost of plant asset (cost minus salvage) to each accounting period in its useful life. *(pp. 101 & 332)*

Straight-line bond amortization Method allocating an equal amount of bond interest expense to each period of the bond life. *(p. 418)*

Subsidiary Entity controlled by another entity (parent) in which the parent owns more than 50% of the subsidiary's voting stock. *(p. C-8)*

Subsidiary ledger List of individual subaccounts and amounts with a common characteristic; linked to a controlling account in the general ledger. *(p. E-6)*

Supplementary records Information outside the usual accounting records; also called *supplemental records*. *(p. 164)*

Supply chain Linkages of services or goods extending from suppliers, to the company itself, and on to customers.

T-account Tool used to show the effects of transactions and events on individual accounts. *(p. 57)*

Temporary accounts Accounts used to record revenues, expenses, and withdrawals (dividends for a corporation); they are closed at the end of each period; also called *nominal accounts*. *(p. 110)*

Term bonds Bonds scheduled for payment (maturity) at a single specified date. *(p. 428)*

Time period assumption Assumption that an organization's activities can be divided into specific time periods such as months, quarters, or years. *(pp. 11 & 96)*

Times interest earned Ratio of income before interest expense (and any income taxes) divided by interest expense; reflects risk of covering interest commitments when income varies. *(p. 384)*

Total asset turnover Measure of a company's ability to use its assets to generate sales; computed by dividing net sales by average total assets. *(p. 347)*

Trade discount Reduction from a list or catalog price that can vary for wholesalers, retailers, and consumers. *(p. 160)*

Trademark or **trade (brand) name** Symbol, name, phrase, or jingle identified with a company, product, or service. *(p. 345)*

Trading on the equity See *financial leverage.*

Trading securities Investments in debt and equity securities that the company intends to actively trade for profit. *(p. C-4)*

Transaction Exchange of economic consideration affecting an entity's financial position that can be reliably measured.

Treasury stock Corporation's own stock that it reacquired and still holds. *(p. 472)*

Trial balance List of accounts and their balances at a point in time; total debit balances equal total credit balances. *(p. 67)*

Unadjusted trial balance List of accounts and balances prepared before accounting adjustments are recorded and posted. *(p. 108)*

Unclassified balance sheet Balance sheet that broadly groups assets, liabilities, and equity accounts. *(p. 115)*

Unearned revenue Liability created when customers pay in advance for products or services; earned when the products or services are later delivered. *(pp. 54 & 102)*

Unit contribution margin Amount a product's unit selling price exceeds its total unit variable cost.

Units-of-production depreciation Method that charges a varying amount to depreciation expense for each period of an asset's useful life depending on its usage. *(p. 333)*

Unlimited liability Legal relationship among general partners that makes each of them responsible for partnership debts if the other partners are unable to pay their shares. *(p. D-3)*

Unrealized gain (loss) Gain (loss) not yet realized by an actual transaction or event such as a sale. *(p. C-4)*

Unsecured bonds Bonds backed only by the issuer's credit standing; almost always riskier than secured bonds; also called *debentures*. *(p. 428)*

Unusual gain or loss Gain or loss that is abnormal or unrelated to the company's ordinary activities and environment. *(p. 580)*

Useful life Length of time an asset will be productively used in the operations of a business; also called *service life* or *limited life*. *(p. 331)*

Vendee Buyer of goods or services. *(p. 273)*

Vendor Seller of goods or services. *(p. 272)*

Vertical analysis Evaluation of each financial statement item or group of items in terms of a specific base amount. *(p. 558)*

Voucher Internal file used to store documents and information to control cash disbursements and to ensure that a transaction is properly authorized and recorded. *(p. 259)*

Voucher register Journal (referred to as *book of original entry*) in which all vouchers are recorded after they have been approved. *(p. 274)*

Voucher system Procedures and approvals designed to control cash disbursements and acceptance of obligations. *(p. 258)*

Wage bracket withholding table Table of the amounts of income tax withheld from employees' wages. *(p. 392)*

Warranty Agreement that obligates the seller to correct or replace a product or service when it fails to perform properly within a specified period. *(p. 380)*

Weighted average Method to assign inventory cost to sales; the cost of available-for-sale units is divided by the number of units available to determine per unit cost prior to each sale that is then multiplied by the units sold to yield the cost of that sale. *(pp. 212 & 227)*

Weighted-average method See *weighted average.*

Wholesaler Intermediary that buys products from manufacturers or other wholesalers and sells them to retailers or other wholesalers. *(p. 158)*

Withdrawals Payment of cash or other assets from a proprietorship or partnership to its owner or owners. *(p. 55)*

Work sheet Spreadsheet used to draft an unadjusted trial balance, adjusting entries, adjusted trial balance, and financial statements. *(p. 125)*

Working capital Current assets minus current liabilities at a point in time. *(p. 567)*

Working papers Analyses and other informal reports prepared by accountants and managers when organizing information for formal reports and financial statements. *(p. 125)*

Credits

Chapter 1
Page 3 © Gabriela Hasbun Photography
Page 9 © Hiroko Masuike/Getty Images
Page 10 © Martin Shields/Getty Images/Photographer's Choice
Page 11 © Scott Boehm/Getty Images
Page 16 © PAUL J. RICHARDS/AFP/Getty Images
Page 23 Map adapted from E. Maimon, J. H. Peritz, and K. B. Yancey, *A Writer's Resource,* 4/e. New York: McGraw-Hill, 2012.

Chapter 2
Page 51 Laura Boyd/Courtesy of CitySlips
Page 54 Laura Boyd/Courtesy of CitySlips
Page 55 © Sports Illustrated/Getty Images
Page 56 © Jed Jacobsohn/Getty Images

Chapter 3
Page 95 © John Keatley/Redux
Page 97 Ezio Petersen/UPI/Landov
Page 116 © Cameron Spencer/Getty Images

Chapter 4
Page 157 © Asia Kepka Photography
Page 158 Courtesy of Lim Ching, Singapore
Page 163 © Christie & Cole/photolibrary

Chapter 5
Page 205 © 2010 Fitness Anywhere, Inc. Used under license
Page 207 © Blend Images/Alamy

Chapter 6
Page 249 Courtesy of New Belgium Brewing Company
Page 252 © Lawrence Lawry/Getty Images/Photodisc

Chapter 7
Page 293 Courtesy of Dave Green/Johnny Cupcakes, Inc.
Page 296 © Ken Reid/Getty Images/Photographer's Choice
Page 297 © Stan Honda/AFP/Getty Images

Chapter 8
Page 327 Courtesy Emily O'Brien/Games2U
Page 330 Getty Images
Page 332 © Bradley C. Bower/Bloomberg via Getty Images

Page 337 ©Streeter Lecka/Getty Images
Page 342 ©Digital Vision/Getty Images
Page 344 ©Hunter Martin/Getty Images

Chapter 9
Page 369 Courtesy of Snorg Tees
Page 373 Dove Shore/Getty Images
Page 375 Adam Gault/Getty Images/OJO Images
Page 380 © Jeff Zelevansky/Getty Images
Page 383 ©John Burcham/National Geographic/Getty Images

Chapter 10
Page 413 © Josh Cogan
Page 416 Courtesy of Dow Chemicals

Chapter 11
Page 457 Courtesy of Clean Air Lawn Care
Page 460 Courtesy of Green Bay Packers, Inc.

Chapter 12
Page 501 © David Johnson
Page 502 AP Images/Brian Kersey

Chapter 13
Page 555 Carrie Devorah/WENN.com/newscom
Page 569 Stelios Varias/Reuters/Landov
Page 574 © Comstock Images/Jupiter Images

Appendix C
Page C-1 Courtesy of Scripophily.com

Appendix D
Page D-1 © Martin Harvey/Getty Images/Photodisc
Page D-2 AP Images/Frank Franklin II
Page D-3 © Royalty Free/Corbis

Appendix E
Page E-1 AP Images/Eric Risberg
Page E-2 ©Royalty-Free/Corbis
Page E-3 ©Jody Dole/Getty Images/The Image Bank
Page E-4 ©Nick Koudis/Getty Images/PhotoDisc

Index

Note: Entries and page numbers in **boldface type** indicate defined terms. Page numbers followed by *n* indicate material in footnotes.

Abbott-Langer.com, 7
Abercrombie & Fitch, 294
Ability to pay debts, 119–120, 130
Abnormal balance, 61, 129
Accelerated depreciation methods, 334–335
Account(s), 53–56, 76
  adjusting (*See* Adjusting accounts)
  asset accounts, 53–54, 113, 511–512
  balance column accounts, 60–61
  cash accounts, 53, 265, 268, 506–507
  chart of, 22, 55–56, 76, CA–CA-1
  cleared (*See* **Closing process**)
  contra accounts, 55, 101, 299, 338, 343
  equity accounts, 55–56, 113
  expense accounts (*See* Expense accounts)
  liability accounts, 54–55, 55*n,* 113
  noncash accounts, 507–508
  permanent accounts, 110, C-4
  prepaid, 53–54
  Retained Earnings account, 112
  revenue accounts (*See* Revenue accounts)
  T-accounts (*See* **T-account(s)**)
  temporary, 110, 111, C-4, C-7
  zero balances of, 57, 111, 473
Account balance, 57
Account form of balance sheet, 22, 70
Accounting, 2–30
  accounting equation (*See* **Accounting equation**)
  defined, 4
  financial accounting, 6
  financial statements (*See* Financial statement(s); *specific statements*)
  fundamentals of, 8–14, 254
  global view of (*See* Global view of accounting)
  importance of, 4–7, 29, 502, 556
  managerial accounting, 6
  off-balance sheet, 423
  principles-based, 10, 23, 118
  private vs. public, 6–7
  rules-based, 23, 118
  transaction analysis (*See* Transaction analysis)
Accounting assumptions, 11–12
Accounting constraints, 13
Accounting cycle, 114–115, 114*n,* 129
Accounting distribution, 275
Accounting equation, 15–16, 29, 53
  analysis of, 65–66
  business activities and, 28–29
  double-entry accounting and, 57
  elements of, 15
  expanded, 15, 57–58
  in preparing statement of cash flows, 507–508
  in transaction analysis, 16–20

Accounting errors, 68, 68*n,* 261–262, 265–266
Accounting period(s), 96, 96–97, 111, 160, 179
Accounting policies, A-9–A-12
Accounting principles, 10–11
  changes in, 581–582
  GAAP vs. IFRS on, 22
  generally accepted (GAAP), 9, 29, 504, C-6
  principles-based accounting, 10, 23, 118
Accounting year, 69
Accounts payable, 18–19, 54, 63
  adjustments for changes, 512
  as known liability, 372
  replacing with notes payable, 374
Accounts receivable, 53, 294–303, 298, 312
  adjusting entries for, 301, 311–312
  adjustments for changes in, 510–511
  aging of, 302–303, 312
  demonstration problem, 310–312
  note regarding, A-9–A-10
  ratio analysis, 309–310, 310*n*
  recognizing, 294–297, 308
  reconstruction analysis of, 527–528
  schedule of, 295
  transaction analysis, 18
  valuation of, 297–300, 308, 312
Accounts receivable ledger, 295
Accounts receivable methods of estimating bad debts, 301
Accounts receivable turnover ratio, 309–310, 310*n,* 312, 313, 569, 575, 580
Account titles, 55, 55*n,* 59
Accrual basis accounting, 97, 129, 527
Accrued expenses, 55, 103–105, 129, 371
  ethical issues with recording, 107, 130
  financial statement links, 107
  interest expense, 104–105, 437–438, 440
  reversing entries for, 128
Accrued revenues, 105–106, 129, 130
Accumulated deficit, 465
Accumulated Depreciation account, 101
Accumulated other comprehensive income, C-9
ACFE (Association of Certified Fraud Examiners), 251, 254
Acid-test (quick) ratio, 174, 177–178, 184, 568–569, 575, 580
"Acts of God," 580
Additions, 339
Adelphia Communications, 13
adidas, 332, 420–421, 422, 435
Adjusted bank balance, 266
Adjusted trial balance, 108, 109, 129
  closing entries prepared from, 112, 175, 177
  financial statements prepared from, 122–123, 175–177
  preparing from work sheet, 126–127

Adjusting accounts, 98–108, 118
  accrued expenses, 103–105
  accrued revenues, 105–106, 130
  adjusted trial balance and, 108
  closing process and (*See* **Closing process**)
  ethical issues, 107, 130
  financial statement preparation and, 108–110
  framework for, 98–99
  links to financial statements, 107, 129
  prepaid (deferred) expenses, 99–102, 130
  unearned (deferred) revenues, 102–103
Adjusting entries, 98–99, 108, 120–121, 129
  accounts receivable, 301, 311–312
  for income tax liabilities, 393
  for investments (demonstration), C-12
  keying adjustments, 126–127
  for merchandisers, 168, 184
  periodic inventory system, 180–182, 181*n*
  prepaid expenses, 99–102, 130
  prepared from bank reconciliation, 267–268, 271
  for prepayments, 123–125
  reporting AFS securities, C-5
  reversing entries, 127–129
  for straight-line depreciation, 332
  for unearned revenues, 102–103
Adjusting entry method, 181*n*
Adjustments, 126–127, 475
  in cash flow reporting, 510–514
  end-of-period, 306–307, 375, 381
Advertising costs, A-12
AFS (available-for-sale) securities, C-2, C-5–C-6, C-9, C-10, C-18
Aging of accounts receivable, 302–303, 312
Aging schedule, 302
AICPA (American Institute of Certified Public Accountants), 9
Alcoa, 342
Allowance for Doubtful Accounts, 299
Allowance method, 298–300, 312
Altered checks, 265
Altria Group, 478
Amazon.com, 253, 438, 463, 466, 478, 501
American Express, 296, 300, 503
American Greetings, 461
American Institute of Certified Public Accountants (AICPA), 9
Amortization, 343
  bonds
    effective interest method, 429, 431–432, 434–436
    straight-line method, 418–421
  intangible assets, 343–344, 345, 350
Amortization tables, 430–431
Analysis period, 559

Andreesen, Marc, 459
"Angel" investors, 460
Animoto, 501
Animoto.com, 501
Annual Federal Unemployment Tax Return **(Form 940), 387**
Annual financial statements, 96
Annual interest rate, 162*n,* 434
Annual report(s), 70, A-1
  Apple, Inc., A-1, A-19–A-23
  Nokia, A-1, A-29–A-33
  Palm, A-1, A-24–A-28
  Research in Motion (RIM), A-1–A-18
Annual Statement Studies (The Risk Management Association), 24
Annual Statement Studies (Robert Morris Associates), 567
Annuity(ies), 433, B-1
  future value *(f)* of, B-6–B-7, B-11
  present value *(p)* of, 425, 426*n,* 433–434, B-5, B-7, B-11
Annuity table, 434, B-11
AOL Time Warner, 13
Apple, Inc., 4, 55*n,* 70, 309–310, 337, 371, 461, C-9
  consolidated financial statements of, A-1, A-19–A-23
  balance sheets, A-20
  statements of cash flows, A-23
  statements of operations, A-21
  statements of shareholders' equity, 475, A-22
  financial statement analysis, 556, 562, 566–574
Appropriated retained earnings, 474
Arm's-length transactions, 308
Asset(s), 15, 53–54, 174, 255, 440
  accrued (*See* **Accrued revenues**)
  book value of (*See* **Book value** of assets)
  classification of, 338
  current (*See* **Current assets**)
  custody of, 252, 256
  fixed (*See* **Plant asset(s)**)
  impairment of value, 336, 338, 344, 346, A-11
  intangible (*See* **Intangible assets**)
  keeping only necessary levels of, 256
  misappropriation of, 102, 307, 343, 346, 516
  noncash assets, 464, 510–512
  noncurrent, 515–516
Asset accounts, 53–54, 113, 511–512
Asset-backed securitization, 14
Asset book value. *See* **Book value** of assets
Asset disposals
  intangible assets, 343
  plant assets (*See* Plant asset disposals)
  receivables, 307–308, 309, 312

Asset management, 28
Association of Certified Fraud Examiners (ACFE), 251, 254
ATM cards (debit cards), 296
ATMs (automated teller machines), 264, 265
Audit, 13
Auditors, 8, 13, 250, 275
    independent (external), 5, 556, A-3–A-4
    internal, 7, 252–253, 556
    reports of, A-3–A-4
Authorized stock, 461
Automated teller machines (ATMs), 264–265
Automatic payments, 265
Available-for-sale (AFS) securities, C-2, **C-5,** C-18
    fair value changes, C-9
    global view of, C-10
    selling, C-6
    valuing and reporting, C-5–C-6
Average collection period, 310n, 570
Average cost method. *See* **Weighted average (WA)**
Average days' sales uncollected, 310n
Average values, comparison to, 559
Avia, 436–437

Baby bond, 416n
Bad debts, 297
    allowance method, 298–300, 312
    direct write-off method, 297–298, 312
    estimating bad debts expense, 300–303, 312
      aging of receivables method, 302–303, 312
      percent of receivables method, 301
      percent of sales method, 300–301, 312
      summary of methods, 303
    notes regarding, 298, 308
Balance column accounts, 60–61
Balance per bank, 266
Balance per book, 266
Balance sheet, 20–22, 27, 423, 439n
    account form of, 22, 70
    cash and cash equivalents combined, 255
    classification of liabilities, 370–371
    classified, 115–117, 172–173
    common-size, 563–564
    comparative, 510, 518, 521, 560–561, 578–579
    consolidated, examples of, A-5, A-20, A-25, A-30
    effects of inventory errors, 218
    GAAP vs. IFRS regulations, 118
    long-term investments, C-14–C-15
    preparation of
      from adjusted trial balance, 123
      global issues, 173
      from trial balance, 69–70, 75, 109–110
    presentations, 342, 420, 480
    uses of, 22, 30
Balance sheet expenditures, 338
Balance sheet methods of estimating bad debts, 301
Banana Republic, C-8
Bank account, 262
Bank errors, 265–266
Banker's rule, 105, 305, 374
Banking activities, 262–268
    bank examiners, 571
    bank reconciliation (*See* **Bank reconciliation**)

bank statement, 264–265
basic services, 262–264, 265
federal depository banks, 387
global view of, 269
notes given by borrowers, 374–375, 424–427
online banking, 262
payroll bank account, 392
Bank of America, 503
Bank reconciliation, 265–268, 270–271, 277
    adjusting entries prepared from, 267–268, 271
    error testing and correction, 266, 271
    illustration of, 266–267
    purpose of, 265–266
Bank service charges (fees), 265
Bank statement, 264–265
Bar code scanners, 207
Bare Escentuals, 164
Barnes & Noble, 184
Base amount, 563
Base period, 561
Basic earnings per share, 477, 477n
Basket purchases, 330
Baskin-Robbins, 375
Bearer bond(s), 428
Bear market, 572
Benchmarks (standards), 558, 582
Berkshire Hathaway, 468
Best Buy, 24, 294, 373, 381, 462
Betterments, 339
Beyoncé, 372
BMX, 479
Boanson, Jacqueline, 254
Board of directors, 5, 12, 459, 465, 556
Bond(s), 414–415, 428
    baby bonds, 416n
    bond financing, 414–415, 440
    bond quote, 415, 422
    book (carrying) value of, 418–419, 424
    callable, 423–424, 428
    corporate, high-risk, 28
    debenture bonds, 428–429, 441
    debt features, 428, 440
    demonstration problems, 429–432
    effective interest amortization, 434–436
      demonstration problem, 429, 431–432
      discount bonds, 434–435
      premium bonds, 435–436
    global view of, 427
    issuances, 416–423, 440
      accrued interest expense, 437–438, 440
      at discount, 417–419
      between interest dates, 436–438
      at par, 416–417
      at premium, 420–421
      pricing, 422
    issuing procedures, 416, 416n
    junk bonds, 424
    kinds of, 428
    present values of, 432–434
      annuities, 433–434, B-11
      applying present value tables, 433
      compounding periods, 434
      present value concepts, 422, 432, 440
      present value tables, 433, B-10
    retirement of, 440–441
      by conversion, 424
      journal entries for, 431–432
      at maturity, 423
      before maturity, 423–424
    return and risk analysis, 28
    straight-line amortization, 418–419, 421, 429–431

Bond certificate, 416, 416n
Bond indenture, 416
Bonding of employees, 251
Bond interest expense, 417, 421, 437–438
Bond issue, 415
Bond rating, 419, 438, 441
Bond redemption, 423–424
Bonds payable, 417–419
    amortizing bond discount, 418–419, 440
    effective interest amortization, 434–435
    mortgage bonds and notes, 426–427
    present value of, 422, B-10–B-11
    straight-line bond amortization, 418–419
Bonus plans, 380
Bookkeeping, 4
Book of original entry. *See* **Journal(s)**
Book value of assets, 101–**102, 333–334**
    impairment of asset value, 338
    recording up-to-date, 340
    sale of asset and, 341
Book (carrying) value of bonds, 418–419, 424
Book value of investment, C-7
Book (carrying) value of notes, 424
Book value per common share, 478–479, 483
Book value per preferred share, 478–479, 483
Book value per share, 477
Boston Beer, 328, 347, 375
Boston Celtics, 102, 382
Bot-networking, 254
Bottom line items, 173, 506
Bowl America, 371
Brand names, 345
Bristol-Myers Squibb, 13
Brokers, 557
Brown, Warren, 413
Brunswick, 339, C-8
Building blocks of financial statement analysis, 557, 567, 582
Buildings, 54, 329, 330
Bulk purchases, 330
Bull market, 572
Business activities, 4, 28–29
    financing (*See* **Financing activities**)
    investing (*See* **Investing activities**)
    operating (*See* **Operating activities**)
Business entity assumption, 11–12, 458
Business segments, 580, A-18
BusinessWeek magazine, 13
Bylaws, corporate, 459

Cake Love, 413
CakeLove.com, 413
Calculators, 422
Calendar-year companies, 69
Callable bond(s), 423–424, 428
Callable preferred stock, 471
Callaway Golf, 294, 344
Call option, 423
Call premium, 423
Call price, 471
Cameron, Andrew, 254
Canceled checks, 265
Capital, 15, 458, 460, 471
    minimum legal capital, 461
    paid-in capital, 462
    paid-in capital in excess of par value, 463, 464, 467
    working capital, 567–568
Capital expenditures, 338, 339, 352
"Capitalization policy," 339
Capital leases, 345, 427, **439,** 439n

Capital stock, 461–462, A-15–A-16. *See also* **Common stock**
Capital structure, 477n
Career opportunities in accounting, 6–7, 29
Carrying (book) value of bonds, 418, 419, 424
Carrying (book) value of notes, 424
Cash, 255, 257, 276–277, 417, 508
    excess, investing, 256, C-1
    misappropriation of, 307, 516
    notes regarding, A-9, A-13
    sources and uses of, 520
Cash accounts, 53, 265, 268, 506–507
Cash basis accounting, 97, 527
Cash budget, 258
Cash controls, 255–262
    banking activities as (*See* Banking activities)
    cash, cash equivalents, and liquidity, 255
    cash disbursements, 258–262, 277, 516
    cash management, 255–256
    cash receipts, 256–258, 277
    days' sales uncollected ratio, 269, 277, 310n, 569–570, 575, 580
    global view of, 268
    misappropriation of cash, 307, 516
Cash coverage of debt ratio, 521, 575
Cash coverage of growth ratio, 521, 575
Cash disbursements, 258–262, 277, 516
Cash discount, 161
Cash dividends, 465, 465n, 483, C-7
    deficits and, 465–466
    liquidating dividend, 466
    transaction analysis, 19, 63
Cash equivalents, 255, 276–277, 503, A-9
Cash flow(s), 502–503
    for bonds, 418, 420
    classification of, 503–504, 506–507
    free cash flows, 520, 575
    net cash inflow, 503, 506, 532
    net cash outflow, 503
Cash flow analysis, 520–521, 532, 575
Cash flow on total assets ratio, 520–521, 532, 575
Cash flow reporting, 500–532, 515–516. *See also* **Statement of cash flows**
    adjustments in (*See* **Indirect method** of reporting operating cash flows)
    basics of, 502–508
      classification, 503–504
      importance of, 502–503
      measurement, 503
      noncash investing and financing, 505, 532
      purpose of, 502
    demonstration problem, 521–524
    financing cash flows, 517–519
      equity analysis, 518
      noncurrent liabilities, 517
      proving cash balances, 519
      three-stage analysis, 517
    global view of, 519
    IFRS on, 531
    investing cash flows, 21, 22, 515–516, 532
      global view of, 519
      noncurrent assets, 515–516
      other assets, 515–516
      three-stage analysis, 515
    operating cash flows
      direct method (*See* **Direct method** of reporting operating cash flows)
      indirect method (*See* **Indirect method** of reporting operating cash flows)

312 Paid-in capital in excess of stated value,
No-par common stock
313 Paid-in capital from retirement of common stock
314 Paid-in capital, Treasury stock
315 Preferred stock
316 Paid-in capital in excess of par value,
Preferred stock

Retained Earnings

318 Retained earnings
319 Cash dividends (or Dividends)
320 Stock dividends

Other Equity Accounts

321 Treasury stock, Common
322 Unrealized gain—Equity
323 Unrealized loss—Equity

Revenues

401 _____ fees earned
402 _____ fees earned
403 _____ services revenue
404 _____ services revenue
405 Commissions earned
406 Rent revenue (or Rent earned)
407 Dividends revenue (or Dividend earned)
408 Earnings from investment in _____
409 Interest revenue (or Interest earned)
410 Sinking fund earnings
413 Sales
414 Sales returns and allowances
415 Sales discounts

Cost of Sales

Cost of Goods Sold

502 Cost of goods sold
505 Purchases
506 Purchases returns and allowances
507 Purchases discounts
508 Transportation-in

Manufacturing

520 Raw materials purchases
521 Freight-in on raw materials
530 Factory payroll
531 Direct labor
540 Factory overhead
541 Indirect materials
542 Indirect labor
543 Factory insurance expired
544 Factory supervision
545 Factory supplies used
546 Factory utilities
547 Miscellaneous production costs
548 Property taxes on factory building
549 Property taxes on factory equipment
550 Rent on factory building
551 Repairs, factory equipment
552 Small tools written off
560 Depreciation of factory equipment
561 Depreciation of factory building

Standard Cost Variance

580 Direct material quantity variance
581 Direct material price variance
582 Direct labor quantity variance
583 Direct labor price variance
584 Factory overhead volume variance
585 Factory overhead controllable variance

Expenses

Amortization, Depletion, and Depreciation

601 Amortization expense—_____
602 Amortization expense—_____
603 Depletion expense—_____
604 Depreciation expense—Boats
605 Depreciation expense—Automobiles
606 Depreciation expense—Building _____
607 Depreciation expense—Building _____
608 Depreciation expense—Land
improvements _____
609 Depreciation expense—Land
improvements _____
610 Depreciation expense—Law library
611 Depreciation expense—Trucks
612 Depreciation expense—_____ equipment
613 Depreciation expense—_____ equipment
614 Depreciation expense—_____
615 Depreciation expense—_____

Employee-Related Expenses

620 Office salaries expense
621 Sales salaries expense
622 Salaries expense
623 _____ wages expense
624 Employees' benefits expense
625 Payroll taxes expense

Financial Expenses

630 Cash over and short
631 Discounts lost
632 Factoring fee expense
633 Interest expense

Insurance Expenses

635 Insurance expense—Delivery equipment
636 Insurance expense—Office equipment
637 Insurance expense—_____

Rental Expenses

640 Rent expense
641 Rent expense—Office space
642 Rent expense—Selling space
643 Press rental expense
644 Truck rental expense
645 _____ rental expense

Supplies Expenses

650 Office supplies expense
651 Store supplies expense
652 _____ supplies expense
653 _____ supplies expense

Miscellaneous Expenses

655 Advertising expense
656 Bad debts expense
657 Blueprinting expense
658 Boat expense
659 Collection expense
661 Concessions expense
662 Credit card expense
663 Delivery expense
664 Dumping expense
667 Equipment expense
668 Food and drinks expense
671 Gas and oil expense
672 General and administrative expense
673 Janitorial expense
674 Legal fees expense
676 Mileage expense
677 Miscellaneous expenses
678 Mower and tools expense
679 Operating expense
680 Organization expense
681 Permits expense
682 Postage expense
683 Property taxes expense
684 Repairs expense—_____
685 Repairs expense—_____
687 Selling expense
688 Telephone expense
689 Travel and entertainment expense
690 Utilities expense
691 Warranty expense
695 Income taxes expense

Gains and Losses

701 Gain on retirement of bonds
702 Gain on sale of machinery
703 Gain on sale of investments
704 Gain on sale of trucks
705 Gain on _____
706 Foreign exchange gain or loss
801 Loss on disposal of machinery
802 Loss on exchange of equipment
803 Loss on exchange of _____
804 Loss on sale of notes
805 Loss on retirement of bonds
806 Loss on sale of investments
807 Loss on sale of machinery
808 Loss on _____
809 Unrealized gain—Income
810 Unrealized loss—Income
811 Impairment gain
812 Impairment loss

Clearing Accounts

901 Income summary
902 Manufacturing summary

A Rose by Any Other Name

The same financial statement sometimes receives different titles. Following are some of the more common aliases.*

Balance Sheet	Statement of Financial Position Statement of Financial Condition
Income Statement	Statement of Income Operating Statement Statement of Operations Statement of Operating Activity Earnings Statement Statement of Earnings Profit and Loss (P&L) Statement
Statement of Cash Flows	Statement of Cash Flow Cash Flows Statement Statement of Changes in Cash Position Statement of Changes in Financial Position
Statement of Stockholders' Equity	Statement of Shareholders' Equity Statement of Changes in Shareholders' Equity Statement of Stockholders' Equity and Comprehensive Income Statement of Changes in Owner's Equity Statement of Changes in Owner's Capital Statement of Changes in Capital Accounts

* The term **Consolidated** often precedes or follows these statement titles to reflect the combination of different entities, such as a parent company and its subsidiaries.

We thank Dr. Louella Moore from Arkansas State University for suggesting this listing.

SELECTED TRANSACTIONS AND RELATIONS

① Merchandising Transactions Summary

Merchandising Transactions		Merchandising Entries	Dr.	Cr.
Purchases	Purchasing merchandise for resale.	• Merchandise Inventory	#	
		Cash or Accounts Payable		#
	Paying freight costs on purchases; FOB shipping point.	• Merchandise Inventory	#	
		Cash		#
	Paying within discount period.	• Accounts Payable	#	
		Merchandise Inventory		#
		Cash		#
	Recording purchase returns or allowances.	• Cash or Accounts Payable	#	
		Merchandise Inventory		#
Sales	Selling merchandise.	• Cash or Accounts Receivable	#	
		Sales		#
		• Cost of Goods Sold	#	
		Merchandise Inventory		#
	Receiving payment within discount period.	• Cash	#	
		Sales Discounts	#	
		Accounts Receivable		#
	Granting sales returns or allowances.	• Sales Returns and Allowances......	#	
		Cash or Accounts Receivable		#
		• Merchandise Inventory	#	
		Cost of Goods Sold		#
	Paying freight costs on sales; FOB destination.	• Delivery Expense	#	
		Cash		#

Merchandising Events		Adjusting and Closing Entries		
Adjusting	Adjusting due to shrinkage (occurs when recorded amount larger than physical inventory).	Cost of Goods Sold	#	
		Merchandise Inventory		#
Closing	Closing temporary accounts with credit balances.	Sales	#	
		Income Summary		#
	Closing temporary accounts with debit balances.	Income Summary	#	
		Sales Returns and Allowances		#
		Sales Discounts		#
		Cost of Goods Sold		#
		Delivery Expense		#
		"Other Expenses"		#

② Merchandising Cost Flows

③ Credit Terms and Amounts

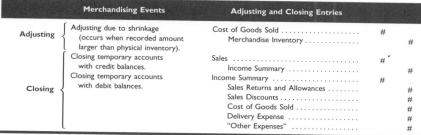

④ Bad Debts Estimation

⑤ Bond Valuation

Bond Sets	Market Sets	Bond Price Determined
Contract rate	Market rate	Contract rate > Market rate → Bond sells at Premium
		Contract rate = Market rate → Bond sells at Par
		Contract rate < Market rate → Bond sells at Discount

⑦ Dividend Transactions

Account Affected	Type of Dividend		
	Cash Dividend	Stock Dividend	Stock Split
Cash	Decrease	—	—
Common Stock	—	Increase	—
Retained Earnings ..	Decrease	Decrease	—

⑥ Stock Transactions Summary

Stock Transactions		Stock Entries	Dr.	Cr.
Issue Common Stock	Issue par value common stock at par (par stock recorded at par).	Cash	#	
		Common Stock		#
	Issue par value common stock at premium (par stock recorded at par).	Cash	#	
		Common Stock		#
		Paid-In Capital in Excess of Par Value, Common Stock		#
	Issue no-par value common stock (no-par stock recorded at amount received).	Cash	#	
		Common Stock		#
	Issue stated value common stock at stated value (stated stock recorded at stated value).	Cash	#	
		Common stock		#
	Issue stated value common stock at premium (stated stock recorded at stated value).	Cash	#	
		Common stock		#
		Paid-In Capital in Excess of Stated Value, Common Stock		#
Issue Preferred Stock	Issue par value preferred stock at par (par stock recorded at par).	Cash	#	
		Preferred Stock		#
	Issue par value preferred stock at premium (par stock recorded at par).	Cash	#	
		Preferred Stock		#
		Paid-In Capital in Excess of Par Value, Preferred Stock		#
Reacquire Common Stock	Reacquire its own common stock (treasury stock recorded at cost).	Treasury Stock, Common	#	
		Cash		#
Reissue Common Stock	Reissue its treasury stock at cost (treasury stock removed at cost).	Cash	#	
		Treasury Stock, Common		#
	Reissue its treasury stock above cost (treasury stock removed at cost).	Cash	#	
		Treasury Stock, Common		#
		Paid-In Capital, Treasury		#
	Reissue its treasury stock below cost (treasury stock removed at cost; if paid-in capital is insufficient to cover amount below cost, retained earnings is debited for remainder).	Cash	#	
		Paid-In Capital, Treasury	#	
		Retained Earnings (if necessary)	#	
		Treasury Stock, Common		#

⑧ A Rose by Any Other Name

The same financial statement sometimes receives different titles. Following are some of the more common aliases.*

Balance Sheet	Statement of Financial Position Statement of Financial Condition
Income Statement	Statement of Income Operating Statement Statement of Operations Statement of Operating Activity Earnings Statement Statement of Earnings Profit and Loss (P&L) Statement
Statement of Cash Flows	Statement of Cash Flow Cash Flows Statement Statement of Changes in Cash Position Statement of Changes in Financial Position
Statement of Stockholders' Equity	Statement of Shareholders' Equity Statement of Changes in Shareholders' Equity Statement of Stockholders' Equity and Comprehensive Income Statement of Changes in Owner's Equity Statement of Changes in Owner's Capital Statement of Changes in Capital Accounts

* The term **Consolidated** often precedes or follows these statement titles to reflect the combination of different entities, such as a parent company and its subsidiaries.

FUNDAMENTALS

① Accounting Equation

Assets		=	Liabilities		+	Equity	
↑	↓		↓	↑		↓	↑
Debit for increases	Credit for decreases		Debit for decreases	Credit for increases		Debit for decreases	Credit for increases

Contributed Capital* + Retained Earnings

Common Stock		−	Dividends		+	Revenues		−	Expenses	
Dr. for decreases	Cr. for increases		Dr. for increases	Cr. for decreases		Dr. for decreases	Cr. for increases		Dr. for increases	Cr. for decreases

☐ Indicates normal balance.

*Includes common stock and any preferred stock.

② Accounting Cycle

③ Adjustments and Entries

Type	Adjusting Entry	
Prepaid Expenses	Dr. Expense	Cr. Asset*
Unearned Revenues	Dr. Liability	Cr. Revenue
Accrued Expenses	Dr. Expense	Cr. Liability
Accrued Revenues	Dr. Asset	Cr. Revenue

*For depreciation, credit Accumulated Depreciation (contra asset).

④ 4-Step Closing Process

1. Transfer revenue and gain account balances to Income Summary.
2. Transfer expense and loss account balances to Income Summary.
3. Transfer Income Summary balance to Retained Earnings.
4. Transfer Dividends balance to Retained Earnings.

⑤ Accounting Concepts

Characteristics	Assumptions	Principles	Constraints
Relevance	Business entity	Measurement (historical cost)	Cost-benefit
Reliability	Going concern	Revenue recognition	Materiality
Comparability	Monetary unit	Expense recognition	Industry practice
Consistency	Periodicity	Full disclosure	Conservatism

⑥ Ownership of Inventory

	Ownership Transfers When Goods Passed To	Transportation Costs Paid By
FOB Shipping Point	Carrier	Buyer
FOB Destination	Buyer	Seller

⑦ Inventory Costing Methods

- Specific identification
- First-in, first-out (FIFO)
- Weighted-average
- Last-in, first-out (LIFO)

⑧ Depreciation and Depletion

Straight-line: $\dfrac{\text{Cost} - \text{Salvage value}}{\text{Useful life in periods}} \times \text{Periods expired}$

Units-of-production: $\dfrac{\text{Cost} - \text{Salvage value}}{\text{Useful life in units}} \times \text{Units produced}$

Declining-balance: Rate* × Beginning-of-period book value
*Rate is often double the straight-line rate, or 2 × (1/Useful life)

Depletion: $\dfrac{\text{Cost} - \text{Salvage value}}{\text{Total capacity in units}} \times \text{Units extracted}$

⑨ Interest Computation

Interest = Principal (face) × Rate × Time

⑩ Accounting for Investment Securities

Classification*	Accounting
Short-Term Investment in Securities	
Held-to-maturity (debt) securities	**Cost** (without any discount or premium amortization)
Trading (debt and equity) securities..........	**Fair value** (with fair value adjustment to income)
Available-for-sale (debt and equity) securities...	**Fair value** (with fair value adjustment to equity)
Long-Term Investment in Securities	
Held-to-maturity (debt) securities	**Cost** (with any discount or premium amortization)
Available-for-sale (debt and equity) securities...	**Fair value** (with fair value adjustment to equity)
Equity securities with significant influence......	Equity method
Equity securities with controlling influence.....	Equity method (with consolidation)

*A *fair value option* allows companies to report HTM and AFS securities much like trading securities.

ANALYSES

① Liquidity and Efficiency

Current ratio $= \dfrac{\text{Current assets}}{\text{Current liabilities}}$ — pp. 119 & 567

Working capital = Current assets − Current liabilities — p. 567

Acid-test ratio $= \dfrac{\text{Cash} + \text{Short-term investments} + \text{Current receivables}}{\text{Current liabilities}}$ — p. 174

Accounts receivable turnover $= \dfrac{\text{Net sales}}{\text{Average accounts receivable, net}}$ — pp. 309 & 569

Credit risk ratio $= \dfrac{\text{Allowance for doubtful accounts}}{\text{Accounts receivable, net}}$ — p. 309

Inventory turnover $= \dfrac{\text{Cost of goods sold}}{\text{Average inventory}}$ — pp. 219 & 569

Days' sales uncollected $= \dfrac{\text{Accounts receivable, net}}{\text{Net sales}} \times 365*$ — p. 569

Days' sales in inventory $= \dfrac{\text{Ending inventory}}{\text{Cost of goods sold}} \times 365*$ — pp. 219 & 570

Total asset turnover $= \dfrac{\text{Net sales}}{\text{Average total assets}}$ — pp. 347 & 570

Plant asset useful life $= \dfrac{\text{Plant asset cost}}{\text{Depreciation expense}}$ — p. 347

Plant asset age $= \dfrac{\text{Accumulated depreciation}}{\text{Depreciation expense}}$ — p. 347

Days' cash expense coverage $= \dfrac{\text{Cash and cash equivalents}}{\text{Average daily cash expenses}}$ — p. 256

*360 days is also commonly used.

② Solvency

Debt ratio $= \dfrac{\text{Total liabilities}}{\text{Total assets}}$ Equity ratio $= \dfrac{\text{Total equity}}{\text{Total assets}}$ — pp. 72 & 571

Debt-to-equity $= \dfrac{\text{Total liabilities}}{\text{Total equity}}$ — pp. 429 & 571

Times interest earned $= \dfrac{\text{Income before interest expense and income taxes}}{\text{Interest expense}}$ — pp. 384 & 572

Cash coverage of growth $= \dfrac{\text{Cash flow from operations}}{\text{Cash outflow for plant assets}}$ — p. 521

Cash coverage of debt $= \dfrac{\text{Cash flow from operations}}{\text{Total noncurrent liabilities}}$ — p. 521

③ Profitability

Profit margin ratio $= \dfrac{\text{Net income}}{\text{Net sales}}$ — p. 119

Gross margin ratio $= \dfrac{\text{Net sales} - \text{Cost of goods sold}}{\text{Net sales}}$ — p. 174

Return on total assets $= \dfrac{\text{Net income}}{\text{Average total assets}}$ — pp. 24 & 572

$= \text{Profit margin ratio} \times \text{Total asset turnover}$ — p. 573

Return on common stockholders' equity $= \dfrac{\text{Net income} - \text{Preferred dividends}}{\text{Average common stockholders' equity}}$ — p. 573

Book value per common share $= \dfrac{\text{Stockholders' equity applicable to common shares}}{\text{Number of common shares outstanding}}$ — p. 478

Basic earnings per share $= \dfrac{\text{Net income} - \text{Preferred dividends}}{\text{Weighted-average common shares outstanding}}$ — p. 477

Cash flow on total assets $= \dfrac{\text{Cash flow from operations}}{\text{Average total assets}}$ — p. 520

Payout ratio $= \dfrac{\text{Cash dividends declared on common stock}}{\text{Net income}}$ — p. 478

④ Market

Price-earnings ratio $= \dfrac{\text{Market value (price) per share}}{\text{Earnings per share}}$ — pp. 477 & 573

Dividend yield $= \dfrac{\text{Annual cash dividends per share}}{\text{Market price per share}}$ — pp. 478 & 574

Residual income = Net income − Target net income

FINANCIAL REPORTS

Income Statement*
For _period_ Ended _date_

Net sales (revenues)		$ #
Cost of goods sold (cost of sales)		#
Gross margin (gross profit)		#
Operating expenses		
Examples: Depreciation, salaries,	$ #	
wages, rent, utilities, interest,	#	
amortization, advertising, taxes	#	
Total operating expenses		#
Nonoperating gains and losses		#
Net income (net profit or earnings)		$ #

* A typical chart of accounts is at the end of the book and classifies all accounts by financial statement categories.

Balance Sheet
Date

ASSETS

Current assets
Examples: Cash, Cash equivalents, Short-term investments,		
Accounts receivable, Current portion of notes	$ #	
receivable, Inventory, Prepaid expenses	#	
Total current assets		$ #

Long-term investments
Examples: Investment in stock, Investment in bonds,	#	
Land for expansion	#	
Total long-term investments		#

Plant assets
Examples: Equipment, Machinery, Buildings, Land	#	
Total plant assets, net of depreciation		#

Intangible assets
Examples: Patent, Trademark, Copyright, License, Goodwill	#	
Total intangible assets, net of amortization		#
Total assets		$ #

LIABILITIES AND EQUITY

Current liabilities
Examples: Accounts payable, Wages payable, Salaries	$ #	
payable, Current notes payable, Taxes payable,	#	
Interest payable, Unearned revenues	#	
Total current liabilities		$ #

Long-term liabilities
Examples: Notes payable, Bonds payable, Lease liability	#	
Total long-term liabilities		#
Total liabilities		#

Equity
Common stock		#
Paid-in capital in excess of par or stated value		#
Retained earnings		#
Less treasury stock		(#)
Total liabilities and equity		$ #

Statement of Cash Flows
For _period_ Ended _date_

Cash flows from operating activities		
[Prepared using the indirect (see below)† or direct method]		
Net cash provided (used) by operating activities		$ #
Cash flows from investing activities		
[List of individual investing inflows and outflows]		
Net cash provided (used) by investing activities		#
Cash flows from financing activities		
[List of individual financing inflows and outflows]		
Net cash provided (used) by financing activities		#
Net increase (decrease) in cash		$ #
Cash (and equivalents) balance at beginning of period		#
Cash (and equivalents) balance at end of period		$ #

Attach separate schedule or note disclosure of "Noncash investing and financing transactions."

†Indirect Method: Cash Flows from Operating Activities

Cash flows from operating activities		
Net income		$ #
Add: Decreases in noncash current assets	$ #	
Increases in current liabilities	#	
Expenses with no cash outflows (examples: depreciation,		
and amortization of both intangibles and bond discounts)	#	
Nonoperating losses (examples: losses from asset sales		
and from debt retirements)	#	#
Less: Increases in noncash current assets	#	
Decreases in current liabilities	#	
Revenues with no cash inflows (examples:		
amortization of bond premiums)	#	
Nonoperating gains (examples: gains from asset sales		
and from debt retirements)	#	#
Net cash provided (used) by operating activities		$ #

Statement of Retained Earnings
For _period_ Ended _date_

Retained earnings, beginning		$ #
Add: Net income		#
		#
Less: Dividends declared		#
Retained earnings, ending		$ #

Statement of Stockholders' Equity†
For _period_ Ended _date_

	Common Stock	Capital in Excess of Par	Retained Earnings	Treasury Stock	Total
Balances, beginning	$ #	$ #	$ #	$ #	$ #
Net income					
Cash dividends					
Stock issuance					
Treasury stock purchase					
Treasury stock reissuance					
Other					
Balances, ending	$ #	$ #	$ #	$ #	$ #

† Additional columns and account titles commonly include number of shares, preferred stock, unrealized gains and losses on available-for-sale securities, foreign currency translation, and comprehensive income.

Premium Bond Amortization (Straight-Line) Table†

Semiannual Period-End	Unamortized Bond Premium*	Bond Carrying Value**
Bond life-start	$ #	$ #
. . . .		
Bond life-end	0	par

† Bond carrying value is adjusted to par and its amortized premium to zero over the bond life (note: carrying value less unamortized bond premium equals par).
* Equals total bond premium less its accumulated amortization.
** Equals bond par value plus its unamortized bond premium.

Discount Bond Amortization (Straight-Line) Table†

Semiannual Period-End	Unamortized Bond Discount*	Bond Carrying Value**
Bond life-start	$ #	$ #
. . . .		
Bond life-end	0	par

† Bond carrying value is adjusted to par and its amortized discount to zero over the bond life (note: unamortized bond discount plus carrying value equals par).
* Equals total bond discount less its accumulated amortization.
** Equals bond par value less its unamortized bond discount.

Effective Interest Amortization Table for Bonds with Semiannual Interest Payment

Semiannual Interest Period-End	Cash Interest Paid^A	Bond Interest Expense^B	Discount or Premium Amortization^C	Unamortized Discount or Premium^D	Carrying Value^E
#	#	#	#	#	#

^A Par value multiplied by the semiannual contract rate.
^B Prior period's carrying value multiplied by the semiannual market rate.
^C The difference between interest paid and bond interest expense.
^D Prior period's unamortized discount or premium less the current period's discount or premium amortization.
^E Par value less unamortized discount or plus unamortized premium.

Installment Notes Payment Table

Period Ending Date	Beginning Balance	Debit Interest Expense	+	Debit Notes Payable	=	Credit Cash	Ending Balance
#	#	#		#		#	#

Bank Reconciliation
Date

Bank statement balance	$#	Book balance		$#
Add: Unrecorded deposits	#	Add: Unrecorded bank credit		
		memoranda		#
Bank errors understating		Book errors understating		
the balance	#	the balance		#
	#			#
Less: Outstanding checks	#	Less: Unrecorded bank debit		
		memoranda		#
Bank errors overstating		Book errors overstating		
the balance	#	the balance		#
Adjusted bank balance	$#	**Adjusted book balance**		$#

Balances are equal (reconciled)